Ammonius and the Seabattle
Texts, Commentary, and Essays

Peripatoi

Philologisch-historische Studien zum Aristotelismus

Herausgegeben von
Wolfgang Kullmann,
Robert W. Sharples, Jürgen Wiesner

Band 18

2001
Walter de Gruyter · Berlin · New York

Ammonius and the Seabattle

Texts, Commentary, and Essays

Edited by
Gerhard Seel

In collaboration with
Jean-Pierre Schneider and Daniel Schulthess

Ammonius on Aristotle: De Interpretatione 9 (and 7, 1-17)
Greek Text established by A. Busse, reprint from CAG IV/v
English translation by David Blank, revised by
J.-P. Schneider and Gerhard Seel
Philosophical Commentary by Gerhard Seel
Essays by Mario Mignucci and Gerhard Seel

2001
Walter de Gruyter · Berlin · New York

Earlier versions of the chapter by Mario Mignucci were published in *Rationality in Greek thought*, edited by Michael Frede and Gisela Striker, Oxford: Clarendon Press, 1996 ((c) the several contributors and in this volume Oxford University Press 1996) and, together with an earlier version of David Blank's translation of Ammonius' commentary on *De interpretatione 9*, in *Ammonius, On Aristotle On Interpretation 9, translated by David Blank, with Boethius, On Aristotle On Interpretation 9, first and second commentaries, translated by Norman Kretzmann, with essays by Richard Sorabji, Norman Kretzmann and Mario Mignucci*, published in the series *Ancient commentators on Aristotle* by Duckworth, London, 1998 (translation of Ammonius (c) 1998 by David Blank, ch.4 (c) 1998 by Mario Mignucci.

♾ Printed on acid-free paper which falls within the guidelines of the ANSI to ensure permanence and durability.

Library of Congress Cataloging-in-Publication Data

Ammonius and the seabattle / edited by Gerhard Seel ; in collaboration with Jean-Pierre Schneider and Daniel Schulthess.
   p.   cm. – (Peripatoi ; Bd. 18)
Includes bibliographical references and index.
ISBN 3-11-016879-0
   1. Ammonius, Hermiae. In Aristotelis De interpretatione commentarius. Kephalaia 9. 2. Free will and determinism. 3. Fate and fatalism. I. Seel, Gerhard, 1940–   . II. Schneider, Jean-Pierre. III. Schulthess, Daniel, 1954–   . IV. Series.
   B439 .A9785 2000
   160–dc21
                            00-050847

Die Deutsche Bibliothek – Cataloging in Publication Data

Ammonius and the seabattle : texts, commentary and essays / ed. by Gerhard Seel. In collab. with Jean-Pierre Schneider and Daniel Schulthess. – Berlin ; New York : de Gruyter, 2000
   (Peripatoi ; 18)
   ISBN 3-11-016879-0

CONTENTS

Part I

Preliminaries

Acknowledgements
Explication of the Terminology and Symbols
List of Symbols
List of Principles and Formulas

I.1 ACKNOWLEDGEMENTS

This book is the fruit of a long lasting co-operation of scholars from different countries who contributed to it either directly or by their most helpful advice. The work started more than ten years ago when the "Centre d'études de la pensée antique et médiévale" at the university of Neuchâtel set out to translate Ammonius' commentary on *De interpretatione* 9 into French. The scholars who participated in this endeavour were F. Brunner, W. Spoerri, A. Schneider, D. Schulthess, G. Seel, B. Decorvet , J.-P. Schneider and A.-S. Cochand. To give a fresh impulse to this enterprise, the founder and first president of this research-centre, Fernand Brunner, organised in 1989 a workshop to which he invited D. Blank, P.-L. Donini, M. Erler, D. O'Meara, M. Mignucci and R. Sorabji. From this time on these scholars were associated with our task and all contributed to it in one way or the other.

I should mention especially D. Blank, M. Mignucci and R. Sorabji. The latter was not only prepared to discuss with me special problems whenever I needed advice, but he wrote also a penetrating criticism of my articles that led to considerable improvements. M. Mignucci wrote a most valuable contribution to this volume and moreover he was a constant philosophical companion for more then ten years from whom I learnt many logical subtleties and clarifications. When CEPAM began the work on the French translation D. Blank was preparing his translation of Ammonius' entire commentary on *De Interpretatione* which is now published in the series 'Ancient Commentators on Aristotle' edited by R. Sorabji. So it was quite natural and most profitable for both sides to work hand in hand. The English version of Ammonius' text published in this volume is in fact a revision of D. Blank's translation made by J.-P. Schneider and myself. I thank D. Blank, R. Sorabji and the publisher G. Duckworth for their generous permission. I should also thank D. Blank for translating my articles into English and for so many helpful discussions.

I had the opportunity to discuss special points of my interpretation with M. Frede, J. Brunschwig, H. Weidemann, F. Zimmermann, S. Broadie, G. Fine, R. Sharples, D. Sedley, A. Long, S. Knuutila, J. Barnes, D. Charles and S. Bobzien. From the latter I learnt a lot about Stoic theory of modalities and determinism.

I am especially grateful to G. Bayer who translated my commentary from French to English. His philosophical understanding of the matter was of great help when I formulated the final version of the commentary.

I should like to thank the editors of 'Peripatoi', W. Kullmann, R. Sharples and J. Wiesner who accepted this volume for this series and made many helpful criticisms and suggestions. R. Sharples deserves special thanks for making the final corrections and creating the layout of the volume.

The typing was done by B. Wallmark, the bibliography and the indices were put together by D. Scheidegger and H. Plüss, the English of my introduction was checked by M. Ruskin. We received a financial aid from the Swiss National Foundation (FNS). I thank all of them.

Finally I would like to thank my co-editors D. Schulthess and J.-P. Schneider. D. Schulthess after taking over the presidency of CEPAM from Fernand Brunner managed the French translation and took part in all our main discussions. J.-P. Schneider was my closest collaborator and never-failing help both in establishing the commentary and in getting the translation right.

Bern, May 2000   Gerhard Seel

I.2 EXPLICATION OF THE TERMINOLOGY AND SYMBOLS

While the problems treated by Ammonius are extremely complex, he uses a language—ordinary Greek, enriched with philosophical terms—which is far from adequate to this complexity. The result is that important statements in his text are ambiguous. The interpreter, however, must be able to express these different meanings in a differentiated way. For this reason we introduce here a language modelled on the modern formal languages of sentence and modal logic. So the purpose of the symbolism we introduce is neither to provide a formal reconstruction of Ammonius' theory nor to symbolise Ammonius' own theses, but rather to allow a clear formulation of our interpretation of his theory and possible alternative interpretations in terms of contemporary logic.

It is a feature of the Greek language that an expression which assigns a predicate to a subject also qualifies the state of affairs described thereby as a fact, i.e., it says that this state of affairs is the case. In order to avoid ambiguity, however, one must allow these two operations (the attribution of properties and the assertion of facts) to be carried out by two different expressions. Therefore, we use the small letters a, b, c, etc. to symbolise states of affairs, while operators consisting of one or two capital letters C, CC, NC, etc., when they are attached to symbols for states of affairs, indicate that the state of affairs is the case or is the case in a certain mode.

Modes play a large role in the problems treated by Ammonius. He expresses these modes by means of adverbs (e.g. ἀναγκαίως), prepositional phrases (e.g. ἐξ ἀνάγκης), or constructions with modal substantives and infinitives. Since these are modalisations of something's being the case, we express these modes by pairs of capital letters, e.g. PC (it is possibly the case that) or NC (it is necessarily the case that), which are added to expressions for states of affairs so that modal sentences such as PCa or NCb arise. To express that a state of affairs is really the case, i.e., for the mode of reality, we use the double capitals CC. In contexts without time indices, we write C as an abbreviation for CC.

The Greek language also has another source of ambiguities. For a predicate expression accomplishes another function in addition to those already mentioned: it indicates the time (relative to the speech-act) at which the state of affairs is the case. This indication is ambiguous in several respects: 1) it is ambiguous because of the relativity regarding the time of the speech-act. Since in written formulations of the sentences the speech-act is not identified, written sentences are in principle ambiguous in this respect; 2) the past and future inflections of verbs contain—because of the relativity regarding what is in each case the present time of the speech-act—not one, but two indications of time, the second of which concerns not a point of time, but a period of time; 3) because of the ambiguity of the copula, it is undecided whether these time indications represent a temporal characterisation of the state of affairs itself or whether they delimit the time at which the state of affairs is the case. To remove these ambiguities, we attach time indices to the modal operators. In this way we can express that the time of the mode and the time of the being the case are different. The expression '$N_{t'}C_{t''}a$', for example, says that at time t' it is necessary that the state of affairs a is the case at time t''. I should emphasise, however, that in expressions with time indices and in expressions without time indices we deal with two different kinds of states of affairs. We may characterise the latter as an entity that either is the case or is not. In order to fulfil this condition the description of the state of affairs must include temporal determinations. On the other hand, a state of affairs that belongs to the former kind does not include any temporal determination. Therefore one can not characterise it as an entity that either is the case or is not. It rather is an entity that at each moment either is the case or is not the case. Thus the expressions Ca and $C\tau_1 b$ can be used to state the same fact in different ways. Whenever the different ways of stating a fact are irrelevant for the argument we use the term 'proposition' and the symbols X, Y, Z instead of either of the former expressions and the symbols P, Q, R for variables of propositions (cp. Mario Mignucci's article).

Ammonius uses the expression πρᾶγμα to signify facts or states of affairs. He has a raft of expressions to speak of sentences, the items which are the subject of the debate: ἀπφαντικὸς λόγος, λόγος, ἀπόφανσις, πρότασις, etc. In our commentary we use 'sentence' (assertive sentence) for all these expressions. In Mario Mignucci's article, however, the term 'proposition' is used as well. Only in contexts where it is important to distinguish type-sentences from token-sentences do we use 'sentence' for the former and 'statement', 'assertion', utterance' for the latter. It must be stressed, however, that Ammonius understands the items in question as tokens and not as types (cp. our article in this volume). Thus, he is dealing with individual speech events. We form names for these speech events by putting the symbols for facts or modalised facts in angle brackets. In certain sentences, however, beside the names of these speech events, we also need sentences which say that the speech event took place at a certain point in time. In order to form these sentences, we add a time index to the expressions in angle brackets; $[Cp]_{t'}$ therefore means that [Cp] was uttered at time t'. Using the names of sentences we also form another group of expressions, which ascribe a certain truth-value to those sentences. [Cp] is thus the name of an expression, while $[Cp]_{t'}$, T[Cp] and $T[Cp]_{t'}$ are expressions about that expression. For a detailed list see the table of formulae which follows.

I.3 LIST OF SYMBOLS

a, b, c	constants for states of affairs
p, q, r	variables for state of affairs
~p	negation of a variable for state of affairs
X, Y, Z	constants for propositions
P, Q, R	variables for propositions
[P], [Q], [R]	names of variables for propositions
l, (k), m, n	sentence constants
Cp	it is the case that p / p is the case
C~p	it is the case that ~p / ~p is the case
[Ca]	name of the sentence 'it is the case that a'
[Cp]	name of the open sentence 'it is the case that p'
¬Cp	it is not the case that p
T[P]	P is simply true
F[P]	P is simply false
T[Cp]	the sentence 'it is the case that p' is simply true
F[Cp]	the sentence 'it is the case that p' is simply false
T_i[Cp]	the sentence 'it is the case that p' is true in an indefinite way
F_i[Cp]	the sentence 'it is the case that p' is false in an indefinite way
T_d[Cp]	the sentence 'it is the case that p' is true in a definite way
F_d[Cp]	the sentence 'it is the case that p' is false in a definite way
$\rho, \sigma, \tau, \tau_1, \tau_2, \tau_3$	constants for moments of time
t', t'', t'''	variables for moments of time
tn	now (nunc)
tp, tf	constants for past, constants for future periods of time
t' < t''	t' is prior to t'' in time
t' ≤ t''	t' is prior to t'' in time or is simultaneous
t' > t''	t' follows t'' in time
$S_1, S_2, S_3, \dots$	constants for nodes
$Lv(S_i)$	the level of the node S_i
$Dev(S_j, S_i)$	the node S_j is a development of the node S_i

$\text{Ass}([P], S_i)=1$	the truth-value 1 is assigned to P in the node S_i
$\text{Ass}([P], S_i)=0$	the truth-value 0 is assigned to P in the node S_i
$S_i \in \mathbf{R}$	the node S_i belongs to the path $\mathbf{R}$ constituting the "real" history of the world
$T^*([P], S_i)$	P has the assigned truth-value 1 in the node S_i
$F^*([P], S_i)$	P has the assigned truth-value 0 in the node S_i
$C\tau_1 p$	at the moment τ_1 it is the case that p
$C_{t'}p$	at the moment t' it is the case that p
$C_{t'}C_{t''}p$	at the moment t' it is the case that at moment t" it is the case that p
DCp	it is decided that p is the case
UCp	it is undecided whether p is the case
$D_{tn}C_{t'}p$	it is now decided that p is the case at t'
$U_{t'}C_{t''}p$	it is undecided at t' whether p is the case at t"
PCp	it is possible that p be the case
NCp	it is necessary that p be the case
$N_{t'}C_{t''}p$	it is necessary at moment t' that p be the case at moment t"
KCp	it is contingent (possible, but not necessary) that p be the case
$K_{t'}C_{t''}p$	it is contingent at moment t' that p is the case at instant t"
$N_a Cp$	it is absolutely necessary that p be the case
$N_b Cp$	it is conditionally necessary that p be the case
$NT[Cp]$	the sentence 'p is the case' is necessarily true
$NF[Cp]$	the sentence 'p is the case' is necessarily false
$KF[Cp]$	it is contingent that the sentence 'p is the case' be false
$N_a T[Cp]$	it is absolutely necessary that the sentence 'p is the case' be true
$T_{t'}[C_{t''}p]_{t'''}$	the sentence 'p is the case at moment t"' uttered at moment t''' is true at moment t'
$T_d([P], S_i)$	P is definitely true in the node Si
$T_i([P], S_i)$	P is indefinitely true in the node Si
$T_d^*[P]$	P is definitely true in the sense used by Alexander of Aphrodisias
(x)	universal quantification
$\exists x$	existential quantification
$\bullet$	and
$\succ\!\!\!-\!\!\!\prec$	or (exclusive)
$\vee$	or
$\rightarrow$	if ... then ...

| G,H | predicates |
| SFCS | singular future contingent sentence |

I.4 LIST OF PRINCIPLES AND FORMULAS[1]

A. *Principles of Correspondence*

C(01)   N{(T[Cp] ↔ Cp) • (T[C~p] ↔ C~p) • (F[Cp] ↔ ¬Cp) •
(F([C~p] ↔ ¬C~p)}

C(02)   (Cp→T_d[Cp]) • (C~p→T_d[C~p])

C(03)   N{(T[Cp] → Cp) • (T[C~p] → C~p) • (F[Cp] → ¬Cp) •
(F[C~p] → ¬C~p)}

C(04)   N{(Cp → T[Cp]) • (C~p → T[C~p]) • (¬Cp → F[Cp]) •
(¬C~p → F[C~p])}

C(11)   (t′)(t″)(p){(t″≤ t′• T_{t′}[C_{t′}p]) → C_{t′}·C_{t′}p}

C(12)   (t′)(t″)(p){(t″≤ t′ • T_{t′}[C_{t′}p]) → ¬ C_{t′}¬ C_{t′}p}

C(13)   (t′)(t″)(p){(t″< t′• C_{t′}p • [C_{t′}p]_{t″}) → T_{t′}[C_{t′}p]}

C(21)   (T[Cp] → NCp) • (T[C~p] → NC~p) • (F[Cp] → N¬Cp) •
(F[C~p] → N¬C~p)

C(22)   (T_d[Cp] → NCp) • (T_d[C~p] → N(C~p) • (F_d[Cp] → N¬Cp) •
(F_d[C~p] → N¬C~p)

C(23)   (NCp→T_d[Cp]) • (NC~p→T_d[C~p]) • (N¬Cp→F_d[Cp]) •
(N¬C~p→F_d[C~p])

C(24)   (NT[Cp] → NCp) • (NT[C~p] → NC~p) • (NF[Cp] → N¬Cp) •
(NF[C~p] → N¬C~p)

C(25)   (T_d[Cp] ↔ NCp) • (T_d[C~p] ↔ NC~p) • (F_d[Cp] ↔ N¬Cp) •
(F_d[C~p] ↔ N¬C~p)

C(26)   (KCp ↔ KT[Cp])

C(28)   (N_aT[Cp] ↔ N_aCp) • (N_aT[C~p] ↔ N_aC~p) • (N_aF[Cp] ↔ N_a¬Cp) •
(N_aF[C~p] ↔ N_a¬C~p)

C(29)   (N_bT[Cp] ↔ N_bCp) • (N_bT[C~p] ↔ N_bC~p) • N_bF[Cp] ↔ N_b¬Cp) •
(N_bF[C~p] ↔ N_b¬C~p)

C(30)   (t′)(t″){t″≤ t′→ (N_{t′}T_{t′}[C_{t′}p]_{t′} ↔ N_{t′}C_{t′}p)}

C(31)   {(T[Cp] • F[C~p]) ⟩–⟨ (T[C~p] • F[Cp])} → (NCp ⟩–⟨ NC~p)

C(32)   {(T[Cp] • F[C~p]) ⟩–⟨ (T[C~p] • F[Cp])} → N(Cp ⟩–⟨ C~p)

---

[1]   N.B.: These are not Principles and Formulas that the authors of the texts hold in
each case, but rather tools used to clarify the different positions attributed to ancient
philosophers.

C(33) $\{(T[Cp] \succ\!\!\prec T[C\!\sim\!p]) \bullet (F[Cp] \succ\!\!\prec F[C\!\sim\!p])\} \rightarrow (NCp \succ\!\!\prec NC\!\sim\!p)$

C(34) $N(\{(T[Cp] \bullet F[C\!\sim\!p]) \succ\!\!\prec (T[C\!\sim\!p] \bullet F[Cp])\} \rightarrow (Cp \succ\!\!\prec C\!\sim\!p))$

C(40) $(t')(t'')(p)\{(t'' < t' \bullet C_t p \bullet [D_{t'}C_t p]_{t'}) \rightarrow T_{t'}[D_{t'}C_t p]\}$

C(41) $(t')(t'')(p)\{(t'' < t' \bullet C_t p \bullet [N_{t'}C_t p]_{t'}) \rightarrow T_{t'}[N_{t'}C_t p]\}$

C(42) $(t')(t'')(p)\{N_a C_{t'}p \rightarrow N_a T_{t'}[C_t p]_{t'}\}$

(T) $T[C_\tau p] =_{df} \exists S_i (S_i \in \mathbf{R} \bullet T^*([C_\tau p], S_i))$

(F) $F[C_\tau p] =_{df} \exists S_i (S_i \in \mathbf{R} \bullet F^*([C_\tau p], S_i))$

B. Principles of Truth

T(04) $\neg P(F[Cp] \bullet F[C\!\sim\!p])$

T(05) $\neg P(T[Cp] \bullet T[C\!\sim\!p])$

T(09) $(T_d[Cp] \succ\!\!\prec F_d[Cp]) \bullet (T_d[C\!\sim\!p] \succ\!\!\prec F_d[C\!\sim\!p])$

T(10) $N\{(T[Cp] \succ\!\!\prec F[Cp]) \bullet (T[C\!\sim\!p] \succ\!\!\prec F[C\!\sim\!p])\}$

T(11) $N\{(T[Cp] \succ\!\!\prec T[C\!\sim\!p]) \bullet (F[Cp] \succ\!\!\prec F[C\!\sim\!p])\}$

T(12) $\neg P(T[Cp] \bullet T[C\!\sim\!p]) \bullet \neg P(F[Cp\} \bullet F[C\!\sim\!p])$

T(13) $N\{(T[Cp] \bullet F[C\!\sim\!p]) \succ\!\!\prec (F[Cp] \bullet T[C\!\sim\!p])\}$

T(14) $N(T_d[Cp] \succ\!\!\prec T_d[C\!\sim\!p])$

T(15) $N\{(T_d[Cp] \bullet F_d[C\!\sim\!p]) \succ\!\!\prec (T_d[C\!\sim\!p] \bullet F_d[Cp])\}$

T(16) $N\{(T[Cp] \leftrightarrow F[C\!\sim\!p]) \bullet (F[Cp] \leftrightarrow T[C\!\sim\!p])\}$

T(17) $NT[Cp] \rightarrow N_a T[Cp]$

T(18) $(t')(t'')([Cp])\{(t' \leq t'' \bullet T_{t'}[C_t p]_{t'}) \rightarrow NT_{t'}[C_t p]_{t'}\}$

T(19) $(t')(t'')(t''')([Cp])\{(t''' < t' \leq t'' \bullet N_a T_{t'}[C_t p]_{t'}) \rightarrow N_a T_{t''}[C_t p]_{t''}\}$

T(20) $(t')(t'')([Cp])\{(t' > t'' \bullet T_{t'}[C_t p]_{t'}) \rightarrow NT_{t'}[C_t p]_{t'}$

T(21) $(t')(t'')(t''')([Cp])\{(t''' < t' \leq t'' \bullet T_{t'}[C_t p]_{t'}) \rightarrow (NT_{t'}[C_t p]_{t'} \bullet NT_{t'''}[C_t p]_{t'''})\}$

T(22) $(t')(t'')(t''')([Cp])\{(t''' < t' \leq t'' \bullet T_{t'}[C_t p]_{t'}) \rightarrow T_{t''}[C_t p]_{t''}\}$

(EM) $T[P] \vee \neg T[P]$ Extended Law of the Excluded Middle

(PB) $T[P] \vee F[P]$ Principle of Bivalence

(PB†) $T[P] \vee T[\neg P]$ Principle of Bivalence

(PB*) $T_d^* [P] \vee T_d^* [\neg P]$

(T*) $T^*([C_\tau p], S_i) =_{df} Ass([C_\tau p], S_i) = 1$

(F*) $F^*([C_\tau p], S_i) =_{df} Ass([C_\tau p], S_i) = 0$

(PA) $T^*([C_\tau p], S_i) \vee F^*([C_\tau p], S_i) \rightarrow Lv(S_i) \geq \tau$

(AT) $T^*([C_\tau p], S_i) \rightarrow (S_j)(Dev(S_j, S_i) \rightarrow T^*([C_\tau p], S_j))$

(AF) $F^*([C_\tau p], S_i) \rightarrow (S_j)(Dev(S_j, S_i) \rightarrow F^*([C_\tau p], S_j))$

(AP) $Lv(S_i) \geq \tau \to T^*([C_\tau p], S_i) \vee F^*([C_\tau p], S_i)$

(APA) $Lv(S_i) \geq \tau \leftrightarrow T^*([C_\tau p], S_i) \vee F^*([C_\tau p], S_i)$

(T$_D$) $T_d([C_\tau p], S_i) =_{df} T^*([C_\tau p], S_i) \bullet S_i \in \mathbf{R}$

(T$_D$†) $T_d([C_\tau p], S_i) =_{df} T([C_\tau p] \bullet T^*([C_\tau p], S_i)$

(T$_I$) $T_i([C_\tau p], S_i) =_{df} T([C_\tau p] \bullet \exists S_j (Dev(S_j, S_i) \bullet F^*[C_\tau p], S_j)$

C. Principles of Facts

F(03) $(t')(t'')(p)\{(t'' < t' \bullet C_t p) \to N_{t'} C_t p\}$

F(04) $(t')(t'')(p)\{(t'' \geq t' \bullet C_t p) \to N_{t'} C_t p\}$

F(10) $Cp \to NCp$

F(11) $N(Cp \succ\!\!\prec C{\sim}p)$

F(12) $NCp \succ\!\!\prec NC{\sim}p$

F(13) $(p)(t')\{(C_{t'} p \to N_{t'} C_{t'} p) \bullet (C_{t'}{\sim}p \to N_{t'} C_{t'}{\sim}p)\}$

F(14) $(p)(t')\{(\neg C_{t'} p \to \neg P_{t'} C_{t'} p) \bullet (\neg C_{t'}{\sim}p \to \neg P_{t'} C_{t'}{\sim}p)\}$

F(15) $(t')(t'')(p)(\neg C_{t''} \neg C_{t'} p \leftrightarrow C_{t'} C_{t'} p)$

F(16) $C{\sim}p \leftrightarrow \neg Cp$

(EM*) $P \vee \neg P$ Law of the Excluded Middle

D. Modal Principles

M(5) $(t')(t'')(p)(\{(t'' < t' \bullet D_{t'} C_t p) \to N_{t'} C_t p\}$

M(11) $NC{\sim}p \leftrightarrow \neg PCp$

M(12) $NCp \to \neg KCp$

M(13) $\neg PCp \to \neg KCp$

M(14) $(T[Cp] \to Cp) \to (NT[Cp] \to NCp)$

M(21) $([Cp])(NT[Cp] \to N_a T[Cp])$

Part II

Introduction

II Introduction. Future Contingencies: The problem and its possible solutions

by Gerhard Seel

II.1 Aristotle

It all began with a great insight. In Book IV of the *Metaphysics*, Aristotle formulates and defends the following logical and semantic principles:

1. An assertive sentence is true if and only if what it asserts is the case, false if it is not the case.
2. Every assertive sentence is either true or false.[2]
3. Two contradictory assertive sentences cannot both be true.
4. Two contradictory assertive sentences cannot both be false.

Today, we call the first of these 'the correspondence principle of truth' (cp. C(01) in our list of principles), the second is called 'the principle of bivalence' (cp. T(10) in our list of principles of truth), the third is called 'the principle of non-contradiction' (cp. T(05)) and the last is called 'the principle of the excluded middle' (cp. T(04)). The same principles are found in other important texts, for example, the *Categories*, the *De Interpretatione* and the *Analytics*.

In the *Metaphysics*, Aristotle first introduces and defends the third of these principles (1005b5-1011b22)[3], qualifying it as the 'best established of all principles' (1005b18-19; b22-23); he then formulates the fourth principle (1011 b23-25), making use, in one of the arguments in its defence, of the first and the second principles, i.e. the correspondence principle and the principle of bivalence (1011b26-29). In modern propositional logic, principles 2, 3 and 4 are equivalent, given the definition of the negator as the operator which, when added, changes a true proposition into a false proposition and vice versa. Aristotle himself might have held a similar position (as we believe), but the issue is far from settled.

---

[2] Since for Aristotle and for philosophers of the Hellenistic period an assertive sentence can in principle change its truth-value, the principle must be understood as meaning: at any time any assertive sentence is either true or false.

[3] The principle is first formulated as an ontological principle (1005b19-22), then as a law of thinking (1005b23-32) and finally as a principle of logic (1011b13-15). It is on the last of these that we focus in the following pages.

Aristotle's theory seems to be clearly articulated and to be defended on solid grounds. Difficulties began, however, when Aristotle discovered (or developed) a certain kind of argument that deduced from the four above- mentioned principles that every event in the world is a necessary event. This theory is called 'logical determinism', since it reaches a deterministic conclusion from purely logical and semantic premises. Determinism[4] was a problem for Aristotle, and for many others, because it seemed to make free human action impossible and moral judgement pointless.

The 'locus classicus' of logical determinism is the famous chapter 9 of the *De Interpretatione*. Here, Aristotle describes two deterministic arguments. Both conclude from the truth of a statement that predicts a future event the necessity of that event. The way the conclusion is reached is different in each case, but both arguments rely on the four fundamental logical and semantic principles.[5] Most of the critical literature focuses on the second of these arguments; it consists of the following steps:[6]

1. Let us claim that a state of affairs p is the case at the present instant t_n.
2. Then at each moment of the past it was true to affirm that p will be the case at t_n.
3. Therefore at each moment of the past it was not the case that p does not occur at t_n.
4. Therefore at each moment of the past it was not possible that p will not be the case at t_n.
5. So at each moment of the past it was necessary that p will be the case at t_n.

The step from (1) to (2) is made by the principle of the retrogradation of truth, C(13). The next step uses the principle of the simultaneity of the truth of a statement and the corresponding fact, C(11), C(12). The third step applies the principle of the necessity of facts (conditional necessity), F(13) and F(14), to these past facts. The final step consists of a simple transformation of modalities. This argument creates a puzzle for Aristotle, i.e. an ἀπορία, in the technical sense of the term given by Hellenistic Philosophy.[7] According to this conception, an ἀπορία was a set of evident assertoric sentences, the members of which cannot be true together; there was usually a technical demonstration showing that a given set

---

[4]   Determinism is the position that every event or occurrent in the real world is predetermined from eternity in such a way that there is no moment in the history of the world at which it is undecided whether or not the event will occur. In the case of Aristotle, determinism is a consequence of necessitarianism. Necessitarianism is the position that there are no contingent states of affairs. Cp. p.19 below.

[5]   For the details see our Commentary pp.171-175 and 182-185.

[6]   For further details see our comments on paragraph 16 of Ammonius' Commentary, pp.182-185. For the first proof see our Commentary on the second lemma pp.171-176.

[7]   For the meaning of the term ἀπορία in the Hellenistic period see G. Seel 1993, 295–301.

of sentences was inconsistent in this way. The demonstration consisted of choosing one of the sentences of the set, taking the other sentences as premises and deducing from these the contradictory of the chosen sentence. The ἀπορία, which literally means a situation when there is 'no way out', results from the fact that on the one hand the inconsistency of the set necessitates the rejection of at least one of its members, while on the other hand, since all the sentences are evident, none can be rejected. ἀπορίαι were usually the object of a special procedure called a λύσις, i.e. a resolution. This consisted either in arguing that one of the seemingly evident sentences was in fact false or in showing that the proof of inconsistency was unsound.

We can interpret chapter 9 of the *De Interpretatione* as a genuine ἀπορία in the above sense. The set of sentences that were evident to Aristotle were the four logical and semantic principles and the thesis that there are contingent events in the world. That this set is inconsistent is shown by the two demonstrations of universal necessitarianism that use the four logical and semantic principles as premises and have as their conclusion the contradictory of the thesis. It is therefore plausible to take the rest of chapter 9 as Aristotle's attempt to resolve this ἀπορία. How could this be achieved?

A possible solution, and indeed the most likely, would be to dispense (either totally or partially) with the principles that cause the trouble. To find out whether Aristotle actually took this step, a first group of interpreters concentrated their attention on the four logical and semantic principles. It is hard to see, however, how Aristotle could possibly have rejected a principle that he considered the best established and most fundamental of all. It would of course be more likely that, instead of completely giving up one or other of those principles, Aristotle simply restricted their scope. Since determinism results only when these principles are applied to future tense sentences, Aristotle could restrict their application to sentences in the present or past tense. It is especially the principle of bivalence that creates the trouble. So a possible solution to the ἀπορία would be to argue that sentences about future contingent facts are neither true nor false, i.e. to exempt them from the principle of bivalence. This would also entail certain modifications to the principles of non-contradiction and of the excluded middle. These need to be conditioned in the following way: If and only if two contradictory sentences have truth-values, then one is true and the other false. These principles would thus apply only to those sentences that actually have truth values. This means that sentences about future contingent events would not fall under these principles. Thus the deterministic arguments would not be sound any more. This solution is called 'the standard solution' and the belief that Aristotle employed the standard solution is called 'the standard interpretation'.[8]

---

[8]   Sometimes (cp. N. Kretzmann 1998, 24-25) the standard interpretation is identified with Lukasiewicz's interpretation, according to which Aristotle not only limited the scope of the principle of bivalence, but also introduced a third truth value, i.e. the value 'neither true nor false', that is supposed to be the value of future contingent sentences.

However, it is highly controversial whether Aristotle actually made this move. The thesis that he did not is known as 'the non-standard interpretation'.[9] There is, of course, more than one version of the non-standard interpretation. They all attempt to prove that instead of limiting the scope of the principle of bivalence Aristotle either limited the scope of one of the other principles used in the proof of determinism or else tried to show that the proofs were unsound. Obvious candidates for the first procedure are the principle of the necessity of facts, F (10), and the truth-to-necessity-principle, C (21). Some interpreters believe that Aristotle denied the validity of these principles for certain future facts and for sentences about this kind of fact. Those who hold that Aristotle found the proofs unsound argue that they rely on a confusion of *necessitas consequentiae* and *necessitas consequentis* and that Aristotle criticises this confusion in the final remarks of chapter 9.[10]

Defenders of the standard interpretation could argue, and some did, that the standard solution is nothing but a consequence of Aristotle's principle of correspondence.[11] According to this principle, an assertoric sentence is true if and only if there is a fact in the real world corresponding to the assertion made in the sentence. In today's semantics, we call this fact the sentence's 'truth- maker'. It could be doubted that sentences about future contingent types of event can have a truth-maker. Firstly, the fact asserted in a future tense sentence is, at the time of the utterance of the sentence, a future fact. Secondly, future contingent facts are undecided at the time of the utterance of the sentence, i.e. at that moment, it is completely open whether or not the corresponding type of event will occur. Therefore, sentences asserting future contingent facts lack both a simultaneous correspondent fact and a decided correspondent fact. If the principle of correspondence states that each sentence needs a simultaneous and a decided correspondent fact in order for that sentence to be true, then there are good reasons to deny that sentences about future contingent types of events can be either true or false. Of course, it is not certain that Aristotle actually understood the principle in this way, but, if he did, it would be quite natural for him to adopt the standard solution. Defenders of the non-standard solution argue that the standard solution is unnecessarily radical. Aristotle did not need to deny the existence of future facts and the truth of sentences about those future facts. He could simply doubt that those facts are necessary in each case and that the truth of the correspondent sentences implies the necessity of those facts.

However, there is no evidence in Aristotle that he ever thought of such a truth value.

[9] This expression was first used by N. Rescher 1963, 139f.

[10] Cp. J. Pacius 1597b, 82; M. Lowe 1980, 55-57; G. Fine 1984, 23, 36-38.

[11] Cp. D. Frede 1985, 75, and H. Weidemann 1994, 294.

II.2 The Dialectical School (Diodorus Cronus)

After Aristotle, the dispute about logical determinism continued on a more complicated level. Members of the so-called 'Dialectical School', and then the Stoics, introduced different semantics for the modalities and on that basis constructed new arguments. The new logical and semantic presuppositions of the Hellenistic debate make it necessary to distinguish clearly between determinism, necessitarianism and fatalism. As I understand it, determinism is the thesis that for every event[12] in the real world there is, in a past-to-future perspective, no moment in the history of the world at which it is undecided whether that event will or will not occur. Thus, every event is predetermined from eternity. We saw in the case of *De Interpretatione* 9 that determinism is a consequence of necessitarianism. The latter is the thesis that every fact is a necessary fact or that there are no contingent states of affairs. However, a determinist need not be a necessitarian; as we shall see, there are semantics of the modalities that avoid this implication. Moreover, determinism follows from fatalism as well, but fatalism does not include necessitarianism. That these positions do not entail one another is clearly shown by the case of Chrysippus, who was certainly a fatalist, but who did not accept necessitarianism. By fatalism I intend the thesis that for every event at any moment before its occurrence there is a nexus of causal factors that ineluctably brings it about.[13]

Scholars usually consider Diodorus Cronus as the first and most prominent Hellenistic defender of determinism. Although he was not a necessitarian, he grounded his determinism on semantics of the modalities. Let us see how this was achieved. In Diodorus' semantics, the so called 'Master Argument' seems to have played an important role. This argument also starts from an ἀπορία. As Epictetus[14] reports, the ἀπορία consisted of the following three principles:

1. Every past truth is necessary.
2. Something impossible does not follow from something possible.
3. There is something possible which neither is nor will be true.

Epictetus goes on to tell us that Diodorus "saw this conflict (the conflict between the three principles) and exploited the convincingness of the first two to establish the conclusion that

'Nothing which neither is nor will be true is possible'."

---

[12] S. Bobzien 1998a, 26-27 introduced the term 'occurrent' for the entities we are talking about.
[13] This is our formulation. For the exact way Chrysippus in particular and the Stoics in general defined the principle of fate see S. Bobzien 1998a, 56-58; 301-314.
[14] Epictetus *Diss.* 2.19,1-10=*FDS* 993, transl. A. Long and D. Sedley 1987, vol. 1, 230-1.

The principle given in the conclusion is clearly contradictory to the third principle, and the fact that this conclusion is demonstrated by the first two principles proves that the original set of three principles was inconsistent. Diodorus' solution to the ἀπορία was to reject the third principle and replace it with the conclusion of the proof. Unfortunately we do not know exactly how Diodorus proceeded in his proof. There are a lot of reconstructions, but so far none has been universally accepted.

It is, however, clear that Diodorus somehow made use of his first principle to show that from something possible (according to the third principle) something impossible would follow, i.e. exactly what the second principle denies. It seems that in showing this he must have made tacit use of at least one further principle, but it is unclear exactly what this was. In one of my articles,[15] I have tried to reconstruct Diodorus' argument, supposing that he made use of the principle of conditional necessity as an additional premise. This principle, F(10), states that if a state of affairs p is the case, then it is necessary that p is the case. With this principle it can easily been shown that the possibility of something that neither is nor will be implies a contradiction and thus something impossible. I argued that Diodorus could have arrived at F(10) by tacitly widening the scope of premise (1) from past facts to all facts. To that R. Gaskin has—rightly— objected[16] that the scope of premise (1) cannot be widened because it explicitly restricts conditional necessity to past facts. However, Diodorus could have meant to include past facts concerning future events. He could have argued that if it is a fact (now) that p neither is nor will be the case, it has always been a fact in the past that from now on it will not be the case. If this is so, we do not need to widen the scope of premise (1). We can deduce directly from the original premise (1) that it has always been necessary that the state of affairs, the possibility of which is in question, neither is the case nor will be the case. This is the reconstruction given by Long and Sedley.[17]

Let me briefly return to R. Gaskin's reconstruction, which will be very useful for the interpretation of an argument discussed below. In his reconstruction Gaskin uses a principle that he calls the principle of "relativity of modality to the facts" (1995,288-299). By this he understands a "self-evident meaning rule for the modal operators" that requires (in the present case) anything possible to be coherent with the given facts. Now, the possibility of something that neither is nor will be the case is, according to Gaskin, not coherent with the facts. This is shown in the following way. Suppose p to be possible, but never the case from now on; we then get ¬Cp as a given fact. If we then suppose the actuality of p in order to test its possibility according to the second premise, we get as the hypothetical outcome Cp • ¬Cp, which is clearly a contradiction. Is the reconstruction sound?

---

[15]   G. Seel, Diodore domine-t-il Aristote? (1982b, 293-313)
[16]   R. Gaskin 1995, 294 n.19.
[17]   Cp. A. Long and D. Sedley 1987, vol. 1, 234.

I think not. By making the hypothesis that p is the case we make the implicit hypothesis that its contradictory is not the case. The given fact that the latter is the case does not, of course, prevent us supposing, as a mere hypothesis, its not being the case. Gaskin holds that the notion of modality relative to the facts does not allow this. In my opinion, however, the only situation that could prevent this would be the necessity of the fact that ~p. It is thus clear that some version of the principle of conditional necessity is needed in order to deduce a contradiction.[18]

The definition of the impossible (i.e. that which neither is nor will be true) given in the conclusion of Diodorus' demonstration forms the core of the system of Diodorean modalities:[19]

necessary	contingent	impossible
that which from now on		
is and always will be true	is sometimes true and sometimes false	is and will be always false

These definitions show that Diodorus was not a necessitarian, because he admits contingent states of affairs. At first glance, this leaves unanswered whether he was a determinist. One may doubt that he was, because his definition of the possible seems to allow that the exact moment of the realisation of a possible state of affairs is undecided at any time before its realisation. However, as soon as we apply Diodorean modalities to sentences that predict the occurrence of a type of event at a precise time, we see that deterministic consequences follow from the definitions of these modalities.[20] Sentences of that kind are always true if they are once true.[21] It is doubtful, however, that Diodorean modalities were to be applied to this kind of sentence. They are rather an example of what I have called 'omnitemporal' modalities.[22] They apply to entities that can exist at any moment from now on and to sentences about those entities.

The question whether or not all future events are predetermined was answered by another argument developed by the Dialectical School, the so called

---

[18]   R. Gaskin 1995, 288 note 12 claims that his interpretation of Aristotle's definition of possibility that includes relativity to the facts coincides with mine (as stated in 1982a, 334 - 336). He does not see that I emphasise (in 1982a, 335 note 82a) that any deduction of a contradiction of the kind used in the Master Argument presupposes the principle of conditional necessity, a principle that Aristotle accepted for present and past facts.

[19]   Cp. S. Bobzien 1993, 83-84.

[20]   This is probably the sense of Cicero's testimony about Diodorus in *De fato* 13.

[21]   There is, however, a problem in that the ancients did not use speaker-independent time indices. So the only examples they could give were sentences about types of events that cannot occur more than once, such as being born and dying. Cp. S. Bobzien 1998a, 98-101.

[22]   Cp. G. Seel 1982a, 218ff. where these are called 'nichtzeitgebundene Modalbegriffe'.

'Reaper Argument'. This could have been a corollary argument to the 'Master Argument', meant to close a loophole left open by the latter. The Reaper Argument is also based on an *ἀπορία*. In the simplest and possibly oldest version of the argument this *ἀπορία* consisted of the following four sentences:

1.   If you are going to reap, it is not undecided whether you will reap or will not reap; it is decided that you will reap.
2.   If you are not going to reap, it is not undecided whether you will reap or will not reap; it is decided that you will not reap.
3.   It is necessary that you are either going to reap or not going to reap.
4.   It is undecided whether you will reap or will not reap.

By taking sentences (1), (2) and (3) as premises and by deducing from them the contradictory of (4), the inventor of the Reaper Argument demonstrated both the inconsistency of the original set of four sentences and the truth of determinism.

In the version we find in Ammonius' commentary a second proof is added. This second proof has the conclusion of the first proof as its first premise. Its second premise is the principle that contingency presupposes undecidedness. From these two premises it is deduced that there are no contingent facts. Thus, while one version of the Reaper Argument is just a demonstration of determinism, the more complex version appears to be a proof of necessitarianism.[23]

II.3 The Stoics

How did Hellenistic philosophers react to these arguments? One would imagine that not all would accept the deterministic or necessitarian solutions to the two *ἀπορίαι*. Let us first see what happened in the Stoic school. Epictetus tells us that Cleanthes, followed by Antipater, resolved the *ἀπορία* of the Master Argument by rejecting premise (1) and keeping the other two. They thus preserved the position commonly held by the Stoics that there are types of events which have the possibility to happen but nonetheless never happen. Epictetus then tells us that Chrysippus' solution to the *ἀπορία* was different, namely the rejection of the second principle in order to keep the first and the third. Chrysippus' argument was as follows. Take the true conditional 'If Dio is dead, this one is dead'. Since this is a true conditional the second proposition (*ἀξίωμα*) follows from the first.[24] However, the first proposition (*ἀξίωμα*) is possible while the second is impossible, because according to Stoic semantics the deiktical expression 'this

---

23   Cp. G. Seel 1993, 318. In this paper I argue that the second premise of the second proof uses a notion of contingency that is different from that of Diodorus and that it is probable therefore that the second proof was added at a later date by people who understood determinism in terms of necessitarianism.

24   Like most scholars we translate the Stoic term *ἀξίωμα* by 'proposition' and not by 'sentence'. Note, however, that what the Stoics called *ἀξίωμα* differs in several respects from the modern proposition.

one' can be used only of someone existing at the present moment, and when Dio is dead, he no longer exists. So according to Chrysippus, in this example, something impossible follows from something possible. This means that the second principle of the Master Argument is false.

We know from several sources that the Stoics also attacked the Reaper Argument, but while we are aware of their general line of argument, we do not definitely know which of the premises of the argument they tried to refute. There is, however, some indirect evidence to suggest that they must have attacked the second premise of the second part of the argument. As we shall see, the Stoics accepted premises (1), (2) and (3). They must therefore have accepted the conclusion of the first stage, i.e. that there are no undecided future events, a thesis which is perfectly in line with Stoic determinism.[25] On the other hand, the Stoics could not have accepted the conclusion of the second stage of the argument, i.e. that there are no contingent states of affairs: their semantics of the modalities prove that there are contingent states of affairs.[26] The Reaper Argument demonstrates the contrary by stating – in the second premise of the second part of the argument – that contingency presupposes undecidedness.

Let us investigate these points one after the other. The Stoics accepted the principles of bivalence and of the excluded middle for the same reasons that they would have accepted premises (1), (2) and (3) of the Reaper Argument. In *Fat.* 20-21, Cicero reports an argument by which Chrysippus deduced fatalism by using the principle of bivalence as one of the premises. Cicero goes on to say that Chrysippus used various arguments to support this principle, but unfortunately he omits to tell us what these arguments were. His testimony is, however, sufficient to show that Chrysippus accepted the principle of bivalence.[27] Given the Stoic conception of negation this implies the principle of the excluded middle.[28]

The way Chrysippus deduced fatalism from the principle of bivalence allows us to understand how he conceived the truth-maker of future tense propositions ($\dot{\alpha}\xi\iota\dot{\omega}\mu\alpha\tau\alpha$).The argument has the following overall structure:[29]

Step one

(P1) The Principle of Bivalence implies the General Causal Principle.

---

[25]   This is probably the reason why the Anonymous Commentator on the *De Interpretatione* (Tarán) 54,8-55,5 (*FDS* 1253, 4) thought that the Stoics themselves used the Reaper Argument to refute contingency, but this is certainly not the case.

[26]   In 1993, 318 I claim that Chrysippus' definition of the contingent excludes determinism. This, however, is correct if and only if 'determinism' means 'necessitarian determinism', as supposed in the article. It is, of course, incorrect if determinism is understood in the sense given above.

[27]   That the Stoics generally accepted the principle of bivalence is well attested. Cp. besides Cicero, *Fat.* 20-21, Cicero, *Ac. pr.* 30,95; Simplicius, *In Arist. Cat.* 406,21ff. Cp. also M. Frede 1974, 40-44.

[28]   Cp. Alexander of Aphr., *In Arist. Anal. pr.*, 402,33-35.

[29]   I use the reconstruction given by S. Bobzien 1998a, 85.

(P2) The Principle of Bivalence holds.
(C1) Therefore the General Causal Principle holds as well.

Step two

(P4) The General Causal Principle implies the Fate Principle.
(C1/P3) The General Causal Principle holds.
(C2) Therefore the Fate Principle holds as well.

The General Causal Principle is that there is no motion without cause. The Fate Principle is that everything happens in accordance with fate.

For our present purposes, only the first step is important. What, according to Chrysippus, is the relation between the truth of propositions (ἀξιώματα) and the causation of events? It should firstly be noted that the Stoics held a kind of correspondence theory of truth, articulated in a special technical vocabulary. According to this theory, a proposition (ἀξίωμα) is true when it is actualised and false when it is not actualised (Sextus Empiricus, *M.* VIII 10): a proposition (ἀξίωμα), for example 'Dio is walking', is actualised when the predicate 'is walking' is actualised in the real object Dio or when Dio is actually walking. This is to say that a proposition (ἀξίωμα) is true if and only if the correspondent state of affairs is the case (Diog. Laert. VII,65).[30] This principle is unproblematic in the case of propositions (ἀξιώματα) about present states of affairs, because for each of these propositions (ἀξιώματα) there is a simultaneous fact that makes the proposition true or false. However, when a proposition (ἀξίωμα) is about an event that will occur at some time in the future, it may be asked whether there is anything at all that makes it true or false. If one assumes, as the Stoics seem to, that the truth-maker of a proposition must be simultaneous with the utterance of the proposition, then the event predicted by a future tense proposition cannot be its truth-maker because it is not simultaneous with the utterance of the proposition. We have already seen that this could have been a reason to adopt the standard solution and to restrict the principle of bivalence. If, however, Chrysippus had wanted to retain the principle of bivalence, he had somehow to identify the truth-maker of future tense propositions (ἀξιώματα) and show how it establishes their truth. Let us see how this was done.

As Cicero (*Fat.* 20-21) tells us, Chrysippus used the following principle to defend (P1):

(P5) That which will have no causes to bring it about, will be neither true nor false.

In order to see exactly what Chrysippus meant S. Bobzien rephrased (P5), in my opinion rightly, as follows:

---

30   I find this interpretation of the Stoic theory most convincing, but I do not exclude that a semantic theory (Tarski style) or a redundancy theory of truth (Ramsey style) would also square with the evidence.

If a motion had no causes, a proposition (ἀξίωμα) correlated to that motion would be neither true nor false.

Why is that so ? Unfortunately Cicero omits to tell us Chrysippus' exact reasons; we can only conjecture what they might have been. Let us consider the proposition (ἀξίωμα) 'Dio will walk'. In order to be either true or false this proposition needs a determinate truth-maker or falsity-maker, i.e. some fact that makes it true and its negation false or vice versa. According to the Stoic correspondence theory of truth, the truth-maker must consist of the actualisation of some predicate in some existing object or of some fact. In the case of our proposition this must be a fact about a future motion. We must ask, however, whether for Chrysippus, this is a present fact about a future motion or a future fact about a (then) present motion. In other words, which of the following modern technical affirmations better expresses what Chrysippus had in mind: 'It is a fact now that Dio will walk' or ' It will be a fact that Dio is walking' ?

Although there is no direct evidence to answer this question, there is some indication that Chrysippus rather meant the former. Firstly, there is a passage in Sextus Empiricus (M. VIII 254-5; SVF II 221, part) that clearly shows that the Stoics considered propositions about future events as either true now or false now: in the case of the conditional 'If this man has been wounded in the heart, this man will die', the proposition (ἀξίωμα) 'this man will die' is said about something happening in the future, but 'is present and true even now'. Given the close link between the truth of a proposition and the actualisation of the state of affairs functioning as the proposition's truth-maker (cp. again Sextus Empiricus, M. VIII 10) it is highly likely that what makes these present propositions true is the present actualisation of a future state of affairs and not the future actualisation of a (then) present state of affairs. Moreover, it is unlikely that Chrysippus would have spoken of a future actualisation of something, because he considered only the present as 'actualised'.[31] Given this, he would hardly have accepted a future fact as the truth-maker of a present proposition (ἀξίωμα).

The crucial question for Chrysippus must have been whether a future motion that has no causes could be considered as already actualised in the present. Of course, this was denied. For, according to his theory, what decides whether a future type of event is actualised already now, can only be the present causes that bring it about and thus prevent it from not being actualised. So if there were some event without a cause, its occurrence would be undecided during the time before it occurs. During this time it could not be said that the event is actualised, nor that its contradictory is actualised. So propositions that predict this event will have no truth-maker and no falsity-maker and thus would be neither true nor false.[32] On

---

31   Cp. Stobaeus, Ecl. 1.106,5-23 (W) = SVF II,509; Plutarch, Comm. not. 1081C-1082A; cp. also A.C. Lloyd 1978, 294.

32   S. Bobzien 1998a, 65 has a different explanation of why a proposition (ἀξίωμα) about an event that has no causes is neither false nor true: "It would not be false, since it is actualised. It would not be true, since the motion to which it correlates has

the other hand, if the future event has present causes that bring it about, it is already decided that it will occur. There is therefore a present fact about the future event. The implication of this is that the present proposition already has a definite truth-value at the present time.

Chrysippus' principle (P1), along with the principle of bivalence, has clear deterministic consequences, since the causes in question are, in modern terminology, sufficient causes. However, as already mentioned, Chrysippus was not a necessitarian, i.e. he admitted contingent states of affairs. He was able to do this without giving up his belief in determinism because of his definition of the modalities, which differs significantly from that of Diodorus. S. Bobzien has shown that the system of Chrysippean modalities had the following structure:

necessary	contingent	impossible
that which		
is not internally capable of ever being false or is externally hindered from being false at all times from now on	is internally capable of being true and of being false and nothing external hinders either from being true or from being false at some time from now on	is not internally capable of ever being true or is externally hindered from being true at all times from now on

These definitions allow for the responsible decisions of human agents that are, on the one hand, determined by an eternal chain of causes and yet are, on the other hand, contingent.[33]

II.4 Epicurus

The deterministic arguments developed in the Dialectical School were a challenge not only to the Stoics but also, and even more so, to the Epicureans. There is no evidence of a refutation of the Master Argument by the Epicureans, but Cicero tells us (*Fat.* 21) that Epicurus refuted a deterministic argument very similar to the Reaper Argument.[34] This he did by denying the third premise of that argument, i.e.

---

no causes". To this one may object that if a motion that is actualised prevents a proposition (ἀξίωμα) from being false, it must also make that proposition (ἀξίωμα) true. I rather think that for the Stoics a motion that has no causes is not actualised. To think otherwise would be to contradict the Stoic correspondence theory of truth.

[33]   Cp. S. Bobzien 1998a, 112-119.

[34]   In G. Seel 1993 I argue that the argument refuted by Epicurus was in fact a version of the Reaper Argument.

the Principle of the Excluded Middle.[35] By contrast, *Fat.* 37 suggests that he accepted a version of this principle, i.e. the truth of 'Cp ∨ ¬Cp', but rejected the Principle of Bivalence. Cicero criticises Epicurus for his 'pitiful ignorance of logical discourse'; he might, however, have meant that in the case of future contingent sentences, although only one of a pair of contradictory sentences can and will finally 'come true', neither is true now.[36] If this were the case, it would mean that Epicurus or some Epicurean followed the standard solution to Aristotle's ἀπορία.

Where Cicero reports Epicurus' worries about fatalism at *Fat.* 21 one easily gets the impression that by denying the Principle of Bivalence Epicurus also wanted to refute Chrysippus' proof of fatalism. For, after the presentation of Chrysippus' argument, Cicero continues: 'Epicurus is afraid that, if he grants this (i.e. the Principle of Bivalence), he will have to grant that whatever comes about does so through fate.' If this were correct, Epicurus must have accepted Chrysippus' (P1). This is indeed what a number of scholars have argued,[37] but the issue is far from settled.[38] All the evidence we have is that Epicurus denied the principle that every motion has a cause – or at least this is how later authors such as Cicero understood him: he, in fact, reports that Epicurus allowed motions without preceding causes and that in defence of this position he invented the theory of the swerve (*Fat.* 22; 48).[39]

However that may be, the only point of importance for our purposes is whether Epicurus or the Epicureans developed any new conception of the truth-maker of future tense sentences. The answer is obviously not. There is no evidence for such an innovation. On the contrary, if the Epicureans accepted the standard solution, they must have done so on the basis of the standard conception of the truth-maker.[40]

---

[35] Cp. Cicero, *Fat.* 37; *Nat. Deor.* I 70; *Acad.* II 97.

[36] Cp. S. Bobzien 1998a, 82-83

[37] Cp. J. Vuillemin 1984, 232; J. Talanga 1986a, 112.

[38] Cp. S. Bobzien 1998a, 86. The only passage that supports this interpretation is *Fat.* 19, where Cicero says that Epicurus could grant the Principle of Bivalence without fearing that all things must necessarily come about by fate and then explains the term 'fate' according to the Chrysippean Principle of Fate. However, this could well be Cicero's own view of the meaning of 'fate'.

[39] It is not settled, however, whether Epicurus considered the swerve a motion without cause. He could equally well have understood that it had no sufficient cause.

[40] If Sextus Empiricus, *M.* VII 211-16 (Usener 247) is a reliable report of the Epicurean conception of truth (which is doubtful, cp. D. Sedley 1982, 239-72) it supports our interpretation. According to Sextus, the Epicureans held that an opinion is true if it is attested or uncontested by self-evidence and false if it is contested or unattested by self-evidence. So it can be true only if it is not contested by self-evidence. However, as the Plato example shows, a future contingent sentence that is later contested by self-evidence is false.

II.5 Carneades

A completely new conception of truth and the truth-maker, and hence a new solution to Aristotle's ἀπορία, was discovered by Carneades of the New Academy. According to him, as reported by Cicero, the truth and falsity of a sentence does not depend upon an eternal chain of causes that bring about the correspondent fact, but simply upon the fact itself.[41] The question is, however, whether in the case of future contingent sentences this fact is to be seen as a present fact about a future event or as a future fact about a (then) present event.[42] Unfortunately, Cicero's imprecise language does not allow a definite answer to this question, but the absence of any evidence to the contrary leads us to suppose that Carneades meant the less technical second version. His new conception of the truth-maker of future tense sentences allows him to reject Chrysippus' (P1) and also to admit future contingent events. He could also, of course, avoid the deterministic consequences of both Aristotle's Truth-to-Necessity-Argument and the Reaper-Argument, without giving up the Principle of Bivalence. Defenders of the non-standard interpretation argue that Aristotle himself followed this line of argument.

II.6 The Peripatetic school of Alexander of Aphrodisias

Carneades was not the only philosopher who tried to avoid Stoic fatalism while preserving, along with the Stoics, the principle of bivalence. Most of the later opponents of Stoicism followed Carneades in rejecting the Stoic thesis that fatalism does not imply necessitarianism. Consequently, they understood the Stoics to be necessitarians.[43] It is impossible to discuss here all the details of the debate. I shall rather concentrate on one particular school that found a new solution to Aristotle's ἀπορία, or so it seems, i.e. the Peripatetic School of Alexander of Aphrodisias.

I shall argue that it was this school that discovered a vital distinction that would later allow the neoplatonic commentators, Ammonius and Boethius, to develop a new solution to Aristotle's ἀπορία. As we shall see, they argued that sentences about future contingent events are either true or false, but not definitely so. They tried to show that deterministic consequences would follow only if all assertoric sentences were either definitely true or definitely false, but in fact some

---

41   Cp. Cicero, *Fat.* 19 *quod ita cecidit certe casurum, sicut cecidit, fuit*; *Fat.* 27 *ut praeterita ea vera dicimus quorum superiore tempore vera fuerit instantia, sic futura quorum consequenti tempore vera erit instantia, ea vera dicemus.*
42   Cp. H. Weidemann 1994, 256-259 who seems to opt for the second possibility.
43   For Alexander of Aphrodisias cp. R. Sharples, 1983a, 20-21.

are either indefinitely true or indefinitely false. In this way, the principle of bivalence was preserved and determinism avoided.

Unfortunately, the exact meaning of the terms 'definitely true' and 'indefinitely true' is unclear in the texts of the neoplatonic commentators and is even less clear in the texts of the School of Alexander. Consequently, there is much scholarly debate concerning this new solution to the ἀπορία, as to whether it is a version of the standard solution or of the non-standard solution.

We know little or nothing about Alexander's position concerning the principle of bivalence. In chapter 10 of his *De Fato*, where he discusses Aristotle's example of tomorrow's sea-battle, his main concern is the theory of the Stoics who, of course, accepted the principle of bivalence. However, he never clearly states whether he himself believes that future contingent sentences are either true or false; all he seems to admit is that, if these sentences are true, then the events they predict occur necessarily.[44] However, we do have two important testimonies that seem to show that members of his school accepted the principle of bivalence for future contingent sentences and that they made a distinction between 'definitely true' and 'indefinitely true'. The first piece of evidence is a passage from Simplicius' *Commentary* on Aristotle's *Categories*. Simplicius reports (*in Cat.* 406, 13-16) that a certain Nicostratus[45] denied that future contingent sentences have any truth-values at all. He then contrasts this position with that of the Peripatetics, saying:

> But the Peripatetics say that the contradiction regarding the future is true or false, while it is by nature unseizable and uncertain which part of it is true and which part is false. For nothing prevents us from saying the contradiction with respect to any time, as for instance 'it will be or it will not be', and each of the two parts contained in it, as for instance 'it will be' or 'it will not be', is already (ἤδη) true or false in a definite way (ἀφωρισμένως) with respect to the present or past time. But those parts of a contradiction which are said with respect to the future are not yet (ἤδη) true or false, and they will be true or false. Let these things be sufficient against (πρὸς) Nicostratus.

Of course, we do not know the definite identity of the Peripatetics referred to by Simplicius, but it is possible, and even plausible, that he is referring to the school of Alexander, because the above theory could very well have been a direct reaction to Nicostratus' view, and he lived in the middle of the second century AD.[46]

However this may be, we learn two important things from this passage:

1.   According to the Peripatetics, the principle of bivalence holds for future contingent sentences. In my opinion, this is obvious from the first sentence of the above text, and is confirmed by the fact that the

---

[44]   See also C. Natali 1996, 243 and R. Sharples 1978a, 264.
[45]   Probably a Platonic philosopher of the second century AD. Cp. M. Mignucci in this volume, 280.
[46]   See also M. Mignucci in this volume, 281-284, who is more hesitant about this.

Peripatetic position is said to be opposed to that of Nicostratus, who denied this.

2. The Peripatetics used the distinction between 'already true or false in a definite way' and 'not yet true or false' to characterise the different ways in which sentences about the present or the past and sentences about the future have their truth-values.

Supporters of the standard interpretation could, of course, understand the expression 'not yet true or false' as meaning that future contingent sentences 'have no truth-value at the moment of their utterance'. In this case, the expression 'already true or false in a definite way' would simply mean that sentences about the present or the past 'already have a truth-value'. This, however, would contradict our first point which is well confirmed.

It should not be forgotten that the distinction is between 'already' and 'not yet', and not between 'in a definite way' and 'in an indefinite way'. It is therefore plausible to suppose that the expression following 'not yet' has the same value as the expression following 'already'. In support of this interpretation, M. Mignucci has argued that ἀφωρισμένως can very well be connected to ἤδη μὲν οὐκ ἔστιν ἀληθῆ ἢ ψευδῆ at 407,12-13.[47] If so, there is no longer a contradiction in the text. It says that, according to the Peripatetics, future contingent sentences are either true or false, but not in a definite way, at the time of their utterance. However, we still do not know what the expression 'already in a definite way' as opposed to 'not yet in a definite way' exactly means. To find out, we need a text in which the expression is used to solve Aristotle's ἀπορία.

Luckily for us, such a text does exist, though transmitted in rather poor shape. I am referring to a passage found in *Quaestio* I,4, attributed to Alexander. We cannot be sure that Alexander himself is the author, but it certainly comes from his school.[48] Although the text is not without ambiguities, it helps clarify the meaning of the expression 'definitely true'. We are told that certain (unnamed) people argue the following:

> If that is possible from which, if it is supposed that it is the case, nothing impossible results, and if from everything of which the contradictory is truly said beforehand, there results, if it is supposed that it is the case, the impossibility that the same thing both is and is not at the same time, then none of those things, of which one part of the contradictory disjunction referring to the future is definitely true, would be contingent. But, as they say, in all cases one part of the contradictory disjunction is definitely true. ... So nothing is contingent.[49]

The argument is clearly meant to be a proof of necessitarianism. The author apparently uses it to show that the Stoics cannot avoid necessitarianism. There are two stages to the argument:

---

47   Cp. M. Mignucci in this volume, 281.
48   Cp. R. Sharples 1978a, 264.
49   The translation is R. Sharples' 1992, 34 slightly modified.

Step one

The overall structure of the first step is the following:

(PI)   If A and B then C
(PII)   Now A and B
(C)   Therefore C

The first premise states that C follows logically from A and B. This is shown by proving that A and B are incompatible with the contradictory of C. Let us analyse this in detail.

> C   'None of those things, of which one part of the contradictory disjunction referring to the future is definitely true, is contingent.'

If p is a variable of future states of affairs, we get:

> C1 $(p)(T_d[Cp] \rightarrow \neg KC\sim p)$

C1 can be transformed into C2.

> C2 $(p) \neg(T_d[Cp] \bullet KC\sim p)$

The contradictory of this is

> D   There are things (states of affairs) such that one part of the contradictory disjunction referring to the future is definitely true and the contradictory state of affairs is contingent.
> $\exists p (T_d[Cp] \bullet KC\sim p)$

That D is not compatible with A and B results from a *reductio* of D with the help of A and B.

> A   (Only) that is possible from which, if it is supposed to be the case, nothing impossible results.

A relies on the principle (P1) and its conversion (P2).

> (P1) If Cp is possible and Cp implies Cq then Cq is possible too.[50]
> (P2) If Cq is impossible and Cp implies Cq then Cp is impossible too.

A also states that something considered to be possible can be tested by supposing its actuality and seeing whether from this hypothesis an impossibility results. If an impossibility does result, it was wrongly considered possible. The state of affairs ~p that, according to D, is contingent and therefore possible is subjected to this test. The inevitable result of the test is stated in B.

---

[50]   This principle is first found in Aristotle (*Metaph.* IX, 3, 1047a24-26; *An. Pr.* I, 13, 32a18ff); it also features as the second premise of the Master Argument. For a commentary see G. Seel 1982a, 329ff.; cp. also G. Seel 1982b.

B   'From everything of which the contradictory is truly said beforehand, there results, if it is supposed that it is the case, the impossibility that the same thing both is and is not at the same time.'

The reasoning underlying B is that according to D [Cp] is true now and therefore, according to the principle of correspondence, it is the case now that p will occur at a precise moment in the future. Furthermore, and still according to D, it is possible now that ~p will occur at the same moment. If one supposes that this possibility is actualised one gets that it is the case now that p will occur at a precise future moment and that it is the case now that ~p will occur at that same moment. This, however, is a contradiction and, as the text states, an impossibility. This means that D is incompatible with both A and B and that its contradictory, C, can be deduced from A and B. This can be shown directly in the following way.

B may be formalized as follows:

B $T[Cp] \rightarrow \{C{\sim}p \rightarrow (Cp \bullet C{\sim}p)\}$

From B, by using the principle of correspondence, one gets the following tautology:

B′ $Cp \rightarrow \{C{\sim}p \rightarrow (Cp \bullet C{\sim}p)\}$

By applying the impossibility test according to (P2) to C~p, from B one gets:

B″   If [Cp] is true, then C~p is impossible.

By using the usual intermodal relations and by substituting 'definitely true' for 'true', as the text has it, B″ can be transformed into C.

C   If [Cp] is definitely true C~p is not contingent.

According to this argument, C in fact follows from A and B. Apparently, the authors of the argument accepted A and B and thus C, because in the following step they use C along with E to deduce F.

Step two

The first premise is an enlarged version of C that we call C3.

C3   If [Cp] is definitely true now C~p is not contingent now and if [C~p] is definitely true now C~p is not contingent now.

As a second premise the authors of the argument add a version of the principles of non-contradiction and of the excluded middle.

E   Either [Cp] is definitely true or [C~p] is definitely true.

From C3 and E they deduce F.

F   Neither Cp nor C~p is contingent.

Of course, F does not follow directly from C3 and E. Therefore, in the passage following our quotation, the authors show that if one part of the contradiction is impossible the other, being necessary, cannot be contingent. So the argument is a proof of necessitarianism, as we said at the beginning. But is it a sound argument?

The answer to this question depends on the meaning of the expression 'definitely true'. It is interesting to note that this expression occurs only in C and D, but we may surmise that the expression 'true' or 'truly' in B must mean 'definitely true'. If ' [Cp] is definitely true' simply meant that the sentence has a truth value and this is the value 'true', as the supporters of the standard interpretation argue, then the deduction in B would be nothing but a fallacy. For if [Cp] is true and one supposes that C~p, one supposes by the same token that [Cp] is not true. The truth of [Cp] does not prevent us supposing that [Cp] is not true, as long as [Cp] could not be true. Therefore, from supposing that C~p no contradiction results.[51]

This is quite different, if 'definitely true' has a modal meaning in the sense of P (3), as stated by the non-standard interpretation.

P(3) If [Cp] is definitely true, then it is necessary that [Cp] is true.

In this case, if [Cp] is definitely true one can no longer reasonably suppose that it is false. This means that the hypothesis that ~p is the case indeed leads to the contradictory assumption of Cp • C~p. Thus, the argument is valid, if the authors understood 'definitely true' in the sense of P(3), while it clearly is a fallacy, if they understood it in the first sense. This is a strong indirect argument in favour of the non-standard interpretation. Only the latter safeguards the authors from the charge of failure.

R. Gaskin (1995, 373-74) gives an alternative reconstruction of the argument. He supposes that the authors adhere to the doctrine of modality relative to the facts.[52] However, there is no trace of this doctrine in the text.

In the solution given at 13, 2-6 the expression 'definitely true' reappears:

> But it is alike possible for the same thing to come to be and not to come to be, how is it not absurd to say, in the case of these things, that one part of the contradiction uttered beforehand is true definitely (ἀφωρισμένως ἀληθές), and the other false, when the thing in question is alike capable of both?[53]

This clearly means that the existence of contingent events prevents us stating that of all contradictory future sentences one is definitely true (and the other definitely false). That is to say that necessitarian consequences follow if and only if all sentences have their truth-values in a definite way.

What then can we conclude as to the meaning of the expression 'definitely true'? Does it mean that a sentence simply has the value 'true', or does it mean that a sentence has the value 'true' in a way that it could not lack it? As we have seen, the argument is sound if and only if the expression 'definitely true' has the latter meaning. I therefore opt for this interpretation. In his paper (p.283 below)

---

[51]   For this objection see also R. Sharples 1992, 34 n. 80.
[52]   See above p.20.
[53]   Here again I follow R. Sharples' translation 1992, 36, slightly modifying it.

M. Mignucci, however, refuses to give a definite answer. His main reason for this is that in the present passage it is not said to what ἀφωρισμένως ἀληθές is opposed; it might be opposed either to what is indefinitely true or to what is not yet true. I feel, however, that Mignucci is being somewhat over-cautious. For, as we have seen, only the first conjecture leaves the argument reported and criticised by the Peripatetics sound. Moreover, the expression οὐκ ἤδη does not occur in the text, and it is surely more natural to oppose ἀφωρισμένως ἀληθές to οὐκ ἀφωρισμένως ἀληθές. It is true, however, that οὐκ ἀφωρισμένως ἀληθές does not occur in the text either and, even if it did, it could have the same meaning as οὐκ ἤδη ἀληθές, but this is speculation for which there is no evidence in the text.

Taken together, these two testimonies (Simplicius' *Commentary* and *Quaestio* 1.4) make it plausible that the Peripatetics of Alexander's School were the first to use the distinction between 'definitely true' and 'indefinitely true' to resolve Aristotle's ἀπορία. Moreover, both testimonies speak in favour of the non-standard interpretation. It is still, however, an open question whether Alexander himself adopted that solution.[54]

II.7 The neoplatonic commentators Ammmonius and Boethius

As we have said, the distinction between 'definitely true' and 'indefinitely true' plays a crucial role in the solution to Aristotle's ἀπορία proposed by the neoplatonic commentators, Ammonius and Boethius. Both argue that sentences about future contingent events are not definitely true or definitely false but only indefinitely true or indefinitely false,[55] and that deterministic consequences follow only if the sentence under consideration is definitely true. In order to understand this solution fully, we again need to know what these authors meant by 'definitely true' and 'indefinitely true'. This is a highly controversial issue.

There is one group of scholars who believe that if a sentence is indefinitely true now it has no truth-value at the present moment and is therefore neither true nor false. On this view, the solution of Ammonius and Boethius is identical, or at least very similar, to the standard solution.[56]

There is a second group of scholars, including Norman Kretzmann and Richard Gaskin, who think that although Ammonius and Boethius agree with the standard solution on a fundamental point, there is still what one might call a 'rhetorical' difference. Both argue that one should distinguish what Kretzmann calls 'narrow and broad bivalence'.[57] The principle of bivalence in the narrow sense is that at any given time every sentence has exactly one of these two truth values, true or false. The principle of bivalence in the broad sense is that at any

---

54   See again R. Sorabji 1980, 92-93 and R. Sharples 1983a, 11-12; 1978a, 264.
55   For Boethius cp. *In Int.* ed. pr. 106.30; ed. sec. 191.5, 208.11ff, 245.9, 249.25-250.1.
        For Ammonius see *In Int.* 130.20-26, 131.2-4, 138.13-17, 139.14-15, 154.34-155.3.
56   Cp. H. Weidemann 1994, 300ff.; D. Frede 1985, 75.
57   Cp. N. Kretzmann 1998, 36.

given time every sentence eventually has exactly one of these two truth values, true or false; and so at any time at which it does not yet have one of those truth values it has the disjunctive property either-true-or-false.

This disjunctive property cannot be understood truth-functionally, as Gaskin (1995, 149) rightly emphasises, nor is it, according to Gaskin, a third truth value.[58] It only means that the values true and false "exhaust the possibilities of which one is to be realised for each such proposition". Kretzmann and Gaskin think that by attributing the broad principle of bivalence to Aristotle, Ammonius and Boethius tried to protect him against the Stoic charge of having abandoned the principle of bivalence. But could Aristotle really be defended in this way? The Stoic point was that Aristotle gave up the principle of bivalence in the narrow sense, and, according to Kretzmann and Gaskin, Ammonius and Boethius admitted that he did. So it is doubtful that this 'second oldest interpretation' differs any more than 'rhetorically' from the oldest one.[59]

A third group of scholars rejects both these interpretations of Ammonius and Boethius;[60] they argue instead that the Neoplatonic solution did not give up the principle of bivalence in the narrow sense. According to this view, Boethius and Ammonius, by characterising a sentence as 'indefinitely true', do not say that it has as yet no truth value, but that the truth value it has is not predetermined by any kind of general law or fatalistic necessity. The solution to the ἀπορία lies in the fact that this kind of truth does not imply necessity.

We are convinced that the general line of interpretation the third group adopts is in fact the correct one. If so, one doubtful point remains, however, to clarify. It is obvious that the solutions of both Carneades and the neoplatonic commentators avoid necessaritarianism. However it is not at all clear that they also avoid determinism, as I define it. For it seems that for all times (t) and all types of events (p) it is settled, at each moment in the history of the world, whether or not p will occur at t, if the sentence predicting that event as a contingent event are true at each moment before t. How then can we call the position of these philosophers 'indeterministic'?

One should keep in mind that determinism, as I define it, is a thesis about the real course of the world process: if one looks from the present to the future there is at each future moment a determined event that is going to happen. Indeterminism, on the other hand, is the position that, from the point of view of the present, it is still open and undecided which of several different types of event will actually occur at each future moment. How is the latter compatible with the present truth of sentences about future events? It is important to see that these sentences have their truth-values not from the point of view of the present but

---

[58]   M. Mignucci, however, considers it to be a third truth-value (cp. his article in this volume, 251).

[59]   That is how N. Kretzmann characterises the Neoplatonic solution. R. Gaskin 1995, 167 explicitly admits that D. Frede's interpretation "broadly coincides" with his.

[60]   R. Sorabji, 1980, 92-93; 1998, 8ff; R. Sharples, 1978a, 263-64; M. Mignucci, 1994; 1998, 53ff.

from the point of view of the future or of eternity. The sentences are true because, from a timeless point of view, there is an event that makes them true. This event presents the outcome of the open course of the world process. It is because, from a timeless point of view, the open course has this outcome that there is a present fact about this outcome and a present truth of the sentence predicting it. Therefore, present facts about future events and the present truth of sentences about those events do not exclude the openness of the course leading to those future events.[61]

The development of the debate about future contingents in antiquity may be summarised in the table given opposite. If we look back at the different solutions given to Aristotle's ἀπορία during antiquity we find two major groups of solutions: (a) those which accept some kind of determinism (Aristotle's adversaries, Diodorus Cronus and the Stoics) and (b) those which avoid determinism (Aristotle, Epicurus, Carneades, the School of Alexander and the Neoplatonic Commentators). Among the latter, as we have seen, the solution which consisted in the rejection of the principle of bivalence is called 'the standard solution';[62] all other solutions should therefore be called 'non-standard'.[63] This is the terminology adopted in the present volume. Nevertheless, there is an important difference between the various non-standard solutions, concerning both the conception of the truth-maker and the modalisation of truth values. While Carneades considers the future events themselves to be the truth-makers of future contingent sentences, Ammonius, as we shall argue, considers present facts about future events to be the truth-makers of this kind of sentence. Furthermore, Carneades did not distinguish between 'definite' and 'indefinite' truth-values, whereas, as we have seen, the difference between 'definitely true' and 'indefinitely true' played a vital role in the interpretations of Ammonius and Boethius.

The crucial question, however, is whether sentences that are 'indefinitely true' are at the moment of their utterance *not yet true* or *simply true*. To hold the former is to follow the standard interpretation; to hold the latter is to follow a non-standard-interpretation. The first and the second group of scholars, discussed above, attribute to Ammonius and Boethius the standard interpretation, whatever other differences they might have discovered between the 'oldest' and the 'second oldest' solutions. In our opinion, however, Ammonius believed that what is indefinitely true is also true. He is thus to be seen as a defender of the non-standard interpretation, hence the difference between Carneades and Ammonius and Boethius in this respect is not fundamental. The major difference between them concerns the explanation of why Aristotle's adversaries and other

---

61   M. Mignucci (cp. below, p.276), though not admitting present facts about future events, comes to a similar solution.

62   Sometimes called 'the traditional solution' (cp. J. Hintikka 1973, 461-92; R. Sorabji 1980, 92) or 'the oldest solution' (cp. N. Kretzmann 1998, 24).

63   Also called 'the non-traditional solution' or 'the second oldest solution'.

	Is the principle of bivalence valid for future contingent sentences?	What is the truth-maker of future contingent sentences?	Ontological position
Aristotle's adversaries	yes	the predicted future event	necessitarian determinism
Aristotle (on the standard interpretation)	no	there is no truth-maker at the present moment	indeterminism
Diodorus Cronus	yes	present facts about future events	non-necessitarian determinism
Chrysippus	yes	present facts about the predicted event established by present causes of that event	non-necessitarian fatalistic determinism
Epicurus	no	there is no truth-maker at the present moment	non-necessitarian anti-fatalistic indeterminism
Carneades	yes	the predicted future event	non-necessitarian indeterminism
Alexander's School	yes	?	non-necessitarian indeterminism
The Neoplatonic Commentators (on my interpretation)	yes: not, however, the modalised principle with definite truth-values	The present fact that the predicted event will happen	non-necessitarian indeterminism

determinists accepted the truth-to-necessity argument as valid. Ammonius and Boethius explain this error by pointing out that the determinists failed to distinguish 'definitely true' and 'indefinitely true' and that they thus thought that what holds only for definitely true sentences would hold for all true sentences. Carneades, however, at least the Carneades presented by Cicero, made no attempt to explain the error of the determinists; for him, it was sufficient simply to show that it was an error. He had no need therefore of the distinction that proved so important to the Neoplatonists.

In this volume we try to present all the available evidence to show that Ammonius did not follow the standard interpretation. We are convinced that the same is true of Boethius. However, his is a more complicated case and needs a separate study. For a discussion of Boethius, the reader may like to refer to the article of Mario Mignucci.

Part III

Ammonius On Aristotle:
De Interpretatione 9
(and 7, 1-17)

Greek text established by A. Busse,
reprint from *CAG* (IV/v)
English translation by David Blank, revised by
J.-P. Schneider and Gerhard Seel

AMMONII IN L. DE INTERPRETATIONE c. 7 [Arist. p. 17ᵃ38.ᵇ12]

p. 17ᵃ38 Ἐπεὶ δέ ἐστι τὰ μὲν καθόλου τῶν πραγμάτων τὰ δὲ **20**
καθ' ἕκαστον (λέγω δὲ καθόλου μὲν ὃ ἐπὶ πλειόνων πέφυκε
κατηγορεῖσθαι, καθ' ἕκαστον δὲ ὃ μή, οἷον ἄνθρωπος μὲν τῶν
καθόλου, Καλλίας δὲ τῶν καθ' ἕκαστον), ἀνάγκη δὲ ἀποφαί- **25**
15 νεσθαι ὡς ὑπάρχει τι ἢ μὴ ὁτὲ μὲν τῶν καθόλου τινὶ ὁτὲ δὲ
τῶν καθ' ἕκαστον, ἐὰν μὲν | καθόλου ἀποφαίνηται ἐπὶ τοῦ **70ʳ**
καθόλου ὅτι ὑπάρχει τι ἢ μή, ἔσονται ἐναντίαι αἱ ἀποφάνσεις
(λέγω δὲ ἐπὶ τοῦ καθόλου ἀποφαίνεσθαι καθόλου οἷον 'πᾶς
ἄνθρωπος λευκός — οὐδεὶς ἄνθρωπος λευκός'), ὅταν δὲ ἐπὶ
20 τῶν καθόλου μέν, μὴ καθόλου δέ, αὗται μὲν οὐκ εἰσὶν ἐναντίαι, **5**
τὰ μέντοι δηλούμενα ἔστιν εἶναί ποτε ἐναντία. λέγω δὲ τὸ μὴ
καθόλου ἀποφαίνεσθαι ἐπὶ τῶν καθόλου οἷον 'ἔστι λευκὸς ἄνθρωπος — οὐκ ἔστι λευκὸς ἄνθρωπος'· καθόλου γὰρ ὄντος τοῦ
ἄνθρωπος οὐχ ὡς καθόλου κέχρηται τῇ ἀποφάνσει· τὸ γὰρ πᾶς **10**
25 　　　　　οὐ τὸ καθόλου σημαίνει, ἀλλ' ὅτι καθόλου.

Ἄρχεται μὲν ἐντεῦθεν τὸ δεύτερον τοῦ βιβλίου κεφάλαιον, ὅπερ ἐλέγομεν εἶναι περὶ τῶν ἐξ ὑποκειμένου καὶ κατηγορουμένου προτάσεως ἢ
ἀποφάνσεων· δεῖ δέ γε ἡμᾶς πρὸ τῆς ἐξηγήσεως τῶν διὰ τοῦ ῥητοῦ λεγο- **15**
μένων θεωρῆσαι τὰ πρὸς κατανόησιν τοῦ κεφαλαίου παντὸς ἀναγκαῖα·
30 ταῦτα δέ ἐστι πρῶτον μὲν τίνα τρόπον ἐκ τῶν καταφάσεων τούτων ποιοῦ-

---

11 ante lemma add. ἀρχὴ τοῦ δευτέρου τμήματος AF: τμῆμα δεύτερον G²:
περὶ τοῦ δευτέρου τμήματος M: Ἀρχὴ τοῦ δευτέρου τμήματος. Περὶ τῶν ἐξ ὑποκειμένου καὶ
κατηγορουμένου προτάσεων a: om. G¹　　12 καθέκαστα a　　　λέγω — καθόλου (25) om.
Ma　　14 καθέκαστα G　　　ἀνάγκη — καθόλου (25) om. G　　16 μὲν οὖν b
17 αἱ om. A　　18 ἀποφαίν.] ἀπόφανσιν F　　20 αὗται μὲν om. F　　21 μέντι A
ἐναντ. ποτέ colloc. b　　24 ἀποφάσει F　　26 μὲν οὖν Ma　　26. 27 ἐλέγομεν]
p. 8,14　　27 ἢ — ἐξηγήσεως τῶν (28) suppl. G²　　28 ἀποφάσεων A　　ἐξηγή-
σεως] ἐξετάσεως A¹M　　30. p. 87,1 ποιούμεθα a

<CHAPTER 7>

(17a38 – 17b12) Since some things are universal and others are singular (by 'universal' I mean what is according to its nature such as to be predicated of several things, by 'singular' what is not such, for example, 'man' belongs to the universals, and 'Callias' to the singulars), it is necessarily sometimes of one of the universals and sometimes of one of the singulars that one asserts that something holds or does not hold. Now, if one asserts universally of a universal that something holds of it or <in the other case> that it does not, then these assertions will be contraries (by 'to assert universally of a universal' I mean, e.g. 'Every man is pale – No man is pale'). But if one asserts something of universals, but not universally, these assertions are not themselves contraries, but the things they indicate can sometimes be contraries. By 'to assert not universally of universals' I mean, e.g. 'Man is pale – Man is not pale', for, although 'man' is universal, the assertion is not used in a universal way; for the word 'every' signifies not the universal, but that <it is used> universally.

<Introduction to the second main section of the book>

1. Here begins the second main section of the book[63], which we said (8,13-16) was about the sentences or assertions <consisting> of a subject and predicate. But before the explanation of what is said in the text, we must examine the points which are necessary for the understanding of the entire section. These are: (a) first, how do we make negative sentences out of affirmative sentences; (b) next, how should we get by division all the

---

63   cp. *infra*, p. 133 of the commentary.

μεν τὰς ἀποφάσεις, ἔπειτα πῶς ἂν λάβοιμεν ἐκ διαιρέσεως ἁπάσας τὰς ἐξ 20
ὑποκειμένου καὶ κατηγορουμένου προτάσεις, ἵνα θαρροῦντες ἀποφαινώμεθα
ὡς οὐκ ἂν εἴη κατὰ τοῦτο τῶν προτάσεων τὸ εἶδος ἄλλη παρὰ ταύτας
πρότασις, καὶ ἐπὶ τούτοις τίνες μέν εἰσιν ἐν αὐταῖς αἱ ἀντιφατικῶς ἀλλή-
5 λαις ἀντικείμεναι, τίνες δὲ αἱ δοκοῦσαι μὲν ἀντιφάσκειν, κατὰ ἀλήθειαν δὲ 25
οὐκ ἀντιφάσκουσαι, καὶ πῶς τὰς ἐκείνων πρὸς ἀλλήλας ἀντιθέσεις προσα-
γορευτέον.

Ὅτι μὲν οὖν ἡ κατάφασις τὸ ἀρνητικὸν προσλαβοῦσα μό|ριον ἀπό- 70ᵛ
φασις γίνεται, φανερόν. ποῦ δὲ τῆς καταφάσεως αὐτὸ θετέον, ἵνα τὴν
10 ἀπόφασιν ποιήσωμεν, καὶ διὰ τί τοῦτο, διορίσασθαι χρή. φημὶ τοίνυν ὡς
οὐ τῷ ὑποκειμένῳ αὐτὸ συντακτέον, ἀλλὰ τῷ κατηγορουμένῳ, πρῶτον μὲν 5
διότι κυριώτερόν ἐστι τὸ κατηγορούμενον, ὡς εἴρηται, καὶ πρότερον τοῦ
ὑποκειμένου, ὅθεν καὶ ὅλος ὁ λόγος καλεῖται κατηγορικός (βουλομένους
οὖν ἡμᾶς ἀνελεῖν τὴν κατάφασιν καὶ ποιῆσαι ἀπόφασιν οὐ χρὴ τὸ ἀρνητι-
15 κὸν μόριον τὸ τῆς ἀναιρέσεως αἴτιον τῷ ἀκυροτέρῳ τῶν μορίων ἐπιφέρειν 10
ἀλλὰ τῷ κυριωτέρῳ, ἐπεὶ καὶ τῶν ζῴων μᾶλλον δὲ πάντων τῶν ἐμψύχων
οὐ τὸ τυχὸν τῶν μορίων ἀναιρεθὲν ἔφθειρε τὸ ὅλον ἀλλά τι τῶν κυριω-
τέρων), ἔπειτα ὅτι τὴν κατάφασιν κατὰ τὸ λέγειν τι ὑπάρχειν ἔφαμεν χαρα-
κτηρίζεσθαι, τοῦτο δὲ ἔτι λέγει ἡ πρότασις ἡ συντάξασα τὸ ἀρνητικὸν 15
20 μόριον τῷ ὑποκειμένῳ· ὁ γὰρ εἰπὼν 'οὐ Σωκράτης περιπατεῖ' οὐ τὸ περιπατεῖν ἀνεῖλεν ἀπὸ τοῦ Σωκράτους, ὅπερ ἔδει ποιεῖν τὸν ἀπόφασιν εἰπεῖν
προθέμενον, ἀλλ' ἄλλον τινὰ παρὰ τὸν Σωκράτην φησὶ περιπατεῖν· πῶς 20
οὖν ἂν εἴη ἀπόφασις τῆς 'Σωκράτης περιπατεῖ' ἡ μήτε περὶ τοῦ αὐτοῦ
ὑποκειμένου διαλεγομένη καὶ ἄλλῳ τὸ περιπατεῖν λέγουσα ὑπάρχειν;
25 ἀνάγκη ἄρα πρὸς τῷ κατηγορουμένῳ μόνως τιθεμένην τὴν ἄρνησιν
ἀπόφασιν ποιεῖν, ὡς ἔχει ἡ λέγουσα πρότασις 'Σωκράτης οὐ περιπατεῖ'. 25
ἡ ἄρα 'οὐ Σωκράτης περιπατεῖ' ἐπειδὴ δέδεικται μὴ οὖσα ἀπόφασις, πᾶσα
δὲ πρότασις ἢ ἀπόφασίς ἐστιν ἢ κατάφασις, κατάφασις ἔσται ἀόριστον
ἔχουσα τὸ ὑποκείμε|νον (τὸ γὰρ ὄνομα τὸ ἀρνητικὸν μόριον προσλαβὸν 71ʳ
30 ἀόριστον προσαγορεύομεν ὄνομα), καὶ ταύτης ἀπόφασιν κατὰ τὸν αὐτὸν
λόγον εὑρήσομεν οὖσαν τὴν 'οὐ Σωκράτης οὐ περιπατεῖ', πρὸς τῷ κατη-

2 ἀποφήν. F   4 πρότασις G: τὰς προτάσεις AFMa   10 διὰ τί om. F   χρή]
δεῖ F   12 διότι om. M   ὡς εἴρηται] p. 70,4 sq.   post εἴρηται add. ἔνθα ἔλεγεν·
ἀνάγκη δὲ πάντα λόγον ἀποφαντικὸν ἐκ ῥήματος εἶναι ἢ πτώσεως ῥήματος. καὶ ὁ πορφύριος
φησὶν ὡς ἐν τῷ κατηγορικῷ εἴδει τοῦ ἀποφαντικοῦ λόγου τὸ κῦρος ἔχει μάλιστα τὸ κατηγορούμενον ὡς τὴν ὕπαρξιν τῆς ἀποφάσεως σημαῖνον G et in mrg. A   ὡς πρότερον G   13 ὅλος om. AM   καλεῖται om. F   15 ἀναιρέσεως] ἀρνήσεως G
ἀκυριωτέρῳ A: ἀκυρωτέρῳ FMa   τῶν μορίων — κυριωτέρῳ (16)] προστιθέναι F:
om. M   17 καιριωτέρων G   18 κατά] καὶ G   τι] τὸ M   ἔφαμεν]
p. 17,2   20 οὐ (prius) ὁ M   21 ἀπὸ om. AM   τόν] τὴν G¹   22 ἄλλα A¹
σωκράτη utrobique A   23 ἂν οὖν colloc. Ma   περιπατεῖν F   an περιπ. ⟨προτά-
σεως⟩?   ἡ om. AGMa   περὶ suppl. G²   24 ἄλλως G   29 μόριον
om. G   30 ἀόριστον om. A   προσηγόρευεν G¹: προσηγορεύομεν G²   αὐτὸν om. F
31 εὑρήσωμεν F   οὐ (ante περιπ.) om. M   τῷ] τὸ A

sentences <consisting> of subject and predicate, so that we may confidently assert that there is no other sentence of this kind besides these; (c) and after that, which sentences among these form contradictory oppositions, which sentences <only> seem to contradict, without actually contradicting, and how must we speak of their oppositions with one another.

<(a) On the placement of the negative particle>

2. Now, that the negative sentence arises when the affirmative sentence takes on the negative particle, is clear. But where in the affirmative sentence one must place it, in order to make the negative sentence, and why this is so, we must determine. I say, therefore, that one must not join it to the subject, but to the predicate; first, because the predicate is more important, as has been said (70,4f.), and prior to the subject, which is also why the whole sentence is called 'predicative' (so, if we want to deny the affirmative sentence and make a negative sentence, we must not attach the negative particle, which is the cause of the destruction, to the less important of the parts, but to the more important, since in animals too, or better in any living being, the whole does not perish if just any part is denied, but only if one of the more important parts <is denied>); next, because we said the affirmative sentence is characterised as <a sentence> saying that something is the case, but the sentence which combines the negative particle with the subject still says this, for one who has said 'Not Socrates walks' did not remove the walking from Socrates, which one intending to say a negative sentence had to do, but says that someone other than Socrates is walking, and how could it be a negation of 'Socrates walks' if it does not speak about the same subject and says that walking belongs to another <subject>? Thus, it is necessary that the negative particle make a negative sentence only when added to the predicate, as in the sentence 'Socrates does not walk'. So, the <sentence> 'Not Socrates walks', since it has been shown not to be a negative sentence and every sentence is either a negative sentence or an affirmative sentence, will be an affirmative sentence with an indefinite subject (for we call the name which has added the negative particle an 'indefinite name'), and we shall find, by the same reasoning, that the corresponding negative sentence is 'Not Socrates does not walk', which places the negative particle with the predicate of the

γορουμένῳ ἐν τῇ καταφάσει τὸ ἀρνητικὸν τιθεῖσαν μόριον. ὥστε περὶ τὸ 5
αὐτὸ ὑποκείμενον δύο γίνονται ἀντιφάσεις, μία μὲν ὡς ὡρισμένῳ αὐτῷ
χρωμένη, ἑτέρα δὲ ὡς ἀορίστῳ.

Τούτων οὖν οὕτως ἐχόντων ἑξῆς ἐπισκεψώμεθα τὰς διαιρέσεις, ἀφ'
5 ὧν οἷόν τε τὸν ἀριθμὸν τῶν ἐξ ὑποκειμένου καὶ κατηγορουμένου προτάσεων 10
ἑλεῖν, καὶ πρότερον τὰς γινομένας ἐν αὐταῖς ἀντιφάσεις ἀριθμήσωμεν·
φανερὸν γὰρ ὅτι αἱ προτάσεις διπλασίους ἔσονται τῶν ἀντιφάσεων. ἐπεὶ
οὖν αἱ προτάσεις αὗται δύο τε μόνον ὅρους ἔχουσι, τὸν ὑποκείμενον καὶ τὸν
κατηγορούμενον, καὶ ἔτι τὴν σχέσιν τοῦ κατηγορουμένου πρὸς τὸν ὑποκεί- 15
10 μενον καὶ οὐδὲν ἄλλο παρὰ ταῦτα, πᾶσα ἀνάγκη καὶ τὰς διαιρέσεις αὐτῶν
ἢ ἀπὸ μόνου γίνεσθαι τοῦ ὑποκειμένου ἢ ἀπὸ μόνου τοῦ κατηγορουμένου
ἢ ἀπὸ τῆς σχέσεως τοῦ κατηγορουμένου πρὸς τὸν ὑποκείμενων. λέγω
δὲ σχέσιν καθ' ἣν ὁ κατηγορούμενος ἢ ἀεὶ ὑπάρχει τῷ ὑποκειμένῳ, ὡς 20
ὅταν εἴπωμεν τὸν ἥλιον κινεῖσθαι ἢ τὸν ἄνθρωπον ζῷον εἶναι, ἢ οὐδέποτε
15 ὑπάρχει, ὡς ὅταν εἴπωμεν τὸν ἥλιον ἑστάναι ἢ τὸν ἄνθρωπον πτερωτὸν
εἶναι, ἢ ποτὲ μὲν ὑπάρχει ποτὲ δὲ οὐχ ὑπάρχει, ὡς ὅταν εἴπωμεν τὸν 25
Σωκράτην βαδίζειν ἢ ἀναγινώσκειν. ταύτας δὲ τὰς σχέσεις καλοῦσιν, οἷς
ἐμέλησε τῆς τούτων τεχνολογίας, τῶν προτάσεων ὕλας, καὶ εἶναι αὐτῶν
φασι τὴν μὲν ἀναγκαίαν τὴν δὲ ἀδύνατον τὴν δὲ ἐνδεχομένην. | καὶ τούτων 71ᵛ
20 μὲν τῶν ὀνομάτων ἡ αἰτία προφανής, ὅλως δὲ καλέσαι τὰς σχέσεις ταύτας
ὕλας ἠξίωσαν, ὅτι τοῖς ὑποκειμένοις ταῖς προτάσεσι πράγμασι συναναφαί-
νονται καὶ οὐκ ἀπὸ τῆς ἡμετέρας οἰήσεως ἢ κατηγορίας ἀλλ' ἀπ' αὐτῆς 5
τῆς τῶν πραγμάτων λαμβάνονται φύσεως· τὸ γὰρ οὕτως ἔχον ὡς ἀεὶ ὑπάρχειν φαμὲν τὴν ἀναγκαίαν ὕλην ποιεῖν, καὶ τὸ ἀεὶ μὴ ὑπάρχον τὴν ἀδύ-
25 νατον, καὶ τὸ ἐπαμφοτερίζον κατὰ τὸ ὑπάρχειν ἢ μὴ ὑπάρχειν τὴν ἐνδεχομένην. ἐπεὶ οὖν τὰ πράγματα ταῖς προτάσεσιν ὑπόκεινται, τὸ δὲ ὑπο- 10
κείμενον πανταχοῦ ἢ ὕλην εἶναί φαμεν ἢ ὕλης λόγον ἔχειν πρὸς ἐκεῖνο ᾧ
ὑπόκειται, διὰ τοῦτο ὕλας αὐτὰς προσαγορεύειν ἠξίωσαν.

Ἡ μὲν οὖν ἀπὸ τοῦ ὑποκειμένου διαίρεσις τοῦτον γίνεται τὸν τρόπον·
30 ὁ ὑποκείμενος ἐν τῇ προτάσει ἤτοι καθ' ἕκαστά ἐστιν ἢ καθόλου. καὶ 15
ἔστιν ἄμεσος ἡ διαίρεσις· μίαν μὲν γάρ, ὡς ἐλέγομεν, εἶναι χρὴ φύσιν
τὴν ὑπὸ τοῦ ὑποκειμένου σημαινομένην, καθάπερ καὶ τὴν ὑπὸ τοῦ κατηγορουμένου, εἴπερ μέλλοι μία ὄντως εἶναι ἡ πρότασις. ταύτην δὲ τὴν 20
μίαν φύσιν ἀναγκαῖον ἤτοι κατά τινων πλειόνων κατηγορεῖσθαι ἢ καθ' ἑνὸς
35 μόνου. καὶ εἰ μὲν εἴη τῶν καθ' ἑνὸς μόνου κατηγορουμένων τὸ ὡς ὑποκείμενον παραληφθὲν οἷον Σωκράτης ἢ Πλάτων, δῆλον ὅτι καθ' ἕκαστα

---

1. 2 τὸν αὐτὸν G   4 οὖν om. G   6 ἀριθ.] θεωρήσωμεν G¹   8 αὗται om. F
τε] γε A: om. G   μόνους G   11 γίγν. AMa   13 τῷ] τῶν A   15. 16 ὑπάρχειν (ter) G   20 ταύτας] αὐτῶν A: αὐτὰς M   21 ante ταῖς additum ἐν del. G²
24 ὑπάρχειν G²   27 ὅλην G¹   ἔχον G   28 αὐτὰς F: αὐτὰ AGMa
29 τὸν τρ. γίν. colloc. M   30 ἐν τῇ iter. G   31 ἐλέγομεν] λέγομεν G (cf.
p. 73,4 sq.)   32 prius ὑπὸ om. AM   alterum τοῦ om. F   33 ὄντως om. F
34 τινων om. A   35 post prius μόνου add. ὑποκειμένου AMa

affirmative sentence. Thus, two pairs of contradictorily opposed sentences arise concerning the same subject term, one using it as definite, and the other as indefinite.

<*(b) Division of the types of sentences consisting of subject and predicate*>

3. These things being so, let us in turn examine the divisions from which it is possible to get the number of sentences which consist of a subject and predicate; and first, let us enumerate the pairs of contradictorily opposed sentences which are produced among them. For it is clear that there will be twice as many sentences as pairs of contradictorily opposed sentences. So, since these sentences contain only two terms, the subject term and the predicate term, and also the relation of the predicate term to the subject term, and nothing else besides these, it is absolutely necessary that the divisions of these <sentences> too are based either only on the subject term or only on the predicate term or on the relation of the predicate term to the subject term. I am talking about the relation according to which the predicate term either always holds of the subject term, as when we say 'The sun moves' or 'Man is an animal', or never holds <of it>, as when we say 'The sun stands still' or 'Man is winged', or sometimes holds and sometimes does not hold, as when we say 'Socrates walks' or 'reads'. Those who care about a technical treatment for these things call these relations the 'matters' of the sentences, and they say that one of these matters is necessary, another impossible, and the third contingent. The reason for these names is obvious: indeed they found it appropriate to call these relations 'matters' in the first place because they show themselves together with the things which underlie the sentences <as reference> and are not obtained from our believing or saying, but from the very nature of the things. For we say that what is such as always to obtain makes the necessary matter, what always does not obtain makes the impossible, and what is ambivalent about obtaining or not obtaining makes the contingent. So, since the things underlie the sentences <as reference> and we say that always what underlies either is matter or has the rôle of matter for that which it underlies, for this reason they found appropriate to call them 'matters'.

<*The division based on the subject term*>

4. Now, the division on the basis of the subject term arises in this way. The subject term in a sentence is either singular or universal. And the division is immediate: for, as we said, the nature signified by the subject term must be one, just as that signified by the predicate too, if the sentence is really going to be one. But it is necessary that this one nature be said either of several things or only of one. If what is used as subject term is something said of one thing only, such as 'Socrates' or 'Plato', it is clear that the sentence will be singular, but if it is something said of several things, such as 'man' or 'animal', the sentence will be universal; and besides these there is <no other possibility>. But if it is universal, it is

ἔσται ἡ πρότασις, εἰ δὲ τῶν κατὰ πλειόνων οἷον ἄνθρωπος ἢ ζῷον, 25
καθόλου· καὶ παρὰ ταῦτα οὐκ ἔστιν. εἰ δὲ καθόλου εἴη, ἀναγκαῖον αὐτὸν
ἤτοι δίχα προσδιορισμοῦ λέγεσθαι ἢ μετὰ προσδιορισμοῦ. προσδιορισμοὶ
δὲ λέγονται προσρή‖ματά τινα τὰ συνταττόμενα τοῖς ὑποκειμένοις καὶ 72ʳ
5 δηλοῦντα ὅπως ἔχει τὸ κατηγορούμενον πρὸς τὸ πλῆθος τῶν ἀτόμων τῶν
ὑπὸ τὸ ὑποκείμενον, εἴτε ὡς ὑπάρχον εἴτε ὡς μὴ ὑπάρχον λαμβάνοιτο·
διὸ καὶ τέτταρές εἰσι τὸν ἀριθμόν, πᾶς καὶ οὐδείς, τίς καὶ οὐ πᾶς, δύο 5
μὲν καθόλου ὁ πᾶς καὶ ὁ οὐδείς, δύο δὲ μερικοὶ ὁ τίς καὶ ὁ οὐ πᾶς. καὶ
τῶν καθόλου ὁ μὲν καταφατικὸς ὁ πᾶς, οἷον 'πᾶς ἄνθρωπος ζῷον,' σημαί-
10 νων ὡς πᾶσι τοῖς ἀτόμοις τοῖς ὑπὸ τὸν ἄνθρωπον ὑπάρχει τὸ ζῷον, ὁ δὲ 10
ἀποφατικὸς ὁ οὐδείς, οἷον 'οὐδεὶς ἄνθρωπος πτερωτός,' σημαίνων ὡς οὐδενὶ
τῶν καθ᾽ ἕκαστα ἀνθρώπων τὸ κατηγορούμενον ὑπάρχει. καὶ τῶν μερικῶν
πάλιν ὁ μὲν καταφατικὸς ὁ δὲ ἀποφατικός· καταφατικὸς μὲν ὁ τίς, οἷον
'τὶς ἄνθρωπος λευκός,' σημαίνων ὅτι τὸ κατηγορούμενον ἑνί γέ τινι τῶν 15
15 ὑπὸ τὸ ὑποκείμενον ἀτόμων ὑπάρχει, ἀποφατικὸς δὲ ὁ οὐ πᾶς, οἷον 'οὐ
πᾶς ἄνθρωπος δίκαιος,' ἀναιρετικὸς ὢν τοῦ πᾶς καὶ σημαίνων ὡς οὐκ ἀληθὲς τὸ πᾶσι τοῖς ὑπὸ τὸ ὑποκείμενον ἀτόμοις τὸ κατηγορούμενον ὑπάρχειν.
οὐ μόνον μέντοι ἐπὶ ἀτόμων ποιοῦνται τοὺς εἰρημένους ἀφορισμοὺς οἱ 20
προσδιορισμοί, ἀλλ᾽ εἴπερ τύχοι γένος ὂν τὸ ἐν τῇ προτάσει ὑποκείμενον,
20 προηγουμένως μὲν ἁρμόσουσιν ἐπὶ τῶν ὑπὸ τὸ γένος ἐκεῖνο ἀναφερομένων
εἰδῶν, ὅταν οὐσιῶδές τι ᾖ τὸ κατ᾽ αὐτοῦ κατηγορούμενον, κατὰ δεύτερον 25
δὲ λόγον καὶ τῶν ὑπὸ τὰ εἴδη ἐκεῖνα ἀτόμων, ἐπεὶ οὐδὲ ἄλλως μετέχειν
τὰ ἄτομα τοῦ γένους δυνατόν, εἰ μὴ διὰ μέσων τῶν οἰκείων εἰδῶν. ὅταν
οὖν εἴπωμεν 'πᾶν ζῷον οὐσία' ἢ 'τὶ ζῷον πτηνόν', ἐπεὶ | κατ᾽ οὐσίαν τοῖς 72ᵛ
25 ὑποκειμένοις τὰ κατηγορούμενα ὑπάρχει, τὴν μὲν οὐσίαν προηγουμένως
κατηγορεῖσθαι φήσεις πάντων ἁπλῶς τῶν εἰδῶν τοῦ ζῷου, τὸ δὲ πτηνὸν
τῶν μετέχειν αὐτοῦ πεφυκότων, καὶ δι᾽ ἐκεῖνα τῶν ὑπὸ τὰ εἴδη ἀτόμων. 5
ἐνίοτε δὲ περὶ μόνων εἰδῶν ποιούμεθα τὴν ἀπόφανσιν, ὡς ὅταν εἴπωμεν
πᾶν εἶδος τοῦ ποσοῦ τοῦ συνεστῶτος ἐκ θέσιν ἐχόντων τῶν μορίων καὶ
30 τοῦ συνεχοῦς ἐστιν εἶδος᾽ ἢ 'πᾶν φυσικὸν εἶδος ἐν τῷ κόσμῳ ἔχει τὴν
οἰκείαν ὑπόστασιν.' δῆλον δὲ ὅτι τὰ συμβεβηκότα ἐπεισοδιώδη τε ὄντα καὶ 10
πεφυκότα τῷ αὐτῷ ὑπάρχειν τε καὶ μὴ ὑπάρχειν τῶν μὲν ἀτόμων προηγουμένως ἐροῦμεν κατηγορεῖσθαι παντοδαπῶς κατά τε ταῦτα καὶ κατὰ τὴν
οὐσίαν μεταβάλλεσθαι πεφυκότων, οὐ μέντοι κυρίως τῶν εἰδῶν τῶν οὐδὲ 15
35 τὴν ἀρχὴν διὰ τὴν ἀσώματον καὶ ἄτρεπτον ἑαυτῶν φύσιν μετέχειν αὐτῶν
δυναμένων.

---

1 ἢ om. FG   2 αὐτὸν] an αὐτό?   3 δίχα] χωρὶς F   4 ante προσρήμ. add. οἱονεὶ a
τὰ om. Aa: ante τινα colloc. M   συνταττ.] ταττ. M   7 καὶ (ante οὐδείς et οὐ) om. M
9 τῶν μὲν καθόλου ὁ μὲν Ma   ὡς ὁ πᾶς AFG   11 ὡς ὁ οὐδείς A: ὡς οὐδείς M   15 ὁ
om. A   16 σημαῖνον A   18 ἐπὶ supra scr. A   εἰρημ.] ὁρισμένους a
19 ὑποκειμένου F   20 μὲν post ἁρμ. colloc. M   τὸ om. M   22 ἐπὶ τῶν G²   25 ὑπάρχειν F   27 ἐκείνων G   28 ἀπόφασιν AF   29 τῶν om. FG   30 εἶδός ἐστιν M
33 ταῦτα G

necessarily said either without additional determination or with additional determination. 'Additional determinations' are what we call certain additional words which are combined with the subject terms and indicate how the predicate relates to the multitude of individuals under the subject term, whether it is taken as holding or as not holding. Hence, they too are four in number, 'every' and 'none', 'some' and 'not every': two universal ('every' and 'none'), and two particular ('some' and 'not every'). And of the universal ones, 'every' is affirmative, e.g. 'Every man is an animal', signifying that 'animal' belongs to all individuals under man, and 'none' is negative, e.g. 'No man is winged', indicating that the predicate term belongs to none of the singular men. And of the particular ones, again one is affirmative and one negative: 'some' is affirmative, e.g. 'Some man is pale', signifying that the predicate term belongs to at least some one of the individuals under the subject term; and 'not every' is negative, e.g. 'Not every man is just', which is destructive of 'every' and signifies that it is not true that the predicate term belongs to all the individuals under the subject term. However, the additional determinations do not make the aforementioned distinctions only in the case of individuals, but if the subject term in the sentence happens to be a genus, the additional determinations will fit primarily for the species occurring under that genus, when what is predicated of it is something essential, but secondarily also for the individuals under those species, since it is not even possible for the individuals to participate in the genus in any other way except through the intermediaries of the appropriate species. So, when we say 'Every animal is a substance' or 'Some animal is winged', since the predicate terms belong to their subjects essentially, you will say that 'substance' is primarily predicated of absolutely all the species of animal, and 'winged' of those <species of animal> which are such as to participate in it, and, because of them, of the individuals under the species. But sometimes we make an assertion concerning species alone, as when we say 'Every species of that quantity which consists of parts which have position is also a species of the continuous', 'Every natural species in the world has its own mode of existence'. But it is clear that we shall say that accidents, which are episodic and such as both to belong and not to belong to the same thing, are primarily predicated of individuals, which are such as to be changing in every way both with regard to these <accidents> and to their essence, but <that accidents are> not properly <predicated> of the species which, because of their incorporeal and unchanging nature, can absolutely not participate in them.

Εἰ μὲν οὖν μηδεὶς τῶν προσδιορισμῶν προσκέοιτο τῷ ὑποκειμένῳ, λέγεται ἡ πρότασις ἀπροσδιόριστος, οἷον ʽ ἄνθρωπος ὑγιαίνει,ʼ εἰ δὲ προσδιορισμόν τινα ἔχει, λέγεται ἡ πρότασις προσδιωρισμένη. ἀλλ' εἰ μὲν τῶν 20 καθόλου εἴη ὁ προσδιορισμός, λέγεται καθόλου, εἰ δὲ τῶν μερικῶν, μερική.

5 ἀναφαίνονται οὖν ἡμῖν ἐκ τῆς διαιρέσεως τοῦ ὑποκειμένου τέτταρα εἴδη τῶν ἐν προτάσεσιν ἀντιθέσεων, τῶν καθ' ἕκαστα, τῶν ἀπροσδιορίστων, τῶν 25 καθόλου ἤτοι καθόλου ὡς καθόλου (καλοῦσι γὰρ αὐτὰς καὶ οὕτως διακρίνοντες τῶν ἄλλων τῶν ὁμοίως ταύταις ὑποκειμένῳ καθόλου χρωμένων τῷ ἐπὶ τούτων συντετάχθαι | τοὺς καθόλου προσδιορισμοὺς τοῖς καθόλου ὑπο- 73ʳ 10 κειμένοις), καὶ ἐπὶ ταύταις τῶν μερικῶν ἤτοι καθόλου ὡς μερικῶν (ἔχουσι γὰρ αὗται τοὺς μερικοὺς προσδιορισμοὺς συντεταγμένους τοῖς καθόλου ὑποκειμένοις, διὸ καὶ οὕτω προσαγορεύονται· διαφέρουσι δὲ τῶν καθ' ἕκαστα 5 αἱ μερικαὶ τῷ τὰς μὲν καθ' ἕκαστα ἐπί τινος ἑνὸς ὡρισμένου ̄ ποιεῖσθαι τὴν ἀπόφανσιν, οἷον Σωκράτους, τὰς δὲ μερικάς, εἰ καὶ πρὸς ἕν τι βλέ- 15 πουσαι ἀποφαίνοιντο, μηδὲν ὡρισμένον σημαίνειν ἀλλ' ἐπί τινος τοῦ τυχόντος 10 δύνασθαι ἀληθεύειν, ὡς ὅταν εἴπωμεν ʽτὶς ἄνθρωπος δίκαιός ἐστιν'· οὐδὲν γὰρ μᾶλλον Σωκράτους χάριν ἀληθεύει ἡ πρότασις ἢ Πλάτωνος ἢ Ἀριστείδου· διόπερ ὀρθῶς ὁ Θεόφραστος τὴν μὲν καθ' ἕκαστα ὡρισμένην καλεῖ τὴν δὲ μερικὴν ἀόριστον), καὶ ἀντιδιαιρεῖται πρὸς μὲν τὴν ἁπλῶς καθόλου 15 20 ἡ καθ' ἕκαστα, πρὸς δὲ τὴν καθόλου ὡς καθόλου ἡ μερική.

Τοιαύτη μὲν οὖν ἡ ἀπὸ τοῦ ὑποκειμένου τῶν προτάσεων διαίρεσις· ἀπὸ δέ γε τοῦ κατηγουμένου ταῦτα πάντα τὰ τέτταρα εἴδη τριπλασιάζεσθαι ῥητέον· ἐπεὶ γὰρ ἀνάγκη τὸν κατηγορούμενον ῥῆμα εἶναι, τὸ δὲ ῥῆμα 20 προσσημαίνειν ἐλέγομεν χρόνον, ὁ δὲ χρόνος λαμβάνεται τριχῶς, κατὰ τὸ 25 παρεληλυθὸς τὸ ἐνεστὸς τὸ μέλλον, δῆλον ὅτι τῶν τεττάρων εἰδῶν τῶν προτάσεων ἕκαστον τριχῶς ποικίλλειν ἀπὸ τοῦ κατηγορουμένου δυνατόν, οἷον ἐπὶ τῶν καθ' ἕκαστα λέγοντας ʽΣωκράτης ὑγίανε' ʽΣωκράτης ὑγιαίνει' 25 ʽΣωκράτης ὑγιανεῖ', ὥστε διὰ τοῦτο δώδεκα γίνεσθαι τὰ τῶν ἐν προτάσεσιν ἀντιθέσεων εἴδη· ὅτι γὰρ ποτε καὶ παρὰ τοὺς χρόνους γίνεταί τις τῶν 30 προτάσεων διαφορά, | διδάσκοντος ἀκουσόμεθα τοῦ Ἀριστοτέλους. ἐπεὶ 73ᵛ δὲ ἑκάστην τῶν δώδεκα τούτων ἀντιθέσεων τριχῶς λαμβάνεσθαι δυνατὸν κατὰ τὰς τρεῖς ὕλας, ἓξ καὶ τριάκοντα γίνεσθαι συμβαίνει τὰς πάσας αὐτῶν ἀντιθέσεις ὡρισμένου ὄντος τοῦ ὑποκειμένου. ταύταις δὲ ἴσας ἀνάγκη 5 γίνεσθαι τὰς ἐξ ἀορίστου τοῦ ὑποκειμένου (καθ' ἑκάστην γὰρ τῶν ὁρισμένῳ

---

2. 4 λέγοιτο AM   7 post ὡς καθόλου add. καὶ τῶν καθόλου μὴ καθόλου a   8 ὑποκειμένων G   13 ἑνὸς· om. F   14 ἀπόφασιν AG   καὶ εἰ colloc. FG   15 ἀποφαίνοιτο F   τυχόντων F   17 ἀληθεύσει G   πλάτων G¹   ἀριστίδου A   18 Θεόφραστος] fr. 57ᶜ (p. 428 ed. Wimmer)   18. 19 τὴν μὲν μερ. ἀόρ. καλεῖ τὴν δὲ καθ' ἕκ. ὡρ. colloc. F   21 ἡ ante διαίρ. colloc. G   post ἀπὸ τοῦ add. ὑπὸ τοῦ F   22 πάντα] γε A: τε M: om. (sed post ῥητέον add. ἅπαντα) G   23 τὸ κατ. G   24 λέγομεν F (cf. p. 47,6)   25 ἐνεστὼς AF   27 λέγοντος M   ante Σωκρ. add. οἷον F   30 διδ. ἀκουσ. τοῦ Ἀρ.] p. 18ᵃ28   ἀκουσώμεθα A   32. 33 πάσας τῶν ἀντιθέσεων A   33. 34 ταύταις—ὑποκειμένου om. FM   34 τοῦ om. Aa

<The four species of opposition based on the subject term>

5. Now, if none of the additional determinations is added to the subject tem, the sentence is called 'undetermined', e.g. 'Man is healthy', and if it has some additional determination, the sentence is called 'determined'. But if the additional determination is universal, it is called 'universal' <i.e general>, and if particular, 'particular'. So, from the division of the subject term, we see four species of oppositions among sentences: the singular; the undetermined; the universal, or universal as universal <i.e. general> (for they call them this too, distinguishing them from the others which, like these, use a universal subject by the fact that, in these instances, the universal additional determinations have been combined with universal subject terms); and in addition to these the particular or universal as particular (for these have particular additional determinations combined with universal subject terms, and for this reason are so called). And the particular sentences differ from the singular in that singular sentences make their assertion about some one definite thing, e.g. Socrates, while particular sentences, even if they are asserted with reference to one thing, signify nothing definite, but can be true of any chance thing, as when we say 'Some man is just': for this sentence is no more true on account of Socrates than of Plato or Aristides. Hence Theophrastus[64] correctly calls the singular sentence 'definite' and the particular 'indefinite'. And on the one hand the singular sentence is contrasted with the sentence which is simply[65] universal, and on the other the particular is contrasted with the universal as universal <i.e. the general>.

<The division of sentences based on the predicate term; their sum total>

6. Now, such is the division of sentences on the basis of their subject term. But on the basis of their predicate term one must say that all these four kinds are multiplied by three. For, since it is necessary that the predicate term be a verb, and we said (47,23) that the verb additionally signifies time, but time is understood in three ways, according to the past, present and future, it is clear that it is possible to vary each of the four kinds of sentence on the basis of the predicate term, saying, for example, in the case of singular sentences, 'Socrates was healthy', 'Socrates is healthy', 'Socrates will be healthy', so that for this reason the kinds of opposition in sentences become twelve. For we shall hear Aristotle teach that sometimes a difference arises among sentences due to the times as well (18a28 [ch. 9]). But, since it is possible to understand each of these twelve oppositions in three ways according to the three matters, it happens that all their oppositions total thirty-six, if the subject term is definite. And it is necessary that those containing an indefinite subject term be equal to these (for you will make the indefinite one for each of those which use a definite subject term by adding the negative particle to the subject), so

---

[64]   cp. A. Graeser, *Die logischen Fragmente des Theophrast*, Berlin/New York, 1973, Fr. 4 (with other parallels and a commentary); *Theophrastus of Eresus, Sources for his Life, Writings, Thought and Influence*, ed. by W.W. Fortenbaugh and al., Part One, Leiden/New York/Cologne, 1992, 82E (with other parallels).

[65]   i.e. without regard to its qualification as undetermined, general or particular.

χρωμένων τῷ ὑποκειμένῳ τὸ ἀρνητικὸν μόριον τῷ ὑποκειμένῳ προσθεὶς τὴν
ἐξ ἀορίστου ποιήσεις), ὥστε δύο καὶ ἑβδομήκοντα γίνεσθαι τὰς πάσας ἀντι- 10
θέσεις τε καὶ ἀντιφάσεις τῶν προκειμένων ἡμῖν εἰς ἐπίσκεψιν προτάσεων.

Ἀλλ' ἐπεὶ τὸν ἀριθμὸν αὐτῶν παραδεδώκαμεν, ἀκόλουθόν ἐστιν
5 ἐφεξῆς ἐπικέψασθαι τίνες ἐν ταῖς ἀπηριθμημέναις ἀντιθέσεσιν αἱ ἀντιφατικῶς ἀλλήλαις ἀντικείμεναι προτάσεις, τίνες δὲ οὔ, καὶ τίνες μὲν αἱ πρὸς 15
ἀλλήλας σχέσεις τῶν μὴ ἀντικειμένων ἀντιφατικῶς, τίς δὲ ἡ πρὸς ἑκατέραν τῶν ἐν αὐταῖς προτάσεων ἀντιφατικῶς μαχομένη· προείληπται γὰρ
ὡς πάσῃ καταφάσει ἐστὶν ἀπόφασις ἀντιφατικῶς ἀντικειμένη καὶ πάσῃ 20
10 ἀποφάσει κατάφασις. ὅτι μὲν οὖν αἱ καθ' ἕκαστα μάχονται ἀντιφατικῶς,
παρὰ πᾶσιν ὡμολόγηται (παρέχει δέ τινα ἀπορίαν ἡ κατὰ τὸν μέλλοντα
χρόνον αὐτῶν λῆψις, ἣν ἐν τοῖς ἑξῆς καὶ ἐκθήσεται καὶ ἐπιλύσεται ὁ Ἀριστοτέλης), τὰ δὲ περὶ τῶν ἀπροσδιορίστων διαφωνεῖται μὲν παρὰ τῶν 25
ἀποφηναμένων τι περὶ τούτου τοῦ θεωρήματος, ὅπῃ δὲ τὸ ἀληθὲς ἔχει
15 μαθεῖν ἀμήχανον, πρὶν ὅπως ἔχει τὰ περὶ τῶν προσδιωρισμένων ἐπισκε-
ψώμεθα, περὶ ὧν οὐδεμία ἢ γέγονεν ἢ γέ|νοιτο ἂν ἀμφισβήτησις· ὥστε 74r
πρότερον περὶ τούτων ῥητέον.

Ἐπεὶ τοίνυν ὡριζόμεθα τὴν ἀντίφασιν μάχην καταφάσεως καὶ ἀποφάσεως ἀεὶ διαιρουσῶν τὸ ἀληθὲς καὶ τὸ ψεῦδος, δῆλον ὅτι ἃς ἂν εὕρωμεν
20 προτάσεις ἢ συμψευδομένας ποτὲ ἢ συναληθευούσας, ταύτας οὐκ ἂν εἴποιμεν 5
ἀντιφατικῶς ἀντικεῖσθαι πρὸς ἀλλήλας. αἱ μὲν οὖν καθόλου ὡς καθόλου
λεγόμεναι ὡς συμψευδόμεναι κατὰ τὴν ἐνδεχομένην ὕλην οὐκ ἂν λέγοιντο
ποιεῖν ἀντίφασιν. οὐ μὴν ἀλλ' οὐδὲ τὰς μερικὰς ἀντιφάσκειν ἐροῦμεν ὡς 10
ἐπὶ τῆς αὐτῆς ὕλης συναληθευούσας. καίτοι καθ' ἑκατέραν τῶν λοιπῶν
25 ὑλῶν διαιροῦσιν ἄμφω τό τε ἀληθὲς καὶ τὸ ψεῦδος· ἐπὶ μὲν γὰρ τῆς
ἀναγκαίας ὕλης αἱ μὲν καταφάσεις ἄμφω λέγουσαι εἶναι τὸ ἐξ ἀνάγκης
ὑπάρχον ἀληθεῖς, αἱ δὲ ἀποφάσεις ἀναιρεῖν αὐτὸ πειρώμεναι ψευδεῖς, ἐπὶ 15
δὲ τῆς ἀδυνάτου λεγομένης ἔμπαλιν εἰκότως ἔχουσιν· αἱ μὲν γὰρ ἀποφάσεις
τὸ ἀδύνατον καὶ διὰ τοῦτο μηδέποτε ὑπάρχον λέγουσαι μὴ ὑπάρχειν
30 ἀληθεῖς, αἱ δὲ καταφάσεις ὑπάρχειν αὐτὸ ἀποφαινόμεναι ψευδεῖς. ἐπὶ δὲ 20
τῆς ἐνδεχομένης ἄμφω μὲν αἱ καθόλου ψευδεῖς, ἄμφω δὲ αἱ κατὰ μέρος
ἀληθεῖς, διότι τὰ κατὰ ταύτην τὴν ὕλην κατηγορούμενα ποτὲ μὲν ὑπάρχειν
τοῖς ὑποκειμένοις πεφύκασι ποτὲ δὲ μὴ ὑπάρχειν, καὶ τισὶ μὲν αὐτῶν
ὑπάρχειν τισὶ δὲ μὴ ὑπάρχειν, οἷον 'πᾶς ἄνθρωπος λευκός — οὐδεὶς 25
35 ἄνθρωπος λευκός· (αὗται ψευδεῖς ἄμφω, ἡ μὲν κατάφασις διὰ τοὺς Αἰθίο-

---

1 prius τῷ om. FG   4 ἐστιν om. G   5 post ἀντιθέσεσιν add. εἰσὶν G   6 προτάσεσι G   7 ἄλληλα F   8 αὐτοῖς G   προείληπται] p. 84,2   12 ἐκθήσεται
καὶ ἐπιλ. ὁ Ἀρ.] p. 18 a 33   13 παρά] περὶ FG   14 ἔχειν A   15 πρὶν] πλὴν
G²a   15. 16 ἐπισκεψόμεθα FG   16 οὐδεμία] οὐ G   prius ἢ om. GM   18 ὡριζ.
scripsi: ὁριζ. libri (cf. p. 81,14)   19 διαιροῦσαν AMa   20 συμψευδ.] ψευδ. F
23 ἀλλ' om. AF   24 συναληθ.] ἀληθ. G   25 ὑλῶν om. M   γάρ] οὖν Ma
26 μὲν om. F   λέγουσιν A¹G   32 ταύτην τὴν] αὐτὴν A: αὐτὴν τὴν Ma
35 αὗται δέ F

that all the oppositions and contradictions of the sentences which we are here examining total seventy-two.

<(c) Which oppositions are contradictory and which are not?>

7. But, since we have given their number, it follows in turn that we should examine which sentences among the enumerated oppositions oppose one another contradictorily, and which do not, and, further, what <logical> relations do those not opposed contradictorily bear to one another, and which is the sentence that conflicts contradictorily with each of the sentences among the latter, <i.e. the sentences not contradictorily opposed to one another>. For it has been assumed that for every affirmative sentence there is a contradictorily opposed negative sentence, and for every negative sentence an affirmative sentence. Now, everyone agrees that singular sentences are opposed <to each other> in the manner of contradiction (although taken in the future tense they give rise to a certain aporia that Aristotle goes on to explain and resolve in what follows [ch. 9]), but about the undetermined sentences there is disagreement among those who have said something about this topic, and it is impossible to learn the truth until we have examined how things stand with the determined sentences, concerning which no dispute either has arisen or could arise. Thus, we must first speak about these.

<Which determined sentences contradict one another and which do not?>

8. Since, therefore, we defined contradiction (81,13-15) as a conflict of an affirmative sentence and a negative sentence in each case dividing the true and the false, it is clear that whatever sentences we find either sometimes simultaneously false or simultaneously true, we should not say that these are opposed contradictorily to one another. Now, the universal sentences said as universal <i.e. the general> should not be said to make a contradiction, since they are simultaneously false in the contingent matter. Nor, indeed, shall we say that the particular sentences contradict each other, for they are simultaneously true in that same matter. However, in each of the remaining matters both oppositions divide the true and the false. For in the necessary matter, both affirmative sentences saying that what necessarily holds is so are true, and the negative sentences which attempt to deny it are false; but in the so-called impossible matter, these are properly reversed, for the negative sentences, which say that what is impossible and for this reason never holds does not hold, are true, while the affirmative sentences, which assert that it holds, are false. In the contingent matter both the general sentences are false, but both the particular sentences are true, because things predicated of this matter are such as sometimes to hold of their subjects and sometimes not to hold of them, and to hold of some but not of others, e.g. 'Every man is pale – No man is pale' (these are both false, the affirmative sentence because of the Ethiopians, and the negative sentence because of, say, the Scythians),

πᾶς, ἡ δὲ ἀπόφασις, εἰ τύχοι, διὰ τοὺς Σκύθας), 'τὶς ἄνθρωπος λευκός —
οὐ πᾶς ἄνθρωπος λευκός'· | αὗται δῆλον ὅτι συναληθεύουσι.   74ᵛ

Τὰς μὲν οὖν καθόλου ὡς καθόλου δείξαντες μὴ ἀντιφασκούσας ὀνο-
μάζουσιν ἐναντίας, ὅτι τῶν ἐναντίων εἰς ἄμεσα διαιρουμένων καὶ ἔμμεσα
5 αἱ προτάσεις αὗται κατὰ μὲν τὴν ἀναγκαίαν καὶ τὴν ἀδύνατον ὕλην τοῖς ⁵
ἀμέσοις ἐναντίοις ἐοίκασιν, ὧν τό τε ἕτερον ἐξ ἀνάγκης πάρεστι τῷ ὑποκειμένῳ καὶ αὗται τὴν ἑτέραν τῶν προτάσεων ἔχουσιν ἀληθῆ καὶ διὰ τοῦτο
μιμουμένην τὴν τοῦ πράγματος ὕπαρξιν, ὥσπερ τὸ ψεῦδος εἰκών ἐστι τῆς
ἀνυπαρξίας, κατὰ δὲ τὴν ἐνδεχομένην τοῖς ἐμμέσοις, ὧν δυνατὸν μηδέτερον ¹⁰
10 παρεῖναι τῷ ὑποκειμένῳ. ἢ ἐπεὶ τὸ εἶναι ἄμεσά τινα τῶν ἐναντίων ἀμφι-
σβητήσιμον, ὅπερ ὡς ὁμολογούμενον ἀξιοῦσι λαμβάνειν οἱ κατὰ τὸν προειρημένον τρόπον ἀποδιδόντες τὴν αἰτίαν τῆς ποσηγορίας τῶν ἐναντίων καλου- ¹⁵
μένων προτάσεων, μᾶλλον ῥητέον ὅτι τὰ ἐναντία συνυπάρχειν μὲν ἀλλήλοις
κατ' ἐνέργειαν ἐπὶ τοῦ αὐτοῦ ὑποκειμένου ἀδύνατον, ἅμα δὲ αὐτοῦ ἀπεῖναι
15 δυνατόν· αἱ οὖν προτάσεις αὗται οὐδέποτε μὲν συναληθεύουσαι ποτὲ δὲ ²⁰
καὶ συμψευδόμεναι καὶ ταύτῃ τὰ ἐναντία μιμούμεναι λέγοιντο ἂν εἰκότως
ἐναντίαι. δυνατὸν δὲ λέγειν ὅτι καὶ ὡς τὴν πλείστην ἀλλήλων ἀφεστῶσαι
διάστασιν ἐναντίαι προσαγορεύονται· τὰ γὰρ ἐναντία πλεῖστον ἀλλήλων διέ-
στηκε τῶν ὑπὸ τὸ αὐτὸ γένος· οὕτω δὲ καὶ αὗται πρὸς ἀλλήλας ἔχουσιν, ²⁵
20 εἴπερ ἡ μὲν ἅπασί φησι τοῖς ὑπὸ τὸ ὑποκείμενον ἀτόμοις τὸ κατηγορούμενον ὑπάρχειν, ἡ δὲ οὐδενί. τὰς δέ γε μερικὰς καλοῦσιν ὑπεναντίας, ὡς
ὑπὸ ταῖς ἐναντίαις τεταγμένας | κἀκείναις ἀκολουθούσας· ὅταν γὰρ ἡ ἑτέρα 75ʳ
τῶν καθόλου ἀληθεύῃ, τότε καὶ ἡ ὑπ' αὐτὴν τεταγμένη μερικὴ πρότασις
ἀληθεύσει, ὡς οἷον μέρος αὐτῆς οὖσα καὶ περιεχομένη ὑπ' αὐτῆς· διὸ
25 καὶ ὑπαλλήλους καλοῦσι τάς τε καταφάσεις, τὴν μερικὴν καὶ τὴν καθόλου, ⁵
καὶ τὰς ἀποφάσεις ὁμοίως. αἱ μὲν οὖν κατὰ μέρος οὐδ' ἂν ἀντικεῖσθαι
πρὸς ἀλλήλας κυρίως λέγοιντο· ποῖον γὰρ αὐταῖς εἶδος ἁρμόσει τῶν ἀντικειμένων; εἰ δὲ τὰς ἀντιφατικῶς ταύταις ἀντικειμένας ζητοίης, εὑρήσεις
ἀντιφασκούσας ταῖς καθόλου τὰς κατὰ μέρος μετὰ τῆς κατὰ τὸ ποιὸν ἀντι- ¹⁰
30 θέσεως, τοῦτ' ἔστι τῇ μὲν καθόλου καταφάσει τὴν μερικὴν ἀπόφασιν, τῇ
δὲ καθόλου ἀποφάσει τὴν μερικὴν κατάφασιν· ὥστε κατὰ τὸ ὑποκείμενον
διάγραμμα τὰς διαγώνιον θέσιν πρὸς ἀλλήλας ἐχούσας τῶν προσδιωρι- ¹⁵
σμένων προτάσεων ταύτας ἀντιφάσκειν ἀλλήλαις· ἀεὶ γὰρ αὗται διαιροῦσι
τό τε ἀληθὲς καὶ τὸ ψεῦδος. καὶ τοῦτο εἰκότως· αἱ μὲν γὰρ ἐναντίαι
35 καὶ ὑπεναντίαι κατὰ τὸ ποιὸν διαφέρουσαι τὸ ποσὸν τὸ αὐτὸ ἔχουσιν,

6 τε om. AGM   παρέστη F   9. 10 μηδ. παρ. δυν. colloc. G   10. 11 ἀμφισβητήσεων
G¹: ἀμφισβητήσιμα M   11 ὡς om. A   14 alterum αὐτοῦ om. F   15 συναληθεύουσι M   18 πλείστων Ma   18. 19 διεστηκότα A   19 τὸ γένος τὸ αὐτὸ A:
τὸ γένος αὐτὸ M   20 ἡ μὲν om. A   πᾶσι F   21 γε om. F   22 τεταγμέ-
ναις G   κἀκείνας A   26 ἂν om. AGMa   29 μετὰ om. G   30. 31 καθόλου
καταφάσει—τῇ δὲ om. F   30 καθ. καταφ.] καθέκαστα φασὶ A¹   καταφάσει] καφα-
τικῇ M   32 πρὸς ἀλλήλαις A   33 ταύταις M   34 καὶ (post ἀληθὲς)]
ἢ A

<and> 'Some man is pale – Not every man is pale', it being clear that these are true together.

<Contraries, subcontraries, subalterns>

9. Now, having shown that the universal as universal <i.e. the general> sentences are not contradictory, they[66] call them contraries, because, given that contrary <predicates> are divided into immediate and mediated,[67] these sentences, in the necessary and the impossible matter, resemble immediate contrary <predicates>: just as one of the latter necessarily is present in the subject, so these <oppositions> have one of their sentences true, which, because of this, imitates the existence of the thing, just as the false is an image of non-existence; but in the contingent matter <they resemble> mediated contrary <predicates>, of which it is possible that neither is present in the subject. Or, since it is disputed[68] whether some of the contrary <predicates> are immediate, which those who give the cause of the appellation of the so-called 'contrary' sentences in the manner just mentioned want to assume as agreed, we should rather say that it is impossible for contraries actually to obtain simultaneously with one another with regard to the same subject, but that it is possible for them to be simultaneously absent from it. So, these sentences which are never simultaneously true, but are sometimes simultaneously false, and in this way mimic the contrary <predicate>, would reasonably be called 'contraries'. It is possible to say that these sentences are called 'contraries' also because they have the greatest distance from one another. For of predicates under the same genus, contraries are most distant from one another, and so do these sentences too relate to one another, since the one says that the predicate belongs to all individuals under the subject, and the other to none. And they call the particular sentences 'subcontraries' as ordered under the contraries and consequent upon them. For, if one of the general sentences is true, then the particular sentence placed under it will be true as well, insofar as it is like a part of it and is contained in it. Hence they also call the affirmative sentences, the particular and the general, and similarly their negative sentences, 'subaltern'. Now, the particular sentences should not even properly be said to be 'opposed' to one another[69]. For what species of opposition will fit them? If you seek those contradictorily opposed to these, you will find that particular sentences contradict the general sentences that are opposed to them in respect of <their> quality, that is, the particular negative sentence is contradictorily opposed to the general affirmative sentence, while the particular affirmative sentence contradicts the general negative sentence. Thus, according to the diagram given below, those of the determined sentences that occupy a diagonally opposite place one to the other contradict one another, for they always divide the true and the false. And that is reasonable, for the contraries and subcontraries, while differing in their quality, have the

---

66   i.e. the specialists in the field of logic (cp. 88,17-18).
67   cp. Arist. *Cat.* 10, 11b38 – 12a25 and *infra*, p. 143 of the commentary.
68   For some difficulties about immediate contraries, cp. Simpl. *In Cat.* 386,6-15 (Kalbfleisch).
69   For they can be true together.

αἱ δὲ ὑπάλληλοι κατὰ τὸ ποσὸν διαφέρουσαι τὸ ποιὸν τὸ αὐτὸ ἔχουσιν, αὗται 20
δὲ κατ' ἄμφω μαχόμεναι τελείαν ἔχουσι τὴν πρὸς ἀλλήλας διαφοράν. διὸ
καὶ ἀδύνατον αὐτὰς ἢ συμψεύδεσθαι ἢ συναληθεύειν· ὅτι μὲν γὰρ ἐπὶ τῆς
ἀναγκαίας ὕλης ἀληθευουσῶν τῶν καταφάσεων ψευδεῖς εἰσιν αἱ ἀποφάσεις,
5 ἐπὶ δὲ τῆς ἀδυνάτου τοὐναντίον, προφανὲς ἐκ τῶν πρότερον εἰρημένων. 25
ἐπὶ δὲ τῆς ἐνδεχομένης ψευδομένης τῆς καθόλου καταφάσεως ἡ μερικὴ
ἀπόφασις ὡς ἀντιφάσκουσα πρὸς αὐτὴν ἀληθής, καὶ ψευδομένης τῆς καθόλου
ἀποφάσεως | ἡ μερικὴ κατάφασις ὡς ἀντιφάσκουσα πρὸς αὐτὴν ἀληθής· 75ᵛ
διὸ ἐκείνων ἅμα ψευδομένων αὗται ἀληθεύουσιν.

10   καθ' ἕκαστα
            Σωκράτης περιπατεῖ   Σωκράτης οὐ περιπατεῖ
                                    ἀπροσδιόριστοι
            ἄνθρωπος περιπατεῖ   ἄνθρωπος οὐ περιπατεῖ
                                 ⟨προσδιωρισμέναι⟩
                                            καθόλου
15   πᾶς ἄνθρωπος περιπατεῖ ἐναντίαι   οὐδεὶς ἄνθρωπος περιπατεῖ

                            ἀντί   φασις
        καταφατικαί   ἀποφατικαί
        ὑπάλληλοι   ἀντί   φασις   ὑπάλληλοι

                                       μερικαί
        τὶς ἄνθρωπος περιπατεῖ ὑπεναντίαι οὐ πᾶς ἄνθρωπος περιπατεῖ

    Ἐπεὶ δὲ θορυβεῖν εἴωθε τοὺς ἁπλουστέρους ἡ μερικὴ ἀπό|φασις ἐπὶ 76ʳ
20 τῆς ἀδυνάτου ὕλης συμψεύδεσθαι δοκοῦσα τῇ καθόλου καταφάσει, ὡς ὅταν
εἴπωμεν 'οὐ πᾶς ἄνθρωπος πτερωτός', διὰ τὸ δοκεῖν τῷ οὐ πᾶς συνεισά-
γεσθαι τὸ ἀλλὰ τὶς μὲν τὶς δὲ οὔ, ὅπερ ἐστὶν ἐναργῶς ἐπὶ τῶν ἀδυνάτων 5
ψεῦδος, ῥητέον τι καὶ περὶ τούτων. ἔξεστι μὲν οὖν ἐκ τῶν πρότερον εἰρημένων περὶ τοῦ οὐ πᾶς προσδιορισμοῦ προχείρως ἀποδοῦναι τῆς ἀπορίας
25 τὴν λύσιν· ἐλέγομεν γὰρ ὅτι τὸ οὐ πᾶς αὐτὸ μόνον καθ' αὑτὸ ληπτέον
ὡς ἰδίαν ἔχον δύναμιν, καθ' ἣν τὸν πᾶς προσδιορισμὸν ἀναιρεῖ, μηδὲν 10
ἕτερον ἐπισυρόμενον. ἐφ' ὧν οὖν πραγμάτων τὸ πᾶς φαίνεται ψευδόμενον,
ἐπὶ τούτων τὸ οὐ πᾶς ἀληθές· ὥστε καὶ ἐπὶ τῶν προχειμένων ἐπειδὴ ὁ
λέγων 'πᾶς ἄνθρωπος πτερωτός' ψεύδεται, ἀληθεύσει ὁ λέγων 'οὐ πᾶς
30 πτερωτός'· ἢ γὰρ πᾶς ἢ οὐ πᾶς, ἀλλὰ τὸ πᾶς ψεῦδος, τὸ ἄρα οὐ πᾶς 15
ἀληθές. ἵνα δὲ μᾶλλον αὐτῶν τὴν ἀπορίαν ἀποπληρώσωμεν, ῥητέον ὅτι

1 αἱ δὲ—ἔχουσιν om. M   3 καὶ om. FGMa   ἢ (prius) om. A   5 εἰρ. πρ.
colloc. G¹   9 post αὗται add. ἄμα Ma   10 figuram recepi ex G, nisi quod προσδιωρισμέναι et ἐναντίαι om. et ἀντιφατικαί pro καταφατικαί habet. προσδιωρισμέναι addidi,
reliqua ex ceteris libris correxi, quorum F paululum differt, Ma plus distant, figuram
om. A   21 τῶ δοκεῖν τὸ δοκεῖν (sic) A   τὸ οὐ πᾶς συνεισάγειν (συνάγειν M)
AMa   23 τι] τε a   25 λέγομεν AMa (cf. 89,15)   post πᾶς add. καθόλου ὡς
μερικόν F   26. 27 μηδέτερον M   27 ἐπισυρ.] ἐπιφερ. F   φαίνεσθαι A
29 λέγων ὡς F   31 ἀποπληρ.] ἀποκλείσωμεν F: ἀποπλήσωμεν G

same quantity, but the subalterns differ in quantity, while having the same quality; but these, which conflict in both respects, are completely different from one another. Hence, it is impossible for them to be either simultaneously false or true. For the fact that in the necessary matter, when the affirmative sentences are true, the negative sentences are false, and in the impossible matter the opposite, is obvious from what was said earlier. On the other hand, in the contingent matter, given that the general affirmative sentence is false, the particular negative sentence is true, since it contradicts it, and the general negative sentence is false, the particular affirmative sentence is true, as contradicting it. Hence, when the former are false, the latter are true.

<Diagram of the opposed sentences>

SINGULAR

Socrates is walking   Socrates is not walking

UNDETERMINED

Man is walking   Man is not walking

<DETERMINED>

General

Every man is walking   No man is walking

contraries

Affirmative   Negative
subalterns   subalterns

~~Contradiction~~
~~Contradiction~~

Particular

Some man is walking   Not every man is walking

subcontraries

<Particular negative sentences: A problem>

10. Since the particular negative sentence tends to unsettle simpler people, seeming in the impossible matter to be false simultaneously with the general affirmative sentence, as when we say 'Not every man is winged', because it seems that in 'not every' are included 'but someone and someone not', which is manifestly false in the case of impossibles, we must say something about these too. Now, it is possible from what has been said earlier about the additional determination 'not every', readily to give the solution of this aporia. For we said (89,15) that 'not every' must be taken just by itself, having a proper force, according to which it denies the additional determination 'every', without dragging in anything else. So, for those things where 'every' is seen to be false, there 'not every' is true. Thus, in the case under discussion too, since he who says 'every man is winged' speaks falsely, he who says 'not every <man> is winged' will speak truly, for: either 'every' or 'not every', but 'every' is false, thus 'not every' is true. So, in order to resolve further the aporia they have got, we should say that the particular negative sentence has a

ἡ μερικὴ ἀπόφασις παραπλησίαν ἔχει δύναμιν τῇ μερικῇ καταφάσει, κατ'
αὐτό γε τὸ μερικόν· ὅπως ἂν οὖν ἔχῃ ἀληθείας ἡ μερικὴ κατάφασις, εἴτε 20
ὡς ἀεὶ τῇ μερικῇ ἀποφάσει συντρέχουσα εἴτε μή, τὸν αὐτὸν ἕξει δῆλον
ὅτι τρόπον καὶ ἡ μερικὴ ἀπόφασις· ἐπεὶ οὖν αἱ μὲν καταφάσεις ἕξεσί τισιν
5 ἀνάλογοί εἰσιν αἱ δὲ ἀποφάσεις στερήσεσι, γνωριμώτεραι δὲ τῶν στερήσεων
αἱ ἕξεις, ἀπὸ τῆς καταφάσεως ὡς γνωριμωτέρας τὸ κατὰ τὴν ἀπόφασιν 25
θεωρητέον. τῆς οὖν καθόλου καταφάσεως κατὰ μόνην τὴν ἀναγκαίαν ὕλην
ἀληθευούσης τὴν μερικὴν κατάφασιν ἐπὶ δύο μὲν ὑλῶν ἀληθεύουσαν ὁρῶμεν,
ταύτης τε καὶ τῆς ἐνδε|χομένης, οὐ μὴν ἐπ' ἀμφοτέρων κατὰ τὸν αὐτὸν 76ʳ
10 τρόπον, ἀλλ' ἐπὶ μὲν τῆς ἐνδεχομένης δι' ἑαυτήν, ὥστε τὸ κατηγορούμενον τινὶ μὲν ὑπάρχειν τῷ ὑποκειμένῳ τινὶ δὲ μὴ ὑπάρχειν, (ὅτε καὶ συντρέχει ἡ μερικὴ κατάφασις τῇ μερικῇ ἀποφάσει, πρὸς δὲ τὴν καθόλου 5
κατάφασιν διαφωνεῖ), ἐπὶ δὲ τῆς ἀναγκαίας οὐκέτι δι' ἑαυτὴν ἀλλὰ διὰ τὴν
καθόλου· διὸ καὶ οὐ συντρέχει τότε τῇ μερικῇ ἀποφάσει· τὸ γὰρ 'τὶς ἄν-
15 θρωπος ζῷον' διὰ τὸ πᾶς ἀληθές, οὐκέτι μέντοι τὸ οὐ πᾶς ἀληθές, ὥσπερ 10
ἐπὶ τῆς ἀδυνάτου διὰ τὴν καθόλου κατάφασιν ψευδομένην καθ' ὅλην ἑαυτὴν
καὶ ἡ μερικὴ κατάφασις ψευδής, ὡς ὅταν εἴπωμεν 'τὶς ἄνθρωπος πτερωτός'·
οὐδὲ γὰρ αὕτη δι' ἑαυτὴν ψευδής. τὸν αὐτὸν οὖν τρόπον καὶ τῆς καθόλου
ἀποφάσεως κατὰ μόνην τὴν ἀδύνατον ὕλην ἀληθευούσης τὴν μερικὴν ἀπό- 15
20 φασιν ἐπὶ δύο ὑλῶν ἀληθεύειν ἀνάγκη, τῆς τε ἐνδεχομένης καὶ μήτε συμ-
φυοῦς μήτε παντελῶς ἀλλοτρίας (ὥστε καὶ δι' ἑαυτὴν ἔσται ἀληθὴς καὶ
συντρέχει τῇ μερικῇ καταφάσει, διαφωνήσει δὲ πρὸς τὴν καθόλου ἀπόφασιν)
καὶ ἔτι τῆς ἀδυνάτου, καθ' ἣν συνέσεται μὲν τῇ καθόλου ἀποφάσει ἅτε δι' 20
ἐκείνην ἔχουσα τὸ ἀληθεύειν, διαφωνήσει δὲ πρὸς τὴν μερικὴν κατάφασιν.
25 περὶ μὲν οὖν τούτων πλείω τῆς ἀξίας ἐνδιατέτριφεν ὁ λόγος, ὅλως δὲ περὶ
αὐτῶν τῶν ἀποφατικῶν προσδιορισμῶν, ὅσα γλαφυρωτέραν ἔχοντα θεωρίαν 25
ὁ φιλόσοφος παραδίδωσι Πορφύριος, πειραθῶμεν εἰπεῖν, προσεπινοοῦντες εἴ
τι δυνάμεθα καὶ αὐτοὶ πρὸς τὴν σαφεστέραν περὶ αὐτῶν διδασκαλίαν.

Ἀπορήσειε γὰρ ἄν τις πῶς | ἐκ τῶν προσδιωρισμένων καταφάσεων 77ʳ
30 τὰς ἀποφάσεις ποιοῦντες οὐ τοῖς κατηγορουμένοις, ὥσπερ ἔμπροσθεν ἠξιοῦ-
μεν, συντάττομεν τὰς ἀρνήσεις ἀλλ' αὐτοῖς τοῖς προσδιορισμοῖς, οἳ γίνονται
μέρη τῶν ὑποκειμένων, οὐ τῶν καθ' αὑτοὺς λεγομένων ἀλλὰ τῶν ὥσπερ 5
εἰδοποιηθέντων ὑπ' αὐτῶν, κατηγοροῦνται δὲ οὐδαμῶς, εἴ γε ὑποκείμενον
μέν ἐστι περὶ οὗ ὁ λόγος, κατηγορούμενον δὲ τὸ περὶ ἐκείνου λεγόμενον·

1 ἡ μερικὴ—δύναμιν om. F   1. 2 κατὰ τοῦτό γε ΑΜ   5 στέρησιν F
8 ἀληθευούσης] ἀληθοῦς οὔσης FMa   κατάφ.] ἀπόφασιν F   μὲν om. AFMa
ἀληθεύουσαν — ὑλῶν (20) in mrg. suppl. F   9. 10 οὐ μὴν—ἐνδεχομένης iter. A
11 ὑπάρχει (pr. l.) A   τῷ ὑποκ.] ὑποκειμένων F   12 πρός] ἀπό F   13 οὐχ
ἔστι a   14 οὐ suppl. G²   17 ὡς—ψευδής (18) om. M   18 οὐδὲ] οὐ F
αὕτη] αὐτή AFMa   19 ἀληθ.] ἀληθινῆς οὔσης G   21 ἐστιν F   ἀληθές A
23 ἀδυν. ὕλης a   συνέσται a   25 πλεῖον G   26 ἀποφαντικῶν (sed ν
induct.) G   ὅσω G   28 δυναίμεθα G   29 ἀπορήσῃ F   προσδιορ Μ
30 ἔμπροσθεν] p. 87,10   31 γίγνονται A: λέγονται a

force similar to the particular affirmative sentence, with regard to their very particularity. So, however the particular affirmative sentence has its truth, whether it always goes along with the particular negative sentence or not, clearly the particular negative sentence will also have it in the same way. Now, since affirmations are analogous to dispositions (literally 'havings') and negations to privations, and dispositions are better known than privations, the examination of negation must be undertaken starting from the affirmation, since it is better known. We see that, whereas the general affirmative sentence is true only in the necessary matter, the particular affirmative sentence is true in two matters, the necessary and the contingent – not in both in the same way, but in the contingent matter <it is true> because of itself, so that the predicate belongs to one subject but not to another (when the particular affirmative sentence also goes along with the particular negative sentence, but is at odds with the general affirmative sentence), on the other hand in the necessary matter <it is> no longer <true> because of itself, but because of the general affirmative sentence, and hence it does not then go along with the particular negative sentence. For 'Some man is an animal' is true because of the 'every', but the 'not every' is no longer true, just as occurs in the impossible matter: because the general affirmative sentence is false entirely on its own, the particular affirmative sentence is also false, as when we say 'some man is winged'; for not even this is false because of itself. So, in the same way, since the general negative sentence too is true only in the impossible matter, the particular negative sentence must be true in two matters, the contingent, which is neither congenital nor completely foreign (so it will both be true because of itself and go along with the particular affirmative sentence, but it will be at odds with the general negative sentence), and the impossible, in which it will accord with the general negative sentence, since it is because of that one that it has its truth, but it will be at odds with the particular affirmative sentence. Now, our discussion has dwelt on these matters longer than it should, but let us now attempt to speak generally about the negative additional determinations themselves, which the philosopher Porphyry teaches with a rather elegant theory, ourselves adding anything we can to make the lesson about them more clear.

<The negation is added to the additional determination of a determined affirmative sentence>

11. For there is a problem about how, making negative sentences from determined affirmative sentences, we combine the negative particles not with the predicates, as we advised earlier (87,10), but with the additional determinations themselves, which become parts of the subjects, not the subjects said by themselves, but those which are, so to speak, specified by the <additional determinations>, and are not predicated at all, if the subject is that which the sentence is about and the predicate that which is said about the first. For we assert of every man that he is an animal, but not that a man is every animal (this after all

ἀποφαινόμεθα γὰρ περὶ παντὸς ἀνθρώπου ὅτι ζῷόν ἐστιν, οὐ μὴν ὅτι ἄνθρωπος πᾶν ζῷόν ἐστι (τοῦτο γοῦν καὶ ψεῦδὸς καὶ ἀδύνατον ὀλίγον ὕστερον 10 ἀποδειχθήσεται), καὶ περὶ τοῦ τινὸς ἀνθρώπου ὅτι λευκός ἐστιν, οὐ μὴν ὅτι τὸ λευκὸν τὶς ἄνθρωπός ἐστι. πῶς οὖν οὐ φαμεν ἀπόφασιν τῆς 'πᾶς
5 ἄνθρωπος περιπατεῖ' τὴν 'πᾶς οὐ περιπατεῖ' ἀλλὰ τὴν 'οὐ πᾶς περιπατεῖ', 15 καὶ τῆς 'τὶς περιπατεῖ' τὴν 'τὶς οὐ περιπατεῖ' ἀλλὰ τὴν 'οὐδεὶς περιπατεῖ', καὶ τοῦτο τὸ οὐδεὶς ποίαν ποτὲ δύναμιν ἔχει, λεκτέον. ἄνωθεν οὖν πρὸς τὴν ἀπορίαν ἀπαντῶντες ἐροῦμεν κατὰ τοὺς πρότερον παραδεδομένους κανόνας τῷ κυριωτέρῳ πανταχοῦ τῆς προτάσεως μέρει δεῖν προσάγεσθαι 20
10 τὰς ἀρνήσεις, ἵνα τὰς ἀποφάσεις ποιήσωμεν· ἐπὶ μὲν οὖν τῶν καθ' ἕκαστα προτάσεων καὶ τῶν ἀπροσδιορίστων κυριώτερον ὁρῶντες τὸ κατηγορούμενον τοῦ ὑποκειμένου καὶ τούτου κυριώτερον οὐδὲν εὑρίσκοντες ἐν ταῖς τοιαύταις προτάσεσιν, εἰκότως αὐτῷ προσήγομεν τὸ ἀποφατικὸν μόριον, ἐπὶ δέ γε 25 τῶν προσδιωρισμένων τὸ κυριώτατόν ἐστιν ὁ προσδιορισμός· διὸ καὶ ἐντεῦθεν
15 ἡ πρότασις ὀνομάζεται προσδιωρισμένη· καὶ γὰρ εἰ συντάττονται τοῖς ὑποκειμένοις | οἱ προσδιορισμοὶ καὶ γίνονται αὐτῶν, ὡς εἴρηται, μέρη, ἀλλ' 77ᵛ ἐφάπτονταί πως καὶ τῶν κατηγορουμένων δηλοῦντες εἴτε ἑνὶ τῶν ὑπὸ τὸ ὑποκείμενον εἴτε πᾶσιν ὑπάρχει τὸ κατηγορούμενον, ἐπειδὴ τὸ πλείοσι μὲν μὴ πᾶσι δὲ περιορίσαι δίχα τοῦ τὸν ἀριθμὸν προσθεῖναι οὐκ ἔστι. διὰ 5
20 ταῦτα μὲν οὖν τούτοις εἰκότως τὸ ἀρνητικὸν συντάττεται μόριον καὶ αἱ τοῦτον τὸν τρόπον γινόμεναι ἀποφάσεις ἀντιφατικῶς ἀντίκεινται ταῖς καταφάσεσι, τῶν δὲ συντατττουσῶν αὐτὸ τῷ κατηγορουμένῳ ἡ μὲν ἐπὶ τῆς 10 καθόλου καταφάσεως τοῦτο ποιοῦσα τῇ καθόλου ἀποφάσει τὴν αὐτὴν ἔχει δύναμιν (τὸ γὰρ 'πᾶς οὐ περιπατεῖ' ταὐτὸν σημαίνει τῷ 'οὐδεὶς περιπατεῖ'),
25 ἡ δὲ ἐπὶ τῆς μερικῆς τῇ μερικῇ ἀποφάσει· τί γὰρ ἄλλο σημαίνει τὸ 'τὶς οὐ περιπατεῖ' ἢ ὅτι οὐ πᾶς περιπατεῖ; ὥστε ἐπὶ ταύτης συντρέχειν ἀλλή- 15 λαις τὰς καθ' ἑκάτερον τὸν τρόπον γινομένας ἀποφάσεις.

Τὸ μὲν οὖν οὐ πᾶς ὅτι σύνθετον ἔκ τε τοῦ πᾶς καὶ τοῦ ἀναιροῦντος αὐτὸ μορίου, φανερόν· τὸ δέ γε οὐδείς πόθεν ἐροῦμεν ἐσχηκέναι τὴν γένε-
30 σιν; ἐχρῆν γὰρ 'οὐχὶ τίς' εἶναι τὴν προτιθεῖσαν τοῦ τίς προσδιορισμοῦ τὸ 20 ἀρνητικὸν μόριον ἀπόφασιν. ἢ ῥητέον ὅτι οὐδὲν ὡρισμένον κατὰ τὸ ποσὸν ἐσήμηνεν ἂν οὕτως λεγομένη, καὶ γὰρ μηδενὸς περιπατοῦντος καὶ πλειόνων περιπατούντων ἀληθὲς τὸ 'οὐχὶ τὶς περιπατεῖ'. καὶ ἔτι σαφέστερον ταῦτα 25

---

1 γὰρ scripsi: δὲ libri   περὶ] παρὰ M   1. 2 ante ἄνθρ. add. ὁ F: πᾶς a
2 γοῦν] γὰρ F   an ἀδύνατον ⟨ὂν⟩?   δ' ὕστερον a   3 τοῦ τὶς ἄνθρωπος F
ἐστιν om. FG   4 τὸ om. F   οὐ om. G   5 an ἄνθρ. περιπ. ⟨προτάσεως⟩?   ante
οὐ περιπ. add. ἄνθρωπος a   6 τῆς] τὴν G²   τὴν τις — οὐδεὶς περιπατεῖ suppl. G²
7 τὸ οὐδεὶς] οὐδεὶς A: οὖν F   8 πρότερον παραδ.] p. 87,14   10 οὖν] αὖ A
13 ἀποφαντικὸν AFM   15 ὀν. ἡ πρότ. colloc. M   καὶ γὰρ εἰ καὶ a   16 ὡς
εἴρηται] p. 94,31   18 ἐπειδὴ G: ἐπεὶ δὲ AFMa   19 περιορίσασθαι M   20 μόριον
συντ. colloc. AM   21 ἀντίκειται G   22 αὐτὸν F   24 τῷ] τὸ A
27 ἑκάτερον] ἕτερον AF   τῶν τρόπων M   τὸ μὲν οὖν — εἷς (p. 96,14) eicias (cf.
p. 96,15 sq.)   28 τε om. G   30 προστιθεῖσαν FMa   32 ἐσήμανεν FM

will be proved both false and impossible a little later), and of some man that he is pale, but not that the pale is some man. So, why don't we form the corresponding negative sentence to 'Every man walks' by saying 'Every <man> does not walk', but rather by saying 'Not every <man> walks', and to 'Some <man> walks' by saying 'Some <man> does not walk', but rather by saying 'No <man> walks'? And we must also say what force this 'none' could possibly have. Now, answering the objection over again, we shall say according to the rules given earlier (87,14) that the negative particle must be added in every case to the more important part of the sentence in order to make the negative sentences. Now, for the singular sentences and the undetermined ones, seeing that the predicate is more important than the subject and finding nothing more important than this in such sentences, we rightly added the negative particle to it, but in determined sentences the most important part is the additional determination, which is why the sentence is named for it: 'determined'. In fact, if the additional determinations are combined with the subjects and become, as was said (94,31), parts of them, still, they somehow touch upon the predicates too, indicating whether the predicate belongs either to <at least> one of the things which fall under the subject or to all, since to specify that it belongs to more <than one> but not to all is impossible unless one adds a number. So, for these reasons the negative particle is rightly combined with these, and the negative sentences arising in this way are contradictorily opposed to the affirmative sentences; but of the <sentences> combining the negative particle with the predicate, that which does this in the case of the general affirmative sentence has the same force as the general negative sentence (for 'Everyone does not walk' signifies the same thing as 'No one walks'), and that <which does it> in the case of the particular <affirmative sentence has the same force> as the particular negative sentence; for what does 'Some <man> does not walk' mean, other than 'Not every <man> walks'? And so, in this case, the negative sentences which arise in both ways go together with one another.[70]

<On 'none'>

12. Now, that 'not every' is a compound of 'every' and the particle which denies it, is clear. But whence shall we say that 'none' has its origin? For the negation which set the negative particle before the additional determination 'some' should have been 'not some'. Or should we say that it would have signified nothing definite in regard to quantity, if it were said in this way, since in fact 'Not some<one> walks' is true if no one is walking and if several people are walking? And this fate would have been even more clearly suffered by 'Not some<one> walks' than by 'not-some',[71] which arises by contraction from it. So,

---

70   ἀλλήκαις in Busse's text is a misprint for ἀλλήλαις (William of Moerbeke translates *invicem*).
71   We adopt Busse's suggestion of correcting the οὐχ εἶς of the manuscripts to οὔτις.

ἔπασχεν ἂν τὸ 'οὐχὶ τὶς περιπατεῖ' ἢ τὸ κατὰ τὴν ἀπὸ τούτου συναλοιφὴν
γινόμενον οὐχ εἷς. βουλόμενοι οὖν ἐμφῆναι ὡς οὔτε πᾶσιν οὔτε πλείοσι
μὲν οὐ πᾶσι δὲ οὔτε ἑνὶ γοῦν τῶν ὑπὸ τὸ καθόλου ὑποκείμενον | ὑπάρχει 78ʳ
τὸ κατηγορούμενον λέγομεν τὸ οὐδείς σύνθετον ἐκ τριῶν τοῦ λόγου μερῶν,
5 τοῦ οὐ ἀρνητικοῦ μορίου, τοῦ δέ συνδέσμου (εἴτε συμπλεκτικοῦ πρὸς τὸ
μηδὲ πάντας μηδὲ πολλοὺς ὄντος εἴτε, ὡς ὁ φιλόσοφος ἀξιοῖ Πορφύριος, 5
ἐπὶ φυλακῇ καὶ διαιρέσει τῆς ἀμφιβολίας εἰλημμένου), καὶ ἐπὶ τούτοις τοῦ
εἷς ἀριθμητικοῦ ὀνόματος, ὃ καὶ κλινόμενον ὁρῶμεν 'οὐδενὸς περιπατοῦντος'
λέγοντες καὶ κατὰ τὰς διαφορὰς τῶν τριῶν γενῶν ἀποδιδόμενον 'οὐδεμία
10 περιπατεῖ' καὶ 'οὐδὲν περιπατεῖ'. τὸ μὲν οὖν οὐδείς ἀπὸ τοῦ δέ συν- 10
δέσμου κατὰ συναλοιφὴν τὴν ἀπὸ τοῦ οὐ δὲ εἷς γέγονεν, ὁμοίως ἔχον τῷ
μηδ' ὅντινα γαστέρι μήτηρ
καὶ ἀποκρινομένῳ τὸ παράπαν οὐδὲ γρῦ, τὸ δὲ οὐθείς ἀπὸ τοῦ τέ κατὰ
συναλοιφὴν τοῦ οὔ τε εἷς.
15 Ἀλλὰ πῶς τῆς καταφάσεως τίς εἰπούσης ἐν τῇ ἀναιρούσῃ αὐτὴν ἀπο- 15
φάσει τὸ οὐδείς λέγομεν; ἢ φήσομεν ὅτι τὸ εἷς ἁπλῶς μὲν θεωρούμενον
τοῦ τίς ἐπὶ πλέον λαμβάνεται· τοῦ γὰρ τίς ἀεὶ βουλομένου συμπλέκεσθαι
τῷ ὑποκειμένῳ, καθάπερ καὶ τῶν ἄλλων προσδιορισμῶν ἑκάστου διὰ τὸ 20
σημαίνειν αὐτοὺς ὅπως ἔχουσι τὰ ὑπὸ τὸ ὑποκείμενον πρὸς τὸ μετέχειν ἢ
20 μὴ τοῦ κατηγορουμένου, τὸ εἷς λαμβάνεται μὲν καὶ τοῦτον τὸν τρόπον
ἐν τῷ
εἷς δέ τις ἀρχὸς ἀνὴρ
καὶ τῷ
εἷς κοίρανος ἔστω,
25 λαμβάνεται δὲ καὶ ὡς κατηγορούμενον οὐ μόνον ἐπὶ τῶν μοναδικῶς λεγο- 25
μένων, οἷον ὅταν λέγωμεν 'ἥλιος εἷς ἐστι' ἢ 'κόσμος εἷς ἐστιν', ὅτε καὶ
τὸ μόνος ἢ κατ' ἐνέργειαν ἢ πάντως κατὰ δύναμιν αὐτῷ προστίθεμεν,
ἀλλὰ καὶ ἁπλῶς ἐπὶ ἑκάστου τῶν ὁπωσοῦν ὄντων, | ἵνα καὶ τὸ πλῆθος 78ᵛ
αὐτῶν ὑπόστασιν ἔχῃ, τῶν προσδιορισμῶν οὔτε καθ' ἑαυτοὺς κατηγορεῖσθαι
30 δυναμένων οὔτε ἄλλοις κατηγορουμένοις εὐλόγως συνδυαζομένων, ὡς διὰ
τῶν ἑξῆς ὁ λόγος ἡμῖν ἐπιδείξει· διὰ ταῦτα μὲν οὖν τὸ εἷς, ὅπερ ἐλέγομεν, 5
τοῦ τίς ἐπὶ πλέον λαμβάνεται, συντρέχοντα δὲ ἀλλήλοις ἐν τῷ συμπλέ-

---

1 τὶς] εἷς FG   τὸ (alt.)] τὴν G   1. 2 γιν. συναλ. colloc. F   2 οὐχ εἷς] corrigas
οὔτις   3 ὑποκειμένῳ Ma   4 τὸ (ante κατηγ.) suppl. G²   an σύνθετον ⟨ὄν⟩?
τῶν τριῶν G   τοῦ om. FG   5 οὐ om. FG   6 μηδὲ (prius)] μηδὲν G
ὄντας Μ   7 καὶ (ante ἐπὶ) om. Μ   9 τριῶν om. FG   οὐδεμίαν F
10 καὶ οὐδὲν περιπατεῖ om. F   11. 14 συναλιφὴν F   τήν] τῶν Ma   τῷ]
τὸ G   12 μηδ' ὅντινα . .] Hom. Ζ 58   13 ἀποκρινομένου Ma   γρῦ ex χρῆ
corr. F   15 τῆς καταφ. τῆς a   ante εἰπούσης add. καὶ μὴ εἷς Μ   16 ante
τὸ οὐδείς add. μὴ τὸ οὐ τὶς ἀλλὰ Ma   17 τοῦ βουλ. G   20 τοῦ om. Μ   εἷς ex
τὶς corr. A   μὲν om. Α   καὶ τοῦτον] κατὰ G¹   22 εἷς δέ τις . .] Hom. A 144
23 τῷ] τὸ AF   24 εἷς κοίρ. ἔστω] Hom. Β 204   25 μοναδικῶν AFGM   26 ἢ]
καὶ FG   27 πάντων G¹   30 ἀλόγως G   διὰ] δὴ Μ   31 ὅπερ] ἅπερ G¹:
καθάπερ G²   32 λαμβάνομεν A¹Fa

wanting to indicate that the predicate belongs to neither all, nor most but not all, nor indeed to one of the things under the universal subject, we say 'none' (οὐδείς), which is a compound of three parts of speech: the negative particle 'not' (οὐ), the conjunction 'even' (δέ) (whether that is a connective regarding <the fact that holds of> neither all nor many, or whether, as the philosopher Porphyry thinks, it is taken as guarding against and distinguishing the ambiguity), and in addition to these the numerical name 'one' (εἷς) – which we also see declined, when we say 'with no one (οὐδένος) walking', and rendered according to the differences of the three genders: 'no (feminine) one walks' and 'nothing walks'. So, 'none' (οὐδείς) arose from the conjunction by the contraction of 'not-even-one' (οὐ δὲ εἷς), and is similar to

'not even whom (μηδ' ὅντινα) a mother in her belly ...' (Hom., *Il.* VI 58)

or to one responding 'Absolutely not even a whit' (τὸ παράπαν οὐδὲ γρῦ),[72] and οὐ ('none') arose from 'and' (τε) by contraction of 'and-not-one' (οὔ τε εἷς).

< 'One' vs. 'some' >

13. But why, when the affirmative sentence says 'some' (τις), do we say 'none' (οὐδείς) in the negative sentence which denies it? Shall we not say that 'one' (εἷς), considered on its own, is understood in more ways than 'some' (τις)? For, while 'some' always wants to be joined to the subject, like each of the other additional determinations too, since they signify how the things under the subject stand with respect to participating in the predicate or not, the word 'one' is understood in this way, as in:

'but one certain (εἷς δέ τις) leading man' (Hom. *Il.* I 144)

and in:

' ... one (εἷς) chief let there be' (Hom. *Il.* II 204),

but it is also understood as predicated not only of things expressed as unique—as when we say 'The sun is one' or 'The world is one', when we also add 'alone' to it, either in actuality or at any rate in potentiality—but also absolutely of each of however many, to the effect that the multitude of those ones also has existence, whereas the true additional determinations are neither able to be predicated on their own nor are they reasonably coupled with other predicates, as the discourse will show us in what follows. So, for these reasons the word 'one', as we said, is understood in more ways than 'some'. But, as they go along with one another in being combined with subjects—not with singular subjects because there is no part of them, but with subjects which are such as to be said of several things – there seems even so to be some difference between them. For since each of the

---

[72] cp. Aristophanes, *Plutus* 17.

κεσθαι τοῖς ὑποκειμένοις, οὐ τοῖς καθ' ἕκαστα διὰ τὸ μηδὲν εἶναι αὐτῶν
μέρος, ἀλλὰ τοῖς κατὰ πλειόνων κατηγορεῖσθαι πεφυκόσιν, ἐοίκασιν ἔχειν
τινὰ καὶ τότε πρὸς ἄλληλα διαφοράν· ἐπεὶ γὰρ τῶν πολλῶν ἕκαστον καὶ 10
ὅλον τί ἐστι καὶ οἷον μέρος τοῦ κοινῶς κατ' αὐτῶν κατηγορουμένου, ὡς
5 μὲν ὅλον τι ὄν, κἂν ἄτομον εἴπῃς, ἀντιδιαστελλόμενον πρὸς τὰ ὁμοειδῆ
τὴν τοῦ ἑνὸς ἐπιδέχεται πρὸς αὐτὸ συμπλοκήν, ὡς δὲ μέρος πως τοῦ κοινοῦ
τυγχάνον τὴν τοῦ τινός· διὸ τῶν μόνως ὅλων οὐδὲ ἕν τι φάναι δυνατόν. 15
καὶ ἔχει ταύτην τὸ ἕν πρὸς τὸ τί τὴν διαφορὰν ἐπὶ τῶν μερικῶν, ἥνπερ
καὶ τὸ ἑνικὸν ἄρθρον πρὸς τὸ πᾶς ἐπὶ τῶν καθόλου· καὶ γὰρ 'ὁ ἄνθρωπος
10 ζῷον' εἴποις ἂν καὶ 'πᾶς ἄνθρωπος ζῷον'· τὸ γὰρ ἄρθρον τὴν δύναμιν 20
ἔχει τοῦ καθόλου προσδιορισμοῦ, ὡς μαθησόμεθα πρὸς τῷ πέρατι τοῦ
βιβλίου. ἀλλὰ τὸ μὲν ἄρθρον τῇ ἑνώσει προσήκει τοῦ καθόλου ὑποκειμένου (διὸ καὶ τῶν μοναδικῶν ἑκάστῳ καὶ τῶν ἀτόμων συντάττεται· καὶ
γὰρ 'ὁ ἥλιος' λέγομεν καὶ 'ὁ Σωκράτης'· ἐνίοτε δὲ καὶ ἐπὶ τοῦ ὑπερέ- 25
15 χοντος λέγεται τῶν ὁμοστοίχων, ὡς ὅταν 'ὁ ποιητής' εἴπωμεν ἢ 'ὁ
ῥήτωρ'), τὸ δὲ πᾶς τῷ πλήθει τῶν ὑπ' αὐτὸ ἀναφερομένων. ὅταν μὲν
οὖν ὡς κατηγορούμενον τὸ εἰς ἀναιρῶμεν, τότε τὴν ἄρνησιν | οὐχ αὐτῷ 79ʳ
συμπλέκομεν, ἀλλὰ τῷ ἐστί τῷ κατ' ἐνέργειάν τε πάντως ἐν τῇ τοιαύτῃ
προτάσει λεγομένῳ καὶ συνδεῖν τὸ κατηγορούμενον πρὸς τὸ ὑποκείμενον
20 πεφυκότι· τῆς γὰρ καταφάσεως εἰπούσης λόγου χάριν 'ὅδε ὁ λίθος εἰς 5
ἐστιν' ἡ ἀπόφασις ἐρεῖ ὅδε ὁ λίθος εἰς οὐκ ἔστιν'. ὅταν δὲ ὡς συμ-
πλεχόμενον τῷ ὑποκειμένῳ τὸ εἰς ἢ τὸ τίς ἀναιρῶμεν τὴν ἀντιφάσκουσαν
ἀπόφασιν τῇ μερικῇ καταφάσει ποιοῦντες, τὸ οὐδείς ἢ οὗτις λέγομεν, ἀλλ'
ὅταν μὲν τὸ οὐδείς λέγωμεν, οὐχ ὡς πρὸς τὸ τίς ἀλλ' ὡς πρὸς τὸ εἰς
25 ἀπαντῶμεν καὶ τὸ μὲν οὐχ εἰς ὡς ἀμφίβολον παραιτησάμενοι τὸ δὲ οὐ 10
εἰς ὡς πρὸς τῷ ἀμφιβόλῳ καὶ κακόφωνον τὸ οὐδείς ἢ οὐθείς λέγομεν.
πρὸς δέ γε τὸ τίς ἐοίκαμεν τότε κυρίως ἀπαντᾶν, ὅταν τὸ οὗτις λέγωμεν,
οὐκ ἐπὶ τοῦ 'τις' τιθεμένης τῆς ὀξείας (οὐ γὰρ οἶδε τὴν τοιαύτην προφορὰν 15
ἡ Ἑλληνικὴ χρῆσις) ἀλλ' ἐπὶ τοῦ οὗ, καθάπερ ἔχει τὸ
30   οὗτις ἐμεῦ ζῶντος
καὶ
                    μήτις νῦν ἐνάρων.
ἀλλὰ τοῦτο μὲν τῇ ποιητικῇ τὸ δὲ οὐδείς τῇ κοινῇ χρήσει μᾶλλον
σύνηθες.

---

1 καθέκαστα μὲν G²: κατηγορουμένοις G¹   5 κἂν] οὐκ ἂν M   εἴποις GM
6 ὑποδέχεται F   πως] τι M   7 ἐπὶ τῶν μόνως Fa   7. 8 ἕν — δυνατὸν καὶ
om. F   7 ἕν τι φάναι] ἀντιφάναι a   8 ταύτην] ταύτῃ a: om. F   ὡς ἐπὶ
τῶν μερ. καθάπερ καὶ F   10 post prius ζῷον add. καὶ AMa   τὸ γὰρ] καὶ τὸ
AFM   16 αὐτὸ G: αὐτοῦ AFMa   21 ὅδε ὁ] ὁ δὲ F   22 τὸ (post ὑποκειμ.)]
τῶ A²   post ἀναιρ. add. ἤτοι Ma   23 τὸ οὐδεὶς ἢ τὸ τίς F: τὸ τίς ἢ οὐδεὶς G
25. 26 οὐ εἰς] οὐδεὶς A   26 καὶ om. M   οὐθεὶς ἢ οὐδεὶς G   27 τὸ (ante τίς)
suppl. G²   οὗτις] οὕτως M   29 ἐπὶ τὸ οὗ F   30 οὗτις ἐμεῦ ζ.] Hom. A 88
32 μήτις νῦν ἐν.] Hom. Z 68   ἐνάρων] ἐράνων F
Comment. in Arist. IV 5. Ammon. in Interpr.   7

many is both a whole and like a part of what is predicated of them in common, as a whole (even if you call it an 'individual'), set apart from those of the same species, it accepts being combined with 'one', and as being in a way a part of what is common <to the many>, <it accepts being combined with> 'some'; hence, it is not even possible to say 'some one' of what are only wholes. And 'one' has the same difference from 'some' in the case of particular sentences as the singular article has from 'every' in the case of general sentences. That is, you could say 'Man is an animal' and 'Every man is an animal' for the article has the force of the universal determination, as we shall learn near the end of the book (ch. 14, 24a3ff.). However, the article fits the unity of the universal subject (hence, it is also combined with each of the singulars and the individuals, for we say 'the sun' and '[the] Socrates'; but sometimes it is also said of what is outstanding in its field, as when we say 'the Poet' or 'the Orator'), but 'every' <fits> the multitude of <things> subsumed under <the universal>. So, when we deny 'one' as predicate, then we join the negative particle not to it, but to the 'is', which is always actually said in this sort of sentence and is such as to bind the predicate with the subject; for, when the affirmative sentence says, for example, 'this stone is one', the negative will say 'this stone is-not one'. But, when we deny the 'one' or the 'some' as joined with the subject and make the negative sentence which contradicts the particular affirmative sentence, we say 'none' (οὐδείς) or 'not some' (οὔτις), and when we say 'none', we are responding not to the 'some' (τις), but to the 'one' (εἷς), and rejecting 'not one' (οὐχ εἷς) as ambiguous, and 'no(t) one' (οὐ εἷς) as not only ambiguous but ugly as well, we say 'none' in either of its forms (οὐδείς or οὐθείς). But it is to the 'some' (τις) that we then seem properly to respond when we say 'not some' (οὔτις), with an acute accent not on the 'some' (for this pronunciation is unknown to Greek usage), but on the 'not', as it is in:

'no one (οὔτις) while I live ...' (Hom. *Il.* I 88)

and in:

'no one (μήτις) now of the spoils ...' (Hom. *Il.* VI 68).

But this is more common in poetic and 'none' (οὐδείς) <is more frequent> in common usage.

Τοσαῦτα μὲν περὶ τῶν προσδιωρισμένων προτάσεων εἴχομεν λέγειν· 20
αἱ δὲ ἀπροσδιόριστοι πῶς ἔχουσι πρὸς τὸ ἀντιφάσκειν ἢ μή, τοῦτο δέ ἐστιν
εἴ τισι τῶν προσδιωρισμένων τὸ αὐτὸ δύνανται, διὰ τῶν ἑξῆς τῷ Ἀριστοτέλει συνοδεύοντες ζητήσωμεν.

5 Ἐπὶ τούτοις οὖν τὴν ῥῆσιν αὐτὴν ἐπισκεψώμεθα, δι᾽ ἧς παραδιδοὺς 25
ἡμῖν τὴν εἰρημένην ἀπὸ τοῦ ὑποκειμένου τῶν προτάσεων διαίρεσιν καὶ
διακρίνας τὰ καθ᾽ ἕκαστα τῶν καθόλου τοῦτό φησιν εἶναι καθόλου ὃ ἐπὶ
πλειόνων πέφυκε κατηγορεῖσθαι, τῶν ὁμωνύμως κατὰ | πλειόνων 79ᵛ
κατηγορουμένων τὰ καθόλου διακρίνων τῷ πεφυκέναι κατὰ πολλῶν κατη-
10 γορεῖσθαι, τοῦτο δέ ἐστι μὴ νόμῳ τινὶ καὶ θέσει, καθάπερ τὸ Αἴας καὶ
τὸ Ἀλέξανδρος, ἀλλὰ τῷ φύσιν μίαν δηλοῦν, ἥτις ἑκάστῳ τῶν πλειόνων 5
ὑπάρχουσα ποιεῖ καὶ τὸ σημαῖνον αὐτὴν ὄνομα κατ᾽ αὐτῶν κατηγορεῖσθαι.
ὅλως δὲ περὶ φωνῶν διαλεγόμενος τῶν πραγμάτων ποιεῖται τὴν διαίρεσιν,
διότι περὶ φωνῶν τοῖς φιλοσόφοις ὁ λόγος οὐ προηγουμένως, καθάπερ
15 ῥήτορσί τε καὶ γραμματικοῖς, ὡς καὶ πρότερον ἐλέγομεν, ἀλλὰ τῆς τῶν 10
πραγμάτων καταλήψεως ἕνεκεν. διελόμενος οὖν τὰ εἴδη τῶν προτάσεων
εἴς τε τὰς καθόλου καὶ τὰς καθ᾽ ἕκαστα, προστίθησι τὴν τῶν καθόλου
διαίρεσιν εἴς τε τὰς καθόλου ὡς καθόλου λεγομένας καὶ τὰς ἀπροσδιο- 15
ρίστους· τῶν γὰρ μερικῶν ἐφεξῆς ποιήσεται μνείαν. ἐν δέ γε τούτοις τὰς
20 μὲν καθόλου ἐπὶ τῶν καθόλου ἀποφάνσεις ἐναντίας εἶναί φησι, δι᾽ ἃς ἐλέγομεν αἰτίας, τὰς δὲ ἐπὶ τῶν καθόλου μὴ καθόλου δέ, τοῦτ᾽ ἔστι τὰς
ἀπροσδιορίστους, αὐτὰς μὲν μὴ εἶναι ἐναντίας, τὰ μέντοι δηλούμενα ὑπ᾽ 20
αὐτῶν δύνασθαί ποτε εἶναι ἐναντία. ὅτι μὲν οὖν καθόλου μὴ καθόλου
τὰς ἀπροσδιορίστους καλεῖ, καὶ τὰ παρατιθέμενα παρ᾽ αὐτοῦ παραδείγματα
25 σαφῶς σημαίνουσιν, ῾ἄνθρωπος λευκός ἐστι᾽ καὶ ῾ἄνθρωπος λευκὸς οὐκ ἔστι᾽.
καλεῖ δὲ αὐτὰς οὕτως διὰ τὸ μὴ προσκεῖσθαι ἐπ᾽ αὐτῶν τῷ καθόλου ὑπο- 25
κειμένῳ τοὺς καθόλου προσδιορισμούς, ὅπερ εἰ καὶ ἐπὶ τῶν μερικῶν
ἁρμόζειν δυνατόν, ἀλλ᾽ ἔχουσί τι ἴδιον ἐκεῖναι, τοὺς μερικοὺς προσδιορισμούς,
ὅθεν καὶ | ὀνομάζονται. πῶς δὲ λέγονται μὴ εἶναι μὲν ἐναντίαι, σημαίνειν 80ʳ
30 δέ ποτε ἐναντία, τοῦτο ἤδη πολλὰ τοῖς ἐξηγηταῖς πράγματα παρέσχε· μή-
ποτε δὲ ταῖς ῥήσεσιν αὐταῖς προσφυὲς ἢ τὸ λέγειν ὅτι βούλεται μὲν ὁ
Ἀριστοτέλης τὰς ἀπροσδιορίστους προτάσεις συναληθεύειν ἀλλήλαις, ὡς 5
ἔσται διὰ τῶν ἑξῆς φανερόν, καὶ διὰ τοῦτο εἰκότως ἀποφαίνεται μὴ εἶναι
αὐτὰς ἐναντίας· οὐ γὰρ ἐναντίων τὸ συνυπάρχειν ἀλλήλαις.

35 Ἀλλ᾽ ἐπεὶ δυνατόν ποτε τὴν ἀπόφασιν ἐπὶ τῆς τοῦ ἐναντίου καταφά- 10
σεως ἀληθεύουσαν παρασχεῖν τισιν ὑποψίαν, ὅτι ἐναντίας χρὴ τότε καλεῖν
ταύτας τὰς προτάσεις, ἅτε ἐναντία τινὰ σημαινούσας, διὰ τοῦτο προστίθησι
τὸ αἴτιον τοῦ παραλογισμοῦ τοῖς οὕτως ὑπολαμβάνουσι, τὰ αὐτὰ λέγων

---

1 ἔχομεν M   3 εἴ τισι] τίσι F   ἐφεξῆς A   4 ζητήσομεν FG   10 τινι
om. F   11 τὸ φύσιν F   ἑκάστη AM   13. 14 διαλεγ.—φωνῶν om. F
15 πρότερον ἐλέγομεν] p. 66, 7   19 τούτοις om. M   20. 21 ἐλέγομεν] p. 92,4
23 ἐναντ. εἶναι colloc. G   26 περικεῖσθαι Ma   32 τὰς om. A   34 ἐναντίον
(alt. l.) a   ἀλλήλοις F   35 ἐπὶ] ἀπὸ A   36 τότε om. M

<*Which undetermined sentences contradict one another?*>

14. So much did we have to say about the determined sentences. But how the undetermined sentences relate to contradicting or not, i.e. whether they have the same force as some of the determined sentences, let us examine in what follows, travelling along with Aristotle.

<*Return to Aristotle's text. Undetermined sentences*>

15. Concerning this, let us examine the text itself, in which <Aristotle>, having taught us the division just discussed of the sentences on the basis of their subject and distinguished the singular <terms> from the universal <terms>, says: this is *'universal, what is according to its nature such as to be predicated of several things'*, distinguishing the universal <terms> from <terms> predicated homonymously of several things by their being naturally such as to be predicated of several things, that is, not by some convention or imposition, such as the terms 'Ajax' and 'Alexander',[73] but by revealing one nature, which, by belonging to each of the several, makes the name which signifies it also be said of them. And, in general, although speaking about vocal sounds, he makes the distinction between things. because for philosophers discourse is not primarily about vocal sounds, as we said earlier (65,2ff.) that it is for rhetoricians and grammarians, but <it is> rather for the sake of understanding the things. So, having divided the species of sentences into the universal and the singular, he adds the division of the universal into those called 'universal as universal' <i.e. the general> and the undetermined; he will mention the particular ones next (17b16ff.). And in these words he says that the universal assertions about universals <i.e. the generals> are contraries, for the reasons we stated (92,3ff.), while those about universals but not universally, i.e. the undetermined ones, *are not themselves contraries, but the things they indicate can sometimes be contraries*. That by 'universal not universally' he means the undetermined sentences, is also clearly shown by the examples he gives, 'Man is pale' and 'Man is not pale'. And he calls them thus because in them the universal additional determinations are not added to the universal subject; and even though <this reason> can also apply to particular sentences, those still have a peculiarity, namely the particular additional determinations from which they take their name. And why are they said not to be contraries, but sometimes to signify contrary <things>? This has already caused many problems for interpreters;[74] perhaps however it fits the text as it stands to say that Aristotle wants the undetermined sentences to be true simultaneously with one another, as will be obvious in what follows, and for this reason rightly asserts that *they are not contraries*: for obtaining simultaneously with one another does not belong to contraries.

<*'but the things they indicate can sometimes be contraries.' Porphyry's account*>

16. Since, however, the fact that sometimes the negation <of a predicate> is true because of the affirmation of its contrary[75] might possibly make some people suspect that these sentences would then have to be called 'contraries', since they signify contrary <things>, for this reason <Aristotle> adds[76] the cause of the paralogism for those who make this

---

73   These terms signify Ajax the son of Telamon and Ajax the son of Oileus, Alexander the son of Priam and Alexander the Great.

74   We can learn the history of these interpretations from Boethius (*In De Int. editio secunda* 157,30ff.).

75   *E.g.* "(man) is not healthy" is true because of the truth of "(man) is ill" and "(man) is not white" because of the truth of "(man) is black."

76   i.e. "but the things they indicate can sometimes be contraries."

τοῖς ἐν τῷ τελευταίῳ θεωρήματι τοῦ βιβλίου ῥηθησομένοις· τὸ μὲν δὴ 15
τούτῳ οἴεσθαι τὰς ἐναντίας δόξας ὡρίσθαι, τῷ τῶν ἐναντίων
εἶναι, ψεῦδος· τοῦ γὰρ ἀγαθοῦ ὅτι ἀγαθὸν καὶ τοῦ κακοῦ ὅτι
κακόν, ἡ αὐτὴ ἴσως καὶ ἀληθής, εἴτε πλείους εἴτε μία ἐστίν·
5 ἐναντία δὲ ταῦτα, ἀλλ᾽ οὐ τῷ ἐναντίων εἶναι ἐναντία, ἀλλὰ 20
μᾶλλον τῷ ἐναντίως. ὅτι μὲν οὖν κατ᾽ οὐδένα τρόπον προσήκει ταῖς
ἀπροσδιορίστοις τὸ τῶν ἐναντίων ὄνομα, σαφῶς ἀπεφήνατο διὰ τούτων ὁ
Ἀριστοτέλης. πότε δὲ ἔστιν εἶναι τὰ δηλούμενα ἐναντία, καλῶς διήρ-
θρωσεν ὁ φιλόσοφος Πορφύριος· οὐ γὰρ ἀεί, φησί, τῷ καταφασκομένῳ 25
10 ἔστι τι ἐναντίον οὐδὲ τὴν ἀπόφασιν δυνατὸν ἀεὶ λέγειν ἀληθεύεσθαι κατὰ
τοῦ ἐναντίου τῷ καταφαθέντι, ἀλλὰ ποτὲ μὲν κατὰ τοῦ ἐναντίου ποτὲ δὲ
κατὰ | στερήσεως ποτὲ δὲ κατ᾽ οὐδετέρου τούτων, ἀλλ᾽ ἀναιρεῖν μόνον τὸ 80ᵛ
εἰρημένον διὰ τῆς καταφάσεως· τῷ μὲν γὰρ περιττῷ τὸ ἄρτιον καὶ τῷ
λευκῷ τὸ μέλαν ἐναντίον, καὶ κατὰ τούτων ἀληθεύονται τὸ οὐ περιττὸν
15 καὶ τὸ οὐ λευκόν (ἐξ ἀνάγκης μὲν οὖν συνεισφερομένων ταῖς ἀποφάσεσιν 5
ἐπὶ τῶν ἀμέσων εἶναι λεγομένων ἐναντίων, ἐνδεχομένως δὲ καὶ ἐπὶ τῶν
ἐμμέσων), τῷ μέντοι ὁρᾶν τὸ ἀντικείμενον στέρησις ἢ τῆς ἐνεργείας ἢ
καὶ τῆς δυνάμεως, τῆς μὲν ἐνεργείας ὡς ἐπὶ τοῦ μὴ πηροῦ μὲν καθεύ- 10
δοντος δὲ ἢ μύοντος, τῆς δὲ δυνάμεως ὡς ἐπὶ τοῦ τυφλοῦ, ἅπερ σημαίνει
20 τὸ μὴ ὁρᾶν (ἐνίοτε δὲ καὶ τὸ μήπω τὴν δύναμιν τὴν προαγωγὸν τῆς ἐνεργείας ἀπειληφὸς τῇ ἀποφάσει τῆς ἐνεργείας σημαίνομεν ὡς ἐπὶ τοῦ σκυ-
λακίου, καὶ τὸ μηδαμῶς τῆς δυνάμεως δεκτικὸν ὡς ἐπὶ τοῦ ξύλου· καὶ 15
γὰρ τὸ ξύλον λέγομεν μὴ ὁρᾶν), καὶ κατ᾽ οὐδὲν τούτων ἐναντίον εἴποις
ἂν εἶναι τῇ καταφάσει τὸ σημαινόμενον ὑπὸ τῆς ἀποφάσεως, ἀλλὰ ποτὲ
25 μὲν στέρησιν ποτὲ δὲ οὐδὲ στέρησιν ἀλλ᾽ ἑτερότητα μόνον, τῷ δέ γε ζῴῳ
ἢ ἄλλῃ οὐσίᾳ οὔτε ὡς ἐναντίον οὔτε ὡς στέρησιν τοιαύτην εὕροις ἄν ποτέ 20
τι ἀντιτιθέμενον, οὐδὲ τῷ ἀφωρισμένῳ ποσῷ ἢ σχήματι οὐδὲ ταῖς ἐνερ-
γείαις ταῖς μὴ κατά τι τῶν ἐναντίων γινομέναις· τῷ μὲν γὰρ θερμαίνειν
ἐστὶν ἐναντίον τὸ ψύχειν, ἐπεὶ καὶ τῷ θερμῷ τὸ ψυχρόν, οὐ μὴν τῷ
30 νοεῖν ἢ τῷ βαδίζειν εἴη ἄν τι ἐναντίον. διὰ ταῦτα οὖν τὸ ὑπὸ τῆς ἀποφά- 25
σεως σημαινόμενον ποτέ φησιν ἐναντίον εἶναι τῷ ὑπὸ τῆς καταφάσεως

---

1 τοῖς—ῥηθησομένοις] p. 23ᵇ3   2 δόξας om. A   τῷ om. G   3 ψεῦδος] οὐκ
ἀληθές G   ὅτι καὶ ἀγαθὸν A   4 ἴσως ἔσται a: ἀληθὴς ἔσται b   ἀληθές A
5 τῷ AF: τῶν GMa   6 μᾶλλον om. G   post οὖν add. οὐδαμῶς G
τοῖς a   8 εἶναι om. F: post δηλούμ. colloc. a   9 καταφασκ.] κατα
suppl. G²   10 τι] τὸ M   ἀεὶ δυν. colloc. G   λέγειν om. M   ἀληθεύεσθαι]
ἀποφαίνεσθαι G¹   11 καταφανθέντι FGMa   12 ποτὲ δὲ κατ᾽ οὐδετέρου τούτων ποτὲ
δὲ κατὰ στερ. colloc. F   ἀλλ᾽ om. AM   ἀναιρεῖ F   13 μὲν om. a
16 ἐνδεχομένης M   καὶ om. FG   17. 18 ἢ καὶ] καὶ A: ἢ G   18 ἐνεργ. μὲν
colloc. A   21 τοῦ om. FG   22 ὂν δεκτ. G   23 οὐδένα AMa
23. 24 εἴποις ἂν] ἐποίησεν F: ἂν εἴποις G   25 οὐδὲ] οὐ FGMa   26 ποτέ om. F
27 τι] τινα M   ἀντιθέμενον A   ἀφορισμ. Ma   28 γιγνομέναις (ubique) A
29 ψυχραίειν G   τῷ (post μὴν)] τὸ AM   30 τῷ (ante βαδ.) om. AMa   ἂν
om. F   τι om. a

7*

assumption, by saying the same thing as will be said in the last theorem of the book (ch. 14, 23b3-7): *'To think that contrary beliefs are defined in this way, by being of contraries, is false; for the <belief> of the good, that it is good, and of the bad, that it is bad, is perhaps the same <belief> and is true, whether they are one or more than one. These <i.e. the good and the bad> are contraries, but <the beliefs> are not contraries[77] by being of contraries, but rather by being to the contrary effect.'* Now, Aristotle clearly showed in these words that the name 'contraries' in no way fits undetermined sentences. The philosopher Porphyry[78] well analysed <the cases> when *the things they indicate can be contraries*. For, he says, there is not always some contrary <predicate> to what is being affirmed,[79] nor is it possible to say that always the negation <of a predicate> is true according to the contrary of what has been affirmed,[80] but rather sometimes according to the contrary, sometimes according to the privation,[81] and sometimes according to neither of these, merely denying what is said by the affirmative sentence. For the even is contrary to the odd and the dark to the pale, and 'not odd' and 'not pale' are true of these (so they are necessarily brought together with their negations in the case of the so-called 'immediate' contraries,[82] but also contingently in the case of mediate <contraries>).[83] However, the opposite of 'seeing' is a privation, either of the activity or of the capacity as well: of the activity as in one who is not blind, but is sleeping or has his eyes closed, and of the capacity as in the blind person; these are the meanings of 'not seeing' (but sometimes we also signify by the negation of the activity that which has not yet acquired the capacity which brings about the activity, as in the puppy, and also that which is in no way receptive of the capacity, as in wood, for in fact we say that wood does not see). And in neither of these cases would you say that what is signified by the negative sentence is contrary to the affirmative sentence, but rather that it is now a privation, now not even a privation, but merely an otherness. But you would never find something opposed to 'animal' or another substance, either as a contrary or a privation, nor to a definite quantity or shape, nor to the activities which do not arise in respect to some contrary. For cooling is contrary to heating, since the cool is also contrary to the warm, but there would be no contrary to thinking or walking. So, for these reasons he <i.e. Aristotle> says that what is signified by the negative sentence is sometimes contrary to what is indicated by the

---

[77] As the context shows ἐναντία must refer not to things but to beliefs (δόξαι) and therefore we correct it to ἐναντίαι, which in fact one main tradition of Aristotle's manuscripts has and which Minio-Paluello adopted.

[78] cp. Porphyrius, *Fragmenta*, ed. A. Smith, Stuttgart/Leipzig, 1993, fr. 97. Smith thinks that we have here a direct quotation going from 99,9 to the end of the paragraph (100,29).

[79] *e.g.* "is walking" does not have any contrary.

[80] *E.g.* "(man) is not white" is not always true if "(man) is black" is true.

[81] *E.g.* "(man) does not see" is true if "(man) is blind" is true.

[82] Like "odd" and "even".

[83] Like "dark" and "pale".

δηλουμένῳ, τῶν προτάσεων αὐτῶν μηδαμῶς ἀλλήλαις οὐσῶν ἐναντίων. |
τοῦτο δὲ εἰκότως ἐπὶ μόνων τῶν ἀπροσδιορίστων ἐπεσημήνατο, διότι μόναι 81ʳ
αὗται τῶν καθόλου προτάσεων κατὰ τοὺς κατηγορουμένους ὅρους μόνους
ἔχουσι τὰς καταφάσεις καὶ ἀποφάσεις γινομένας, ἀλλ' οὐ κατά τινας προσ- 5
5 διορισμούς, οἳ οὐδ' ἂν ὑποπτευθεῖεν καθ' ἑαυτοὺς λαμβανόμενοι καταφατι-
κῶς καὶ ἀποφατικῶς, οἷον πᾶς, οὐ πᾶς, τίς, οὐδείς, ἐναντιότητα πραγμάτων
σημαίνειν, καθάπερ οἱ κατηγορούμενοι, καὶ μάλιστά γε ὅταν ἐπὶ τῶν ἀμέσων λεγομένων ἐναντίων ποιώμεθα τὴν κατάφασιν καὶ τὴν ἀπόφασιν (ἔργον 10
γὰρ τῶν προσδιορισμῶν, ὡς πολλάκις εἰρήκαμεν, μόνην σημαίνειν τὴν κατὰ
10 τὸ πλῆθος διαφορὰν τῶν ὑπὸ τὸ ὑποκείμενον ἀναφερομένων ὡς μετεχόντων ἢ μὴ μετεχόντων τοῦ ἐν τῇ προτάσει κατηγορουμένου), καὶ ὅτι
προφανῆ τὰ ἐπὶ τῶν ἄλλων ἀντιθέσεων συμβαίνοντα, οἷον ὅτι αἱ καθόλου 15
ὡς καθόλου συμψεύδονται, διὸ ἐναντίαι, ὅτι αἱ μερικαὶ συναληθεύουσι καὶ
οὐδ' ἂν ὑποπτεύσειέ τις προσήκειν αὐταῖς τὸ ὄνομα τῶν ἐναντίων, ὅτι αἱ
15 διαγώνιοι καὶ αἱ καθ' ἕκαστα μερίζουσι τό τε ἀληθὲς καὶ τὸ ψεῦδος· ἐπὶ 20
δὲ τῶν ἀπροσδιορίστων ἐπεὶ μήτε καθ' ἕκαστα καὶ ὡρισμένος οὗτός ἐστιν
ὁ ὑποκείμενος μήτε πρόσκειταί τις αὐτῷ τῶν προσδιορισμῶν, οὐ σφόδρα
ἐστὶ φανερὸς ὁ τῆς ἀντιθέσεως αὐτῶν τρόπος, ἀλλὰ καὶ ὡς ἐναντίας ὑπο-
πτεύσειεν ἄν τις αὐτὰς ἀντικεῖσθαί ποτε. καὶ τοῦτο διισχυρίζεται σημαίνειν 25
20 ὁ ἀπὸ τῆς Ἀφροδισιάδος ἐξηγητὴς τὸ τὰ δηλούμενα ὑπ' αὐτῶν ἐναντία
εἶναί ποτε, καὶ ταῦτα τοῦ Ἀριστοτέλους ἐν τοῖς ἑξῆς βοῶντος ὡς ταῖς
μερικαῖς τὴν αὐτὴν ἔχουσι δύναμιν, | τῶν δὲ μερικῶν ἀπὸ διαμέτρου πρὸς τὰς 81ᵛ
ἐναντίας ἐχουσῶν. καὶ αὐτὸ τοῦτο τὸ τῷ Ἀριστοτέλει δοκοῦν συναληθεύειν
αὐτὰς ἐπί τινος ὕλης ἕτερος ἄν τις οἰηθείη καὶ ἀντιφάσκειν πρὸς ἀλλή-
25 λας, ἀλλ' ὡς παραπλησίως τῇ ἑτέρᾳ τῶν διαγωνίων τῇ τίς καὶ οὐδείς. 5
διὰ ταῦτα τοίνυν ἐν μὲν τοῖς προκειμένοις ὁ Ἀριστοτέλης τοσοῦτον ἐπεσημήνατο μόνον, ὅτι μὴ δίκαιον καλεῖν αὐτὰς ἐναντίας, καὶ εἰ ἐναντίων πραγμάτων γίνοιντό ποτε δηλωτικαί, προϊὼν δὲ καὶ ὅτι συναληθεύουσιν ἀλλ' 10
οὐκ ἀντιφάσκουσι κατασκευάσαι πειράσεται.

30   Τὸ δὲ αἴτιον εἰπὼν τοῦ καθόλου μὴ καθόλου λέγεσθαι τὰς ἀδιορίστους,
ὅτι περὶ τῶν καθόλου ὑποκειμένων οὐ καθόλου ἀποφαίνονται, μὴ συντάττουσαι αὐτοῖς τοὺς καθόλου προσδιορισμούς, οἳ ποιοῦσι καθόλου ἡμᾶς ἀπο- 15
φαίνεσθαι περὶ τῶν καθόλου, αὐτοῦ τούτου πάλιν τὸ αἴτιον ἀποδίδωσι τοῦ
τοιούτων ἀποφάνσεων αἰτίους γίνεσθαι τοὺς καθόλου προσδιορισμοὺς ὡς

1 οὐσῶν] ὄντων M   2 ἐπεσημάνατο F   μόνον G   4 καταφάσεις καὶ om. F
γιγνομένας in mrg. suppl. A   6 καὶ ἀποφατικῶς om. F   9 μόνον G¹   10 ὡς]
ὥστε AFM   13 ante ὅτι add. καὶ G²   14 τὸ] τῶν F   15 αἱ suppl. G²
16 τῶν ἄλλων ἀποσδ. G   μήτε] μὴ G   οὕτως FG   20 τὸ] τῷ AMa
21 ἐν τοῖς ἑξῆς] p. 17ᵇ29   23 τὸ om. Fa   24 τινος ἐνδεχομένης G: τῆς ἐνδεχομένης
M: τινος τῆς ἐνδ. a   οἰηθ.] πεισθείη F   ἀντιφάσκει F   25 ἀλλ' ὡς] ἄλλος
A²FG   27 μὴ om. A   post δίκαιον add. μόνον del. G   αὐτὰς καλεῖν
colloc. M   καὶ εἰ] κἂν AMa   30 τοῦ] τῶν a   τὰς] τοὺς a   31 μὴ om. A
μὴ οὖν M   31. 32 συντάττουσαι δὲ G   32 ἑαυτοῖς G   ἡμᾶς καθ. colloc. F
33 τοῦ] τῶν AM   34 τοσούτων G   ἀποφάσεων GMa   γενέσθαι Ma

affirmative sentence, although the sentences themselves are by no means contraries of one another. But he correctly indicated that this is only so for undetermined sentences, because, among universal sentences, only the latter get their affirmations and negations merely in respect of the predicate terms, and not according to additional determinations, such as 'every', 'not every', 'some', 'none', which, when we take them by themselves as negative or affirmative, would not even be suspected to signify an opposition of things as predicates do, and especially when we make the affirmative sentence and the negative sentence in the case of so-called 'immediate' contraries (for it is the task of the additional determinations, as we[84] have often said, to signify only the difference in quantity of the <things> falling under the subject as participating or not participating in the predicate of the sentence). And <he indicated> that what happens in the case of the other oppositions is obvious, e.g. that the universal sentences <taken> as universal <i.e. the general> are[85] simultaneously false, and hence contraries, that the particular sentences are[86] simultaneously true and one would not even suspect that the name 'contraries' pertained to them, and that the diagonal and the singular sentences divide the true and the false. But in the case of undetermined sentences, since neither is the subject term singular and definite, nor is any of the additional determinations added to it, it is not very clear what the manner of their opposition is, moreover one might even suspect that they are at times opposed as contraries. And the Aphrodisian interpreter <i.e. Alexander> affirms with force that this is what the phrase *'the things they indicate are sometimes contraries'* signifies, and this in spite of the fact that Aristotle shouts in what follows (17b29) that they have the same force as the particular sentences, and in spite of the fact that the particular sentences are diagonally related <i.e. opposed> to the contraries. And someone else might believe[87] both that they are simultaneously true in a certain matter,[88] <i.e.> precisely what was obvious for Aristotle—, and that they contradict one another, but in a way similar to one of the diagonals, that of 'some' and 'none'. For these reasons, then, Aristotle here indicated only this much, that it is not right to call them contraries, even if they sometimes came to indicate contrary things, but going on he will also try to establish (17b28 ff.) that they are simultaneously true,[89] but do not contradict each other.

<' *"Every" signifies not the universal, but that it is used universally* '>

17. Having given the reason why the undetermined sentences are called 'universal not universally', namely that they are not universally stated of universal subjects, since they do not attach to them the universal additional determinations which cause us to make assertions universally about universals, he again gave the reason for this very fact, that the universal additional determinations become causes of such assertions, by couching his

---

84   i.e. Ammonius and the other members of the Neoplatonic school.

85   We must understand "in the contingent matter".

86   We must understand "in the contingent matter".

87   cp. 17b34-36.

88   i.e. in the contingent matter ("Man is pale" – "Man is not pale").

89   We must understand "in a certain matter".

ἐπὶ τοῦ καταφατικοῦ τοῦ πᾶς τὴν διδασκαλίαν ποιούμενος, ὡς ἂν τῶν αὐτῶν
λόγων ἁρμοζόντων καὶ ἐπὶ τοῦ οὐδείς. τί οὖν τούτου τὸ αἴτιον; ὅτι τὸ 20
πᾶς, φησίν, οὐ τὸ καθόλου σημαίνει, ἀλλ᾽ ὅτι καθόλου, τοῦτ᾽ ἔστιν
οὐκ αὐτὴν σημαίνει τὴν τοῦ εἴδους τοῦ καθόλου φύσιν, οἷον τοῦ ἀνθρώπου
5 (τὸ γὰρ εἶδος ἓν κατὰ τὴν ἑαυτοῦ φύσιν ὂν καὶ τὴν ἀεὶ γινομένην ἀπειρίαν
τῶν ἀτόμων συλλαμβάνειν καὶ ἑνοῦν λέγεται· περὶ δὲ ἑνὸς πῶς ἂν ἔχοι 25
χώραν λέγεσθαι τὸ πᾶς;), οὐκ αὐτὸ οὖν τὸ καθόλου σημαίνει τὸ πᾶς, ἀλλ᾽
ὅτι καθόλου, τοῦτο δέ ἐστιν ἀλλ᾽ ὅτι κατὰ πάντων τῶν ὑπὸ τὸ εἶδος
ἀτόμων καταφά|σκεσθαι τὸ κατηγορούμενον ἀποφαινόμεθα.   82ʳ

2 τί] τίς M   τοῦτο A   4 οὐκ] οὐ κατ᾽ AG¹   6 τῶν ἀνθρώπων ἤγουν τῶν
(ἤγουν τῶν in mrg.) ἀτόμων A: ἀνθρώπων ἢ τῶν ἀτόμων M   7. 8 ἀλλ᾽ ὅτι καθόλου
iter. G¹   8 τῶν om. M   9 ἀποφαινόμεθα om. F

lesson in terms of the affirmative 'every', understanding that the same arguments also fit in the case of 'none'. And what is the cause of this? That *'the word "every" '*, he says, *'signifies not the universal, but that <it is used> universally'*, i.e. it does not signify the nature of the universal species itself, e.g. 'man' (for, since the species is one in respect of its own nature, it is also said to gather and unite the infinitude of individuals which constantly arises; but how could 'every' be said of one?), so 'every' does not signify the universal itself, *'but that <it is used> universally'*, that is, 'but that we assert that the predicate is predicated of all the individuals under the species'.

AMMONII IN L. DE INTERPRETATIONE c. 9 [Arist. p. 18ᵃ28. 33]

15 p. 18ᵃ28 Ἐπὶ μὲν οὖν τῶν ὄντων καὶ γενομένων ἀνάγκη τὴν κα-
τάφασιν ἢ τὴν ἀπόφασιν ἀληθῆ ἢ ψευδῆ εἶναι, καὶ ἐπὶ | μὲν 103ᵛ
τῶν καθόλου ὡς καθόλου ἀεὶ τὴν μὲν ἀληθῆ τὴν δὲ ψευδῆ, καὶ
ἐπὶ τῶν καθ' ἕκαστα ὥσπερ εἴρηται, ἐπὶ δὲ τῶν καθόλου λεχ-
θέντων μὴ καθόλου οὐκ ἀνάγκη· εἴρηται δὲ καὶ περὶ τούτων.
20   ἐπὶ δὲ τῶν καθ' ἕκαστα καὶ μελλόντων οὐχ ὁμοίως.   5

    Παραδοὺς ἡμῖν διὰ τῶν προλαβόντων ὁ Ἀριστοτέλης τὴν ἀπὸ τοῦ
ὑποκειμένου τῶν προτάσεων διαίρεσιν καὶ διακρίνας τάς τε συναληθεύειν ἢ
συμψεύδεσθαί ποτε δυναμένας προτάσεις καὶ τὰς ἀεὶ διαιρούσας τό τε ἀλη- 10
θὲς καὶ τὸ ψεῦδος, διὰ τούτων προστίθησι τὴν ἀπὸ τοῦ κατηγορουμένου
25 γινομένην ἐν αὐταῖς διαφορὰν πρὸς τὸ διαιρεῖν πάλιν ἢ μὴ διαιρεῖν τὸ
ἀληθὲς καὶ τὸ ψεῦδος· ἐπεὶ γὰρ τὸ κατηγορούμενον ἐν ταῖς προτάσεσι ῥῆμα
εἶναι ἀναγκαῖον τὸ δὲ ῥῆμα χρόνον ἐλέγομεν προσσημαίνειν τὸν δὲ χρόνον 15
τριχῇ διαιροῦμεν εἴς τε τὸ παρεληλυθὸς καὶ τὸ ἐνεστὸς καὶ τὸ μέλλον,
ἀνάγκη τῶν προτάσεων ἑκάστην καθ' ἕνα τῶν τριῶν λαμβάνεσθαι χρόνων.
30 τεττάρων οὖν οὐσῶν ἐν ταῖς προτάσεσιν ἀντιθέσεων κατὰ τὴν ἀπὸ τοῦ 20
ὑποκειμένου διαίρεσιν, δύο μὲν τῶν διαγωνίων, τῆς πᾶς πρὸς τὴν οὐ πᾶς
καὶ τῆς τὶς πρὸς τὴν οὐδείς, τρίτης δὲ τῆς τῶν ἀπροσδιορίστων, καὶ ἐπὶ

---

                                                  15 γινομ. G   16 τὴν (ante
ἀπόφ.) om. FM   ἀληθῆ — ὁμοίως (20) om. M   καὶ ἐπὶ—ὁμοίως (20) om. a
καὶ om. A   μὲν—καὶ ἐπὶ (17.18) om. G   μὲν om. F   17 τῶν] τοῦ F
ψευδῆ εἶναι b   18. 19 μὴ καθ. λεχθ. colloc. b   19 καὶ μὴ καθ. G   24 προ-
τίθ. F   27 ἀνάγκη G   ἐλέγομεν] p. 48,3   28 τε om. AFM   ἐνεστὼς AM
καὶ (alt.) om. G   30 οὖν] τοίνυν Fa   τὴν τοῦ ἀπὸ τοῦ M   31 ante τῶν διαγ. III
litt. eras. A   32 τῆς (ante τίς)] τὴν AG²

<CHAPTER 9>

18a28 *Now, in the case of things which are or have happened it is necessary that the affirmative sentence or the negative sentence be true or false; and in the case of universals taken universally <it is necessary that> one is always true and the other false, and also in the case of singulars, as has been said, while for universals not said universally it is not necessary, but these too have been discussed. But in the case of future singulars it is not the same.*

<The division of sentences based on their predicate>

1. Having taught us through what has preceded (ch. 7, 17a38ff.) the division of sentences based on their subject and having distinguished the sentences which can in some cases be true together or false together from those which always divide the true and false, Aristotle in these lines adds the difference which arises among sentences based on their predicate with regard once again to dividing or not dividing the true and false. For since the predicate in sentences must be a verb, and we said (48,3) that a verb additionally signifies time, and we divide time three ways, into the past, present, and future, it is necessary to take each of the sentences in one of the three times. Now, there being four oppositions among sentences according to the division based on their subject, those of the two diagonals on the one hand, <i.e.> the 'every' to the 'not every' and the 'some' to the

ταύταις τῆς τῶν καθ᾽ ἕκαστα, πάνυ προσεκτικῶς τὰ μὲν τρία τῶν ἐν ταῖς
προτάσεσιν ἀντιθέσεων εἴδη κατὰ πάντα χρόνον ὁμοίως ἔχειν φησὶ πρὸς 25
τὸ διαιρεῖν τὸ ἀληθὲς καὶ τὸ ψεῦδος ἢ συναληθεύειν, λέγω δὴ τάς τε διαγωνίους καὶ τὰς ἀπροσδιορίστους, τὰς δὲ καθ᾽ ἕκαστα οὐκέτι.

5   Γινέσθω δὲ ἡμῖν ὁ λόγος ἐπὶ μιᾶς | τῶν εἰρημένων τριῶν ἀντιθέ- 104ʳ
σεων, ἵνα καὶ ὅπη διαφέρουσιν αὐτῶν κατὰ τὸν εἰρημένον τρόπον αἱ καθ᾽
ἕκαστα προτάσεις γένηται φανερόν, τῶν αὐτῶν ἁρμόσαι ἡμῖν δηλονότι
δυναμένων πρὸς τὴν διάκρισιν τῶν καθ᾽ ἕκαστα προτάσεων ἀπὸ τῶν λοιπῶν 5
δύο ἀντιθέσεων. εἰλήφθωσαν οὖν ἥ τε μερικὴ κατάφασις καὶ ἡ καθόλου
10 ἀπόφασις. ταῦτα τοίνυν εἰ μὲν κατὰ τὴν ἀναγκαίαν ὕλην λαμβάνοις, ἀεὶ
τὴν μὲν κατάφασιν ἀληθεύουσαν εὑρήσεις τὴν δὲ ἀπόφασιν ψευδομένην,
εἰ δὲ κατὰ τὴν ἀδύνατον, τὴν μὲν κατάφασιν ψευδομένην τὴν δὲ ἀπόφασιν 10
ἀληθεύουσαν· ἐπὶ δὲ τῆς ἐνδεχομένης τὴν μὲν κατάφασιν ἅτε ἐπὶ μέρους
εἶναι τὸ ἐνδεχόμενον λέγουσαν, ὥσπερ καὶ πέφυκεν ὑπάρχειν, ἀληθεύουσαν
15 πάλιν εὑρήσεις, τὴν δὲ ἀπόφασιν παντελῶς ἀναιροῦσαν τὸ ἐνδεχόμενον τὸ 15
τισὶ μὲν πεφυκὸς ὑπάρχειν τισὶ δὲ μὴ ὑπάρχειν ἐξ ἀνάγκης ψευδομένην·
ὥσπερ γὰρ κατὰ τὸν ἐνεστῶτα χρόνον τὸ μὲν 'τὶς ἄνθρωπος λευκός ἐστιν'
ἀληθὲς τὸ δὲ 'οὐδεὶς ἄνθρωπος λευκός ἐστι' ψεῦδος, οὕτω καὶ ἐπὶ τοῦ
παρεληλυθότος τὸ μὲν 'τὶς ἄνθρωπος λευκὸς ἦν' ἀληθὲς τὸ δὲ 'οὐδεὶς 20
20 ἄνθρωπος λευκὸς ἦν' ψεῦδος, καὶ ἐπὶ τοῦ μέλλοντος ὡσαύτως τὸ μὲν
'τὶς ἄνθρωπος λευκὸς ἔσται' ἀληθὲς τὸ δὲ 'οὐδεὶς ἄνθρωπος λευκὸς ἔσται'
ψεῦδος. ὁ δὲ αὐτὸς δηλονότι λόγος ἁρμόσει καὶ ἐπὶ τῆς ἑτέρας τῶν δια- 25
γωνίων ἀντιθέσεων, τῆς πᾶς καὶ οὐ πᾶς· καὶ γὰρ ἐκείνης τὰ μόρια καθ᾽
οἵαν ἂν ὕλην ληφθῶσι, παραπλησίως ἔχοντα κατὰ πάντα χρόνον πρὸς τὸ
25 διαιρεῖν τὸ ἀληθὲς καὶ τὸ ψεῦδος καταλαμβάνονται. καὶ τὰς | ἀπροσδιο- 104ᵛ
ρίστους μέντοι λεγομένας προτάσεις εἰ μὲν ἐπὶ τῆς ἀναγκαίας ἢ τῆς ἀδυνάτου ὕλης θεωροίης, ὄψει κατὰ πάντα χρόνον ὁμοίως διαιρούσας τό τε
ἀληθὲς καὶ τὸ ψεῦδος· ἐπὶ δὲ τῆς ἐνδεχομένης εἴτε συναληθεύοιεν, ὡς 5
ἐλέγετο πρότερον, κατὰ πάντα χρόνον ὑπάρξει αὐταῖς τὸ συναληθεύειν, καὶ
30 οὐ κατὰ μὲν τὸν ἐνεστῶτα, εἰ τύχοι, συναληθεύουσι κατὰ δὲ τὸν παρεληλυθότα ἢ τὸν μέλλοντα οὐχ οὕτως ἕξουσιν, εἴτε διαιροῖεν τὸ ἀληθὲς καὶ
τὸ ψεῦδος, τῆς ἀδιορίστου ἀποφάσεως οὐ τῇ μερικῇ ἀποφάσει ταὐτὸν 10
φθεγγομένης ἀλλὰ τῇ καθόλου, κατὰ πάντα πάλιν χρόνον ἕξουσι τὸ ἀντιφάσκειν πρὸς ἀλλήλας παραπλησίως τῇ τῆς μερικῆς καταφάσεως πρὸς τὴν
35 καθόλου ἀπόφασιν ἀντιθέσει.

3 καὶ τὸ ψεῦδος om. F   δὴ] δὲ G   6 καὶ om. F   διαφέρωσιν A
8 τὴν om. G   9. 10 μερικὴ ἀπόφασις καὶ ἡ καθ. κατάφασις M   13 τὴν μὲν—
εὑρήσεις (15) om. F   post κατάφασιν add. παντελῶς G   15 ὡς παντ. F
20 καὶ ἐπὶ—ψεῦδος (22) om. F   22 δηλονότι om. G   23 ἀντιθέσεως Ma
τῆς] τὴν G¹   ἐκεῖνα F   24 ἂν om. AG   κατὰ—χρόνον om. G   27 θεωροῦν-
τες G   τε om. F   29 ἐλέγετο πρότερον] p. 111,15   30 συναληθεύσουσι G
31 οὐχ οὕτως] ἐναντίως (superscr. οὐχ ὁμοίως) G   34 τῇ τῆς] τῆς τε G   κατα-
φάσεως] ἀποφάσεως Ma

'none', then as a third opposition that of the undetermined sentences, and in addition to these that of the singulars, Aristotle very carefully says that three of the kinds of oppositions among sentences divide the true and false or are true together in the same way in every time, I mean the diagonals and the undetermined <sentences>, but not the singulars.

<The oppositions in various matters and times>

2. Let us discuss one of the aforementioned three oppositions, so as to make clear how the singular sentences differ in the stated manner from them, since the same <points> are obviously able to help us distinguish <the case of> the singular sentences from the remaining two oppositions. So let us take the particular affirmative sentence and the universal negative sentence. If, then, you take these in the necessary matter, you will find that the affirmative sentence is always true and the negative sentence false; if in the impossible matter, that the affirmative sentence is false and the negative sentence true. But in the contingent matter you will again find that the affirmative sentence is true, since it says that the contingent holds for some cases, exactly as is its nature to hold, but the negative sentence is necessarily false, as it completely denies the contingent, which is such as to hold of some and not of others. For just as in the present time 'Some man is pale' is true while 'No man is pale' is false, so too in the past 'Some man was pale' is true while 'No man was pale' is false, and similarly in the future 'Some man will be pale' is true while 'No man will be pale' is false. The same argument will obviously apply also in the other diagonal opposition, that between 'every' and 'not every'. In fact, in whichever matter the parts of that opposition are taken, they are understood as behaving the same in every time with regard to dividing the true and false. If, however, you examine the so-called 'undetermined' sentences in the necessary or the impossible matter, you will see that in every time they divide the true and false in the same way: if in the contingent matter they are true together, as was said before (111,15), it will hold for them that they will be true together in every time, and not that they will be true together in, say, the present time but not in the past or the future, and if they divide the true and false, since the undetermined negative sentence expresses the same <thing> as the universal and not as the particular negative sentence, they will again contradict one another in every time similarly to the opposition of the particular affirmative sentence to the universal negative sentence.

Τῶν οὖν εἰρημένων τριῶν ἀντιθέσεων κατὰ πάντα χρόνον ὁμοίως 15
ἐχουσῶν κατὰ τὸ ποιεῖν ἀντίφασιν ἢ μὴ ποιεῖν, τὰς καθ᾽ ἔκαστα προτάσεις φησὶν ὁ Ἀριστοτέλης ἐπὶ μὲν τῆς ἀναγκαίας ὕλης καὶ τῆς ἀδυνάτου
διαιρεῖν ὁμοίως ταῖς ἄλλαις κατὰ πάντα χρόνον ὡρισμένως τὸ ἀληθὲς καὶ
5 τὸ ψεῦδος (κατὰ μὲν γὰρ τὴν ἀναγκαίαν ὕλην τὴν μὲν κατάφασιν ἀληθεύειν 20
ἀνάγκη τὸ ἀναγκαίως ὑπάρχον ὑπάρχειν λέγουσαν, τὴν δὲ ἀπόφασιν ψεύδεσθαι ἅτε ἀναιροῦσαν τὸ ἀναγκαίως ὑπάρχον, κατὰ δὲ τὴν ἀδύνατον τὴν
μὲν κατάφασιν ψεύδεσθαι τὸ ἀδύνατον ὑπάρχειν λέγουσαν, τὴν δὲ ἀπό- 25
φασιν ἅτε ἀναιροῦσαν αὐτὸ ἀληθεύειν), κατὰ δέ γε τὴν ἐνδεχομένην ὕλην
10 οὐκέτι φησὶν ὁμοίως αὐτὰς ἔχειν κατὰ πάντα χρόνον λαμβανομένας πρὸς
τὴν διάκρισιν τοῦ τε ἀληθοῦς καὶ τοῦ ψεύδους· ἐπὶ μὲν | γὰρ τοῦ παρε- 105ʳ
ληλυθότος καὶ τοῦ ἐνεστῶτος, ἅτε δὴ τοῦ πράγματος ἐκβεβηκότος περὶ
οὗ ὁ λόγος, φανερὰν εἶναι τῶν καθ᾽ ἔκαστα προτάσεων τήν τε ἀληθεύουσαν
καὶ τὴν ψευδομένην· εἰ γὰρ τύχοι λουόμενος ἢ λουσάμενος χθὲς ὁ Σω- 5
15 κράτης, ἡ μὲν κατάφασις ἀληθεύσει ἡ λέγουσα ʽΣωκράτης λούεταιʼ ʽΣωκράτης χθὲς ἐλούσατοʼ, ἡ δὲ ἀπόφασις ἀναιρεῖν πειρωμένη τὸ ὑπάρχον ἢ
ὑπάρξαν δῆλον ὅτι ψευδὴς ἔσται, καὶ εἰ τύχοι μὴ λουόμενος ἢ μὴ λελου-
μένος τῇ προτεραίᾳ, δῆλον ὅτι τὴν μὲν ἀπόφασιν κατὰ τὸν ἐνεστῶτα χρόνον 10
καὶ τὸν παρεληλυθότα λαμβανομένην ἀληθεύειν ἀνάγκη, τὴν δὲ κατάφασιν
20 ὑπάρχειν ἢ ὑπάρξαι λέγουσαν τὸ μὴ ἐκβεβηκὸς ψεύδεσθαι. κατὰ δέ γε
τὸν μέλλοντα χρόνον διαιρεῖν μὲν καὶ οὕτως φησὶ τὰς καθ᾽ ἔκαστα προτάσεις τό τε ἀληθὲς καὶ τὸ ψεῦδος, οὐκέτι μέντοι ὁμοίως ταῖς κατὰ τὸν 15
ἐνεστῶτα χρόνον ἢ τὸν παρεληλυθότα λαμβανομέναις· οὐ γὰρ ἔτι ὡρισμένως ἔστιν εἰπεῖν ποτέρα μὲν αὐτῶν ἀληθεύσει ποτέρα δὲ ψεύσεται,
25 μήπω τοῦ πράγματος ἐκβεβηκότος δυναμένου δὲ καὶ ἐκβῆναι καὶ μὴ 20
ἐκβῆναι.

Τοῦτο μέντοι τὸ θεώρημα τὸ νῦν ὑπὸ τοῦ Ἀριστοτέλους κινούμενον
δοκεῖ μὲν εἶναι λογικόν, κατὰ ἀλήθειαν δὲ πρὸς πάντα τὰ μόρια τῆς φιλο-
σοφίας ἐστὶν ἀναγκαῖον· κατά τε γὰρ τὴν ἠθικὴν φιλοσοφίαν πᾶσαν ἀνάγκη
30 προσλαμβάνειν ὡς οὐ πάντα ἔστι καὶ γίνεται ἐξ ἀνάγκης, ἀλλ᾽ ἔστι τινὰ 25
καὶ ἐφ᾽ ἡμῖν, ἐπείπερ κύριοι πράξεών τινων ὄντες καὶ ἐφ᾽ ἡμῖν ὂν ἑλέσθαι
ἢ μὴ ἑλέσθαι τάδε τινὰ καὶ πρᾶξαι ἢ μή, τὰς μὲν ἐπαινετὰς τὰς δὲ
ψεκτὰς εἶναι τῶν τε | προαιρέσεων καὶ τῶν πράξεων λέγομεν, καὶ προ- 105ᵛ
τρέπειν μὲν τοὺς πέλας ἀξιοῦμεν ἐπὶ τὰς καλὰς καὶ ἀγαθὰς πράξεις ἀπο-
35 τρέπειν δὲ ἐκ τῶν ἐναντίων. καὶ μέντοι καὶ πρὸς φυσιολογίαν φαίνεται
χρήσιμον τὸ θεώρημα· ζητήσει γὰρ καὶ ὁ φυσιολόγος εἴτε πάντα ἐξ ἀνάγκης 5

---

4 ὡρισμένον G¹   9 γε om. FG   10 οὐκέτι] οὐκ ἔστι F   αὐτὰς ὁμοίως colloc.
GM   11 ψευδοῦς AG¹Ma   12 δὴ] ἤδη F   13 φανερὸν AGM   15 ἀληθεύει Ma   alt. ἡ om. F   16 ἢ om. G   20 γε om. F   22 τε om. G
μέντοι om. A   23 ἢ τὸν ex εἴ τοι corr. A   παρελ.] παρωχηκότα Fa   24 ἔστιν
om. G   ἀληθεύει .. ψεύδεται G   25 οὔπω Fa   ἐκβεβηκότως A
δὲ] μέντοι Fa   27 τοῦ om. G   28 δὲ] μέντοι F   30 ἔστι τε καὶ Fa
31 ὡς κύριοι F   33 ψεκτὰς] ψευκτὰς F   εἶναι om. G   34 τοὺς πέλας ἀξιοῦμεν
om. G   35. 36 χρ. φαίν. colloc. a   36 ζητήσοι F

<*Future singular contingent sentences do not divide the true and false
in a definite manner*>

3. Since the three oppositions discussed are similar in every time with regard to making a
contradiction or not, Aristotle says that the singular sentences in the necessary and the
impossible matter divide the true and false in every time in a definite manner, in the same
way as do the others (for in the necessary matter the affirmative sentence, since it says that
what necessarily holds does hold, must be true, while the negative sentence must be false,
since it denies what necessarily holds; in the impossible matter the affirmative sentence
must be false, as saying that what is impossible holds, while the negative sentence, since it
denies it, must be true). In the contingent matter, however, he says they no longer behave
in the same way with regard to the assignment of the true and false when they are taken in
each time. For in the past and present, inasmuch as the thing about which one is speaking
has already occurred, the true and false singular sentences are obvious: if, say, Socrates
happens to be bathing or to have bathed yesterday, the affirmative sentence 'Socrates is
bathing' <or> 'Socrates bathed yesterday' will be true, while the negative sentence which
attempts to deny what holds or held will clearly be false, and if he happens not to be
bathing or to have bathed on the previous day, it is clear that the negative sentence taken in
the present or the past must be true, while the affirmative sentence, since it says that what
has not occurred either holds or held, must be false. In the future time, on the other hand,
he says that the singular sentences still divide the true and false even so, but no longer in
the same way as the sentences taken in the present or past time: it is no longer possible in a
definite manner to say which of them will be true and which will be false, since the thing
has not already occurred but can both occur and not occur.

<*This study bears on all the parts of philosophy*>

4. Although this study now advanced by Aristotle seems to be a logical one, it is actually
necessary for all the parts of philosophy. For, in all of ethical philosophy it is necessary to
admit that not all things are or come to be of necessity, but that there are also some things
which are up to us, since indeed, being masters of some actions and it being up to us to
choose or not to choose certain things and to do or not to do them, we say that some
choices and actions are praiseworthy and others blameworthy and we think we should
exhort our neighbours to the fine and good actions but dissuade them from their opposites.
Further, this study is also seen to be useful for natural philosophy, since the natural
philosopher too will investigate whether all that comes to be arises of necessity or whether
some things arise from chance and spontaneously. And similarly regarding the discipline

γίνεται τὰ γινόμενα, εἴτε τινὰ ἀπὸ τύχης καὶ ἐκ ταὐτομάτου. καὶ πρὸς
τὴν λογικὴν μέθοδον ὡσαύτως· αὐτὸ γοῦν τοῦτό ἐστι τὸ νῦν ζητούμενον
εἴτε πᾶσα ἀντίφασις ἀφωρισμένως διαιρεῖ τὸ ἀληθὲς καὶ τὸ ψεῦδος εἴτε 10
ἔστι τις καὶ ἀορίστως ταῦτα διαιροῦσα. ἐκτεινόμενον δὲ τὸ θεώρημα καὶ
5 ἐπὶ τὴν πρώτην φιλοσοφίαν εὑρήσεις· ζητήσει γὰρ καὶ ὁ θεολόγος κατὰ
τίνα τρόπον ὑπὸ τῆς προνοίας διακυβερνᾶται τὰ ἐν τῷ κόσμῳ πράγματα,
καὶ εἴτε πάντα ὡρισμένως καὶ ἐξ ἀνάγκης γίνεται τὰ γινόμενα, καθάπερ 15
τὰ ἐπὶ τῶν ἀιδίων ὑπάρχοντα, ἢ ἔστι τινὰ καὶ ἐνδεχομένως ἐκβαίνοντα, ὧν
τὴν γένεσιν ἐπὶ μερικὰς δηλονότι καὶ ἄλλοτε ἄλλως ἐχούσας αἰτίας ἀνάγειν
10 ἀνάγκη. καὶ οὐδὲ τοὺς πάνυ ἰδιωτικῶς διακειμένους τῶν ἀνθρώπων εὑρή- 20
σεις ἀμελοῦντας τῆς περὶ τούτου τοῦ θεωρήματος ἐννοίας, ἀλλὰ τοὺς μὲν
ὡς πάντων ἐξ ἀνάγκης γινομένων τὰς αἰτίας ὧν ἁμαρτάνουσιν ἐπὶ τὴν
εἱμαρμένην ἢ τὴν πρόνοιαν τήν τε θείαν καὶ τὴν δαιμονίαν ἀναφέρειν
πειρωμένους, καθάπερ ὁ ἀπαιδεύτως παρ' Ὁμήρῳ λέγων   25
15   ἐγὼ δ' οὐκ αἴτιός εἰμι,
          ἀλλὰ Ζεὺς καὶ Μοῖρα καὶ ἠεροφοῖτις Ἐρινύς,
τοὺς δὲ ὡς ὄντων τινῶν καὶ ἐφ' ἡμῖν ἀπομαχομένους μὲν τοῖς πάντα
ἀναγκάζουσιν ἀξιοῦντας δὲ ἡμᾶς ὡς αὐτο|κινήτους παιδείας τε καὶ ἀρετῆς 106ʳ
ἐπιμέλειαν ποιεῖσθαι.
20   Τοσαύτην οὖν δύναμιν ἔχοντος τοῦ θεωρήματος πρὸς πάντα ἡμῶν
τὸν βίον ἀναγκαῖον ἡγοῦμαι τῶν πάντα ἀναγκάζειν πειρωμένων λόγων τοὺς
δοκοῦντας παρέχειν τινὰ τοῖς ἀκούουσιν ἀπορίαν ἐκθέσθαί τε καὶ διαλῦσαι. 5
δύο δὲ τούτων ὄντων, τοῦ μὲν λογικωτέρου τοῦ δὲ πραγματειωδεστέρου,
ὁ μὲν λογικώτερος προάγεται ὡς ἐπί τινος ἡμῶν ἐνεργείας, οἷον τῆς κατὰ
25 τὸ θερίζειν, τὸν τρόπον τοῦτον· εἰ θεριεῖς, φησίν, οὐχὶ τάχα μὲν θεριεῖς 10
τάχα δὲ οὐ θεριεῖς, ἀλλὰ πάντως θεριεῖς, καὶ εἰ μὴ θεριεῖς, ὡσαύτως
οὐχὶ τάχα μὲν θεριεῖς τάχα δὲ οὐ θεριεῖς, ἀλλὰ πάντως οὐ θεριεῖς· ἀλλὰ
μὴν ἐξ ἀνάγκης ἤτοι, θεριεῖς ἢ οὐ θεριεῖς· ἀνῄρηται ἄρα τὸ τάχα, εἴπερ
μήτε κατὰ τὴν ἀντίθεσιν τοῦ θεριεῖν πρὸς τὸ μὴ θεριεῖν ἔχει χώραν, ἐξ 15
30 ἀνάγκης τοῦ ἑτέρου τούτων ἐκβαίνοντος, μήτε κατὰ τὸ ἑπόμενον ὁποτεροῦν
τῶν ὑποθέσεων· τὸ δὲ τάχα ἦν τὸ εἰσφέρον τὸ ἐνδεχόμενον· οἴχεται ἄρα
τὸ ἐνδεχόμενον. πρὸς τοῦτον οὖν τὸν λόγον ῥᾴδιον ἀπαντᾶν λέγοντας ὡς
ὅταν φάσκητε τὸ 'εἰ θεριεῖς, οὐχὶ τάχα μὲν θεριεῖς τάχα δὲ οὐ θεριεῖς, 20
ἀλλὰ πάντως θεριεῖς', πῶς ἀξιοῦτε ὑποτίθεσθαι τὸ θεριεῖν ὡς ἀναγκαῖον

1 γίνονται G   εἴτε] ἢ F   τινὰ καὶ ἀπὸ FG   ἐκ] ἀπὸ G   2 ζητοῦμεν A
4 καὶ (post τις) om. G   ἀδιορίστως G   δὲ suppl. G²   7 γίνονται G   8 τὰ] καὶ
G: om. M   ἢ] εἰ A   ἐνδεχομένως F: ἐπὶ ἐνδεχομένων AMa: ἐπὶ τῶν ἐνδεχομένων G
ἐκβαίνοντος F   ὧν] τῶν A   9 μερικῆς M   καὶ ἄλλοτε iter. A   καὶ
om. F   10 τοὺς] τὰς FG   ἰδιωτικὰς G¹   διακειμένας G   14 παρ' Ὁμήρῳ]
T 86. 87   15 οὐκ] οὐκέτι A: οὐκ ἂν G: οὐκέτι ἂν M   21 ante τῶν πάντα add.
τὸν πάντα A   23 πραγματιωδ. A   26 καὶ] ὡς AM   καὶ—ὡσαύτως] ὡσαύτως
εἰ οὐ θεριεῖς F   27 τάχα (prius)] ταῦτα F: τὰ M   28 ἤτοι] εἴ τι A   εἴπερ
οὖν F   31 εἰσφερόμενον G¹   οἴχεται—ἐνδεχόμενον (32) om. G   33 φάσκηται ΑΜ
οὐχὶ] οὐ M   34 ἀξιοῦται A: ἀξιοῖτε Ma

of logic, since this is actually the object of the present investigation: whether every contradiction divides the true and false in a definite manner or whether there is also a contradiction which divides them in an indefinite manner. You will also find that this study extends to first philosophy. For the theologian too will investigate how the things in the world are governed by providence, and whether all that comes to be arises in a definite manner and of necessity, like what holds in the case of eternal things, or whether there are also some things which occur contingently, whose coming to be one must ascribe to causes which are, obviously, particular and at each time different. You will not find even the most inexpert of people neglecting to think about this study, but some try to ascribe the fault for their errors to fate or to divine or demonic providence, as though all things occurred of necessity, like the man who ignorantly says in Homer:

> ... but it is not I who am responsible,
> but Zeus and Fate and Fury, who comes in the mists (*Iliad* XIX 86-7)

while others, assuming that there are also some things which are up to us, fight off those who make everything necessary and they hold that we should take care for our upbringing and virtue as self-movers.

<The 'reaper' argument>

5. Now, since this study has such great force in regard to our entire life, I consider it necessary to set out and resolve those of the arguments attempting to make all things necessary which are thought to pose an aporia for those who hear them. Of these two, one more based on the meaning of words and the other more based on the nature of the things, the more logical one proceeds as in the case of some activity of ours, e.g. our activity of reaping, in the following manner: 'If you will reap,' it says, 'it is not the case that perhaps (τάχα) you will reap and perhaps you will not reap, but you will reap, in any case (πάντως); and if you will not reap, in the same way it is not the case that perhaps you will reap and perhaps you will not reap, but, in any case, you will not reap. But in fact, of necessity, either you will reap or you will not reap.' Therefore the 'perhaps' has been negated, given that it has no place either in the opposition of reaping to not reaping, since it is necessary that one of these occurs, or in what follows from either of the hypotheses. But the 'perhaps' was what introduced the contingent. Therefore, the contingent is gone. Now, against this argument it is easy to answer that 'whenever you say "If you will reap, it is not so that perhaps you will reap and perhaps you will not reap, but you will reap, in any case," how do you think that the future reaping is presupposed, as necessary or as contingent?' If it is as contingent, we have what we are seeking, and if it is as necessary,

ἢ ὡς ἐνδεχόμενον; εἰ μὲν γὰρ ὡς ἐνδεχόμενον, ἔχομεν τὸ ζητούμενον, εἰ δὲ ὡς ἀναγκαῖον, πρῶτον μὲν αὐτὸ αἰτεῖσθε τὸ ἐξ ἀρχῆς ζητούμενον 25 συγχωρεῖσθαι ὑμῖν ὡς ἐναργές, ἔπειτα ἀληθὲς μὲν ἔσται τὸ πάντως θεριεῖν, οὐκέτι μέντοι χώραν ἕξει τὸ λέγειν ʽἀλλὰ μὴν ἤτοι θεριεῖς ἢ οὐ θεριεῖςʼ·
5 πῶς γὰρ τοῦ ἑτέρου τούτων ἐκβαίνοντος ἀναγκαίως τοῦ δὲ ἑτέρου | δηλον- 106ᵛ ὅτι ἀδυνάτου ὄντος χώραν ἔχει τὸ λέγειν ʽἀλλὰ μὴν ἢ τόδε ἔσται ἢ τόδεʼ; ὥστε οὐ πρόεισιν αὕτη τέως αὐτοῖς ἡ ἐπιχείρησις.

ʽΟ δέ γε ἕτερος τῶν λόγων οὕτως ὢν πραγματειώδης καὶ δυσαντίβλε-πτος, ὥστε καὶ πολλοὺς τῶν ἐπιστατικωτέρων εἶναι δοκούντων ἀπάγεσθαι 5
10 πρὸς τὴν ἀναιροῦσαν τὸ ἐνδεχόμενον δόξαν, πρόεισιν ἐκ διαιρέσεως τοιαύτης· οἱ θεοί, φασίν, ἤτοι ὡρισμένως ἴσασι τὴν ἔκβασιν τῶν ἐνδεχομένων ἢ παν-τάπασιν οὐδεμίαν αὐτῶν ἔχουσιν ἔννοιαν ἢ καθάπερ ἡμεῖς ἀόριστον αὐτῶν 10 ἔχουσι τὴν γνῶσιν. ἀλλ' ἀγνοεῖν μὲν οὐδὲν τῶν ὄντων αὐτοὺς ἐνδέχεται τὰ πάντα παράγοντάς τε καὶ διακοσμοῦντας νοῦς τε παντελῶς ἀμιγεῖς πρὸς
15 ὕλην ὄντας, μᾶλλον δέ (εἰ χρὴ τὸ ἀκριβέστερον φάναι) καὶ ὑπὲρ τὴν νοερὰν αὐτὴν ἰδιότητα τὴν ὄντως ἑαυτῶν ὕπαρξιν ἱδρυμένους· οὔτε γὰρ 15 αὐτόματον ἐροῦμεν εἶναι τῶν ὄντων τὴν φύσιν τε καὶ τάξιν, οὔτε τοὺς θεοὺς εὔλογον ἢ ἀγνοεῖν ἅπερ παράγουσιν ἢ ὥς τινας ἀφερεπόνους κατο-λιγωρεῖν τῆς τε γνώσεως αὐτῶν καὶ τῆς διακοσμήσεως· τὸ γὰρ ὑπολαμ-
20 βάνειν ὡς ἐργώδη τε καὶ ἄσχολον ποιοῦμεν τὸν τῶν θεῶν βίον καὶ ἄμοι- 20 ρον τῆς τοῖς θεοῖς προσηκούσης ἔμφρονος ῥᾳστώνης, ἐπιμελεῖσθαι τῶν κατὰ μέρος αὐτοὺς ἀποφαινόμενοι, μὴ συνεωρακότων ἐστὶ τὴν ὑπεροχὴν τῆς τῶν θεῶν γνώσεώς τε καὶ δυνάμεως πρὸς τὴν ἡμετέραν καὶ διὰ τὴν ἄγνοιαν ταύτην ἀξιούντων ἐκ τῶν περὶ ἡμᾶς τὰ κατὰ τοὺς θεοὺς σταθμᾶ- 25
25 σθαι καὶ τὴν ἡμετέραν ἀσθένειαν ἐπ' ἐκείνους μεταφέρειν, ὡς τοῦ μὲν βασιλέως ἡλίου ἅπαντα ἅμα τὰ ἐν τῷ κόσμῳ καταλάμπειν δυναμένου, πλὴν εἰ | μή τισιν ἀντιφράττοι ποτέ τινα τῶν μὴ διαφανῶν ἀλλὰ στερεῶν 107ʳ σωμάτων, τῆς δὲ ἀσωμάτου καὶ παντάπασιν ἀΰλου τῶν θεῶν δυνάμεως οὐ δυναμένης ἀπαραποδίστως τε καὶ ἀθρόως ἅπασιν ἅμα παρεῖναι τοῖς 5
30 οὖσιν, οὐδενὸς ἀντιφράττειν αὐτῇ δυναμένου πλὴν τῆς ἡμετέρας ἀνεπιτη-δειότητος, οὐδὲ τότε κατὰ ἀλήθειαν τῆς προνοίας τῶν θεῶν παραποδιζο-μένης ἢ πρὸς τὴν γνῶσιν τῶν καθ' ἡμᾶς ἢ πρὸς τὴν ἐπιμέλειαν, ἀλλ' ἡμῶν αὐτῶν παραπλήσια πασχόντων τοῖς ὑπὸ τὸ φῶς τὸ ἡλιακὸν καθεύ- 10

---

1 γὰρ om. FM   2 αἰτεῖσθαι A   4 ἤτοι] εἴ τι A: εἴτε a   5. 6 δηλονότι om. F   6 ἀδ. ὄντος] ἀδυνατοῦντος F   ἔσται] ἐστὶν AGMa   7 αὕτη] αὐτὴ G 8 οὕτως] ὄντως AG¹   ὢν iter. G   πραγματιώδ. A   8. 9 δυσαντίβλ.] scribas δυσαντίλεκτος   9 εἶναι om. G   δοκοῦντας F   ἐπάγεσθαι G   11 φησίν A 12. 13 ἔχουσιν αὐτῶν G   14 παραγαγόντας a   νοῦς] νόας F   ἀμιγῆ A   16 ἰδρυ-σαμένους AM   17 τὴν τῶν ὄντ. φύσιν M   φύσιν τε καὶ] φυσικὴν F   18 τινες A ἀφεροπόν. G¹   18. 19 κατολιγορεῖν F   19. 20 ὑπολαμβάνειν] αἰνίττεται τὸ ἔπος μενάνδρειον· τοσαύτην τοὺς θεοὺς ἄγειν σχολήν καὶ ἑξῆς in mrg. A: αἰν. τὸ μενάνδρειον ἔπος in mrg. G² (cf. fr. 174 Com. Att. fr. ed. Kock III p. 51)   20 ἀργώδη F¹   21 τῆς om. AG   τοῖς om. F   μὴ προσηκ. Ma   ἔμφρονος Ma   24 τοὺς om. M 27 ἀντιφράττοιτο Ma   29 ἀπαρεμποδ. G   33 παραπλήσιον G

then, first, you are asking that we grant you as evident just what you have been seeking from the beginning, and second, 'you will reap, in any case' will be true, but there will no longer be room to say 'but in fact either you will reap or you will not reap'—for, if one of these occurs necessarily and the other, obviously, is impossible, how is there room to say 'but in fact either this will be or this'? Thus, this argument does not work for them so far.

<The argument from divine foreknowledge>

6. The other argument, which is based on the nature of the things and so difficult to face that even many of those who are thought most expert are led off to the belief which denies the contingent, proceeds from the following sort of division: 'The gods,' they say, 'either know in a definite manner the outcome of contingent things or they have absolutely no notion of them or they have an indefinite knowledge of them, just as we do.' Yet it is not possible for them to be ignorant of anything which exists, since they bring about and arrange all things and are intelligences wholly unmixed with matter, or rather (to speak more accurately) even establish their own real existence on a level above the very character of the intellectual itself. For neither shall we say that the nature and order of the things which exist is spontaneous, nor is it reasonable <to say> either that the gods are ignorant of the very things they bring about or that they neglect the knowledge and arrangement of these things as though they were careless. The assumption that we make the life of the gods toilsome, 'unleisured', and lacking the 'wise ease' which befits the gods. when we state that they care for particular things, belongs to those who have not grasped the transcendence of the gods' knowledge and power in comparison to our own, who think because of their ignorance that divine things can be measured by our standards, and who transfer our weakness to them. <For such men> it is as though on the one hand King Sun were able to illuminate at once everything in the world, except that some non-transparent, solid bodies occasionally block certain things, but on the other hand the incorporeal and totally immaterial power of the gods would not be able unimpededly and instantly to be present at once to all existing things, although nothing is able to block it except our own ineptitude. And even then, the providence of the gods is not truly impeded either in its knowledge of our affairs or in its solicitude, but we ourselves suffer something similar to those who fall asleep or just close their eyes in the sunlight. Just as they receive the warmth which is provided from the sun to things here <on earth>, but they deprive themselves of the sun's illuminating power by their own choice and not because the god's

δουσιν ἢ καὶ μύουσιν· ὥσπερ γὰρ ἐκεῖνοι τῆς μὲν θερμότητος τῆς ἀπὸ
τοῦ ἡλίου τοῖς τῇδε παρεχομένης τυγχάνουσι, τῆς δὲ φωτιστικῆς αὐτοῦ
δυνάμεως ἑαυτοὺς ἀποστεροῦσι διὰ τὴν οἰκείαν αἴρεσιν ἀλλ' οὐ διά τινα
τοῦ θεοῦ μῆνιν ἀναστέλλοντος ἀπ' αὐτῶν τὰς οἰκείας ἀκτῖνας· οὕτω καὶ 15
5 οἱ διά τινα κακοζωΐαν ἔξω τῆς προνοίας τῶν θεῶν λεγόμενοι πίπτειν οὐ
παντάπασίν εἰσιν αὐτῆς ἔξω· οὐ γὰρ ἂν γένοιτό τις, ὅπερ φησὶν ὁ Ἀθηναῖος ξένος, ἢ οὕτω σμικρὸς ὥστε καταδὺς εἰς τὸ βάθος τῆς γῆς λαθεῖν
τὴν ἅπαντα καὶ τὰ σμικρότατα ἐποπτεύουσαν πρόνοιαν, οὐδὲ οὕτως μέγας 20
ὥστε ὑπερπτῆναι τὸν οὐρανὸν καὶ γενέσθαι ἔξω τῆς διακοσμούσης τὰ ὅλα
10 προνοίας, ἀλλὰ τῶν αὐτόθεν νεμουσῶν ἡμῖν τὰ ἀγαθὰ δυνάμεων τῶν θεῶν
ἑαυτοὺς ἀποστερήσαντες τυγχάνουσιν ἀναγκαίως τῶν διὰ τιμωρίας καὶ
κολάσεως περιαγουσῶν αὐτοὺς εἰς τὸ κατὰ φύσιν.   25
      Τούτων οὖν κατά τε τὰς κοινὰς καὶ ἀδιαστρόφους τῶν ψυχῶν ἐννοίας
ὁμολογουμένων ὄντων καὶ ἐν τῷ δεκάτῳ τῶν Νόμων ἐναργῶς ἀποδεδειγ-
15 μένων οὔτε ἀγνοεῖν τὰ ἡμέτερα | τοὺς θεοὺς δυνατὸν οὔτε ἀόριστον αὐτῶν 107ᵛ
γνῶσιν ἔχειν, ὥσπερ εἰκάζοντας περὶ τῶν ἐκβησομένων· πρῶτον μὲν γάρ,
ὡς ὁ Τίμαιος ἡμᾶς ἐδίδαξε καὶ αὐτὸς ὁ Ἀριστοτέλης θεολογῶν ἀποφαίνεται καὶ πρὸ τούτων ὁ Παρμενίδης οὐχ ὁ παρὰ Πλάτωνι μόνον ἀλλὰ καὶ 5
ὁ ἐν τοῖς οἰκείοις ἔπεσιν, οὐδέν ἐστι παρὰ τοῖς θεοῖς οὔτε παρεληλυθὸς
20 οὔτε μέλλον, εἴ γε τούτων μὲν ἑκάτερον οὐκ ὄν, τὸ μὲν οὐκέτι τὸ δὲ
οὔπω καὶ τὸ μὲν μεταβεβληκὸς τὸ δὲ πεφυκὸς μεταβάλλειν, τὰ δὲ τοιαῦτα τοῖς ὄντως οὖσι καὶ μεταβολὴν οὐδὲ κατ' ἐπίνοιαν ἐπιδεχομένοις 10
προσαρμόττειν ἀμήχανον· προηγεῖσθαι γὰρ ἀνάγκη τὸ παντελῶς ἀμετάβλητον τοῦ ὁπωσοῦν μεταβάλλοντος, ἵνα καὶ μένῃ μεταβάλλον. ὥστε
25 ἐπὶ θεῶν ἀρχῆς ἐχόντων πρὸς τὰ ὄντα λόγον τὸ παρεληλυθὸς ἢ τὸ μέλλον
θεωρεῖσθαι ἀδύνατον, ἀλλὰ πάντα παρ' αὐτοῖς ἐν ἑνὶ τῷ νῦν ἐστι τῷ 15
αἰωνίῳ ἱδρυμένα, τῶν χρονικῶν μέτρων ἅμα τῇ ὑποστάσει τοῦ παντὸς
ἀναφαινομένων καὶ μόνα μετρούντων τὰ κατὰ χρόνον ἔχοντα ἢ τὴν ὑπόστασιν ἢ τὴν ἐνέργειαν. ὥστε καὶ τὴν εἰκαστικὴν γνῶσιν πόρρω που τῶν 20
30 θεῶν καὶ ἐν τῇ ἀποπερατώσει τῆς λογικῆς ζωῆς ἀπερρίφθαι ἀναγκαῖον.
ἔπειτα πῶς ἂν δόξαιμεν κατὰ βραχὺ γοῦν σωφροσύνης μετέχειν, τῇ γνώσει τῶν θεῶν μηδὲν πλέον ἀξιοῦντες τῆς ἡμετέρας ἀπονέμειν, ἀλλὰ
τολμῶντες ἀμφίβολον αὐτὴν καὶ ἀόριστον ὁμολογεῖν; τῆς γὰρ αὐτῆς ἔσται 25

---

1 καὶ om. F   τῆς (post θερμ.) om. F   2 παρεχομένοις Α¹Ga   3 αἴρεσιν]
ἀσθένειαν F   4 ἀνατέλλ. Μ   5 πρωνοίας F   πίπτειν] πιστεύειν FG¹
6 εἰσιν suppl. G²   6. 7 ὁ Ἀθηναῖος ξένος] cf. Plat. Leg. X 12 p. 905 A   7 οὕτως
μικρὸς (μικρῶς G) AG   βάθος] μέγεθος F   8 οὔτε F   10 δυναμένων GMa
14 ὡμολογουμ. Α   ἐν τῷ δεκ. τῶν Νόμων] c. 10 p. 899 D sq.   14. 15 παραδε-
δειγμ. G¹   17 ὁ Τίμαιος] Plat. Tim. c. 5 p. 27 C sq.   ὁ Ἀριστοτέλης] Metaph.
Λ 7 p. 1072ᵃ25 sq.   18 ὁ Παρμενίδης] fr. v. 61 (Mullach I p. 120), Plat. Parm. c. 9
p. 137 A sq.   20 μέλλον G¹   εἴ γε] οὔτε AGMa   22 ἐπιδεχ.] δεχ. G
25 ἢ τὸ] ἤτοι G¹   26 ἐστι om. F   27 αἰῶνι Ma   μέτρων] μερῶν G¹
τοῦ παντὸς om. M   28. 29 ἢ τὴν ὑπόστασιν iter. F   29 πόρω Α   31 κατά]
κἂν G

wrath causes him to deflect from them his own rays, in the same way those who are said to fall outside the providence of the gods because of their evil life are not entirely outside of it. For no one, as the Athenian Stranger says ,[90] could be small enough to sink into the depths of the earth and escape the providence which surveys everything, even the smallest things, or so large as to leap over the heavens and come to be outside of the providence which arranges all things; but rather, although they deprive themselves of the powers of the gods, which immediately distribute good things to us, these people necessarily receive the <powers> which bring them through punishment and chastisement back to what is in accordance with nature.

<The gods must have definite knowledge of their creations>

7. Since these points are agreed according to the common and undistorted conceptions of our souls and have been clearly demonstrated in the tenth book of the *Laws* (899d ff.), it is neither possible for the gods to be ignorant of our affairs nor for them to have an indefinite knowledge of them, as though they were conjecturing about their outcomes. First, as Timaeus[91] taught us and as Aristotle himself reveals in his *Theology*,[92] and Parmenides before them—not only <the one who speaks> in Plato,[93] but also in his own verses[94]—there is neither past nor future among the gods, since indeed each of these is not-being: the former is no longer, the latter is not yet; the former is changed, the latter is such as to be changed; and it is impossible for things of this sort to fit with things which truly exist and which cannot even be imagined to admit change. For, what is entirely unchanging necessarily precedes what changes in any way, in order for it also to persist while changing. Thus, in the case of the gods, since they have the rôle of a principle with respect to what exists, it is impossible to think of the past or future; rather, all things among them are established in the one eternal 'now', while temporal measures appear together with the existence of the universe and measure only what has either its existence or its activity in time. Thus, it is also necessary that conjectural knowledge stand banished somewhere far from the gods and at the extreme edge of the rational life. Second, how could we think that we had the least share of wisdom when we believe we should not assign anything more to the gods' knowledge than to our own, but rather dare to agree that it is ambiguous and indefinite? The same thought—or rather, lack of thought—will also compare the knowledge of irrational animals to our own and make them too share in the grasp of universals and intelligibles. In sum, if it is absolutely necessary for the gods to be

---

[90]　Cp. Plat. *Leg.* X 905a.
[91]　Plat. *Tim.* 37d ff.
[92]　Arist. *Metaph.* XII 1072a25ff.
[93]　Plat. *Parm.* 140e ff.
[94]　Parmenides, B 8,5 D.-K.

διανοίας, μᾶλλον δὲ ἀνοίας, καὶ τῶν ἀλόγων ζῴων τὴν γνῶσιν παραβάλλειν
πρὸς τὴν ἡμετέραν μεταδιδόναι τε κἀκείνοις τῆς ἀντιλήψεως τῶν καθόλου
καὶ τῶν νοητῶν. ὅλως δὲ εἰ πᾶσα ἀνάγκη | τῶν ὄντων ἁπάντων αἰτίους 108ʳ
εἶναι τοὺς θεοὺς ἢ προαιτίους, πῶς ἂν ἔχοι λόγον ἢ ἀγνοεῖν αὐτοὺς τὰ
5 οἰκεῖα γεννήματα ἢ τὰ τῶν οἰκείων γεννημάτων ἀποτελέσματα ἢ τὰ ὑπ'
ἐκείνων καθ' οἷον δήποτε τρόπον γινόμενα, ἢ ὥσπερ οὐδὲν αὐτοῖς προση- 5
κόντων οὐδὲ ἐπ' αὐτοῖς κειμένων ἀμφίβολον ἔχειν τὴν γνῶσιν;

Κατ' οὐδετέραν γὰρ τούτων τῶν ὑποθέσεων ἐπιμελεῖσθαι τοὺς θεοὺς
τῶν περὶ ἡμᾶς δυνατὸν κατὰ τὸν τοῖς θεοῖς προσήκοντα τρόπον τῆς προ-
10 νοίας, τοῦτο δέ ἐστιν ἀπ' αὐτῆς τῆς οὐσίας τῶν προνοουμένων ποιουμένους 10
αὐτῶν τὴν ἐπιμέλειαν καὶ ὥσπερ ἐκ πρύμνης αὐτὰ διακοσμοῦντας, οὐ τῷ
βουλεύεσθαι περὶ αὐτῶν, ὡς οἱ ποιηταὶ λέγουσιν (ἔνδεια γὰρ ἡ βουλὴ
φρονήσεως) οὐδὲ τῷ ἄλλοτε ἄλλα βουλεύεσθαι καὶ ποιεῖν (ἀλλότριον γὰρ
τοῦτο τῆς μιᾶς καὶ ἁπλῆς καὶ ἀτρέπτου παντάπασιν αὐτῶν ἐνεργείας καὶ 15
15 μόνοις προσῆκον τοῖς ὑπὸ χρόνου μετρουμένοις καὶ μετὰ προαιρέσεως τὰς
ἐνεργείας ποιουμένοις), ἀλλ' αὐτῷ φασι τῷ εἶναι, καθάπερ ὁ ἥλιος οὐ βου-
λευόμενος οὐδὲ κινούμενος ἀλλὰ τῷ εἶναι, καὶ εἰ μένων ἐπινοηθείη, πληροῖ 20
τὰ μετέχειν δυνάμενα τοῦ οἰκείου φωτός· οὔτε οὖν τὴν πρόνοιαν αὐτῶν
οὕτω γίνεσθαι δυνατὸν οὔτε τὸ εὔχεσθαι καὶ ἱκετεύειν αὐτοὺς ὑπὲρ ὑετοῦ
20 τυχὸν ἢ σωτηρίας καρπῶν ἢ νίκης, ὧν τὴν ἔκβασιν ἀγνοοῦσι, πόρρω ἂν
ἐμπληξίας εἴη. εἰ δὲ ταῦτα καὶ ἀδύνατα καὶ οὔτε λέγειν οὔτε διανοεῖσθαι 25
ὅσια καὶ ὑπ' αὐτῆς ἐλεγχόμενα τῆς πείρας, ὡς αἱ πολύστιχοι τῶν θείων
ἐνεργειῶν πραγματεῖαι καὶ τὰ καθ' ἑκάστην ὡς εἰπεῖν ἡμέραν γινόμενα
τοῖς ἐφιστάνειν αὐτοῖς δυναμένοις | σημαίνουσι, δῆλον ὅτι καὶ διατάττεσθαι 108ᵛ
25 ὑπὸ τῶν θεῶν τὰ ἐνδεχόμενα ῥητέον καὶ ὡρισμένως γινώσκεσθαι αὐτῶν
τὴν ἔκβασιν· μᾶλλον γὰρ ἦν εἰκὸς τὰ ἀΐδια τῶν πραγμάτων περιορᾶσθαι
ὑπ' αὐτῶν ἔρημα τῆς ἐπιβαλλούσης αὐτοῖς προνοίας ἢ τὰ ῥευστὴν ἔχοντα 5
φύσιν, εἴπερ ἐκεῖνα μὲν ἀπὸ τῆς ἑαυτῶν φύσεως τὸ ὡρισμένον ἔχει καὶ
ἄτρεπτον τοιαύτην θεόθεν τὴν ὑπόστασιν εἰληχότα, τὰ δὲ ἐν γενέσει διὰ
30 τὸ ῥευστὸν τῆς οἰκείας ὕλης ἐν παντοδαπῇ μεταβολῇ φέρεσθαι πεφυκότα
οὔτε εἶναι οὔτε συνέχεσθαι καὶ διακοσμεῖσθαι δυνατὸν μὴ πολλῆς τυγχάνοντα 10
τῆς τῶν ἀεὶ ὡσαύτως ἐχόντων δημιουργικῆς τε καὶ προνοητικῆς αἰτίας,
οὐ μόνον τῆς ὁλικωτέρας καὶ ἐξηρημένης ἀλλὰ καί τινος μερικωτέρας καὶ
προσεχεστέρας· ὥσπερ καὶ τῶν ἀνθρώπων τοὺς παῖδας ὁρῶμεν πλείονος 15
35 δεομένους ἐπιμελείας ἢ τοὺς ἄνδρας, καὶ τοὺς ἀνοήτους ἥπερ τοὺς ἔμφρο-

---

1 ἀλόγ.] ἄλλων F   3 τῶν (prius) om. M   4 προσαιτίους Ma   ἢ (alterum) om.
FM   5 γεννημ. FM   8 γὰρ] δὲ a   9 τοῖς om. AMa   11 οὐ τῷ] οὕτω
GM   12 λέγ.] μυθολογοῦσι GM   ἔνδειαν F   13 τῷ] τὸ A   15 μόνης A
χρόνον AF   16 αὐτὸ AGM   16. 17 βουλόμενος AGM   17 τῷ] τὸ M
εἰ] ἀεὶ a   20 οὐκ ἀγνοοῦσι a   21 ἐκπληξίας G   22 καὶ ὑπ' αὐτῆς — σημαι-
νουσι (24) om. F   πολύστοιχοι Ma   25 τῶν om. AFG   αὐτὴν A
26 εἰκότως FGM   ἴδια AG   27 ἐπιβαλούσης G   ἢ τὰ] εἶτα A   29 ἐν
suppl. G²   31 τυχόντα GMa   33 τινὸς καὶ colloc. F   34 καὶ suppl. G²

causes or anterior causes of all existing things, how could it be rational for them to be ignorant of their own creations, or the results of their own creations, or what is brought about in any way whatsoever by them, or for them to have ambivalent knowledge of these things, as though they did not concern them at all or depend upon them?

<Divine foreknowledge abolishes the contingent>

8. On neither of these hypotheses is it possible for the gods to care for our affairs in the providential manner which would befit the gods, that is, that they take care of the very objects of their providence from their very essence and arrange them from the stern, so to speak, not by deliberating about them, as the poets say (for deliberation is a lack of wisdom), nor by deliberating and doing different things at different times (for this is foreign to their single, simple, and wholly unchangeable activity and would befit only beings measured by time, who perform their activities by rational choice), but by their very being, they say, like the sun, which neither deliberating nor moving, but by being, fills what is able to partake of it with its own light, even if it be imagined to be standing still. Neither, then, is it possible for their providence to be such, nor would it be far from madness to pray and supplicate them for, say, rain or the safety of crops or victory, whose outcome they do not know. But if this is impossible, impious either to think or to say, and also refuted by experience, as the lengthy tales of divine activities and what happens, in a manner of speaking, every day show to those who are capable of paying attention to them, then clearly one must say both that contingent things are arranged by the gods and that they know their outcome in a definite manner. For it would be more likely that the gods neglect the eternal things, which would be deprived by the gods of the providence due to them, than the things which have a flowing nature, if the former are indeed definite by their own nature and have received an unchanging existence of this kind from the gods, while the things in genesis, which are such as to undergo any kind of changes because of the flowing of their own matter, can neither exist nor be held together and arranged without receiving the mighty demiurgic and providential cause of those things which are always the same, not merely the cause which is more total and transcendent, but also a more particular and more proximate cause, just as we see that human children require more care than adults and the stupid than the intelligent. But if the gods know contingent things and they know them in a definite manner, so that, as we said, we do not make their knowledge of them indefinite, and they know that 'Only the wooden wall will save Athens from the danger of the barbarians,' and that 'Divine Salamis will destroy the children of

νας. εἰ δὲ γινώσκουσιν οἱ θεοὶ τὰ ἐνδεχόμενα καὶ ὡρισμένως γινώσκουσιν, ἵνα μή, ὅπερ ἐλέγομεν, ἀόριστον αὐτῶν ποιῶμεν τὴν γνῶσιν, καὶ
ἴσασιν ὅτι μόνον τὸ ξύλινον τεῖχος σώσει τὰς Ἀθήνας ἐκ τῶν βαρβαρι- 20
κῶν κινδύνων καὶ ἡ θεία Σαλαμὶς ἀπολεῖ τὰ τέκνα τῶν γυναικῶν καὶ ὁ
5 Κροῖσος τὸν Ἅλυν διαβὰς μεγάλην ἀρχὴν καταλύσει καὶ ὁ Λάϊος παιδο-
ποιῶν ἄρδην ἀνατρέψει πᾶσαν ἑαυτοῦ τὴν οἰκίαν, δῆλον ὅτι οὐχ οἷόν τε
ταῦτα μὴ ἐκβαίνειν, εἰ δὲ μή, ψεύδεσθαι αὐτοὺς ἀναγκαῖον. δυοῖν οὖν 25
θάτερον, ἢ πάντα ἀναγκαίως καὶ ὡς ὑπὸ τῶν θεῶν γινώσκεταί τε καὶ
προλέγεται φήσομεν ἐκβαίνειν καὶ τὸ ἐνδεχόμενον ὄνομα ἔσται | κενόν, 109ʳ
10 ἢ οὔτε γινώσκεσθαι ὑπὸ τῶν θεῶν οὔτε προνοεῖσθαι τὰ τῇδε φήσομεν·
ἀλλὰ μὴν τοῦτο ἀδύνατον· οἴχεται ἄρα τὸ ἐνδεχόμενον.

Πρὸς τοῦτον οὖν τὸν λόγον δυσαντίβλεπτον, ὅπερ ἐλέγομεν, ὄντα καὶ
ὑπ' αὐτῆς δοκοῦντα τῆς ἐναργείας κρατύνεσθαι, ὡς αἱ τῶν μαντειῶν 5
προρρήσεις δηλοῦσιν, ἀπαντῶντες ἡμεῖς κατὰ τὴν τοῦ θείου Ἰαμβλίχου
15 ὑφήγησιν, τὰ διάφορα μέτρα τῶν γνώσεων διαιρεῖν ἀξιώσομεν λέγοντες ὡς
ἡ γνῶσις μέση οὖσα τοῦ τε γινώσκοντος καὶ τοῦ γινωσκομένου, εἴπερ ἐστὶν 10
ἐνέργεια τοῦ γινώσκοντος περὶ τὸ γινωσκόμενον, οἷον τῆς ὄψεως περὶ τὸ
λευκόν, ποτὲ μὲν κρειττόνως γινώσκει τὸ γινωσκόμενον, τῆς αὐτοῦ τοῦ
γνωστοῦ φύσεως ποτὲ δὲ χειρόνως ποτὲ δὲ συστοίχως· ὅταν μὲν γὰρ τὸν
20 νοῦν τὸν ἡμέτερον τὰς πολιτικὰς τῶν πράξεων προχειριζόμενον λέγωμεν 15
γινώσκειν τὰ καθ' ἕκαστα τῶν πραγμάτων, ἀναφέροντα ταῦτα ἐπὶ τὰ καθόλου καὶ δι' ἐκείνων ὡς οἰκείων γινώσκειν αὐτὰ πειρώμενον, δῆλον ὅτι κρείτ-
τονα ἐνταῦθα ἐροῦμεν εἶναι τοῦ γινωσκομένου τὴν γνῶσιν, εἴπερ μεριστὸν
μὲν καὶ ἐν μεταβολῇ τὸ καθ' ἕκαστον, ὁ δὲ λόγος, καθ' ὃν ταῦτα ὁ νοῦς ὁ 20
25 πρακτικὸς γινώσκει, ἀδιαίρετός τε καὶ ἀμετάβλητος. ὅταν δὲ αὐτὸς πρὸς
ἑαυτὸν ἐπιστρεφόμενος καὶ κατὰ τὰς καθαρτικὰς ἐνεργῶν ἀρετὰς τὴν
οὐσίαν τὴν ἑαυτοῦ θεωρῇ, σύστοιχον εἶναι ἀνάγκη τῷ γινωσκομένῳ
τὴν γνῶσιν. ὅταν δέ γε ἀνελθὼν ἐπὶ τὸ ἀκρότατον τῆς ἑαυτοῦ τελειό- 25
τητος καὶ τὰς θεωρητικὰς τῶν ἀρετῶν προχειριζόμενος θεωρῇ τὰ περὶ
30 τῶν θείων διακοσμήσεων καὶ ὅπως ἐκ τῆς μιᾶς τῶν πάντων ἀρχῆς
αὗται παράγονται | καὶ τίς ἑκάστης ἡ ἰδιότης, χείρονα εἶναι ἀνάγκη τοῦ 109ᵛ
γινωσκομένου τὴν γνῶσιν.

---

1. 2 οἱ θεοὶ — γινώσκουσιν om. F   2 ὅπερ ἐλέγομεν] p. 133,15 134,7   3 τὸ ξύλινον
τεῖχος] cf. Herod. VII 141   4 ἡ θεία Σαλαμίς] cf. Herod. VII 141   4. 5 ὁ Κροῖσος]
cf. Herod. I 53 Diod. exc. VII 28   5 καὶ ὁ Λάϊος — οἰκίαν (6) om. F (unde haec Ammon.
hauserit, nescio; cf. Soph. Oed. R. arg. et v. 711 sq. Eur. Phoen. arg. et v. 17—20)
7 οὖν om. G   8 καὶ ὡς om. G   8. 9 γινώσκεσθαι .. προλέγεσθαι AGMa   8 τε
om. FG   10 τῶν om. FG   12 δυσαντιβλ.] scribas δυσαντίλεκτον (cf. p. 132,8)
ὅπερ] ὥσπερ F   ὄντα ὅπερ ἐλέγ. M   13 ματειῶν F   14 ἀπατῶντες G¹
17 οἷον — γινωσκόμενον (18) om. et ante ποτὲ δὲ (19) add. ποτὲ μὲν κρείττων F   18 τοῦ
suppl. G²   19 χείρων F   σύστοιχος F   21 τὰ καθ' ἕκαστα — γινώσκειν (22)
om. F   22 οἰκεῖον A: οἰκεῖα M   22. 23 ἐντ. κρ. (num. corr.) colloc. G
25 πρακτ.] παρεκτικὸς G   27 θεωρεῖ G   29 θεωρεῖ F: θεωρεῖν G   31 παρα-
γίνονται F: προάγονται G   τίς] τῆς F

the women,' and that 'If Croesus crosses the Halys, he will destroy a great empire,' and that 'If Laius begets children, he will utterly destroy his entire house,' then it is clear that it is impossible for these things not to occur; but if not, then they must be lying. Thus, one of the two: either we shall say that all things occur necessarily and as they are both known and foretold by the gods, and the 'contingent' will be an empty name, or we shall say that things here are neither known by the gods nor are they the objects of divine providence. But the latter is certainly impossible; therefore the contingent disappears.

<*Counter argument: Iamblichus' distinction of degrees of knowledge*>

9. Against this argument which, as we have said, is difficult to oppose and appears to be strengthened by its very evidence, as the prophecies of the oracles show, we answer in accordance with the teaching of the divine Iamblichus and we shall think it right to distinguish the various degrees of knowledge by saying that knowledge is intermediate between the knower and the known, since it is the activity of the knower concerning the known—for example, the activity of sight concerning the pale—and it sometimes knows the known in a way better than the nature of the knowable thing itself, sometimes worse, and sometimes on the same level. For when we say that our own intelligence while dealing with political actions knows the individual affairs by referring them to the universals and attempting to know them by means of those, as they are akin to them, it is clear that then we shall say that the knowledge is better than the known, since the individual is divisible and changing, but reason, according to which the practical intelligence knows these things, is indivisible and unchanging. But when intelligence, returning to itself and acting according to the purifying virtues, observes its own essence, its knowledge is necessarily on the same level as what is known. And when intelligence, having risen to the peak of its own perfection and dealing with the theoretical virtues, observes what concerns the divine arrangements, how they are derived from the single principle of all things, and what is the proper quality of each of them, its knowledge is necessarily worse than what is known.

Τούτων οὖν οὕτως ἐχόντων ῥητέον τοὺς θεοὺς γινώσκειν μὲν πάντα
τὰ γεγονότα καὶ τὰ ὄντα καὶ τὰ ἐσόμενα ἢ μέλλοντα τὸν θεοῖς προσήκοντα τρόπον, τοῦτο δέ ἐστι μιᾷ καὶ ὡρισμένῃ καὶ ἀμεταβλήτῳ γνώσει, 5
διόπερ καὶ τῶν ἐνδεχομένων περιειληφέναι τὴν εἴδησιν, ἅτε καὶ πάντα τὰ
5 ἐν τῷ κόσμῳ παράγοντας καὶ τῶν μὲν ἀιδίων οὐσιῶν αἰτίους ὄντας τῶν
δὲ γεννητῶν προαιτίους κατὰ τὰς οἰκείας ἑκάστοις αὐτῶν ἐνεργείας καὶ 10
οἷον ὁρῶντας οὐκ αὐτὰς μόνον τὰς οὐσίας ἀλλὰ καὶ τὰς δυνάμεις αὐτῶν καὶ
τὰς ἐνεργείας τάς τε κατὰ φύσιν καὶ τὰς παρὰ φύσιν, ὅπερ παρὰ φύσιν
συνεισῆλθε τῇ ἀναγκαίᾳ τῆς ὑποβάσεως τῶν ὄντων ὑφέσει τοῖς καὶ τού-
10 του μετέχειν ποτὲ πεφυκόσιν, οὐ προηγουμένως ἀλλὰ κατὰ τὸν λεγόμενον 15
τῆς παρυποστάσεως τρόπον· γινώσκειν μέντοι τὰ ἐνδεχόμενα κρειττόνως
τῆς αὐτῶν ἐκείνων φύσεως, διόπερ ταῦτα μὲν ἀόριστον ἔχειν τὴν φύσιν
δύνασθαί τε καὶ ἐκβαίνειν καὶ μὴ ἐκβαίνειν, ἐκείνους δὲ ἅτε κρειττόνως 20
τῆς φύσεως αὐτῶν τὴν γνῶσιν αὐτῶν προειληφότας ὡρισμένως καὶ ταῦτα
15 εἰδέναι· καὶ γὰρ τὰ μεριστὰ τῶν πραγμάτων ἀμερίστως καὶ ἀδιαστάτως
γινώσκειν αὐτοὺς ἀναγκαῖον, καὶ τὰ πεπληθυσμένα ἑνοειδῶς καὶ τὰ ἔγχρονα
αἰωνίως καὶ τὰ γεννητὰ ἀγεννήτως· οὐ γὰρ δὴ συμπαραθέειν τῇ ῥύσει 25
τῶν πραγμάτων τὴν τῶν θεῶν γνῶσιν ἀνεξόμεθα λέγειν, οὐδὲ εἶναί τι ἐπ'
ἐκείνων ἢ παρεληλυθὸς ἢ μέλλον οὐδὲ λέγεσθαι ἐπ' αὐτῶν, ὡς ἐν Τιμαίῳ
20 παρειλήφαμεν, τὸ | ἦν ἢ τὸ ἔσται μεταβολῆς τινος ὄντα σημαντικά, μόνον 110r
δὲ τὸ ἔστι, καὶ τοῦτο οὐ τὸ συναριθμούμενον τῷ τε ἦν καὶ τῷ ἔσται καὶ
ἀντιδιαιρούμενον αὐτοῖς, ἀλλὰ τὸ πρὸ πάσης χρονικῆς ἐμφάσεως ἐπινοού-
μενον καὶ τὸ ἄτρεπτον αὐτῶν καὶ ἀμετάβλητον σημαῖνον, ὅπερ καὶ ὁ 5
μέγας Παρμενίδης παντὶ τῷ νοητῷ ὑπάρχειν ἀποφαίνεται· 'οὐ γὰρ ἔην
25 οὐδ' ἔσται,' φησίν, 'ὁμοῦ πᾶν, ἔστι δὲ μοῦνον'. καὶ οὐ χρὴ νομίζειν ὅτι
ἀναγκαίαν ἕξει τὴν ἔκβασιν ἃ λέγομεν ἐνδεχόμενα διὰ τὸ ὑπὸ θεῶν γινώσκεσθαι ὡρισμένως· οὐ γὰρ διότι γινώσκουσιν αὐτὰ οἱ θεοί, διὰ τοῦτο ἀναγ- 10
καίως ἐκβήσεται, ἀλλ' ἐπειδὴ φύσιν ἔχοντα ἐνδεχομένην καὶ ἀμφίβολον
πέρας ἕξει πάντως ἢ τοῖον ἢ τοῖον, διὰ τοῦτο τοὺς θεοὺς εἰδέναι ἀναγ-
30 καῖον ὅπως ἐκβήσεται. καὶ ἔστι τὸ αὐτὸ τῇ μὲν φύσει τῇ ἑαυτοῦ ἐνδεχό- 15

---

1. 2 τὰ πάντα τὰ M   2 τὸν] τοῖς a   3 ἀμεταβάτω AGMa   4 τά]
τοὺς F   6 γεννητῶν AFMa   προσαιτίους a   8 ὅπερ παρὰ φύσει AM; hoc
παρὰ φύσιν fort. eicias   9 συνῆλθε GM   ὑποβάσ.] ὑποστάσεως A   ὑφέσει in
mrg. suppl. A   9. 10 τοῦτο F   10 ποτὲ μετέχειν colloc. M   12 ἔχει AG:
ἔχοντα Ma   13 δύναται G   καὶ (post τε) om. M   ἐκεῖνα G²
14 τῆς φύσεως — προειληφότας suppl. G²   αὐτῶν (post γνῶσιν) supra scr. M
16 ἐγχρόνια G   17 γεννητὰ AFMa   ἀγενήτως FMa   συμπαραθεῖν FMa (cf. συνδέειν
p. 126,18)   ῥεύσει Brand.   18 ἀνεξώμεθα A   19 ὡς] καὶ G¹: ὡς καὶ G²   ἐν Τιμαίῳ]
c. 10 p. 37 E   20 τὸ (ante ἦν) om. M   σημ. ὄντα (num. corr.) G   21 τὸ (post οὐ)
om. M   τῶ (ante ἔσται) om. M   23 ὅπερ — μοῦνον (25) om. F   ὥσπερ M
24 Παρμενίδης] fr. v. 61 (Mullach I p. 120)   25 οὐδ'] οὐκ G   μόνον M
26 ἔχει G¹   27 ὡρισμένως om. F   27. 28 ἀναγκαῖον G²   29 πάντως superscr. M   ἢ (prius) om. FG   ἢ τοῖον (alt.) om. F   30. p. 137,1 post ἐνδεχ.
add. καὶ ἀόριστον F

<Only the gods know the contingent in a definite manner>

10. Now, these things being so, we must say: that the gods know everything which has occurred, which is <now>, and which will be (τὰ ἐσόμενα) or is going to be (τὰ μέλλοντα) in the way appropriate for the gods, that is, by one definite and unchanging knowledge; that hence the gods encompass the knowledge of contingents as well, inasmuch as they bring about all things in the world, are on the one hand causes of the eternal essences and on the other anterior causes of generated things according to the actualities proper to each of these things, and since they, so to speak, see not only the essences themselves but also their potentialities and actualities, both those according to and contrary to nature (what is contrary to nature entered along with those things which are such as sometimes to partake of this state, not primarily but in the so-called manner of 'parasitic existence', along with the necessary degradation due to the decline of beings); that, however, they know the contingents in a manner better than the contingents' own nature, which is why these things have an indefinite nature and can both occur and not occur, while the gods, who have pre - conceived the knowledge of the contingents in a manner better than their nature, know these things too in a definite manner. In fact, it is necessary for them to know divisible things indivisibly and without extension, as well as multiplied things by a single act, temporal things eternally, and generated things ungeneratedly. For we shall certainly not allow ourselves to say that the gods' knowledge parallels the flux of things, nor that there is for the gods anything which is either past or future, nor that 'was' or 'will be', which would be significant of some change, are said in the case of the gods, as we have learned in the *Timaeus* (37e), but only 'is', and not the 'is' which counted along with 'was' and 'will be' and is opposed to them, but the 'is' which is conceived before any manifestation of time and which signifies the gods' constancy and immutability. This is also what the great Parmenides declares to belong to the whole intelligible <world>: 'for it was not, nor will it be,' he says,[95] 'all together, but it only is'. Moreover one must not think that the things we are calling 'contingent' will have a necessary outcome because of the fact that they are known in a definite manner by the gods: it is not because the gods know them that they will occur necessarily; but since, having a contingent and ambiguous nature, they will have an end which will in any case be so or so, it is necessary that the gods know how they will occur. And the same thing is contingent in its own nature, but in the gods' knowledge

---

[95]   Cp. B 8,6 D.-K.

μενον, τῇ δὲ γνώσει τῶν θεῶν οὐκέτι ἀόριστον ἀλλ' ὡρισμένον. δῆλον
δὲ ὅτι καὶ τῇ ἡμετέρᾳ γνώσει δυνατὸν ὡρισμένως ποτὲ γινώσκεσθαι τὸ
ἐνδεχόμενον, ὅτε οὐδὲ κυρίως ἔτι ἐστὶν ἐνδεχόμενον ἀλλ' ἐξ ἀνάγκης ἀκολουθεῖ τοῖς προηγησαμένοις αἰτίοις τῆς ἑαυτοῦ γενέσεως· τὴν γοῦν σφαῖ- 20
5 ραν τὴν ἠρεμοῦσαν ἐν παραλλήλῳ τῷ ὁρίζοντι ἐπιπέδῳ δυνατὸν μὲν τοῦ
ἐπιπέδου τὴν αὐτὴν ἔχοντος θέσιν κινεῖσθαί τε ὑπό τινος καὶ μή, τοῦ
μέντοι ἐπιπέδου κλιθέντος μὴ κινηθῆναι ἀδύνατον. διὰ ταῦτα καὶ τοὺς
ἰατροὺς ὁρῶμεν ὁτὲ μὲν οὐδὲν θαρροῦντας ἀποφαίνεσθαι περὶ τῶν ἀρρώ- 25
στων εἴτε ὑγιανοῦσιν εἴτε φθαρήσονται, ὡς ἂν ἐνδεχομένων ὄντων ἀμφοτέ-
10 ρων, ποτὲ δὲ ἀνενδοιάστως περὶ τοῦ ἑτέρου τούτων ὡς τῷ ἀρρώστῳ πάν-
τως τι ὑπάρξοντος | ἀποφαινομένους.   110v

Ἐπεὶ δέ τινες θρασύτερον ἀναστρεφόμενοι περὶ τὴν ζήτησιν τοῦ προκειμένου θεωρήματος οἴονται δεικνύναι μηδὲ τοῖς θεοῖς ὡρισμένην ὑπάρ-
χουσαν γνῶσιν τῶν ἐνδεχομένων χρησμοὺς παράγοντες ἡμῖν περὶ τῶν 5
15 μελλόντων ἀμφιβόλως ἀποφηναμένους, ῥητέον πρὸς αὐτούς, ἅπερ ὁ μέγας
φησὶ Συριανός, ὅτι πρῶτον μὲν ἐφιστάνειν ἐχρῆν ὡς ἄλλη μέν ἐστιν ἡ
τῶν θεῶν γνῶσις καὶ νόησις ἑτέρα δὲ ἡ τῆς προφήτιδος ἐνέργεια, κινη-
θείσης μὲν ἐκ θεοῦ τεκούσης δὲ ἐν αὐτῇ καὶ λόγον μεριστὸν καὶ μέτρα 10
καὶ γνῶσιν ἀμφίβολον· οὐ γὰρ δὴ τὸ ἐλλαμπόμενον τοιοῦτόν ἐστιν οἷον
20 τὸ ἐλλάμπον. ἔπειτα δὲ ὅτι καὶ τοῦ συμφέροντος ἕνεκεν τῶν ἀκουόντων
πολλάκις ἀμφίβολοι δίδονται χρησμοὶ τὴν διάνοιαν αὐτῶν γυμνάζοντες·
χρῶνται γὰρ ἡμῖν ὡς αὐτοκινήτοις οἱ θεοὶ καὶ τοῦτον τὸν τρόπον τὰ περὶ 15
ἡμᾶς κυβερνῶσι καὶ πάντα ἡμῖν κατὰ τὴν ἡμῶν αὐτῶν ἀξίαν ἀπονέμουσιν.
ἀλλὰ ταῦτα μὲν ἴσως καὶ τολμηρὰ καὶ τῶν προκειμένων εἰς ἐξέτασιν
25 μακρὰν ἀποπλανώμενα· ὅλως δὲ ὁ πάντα ἀναγκάζων λόγος πότερον καὶ 20
αὐτὸ τοῦτο ἐξ ἀνάγκης συμβαίνειν τοῖς ἀνθρώποις φησί, τὸ λέγειν ὅτι
πάντα ἠνάγκασται, ἢ ἐφ' ἡμῖν κεῖσθαι τὰς περὶ τοῦ τρόπου τῆς γενέσεως
τῶν πραγμάτων δόξας; εἰ μὲν γὰρ τὸ δεύτερον ἀληθές, οὐκ ἄρα πάντα
ἐξ ἀνάγκης· εἰ δὲ τὸ πρότερον, πῶς δοξάζουσί τινες τὸ ἀντιχείμενον, ὅτι 25
30 πολλά ἐστιν ἐφ' ἡμῖν; τὸ γὰρ ὑπὸ τῆς φύσεως τῆς πάντα ἀναγκαζούσης,
ὡς ὁ ἐκείνων λόγος, κινεῖσθαι παρὰ φύσιν ἡμᾶς ἐπὶ τὸ καταψηφίζεσθαι
τῶν ὑπ' αὐτῆς γινο|μένων παντελῶς ἄλογον καὶ παραπλήσιον ὡς εἴ τις 111r
ἰατρικὴν τέχνην διδάσκων δι' αὐτοῦ τούτου παρεσκεύαζε τοὺς διδασκο-

---

1 οὐκέτι ex οὐκ ἔστι corr. F   2 ἡμετ.] ἑτέρα F   3 ὅτε — ἐνδεχόμενον om. AGM
(in mrg. suppl. AG²)   4 προηγουμένοις F   τῆς] τοῖς A   5 τὴν om. M
5. 6 τοῦ ἐπιπ.] τοῦ ἐπ' ἐλπίδι G¹: ἐπὶ τοῦ ἐπιπ. M   6 τε om. M   7 κινεῖσθαι F
8 ὁτὲ] ὅτι M   θαροῦντας F   9 ὑγιαίνουσιν FM   9. 10 ἀμφ. ὄντ. colloc. G   10 ποτὲ] ὁτὲ a   ἀνενδυάστως A   11 τι om. FG
ὑπάρξαντος G¹   13 τῷ θεῷ F   14 τὴν γνῶσιν FG   προάγ. F
15 ἀμφιβόλους A   ἀποφαινομ. G   17 τοῦ θεοῦ F   καὶ νόησις om. F
20 ὅτι] εἴ τι M   21 δίδ.] δηλοῦνται F   23 ἡμῶν om. F   αὐτῶν om. G
24 ἀλλὰ — ἀποπλανώμενα (25) suppl. G²   26 ὅτι om. F   27 πάντα ἢ a
ἠναγκάσθαι Aa   κεῖται A   29 ἐξ om. F   31 ὁ superscr. A: om. M
33 τέχνην om. F

it is no longer indefinite, but rather definite. It is clearly possible for the contingent sometimes to be known in a definite manner even by our own knowledge, namely when it is no longer contingent properly-speaking, but necessarily follows from the causes leading the way to its own generation: it is possible, for example, for a sphere which rests on a horizontal surface, while the surface keeps the same position, to be moved by something or not, but when the surface is tilted it is impossible for it not to be moved. Hence, we also see that physicians sometimes lack the confidence to pronounce anything about whether their patients will recover or perish, thinking both are possible, while they some times indubitably pronounce about one or the other of these as certainly going to happen to the patient.

<Oracular ambiguity; Are our beliefs necessary?>

11. Since some people who are too bold in their occupation with the investigation of the present theory believe that when they adduce for us oracles which make ambiguous pronouncements about future events they are demonstrating that definite knowledge of contingents does not even belong to the gods, we must say to them just what the great Syrianus says: First, that one must note that the knowledge and understanding of the gods is one thing, and the activity of the prophetess is another, since, although she is moved by the god, she brings to birth in herself speech which has parts, verses, and ambivalent knowledge: surely what is illuminated is not such as that which illuminates it. Second, that it is for the benefit of the listeners that ambiguous oracles are given, which exercise their intelligence: the gods treat us as self-movers and it is in this way that they govern our affairs and distribute all things to us according to our own desert. But perhaps these matters are both audacious and far afield of the investigation of the present issues. In general, does the argument which makes everything necessary also say that this very thing of necessity happens to humans, that they say that everything is necessitated, or does it say that our opinions about the manner of the generation of things are up to us? If the second is true, then not everything is of necessity. If the first, how can some people believe the opposite, that many things are up to us? It is utterly irrational <to say> that we are moved in a way contrary to nature by a nature which necessitates everything, as their argument claims, so that we cast our vote against the things which are brought about by that nature. It is almost as if someone, while teaching the art of medicine, by this very act prepared his

μένους τὰς ἀρχὰς τῆς τέχνης ἧς μετῆεσαν ἀναιρεῖν, καίτοι τὸν μὲν τεχνί-
την εἰκὸς ποιῆσαί τι τῶν παρὰ τὴν τέχνην, οὐ καθ᾽ ὃ τοιοῦτος, οἷον τὸν 5
ἰατρὸν δοῦναι φθόριον ἢ δηλητήριον, ἅτε ψυχὴν αὐτοκίνητον ἔχοντα καὶ
τῆς τέχνης μηδὲν συντελούσης πρὸς αὐτὴν τῆς ψυχῆς τὴν τελειότητα τοῦ
5 δὲ σώματος ἢ τῶν ἐκτὸς ἐπιμελουμένης, τὴν μέντοι φύσιν ὑπεναντίον τι 10
τῷ οἰκείῳ τέλει ποιεῖν ἀμήχανον. οὐ μὴν οὐδ᾽ ὥσπερ τῶν τεράτων, οὕτω
καὶ τῶν δοξῶν πλεονεξίαν τῆς ὕλης ἢ ἔνδειαν αἰτιασόμεθα· οὔτε γὰρ
πλάττειν αὐτοῖς βουλομένοις ῥάδιον ἀποδοῦναι τῶν διαφόρων δοξῶν ἐκ
τῆς κατὰ τὴν ὕλην διαφορᾶς τὰς αἰτίας οὔτε πάντων ἔτι τὴν εἱμαρμένην 15
10 αἰτίαν εἶναι ὁμολογήσουσιν. ἀλλὰ τούτων μὲν ἅλις.

Ἐπανάγοντες δὲ τὸν λόγον ἐπὶ τὴν ἐξήγησιν τῶν ὑπὸ τοῦ Ἀριστοτέλους ἐν τούτοις λεγομένων πρῶτον μὲν ἀκόλουθα εἶναι φήσομεν τὰ διὰ
τούτων παραδιδόμενα τοῖς ὀλίγῳ πρότερον εἰρημένοις· ἐλέγετο γὰρ προσε- 20
χῶς περὶ ἀντιθέσεως καταφάσεώς τε καὶ ἀποφάσεως οὐκ ἀεὶ διαιρουσῶν
15 τό τε ἀληθὲς καὶ τὸ ψεῦδος· τούτοις οὖν ἀκολούθως προστίθησι ποία
κατάφασις πρὸς ποίαν ἀπόφασιν ἀντίκειται οὕτως ὥστε διαιρεῖν μὲν αὐτὰς
ἀεὶ τό τε ἀληθὲς καὶ τὸ ψεῦδος, οὐ μέντοι ἀφωρισμένως ἀλλ᾽ ἀορίστως. 25
παραδίδωσι δὲ πρῶτον μὲν τὰ κοινῶς ὑπάρχοντα ταῖς τε διαγωνίοις ἀντι-
φάσεσι καὶ τῇ τῶν καθ᾽ ἕκαστα, λέγων ὅτι πάσαις αὐταῖς ὑπάρχει τὸ
20 ἀφωρισμένως ταῦτα | μερίζειν κατὰ τὸν ἐνεστῶτα χρόνον καὶ τὸν παρῳ- 111ᵛ
χηκότα (τοῦτο γάρ ἐστι τὸ ἐπὶ τῶν ὄντων καὶ γενομένων τὴν κατάφασιν ἢ τὴν ἀπόφασιν ἀληθῆ ἢ ψευδῆ εἶναι), πρότερον μὲν ὅτι
ταῖς διαγωνίοις τοῦτο ὑπάρχει διδάσκων, ἃς καθόλου ὡς καθόλου 5
προσηγόρευσεν, ὡς ἐχούσας τὴν ἑτέραν τῶν προτάσεων καθόλου, ἔπειτα
25 προστιθεὶς ὅτι καὶ ἐπὶ τῶν καθ᾽ ἕκαστα προτάσεων τὸ αὐτὸ συμβαίνει, ὅπερ
καὶ ἐπὶ τῶν διαγωνίων· τοῦτο γὰρ βούλεται τὸ ὥσπερ εἴρηται. ἐπισημαι-
νόμενος δὲ ὅτι τῶν ἀπροσδιορίστων προτάσεων κατὰ τὴν ἐνδεχομένην ὕλην 10
λαμβανομένων οὐκ ἀνάγκη τὴν μὲν ἀληθῆ τὴν δὲ ψευδῆ εἶναι, ἔπειτα ἐπάγων
τὴν κατὰ τὸν μέλλοντα χρόνον διαφορὰν τῶν καθ᾽ ἕκαστα προτάσεων πρὸς
30 τὰ λοιπὰ τῶν ἀντιφάσεων εἴδη διὰ τοῦ λέγειν ἐπὶ δὲ τῶν καθ᾽ ἕκαστα 15
καὶ μελλόντων οὐχ ὁμοίως, καὶ ἐνδεικνύμενος ἡμῖν διὰ τούτων ὡς
αἱ μὲν ἄλλαι προτάσεις, αἵ τε διαγώνιοι καὶ αἱ ἀπροσδιόριστοι, οὕτως
ἔχουσι κατὰ τὸν μέλλοντα χρόνον, ὥσπερ εἶχον κατά τε τὸν ἐνεστῶτα
χρόνον καὶ τὸν παρεληλυθότα, αἱ δὲ καθ᾽ ἕκαστα οὐκέτι (πάνυ δὲ ἀκρι- 20
35 βῶς τὸ ἴδιον τῶν προτάσεων, περὶ ὧν ὁ λόγος, ἀφοριζόμενος ἐπὶ τῶν

---

1 τὴν ἀρχὴν G   ἧς μετῆεσαν om. F   μετίεσαν A   2 τὴν iter. G
3 φθόρον a   4 αὐτῆς M   5 ἐναντ. G   6 ποιεῖν τέλει colloc. G
οὐδ᾽] δ᾽ A   περάτων AMa   οὕτω δὴ G   8 ἀπόδ. ῥάδ. colloc. M
10 εἶναι om. M   12 πρῶτα G   15 τε om. M   τὸ (ante ψεῦδ.)
om. F   17 τε om. F   18 τε om. A   διαγωνίαις G   21 τῶν γενομ. Ma
21. 22 τὴν μὲν κατάφ. M: ἀνάγκη τὴν κατάφ. b   22 πρῶτον M   23 ὡς καθόλου — καθόλου (24) om. M   24 προηγόρ. Aa   25 προτιθεὶς F   30 διὰ τοῦτο
λέγει F   33 τε om. FM   34 χρόνον om. M

pupils to refute the principles of the art in which they shared; and, although it is likely that
the technician will do something contrary to his art (not qua technician—as when the
doctor administers an abortifacient or a poison, inasmuch as he has a self-moving soul and
the art contributes nothing to the actual perfection of the soul, being instead occupied with
the body or external things), it is impossible for nature to do anything contrary to its
proper end. Nor, indeed, shall we hold an excess or deficiency of matter responsible for
our opinions, as <we do> for monsters: even if they want to exercise their imagination, it
will not be easy for them to explain the causes of the different opinions <as arising> from
the difference in matter, nor will they be agreeing that fate is still the cause of all things.
But enough on this subject.

<Explication of Aristotle's words>

12. Returning our discussion to the explication of what Aristotle says in this passage, we
shall say first that what is taught in these words follows from what was said a bit earlier
(ch. 7, 17b3ff.). He said, namely, just above about the opposition between the affirmative
and the negative sentences, that they do not always divide the true and false. Consequent
to this, then, he adds (18a33-34)[96] what sort of affirmative sentence is opposed to what sort
of negative sentence in such a way that they always divide the true and false, not in a
definite, however, but in an indefinite manner. First, he teaches us what holds in common
of the diagonal contradictions and of the contradiction of the singular sentences, saying
that it holds of all of these <contradictions> that they distribute the true and false in a
definite manner in the present and past time (for this is <the meaning of> *'in the case of
things which are or have come to be [sc. it is necessary] that the affirmative sentence or
negative sentence be true or false'*), teaching first that this holds of the diagonal
<contradictions>, which he called 'universal taken universally' <i.e. general> since these
<contradictions> have one of their two sentences as general, and next adding that the same
thing happens in the case of the singular sentences as in the diagonals, which is the sense
of *'as has been said'*. But he also indicates that, of the undetermined sentences taken in
the contingent matter, it is not necessary for one to be true and the other false, and he then
brings in the difference in the future time between the singular sentences and the
remaining species of contradictions when he says *'But with future singulars it is not the
same,'* and he shows us in these words that, while the other sentences, the diagonals and
the undetermined ones, behave in the future time just as they do in the present and past
time, the singular sentences no longer do so (he defines with great precision what is proper
to the sentences he is speaking about, saying *'with future singulars'* and meaning by

---

[96]   Aristotle says simply: "But in the case of singulars that are going to be it is not the
same (οὐχ ὁμοίως)."

ἕκαστα καὶ μελλόντων εἶπε διὰ τοῦ μελλόντων τὸ ἐπὶ τῆς ἐνδεχομένης ὕλης λαμβανόμενον σημαίνων· ἄλλο γὰρ ἐστιν, ὡς αὐτὸς ἐν τοῖς
Περὶ γενέσεως καὶ φθορᾶς διορίζεται, τὸ μέλλον παρὰ τὸ ἐσόμενον, καὶ τὸ μὲν 25
ἐσόμενον τὸ πάντως ἐκβησόμενον σημαίνει, ὡς ὅταν εἴπωμεν 'ἔσται χειμὼν
5 ἢ θέρος ἢ ἔκλειψις', τὸ δὲ μέλλον τὸ καὶ ἐκβῆναι καὶ μὴ ἐκβῆναι δυνά-
μενον, οἷον 'μέλλω βα|δίζειν, μέλλω πλέειν')· ἐνδεικνύμενος οὖν ὅτι κατὰ 112ʳ
μὲν τὰς ἄλλας ὕλας, τήν τε ἀναγκαίαν καὶ τὴν ἀδύνατον, ὁμοίως ἔχουσιν
αἱ καθ' ἕκαστα προτάσεις, ὥσπερ ἐπὶ τοῦ προλαβόντος χρόνου καὶ τοῦ
ἐνεστῶτος οὕτω δὲ καὶ ἐπὶ τοῦ μέλλοντος κατὰ τὸ ἀφωρισμένως διαιρεῖν 5
10 τὸ ἀληθὲς καὶ τὸ ψεῦδος, κατὰ δὲ τὴν ἐνδεχομένην οὐκέτι, καίτοι τῶν
ἄλλων πασῶν ἀντιφάσεων καὶ ἐπὶ ταύτης τῆς ὕλης ὁμοίως ἐχουσῶν εἰς
τὸν μέλλοντα χρόνον ὥσπερ καὶ ἐπὶ τῶν λοιπῶν, προσέθεικε τὸ οὐχ
ὁμοίως, ἅμα διὰ τούτου σημαίνων κατὰ τί αὗται οὐκέτι ὁμοίως ἔχουσιν 10
ἐπὶ τῆς εἰρημένης ὑποθέσεως λαμβανόμεναι, ὅτι διαιροῦσι μὲν πάντως τὸ
15 ἀληθὲς καὶ τὸ ψεῦδος, οὐ μέντοι ἀφωρισμένως ἀλλ' ἀορίστως· ἀνάγκη μὲν
γὰρ τὸν Σωκράτην λούσασθαι ἢ μὴ λούσασθαι αὔριον, καὶ οὔτε ἄμφω οὔτε 15
μηδέτερον γενέσθαι δυνατόν· πότερον δὲ τούτων ἔσται τὸ ἀληθές, οὐχ
οἷόν τε γνῶναι πρὸ τῆς τοῦ πράγματος ἐκβάσεως, εἴπερ ἑκάτερον αὐτῶν
καὶ γενέσθαι καὶ μὴ γενέσθαι δι' αὐτὴν τὴν τοῦ ἐνδεχομένου φύσιν
20 ἐγχωρεῖ. τοῦτο οὖν βραχέως ἐνεδείξατο ἡμῖν διὰ τοῦ εἰπεῖν οὐχ ὁμοίως. 20

p. 18ª34 Εἰ γὰρ πᾶσα κατάφασις ἢ ἀπόφασις ἀληθὴς ἢ ψευδής,
καὶ ἅπαν ἀνάγκη ὑπάρχειν ἢ μὴ ὑπάρχειν· εἰ δὴ ὁ μὲν φήσει
ἔσεσθαί τι ὁ δὲ μὴ φήσει τὸ αὐτὸ τοῦτο, δῆλον ὅτι ἀνάγκη ἀληθεύειν τὸν ἕτερον αὐτῶν, εἰ πᾶσα κατάφασις ἢ ἀπόφασις ἀληθὴς 25
25 ἢ ψευδής· ἄμφω γὰρ οὐχ ὑπάρξει ἅμα ἐπὶ τοῖς τοιούτοις.

Βούλεται μὲν διὰ τούτων παραστῆναι τῇ δόξῃ τῇ ἀναιρούσῃ τὸ ἐνδε-
χόμενον, ἵνα ὡς οἷόν τέ ἐστι κρατυν|θεῖσαν αὐτὴν διελέγξῃ, τοὺς δὲ προ- 112ᵛ
ισταμένους ταύτης τῆς δόξης διὰ τούτων ὑποκρινόμενος ὥσπερ λημμάτιόν
τι πρῶτον λαμβάνει, ὅτι τῇ μὲν ἀληθείᾳ τῶν λόγων ἔπεσθαι ἀνάγκη τὴν
30 ὕπαρξιν τῶν πραγμάτων, τῷ δὲ ψεύδει τὴν ἀνυπαρξίαν, ὅπερ αὐτῷ βούλε- 5
ται τὸ εἰ γὰρ πᾶσα κατάφασις ἢ ἀπόφασις ἀληθὴς ἢ ψευδής,
καὶ ἅπαν ἀνάγκη ὑπάρχειν ἢ μὴ ὑπάρχειν. ἔπειτα ὁρμᾶται μὲν

---

1 τοῦ suppl. G²: τῶν F   2 λαμβανομένων G   2. 3 ἐν τοῖς Περὶ γεν. καὶ φθ.]
B 11 p. 337ᵇ3   2 ἐν] οὖν M   5 καὶ (prius) ante τὸ colloc. A: om. Ma   7 ὕλας
om. G   10 καίτοι] καί τι F: καίτοι καὶ M   13 οὐκέτι] οὐχ G   17 δὲ]
διὰ G   ἐστὶ F   18 διαγνῶναι G   εἴπερ] εἶπεν M   20 οὖν] δὲ M¹
βραχέος F   21 ἢ ἀπόφασις] καὶ ἀπόφασις F²Gb: om. F¹ (cf. v. 31)   ἢ ἀληθὴς AGM
(cf. v. 31)   22 καὶ ἅπαν — τοιούτοις (25) om. M   εἰ δὴ — τοιούτοις (25)
om. a   εἰ δὴ AG: εἰ δὲ F: ὥστε εἰ b   24 ἢ ἀπόφ.] καὶ ἀπόφ. b   26 προστῆ-
ναι F: παραστῆσαι G²a   τῆς δόξης τῆς ἀναιρούσης F   27 ἔστι om. M
30 αὐτὸ AF   31 ἢ ἀπόφασις om. F: καὶ ἀποφ. b

'*future*' that which is taken in the contingent matter; for what is going to be is different, as he himself makes the distinction in *On Generation and Corruption*,[97] from what will be, since 'what will be' signifies what will occur, in any case, as when we say 'there will be winter,' or ' ... summer,' or ' ... an eclipse,' while 'what is going to be' <signifies> what can either occur or not occur, for example, 'I am going to walk,' 'I am going to sail'). So, showing that in the other matters, i.e. the necessary and the impossible, the singular sentences behave similarly in regard to dividing the true and false in a definite manner (18a31)—just as in the preceding time and the present, so too in the future—but that they no longer do so in the contingent matter, even though all the other contradictions behave the same toward the future in this matter as they do in the other matters too, he has added 'it is not the same,' thereby signifying at the same time in what respect these, when taken on the stated assumption, no longer behave the same, namely that they always divide the true and false, but in an indefinite, not in a definite manner; for it is necessary that Socrates bathe or not bathe tomorrow, and it is impossible that either both or neither happen, but which of these will be the true one it is not possible to know before the outcome of the matter, if indeed each of them can either happen or not happen because of the very nature of the contingent. This, then, is what he concisely showed us by saying 'it is not the same'.

18a34 *For if every affirmative sentence or negative sentence is true or false, it is also necessary that everything be the case or not be the case. Indeed, if one person says something will be and another denies the same thing, it is clearly necessary that one of them is speaking truly—if every affirmative sentence or negative sentence[98] is true or false; for in the case of this kind of things both will not be the case together.*

<Strengthening the case against the contingent>

13. <Aristotle> wants in these words to support the opinion which destroys the contingent, in order to refute it when it is at its strongest, and here, acting the part of those who defend this opinion, he first takes as a kind of assumption that it is necessary that the existence of the things follows upon the truth of the sentences, their non-existence upon falsity, which is the meaning of his '*For if every affirmative sentence or negative sentence is true or false, it is also necessary that everything be the case or not be the case.*' Next, he begins from the axiom of contradiction, saying that, necessarily, of singular contingent sentences

---

[97] *GC* II 11, 337b3-7.

[98] κατάφασις ἢ ἀπόφασις; Minio-Paluello (following most of the manuscripts) has κατάφασις alone.

ἀπὸ τοῦ ἀξιώματος τῆς ἀντιφάσεως λέγων ὅτι ἀνάγκη τῶν καθ᾽ ἔκαστα
καὶ ἐνδεχομένων προτάσεων ἐπὶ τοῦ μέλλοντος χρόνου λαμβανομένων τὴν 10
ἑτέραν ἀληθεύειν, ἐπειδὴ οὔτε ἀμφοτέρας ἅμα ψεύδεσθαι οὔτε ἀληθεύειν
ἀμφοτέρας ἅμα δυνατόν. τούτων δὲ τὸ μὲν ὅτι οὐκ ἀληθεύουσιν ἄμφω
5 λέγεται σαφῶς ἐν τούτοις διὰ τοῦ ἄμφω γὰρ οὐχ ὑπάρξει ἅμα ἐπὶ 15
τοῖς τοιούτοις, τοῦτ᾽ ἔστιν αἱ γὰρ τοιαῦται προτάσεις οὐ πείσονται τὸ
αὐτὸ ταῖς ἀπροσδιορίστοις ταῖς ἐπὶ τῆς ἐνδεχομένης ὕλης λαμβανομέναις
(ἐκείνας μὲν γὰρ συναληθεύειν ἐλέγομεν, ταύτας δὲ συναληθεύειν ἀδύνατον,
ἵνα μὴ τὸ αὐτὸ ἅμα τῷ αὐτῷ καὶ ὑπάρχῃ καὶ μὴ ὑπάρχῃ, οἷον τῷ 20
10 Σωκράτει καὶ τὸ λούσασθαι τῇ ἑξῆς καὶ τὸ μὴ λούσασθαι), τὸ δὲ ὅτι
οὐδὲ ψεύδεσθαι αὐτὰς ἅμα δυνατόν, ἐν τοῖς ἐφεξῆς προσθήσει. τούτων
οὖν ἀνῃρημένων καὶ διὰ τούτου κατεσκευασμένου τοῦ διαιρεῖν αὐτὰς τὸ ἀληθὲς
καὶ τὸ ψεῦδος, ὅτι καὶ ὡρισμένως, φησί, τοῦτο ποιοῦσιν ἐπιδείξομεν, εἰ δύο 25
τινὰς οἷον μαντεύεσθαι προσποιουμένους λάβοιμεν περί τινος τῶν καθ᾽ ἕκα-
15 στα προλέγειν πειρωμένους οἷον ἀρρώστου, τὸν μὲν ὅτι ὑγιανεῖ τὸν | δὲ ὅτι 113ʳ
οὐχ ὑγιανεῖ· δῆλον γὰρ ὅτι τὸν μὲν ἕτερον αὐτῶν ἀληθεύειν ἀνάγκη τὸν δὲ
ἕτερον ψεύδεσθαι. εἰ μὲν οὖν ὁ λέγων ὑγιανεῖν αὐτὸν ἀληθεύοι, ἀνάγκη
αὐτὸν ὑγιᾶναι (προείληπται γὰρ ὅτι τῇ ἀληθείᾳ τῶν λόγων ἕπεται πάν- 5
τως ἡ ἔκβασις τῶν πραγμάτων), εἰ δὲ ὁ τὴν ἀπόφασιν εἰπὼν ἀληθεύοι,
20 δῆλον ὅτι ἀδύνατον αὐτὸν ὑγιᾶναι· ὥστε ἢ ἀναγκαίως ἐκβήσεται τὸ πρᾶγμα
ἢ ἀδύνατον ἕξει τὴν ἔκβασιν· ἀνῄρηται ἄρα τὸ ἐνδεχόμενον.

p. 18ᵃ 39 Εἰ γὰρ ἀληθὲς εἰπεῖν ὅτι λευκὸν ἢ οὐ λευκόν ἐστιν,
ἀνάγκη εἶναι λευκὸν ἢ οὐ λευκόν, καὶ εἰ ἔστι λευκὸν ἢ οὐ λευ- 10
κόν, ἀληθὲς ἦν φάναι ἢ ἀποφάναι· καὶ εἰ μὴ ὑπάρχει, ψεύδεται,
25 καὶ εἰ ψεύδεται, οὐχ ὑπάρχει· ὥστε ἀνάγκη τὴν κατάφασιν ἢ
τὴν ἀπόφασιν ἀληθῆ εἶναι ἢ ψευδῆ. οὐδὲν ἄρα οὔτε ἔστιν
οὔτε γίνεται οὔτε ἀπὸ τύχης οὔτε ὁπότερ᾽ ἔτυχεν, οὐδὲ ἔσται 15
ἢ οὐκ ἔσται, ἀλλ᾽ ἐξ ἀνάγκης ἅπαντα καὶ οὐχ ὁπότερ᾽ ἔτυχεν·
ἢ γὰρ ὁ φὰς ἀληθεύσει ἢ ὁ ἀποφάς· ὁμοίως γὰρ ἂν ἐγίνετο ἢ
30 οὐκ ἐγίνετο· τὸ γὰρ ὁπότερ᾽ ἔτυχεν οὐδὲν μᾶλλον οὕτως ἢ μὴ
οὕτως ἔχει ἢ ἕξει.

Τὸ προειρημένον λημμάτιον κρατῦναι βουλόμενος ὁ Ἀριστοτέλης, ὅτι 20
τῇ ἀληθείᾳ τῶν λόγων ἕπεται ἡ ὕπαρξις τῶν πραγμάτων καὶ τῷ ψεύδει
ἡ ἀνυπαρξία, διὰ παραδειγμάτων ἐπιδείκνυσι τοῦτο οὕτως ἔχον, ἐπείπερ

---

1 ἀπὸ] ἐπὶ F　　3. 4 ἀμφ. ἀλ. colloc. A　　8 ἐκείναις G¹　　9 αὐτῷ] λόγῳ M
ὑπάρχει (utrobique) G: compend. F　　10 τὸ ἑξῆς G　　11 ἐν] ἐπὶ G　　προσθεί-
σει F　　12 διὰ τούτων F　　13 ἐπιδείξωμεν Ma　　14 περί] παρά G　　15 ὅτι
(prius) om. A　　16 ἀλ. αὐτ. colloc. AGa　　17 αὐτ. ὑγ. colloc. AGM　　ὑγιαίνειν AG
21 ἔχει A²　　22 ἢ ὅτι οὐ ab　　ἐστιν—ἕξει (31) om. M　　23 καὶ εἰ—ἕξει (31) om.
Ga　　25 ἀνάγκη ἢ b (recte, cf. p. 141,19. 24)　　25. 26 ἢ τὴν ἀπόφασιν suppl. F²
27 οὐδὲ ὁπότερον A　　32 τὸ γὰρ προειρ. M

taken in the future time, one or the other is true, since it is neither possible for both to be false together nor for both to be true together. The latter of these, that both are not true, is clearly mentioned here in the words *'for in the case of this kind of things both will not be true together'*; that is, such sentences will not undergo the same effect as the undetermined sentences when taken in the contingent matter (we said [129,25-31] that those are true together; but it is impossible for these to be true together, lest the same thing at once hold and not hold of the same thing, for example that both bathing on the next day and not bathing on the next day hold of Socrates). The former case, where it is not even possible for them to be false together, he will add in what follows (18b17). Thus, with these cases excluded and it being established by this that these sentences divide the true and false, that they also do this in a definite manner, he means, we shall show if we take two people e.g. who pretend to be capable of prophecy and attempt to make predictions about some individual, e.g. a sick person, and one says he will get well, the other that he will not get well. Obviously it is necessary that one of them is speaking truly and the other falsely. Now, if the one saying the person will get well is speaking truly, it is necessary that he will get well (for it was assumed beforehand [139,29-30] that the outcome of the facts follows the truth of the sentences, in any case); but if the one who stated the negation is speaking truly, then obviously it is impossible that the person will get well. Thus, the event will either occur necessarily or it will have an impossible outcome. Therefore, the contingent has been denied.

18a39 *For if it is true to say that <such a thing> is pale or that it is not pale, it is necessary that it be pale or not pale, and if it is pale or not pale, it was true to affirm or deny this. If it does not hold, it is false, and if it is false, it does not hold. Thus, it is necessary that either the affirmative sentence or the negative sentence be true or <in the other case> false.*[99] *Therefore, nothing either is or is happening either by chance or however it chances, or will be or will not be, but everything <is or occurs> of necessity and not however it chances. For, either the one who affirms it or the one who denies it will be speaking truly;*[100] *otherwise, it might equally well happen or not happen, since what is however it chances neither is nor will be any more thus than not thus.*

<Confirmation of the relation of facts and sentences>

14. Wanting to strengthen the foregoing assumption, that the existence of the things follows upon the truth of the sentences and non-existence upon their falsity, Aristotle shows by means of examples that this is so, since indeed examples usually clarify arguments which are given without them. Now, the causal connective *'for'* in the phrase

---

[99]   ἀληθῆ εἶναι ἢ ψευδῆ; Minio-Paluello has ἀληθῆ εἶναι alone.
[100] ἀληθεύσει; Minio-Paluello has ἀληθεύει ("speaks truly").

τὰ παραδείγματα σαφεστέρους ποιεῖν εἰώθασι τοὺς χωρὶς αὐτῶν λεγομένους 25
λόγους. παρείληπται μὲν οὖν ὁ γάρ αἰτιολογικὸς σύνδεσμος ἐν τῷ εἰ γὰρ
ἀληθὲς εἰπεῖν πρὸς ἔνδειξιν τῆς προσθέσεως τῶν νῦν λεγομένων, ὅτι τοῦ
προειρημένου θεωρήματος περιέχουσι κατασκευήν. | λέγει δὲ ὅτι εἰ ἀληθὲς 113ᵛ
5 εἰπεῖν περί τινος, οἷον τοῦδε τοῦ ἱματίου, ὅτι λευκόν ἐστιν, ἀνάγκη λευκὸν αὐτὸ εἶναι, καὶ εἰ ὅτι οὐ λευκόν, ἀνάγκη λευκὸν μὴ εἶναι. εἶτα
προστίθησί τι διὰ τούτων τοῖς προειρημένοις ἀντιστρέφειν πρὸς ἑαυτὸ τὸ 5
λημμάτιον ἀξιῶν, λέγω δὲ ὅτι οὐ μόνον τοῖς λόγοις ἀληθεύουσιν ἀκολουθεῖν ἀνάγκη τὴν ὕπαρξιν τῶν πραγμάτων, ἀλλὰ καὶ τῇ ὑπάρξει τὴν ἀλή-
10 θειαν τῶν λόγων· διόπερ φησὶ καὶ εἰ ἔστι λευκὸν ἢ οὐ λευκόν, ἀληθὲς ἦν φάναι ἢ ἀποφάναι, διδάσκων ἡμᾶς ἅμα διὰ τοῦ μὴ εἰπεῖν 10
ἀληθές ἐστι φάναι ἀλλὰ ἀληθὲς ἦν, ὅπερ ἐν τοῖς ἑξῆς σαφῶς προσθήσει,
ὅτι οὐ μόνον κατ᾽ αὐτὸν τὸν χρόνον, καθ᾽ ὃν ἐκβαίνει τὰ πράγματα καὶ
ὑφέστηκεν, ἀληθές ἐστι λέγειν περὶ αὐτῶν ὅτι οὕτως ἔχει ὡς ἔχει, ἀλλὰ
15 καὶ πρὸ τῆς ἐκβάσεως ἀληθής ἐστιν ἡ περὶ αὐτῶν πρόρρησις, ἀναγκαίως 15
τοῦτο προλαμβάνων ὡς ἐσόμενον αὐτῷ χρήσιμον πρὸς τὴν ἀναίρεσιν τοῦ
ἐνδεχομένου καὶ τὴν ὅλην τῆς ἐφόδου δύναμιν, ὡς μαθησόμεθα, συνέχον.
τοῦτο οὖν ὥσπερ ἐκ συλλογισμοῦ συνάγων ἀκολούθως ἐπάγει τὸ ὥστε
ἀνάγκη τὴν κατάφασιν ἢ τὴν ἀπόφασιν ἀληθῆ εἶναι ἢ ψευδῆ, 20
20 προσυπακουμένου δηλονότι τοῦ ἀφωρισμένου. καὶ τοῦτο εἰκότως· εἰ γὰρ
ἀνάγκη τὸ λευκὸν ἢ εἶναι ἢ μὴ εἶναι καὶ παρὰ ταῦτα οὐκ ἔστιν, ἀλλ᾽
ὄντος μὲν αὐτοῦ ἡ περὶ αὐτοῦ προρρηθεῖσα κατάφασις ὡρισμένως ἀληθής
μὴ ὄντος δὲ ἡ ἀπόφασις, εὐλόγως ἄρα ὥσπερ συμπέρασμα ἑπόμενον τοῖς 25
προειρημένοις ἐπήγαγε τὸ ὥστε ἀνάγκη ἢ τὴν κατάφασιν ἢ τὴν ἀπό-
25 φασιν ἀληθῆ εἶναι ἢ ψευδῆ. ἀντιστρεφούσας δὲ ἀλλήλαις ἐπιδεί⟨ξ⟩ας 114ʳ
τήν τε ἀλήθειαν τῶν λόγων καὶ τὴν ὕπαρξιν τῶν πραγμάτων, πρὶν τὸ
εἰρημένον συμπέρασμα ἐπαγαγεῖν, μεταξὺ προστίθησιν ὅτι καὶ τὸ ψεῦδος
τῶν λόγων καὶ ἡ ἀνυπαρξία τῶν πραγμάτων ἀντιστρέφουσι πρὸς ἄλληλα 5
διὰ τοῦ καὶ εἰ μὴ ὑπάρχει, ψεύδεται, καὶ εἰ ψεύδεται, οὐχ
30 ὑπάρχει.
     Τούτων οὖν οὕτως ἐχόντων ἐκ τῶν προειρημένων λαβὼν ὅτι ἀνάγκη
τὴν ἑτέραν τῶν ἀντιφασκουσῶν ἀλλήλαις κατὰ τὸν μέλλοντα χρόνον καθ᾽
ἕκαστα καὶ ἐνδεχομένων προτάσεων ὡρισμένως τὴν μὲν ἑτέραν ἀληθεύειν 10
τὴν δὲ ἑτέραν ψεύδεσθαι, ὡς αὐτόθεν ἑπομένου τοῦ ἀναιρεῖσθαι διὰ τὰ
35 προειλημμένα τὸ ἐνδεχόμενόν φησιν οὐδὲν ἄρα οὔτε ἔστιν οὔτε γίνεται οὔτε ἀπὸ τύχης οὔτε ὁπότερ᾽ ἔτυχε, διὰ τοῦ ἄρα σημαίνων
ὡς ἐκ τῆς ἀνάγκης τῶν προειλημμένων ἀναιρεῖσθαι συμβαίνει τὸ ἐνδεχό- 15

_____

3 προσθέσεως scripsi: προθέσεως libri   5 περί] παρά G   οἷον τοῦδε τοῦ om. G
ἐστιν om. G   6 ὅτι εἰ G: ὅτι (εἰ om.) F   μὴ εἶναι λ. colloc. F   14 ὡς ἔχει om. G
19 ἀνάγκη ἢ b (cf. v. 24)   21 ἢ (prius) om. M   22 ἀληθὲς A   24 ἢ (prius) om.
FG   25 post ψευδῆ add. χρήσιμον αὐτῶ ἐσόμενον πρὸς ἀναίρεσιν τοῦ ἐνδεχομένου (cf.
v. 16) G   28 ἀντιστρέφει a   29 εἰ (prius) om. F   ὑπάρχη A   32 τὴν ἑτέραν
om. G   33 ἑτέραν om. AGMa   35 οὔτε ἔστιν suppl. G²   36 ὁπότερον GMa
διὰ τὸ A¹: διὰ τούτων G   37 ὡς —προειλημμένων om. F   συμβ.] ἐμμένει A

'For if it is true to say' was chosen to explain the addition of what is now being said, namely that it contains a confirmation of the point stated above. He says that, if it is true to say of something, say of this cloak, that it is pale, then it is necessary that it be pale, and if <it is true to say> that it is not pale, then it is necessary that it not be pale. Then he adds something here to what was said before, believing that the assumption is convertible; I mean that it is not only necessary that the existence of the things follow upon the sentences being true, but also the truth of the sentences upon the existence <of the things>. Hence he says *'and if it is pale or not pale, it was true to affirm or deny this,'* teaching us at once by not saying 'it is true to say' but *'it was true ...'* just what he will add clearly in what follows, namely that it is not only in the very time in which the things occur and exist that it is true to say of them that they are such as they are, but even before their occurrence the prediction about them is true; and he necessarily anticipates this, thinking that it will be useful to him for the negation of the contingent and that it contains, as we shall see, the entire force of the attack. So, drawing the conclusion as if from a syllogism, he infers *'Thus, it is necessary that the affirmative sentence or the negative sentence be true or <in the other case> false,'* obviously implicitly understanding 'in a definite manner'. And he is correct in this. For if it is necessary that the pale be or not be, and there is nothing besides these, and if, when it exists, the previous affirmation about it is true in a definite manner, while when it does not exist the negation is, then it is reasonable for him to infer as a conclusion following upon the previous statements: *'Thus, it is necessary that the affirmative sentence or the negative sentence be true or in the other case false.'* Having shown the truth of the sentences and the existence of the things to be interconvertible with one another, before bringing on the stated conclusion, he adds parenthetically that the falsity of the sentences and the non-existence of the things are also interconvertible with one another in the words *'If it does not hold, it is false, and if it is false, it does not hold.'*

<The varieties of the contingent>

15. These things being so, having taken from the preceding that, necessarily, of singular contingent sentences concerning the future which contradict one another one is true in a definite manner and the other false, on the basis that the contingent is denied as an immediate consequence of what has been assumed, he says: *'Therefore, nothing either is or is happening either by chance or however it chances,'* signifying by the *'therefore'* that it follows from the necessity of the assumptions that the contingent is denied. The contingent is divided into three: one is called 'for the most part', for example that a man is born with five fingers or becomes grey with age (for things behaving otherwise are rare);

μενον. οὗπερ εἰς τρία διῃρημένου τὸ μὲν λέγεται ὡς ἐπὶ τὸ πολύ, οἷον
τὸ γενέσθαι ἄνθρωπον πενταδάκτυλον ἢ ἐν γήρᾳ πολιοῦσθαι (σπάνια γὰρ
τὰ μὴ οὕτως ἔχοντα), τὸ δὲ ὡς ἐπ᾽ ἔλαττον, οἷον τὸ τὸν σκάπτοντα
θησαυρῷ περιτυχεῖν, τὸ δὲ ἐπ᾽ ἴσης, οἷον τὸ λούσασθαι καὶ μὴ λούσα- 20
5 σθαι ἢ βαδίσαι καὶ μὴ βαδίσαι. καὶ περὶ μὲν τὸ ὡς ἐπὶ τὸ πολὺ
ἐνδεχόμενον ἔχουσι δύο τινὰ αἴτια, ἥ τε φύσις καὶ ἡ τέχνη· τήν τε γὰρ
φύσιν ὡς ἐπὶ τὸ πολὺ κατορθοῦσαν ὁρῶμεν ἐν τοῖς οἰκείοις ἀποτελέσμασι
(τὰ γὰρ τέρατα σπάνια) καὶ τὰς τέχνας ἐνίοτε μὲν ἀποτυγχανούσας διὰ 25
τὸ ῥευστὸν τῆς ὑποκειμένης αὐταῖς ὕλης, ὡς ἐπὶ τὸ πολὺ μέντοι κατορ-
10 θοῦν ἐπαγγελλομένας· οὐ γὰρ ἄν τις αὐταῖς ἐχρήσατο μὴ τοῦτο ἐπαγγελ|λο- 114ᵛ
μέναις· διόπερ ὅ τε ῥήτωρ ὡς ἐπὶ τὸ πολὺ διαβεβαιοῦται τὸν δικαστὴν
πείσειν καὶ ὁ ἰατρὸς ὡς ἐπὶ τὸ πολὺ τὸν ἄρρωστον ὑγιάσειν, καὶ ἕκαστος
τῶν ἄλλων τεχνιτῶν ὡς ἐπὶ τὸ πολὺ τεύξεσθαι τοῦ οἰκείου τέλους. περὶ
δὲ τὸ ἐπ᾽ ἔλαττον ἐνδεχόμενον δύο ταῦτα ἔχουσιν, ἥ τε τύχη καὶ τὸ 5
15 αὐτόματον. διαφέρουσι δὲ ἀλλήλων, ὅτι τὸ μὲν ἀπὸ τύχης παρυφίστασθαι
παὶ ἐπισυμβαίνειν παρὰ δόξαν καὶ σπανίως λέγεται τοῖς κατὰ προαίρεσιν
γινομένοις, ταὐτὸν δὲ εἰπεῖν τοῖς τῶν ἀνθρώπων ἔργοις (ἐπὶ μόνων γὰρ 10
τῶν ἀνθρώπων ἡ προαίρεσις λέγεται, τῶν βουλεύεσθαι καὶ αἱρεῖσθαι τόδε
πρὸ τοῦδε πεφυκότων, οὔτε τῶν κρειττόνων ἡμῶν βουλῆς δεομένων οὔτε
20 τῶν ἀλόγων ζῴων βουλεύεσθαι δυναμένων), τὸ μὲν οὖν ἀπὸ τύχης παρ-
υφίσταται, ὅπερ ἐλέγομεν, τοῖς κατὰ προαίρεσιν γινομένοις, τὸ δὲ ἀπὸ 15
ταὐτομάτου τοῖς κατὰ φύσιν· εἰ μὲν γάρ τις ἡμῶν προελθὼν ἐπὶ τὸ ἐντυχεῖν τῷ φίλῳ περιτύχοι παρ᾽ ἐλπίδα τινὶ βιβλίον πιπράσκοντι καὶ τοῦτο
ὠνήσαιτο, κατὰ τύχην λέγεται αὐτὸ ὠνήσασθαι, διότι τὸ πρίασθαι τὸ 20
25 βιβλίον προαιρέσει τινὶ τῇ πρὸς τὴν πρόοδον κινησάσῃ ἡμᾶς παρυπέστη
καὶ ἔξωθεν ἐπισυμβέβηκεν, οὐδεμιᾶς αὐτὸ ὡρισμένως ποιησάσης προσε-
χοῦς αἰτίας (καὶ γὰρ ἐπὶ λουτρὸν ἀπιὼν ἐπρίατο ἂν τὸ βιβλίον καὶ εὐξό-
μενος ἢ θέαν τινὰ ὀψόμενος), εἰ δέ γε σεισμοῦ γεγονότος καὶ διαστάντος 25
τινὸς τῆς γῆς μέρους ὕδατος ἀναρραγείη πηγὴ μὴ οὖσα πρότερον ἢ οὖσα
30 ἀφανισθείη, οὐκ ἂν λέγοιτο ἀπὸ τύχης ἡ πηγὴ γεγονέναι ἢ ἀπολωλέναι
ἀλλ᾽ ἐκ τοὐτομάτου. καὶ εἰ ἀπὸ μετεώρου | τινὸς κατενεχθεὶς λίθος 115ʳ
οὕτως ἔχοι θέσεως, ὥστε εἶναι πρὸς καθέδραν, φέρε εἰπεῖν, ἐπιτήδειος,
ἀπὸ ταὐτομάτου καὶ οὐκ ἀπὸ τύχης λέγεται εἶναι καθέδρα, διότι τὸ σύμ-
πτωμα τοῦτο παρυπέστη οὐ προαιρέσει ἀλλὰ τῇ φυσικῇ αὐτοῦ ῥοπῇ, καθ᾽ 5

1. 3 οἷον] ὡς G   3 τὸν om. AFMa   10. 11 οὐ—ἐπαγγελλομέναις om. M
11. 12 ῥήτωρ—καὶ ὁ om. F   12 ὑγιάσει F   13 τεύξεται F   14 τύχη]
τέχνη G¹   15 ὑφίστασθαι A   16 καὶ (ante σπανίως) om. M   καὶ σπανίως
λέγεται iter. G   18 τόδε—τοῦδε (19) om. F   τόδε] τότε M   20. 21 παρυφίστασθαι
Ma   22 προελθὼν F: προσελθὼν G   τὸ] τῷ Ma   23 παρ᾽ ἐλπ. παρατύχοι
(περιτ. G²) G   post πιπρ. add. οὗ πάλαι ἠφίετο (sic) a   24 ὠνήσατο M
αὐτῷ ἐντυχεῖν καὶ ὠνήσασθαι a   26 ὡρισμένης FM   27 καὶ (alt.)] ἢ a
29 ὕδωρ ἀναρραγῇ ἢ πηγὴ μὴ οὖσα πρ. φανῇ F   30 λέγ.] γένοιτο F   31 κατενεχθῇ
A: κατενεχθείη GMa   32 ἔχει a

another is 'for the lesser part', for example that one digging comes upon a hoard of treasure; and the last is 'equally <often>', for example to bathe or not to bathe and to walk or not to walk. Concerning the contingent <which occurs> 'for the most part', there are two causes, nature and art. For we see that nature is for the most part successful in her own products—since monsters are rare—and that the arts sometimes fail because of the flux of their subject matter, although they promise to succeed for the most part (no one would use them if they did not promise this, which is why the orator gives assurances that he will for the most part persuade the juror, the physician that he will for the most part cure the patient, and every other kind of technician that he will for the most part obtain his particular end). Concerning the contingent <which occurs> 'for the lesser part', there are these two <causes>, chance and spontaneity. These differ from one another in that what is by chance is said to exist parasitically or supervene unexpectedly and rarely upon what happens by choice, i.e. upon the works of people (for 'choice' is said only of people, who are such as to deliberate and choose one thing instead of another, given that the beings who are better than we are have no need of deliberation and that the irrational animals are incapable of deliberating), and so what is by chance, as we said, exists parasitically upon what happens by choice, and what is spontaneous upon what happens naturally. For if one of us goes out to meet his friend, unexpectedly encounters someone selling a book and buys it, he is said to have bought it by chance, because <his> buying the book existed parasitically or supervened from outside upon a choice which moved him[101] to <his> outing, since there was no proximate cause which did this in a definite manner (in fact, he could have bought the book while going off to a bath, while intending to offer a prayer, or while intending to observe a spectacle). But if there had been an earthquake and a fissure opened in the earth and a spring of water gushed where previously there was none or an existing spring disappeared, the spring would not be said to have appeared or disappeared by chance, but spontaneously; or if a stone fallen from some height should occupy a position such that it could serve as, say, a seat, it is said to be a seat spontaneously, not by chance, because this event attended not upon a choice, but upon the stone's own natural tendency, according to which it was borne downward from on high. Concerning the contingent <which occurs> 'equally <often>' there is only choice, for example to go out or not to go out, to converse or not. Only this species of the contingent is called *'however it*

---

[101] Ammonius' text reads ἡμᾶς ("moved us") referring to the "us" in "one of us" above. But it seems more natural to adopt our translation.

ἦν ἄνωθεν ἐπὶ τὰ κάτω ἠνέχθη. περὶ δέ γε τὸ ἐπ᾽ ἴσης ἐνδεχόμενον
ἡ προαίρεσις ἔχει μόνη, οἷον τὸ προελθεῖν ἢ μὴ προελθεῖν καὶ τὸ διαλε-
χθῆναι ἢ μή. καὶ τοῦτο μόνον τὸ εἶδος τοῦ ἐνδεχομένου καλεῖται ὁπότερον ἔτυχε, διότι οὐδὲν πλέον οὐδὲ ἔλαττον ἔχει κατὰ τοῦτο ἡ ὕπαρξις 10
5 τῆς ἀνυπαρξίας, ἀλλ᾽ ὁπότερον ἔτυχε μόριον τῆς ἀντιφάσεως ὁμοίως ἐκβῆναι δυνατόν. ἀναιρῶν οὖν, ὅπερ ἐλέγομεν, τὸ ἐνδεχόμενον οὐδὲν ἄρα,
φησίν, οὔτε ἔστιν οὔτε γίνεται οὔτε ἀπὸ τύχης οὔτε ὁπότερ᾽
ἔτυχε, τοῦτ᾽ ἔστιν οὐδὲν ἄρα οὔτε νῦν ἐστιν ἤδη ἐκβεβηκὸς ἢ ὡς ἐπ᾽ 15
ἔλαττον ἐνδεχόμενον ἢ ὡς ἐπ᾽ ἴσης οὔτε ὕστερόν ποτε ἐκβήσεται. εἶτα
10 καὶ κοινὴν ποιούμενος τὴν ἀναίρεσιν παντὸς τοῦ ἐνδεχομένου προσέθηκεν
οὐδ᾽ ἔσται ἢ οὐκ ἔσται· ἅπαν γὰρ ἐνδεχόμενον ταύτῃ διαφέρει τοῦ τε
ἀναγκαίως ἐκβαίνοντος καὶ τοῦ ἀδυνάτου, ὅτι τὸ μὲν μόνως ἔσεσθαι λέγο- 20
μεν καὶ τὸ ἀδύνατον μόνως οὐκ ἔσεσθαι, τὸ δὲ ἐνδεχόμενον ἢ ἔσεσθαι ἢ
μὴ ἔσεσθαι. οὐδὲν οὖν, φησίν, οὔτε ἔστιν οὔτε γίνεται τὸν τῶν ἐνδεχο-
15 μένων τρόπον, ἀλλ᾽ ἐξ ἀνάγκης ἅπαντα καὶ οὐχ ὁπότερ᾽ ἔτυχεν. εἶτα
ὥσπερ ἀναμιμνήσκων ἡμᾶς τῆς ἐφόδου, καθ᾽ ἣν ταῦτα ἔδοξε συμβαίνειν, 25
ἐπάγει ἢ γὰρ ὁ φὰς ἀληθεύσει ἢ ὁ ἀποφάς. εἰ δὲ ὁ ἕτερος τούτων
ὡρισμένως ἀληθεύσει, τῷ δὲ τὴν ἑτέραν πρότασιν τῆς ἀντιφάσεως ὡρι-
σμένως ἀληθεύειν εἵπετο | ἡ ἀναίρεσις τοῦ ἐνδεχομένου, φανερὸν ὅτι 115ᵛ
20 οἰχήσεται τὸ ἐνδεχόμενον ἐκ τῶν ὄντων, τό τε ἄλλο καὶ τὸ οἷον κέντρον
αὐτοῦ τὸ ὁπότερ᾽ ἔτυχεν, ὅπερ ἔλαβεν ἀντὶ τοῦ ἐνδεχομένου παντὸς
ὁ Ἀριστοτέλης. εἰ δέ γε εἶχέ τινα ὑπόστασιν, ὁμοίως ἂν ἐγίνετο ἢ 5
οὐκ ἐγίνετο· τοῦτο γὰρ λέγομεν ὁπότερ᾽ ἔτυχεν ἢ εἶναι ἢ γίνεσθαι,
ὅπερ οὐδὲν μᾶλλον οὕτως ἢ μὴ οὕτως ἔχει ἢ ἕξει, ἐπὶ μὲν τοῦ
25 γεγονότος δηλονότι καὶ ἤδη ἐν ὑποστάσει ὄντος τὸ ἔχει λέγοντες ἐπὶ δὲ
τοῦ γενησομένου τὸ ἕξει.

---

1 τὸ κάτω Fa   γε] τε G¹   2 προσελθεῖν (utrobique) A   ἢ μὴ προελθεῖν om. F   τὸ (alt.) om. AFMa   3. 4 ὁπότερος G¹   4 οὐδὲν] οὐδὲ A
οὐδὲ ἔλαττον om. G   οὐδὲ] οὔτε F   6 ὥσπερ F   ἔλεγον F (cf.
p. 141,34)   7 ὁπότερον A   8 ἤδη om. F   post ἐκβεβ. add.
καὶ G²   11 γὰρ τὸ ἐνδεχ. F   15 πάντα F   16 ἔδοξαν G
18 ἀληθεύει F   20 ὄντων] αὐτῶν M   κέντρον om. G   21 ἔλαβε μὲν
AGMa   22 τινα ὑπόστ. εἶχε colloc. G   23 ἐλέγομεν GM; corrigas λέγει at v. 25
λέγων   γενέσθαι AGMa   24 ἐπὶ — ἕξει (26) om. (in margine partim nunc abs-
ciso suppl.) A   25 δὲ om. G   26 τὸ om. G

chances', because its existence is no more or less <frequent> than its non-existence, but whichever part of the contradiction it chances can equally occur. So it is, as we said, to deny the contingent that he says *'Therefore, nothing either is or is happening either by chance or however it chances'*, i.e. 'therefore nothing contingent, be it of the kind that occurs for the lesser part or of the kind occurring with equal probability, has already occurred or will ever occur in the future.' Accordingly, in order to make the negation of every contingent general he added *'or will be or will not be'*. For every contingent differs in this way from what occurs necessarily and from what is impossible, namely that of the former we say only that it will be and of the impossible only that it will not be, while we say that the contingent either will be or will not be. So, *'nothing,'* he says, *'either is or is happening'* in the way contingents do, *'but everything <is or occurs> of necessity and not however it chances.'* Then as if to remind us of the attack, according to which these things seemed to follow, he infers *'For, either the one who affirms it or the one who denies it will be speaking truly.'* But if one of these will be speaking truly in a definite manner, and the destruction of the contingent followed from the fact that one sentence of the contradiction is true in a definite manner, then it is apparent that the contingent will disappear from among the things which exist, both the rest of it and also its core, so to speak, the *'however it chances'*, which Aristotle used for the whole of the contingent. If, however, it did have any existence, *'it might equally well happen or not happen'* —this is what we say either is or is happening *'however it chances'*, that which *'neither is nor will be any more thus than not thus,'* where we obviously say 'is' of what has happened and is already in existence and 'will be' of what will happen.

p. 18b9 Ἔτι εἰ ἔστι λευκὸν νῦν, ἀληθὲς ἦν εἰπεῖν πρότερον 10
ὅτι ἔσται λευκόν· ὥστε ἀεὶ ἀληθὲς ἦν εἰπεῖν ὁτιοῦν τῶν γινομένων ὅτι ἔστιν ἢ ἔσται. εἰ δὲ ἀεὶ ἀληθὲς ἦν εἰπεῖν ὅτι ἔστιν
ἢ ἔσται, οὐχ οἷόν τε τοῦτο μὴ εἶναι οὐδὲ μὴ ἔσεσθαι· ὃ δὲ μὴ
5 οἷόν τε μὴ γενέσθαι, ἀδύνατον μὴ γενέσθαι· ὃ δὲ ἀδύνατον μὴ 15
γενέσθαι, ἀνάγκη γενέσθαι· ἅπαντα οὖν τὰ ἐσόμενα ἀναγκαῖον
γενέσθαι· οὐδὲν ἄρα ὁπότερ' ἔτυχεν οὐδὲ ἀπὸ τύχης ἔσται·
εἰ γὰρ ἀπὸ τύχης, οὐκ ἐξ ἀνάγκης.

Τὰ διὰ τῶν προλαβάντων ἀσυμφανῶς εἰρημένα πρὸς κατασκευὴν τοῦ 20
10 καὶ εἰς τὸν μέλλοντα χρόνον λαμβανομένας τὰς προτάσεις, περὶ ὧν ὁ λόγος,
ἀφωρισμένως διαιρεῖν τὸ ἀληθὲς καὶ τὸ ψεῦδος, ᾧ αὐτόθεν εἵπετο μηδε-
μίαν ἐν τοῖς οὖσι χώραν ἔχειν τὸ ἐνδεχόμενον, βούλεται διὰ τούτων
σαφέστερον ἡμῖν παραδοῦναι μετὰ πλείονος ἐπεξεργασίας προάγων τὸν 25
λόγον. διὸ ὥσπερ ἀπ' ἄλλης ἀρχῆς ποιούμενος τὴν ἐπιχείρησίν φησιν·
15 ἔτι εἰ ἔστι λευκόν τι νῦν, οἷον παιδίον ἄρτι τεχθέν, ἀληθὲς ἦν εἰπεῖν
τῇ προτεραίᾳ ὅτι τεχθήσεται τῇ ἑξῆς | λευκὸν παιδίον, καὶ οὐ τῇ προ- 116r
τεραίᾳ μᾶλλον ἢ πρὸ οἵου δήποτε χρόνου· τίς γὰρ ἡ ἀποπλήρωσις; ὃ δὲ
ἀεὶ προλέγοντες ὅτι ἔσται ἀληθεύομεν, οὐχ οἷόν τε τοῦτο μὴ ἔσεσθαι,
ὥσπερ οὐδὲ ὃ εἶναι λέγοντες ἀληθεύομεν, οἷόν τε τοῦτο μὴ εἶναι· ἀδύνα- 5
20 τον ἄρα ἦν μὴ γενέσθαι λευκὸν παιδίον, διότι ἡ περὶ αὐτοῦ ἐν τῷ ἀπείρῳ
καὶ προλαβόντι χρόνῳ γεγονυῖα πρόρρησις ἀληθής· ὁ γὰρ μὴ οἷόν τε,
φησί, μὴ γενέσθαι, ἀδύνατον μὴ γενέσθαι, ὃ δὲ ἀδύνατον μὴ
γενέσθαι, ἀνάγκη γενέσθαι, προάγων τὸν λόγον εἰς τὸ πάντα ἀναγ- 10
κάζειν, ὅπερ ἦν αὐτῷ προχείμενον, ἐκ τῶν σαφεστέρων μὲν καὶ μᾶλλον
25 συγχωρουμένων προτάσεων, ἴσον δὲ δυναμένων ταῖς εἰς ἃς μεταλαμβάνον-
ται· τό τε γὰρ οὐχ οἷόν τε τὸ ἀδύνατον σημαίνει καὶ τὸ οὐχ οἷόν τε μὴ
γενέσθαι τῷ ἀδύνατον μὴ γενέσθαι εἰς ταὐτὸν ἔρχεται, τὸ δὲ ἀδύνατον 15
μὴ γενέσθαι τῷ ἀναγκαῖον γενέσθαι, ὥσπερ καὶ τὸ ἀδύνατον γενέσθαι τῷ

2 ὅτι—ἀνάγκης (8) om. M   ὥστε—ἀνάγκης (8) om. a   ἀεὶ om. G   2. 3 ὁτιοῦν
τῶν γινομένων suppl. G²   γενομ. b   3 ἔστιν ἢ om. AF   εἰ — ἔσται (4) suppl. G²
ἀεὶ om. F   ἦν om. G   5. 6 ἀδύν. μὴ γεν.· ὃ δὲ ἀδύν. μὴ γενέσθαι suppl. G²
6 ἅπαντα — γενέσθαι (7) om. G   7 οὐδὲν] οὐδὲ A   8 εἰ—τύχης, οὐκ] ἀλλ' F
10 καὶ om. Ma   παραλαμβ. G   11 ᾧ] οἷς F   an εἵπετο ⟨τὸ⟩?   12 ἔχειν ante
χώραν colloc. A: ante ἐν Fa   14 τὴν ἐπιχ. ποιούμ. colloc. G   15 ἔτι] ὅτι M
τι om. Mab   ἦν om. G   16. 17 τεχθ.—προτεραίᾳ om. F   16 τῇ
(ante ἑξῆς)] καὶ τὰ G   καὶ οὐ] εἰ δὲ τῇ προτεραίᾳ, τί M   17 πρὸ] πρὸς AFG¹
οἵου] ὅσου M   ἀποχλήρωσις FGMa   δ] εἰ AFM   18 ante ἔσεσθαι add. εἶναι
ἀδύνατον ἄρα ἦν μὴ γενέσθαι λευκὸν παιδίον (sed del.) G (cf. v. 19. 20)   19 οὐχ οἷον G
εἶναι (alt.)] ἢ F   21 καὶ] τῷ F   22 ἀδύνατον — ἀνάγκη γενέσθαι (23) om. G
23 τὸν λόγον iter. G   23. 24 ἀναγκάζειν] ἐξ ἀνάγκης Ma   25 εἰς ἃ F: ἴσαις G
25. 26 μεταλαμβανομέναις G   26 τὸ ἀδύν.—οἷόν τε om. G¹a   28 ἀναγκ. μὴ γεν.
(sed μὴ del.) G   γενέσθαι ὥσπερ—ἀναγκαῖον (p. 145,1) om. M

18b9 *Further, if it is pale now, it was true to say earlier that it would be pale; thus, it was always true to say of anything that happens*[102] *that it was or would be.*[103] *But if it was always true to say that it was or would be, it was not such as not to be or not to be going to be; and something that is not such as not to happen cannot not happen; and if it is impossible for something not to happen, it is necessary for it to happen. Therefore, for all things which will be it is necessary to happen. So nothing will be however it chances or by chance: for if it is by chance, it is not of necessity.*

<Strengthening the case for the necessitation of all things>

16. What was said in the foregoing with insufficient clarity to establish that the sentences taken in the future time, about which he is speaking, also divide in a definite manner the true and false, from which it immediately followed that the contingent had no place among existing things, he here wants to show us more clearly, extending his discourse with greater elaboration. Hence, he speaks as though making his argument from a new beginning. *'Further, if something is pale now,'* like a new-born child, *'it was true to say'* on the previous day that tomorrow a pale child would be born—actually, no more on the previous day than at any previous time at all. For what is strange <in this>?[104] If we speak truly each time we say in advance that something will be, *this thing is not such as not to be going to be*, just as neither *is something such as not to be*, if we say truly that it exists. Thus, it was impossible for the pale child not to be born, because the prediction made about it in indefinite preceding time was true. For, *'something that is not such, he says, as not to happen cannot not happen; and if it is impossible for something not to happen, it is necessary for it to happen,'* extending his argument to the necessitation of all things, which was his intention, from sentences which, while they are clearer and more agreed upon, still have the same force as those into which they are transposed. In fact, 'is not such as' means 'impossible', and 'is not such as not to happen' amounts to the same as 'impossible not to happen', and 'impossible not to happen' <is the same as> 'necessary to happen', just as 'impossible to happen' <is the same as> 'necessary not to happen'. We

---

[102] γινομένων. Minio-Paluello (following most of the manuscripts) has γενομένων: "has happened".

[103] ἔστιν ἢ ἔσται; Minio-Paluello has ἔσται alone.

[104] The phrase τίς γὰρ ἡ ἀποκλήρωσις is rather frequent in later Greek. We adopt the reading which most of the manuscripts have (ἀποκλήρωσις). Busse adopted ἀποπλήρωσις ("How, then, is <this argument> perfected?" [Blank]).

ἀναγκαῖον μὴ γενέσθαι. μᾶλλον μέντοι κινούμεθα ὑπὸ τοῦ ἀδύνατον μὴ
γενέσθαι ὡς ἐναργεστέρου ἥπερ ὑπὸ τοῦ ἀνάγκη γενέσθαι, διὸ καὶ ὁ ἰατρὸς
εἰπὼν λόγου χάριν ὅτι ἀνάγκη φλεβοτομηθῆναι τὸν ἄρρωστον, εἴπερ 20
βούλοιτο ὑγιασθῆναι, ὡς κατασκευαστικὸν τούτου καὶ πρὸς τὴν πειθὼ
5 κινῆσαι μᾶλλον ὀφεῖλον προστίθησιν 'ἀδύνατον γὰρ μὴ φλεβοτομηθέντα
αὐτὸν ὑγιᾶναι'. ὥστε εἰκότως, φησίν, ἐλέγομεν ἅπαντα τὰ ἐσόμενα ἐξ
ἀνάγκης γενέσθαι καὶ μηδὲν μήτε ἀπὸ τύχης μήτε καθ' ἕτερον τρόπον τοῦ 25
ἐνδεχομένου.

Ῥητέον δὲ πρὸς ταύτην τὴν ἐπιχείρησιν ὅτι τὸ ἐκβεβηκὸς νῦν καὶ
10 ἤδη γεγονὸς οὐκ ἀληθὲς πρὸ τῆς ἐκβάσεως λέγειν ὅτι ἔσται πάντως λευ-
κόν· οὐ γὰρ | ἐπειδὴ ὁ χρόνος εἰς τὸ εἶναι αὐτὸ ἀποκατέστησε, διὰ τοῦτο 116v
οἴεσθαι χρὴ ἐξ ἀναγκαίας αὐτὸ προκαταβολῆς γεγονέναι. ὥστε τῶν προ-
λεγόντων περὶ αὐτοῦ οὐχ ὁ λέγων ὅτι ἐξ ἀνάγκης ἔσται λευκὸν ἀληθεύσει,
ἀλλ' ὁ τὸ ὅλον τοῦτο ἐνδεχομένως αὐτὸ ἐκβήσεσθαι λέγων· εἰ δὲ τοῦτο, 5
15 δῆλον ὅτι δυνατὸν ἦν αὐτὸ καὶ μὴ ἐκβῆναι· οὐ γὰρ ἂν ἄλλως ἠλήθευε
τὸ ἐνδεχομένως αὐτὸ ἐκβήσεσθαι. μὴ τοίνυν ἀπὸ τοῦ ἤδη ἐκβάντος τὸ
ἔτι μέλλον κρινέτωσαν οἱ ταῦτα λέγοντος, ἀλλὰ φυλάττοντες αὐτὸ μήπω 10
ἐκβεβηκὸς ζητείτωσαν εἰ ἐξ ἀνάγκης ἐκβήσεται· οὐ γὰρ ἕξουσι τοῦτο ἐπιδεῖξαι, ὡς αὐτὸς ἡμᾶς σαφῶς ἐν τοῖς ἑξῆς ὁ Ἀριστοτέλης διδάξει.

20 p. 18b16 Ἀλλὰ μὴν οὐδ' ὡς οὐδέτερόν γε ἀληθὲς ἐνδέχεται
λέγειν, οἷον ὅτι οὔτε ἔσται οὔτε οὐκ ἔσται· πρῶτον μὲν γὰρ 15
οὔσης τῆς καταφάσεως ψευδοῦς ἡ ἀπόφασις οὐκ ἀληθής, καὶ
ταύτης ψευδοῦς οὔσης τὴν κατάφασιν συμβαίνει μὴ ἀληθῆ
εἶναι. καὶ πρὸς τούτοις εἰ ἀληθὲς εἰπεῖν ὅτι λευκὸν καὶ μέγα,
25 δεῖ ἄμφω ὑπάρχειν· εἰ δὲ ὑπάρξει εἰς αὔριον, ὑπάρξειν εἰς αὔριον. εἰ δὲ μήτε ἔσται μήτε μὴ ἔσται αὔριον, οὐκ ἂν εἴη τὸ ὁπό- 20
τερ' ἔτυχεν, οἷον ναυμαχία· δέοι γὰρ ἂν μήτε γενέσθαι ναυμαχίαν αὔριον μήτε μὴ γενέσθαι.

Ἐπειδὴ προείληπται μὲν πρὸς ἀναίρεσιν τοῦ ἐνδεχομένου τὸ τὰς
30 προτάσεις, περὶ ὧν ὁ λόγος, ἀφωρισμένως διαιρεῖν τὸ ἀληθὲς καὶ τὸ ψεῦ- 25
δος, ἔλαβε δὲ τοῦτο διὰ τὸ μὴ δύνασθαι αὐτὰς συναληθεύειν ἀλλήλαις,

---

1 prius μὴ superscr. M   ἀδυνάτου AMa   3 τὸν om. AG   4 βούλ.] μέλλοι G
5 μᾶλλον ante πρὸς (4) colloc. G   7 γίνεσθαι F   8 ἐνδεχ.] ἀντικειμένου F
10 ἤδη om. F   τῆς ἐκβάσεως om. F   11 διὰ om. M   12 αὐτῶ A
13 ante ἔσται add. ὅτι G   15 γὰρ om. G   ἄλλως] ὅλως F   17 μέλλον]
μᾶλλον Ga   18 ζητήτ. F   εἰ om. M   εἰ οὐδ' a   19 αὐτὸ M
σαφ. ἡμᾶς colloc. G   ἐν τοῖς ἑξ. post ἡμᾶς colloc. M: post Ἀρ. a   ὁ Ἀριστοτέλης fort. eicias   21 οἷον — γενέσθαι (28) om. M   ὅτι—γενέσθαι (28) om. a
22. 23 καὶ ταύτης—γενέσθαι (28) om. G   24 λευκὸν ἅμα F   25 ὑπάρξειν] ὑπάρξει
Fb   26 μήτε (prius)] μὴ F   εἰς αὔριον F (cf. p. 146,26)   26. 27 ὁπότερον F
29 ἐπειδὴ] ἔπειτα δὴ M   τὴν ἀναίρ. G

are, however, more moved by 'impossible not to happen', which is more clear, than by 'necessary to happen', which is why the physician too, saying for example that it is necessary for the patient to have his veins opened if he wants to get well, adds 'for it is impossible that he will get well if his veins have not been opened,' <a sentence which> brings this about and ought to do more to persuade the patient. Thus, Aristotle says, we were right to say that everything which will be happens of necessity and nothing either by chance or by another kind of contingency.

<True prediction does not necessitate future events>

17. To this argument one must reply that it was not true of what has occurred now or has already happened to say before the event that it will, in any case, be pale. For we should not think it has happened by a necessary pre-establishment just because time has brought it into being. Thus, of those who make predictions about it, it is not the one who says that of necessity it will be pale who will speak truly, but rather the one who says all of this, <namely> that it will occur in a contingent manner. If this is so, it is clear that it was also possible for it not to occur, since it would not otherwise have been true that it would occur in a contingent manner. Therefore, let those who say this not judge what is still going to be from what has already occurred, but let them keep it as not yet having occurred and inquire whether it will occur of necessity. For they will not be able to show this, as Aristotle himself will teach us clearly in what follows (19a23-29).

18b17 *Nor, however, can one say that neither is true, i.e. that it will neither be nor not be. First, if the affirmative sentence is false the negative sentence is not true, and if the latter is false it occurs that the affirmative sentence is not true. Moreover, if it is true to say that something is pale and large,* [105] *both have to hold; and if they will hold tomorrow, they will have to hold tomorrow.* [106] *But if it will neither be nor not be tomorrow, there would be no <event of the kind> 'however it chances', as for instance a sea battle, since a sea battle would have neither to happen tomorrow* [107] *nor not to happen.*

<Absurd consequences of the argument for necessitation>

18. Since it has been assumed for purposes of the destruction of the contingent that the sentences about which we are speaking divide the true and false in a definite manner—he assumed this because of the fact that they cannot be true together, which was said in the

---

[105] Ammonius, here and in the commentary, has μέγα; Minio-Paluello (following most of the manuscripts) μέλαν ("dark").

[106] εἰ δὲ ὑπάρξει ... ὑπάρξειν; Minio-Paluello has εἰ δὲ ὑπάρξειν ... ὑπάρξει.

[107] ναυμαχίαν αὔριον; Minio-Paluello has ναυμαχίαν alone.

ὅπερ ἐλέγετο διὰ τοῦ ἄμφω γὰρ οὐχ ὑπάρξει ἅμα ἐπὶ τοῖς τοιού-
τοις, ἠδύνατο δέ τις ὑποπτεύειν ὡς οὐκ ἀναγ|καῖον ἢ συναληθεύειν 117ʳ
αὐτὰς ἢ διαιρεῖν τὸ ἀληθὲς καὶ τὸ ψεῦδος (ἐνδέχεσθαι γὰρ καὶ συμψεύδεσθαι), διὰ τοῦτο νῦν προτίθεται δεῖξαι ὅτι οὐδὲ συμψεύδεσθαι δυνατὸν
5 ταύτας τὰς προτάσεις, ὅπερ οὔτε ὀνίνησί τι τὸν οὕτως λέγειν αἱρούμενον 5
πρὸς τὸ εἰσάγειν τὸ ἐνδεχόμενον ἀλλὰ καὶ ἄλλως ἐστὶν ἀδύνατον· δειχθή-
σεται γὰρ καὶ κατ' αὐτὴν τὴν ὑπόθεσιν τὸ αὐτὸ πρᾶγμα καὶ ἀναγκαίως
ἐκβαῖνον καὶ ἀδύνατον ἔχον τὴν ἔκβασιν. φησὶν οὖν ὡς οὐδὲ τοῦτο ἐνδέχεται λέγειν ὅτι αἱ καθ' ἕκαστα καὶ ἐνδεχόμεναι προτάσεις κατὰ τὸν 10
10 μέλλοντα χρόνον συμψεύδονται ἀλλήλαις, ὅπερ ἐσήμηνε διὰ τοῦ οὐδ' ὡς
οὐδέτερόν γε ἀληθές, ἐπεὶ πρῶτον μέν, φησίν, ἀναιρήσομεν τὸ ἀξίωμα
τῆς ἀντιφάσεως, ἀφ' οὗ πάσας προάγομεν τὰς ἀποδείξεις ὡς ὄντος ἐναργε-
στάτου. πρὸς δὲ τούτοις συμβήσεται τὸ πρᾶγμα ἅμα μήτε ἔσεσθαι διὰ 15
τὸ ψεύδεσθαι τὴν λέγουσαν ἔσεσθαι αὐτὸ κατάφασιν καὶ πάλιν ἔσεσθαι
15 διὰ τὸ ψεύδεσθαι τὴν λέγουσαν μὴ ἔσεσθαι αὐτὸ ἀπόφασιν, ὥστε
καὶ ἔσεσθαι αὐτὸ ἐξ ἀνάγκης καὶ μὴ ἔσεσθαι ἐξ ἀνάγκης, οὗ τί ἂν
εἴη τερατωδέστερον; ἵνα δὲ τοῦτο συναγάγῃ, ἀναμιμνήσκει πάλιν ἡμᾶς 20
τοῦ λήμματίου τοῦ λέγοντος ὅτι τῇ ἀληθείᾳ τῶν λόγων ἡ τῶν πραγμάτων ἔκβασις ἀκολουθεῖ, καὶ οὐ κατὰ τὸν ἐνεστῶτα χρόνον μόνον ἀλλὰ
20 καὶ κατὰ τὸν μέλλοντα· εἰ γάρ τις προειπὼν ὅτι τεχθήσεται αὔριον
παιδίον λευκὸν καὶ μέγα ἀληθῶς προλέγοι, δεῖ αὔριον τεχθῆναι παιδίον, 25
ᾧ ἄμφω τὰ προειρημένα ὑπάρξει. σιωπήσας οὖν τὸ τούτων ἀκόλουθον,
ὅτι καὶ τῷ ψεύδει τῶν λόγων ἕπεται τὸ τὰ πράγματα μὴ ὑπάρχειν,
ὡς ἤδη πρότερον αὐτῷ παραδεδομένον, ἅμα τούτῳ | τῷ θεωρήματι 117ᵛ
25 τὸ ἑπόμενον τῷ παραλελειμμένῳ συνάγει λέγων εἰ δὲ μήτε ἔσται μήτε
μὴ ἔσται αὔριον, οὐκ ἂν εἴη τὸ ὁπότερ' ἔτυχε, τοῦτ' ἔστιν εἰ δὴ
συμψεύδονται αἱ τοιαῦται προτάσεις, ἀναιρεθήσεται μὲν καὶ οὕτως τὸ ἐνδεχό- 5
μενον, ἀναιρεθήσεται δὲ διὰ τὸ ἅμα ἀναγκαίως τε ἐκβαίνειν τὸ πρᾶγμα
καὶ ἀδύνατον ἔχειν τὴν ἔκβασιν.

---

1 ἄμφω γὰρ . .] p. 18ᵃ38   οὐχ om. F   3 ἐνδέχεται Fa   4 νῦν
om. A   οὐδὲ suppl. G²   5 ταύτας om. G   τῶν . . αἱρουμένων A
ἠρημένον G   6 ἀλλὰ om. F   8 καὶ] καίτοι G   10 οὐδ' om. G   11 γε]
τε G   15 αὐτὸ μὴ ἔσ. (num. corr.) G   16 μὴ om. F   17 τερατω-
δέστερος G¹   πάλιν om. ed. Ven. Brand.   19 μόνον χρ. colloc. Fa
21 παιδίον om. A   λέγοι F: προλέγει a   22 ἀμφότερα Ma   σκοπήσας A:
σιωπήσασθαι G   23 τὸ om. G   24 αὐτῷ om. G   25 μηδὲ (utrobique) F
26 ὁπότερον F   27 ψεύδονται F   προτ.] προρρήσεις F

words *'for under these circumstances both will not be true together'* (18a38-9)—and one
could suppose that it was not necessary that they either be true together or divide the true
and false, since they could also be false together, for this reason he now proposes to show
that it is not even possible for these sentences to be false together, which not only would
not be useful at all to somebody who chooses to say this in order to introduce the
contingent, but also is in any case impossible anyhow. For it will be shown that, also on
this very hypothesis, the same thing both necessarily occurs and its accomplishment is
impossible. Thus, he says that it is not even possible to say this, that the singular
contingent sentences in the future time are false together, which he signified by the words
'nor ... that neither is true,' since, first, he says, we shall deny the axiom of contradiction,
from which, as most evident, we develop all proofs. In addition, it will happen that the
thing at the same time will not be, because of the falsity of the affirmative sentence which
says that it will be, and on the other hand will be, because of the falsity of the negative
sentence which says that it will not be, so that it will both of necessity be and of necessity
not be: what could be more monstrous than that? In order to conclude this, he reminds us
again of the assumption that the outcome of the affairs follows upon the truth of the
sentences, not just in the present time but also in the future. For, if someone, having
prophesied that tomorrow there would be born a pale, large child, prophesied truly, a child
would have to be born tomorrow of whom both the <properties> foretold would hold. So,
not speaking about the consequence of this, that it also follows upon the falsity of the
sentences that the things do not hold good, since this has already been taught by him
previously, together with this theorem he deduces what follows from the theorem he <had
previously> (cp. 140,10-11) left out, saying *'But if it will neither be nor not be tomorrow,
there would be no <event of the kind> "however it chances"'*, i.e. if such sentences are
indeed false together, even so the contingent will be denied, and it will be denied because
of the fact that the thing at the same time both necessarily occurs and its accomplishment
is impossible.

p. 18b26 Τὰ μὲν δὴ συμβαίνοντα ἄτοπα ταῦτα καὶ τοιαῦτα
ἕτερα, εἴπερ πάσης καταφάσεως καὶ ἀποφάσεως ἢ ἐπὶ τῶν 10
καθόλου λεγομένων ὡς καθόλου ἢ ἐπὶ τῶν καθ᾽ ἕκαστα ἀνάγκη
τῶν ἀντικειμένων εἶναι τὴν μὲν ἀληθῆ τὴν δὲ ψευδῆ, μηδὲν
5 δὲ ὁπότερ᾽ ἔτυχεν εἶναι ἐν τοῖς γινομένοις, ἀλλὰ πάντα εἶναι
καὶ γίνεσθαι ἐξ ἀνάγκης· ὥστε οὔτε βουλεύεσθαι δέοι ἂν οὔτε
πραγματεύεσθαι, ὡς ἐὰν μὲν τοδὶ ποιήσωμεν, ἔσται τοδί, 15
ἐὰν δὲ μὴ τοδί, οὐκ ἔσται τοδί· οὐδὲν γὰρ κωλύει καὶ εἰς
μυριοστὸν ἔτος τὸν μὲν φάναι τοῦτο ἔσεσθαι τὸν δὲ μὴ φάναι,
10 ὥστε ἐξ ἀνάγκης ἔσται ὁπότερον ἦν αὐτῶν ἀληθὲς εἰπεῖν τότε.
ἀλλὰ μὴν οὐδὲ τοῦτο διαφέρει, εἴ τινες εἶπον τὴν ἀντίφασιν ἢ 20
μὴ εἶπον· δῆλον γὰρ ὅτι οὕτως ἔχει τὰ πράγματα, κἂν μὴ ὁ
μὲν καταφήσῃ τι ὁ δὲ ἀποφήσῃ· οὐ γὰρ διὰ τὸ καταφάναι ἢ
ἀποφάναι ἔσται ἢ οὐκ ἔσται, οὐδ᾽ εἰς μυριοστὸν ἔτος μᾶλλον
15 ἢ ἐν ὁποσῳοῦν χρόνῳ. ὥστε εἰ ἐν ἅπαντι χρόνῳ οὕτως εἶχεν, 25
ὥστε τὸ ἕτερον ἀληθεύεσθαι, ἀναγκαῖον ἦν τοῦτο γενέσθαι,
καὶ ἕκαστον τῶν γενομένων ἀεὶ οὕτως εἶχεν, ὥστε ἐξ ἀνάγκης
γενέσθαι· ὅ τε γὰρ ἀληθῶς εἶπέ τις ὅτι ἔσται, οὐχ οἷόν τε μὴ
γενέσθαι, καὶ τὸ γινόμενον ἀλη|θὲς ἦν εἰπεῖν ὅτι ἔσται.   118ʳ

20   Προέκειτο μὲν ἐξ ἀρχῆς σκοπεῖν εἰ πάσης ἀντιφάσεως εἰς τὸν μέλλοντα
χρόνον λαμβανομένης αἱ προτάσεις ὡρισμένως διαιροῦσι τό τε ἀληθὲς καὶ
τὸ ψεῦδος, δέδεικται δὲ διὰ πλειόνων ὡς ἕπεται τούτῳ τὸ ἐκποδὼν γίνε- 5
σθαι τοῦ ἐνδεχομένου τὴν φύσιν, τῶν μὲν ἐξ ἀνάγκης ἐκβαινόντων τῶν δὲ
τὴν ἔκβασιν ἀδύνατον ἐχόντων, καὶ ἐφ᾽ ἡμῖν εἶναι μηδέν, ἅπερ δεῖ λοιπὸν
25 ἐπιδεῖξαι ἄτοπα καὶ τῇ ἐναργείᾳ μαχόμενα. σφίγγων οὖν ἐν τούτοις τὸν 10
πάντα λόγον ὁ Ἀριστοτέλης τοῦ τε προτεθέντος ἐξ ἀρχῆς προβλήματος
ἀναμιμνήσκει καί τινα τὰ ἕπεσθαι αὐτῷ δεδειγμένα προστίθησι, καὶ ἄτοπα
ταῦτα καλεῖ, καίτοι μηδέπω δείξας ὅτι ἐστὶν ἄτοπα, ταῖς τε αὐτοφυέσιν
ἐννοίαις τῶν ψυχῶν ἀποχρώμενος καὶ ὡς εὐθὺς ἐπάξων τὴν κατασκευὴν 15
30 τοῦ ἄτοπον εἶναι τὸν ἀναιρεῖν πειρώμενον τὸ ἐνδεχόμενον λόγον (ὃν ἐλέγχει διχόθεν, νῦν μὲν ἐπιδεικνὺς ὅσα ἕπεται αὐτῷ ἀδύνατα, ὀλίγον δὲ ὕστερον
καὶ τὰ ψευδῶς εἰλημμένα ἐν αὐτῷ διαβάλλων)· ἔδει γὰρ αὐτό τε καθ᾽ αὑτὸ 20

1 τὰ τοιαῦτα G   2 εἴπερ — ἔσται (19) om. a   καταφ.—ἔσται (19) om. M
3 ἕκαστον b   4 μηδὲν—ἔσται (19) om. G   5 ὁπότερον F   5. 6 καὶ εἶναι καὶ F
6 οὐδὲ (pr. l) F   βούλεσθαι A¹F¹   9 prius τὸν] τὸ F   10 ἔσται] ἔσεσθαι b
ὁποτερονοῦν b   αὐτῶν ἀλ. ἦν b   13 τι om. F   οὐ] οὐδὲ b   καταφ.]
φάναι F: καταφαθῆναι b   14 ἀποφαθῆναι b   οὐδ᾽—ἔτος om. F¹ (πράγματα οὐδ᾽
εἰς μ. ἔτος F²)   15 τῶ χρ. (alt. l.) b   17 καὶ ἕκαστον — γενέσθαι (18) suppl. F²
18 εἰ ὅ τε γὰρ A   19 γενόμ. F   εἰπεῖν ἀεὶ b   20 προσέκειτο G¹   ἐξ ἀρχῆς
om. F   21 ὡρισμένως suppl. G²   τε om. G   25 ἐναργείᾳ scripsi: ἐνεργείᾳ
libri (cf. p. 148,3)   30 τὸ] τὸν A   32 ἐν αὐτῶ F: ἑαυτῶ AGMa

10*

18b26 *These and others of the same sort are the absurdities which result if it is necessary,*
for every affirmative and negative sentence either of universals spoken of universally or of
singulars, that one of the opposites be true and the other false, and <consequently> that
nothing that happens be however it chances, but that everything be and happen of
necessity. Thus, there would be no need to deliberate or to take trouble that if we shall do
this, this will happen, but if we do not do this, this will not happen. For nothing prevents
someone from having said even[108] *ten thousand years ago that this would happen and*
someone else that it would not; so that whichever of them it was true to say then will
happen of necessity. Nor, however, does it make a difference whether any people stated
the contradictory sentences or did not state them, since it is clear that the things are this
way even if <it is not the case that> one person affirmed something[109] *and the other*
denied it. For it is not because of the affirming or denying that it will be or not be, nor
<will it> rather be <when> stated ten thousand years ago than at any other time. Hence,
if at all time(s) it was so that one of the two was true, it was necessary for this to happen,
and everything that happens was always such as to happen of necessity. For what
someone has truly said would be so is not such that it does not happen, and of what
happens[110] *it was true to say*[111] *that it would be the case.*

<Nature cannot have vainly made us capable of deliberation>

19. From the beginning it was proposed to see whether the sentences of every
contradiction taken in the future time divide the true and false in a definite manner, and it
has been shown in more than one way that the elimination of the nature of the contingent
follows from this, some things occurring of necessity and the accomplishment of others
being impossible, and that nothing is up to us, which one must still show is absurd and
contrary to the evidence. Now, concentrating in these words his entire argument, Aristotle
reminds us of the problem which was posed at the beginning, adds certain things which
have been shown to follow from it, and calls them 'absurdities', although he has not yet
shown that they are absurd, relying upon the innate concepts of our souls and intending to
bring on immediately the demonstration of the absurdity of the argument which attempts to
deny the contingent (which he refutes in two ways, now by showing all the impossibilities
which follow from it, and a little later by attacking also what has been falsely assumed by
it). For he had to show what, taken by itself, the nature of the thing itself was by saying

---

[108] καί; Minio-Paluello does not have the adverb.
[109] τι; Minio-Paluello does not have the τι.
[110] γινόμενον; Minio-Paluello has γενόμενον.
[111] ἀληθὲς ἦν εἰπεῖν; Minio-Paluello has ἀληθὲς ἦν εἰπεῖν ἀεί ("it was always true to say").

δεικνύναι τὸ πρᾶγμα ὅπως ἔχει φύσεως, λέγοντα ὅτι ἔστιν ἐν τοῖς οὖσι
τὸ ἐνδεχόμενον (πολλὰ γὰρ ἕπεται ἀδύνατα τοῖς ἀναιρεῖν αὐτὸ πειρωμένοις,
καὶ ἡ ἐνάργεια δείκνυσιν αὐτὸ ὑφεστηκός), καὶ ἐπὶ τούτοις σαθρὸν ἐπιδεῖξαι τὸν προειρημένον λόγον τὸν πάντα ἀναγκάζειν πειρώμενον καὶ τὸ 25
5 ἐνδεχόμενον ἐκβάλλειν τῶν ὄντων. διὰ τούτων οὖν τέως παραδιδοὺς
τὰ ἑπόμενα ἀδύνατα τοῖς ἀναιροῦσι τὸ ἐνδεχόμενον, φησὶν ὡς εἴ τις ἀξιοίη
πᾶσαν ἀντίφασιν κατὰ πάν|τα χρόνον ὁμοίως ἔχειν πρὸς τὸ διαιρεῖν τὸ 118ᵛ
ἀληθὲς καὶ τὸ ψεῦδος καὶ μὴ μόνον τὰς διαγωνίους, ἃς καθόλου ὡς καθόλου καλεῖν εἴωθεν, ἀφωρισμένως ἔχειν ἀεὶ τὴν μὲν ἑτέραν τῶν προτά-
10 σεων ἀληθῆ τὴν δὲ ἑτέραν ψευδῆ κατὰ πᾶσαν ὕλην, ἀλλὰ καὶ τὰς καθ' 5
ἕκαστα, ᾧ ἠκολούθει τὸ ἐκποδὼν γίνεσθαι τὸ ἐνδεχόμενον, ματαιοπονίαν
τῆς φύσεως κατηγορήσει βουλευτικοὺς ἡμᾶς ποιησάσης· δῆλον γὰρ ὡς εἰ
μηδέν ἐστιν ἐφ' ἡμῖν, μάτην ἐπιχειρήσομεν βουλεύεσθαι περὶ τῶν οὐκ ἐν
τῇ ἐξουσίᾳ τῇ ἡμετέρᾳ κειμένων, καὶ ὅμοιόν τι ποιήσομεν τοῖς βουλευο- 10
15 μένοις πῶς ἂν ἀνατείλαι ἢ μὴ ἀνατείλαι ὁ ἥλιος. ἀλλὰ μὴν τὸ λέγειν
ὡς μάτην ἡμᾶς ἡ φύσις βουλευτικοὺς ἐποίησε παντελῶς ἄλογον· αὐτό τε
γὰρ καθ' αὑτὸ τοῦτο ἀποδέδεικται γεωμετρικαῖς, φασίν, ἀνάγκαις ὡς οὐδὲν 15
μάτην ὑπὸ τῆς φύσεως γίνεται, καὶ ὑπὸ τῆς ἐναργείας πάσης ἀποδείξεως
μᾶλλον ὁμολογεῖται. καὶ αὐτοὶ μέντοι οἱ πάντα ἀναγκάζοντες καὶ τὸ
20 ἐνδεχόμενον ἐκποδὼν ποιοῦντες πάντως ὁμολογήσουσιν αὐτὴν πάλιν εἶναι
τὴν φύσιν τὴν πάντα, ὡς αὐτοί φασιν, ὡρισμένως καὶ ἐξ ἀνάγκης μάτην 20
δὲ οὐδὲν ποιοῦσαν· ὥστε πῶς οὐ καταγέλαστον τὸ λέγειν τὴν φύσιν καὶ
μηδὲν ἐν τῇ ἐξουσίᾳ τῇ ἡμετέρᾳ καταλιπεῖν καὶ ποιεῖν ἡμᾶς βουλευτικοὺς
ὡς ἂν ὄντας κυρίους τοῦ πρᾶξαί τινα ἢ μὴ πρᾶξαι; εἰ γὰρ λέγοι τις ὅτι
25 χρῆται τῇ διανοίᾳ ὡς ὀργάνῳ πρὸς τὴν ἔκβασιν τῶν πράξεων, ἀλλ' ἐχρῆν, 25
φήσομεν, ὁρμᾶν ἡμᾶς αὐτόθεν ἐπὶ τὰς πράξεις, ἐφ' ἃς ἡ φύσις κατή-
πειγεν, ὥσπερ ἐπὶ τῶν ὄντως ὑπὸ φύσεως κινουμένων συμβαῖνον ὁρῶμεν
ἀνενδοιάστως ἐπὶ τὰ οἰκεῖα | τέλη φερομένων. διὸ καὶ ἡμεῖς ὅταν μιμώ- 119ʳ
μεθα τὴν φύσιν κατὰ τέχνην τινὰ ἐνεργοῦντες, οὐ βουλευόμεθα, εἴπερ
30 τελείαν καὶ πρόχειρον ἔχοιμεν τὴν γνῶσιν τῆς τέχνης, ὅπερ ἀνάγκη ὑπάρχειν τῷ μιμησομένῳ τὴν φύσιν.

Εἰ τοίνυν πάντα ἐξ ἀνάγκης, οὔτε βουλεύεσθαι δέοι ἄν, φησίν, 5
οὔτε πραγματεύεσθαι, τοῦτ' ἔστι ταῖς ἀρχαῖς τῶν πράξεων ἐγχειρεῖν·

---

2 αὐτὰ a   3 ἐνέργεια Α²   3. 4 ἐπιδ. σαθρὸν colloc. Αa   6 ἀξιοῖ G
8. 9 ὡς καθόλου om. Μ   9 εἴωθεν ὁ ἀριστοτέλης F   11 ᾧ] αἷς G   ἀκολουθεῖ F   12 τὴν φύσιν G¹   γάρ ἐστι Μ   14. 15 βουλομένοις FMa
15 ἂν om. ΑGMa   ἀνατείλοι (utrobique) libri   16 ἡμᾶς superscr. G²   παντελῶς
om. F   εὔλογον F   αὐτό τε—τοῦτο (17) om. F   τε] καὶ Α   17 ἀποδέδ. γὰρ F
φησιν Ma   18 ἐναργοῦς Μ   πάσης] μᾶλλον G   19 μᾶλλον] πλέον F   ὡμολόγηται Α: ὁμολογεῖσθαι G   21 ὡρισμ. ante ὡς colloc. G   22 καὶ om. F
23 καταλείπειν G   βουλευτικὰς F   24 τινα] τι Ma   λέγει Ma   25 πράξ.]
πραγμάτων FG   26 ὁρᾶν G¹   26. 27 κατέπειγεν Μ   27 ὄντως] οὕτως ΑGMa
ὑπὸ] ἀπὸ ΑGM   28 ἀνενδοιάστ. Αa   καὶ om. Μ   29 βουλόμεθα ΑG   εἴπερ
εἰπεῖν G¹   31 μιμησαμένῳ FM   33 πράξ.] πραγμάτων F

that the contingent was among the things that exist (since many impossible things follow for those seeking to deny it, and evidence shows that it exists), and in addition he had to show that the aforementioned argument, which tried to make everything necessary and to expel the contingent from the things that exist, was unsound. So, teaching thus far in these words the impossible things which follow for those who deny the contingent, he says that if one should think that every contradiction behaves in the same way in every time with respect to dividing the true and false, and that not just the diagonal contradictions, which he has been calling 'universal as universal', always have in a definite manner one of their sentences true and the other false in every matter, but the singular contradictions as well, <an assertion> from which it would follow that the contingent is eliminated, then one would be accusing nature of vain toil for having made us capable of deliberation. For it is clear that, if nothing is up to us, we shall try in vain to deliberate about what does not lie in our power, and we shall do something similar to those who deliberate as to how the sun will rise or not rise. Moreover, to say that nature vainly made us capable of deliberation is completely illogical: this very thing by itself has been demonstrated 'with geometrical necessity', as they say,[112] that nothing is done by nature in vain, and it is agreed upon for its evidence more than for any proof. Even those who make everything necessary and eliminate the contingent will certainly agree that it is nature herself, again, which does everything, in their words, 'in a definite manner and of necessity' and nothing in vain. So, how can it not be ridiculous to say that nature both has left nothing in our power and makes us capable of deliberation, as though we were masters of our doing or not doing certain things? For, if one would say that <nature> uses our intelligence as a tool to bring about our actions, then, we would reply, it was necessary for us, on the contrary, to be driven immediately toward those actions to which nature forced us, just as in the case of things which are really moved by nature we see it happen that they are unhesitatingly borne to their proper ends. Hence, we too, whenever we imitate nature by acting in accordance with some art, do not deliberate, if we indeed have the perfect and ready understanding of the art which must necessarily belong to him who would imitate nature.

<Deliberation; The relation between prophecy and event>

20. If, then, everything <were> of necessity, *'there would be no need to deliberate,'* he says, *'or to take trouble,'* i.e. to deal with the starting points of our actions. For example, if we intend to sail from Egypt to Athens, we need not go down into the harbour, seek a ship,

---

[112] Cp. Plat. *Resp.* V 458d5.

οἷον εἰ διανοοίμεθα πλεῦσαι ἐξ Αἰγύπτου Ἀθήναζε, οὐ χρὴ κατελθεῖν εἰς
τὸν λιμένα οὐδὲ ναῦν ζητῆσαι οὐδὲ τὰ σκευάρια ἐμβαλέσθαι· καὶ γὰρ μηδὲν 10
τούτων πεπραχότων ἡμῶν ἀνάγκη γενέσθαι ἡμᾶς ἐν Ἀθήναις. εἶτα καὶ
τρόπον, καθ᾽ ὃν βουλεύεσθαι εἰώθαμεν, ὑπογράφων ἡμῖν ὡς ἐὰν μὲν
5 τοδὶ ποιήσωμεν, φησίν, ἔσται τοδί, ἐὰν δὲ μὴ τοδί, οὐκ ἔσται
τοδί· προκειμένου γὰρ φέρε τοῦ ἀπελθεῖν εἰς τόνδε τὸν τόπον, εἰς ὃν 15
δυνατὸν καὶ διὰ νεὼς ἀπελθεῖν καὶ ὑποζυγίῳ χρώμενον, βουλευόμεθα
πότερος τῶν τρόπων τῆς ἐκεῖσε ἀφίξεώς ἐστιν ἡμῖν αἱρετώτερος, τὰ ἑκα-
τέρῳ ἑπόμενα ἀγαθὰ ἢ φαῦλα παρατιθέντες παρ᾽ ἄλληλα καὶ ἀντισηκοῦντες
10 ἀλλήλοις· ὁποτέρῳ γὰρ ἂν αὐτῶν φαίνηται ἢ μεῖζον ἀγαθὸν ἢ ἔλαττον 20
κακὸν ἑπόμενον, ἐκεῖνο μᾶλλον αἱρούμεθα. οὕτω δὲ καὶ ὁ ποιητὴς τὸν
Ἀχιλλέα φησὶν εἰδέναι ὅτι μένων μὲν ἐν τῇ Τροίᾳ καὶ πολεμῶν ὀλιγο-
χρόνιος ἔσται καὶ εὐκλεής, ἀναχωρῶν δὲ τοῦ πολέμου καὶ τὴν ἐν τῇ
πατρίδι διατριβὴν ἀγαπῶν πολυχρόνιος μὲν ἀκλεὴς δέ, καὶ προτιμῆσαι τὴν 25
15 εὔκλειαν τοῦ εἰς γῆρας ἐλθεῖν. εἶτα πάλιν ἀναμνήσας ἡμᾶς τῆς ἐπιχειρή-
σεως τῆς ἀναιρεῖν δοκούσης τὸ ἐνδεχόμενον (λέγω δὴ τοῦ δύο τινῶν
προλεγόντων ἀντίφασιν τὸν | ἕτερον ὡρισμένως ἀληθεύειν καὶ διὰ τοῦτο 119ᵛ
ἐκβαίνειν τὸ ὑπ᾽ ἐκείνου λεγόμενον), ὅπερ ἄν τις ἀπερισκέπτως εἶπεν
ἐλέγχειν οἰόμενος τὴν ἐπιχείρησιν τῷ λέγειν ‘ἀλλ᾽ οὐδὲν γέγονε τοιοῦτον
20 οὐδὲ προεῖπέ τις περὶ τοῦ πράγματος ὡς ἐκβησομένου, ἵνα καὶ ἀληθεύειν 5
ἐκεῖνον συγχωρήσαντες ἀναγκαίως φῶμεν τὸ πρᾶγμα ἐκβεβηκέναι᾽, τοῦτο
θεὶς διαβάλλει καὶ δείκνυσιν οὐκ ὀρθῶς λεγόμενον· οὐ γὰρ διὰ τὸ ἀλη-
θεῦσαι τοὺς πρὸ τῆς ἐκβάσεως τοῦ πράγματος εἰπόντας αὐτὸ ἐκβήσεσθαι
φήσομεν ἐκβαίνειν τὸ πρᾶγμα, ἀλλ᾽ ἔμπαλιν διὰ τὴν τοῦ πράγματος φύσιν 10
25 ἀληθὴς ὁ περὶ αὐτοῦ λεγόμενος λόγος· ὡς γὰρ εἴρηται καὶ ἐν Κατηγορίαις,
εἰ καὶ ἀντιστρέφουσι ταῦτα πρὸς ἄλληλα, ἥ τε τοῦ πράγματος φύσις καὶ ὁ
ἀληθὴς περὶ αὐτοῦ λόγος, ἀλλ᾽ οὐχ ὁ λόγος τῷ πράγματι τοῦ εἶναι αἴτιος 15
ἀλλ᾽ ἡ τοῦ πράγματος ὕπαρξις τοῦ ἀληθεύειν τὸν λόγον αἰτία· ὥστε εἰ
μηδὲν ἔλαττον ἔχει τοῦ πράγματος ἡ ἔκβασις διὰ τὸ μὴ κατ᾽ ἐνέργειαν
30 προειρῆσθαι τὸν ἐκβήσεσθαι αὐτὸ ἀποφαινόμενον λόγον, πᾶσαι αἱ περὶ
τῶν ἐνδεχομένως γινομένων πρὸ τῆς ἐκβάσεως λεγόμεναι προρρήσεις, εἴτε 20
κατ᾽ ἐνέργειαν εἴτε κατὰ δύναμιν, ἀληθεῖς ἔσονται. τούτου δὲ οὕτως
ἔχοντος ἀναγκαίως ἐκβέβηκεν ἕκαστον αὐτῶν, καὶ οὐκ ἐνεδέχετο αὐτὸ μὴ
ἐκβῆναι.

---

2 ἐκβαλ. F   4 ἡμῖν om. F   5 φησίν superscr. A   6 τοδί om. F
7 νηός Ga   8 πρότερος τὸν τρόπον τῆς ἐκ. ἀφ. εἰ ἔστιν F   ἔσται M   8. 9 τὸ
ἑκατέρας G¹   9 ἑπόμ.] ἑσόμ. F   11 ἐκεῖνο] ἐκεῖ M   ὁ ποιητής] Hom. I 412
12 τῇ om. M   13 ἀπὸ τοῦ πολ. G   καὶ τὴν—ἀκλεὴς δέ (14)] τὴν μὲν μακρο-
χρονίαν λάβοι, τὴν δὲ δόξαν ἀπολέσαι F   13 τῇ om. G   14 ἀκλ.] οὐκ εὐκλεὴς G
προτιμήσας F   15 ὑπομνήσ. G   17 τὴν ἀντίφ. F   ἀντίφασιν suppl. G²
18 ἥνπερ F   εἶπεν] εἴπερ G   19 ἐλέγχει F   οἰόμενος τὴν ἐπιχ.] ῥῆσιν F
21 ἐκεῖνο A: ἐκείνῳ a   συγχωρήσαντος AMa   θῶμεν M   23 αὐτὸ suppl. G²
25 ἐν Κατηγορίαις] c. 12 p. 14ᵇ14   29 ἔχειν Aa   30 αὐτῷ a   31 πρὸ τῆς
ἐκβάσεως om. G   33 αὐτῶν suppl. G²

or stow our baggage. In fact, even if we have done none of these things, it is necessary for us to arrive in Athens. Next, sketching for us the manner in which we usually deliberate, he says *'that if we shall do this, this will happen, but if we do not do this, this will not happen.'* For, if the intention is, say, to go off to this place here, to which one can go either by ship or using a cart, we deliberate as to which of the ways of arriving there is preferable for us, comparing and balancing against one another the goods and evils arising from each one, since whichever turns out to entail either the greater good or the lesser evil is the one we choose. So too does the Poet[113] say that Achilles knows that, if he remains at Troy and fights, he will be short-lived but famous, while, if he retires from the war and is content to spend his time in his fatherland, he will be long-lived but without fame, and that he prefers fame to reaching old-age. Then, having reminded us again of the argument which appeared to deny the contingent (I mean, of the fact that, of two people foretelling a contradiction, one speaks the truth in a definite manner and for this reason what is said by him occurs), <Aristotle posits for the sake of argument> what someone would have thoughtlessly said believing that he was refuting the argument by saying 'but nothing of the sort happened, nor did anyone foretell that the thing would occur, to the effect that we are obliged to say, if we have agreed that he speaks truly, that the thing occurred necessarily'; having posited this he attacks it and shows that it is not correctly stated. We shall not say that the thing occurred because those who said before the outcome of the thing that it would occur spoke truly, but, on the contrary, it is because of the nature of the thing that the sentence about it <is> true. As was also said in the *Categories* (14b14), even if these are interconvertible, namely the nature of the thing and the true sentence about it, it is not the sentence which is the cause of the thing's being, but the existence of the thing which is responsible for the sentence being true. Thus, if the occurrence of the thing is no less so for the fact that the sentence declaring that it would occur was not actually said in advance, then all prophecies of what happens contingently which are said before their outcome, whether actually or potentially, will be true. This being so, each of these things occurred necessarily, and it was not possible for it not to occur.

---

[113]   Hom. *Iliad.* IX 412-416.

p. 19ᵃ7 Εἰ δὴ ταῦτα ἀδύνατα· ὁρῶμεν γὰρ ὅτι ἀρχή ἐστι τῶν 25
ἐσομένων καὶ ἀπὸ τοῦ βουλεύεσθαι καὶ ἀπὸ τοῦ πρᾶξαί τι,
καὶ ὅλως ὅτι ἔστιν ἐν τοῖς μὴ ἀεὶ ἐνεργοῦσι τὸ δυνατὸν εἶναι
καὶ μὴ ὁμοίως· ἐν οἷς ἄμφω ἐνδέχεται καὶ τὸ εἶναι καὶ τὸ μὴ
5 εἶναι, ὥστε καὶ τὸ γενέσθαι | καὶ τὸ μὴ γενέσθαι. καὶ πολλὰ 120ʳ
ἡμῖν δῆλά ἐστιν οὕτως ἔχοντα, οἷον ὅτι τοῦτο τὸ ἱμάτιον δυνατόν ἐστι διατμηθῆναι, καὶ οὐ διατμηθήσεται ἀλλ' ἔμπροσθεν
κατατριβήσεται. ὁμοίως δὲ καὶ τὸ μὴ διατμηθῆναι δυνατόν· 5
οὐ γὰρ ἂν ὑπῆρχε τὸ ἔμπροσθεν αὐτὸ κατατριβῆναι, εἴ γε μὴ
10 δυνατὸν ἦν τὸ μὴ διατμηθῆναι. ὥστε καὶ ἐπὶ τῶν ἄλλων γενέ-
σεων, ὅσαι κατὰ δύναμιν λέγονται τὴν τοιαύτην. φανερὸν οὖν
ὅτι οὐχ ἅπαντα ἐξ ἀνάγκης οὔτε ἔστιν οὔτε γίνεται, ἀλλὰ τὰ μὲν 10
ὁπότερ' ἔτυχε, καὶ οὐδὲν μᾶλλον ἡ κατάφασις ἢ ἡ ἀπόφασις
ἀληθής, τὰ δὲ μᾶλλον μὲν καὶ ὡς ἐπὶ τὸ πολὺ θάτερον, οὐ
15 μὴν ἀλλ' ἐνδέχεται γενέσθαι καὶ θάτερον, θάτερον δὲ μή.

Παραδοὺς ἡμῖν διὰ τῶν προλαβόντων ὅσα ἕπεται ἀδύνατα τοῖς ἀναι- 15
ροῦσι τὸ ἐνδεχόμενον, ὅτι τὸ μάτην βουλεύεσθαι μάτην ἐγχειρεῖν ὅλως
ταῖς πράξεσι καὶ ὅσα τούτοις ἐστὶν ἀκόλουθα, οἷον τὸ μάτην αἰτιᾶσθαί
τινας ὡς συμπράττοντας ἡμῖν ἢ ἀντιπράττοντας, μάτην ἐπαινεῖν τινας ὡς
20 ἀγαθοὺς ἢ ψέγειν ὡς κακούς, καὶ ὀνόματα κενὰ εἶναι τὰ πολυθρύλλητα 20
ταῦτα, τὴν ἀρετὴν καὶ τὴν κακίαν (ποῦ γὰρ οἷόν τε ταῦτα χώραν ἔχειν,
μηδενὸς ὄντος ἐφ' ἡμῖν ἀλλ' ἐξ ἀνάγκης ἡμῶν, ὡς ὁ ἐκείνων λόγος, ἐπὶ
τὸ τάδε τινὰ πράττειν ἀγομένων; ἅπερ δηλονότι καὶ ἐναργῶς ἄλογα καὶ
τὸν ὅλον τῶν ἀνθρώπων ἄρδην ἀνατρέπει βίον), προτίθεται διὰ τούτων 25
25 καὶ ἐπ' εὐθείας ἐξ αὐτῆς τῆς ἐναργείας τῶν πραγμάτων ἐπιδεῖξαι ὅτι τε
ἔστιν ἐν τοῖς οὖσι τὸ ἐνδεχόμενον καὶ ἐν τίσιν ἐστίν, ὅτι οὐκ ἐν τοῖς |
ἀϊδίοις ἀλλ' ἐν μόνοις τοῖς ἐν γενέσει καὶ φθορᾷ τὸ εἶναι ἔχουσιν. ὅτι 120ᵛ
μὲν οὖν τό τε βουλεύεσθαι μεγάλην ἔχει πρὸς τὰς πράξεις δύναμιν καὶ
πολλά ἐστιν ἐφ' ἡμῖν τῶν ὄντων, ἃ οὐκ ἂν ἐπράχθη μὴ βουλευσαμένων
30 ἡμῶν καὶ ταῖς ὁδοῖς τῆς ἐκβάσεως αὐτῶν ἐγκεχειρηκότων, δείκνυσιν ἀπὸ 5
τοῦ κατὰ τὸ ἱμάτιον παραδείγματος, ὃ ἐφ' ἡμῖν ἐστιν ἢ διατεμεῖν ἢ σῶον
ἐᾶσαι καὶ ἀδιάτμητον, ἄχρις ἂν ἢ ἐν χρήσει ὂν καὶ φορούμενον κατατριβῇ
ἢ καὶ ἄνευ χρήσεως κείμενον ὑπὸ τοῦ χρόνου κατασαπῇ. δῆλον δὲ ὅτι 10

19a7 *What, then, if this is impossible? For we see that what will be has an origin both in our deliberation and in our doing something, and in general, that* [114] *in those things which are not always actual there is similarly* [115] *the possibility of being and not being; in those both are possible, both to be and not to be, and hence both coming to be and not coming to be. It is clear to us that many things are such, e.g. that it is possible for this cloak to be cut up, and yet it will not be cut up, but will wear out first. Similarly, that it not be cut up is also possible: for it would not have been the case that it would wear out first, unless it was possible for it not to be cut up. Hence, this is also the case for all events which are spoken of with regard to this kind of possibility. Now, it is clear* [116] *that not everything either is or comes to be of necessity, but some things occur however it chances, where the affirmative sentence is no more true than the negative sentence, while for other things one of the two occurs rather or for the most part, although it is possible as well that the other happens and the first does not.*

<It is evident that deliberation is important in actions>

21. Having taught us in the preceding how many impossible things follow for those who deny the contingent—that it is vain to deliberate, vain to deal at all with actions, and everything that follows from these, e.g. that it is vain to hold certain people responsible for co-operating with us or thwarting us, vain to praise certain people as good or blame them as bad, and that these much bandied-about terms, virtue and vice, are empty names (for where can they have a place, if nothing is up to us, but we, as they say, are of necessity brought to do these particular things, <consequences> which, it is clear, are evidently irrational and turn all of human life completely on its head)—he proposes in these words and directly from the evidence of the things itself to show both that the contingent is among the things that exist and among which things it is <found>, namely, that it is not among the eternal things but only among those which have their existence in coming to be and passing away. Now, that deliberation has great force with respect to actions and many things are up to us which would not have been done had we not deliberated and dealt with the means of their occurring, he shows by the example of the cloak, which it is up to us either to cut up or leave whole and uncut until it either wears out from use and being worn or rots with time, even if it lies unused. It is clear that the same arguments will also apply

---

[114] καὶ ὅλως ὅτι; Minio-Paluello has καὶ ὅτι ὅλως ("and that in general").

[115] ὁμοίως; Minio-Paluello does not have the adverb.

[116] φανερὸν οὖν; Minio-Paluello has φανερὸν ἄρα.

καὶ ἐπ' ἄλλων πολλάκις μυρίων οἱ αὐτοὶ ἁρμόσουσι λόγοι· ὥστε φανερὸν
ὅτι πάντων τῶν οὕτω γινομένων κυρίους ἡμᾶς ἐποίησεν ἡ φύσις. ἅπερ
ἐνδεικνύμενος ὁ Ἀριστοτέλης εἶπεν ὅτι ἀρχή ἐστι τῶν ἐσομένων καὶ
ἀπὸ τοῦ βουλεύεσθαι καὶ ἀπὸ τοῦ πρᾶξαί τι, τῷ μὲν ὀνόματι τοῦ 15
5 ἐσομένου ἐπὶ τοῦ μήπω μὲν ἐκβεβηκότος δυναμένου δὲ ἐκβῆναι, εἰ μή
τι κωλύσοι, κοινότερον νῦν χρησάμενος, διὰ δὲ τοῦ πρᾶξαί τι δηλῶν τὸ
ταῖς ἀρχαῖς ἐγχειρῆσαι τῆς πράξεως, ὅπερ πρότερον ἐκάλει πραγματεύεσθαι.

Ἐν τίσι δὲ τῶν ὄντων ἔχει τὴν ὑπόστασιν τὸ ἐνδεχόμενον, συντόμως 20
10 ἐδίδαξεν εἰπὼν ὅτι ἐν τοῖς μὴ ἀεὶ ἐνεργοῦσι, ταὐτὸν δ' εἰπεῖν τοῖς
ποτὲ μὲν οὖσι ποτὲ δὲ μὴ οὖσι· ταῦτα γὰρ μεταξὺ ὄντα τῶν τε ἀεὶ
ὄντων καὶ τῶν ἀεὶ μὴ ὄντων ὡς μὲν ἐνεργοῦντα ὅλως διαφέροι ἂν τῶν
ἀεὶ μὴ ὄντων, ὡς δὲ μὴ ἀεὶ ἐνεργοῦντα διαφέροι ἂν τῶν ἀεὶ ὄντων τε 25
καὶ ἐνεργούντων. ποῖα δέ ἐστι τὰ μὴ ἀεὶ ἐνεργοῦντα, πάλιν συντόμως
15 ἐδίδαξεν εἰπὼν ἐν οἷς ἄμφω ἐνδέχεται καὶ τὸ εἶναι καὶ τὸ μὴ εἶναι,
τοῦτ' ἔστι τοῖς ἐν γενέσει | καὶ φθορᾷ· οὔτε γὰρ τῶν ἀεὶ μὴ ὄντων τι 121ʳ
δύναταί ποτε ἐνεργεῖν (πῶς γὰρ ὃ μηδὲ τὴν ἀρχὴν τοῦ εἶναι πέφυκε
μετέχειν;) οὔτε τῶν ἀεὶ ὄντων τι δύναταί ποτε μὴ ἐνεργεῖν· εἰ γάρ ἐστιν
ἀεὶ ὄν, δῆλον ὡς ἀεὶ τέλειόν ἐστι καὶ τὴν οὐσίαν τὴν ἑαυτοῦ κατὰ φύσιν 5
20 ἔχον (οὐ γὰρ ἂν ἄλλως ἠδύνατο εἶναι ἀίδιον), τοιοῦτον δὲ ὂν ἕξει τινὰ πάντως οὐσιώδη ἐνέργειαν, καθ' ἣν ἀεὶ ἐνεργεῖν αὐτὸ ἀναγκαῖον, ἵνα μὴ καὶ
ὁντιναοῦν χρόνον ἀνενέργητον μένον ματαίαν δεικνύῃ τὴν ἑαυτοῦ φύσιν
καὶ αὐτὸ τηνάλλως ἐγκαταλέγηται τοῖς οὖσιν. ὥστε εἰκότως τὰ ποτὲ μὲν 10
ὄντα ποτὲ δὲ μὴ ὄντα τῶν ὄντων ἐχαρακτήρισεν ἀπὸ τοῦ μὴ ἀεὶ ἐνεργεῖν.
25 πᾶσι μὲν οὖν τοῖς ἐνδεχομένοις τοῦτο ὑπάρχει τὸ δύνασθαι καὶ εἶναι καὶ
μὴ εἶναι· ὥστε καὶ πρὸ τῆς ἐκβάσεως αὐτῶν ὑπάρξει αὐτοῖς τὸ δύνασθαι 15
καὶ γενέσθαι καὶ μὴ γενέσθαι. ἀλλὰ τὰ μὲν αὐτῶν ὁμοίως ἔχει πρός τε
τὸ εἶναι καὶ πρὸς τὸ μὴ εἶναι, διὸ καὶ πρὸς τὸ γενέσθαι καὶ τὸ μὴ γενέσθαι,
ὅσα ἐπὶ τῇ προαιρέσει κεῖται τῇ ἡμετέρᾳ καὶ καλεῖται ὁπότερ' ἔτυχε, τὰ
30 δὲ ἀποκλίνει μᾶλλον ἢ πρὸς τὸ εἶναι καὶ γενέσθαι καὶ λέγεται ὡς ἐπὶ τὸ 20
πολύ, ἢ πρὸς τὸ μὴ εἶναι μηδὲ γενέσθαι καὶ λέγεται ὡς ἐπ' ἔλαττον, ἅπερ
ἀμφότερα κοινῶς σημῆναι βουληθεὶς εἶπε τὰ δὲ μᾶλλον μὲν καὶ ὡς ἐπὶ
τὸ πολὺ θάτερον, οὐ μὴν ἀλλ' ἐνδέχεται γενέσθαι καὶ θάτερον,
θάτερον δὲ μή· ἔχει γὰρ τὸ μὲν οὕτως λεγόμενον ὡς ἐπὶ τὸ πολὺ τὴν 25

---

1 οἱ αὐτοὶ — γινομένων (2) in mrg. suppl. A　　4 βουλεύσασθαι F　　4. 5 τῶν ἐσομένων F　　5 δὲ καὶ ἐκβῆναι F　　6 κωλύσει a　　10 ὅτι μὴ (sed μὴ del.) F
12 μὲν ἀεὶ ἐνεργ. a　　　　διαφέρει G¹　　13 μὴ ὄντων — τῶν ἀεὶ om. F　　　　τε
om. M　　　　16 τι post ποτε (17) colloc. G　　17 δύνασθαι G　　　　ἐνεργεῖν —
ποτε (18) om. M　　18 μετ.] μὴ ἔχειν G　　δύναταί τι G　　ποτε om. F　　19 τὴν
(post οὐσίαν) om. A　　20 ἀεὶ ὂν a　　21 αὐτὸ ἐνεργ. colloc. F　　22 ante ματ.
add. καὶ G¹　　δείκνυσι G　　23 τηνάλλως] τοῖς ἄλλοτε ἄλλως ἔχουσι G
τὰ om. M　　27 τά] τὸ A　　28 πρὸς τὸ suppl. G²　　καὶ τὸ μὴ γενέσθαι om. M
καὶ πρὸς τὸ μὴ A　　30 γίνεσθαι F　　31 γίνεσθαι AFa: λέγεσθαι M　　32 καὶ
om. A　　32. 33. 34 ἐπὶ πολὺ F

to many ten thousands of other cases. Thus, it is obvious that nature made us masters of all things which happen in this way. To show this Aristotle said that *'what will be has an origin both in our deliberation and in our doing some thing,'* using *'what will be'* here in a loose way of what has not yet occurred but can occur unless something prevents it, and indicating by *'doing something'* our dealing with the origins of action, what he previously called *'taking trouble'*.

<What is not always actual>

22. Among which of the existing things the contingent has its existence, he concisely taught by saying *'that <it is> in those things which are not always actual,'* which is the same as saying 'among those which sometimes exist and sometimes do not exist.' Since these are intermediate between the things which always exist and those which always do not exist, insofar as they are actual they would be completely different from those which always do not exist, and insofar as they are not always actual they would differ from those which are always existent and actual. What sort of things are those which are not always actual, he again concisely taught by saying *'in those both are possible, both to be and not to be,'* i.e. those <having their existence> in coming to be and passing away. For, neither is it possible for anything which always does not exist ever to be actual (for how could something <ever be actual>, that according to its nature does not even partake of the principle of being?) nor is it possible for anything which always exists ever not to be actual; for, if it always exists, it is clear that it is always perfect and its own essence is in accordance with nature (it could not otherwise have been eternal) and being such it will have an actuality in perfect conformity with its essence, according to which it must always be actual, lest, remaining inactive for any time at all, it show its own nature to be vain and itself be counted incorrectly among the things that are. Thus, Aristotle was correct to characterise those things which sometimes are and sometimes are not by the fact that they are not always actual. Now, this holds of all contingents, that they can both be and not be, so that even before their occurrence it will hold of them that they can both come to be and not come to be. However, some of them have the same relation both to being and to not being, and therefore also to coming to be and not coming to be, namely all those which depend upon our choice and are called 'however it chances', while others rather incline either towards being and coming to be and are called 'for the most part' or towards not being and not coming to be and are called 'for the lesser part'. Wanting to indicate both of these together he said *'for other things one of the two occurs rather or for the most part, although it is possible as well that the other happens and the first does not'* : for, the very thing that is called in this way 'for the most part' has its accomplishment for the most part,

μὲν ἔκβασιν αὐτὸ τοῦτο ὡς ἐπὶ τὸ πολύ, ἐνδεχόμενον μέντοι καὶ τὸ μὴ
ἐκβῆναι, εἰ καὶ σπανιώτερον τοῦ ἐκβῆναι, τὸ δὲ ἐπ' ἔλαττον τὸ μὲν μὴ
ἐκβαίνειν | ὡς ἐπὶ τὸ πολύ, ἐνδεχόμενον μέντοι καὶ τὸ ἐκβαίνειν, εἰ καὶ 121ᵛ
σπανιώτερον τοῦ μὴ ἐκβαίνειν. ἐπιτρέπων οὖν ἡμῖν τὸ ὡς ἐπὶ τὸ πολὺ
5 θάτερον, τοῦ τε εἶναι δηλονότι καὶ τοῦ μὴ εἶναι, καὶ τὸ τούτῳ ἀντικείμενον καὶ ἐπ' ἔλαττον, ὃ καὶ αὐτὸ προσηγόρευσε θάτερον, μεθαρμόζειν ὡς 5
ἂν ἐθέλωμεν πρός τε τὸ εἶναι καὶ τὸ μὴ εἶναι, διὰ τῶν αὐτῶν λεξειδίων
περιέλαβε τὰ πλεῖστον ἀλλήλων διεστηκότα σημαινόμενα τοῦ ἐνδεχομένου,
τό τε ἐπὶ τὸ πολὺ καὶ τὸ ἐπ' ἔλαττον. δῆλον δὲ ὅτι καὶ τοῖς πράγμα- 10
10 σιν ὁμοίως ἔχουσιν αἱ περὶ αὐτῶν ἀποφάνσεις κατὰ τὸ ἀληθεύειν ἢ
ψεύδεσθαι.

p. 19ᵃ23 Τὸ μὲν οὖν εἶναι τὸ ὄν ὅταν ᾖ, καὶ τὸ μὴ ὄν μὴ εἶναι
ὅταν μὴ ᾖ, ἀνάγκη· οὐ μέντοι οὔτε τὸ ὄν ἅπαν ἀνάγκη εἶναι
οὔτε τὸ μὴ ὄν ἀνάγκη μὴ εἶναι· οὐ γὰρ ταὐτόν ἐστιν τὸ ὄν ἅπαν 15
15 εἶναι ἐξ ἀνάγκης ὅτε ἐστί, καὶ τὸ ἁπλῶς εἶναι ἐξ ἀνάγκης.
ὁμοίως δὲ καὶ ἐπὶ τοῦ μὴ ὄντος. καὶ ἐπὶ τῆς ἀντιφάσεως ὁ
αὐτὸς λόγος· εἶναι μὲν ἢ μὴ εἶναι ἅπαν ἀνάγκη, καὶ ἔσεσθαί
γε ἢ μή· οὐ μέντοι διελόντα γε εἰπεῖν θάτερον ἀναγκαῖον.
λέγω δὲ οἷον ἀνάγκη μὲν ἔσεσθαι ναυμαχίαν αὔριον ἢ μὴ 20
20 ἔσεσθαι, οὐ μέντοι γενέσθαι ναυμαχίαν αὔριον ἀναγκαῖον οὐδὲ
μὴ γενέσθαι, γενέσθαι μέντοι ἢ μὴ γενέσθαι ἀναγκαῖον. ὥστε
ἐπεὶ ὁμοίως οἱ λόγοι ἀληθεῖς ὥσπερ τὰ πράγματα, δῆλον ὅτι
ὅσα οὕτως ἔχει ὥστε ὁπότερ' ἔτυχεν εἶναι καὶ τὰ ἐναντία ἐνδέχε- 25
σθαι, ἀνάγκη ὁμοίως ἔχειν καὶ τὴν ἀντίφασιν. ὅπερ συμβαίνει
25 ἐπὶ τοῖς μὴ ἀεὶ οὖσιν ἢ μὴ ἀεὶ μὴ οὖσι· τούτων γὰρ ἀνάγκη
μὲν θάτερον μόριον τῆς ἀντιφάσεως ἀληθὲς εἶναι ἢ ψεῦδος,
οὐ μέντοι | τόδε ἢ τόδε ἀλλ' ὁπότερ' ἔτυχε, καὶ μᾶλλον μὲν 122ʳ
ἀληθῆ τὴν ἑτέραν, οὐ μέντοι ἤδη ἀληθῆ ἢ ψευδῆ. ὥστε δῆλον
ὅτι οὐκ ἀνάγκη πάσης καταφάσεως καὶ ἀποφάσεως τῶν ἀντικει-
30 μένων τὴν μὲν ἀληθῆ τὴν δὲ ψευδῆ εἶναι· οὐ γὰρ ὥσπερ ἐπὶ 5
τῶν ὄντων, οὕτως ἔχει καὶ ἐπὶ τῶν μὴ ὄντων μὲν δυνατῶν δὲ
εἶναι, ἀλλ' ὥσπερ εἴρηται.

Πρόκειται μὲν ἐν τούτοις αὐτὸν λοιπὸν τὸν λόγον τὸν ἀναιρεῖν
δοκοῦντα τὸ ἐνδεχόμενον σαθρὸν ἐπιδεῖξαι καὶ μηδὲν ἀναγκαῖον συνάγοντα, 10

2 ἐκβαίνειν (pr.) Μ   εἰ] ἢ Α   ἐκβῆναι (alt.) — σπανιώτερον τοῦ (4) om. Μ
ἐπ' om. F   3 ὡς—μὴ ἐκβαίνειν (4) om. F   4. 9 ἐπὶ πολὺ F   5 τούτων AG
6 ἐπ' ἔλ.] ἐπίδηλον G¹   αὐτὸς GMa   7 ἐθέλοιμεν ΑΜα   πρὸς τὸ μὴ εἶναι καὶ
τὸ εἶναι AFa: πρὸς τὸ εἶναι καὶ μὴ εἶναι Μ   12 μὴ ὄν—εἴρηται (32) om. M
13 οὐ — εἴρηται (32) om. G   μέντοι] μὴν b   14 ἀνάγκη om. b   οὐ γὰρ —
εἴρηται (32) om. a   16 ἀντιφ. δὲ F   18 γε (post διελ.) om. F   20 μέντοι
ἔσεσθαί γε αὔριον ναυμ. b   23 εἶναι om. b   31 μὲν suppl. F²: om. AF¹
δυνατὸν Α   33 μὲν οὖν G   τὸν (post λόγον) om. F   34 ἀναγκ.] ἐναντίον G

it being possible, however, for it also not to occur, even if that is more rare than its occurrence; while what is 'for the lesser part' is what 'for the most part' does not occur, it being possible, however, for it also to occur, even if that is more rare than its non-occurrence. Thus, by allowing us to apply as we see fit the 'one of the two', that which is 'for the most part'—evidently concerning being and not being—and its opposite, that which is 'for the lesser part', which he also calls 'one of the two', to being and not being, Aristotle encompassed in the same words the significations of the 'contingent' which differ most from one another, the 'for the most part' and the 'for the lesser part'. It is clear that assertions behave in the same way with regard to truth and falsity as do the things which they are about.

19a23 *Now, it is necessary that what is, is, when it is, and also that what is not, is not, when it is not. However, it is neither necessary that everything which is, is, nor necessary that everything which is not, is not: for that everything which is, is of necessity, when it is, is not the same as that it simply is of necessity; and similarly with what is not. The same account <holds> for the contradiction as well: it is necessary that everything is or is not, and will be or will not be. But one cannot, by dividing them, say that one or the other is necessary. I mean, for example, it is necessary that either there will be a sea battle tomorrow or there will not be; but it is not necessary that a sea battle happen tomorrow or <necessary> that one not happen—even though it is necessary that one happen or not happen. Thus, since the sentences are true in the way that the things are, it is clear that in the case of things which behave in such a way that they exist however it chances and that the contraries are <both> possible, it is necessary that the same holds for <the truth of >the contradiction <of the sentences> as well. This occurs with things which do not always exist or which do not always not exist: with these it is necessary that one <or the other> member of the contradiction is true or <in the other case> false - not, however, this one or that one, but however it chances—and one must be rather true than the other, but not already true or false. Thus, it is clear that it is not necessary that of every affirmative and negative sentence, that are opposed to one another, one be true and the other false. For, things which do not exist, but are possible,* [117] *do not behave in the same way as things which exist; rather, it is as has been stated.*

<*'Absolutely' vs. 'As long as the predicate holds of the subject'*>

23. The intention of these lines is to show that the actual argument which appears to deny the contingent is finally unsound and leads to no necessary conclusion. This argument,

---

[117] δυνατῶν δὲ εἶναι; Minio-Paluello has δυνατῶν δὲ εἶναι ἢ μὴ εἶναι.

προήει δὲ οὗτος ἐκ τῶν ἤδη ἐκβεβηκότων ἀξιῶν κρίνεσθαι τὰ ἔτι μέλλοντα·
λαβὼν γὰρ ὡς εἰ ἔστι τι νῦν λευκόν, ἀνάγκη ἀληθεύειν τὸν αὐτὸ τοῦτο
λέγοντα περὶ αὐτοῦ ὅτι ἔστι λευκόν, καὶ οὐ νῦν μόνον ἀλλὰ καὶ ἐν ἅπαντι
τῷ πρόσθεν χρόνῳ ἀληθὲς ἦν προλέγειν ὅτι ἔσται λευκόν (ὡς οὐδὲν τοῦτο 15
5 ἐκείνου διαφέρον), καὶ ὅτι ὅπερ ἐν παντὶ τῷ πρόσθεν χρόνῳ ἀληθὲς ἦν
εἰπεῖν ὅτι ἔσται λευκὸν ἀνάγκη γενέσθαι, συνάγειν ἠξίου τὸ πάντα ἐξ ἀνάγκης γίνεσθαι τὰ γινόμενα. πρὸς τοῦτον τοίνυν τὸν λόγον ἐνιστάμενος διὰ 20
τούτων ὁ Ἀριστοτέλης πάνυ τεχνικῶς, πρὶν διελέσθαι τὰς εἰς τὸν μέλλοντα
χρόνον γινομένας ἀποφάνσεις, πῶς μὲν ἔχουσι τὸ ἐξ ἀνάγκης ἀληθεύειν
10 πῶς δὲ οὐκ ἔχουσι, διορίζεται πρότερον περὶ τῶν κατὰ τὸν ἐνεστῶτα χρόνον
γινομένων, καὶ τὴν διαφορὰν αὐτῶν ἀπὸ τῆς φύσεως τῶν πραγμάτων 25
λαμβάνων, ἐπειδὴ χρὴ τὸν ἀληθεύοντα λόγον συνάδειν ἐξ ἀνάγκης τῷ
πράγματι περὶ οὗ ἀποφαίνεται, διττὸν εἶναί φησι τὸ ἀναγκαῖον, τὸ μὲν τὸ
ἁπλῶς καὶ κυρίως λεγόμενον, ὅπερ ἐστὶ | τὸ ἀεὶ ὑπάρχον τῷ ὑποκειμένῳ 122ᵛ
15 ὡς οὐδὲ ὑφεστάναι χωρὶς αὐτοῦ δυναμένῳ (τοῦ ἀεὶ ἤτοι κατὰ τὸν ἄπειρον
χρόνον λαμβανομένου ὡς ἐπὶ τῶν ἀιδίων, οἷον ὅταν λέγωμεν ἐξ ἀνάγκης
κινεῖσθαι τὸν ἥλιον ἢ τοῦ τριγώνου τὰς γωνίας δυσὶν ὀρθαῖς ἴσας εἶναι, ἢ 5
ἕως ἂν ὑπάρχῃ τὸ ὑποκείμενον, ὡς ὅταν εἴπωμεν ἐξ ἀνάγκης τόδε τὸ
πῦρ θερμὸν εἶναι ἢ τὸν Σωκράτην ζῷον εἶναι), τὸ δὲ οὐ τοιοῦτον ἀλλὰ μετὰ
20 μὲν προσδιορισμοῦ τοῦ ἕως ἂν ᾖ τὸ κατηγορούμενον ὑπὸ τοῦ λέγοντος
οὕτως αὐτὸ ἔχειν ἀληθεῦον, ἁπλῶς δὲ οὐκέτι, εἴτε ἀίδιον εἴη τὸ ὑποκεί- 10
μενον εἴτε φθαρτόν· τὸ γὰρ ἐξ ἀνάγκης ἐπιπροσθεῖσθαι ὑπὸ τοῦ νέφους
ἢ τῆς σελήνης τὸν ἥλιον, ἕως ἂν ἐπιπροσθῆται, ἀληθές, ἁπλῶς δὲ οὐκέτι,
καὶ τὸ ἐξ ἀνάγκης καθέζεσθαί σε ἢ βαδίζειν, ἕως ἄν τι τούτων ὑπάρχῃ 15
25 σοι, ἀληθές, ἁπλῶς δὲ οὐκέτι· οὔτε γὰρ ἀεὶ βαδίζομεν ἢ καθεζόμεθα,
οὔτε μὴν ἕως ἂν τοῦ εἶναι μετέχωμεν. ὁ δὲ αὐτὸς λόγος καὶ ἐπὶ τοῦ ἐξ
ἀνάγκης μὴ ὄντος· καὶ γὰρ τοῦτο διττόν, τὸ μὲν ἁπλῶς (οἷον τὸ μὴ εἶναι
τὴν διάμετρον σύμμετρον τῇ πλευρᾷ ἢ τὸ μὴ παύεσθαι τῆς κινήσεως τὸν 20
ἥλιον ἢ τὸ μὴ εἶναι τόδε τὸ πῦρ ψυχρόν), τὸ δὲ ἕως ἂν μὴ ᾖ τὸ κατη-
30 γορούμενον, οἷον τὸ ἐξ ἀνάγκης μὴ βαδίζειν, ὅταν μὴ βαδίζῃς· οὐ γὰρ
ἁπλῶς τοῦτο ἀληθές, ἀλλ' ἕως ἂν μὴ βαδίζῃς, ἐπειδὴ ἀδύνατον τὸν μὴ
βαδίζοντα ὅτε μὴ βαδίζει ἅμα καὶ βαδίζειν. καὶ ἔχεις ἐν τούτοις τὴν 25
κατὰ τὰς ὕλας διαφορὰν τῶν προτάσεων παραδεδομένην· τὸ μὲν γὰρ ἁπλῶς
ὂν τὸ ἀναγκαῖον σημαίνει, τὸ δ' ἁπλῶς μὴ ὂν τὸ ἀδύνατον, τὸ δὲ ἔστ'

---

1 προείη AF   2 λευκὸν νῦν colloc. a   5 διαφέρει F   ἅπαντι a
6 λευκόν om. F: del. G   συνάγειν—γίνεσθαι om. M   τὸ] τὰ A: om. a   7 ἱστάμ.
A: ἀνιστάμ. F   9 ἀποφάσεις Ma   13 διττὸν δὲ F   τὸ (post μὲν) om. AG¹
15 χωρὶς αὐτοῦ ὑφ. (num. corr.) G   17 τῆς τρυγώνου (sic) F   δύο AFMa   ἢ
om. M   18 ἕως] ὡς G¹   ὑπάρχει F   ἐξ ἀνάγκης om. G   19 σωκράτη A
20 λέγ.] μέλλοντος F   21 αὐτὸ om. G   22 ὑπὸ νέφους ἢ ὑπὸ τῆς σελ. F   24 καὶ
τὸ—οὐκέτι (25) om. M   25 post ἁπλῶς δὲ add. ἤτοι κυρίως καὶ ἀιδίως a   26 μετέ-
χομεν A   28 τῇ πλ. συμ. colloc. F   29 ἕως] ὡς a   τὸ (ante κατ.) om. G
30 βαδίζῃ Fa: βαδίσῃς G   31 βαδίζῃς] βαδίζῃ Fa   32 ἐν τούτοις om. F

however, proceeded by claiming to judge what is still going to be from what has already occurred. It assumed that, if something is now pale, one who says just this about it, that it is now pale, necessarily speaks truly, and it was true not just now but also in the entire preceding time to predict that it would be pale (as though this were no different from the other); and because the thing which it was true to say during the entire preceding time, that it would be pale, happens necessarily, <the argument> wanted to conclude that everything that happens happens of necessity. Hence, refuting this argument here in a very technical manner, Aristotle, before analysing the statements which bear on the future, <concerning the question> how they do have the <property> of being necessarily true and how they do not, first makes a distinction regarding things which happen in the present time. Taking the distinction of these <sentences> from the nature of the things, since the true sentence must of necessity correspond to the thing about which it is said, he says that there are two kinds of 'necessary' <things>: first, that which is absolutely and primarily so called, namely what always holds of the subject so that the subject cannot exist without it (the word 'always' is understood either as in infinite time, as in the case of eternal things, for example, whenever we say that 'of necessity' the sun moves or the angles of a triangle are equal to two right angles, or as long as the subject exists, as when we say that 'of necessity' this fire is hot or Socrates is an animal); second, what is not <absolutely so called>, but with the qualification 'as long as that is true which is predicated by the one who says that it is so,' and no longer absolutely, no matter whether the subject is eternal or perishable. That the sun is of necessity obscured by a cloud or by the moon, as long as it is obscured, is true, but it is no longer absolutely <necessary>; and that you of necessity are sitting or walking, as long as one of these holds of you, is true, but it is no longer absolutely <necessary>: we are neither walking or sitting always, nor even as long as we partake of existence. The same point <holds> also in the case of that which of necessity does not exist. In fact, this has two kinds as well: first, what is absolutely <necessary> (e.g. that the diagonal is not commensurate with the side <of a triangle> or that the sun does not cease its motion or that this fire is not cold); second, as long as what is predicated does not belong <to the subject> (e.g. that you of necessity are not walking, whenever you are not walking: this is not absolutely true, but as long as you are not walking, since it is impossible for one who is not walking to be walking at the same time as he is not walking). Thus, you have here the distinction of sentences taught according to their matter: what absolutely is signifies the necessary; what absolutely is not signifies the impossible; and what is as long as the predicate belongs to the subject, and what is not as long as it

ἂν ἦ τὸ κα|τηγορούμενον τῷ ὑποκειμένῳ ὂν καὶ ἔστ' ἂν μὴ ἦ μὴ ὂν 123ʳ
τὸ ἐνδεχόμενον.

Ταῦτα διελόμενος ὁ Ἀριστοτέλης παραπλησίως τοῖς ἐπὶ τῶν ὄντων
εἰρημένοις ἔχειν φησὶ τὸ ἀναγκαῖον τὴν ἐν τοῖς λόγοις ἀλήθειαν· τοὺς
5 μὲν γὰρ αὐτῶν ἐξ ἀνάγκης ἀληθεύειν κατὰ τὸ ἁπλῶς λεγόμενον ἀναγ- 5
καῖον, ἐφ' οἵων ἂν λέγωνται πραγμάτων, εἴτε ἀιδίων εἴτε φθαρτῶν εἴτε
ὄντων εἴτε μὴ ὄντων, ὡς τοὺς κατὰ τὴν ὅλην ἀντίφασιν προφερομένους,
οἷον ὅτι Σωκράτης ἢ βαδίζει ἢ οὐ βαδίζει (τὸ γὰρ ὅλον τοῦτο ἀνάγκη 10
εἶναι ἀληθὲς οὐ μόνον ὄντος ἀλλὰ καὶ μὴ ὄντος Σωκράτους) καὶ ὅτι τὸ
10 πῦρ ἢ θερμὸν ἢ οὐ θερμόν, εἰ καὶ συμβαίνει ἐπὶ τῶν τοιούτων διὰ
τὴν τοῦ πράγματος φύσιν θάτερον μόριον τῆς ἀντιφάσεως ἀφωρισμένως
ἀληθεύειν, καὶ οὐ τὴν ὅλην ἀντίφασιν μόνον. τοὺς μὲν οὖν τῶν λόγων 15
οὕτως ἔχειν φησὶ τὸ ἐξ ἀνάγκης ἀληθεύειν κατὰ τὸ ἁπλῶς ἀναγκαῖον,
τοὺς δὲ κατὰ τὸν ἕτερον τρόπον, ἕως ἂν ὑπάρχῃ ἢ μὴ ὑπάρχῃ τὸ κατη-
15 γορούμενον τῷ ὑποκειμένῳ, ὡς τὸ ἐξ ἀνάγκης βαδίζειν ἢ ἐξ ἀνάγκης μὴ
βαδίζειν τὸν Σωκράτην· οὕτως γὰρ ἀνάγκη τὸ ἀληθὲς ἔχειν τοὺς λόγους, 20
ὅπερ φησὶν ὁ Ἀριστοτέλης, ὡς ἔχει φύσεως τὰ ὑπ' αὐτῶν σημαινόμενα
πράγματα, ἐπεὶ καὶ εἰσὶν ἐξηγηταὶ τῶν πραγμάτων οἱ λόγοι καὶ διὰ τοῦτο
μιμοῦνται αὐτῶν τὴν φύσιν, ὡς πρὸ τοῦ Ἀριστοτέλους ὁ Πλάτων ἡμᾶς
20 ἐδίδαξεν. 25

Ἀλλὰ τί ταῦτα φαίης ἂν πρὸς τὸ προκείμενον καὶ πῶς διὰ τούτων
σαλεύεται ὁ ἀναιρεῖν δοκῶν τὸ ἐνδεχόμενον λόγος; ὅτι, φήσω, εἰ μὲν πᾶς
λόγος εἶχε τὸ ἐξ ἀνάγκης ἀληθεύειν κατὰ τὸ ἁπλῶς ἀναγκαῖον, | εἰκότως 123ᵛ
ἐλάμβανον οἱ ἀναιροῦντες τὸ ἐνδεχόμενον ἐκ τοῦ ὁρᾶν ἐξ ἀνάγκης ἀλη-
25 θεύοντας τοὺς λόγους τοὺς οἰκείους τῇ ἐκβάσει τῶν πραγμάτων περὶ τῶν
ἤδη ἐκβεβηκότων ἀποφαινομένους ὅτι καὶ οἱ πρὸ τῆς ἐκβάσεως αὐτῶν 5
διαβεβαιούμενοι ἐκβήσεσθαι αὐτὰ τὸ ἀληθὲς ἐξ ἀνάγκης ἔχουσι, καὶ οὕτως
τῷ ὄντι συνέβαινεν ἀναιρεῖσθαι τὸ ἐνδεχόμενον. ἐπεὶ δὲ τοῦτο τῇ μὲν
ὅλῃ ἀντιφάσει, ὥσπερ ἐλέγομεν, ὑπάρχει, τοῖς δὲ μέρεσιν αὐτῆς, ἐφ' ὧν
30 τὸ κατηγορούμενον ποτὲ μὲν ὑπάρχει τῷ ὑποκειμένῳ ποτὲ δὲ οὐχ ὑπάρ- 10
χει, οὐκέτι, δῆλον ὅτι οὐ συνάγουσιν ὅπερ προτίθενται· οἷον, ὅπερ αὐτός
φησιν, ἀνάγκη πάντως αὔριον ἢ γενέσθαι ἢ μὴ γενέσθαι ναυμαχίαν, οὐ
μέντοι διελόντες καὶ τὸ ἕτερον μόνον μόριον τῆς ἀντιφάσεως εἰπόντες
ἀσφαλῶς ἀποφανούμεθα ὅτι ἔσται πάντως ἢ οὐκ ἔσται πάντως. δῆλον 15
35 ἄρα ὅτι ἀνάγκη τοὺς περὶ τῶν ἐνδεχομένων ἀποφαινομένους λόγους (ὅπερ
ἐσήμηνε τῇ ἀναιρέσει τῶν ἄκρων, τοῦ ἀναγκαίου λέγω καὶ τοῦ ἀδυνάτου,
ὧν τὸ μὲν ἐκάλεσεν ἀεὶ ὂν τὸ δὲ ἀεὶ μὴ ὄν) μὴ πάντως ἔχειν τὸ ἕτερον 20

---

1 τῷ ὑποκειμένῳ om. F   6 λέγονται G   10 ἢ θερμόν ἐστιν Fa   συμβαίνοι Ma
11 μόριον] μόνον A   12 μόνως a   13 ἔχει GMa   16 τῷ σωκράτει F
σωκράτη A   ἔχεις F   18 post λόγοι add. δῆλον F: διὸ G   19 post ὡς add.
καὶ G²   ὁ Πλάτων] Cratyl. c. 3 p. 385 B sq.   27 τὸ ἀλ. ἔχ. ἐξ ἀν. colloc. M: ἐξ ἀν.
τὸ ἀλ. ἔχ. a   29 ἐλέγομεν] v. 7   αὐτοῖς F   31 οὐκέτι om. A   ὅτι ὡς AMa
32 ἢ γενέσθαι αὖρ. colloc. A   33 μόνον om. AG   36 p. 155,6 ἐσήμανε M

does not, signifies the contingent.

<Sentences about the whole contradiction vs. those about its parts>

24. Having made these distinctions, Aristotle says that the <property of being> necessary belongs to the truth in sentences in a manner similar to what he said about existing things. For, some sentences are of necessity true in the absolute sense of 'necessary', no matter what things they are said of—whether of eternal or perishable, existing or non-existent things such as those uttered about the whole of a contradiction, e.g. that Socrates is either walking or not walking (for this whole is necessarily true, not only if Socrates exists, but even if he does not), or that fire is either hot or not hot, even if it happens in such cases that, due to the nature of the thing, just one of the two parts of the contradiction is true in a definite manner, and not only the contradiction as a whole. So, he says that among sentences, some are necessarily true in the absolute sense of 'necessary', but the others in the other sense, i.e. as long as the predicate belongs or does not belong to the subject, such as that Socrates of necessity is walking or of necessity is not walking. For, sentences necessarily have truth in the same way, which is what Aristotle says, as the things signified by them behave according to their nature, since sentences are interpreters of the things and for this reason imitate their nature, as Plato taught us[118] before Aristotle.

<The solution of the aporia>

25. But what, you may ask, has this to do with the present question, and how is the argument which appears to deny the contingent shaken by this? It is, I shall reply, that if every sentence were of necessity true in the absolute sense of 'necessary', then those who deny the contingent, upon seeing that those sentences are necessarily true which, when said about things which have already occurred, are in conformity with the outcome of those things, would have correctly assumed that also those sentences which affirmed before the occurrence of the things that they would occur have truth of necessity, and thus it would have actually happened that the contingent was denied. But, since this holds, as we said, of the whole contradiction, but not of its parts, in which the predicate sometimes holds of the subject and sometimes not, it is clear that they do not reach the conclusion they propose. For example, as Aristotle himself says, it is necessary, whatever happens, that tomorrow a sea battle take place or not take place, but dividing them and stating only one part of the contradiction, we shall not safely announce that it will be so, in any case, or it will not be so, in any case. Therefore, it is clearly necessary for sentences said about contingent <things> (which he indicated by the elimination of the extremes, i.e. the necessary and the impossible, of which he called the one *'what always exists'* and the other *'what always does not exist'*) not in every case to have one member of the contradiction be true in a definite manner—which was what we were to investigate from

---

[118] Plat. *Crat.* 385b.

μόριον τῆς ἀντιφάσεως ἀφωρισμένως ἀληθεῦον, ὅπερ ἦν τὸ ἐξ ἀρχῆς ἡμῖν
εἰς ἐπίσκεψιν προκείμενον, ἀλλ᾿ ἤτοι ἄμφω ὁμοίως δεκτικὰ ψεύδους τε καὶ
ἀληθείας, ὡς τὰ περὶ τῶν ὁπότερ᾿ ἔτυχεν ἐνδεχομένων ἀποφαινόμενα, ἢ
τὸ μὲν ἕτερον μᾶλλον ἀληθεύειν πεφυκὸς τὸ δὲ ἕτερον ψεύδεσθαι μᾶλλον, 25
5 οὔτε μέντοι τὸ ἀληθεῦον ἀεὶ ἀληθεῦον οὔτε τὸ ψευδόμενον ἀεὶ ψευδόμενον,
ὅπερ ἐσήμηνε διὰ τοῦ οὐ μέντοι ἤδη ἀληθῆ ἢ ψευδῆ. δῆλον δὲ ὅτι
ἐπὶ μὲν τοῦ ὡς ἐπὶ τὸ πολὺ | λεγομένου ἡ κατάφασίς ἐστιν ἡ μᾶλλον 124ʳ
ἀληθής, ἐπὶ δὲ τοῦ ὡς ἐπ᾿ ἔλαττον ἡ ἀπόφασις.

---

1 ἀρχῆς] ἀνάγκης F   4 ἕτερον μᾶλλον iteratum del. A   ἀληθ. μᾶλλον colloc. M
5 οὔτε (prius)] οὐ M   ἀεὶ ψευδόμενον om. M   6 ὅτι ὡς M   8 ὡς
om. M

the beginning—but either to have both members equally receptive of truth and falsity, as what is said about contingents which are however it chances, or to have one member which is rather such as to be true and the other rather such as to be false, but not to have that which is true be always true nor that which is false be always false, which he indicated by '*but not already true or false*'. It is clear that, in the case of what is said for the most part, it is the affirmative sentence that is rather true, and in the case of what is for the lesser part, it is the negative sentence.

Part V

Philosophical Commentary

by Gerhard Seel

translated from the French by Greg Bayer

IV.1 Introduction

The commentary of Ammonius[119] on *De Interpretatione* is part of a long tradition.[120] According to available evidence, the following authors wrote commentaries on *De Interpretatione*: Aspasius (1st-2nd century),[121] Herminus (2nd century AD),[122] Galen (129-after 210), Alexander of Aphrodisias (2nd-3rd century),[123] Porphyry (232-309)—after Porphyry, the commentators are linked to the Neoplatonic school—Iamblichus (circa 240-circa 325),[124] Syrianus (died about 437), Proclus (412-485),[125] Ammonius (435/45-517/26),[126] Boethius (480-525 or 526),[127] Philoponus (about 490-after 570),[128] Olympiodorus (495/505-after 565),[129] Elias (2nd half of the 6th century,[130] Stephanus 6th-7th century),[131] and an anonymous commentator (end of the 6th century or beginning of the 7th).[132] Except for the commentaries of Ammonius, Boethius, Stephanus and the anonymous commentary, all these works are lost, and only about twenty scholia of Olympiodorus' commentary survive.[133] Proclus' commentary, a treatise that was a main source of inspiration for Ammonius, was probably never published.

---

[119] Ed. A. Busse, *Commentaria in Aristotelem Graeca* (hereafter *CAG*), IV,5, Berlin, 1897. Our references to the text of Ammonius are given with Busse's pagination.

[120] See also Blank's introduction to the first volume of his translation: D. Blank 1996.

[121] Cp. P. Moraux 1984, 230-5. According to Moraux (p. 231), Aspasius is probably the first commentator on *De Interpretatione*.

[122] Cp. P. Moraux 1984, 374-82. The dates of his life are difficult to establish. Moraux suggests around 120 to 180/190.

[123] Alexander of Aphrodisias was a student of Herminus.

[124] Iamblichus was a student of Porphyry.

[125] Proclus was a student of Syrianus.

[126] Ammonius was a student of Proclus at Athens before teaching in Alexandria.

[127] Boethius wrote (in Latin) two commentaries on *De Interpretatione*, of which the second is more important: *Commentarii in librum Aristotelis Peri Hermēneias*.

[128] The Neoplatonic Christian Philoponus was a student of Ammonius at Alexandria.

[129] Olympiodorus was also a student of Ammonius.

[130] The philosopher Elias, most likely a Christian, was probably a student of Olympiodorus. Some scholia from his commentary have been edited by Busse in *CAG* IV,5, 1897, p. xxvi-xxviii.

[131] Stephanus of Alexandria was appointed to a chair in Constantinople in 610 or shortly after. Ed. M. Hayduck, *CAG* XVIII,3, 1885.

[132] L. Tarán 1978. The beginning of the commentary is lost. The text of the only manuscript (*Parisinus Graecus* 2064) begins in the middle of a discussion of *Int* 16a30.

[133] They are edited by L. Tarán 1978, xxv-xli.

The ancient tradition of commentary on the works of Aristotle extended to the Byzantines, Syrians, Arabs, and the Latin writers of the Middle Ages[134] and the Renaissance. The commentary of Ammonius was translated into Latin in the thirteenth century by William of Moerbeke.[135]

The influence of Ammonius (born between 435 and 445, died between 517 and 526)[136] on the later commentators was immense. He clearly influenced Stephanus' and the anonymous commentaries, where the so-called 'Reaper'[137] Argument is found. P. Courcelle considers Ammonius the principal source for Boethius.[138] Tarán, however, thinks that the two commentaries are independent but use common sources, particularly the lost commentary of Porphyry.[139] According to David Blank[140] and Richard Sorabji,[141] the main sources of Ammonius and Boethius are quite different, though they both used Porphyry's (now lost) commentary on De Interpretatione. In fact, Boethius declares (In Int. ed. sec., 7, 5-9) that he drew as much as possible from Porphyry whereas Ammonius according to his own words (In Int. 1, 6-11) worked out what he remembered of Proclus' exegesis of De Interpretatione. So Ammonius was very much influenced by Proclus and by Syrianus (the predecessor of Proclus)[142] while Boethius' commentary depends directly on Porphyry. These considerations lead us occasionally to turn to the commentaries of Boethius in our discussion of Ammonius'.

Among the commentaries[143] of Ammonius, that on De Interpretatione is the only one that he himself prepared for publication.[144] The other commentaries on Aristotle surviving under Ammonius' name are notes on public courses by students. Hence their titles declare that they are ἀπὸ φωνῆς, i.e. 'from the voice' of the master.[145]

Ammonius divides the whole of De Interpretatione into four principal sections (κεφάλαια), which include the first thirteen chapters of our modern editions,[146] to which he adds, with some doubt about its authenticity, our chapter

---

134   Cp. J. Isaac 1953.
135   *Ammonius, Commentaire sur le Peri Hermeneias d'Aristote, traduction de Guillaume de Moerbeke*, 1961. William's translation is quite literal and we have consulted it often. On William's work, see L. Minio-Paluello 1974, 434-40.
136   Cp. L.G. Westerink 1990, xi-xv.
137   Cp. below, on paragraph 5.
138   P. Courcelle 1948, 264-78.
139   Op. cit., p. VII, n. 10. L. Obertello 1981, 155-6 defends a position close to L. Tarán's. J. Shiel 1990, 349-72, also has this view.
140   Cp. D. Blank 1996, 1-6.
141   Cp. R. Sorabji 1998, 17.
142   For Ammonius' relation to the other members of the Neoplatonic school see D. Blank 1996, 1-6.
143   Cp. H.D. Saffrey 1989.
144   L. Tarán 1981, xv. ff.
145   Cp. M. Richard 1950, 191-222 and again D. Blank, 1996, 2.
146   Cp. *in Int.* 7,15-8,22.

14.[147] This division apparently can be traced back to Proclus or to Ammonius himself;[148] it was adopted by Stephanus,[149] by the anonymous commentator and also by Probha (Probus) of Antioch,[150] a Nestorian writing in Syrian, by al-Farabi and Averroes,[151] but not by Boethius. The sections, in turn, are divided into lemmata that Ammonius in his commentary transcribes in full 'in order to discern what is apparently the most accurate edition' (8,28). Thus our customary division into 14 chapters, which can probably be traced back to Julius Pacius' 1584 edition of the *Organon*,[152] is not to be found here—and so Ammonius nowhere speaks of a 'Chapter 9'. This does not mean, however, that he was unaware of the thematic unity of our chapter 9. Thus, though this part of the text got its denomination 'chapter 9' much later, we are justified in considering it a unity and devoting our commentary exclusively to it. The Aristotelian text of the chapter is divided into eight lemmata, which are found in the second principal section of Ammonius. This section includes our chapters 7 to 9 with the beginning of chapter 10 (17a38-19b19 of Aristotle's text and 86, 26-159,9 in Ammonius' commentary). It discusses 'the simplest propositions, and will be about the proposition or assertion <consisting> of subject and predicate' (*In Int.* 8,14-16). The lemmata of chapter 9 fit neatly into this context. They treat the specific question of whether pairs of opposite assertoric sentences can always divide the values 'true' and 'false', or are singular assertoric sentences about future contingents (henceforth: SFCS's) an exception? Ammonius gives his version of Aristotle's response to this question at in *Int.* 128,21-155,8. This text is the principal focus of our work.

Ammonius understands[153] however that in saying, at the beginning of chapter 9, ὥσπερ εἴρηται 'as has been said', Aristotle is clearly referring to the

---

147   Cp. *in Int.* 8,22-23. Most authors attribute to Aristotle a division of the text into five parts. But Ammonius argues convincingly that he divided it into four units which contain the totality of his doctrine of the simple sentence: (1) the exposition of 'principles' (definitions of noun, verb, affirmation, negation, sentence and contradiction); (2.) the theory of the simplest sentences, i.e. assertoric sentences composed of a subject and predicate; (3) the theory of assertoric sentences composed of a subject, predicate and the verb 'to be'; (4) the theory of modal sentences. Ammonius notes that the last part of Aristotle's treatise (=chapter 14) is either not by Aristotle but one of his disciples, or is Aristotle's but is a dialectical exercise addressed to his readers (*In Int.* 251,25-252,8). He ultimately decides this alternative in favor of the latter saying that it is worthwhile to give commentary on this text, *contra* Porphyry, on the grounds that it is authentic.

148   Cp. L. Tarán 1978, xvii. F.W. Zimmermann 1981, xci, does not exclude the possibility that Iamblichus may be the source of this.

149   Stephanus (*In Int.* 63,4 ff..), like the anonymous commentator (L. Tarán 1978, 115,7ff.), calls chapter 14 'the fifteenth section [τμῆμα]'; he even gives it the name κεφάλαιον (63,11). He notes that this part of *De Interpretatione* 'is not entirely by Aristotle, but has been written in the form of an exercise.'

150   Cp. J.G.E. Hoffman 1869, 94 and *passim*.

151   Cp. E. Meyer 1984, 272 and C. Ehrig-Eggert 1989, 292, and 1990, 45.

152   Cp. H. Weidemann 1994, 59.

153   Cp. *In Int.* 128,1.

theory of oppositions of assertoric sentences (henceforth: sentences) first sketched in chapters 5 and 6 of *De Interpretatione* and developed at length in chapter 7. In fact, according to Ammonius, chapter 9 deals with a special problem that arises from this theory: whether the oppositions of singular sentences in the case of future contingents behave, concerning their truth values, like the other oppositions of singular sentences. Consequently, Ammonius makes use of his commentary on these chapters, especially on chapter 7, to discuss the first lemma of chapter 9. For this reason, before approaching the commentary on chapter 9, we present a summary of the theory of sentence-oppositions and of the logical relations among sentences that is developed by Ammonius in his commentary on chapter 7 (*In Int.* 86,26-101,9). This will make what Ammonius says on chapter 9 regarding oppositions easier to understand. We limit however our commentary to the first lemma of this chapter, which contains the core of the theory of oppositions, leaving aside the other paragraphs, which offer Ammonius the opportunity to discuss more special questions in relation to this theory.

In our commentary, we will follow the division of Aristotle's text into lemmata laid down by Ammonius, and we use the division of Ammonius' text into paragraphs adopted by the modern editor A. Busse. As an aid to reading, we number the paragraphs conforming to Busse's division, beginning at the start of each chapter.

IV.2 Commentary on Chapter 7, 1-17

Lemma 1 (17a38 - b12)

Paragraph 1

For Ammonius, chapter 7 marks the beginning of the second main part of the treatise (τὸ δεύτερον τοῦ βιβλίου κεφάλαιον, 86,26). He begins his commentary with a description of his procedure, proposing three tasks to be accomplished: (a) to make clear how a negative sentence is obtained from an affirmative (in fact, it is the pair of sentences so formed that is called an 'opposition', ἀντίθεσις); (b) to establish a classification of sentences that will serve as the basis for a classification of oppositions between sentences; (c) to determine which oppositions constitute true contradictions and which only have the appearance to do so (86,30-87,7). We will follow the same order in our exposition.

Paragraph 2

(a) The theory of sentence-opposition is based first of all on the distinction between affirmative and negative sentences, a distinction concerning what Ammonius calls the 'quality' (τὸ ποιόν) of sentences. Aristotle mentions this distinction at the beginning of chapter 5 (17a8-9), gives a preliminary account of it in the same chapter (17a20-1), and returns to it at the beginning of chapter 6 (17a25-6): a positive sentence is 'an assertion that attributes something to something', while a negative sentence is 'an assertion that denies something of something'. Thus Aristotle establishes a logico-semantic criterion for distinguishing affirmative from negative sentences. There is also, however, a purely lexico-grammatical criterion (which concerns the λέξις, 'expression' or 'wording', of the sentence): a positive sentence is distinguished from a negative sentence by the fact that the latter includes a sign of negation that is absent from the former. Although this criterion is not mentioned by Aristotle in his definition of negative sentence, it plays an important role in his theory, notably in the formation of oppositions between sentences. It is thus the source of a certain confusion, which gives rise to the series of problems Aristotle attends to in chapter 7.

The fact that there is in Aristotle both a logico-semantic criterion and a purely lexical criterion for the qualitative difference in sentences has not escaped

Ammonius (80,31-5). But he clearly gives precedence to the latter when he asserts that the difference in quality, i.e. between affirmative and negative sentences, depends on the distinction in λέξις, 'expression' (72,15-21; 79,15-17). Consequently, the formation of the oppositions between sentences in Ammonius becomes principally a lexical affair. He informs us a number of times (67,25-7; 70,4-10; 87,8-10) that a negative sentence can be obtained by adding a sign of negation (ἀρνητικὸν μόριον, ἀποφατικὸν μόριον, 'the denying particle', 'the negative particle') to a positive sentence, or more precisely to its predicate. The pairs of sentences Ammonius names ἀντιθέσεις are obtained in this way. Thus these pairs of opposites are not formed by a logico-semantic method, but by a lexico-grammatical one. This is the reason why the analysis undertaken in the last part of chapter 7 is quite indispensable. If the pairs of opposites had been established from logical criteria at the outset, there would be no reason to wonder further about the logical relations holding between the members of each pair. Ammonius, then, is right to treat Aristotle's pairs of opposites as principally lexico-grammatical entities.

This view, however, requires further precision. When Ammonius, following Aristotle, wonders if in the formation of the negative sentence the sign of negation must be added to the subject or to the predicate, he justifies his answer on the basis of the fact that the predicate has a priority[154] over the subject (70,3-10 and 87,12-13). This priority can only be logico-semantic. Ammonius in fact thinks that it is the predicate, and more precisely the copula, that at the same time performs both a descriptive and assertive function.[155] This is the reason why, in order to deny what an affirmative sentence holds, one must add a sign of negation to its predicate.

For the opposition of assertoric sentences according to their λέξις, Ammonius uses the term ἀντίθεσις. An opposition in this sense is a pair of sentences having the same terms in the subject and predicate positions, but distinguished by the fact that in one sentence a negation sign has been added to the predicate.

Considering chapter 6 of De Interpretatione, one has the impression that for Aristotle, unlike Ammonius, the formation of each pair of opposites is, in fact, guided by the (logico-semantic) idea that one of its members denies what the other affirms. Thus Aristotle states:

> So one should be able to deny all that anyone has affirmed, and to affirm all that anyone has denied. Thus it is clear that for every affirmative sentence there is a negative sentence opposed [ἀντικειμένη] to it, and for every negative sentence an affirmative one. And let this be a contradiction [ἀντίφασις]: <<the pair of>> an affirmative sentence and a negative sentence that are opposed to each other. By 'are opposed' I mean that the sentences affirm and deny the same thing of the same thing, but not in a homonymous way, and in

---

154   Cp. τὸ κῦρος (70,5) and κυριώτερον (87,12).
155   Cp. G. Seel's first essay in this volume, 226-227.

accordance with all the other conditions that we add to counter sophistical difficulties' (*Int.* 6, 17a30-7, our translation).

It would be a mistake, however, to consider the lines 17a34-7 as a definition of what Aristotle means by the term ἀντικεῖσθαι. Rather, these lines give the restricted sense that the term has in the definition of ἀντίφασις in the lines preceding. Thus one should read in 17a34: 'I mean here (as an exceptional case)....' As *An. Pr.* 2.15, 63b23-30 clearly shows, Aristotle in fact distinguishes between the opposition 'according to the λέξις' and the opposition 'according to truth'. But on the other hand, he places both contradictions and oppositions between contrary sentences under the opposition according to truth. In chapter 7 of *De Interpretatione*, Aristotle also distinguishes between two modes of opposition: two sentences can be opposed either in a contradictory way (ἀντιφατικῶς) or in a contrary way (ἐναντίως). Thus *Int.* 6, 17a30-7 must be understood as presenting what he means by 'contradiction' and not as a definition of the term 'opposition'.

Paragraph 3

(b) The second task Ammonius has set for himself is to establish a classification (διαίρεσις) of sentences in order to distinguish the different species of opposition. Without abandoning the spirit of the Aristotelian distinctions, he seeks to do this more systematically than Aristotle by following the general principles of classification. He tells us at the beginning of his exposition that because sentences have only two terms, the subject and predicate, they can be classified by differences of the subject, or by differences of the predicate, or by different types of relations between subject and predicate (88,7-12). The classification according to subject will lead to the theory of opposition, the distinction by predicate permits the sorting of sentences according to their verbal tense, and the difference in relations between subject and predicate serves to classify the statements by their modal status.

(1) Ammonius first introduces the classification of sentences according to the last criterion. This is not found in Aristotle, either in chapter 7 or in the first lemma of chapter 9. But since it will be of paramount importance for the commentary Ammonius gives on the latter chapter, we can hardly neglect it.

Ammonius first tells us there are three possible relations between subject and predicate:

(a) the predicate always belongs to the subject;
(b) the predicate never belongs to it;
(c) the predicate sometimes belongs to it and sometimes not (*in Int.* 88,7-19).

Using technical terminology, he tells us that these three relations are called the 'matters of sentences', the first matter being 'necessary', the second 'impossible', and the third 'contingent'. Sentences can then be distinguished as 'sentences in necessary matter', 'in impossible matter' and 'in contingent matter'.

It should be noted that this is not a classification according to the modalities of the sentences themselves, but according to the modal status of the state of affairs asserted by the sentences. Ammonius is careful to stress the point: this classification is not derived 'from our believing or saying, but from the very nature of the things' (88,22-3). Consequently, it is not sentences with modal operators that are classified in this way, but plain non-modal sentences. Ammonius will use this classification to clarify the way sentences behave with regard to their truth values, thus showing himself to be quite original in his approach to Aristotle.

Paragraphs 4-5

(2) The second classification treated by Ammonius is based on differences in the subject, or more precisely differences in the subject's quantity. The division of sentences according to this criterion is introduced and explained by Aristotle in chapter 7 (*Int.* 17a38ff.) together with the theory of opposition. Ammonius presents Aristotle's distinctions in a different order; he in effect constructs a kind of *arbor porphyreana* of genera and species of sentences, as he successively applies three different criteria.

1. The first criterion concerns the type of term functioning as the subject. Terms used as the subject or predicate of a statement are either singular (καθ' ἕκαστα) or universal (καθόλου) (*In Int.* 88,30). According to Aristotle, a universal term is one that can be predicated of many subjects, while a singular term cannot (*Int.* 7, 17a38-b1). As he clearly stresses in *An. Pr.* 1.27, 43a25-43, Aristotle is convinced—and *Int.* 7, 17a40 must be interpreted this way—that *stricto sensu* a singular term like 'Kallias' cannot be predicated at all of any other term. Ammonius, on the other hand, characterizes singular terms as those that can be predicated, but only of single and unique subjects (*In Int.* 88,35). This is an important difference between Ammonius and Aristotle.

2. A universal term can be predicated of a universal term 'either without additional determination (προσδιορισμός) or with additional determination' (89,3). The determinations Ammonius is talking about are adjectives expressing an indefinite quantity, like πᾶς, οὐδείς, τις, οὐ πᾶς ('all ', 'no', 'some', 'not all') that are added to the subject of a sentence. The presence or absence of such adjectives in a sentence is the second criterion used by Ammonius in his classification of sentences.

3. The third criterion arises from the differences among these determinating signs themselves, since they indicate whether the predicate is affirmed (or denied) of the totality of individuals included under the subject, or only of a part of them.

By the first criterion, sentences are divided into singular (καθ' ἕκαστα) and simply (ἁπλῶς) universal. Universal sentences, in turn, are divided according to the second criterion into undetermined (ἀπροσδιόριστοι) and determined (προσδιωρισμένοι). Determined sentences, then, are divided into general (καθόλου) and particular (μερικαί) (90,1-4). The term καθόλου here indicates not that the subject is a universal term, but rather that the predicate is attributed to all the individuals included under the subject, in other words that it is predicated in a general way (ὡς καθόλου); the adjective μερική on the other hand indicates that the predicate is attributed to only a part of the individuals included under the subject, or that it is predicated in a particular way (ὡς μερικαί) (90,5-10). Thus Ammonius obtains the following division:

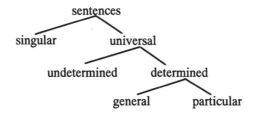

There are thus four species of sentences: singular, undetermined, general and particular. Ammonius concludes that there are just as many species of sentence-oppositions (90,5-10):

1. opposition of singular sentences.
Ex: Socrates is walking - Socrates is not walking.

2. opposition of undetermined sentences.
Ex: Man is walking - man is not walking.

3. opposition of general sentences.
Ex: Every man is walking - every man is not walking;
                    - no man is walking.
4. opposition of particular sentences.

Ex: Some man is walking - some man is not walking;
                    - not every man is walking.

The third and fourth oppositions together form what is called the 'square of opposition', which is found first in the Περὶ ἑρμηνείας of Apuleius of Madaura,[156] although Ammonius and Boethius (ed. pr. 87; ed. sec. 152), probably following Porphyry, have given it its definitive form. Replacing sentences given in the examples with the letters A, E, I, O, as has been customary since medieval times, here is the square as found at in Int. 93,10-18:[157]

---

[156]   Cp. D. Londey and C. Johanson 1987, 86; J.-M. Flamand 1989, 304-307.
[157]   For a history of the square of oppositions, cp. A. Lumpe 1982 and W.L. Gombocz 1988.

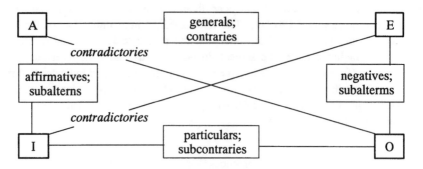

We find the same species of sentences in Aristotle (*Int.* 17b16-34), who also arranges them in four pairs of opposites. But the list of the four pairs is different from Ammonius'. In Aristotle the two pairs of sentences on the diagonals (called simply 'the diagonals' by Ammonius), which in Ammonius' commentary[58] do not count as pairs of opposites, are in effect treated as a species of opposites. Subcontraries, on the other hand, which in Ammonius are treated as a fourth species, are excluded from Aristotle's list. This is because Ammonius strictly applies his definition of a pair of opposites which, as we have seen, is based on their lexico-grammatical relations, while Aristotle, if we follow Ackrill's interpretation (1963,129-30), sets up a list of opposite pairs according to their logical relations. He is, however, not very consistent in his procedure including in his list the undetermined sentences as contradictorily opposed, even though the members of such a pair are sometimes both true, as he himself stresses.

Contrary to Ackrill, Weidemann 1994, 202-3 holds that Aristotle establishes his list on purely grammatical grounds. He maintains that the species of opposite pairs are constituted according to the rule that 'both members of the pair have the same subject and the same predicate and one is affirmative and the other negative.' But according to this rule, which is nowhere stated in Aristotle, the subcontraries should also be included in Aristotle's list—which is not the case. For his interpretation, Weidemann can cite the passage in the *Prior Analytics* (II.15, 63b23-8) in which Aristotle explicitly lists four pairs of opposite sentences according to grammatical form (κατὰ τὴν λέξιν). The subcontraries, which Aristotle says are 'opposed only in their expression' [λέξις], are in fact included in this list, which only contains sentences of the square of opposition.

It must be noted, however, that the rule Weidemann ascribes to Aristotle is not as strong and logical as that of Ammonius. Ammonius not only requires that the subject and predicate of the two sides of a pair be identical and that one be affirmative and the other negative, but also that the sign of negation be attached to the predicate and the sign of quantification be attached to the subject. If this rule is strictly applied, the pairs of opposites ought to be formulated according to the

---

[58]   It must be noted, however, that in his commentary on chapter 9 (*In Int.* 129,31-2) Ammonius, here following Aristotle, actually includes the diagonals, instead of generals and particulars, among the species of sentence-oppositions.

list given on page 139 (making sure that only the sentences of the first line figure under the headings 3 and 4). One can see immediately that only general and particular sentences satisfy this rule, while the diagonals do not have the same expression in the subject position.

Paragraph 6

(3) It remains to be seen how Ammonius classifies sentences according to differences in their predicates. In his procedure, he only takes into consideration one aspect of the predicate: the fact that the predicate always cosignifies time. He thus gets three species of sentences: those in the past tense, those in the present tense, and those in the future tense. This classification is also based on a grammatical criterion, although Ammonius sets aside further tense-distinctions mentioned by Greek grammarians.[159]

It is interesting to note how Ammonius benefits from the results of his tripartite classification of sentences for working out the number of species of opposition pairs. Counting three species according to the modal division, four according to quantity and three according to verbal tense, one arrives at 36 species of opposition pairs, a figure that doubles if one considers that the subject is either determined or undetermined (90,21-91,30).

Paragraphs 7-17

(c) The last part of the commentary on the first lemma of chapter 7 (91,4-101,9) is devoted to determining the logical relations between sentences, relations that form the basis of the different species of opposition and that are partly represented in the square of opposition. Two points in the text of Ammonius are important for understanding his commentary on chapter 9:

1. Ammonius already includes what is going to be at stake in chapter 9, in the context of themes found in the last part of chapter 7: "Everyone agrees that singular sentences are opposed <to each other> in the manner of contradiction (although taken in the future tense they give rise to a certain ἀπορία that Aristotle goes on to explain and resolve in what follows [ch. 9])" (91,10-13). It is particularly interesting that the subject of chapter 9 should be presented here as an ἀπορία. As Seel 1993 suggests, following the Stoic conception (which certainly influenced Ammonius), an ἀπορία is a set of sentences, each of which is evident at first glance, but which together are incompatible. Thus an ἀπορία calls for a resolution (λύσις) that involves either showing that there is no incompatibility between the sentences or proving that at least one of the sentences is false and restoring coherence by replacing it with a true one. If according to Ammonius the

---

[159]   Cp. J. Lallot 1989, 169-77.

subject of chapter 9 amounts to an ἀπορία, we should expect him to point out the sentences of the ἀπορία, analyze the proof that these sentences are incompatible, and explain how Aristotle goes on to resolve the ἀπορία.

2. In determining the logical relations among sentences, Ammonius makes use of a method of analysis not mentioned in Aristotle, at least not in chapter 7. In fact, in order to decide if for a given species of sentence pairs the two sentences have different truth values or are true or false together, Ammonius asks how these sentences behave in the different modal domains. If, for example, the members of a pair are both *de facto* true in a certain modal domain, he concludes that the members of the given species can be true together; but if they are not both true in any modal domain, he concludes they are incapable of this. The same method is later applied in the commentary on chapter 9, where it proves just as fruitful.

Let us first see how Ammonius determines the logical relations between the different species of sentences that he goes on to distinguish. We must note at the outset that, just as Aristotle does, Ammonius disposes only of an incomplete technical terminology for designating these relations. Furthermore these terms are used ambiguously, sometimes referring to the logical relation, and sometimes to the pair of sentences tied by the relation. Further, Ammonius is familiar only with the technical terms for the contradiction and contrariety relations, for which he also gives a truth-functional definition. The other logical relations are not named, but are presented indirectly through the set of truth values that characterize them.[160]

First we shall analyze how Ammonius defines the relations of contradiction and of contrariety:

(1) To designate the contradiction relation Ammonius uses the following terms taken from Aristotle: ἀντίφασις, ἀντιφατικῶς, ἀντικεῖσθαι, ἀντιφάναι. But it is odd that, unlike Aristotle, who at *Int.* 17a31-7 introduced the term ἀντίφασις to denote the pair of contradictorily opposite sentences, Ammonius uses this term most often to denote the *logical relation* present in such a pair (though he also uses the term with the meaning found in Aristotle).

In commenting on *Int.* 17a31-7, Ammonius defines contradiction several times (*In Int.* 81,14-16; 83,3-5; 84,4-6; cp. also 91,18-19). The most complete of these definitions is the first. '[Contradiction] is the conflict [μάχη] between an affirmative and a negative sentence which always divide the true and false

---

160   H. Weidemann 1944, 205 is wrong in supposing that Ammonius uses the terms ὑπεναντίοι and ὑπάλληλοι to designate the logical relations of non-exclusive disjunction and implication. As can be shown at *In Int.* 92,21-2 and 24-6, these terms indicate 'subcontraries' and 'subalterns' not because of their logical relation, but entirely due to their position in the design of the logical square, i.e. due to topological considerations. It is, however, interesting to note, that Aristotle already used the term 'subcontrary' to designate sentences that can be true together, but cannot be false together (cp. *GC* I.7 323b2, b16), though there is no hint that he used the topological tool of the square of oppositions.

between them, so that if one of them is false the other is true, and vice versa'.[161]
One can derive from this definition the following rules:

T(16) $N\{(T[Cp] \leftrightarrow F[C{\sim}p]) \bullet (F[Cp] \leftrightarrow T[C{\sim}p])\}$

T(13) $N\{(T[Cp] \bullet F[C{\sim}p]) {\scriptstyle >-<} (F[Cp] \bullet T[C{\sim}p])\}$

T(13) is the formula made explicit at *In Int.* 121,22-3 where Ammonius, referring
to the definitions Aristotle gives for contradiction in the *Analytics* (*An. Post.* 1.2,
72a12) and in the *Categories* (13a37), explains that according to Aristotle
contradiction is unique among oppositions, because only with contradictories is it
necessarily the case that one is true and the other false. T(13) logically follows
from T(16) and from the principle of bivalence, formulated at *In Int.* 80,24-6,
saying that a statement is either true or false. Ammonius clearly means by this that
no other truth value can be assigned to it:

T(10) $N\{(T[Cp] {\scriptstyle >-<} F[Cp]) \bullet (T[C{\sim}p] {\scriptstyle >-<} F[C{\sim}p])\}$

T(13) is equivalent to the following law:

T(11) $N\{(T[Cp] {\scriptstyle >-<} T[C{\sim}p]) \bullet (F[Cp] {\scriptstyle >-<} F[C{\sim}p])\}$

T(13) and T(11) are both confirmed by *In Int.* 82,26-8 and especially by
123,15-18. In the latter passage Ammonius is commenting on *Int.* 17b38-18a12
and stressing that, according to Aristotle, for each affirmative sentence there is
only one negative sentence, which is opposed to it as a contradictory.

The fact that, in his commentary on chapters 6, 7 and 8, Ammonius holds
T(10), T(11), T(13) and T(16) is crucially important for understanding what he
says on chapter 9 of *De Interpretatione*. For one can scarcely see how he could,
without contradicting himself, assent to these principles and also—in what
concerns SFCSs—adhere to the traditional interpretation.

(2) For the contrariety relation Ammonius uses the terms ἐναντίως
ἀντικεῖσθαι, ἐναντίον εἶναι. A pair of statements opposed as contraries are
indicated by the term ἐναντίαι (προτάσεις) ('contrary sentences'). Unlike
contradiction this relation is not explicitly defined by Ammonius. At *In Int.*
92,3-21, however, he offers an explication of contrary sentences that amounts to
an implicit definition. In this passage he compares this type of sentence pair to
pairs of contrary predicates having intermediates. Since it is impossible for two
predicates of this type to be assigned at the same time to the same subject, but it is
possible for neither to be assigned, it is likewise impossible that two contrary
sentences be both true, but it is possible that neither is. This explication amounts
to a truth-functional definition of the contrariety relation. In effect, it can be
characterized by the fact that it permits every combination of truth values except
for both sentences being simultaneously true.

---

[161]   Our translation differs somewhat from D. Blank's.

But let us come back to the third part of Ammonius commentary on the first lemma of chapter 7. He opens this part with a description of the task he intends to perform (*In Int.* 91,4-8). This involves answering three questions:

(1)   'Which sentences among the enumerated oppositions oppose one another contradictorily and which do not?'
(2)   'What <logical> relations do those not opposed contradictorily bear to one another?'
(3)   'Which is the sentence that conflicts contradictorily with each of the sentences among the latter. <i.e. the sentences not contradictorily opposed to one another>?'

For his answers, he follows the order of pairs of opposed sentences established earlier.

(1)   The pair of singular sentences are contradictorily opposed; everyone is convinced of this. (There is, however, a puzzle concerning SFCSs, which Aristotle will resolve in chapter 9 (91,10-13)).
(2)   It is difficult to know the answer regarding the undetermineds before analyzing the determineds (91,13-17).
(3)   Determined sentences form the logical square already explained. Ammonius lists the following relations among the sentences in the square:

(a)   The pair of universal sentences taken universally (=general sentences) does not form a contradiction, because these sentences are both false at once 'in contingent matter' (91,21-3). But on the other hand, since they cannot be both true at once, Ammonius designates them by the term 'contraries' (92,15-17) which here signifies the logical relation.

(b)   The pair of particular sentences are not a contradiction because they are both true at once in contingent matter (91,30-2), but cannot both be false. Due to their position in the square 'under the contraries', Ammonius calls them ὑπεναντίαι, 'sub-contraries'.

(c)   The logical relation between general and particular affirmative sentences and between general and particular negative sentences (these Ammonius calls ὑπάλληλοι, 'subalterns') is characterized by the fact that 'if one of the general sentences is true, then the particular sentence placed under it will be true as well, insofar as it is like a part of it and is contained in it' (92,22-4); the same could be said of negative sentences as well. Since subaltern sentences can be false together, the only distribution of truth values that is excluded is the case in which the general sentence is true and the particular is false. The subalterns thus form a logical relation that can be characterized by the modern term of implication.

(d)   Under (a), (b) and (c), Ammonius has answered the first two
       questions. It remains for him to answer the third, viz. to
       determine which sentences in the logical square form true
       contradictions. For this one doesn't have to look far: 'The
       particular negative sentence is contradictorily opposed to the
       general affirmative sentence, while the particular affirmative
       sentence contradicts the general negative sentence' (92,30-1).

These answers are confirmed by an analysis of the distribution of truth values in
different modal 'matters'. In necessary matter the A and I sentences are true and
the E and O sentences are false. But in impossible matter the latter are true and
the former false. Finally, in contingent matter the two particular sentences are
both true while the two general sentences are false. Thus there is no matter in
which the sentences located on the diagonal would be true together or false
together.

Ammonius postpones the discussion of undetermined sentences until the end
of his analysis; we can consider it briefly here. This discussion is found in the
commentary on the fourth lemma (*Int.* 17b26-37), i.e. at *In Int.* 110,14-112,29.
Aristotle affirms here that a pair of opposite undetermined sentences are peculiar
in that they 'are not contraries' (17b7-8), and that in this type of opposition, which
here Aristotle for apparently grammatical reasons calls ἀντίφασις, 'it is not always
the case that one sentence is true and the other false' (17b29-30).

Contemporary interpretations explain this strange conception by the fact that
Aristotle considers undetermined sentences as ambiguous signifying (in the
majority of cases) the same thing as particular sentences, but also (though as an
exception) the same as general sentences (cp. Ackrill 1963, 129 and Weidemann
1994, 206). According to them this is the reason why he can say that
undetermineds do not always divide the true and the false.[162] This interpretation,
however, is unacceptable because neither in the first case, where they can be true

---

[162]   This contemporary interpretation has prominent ancient precursors going back at
        least to Herminus, the teacher of Alexander of Aphrodisias, and Alexander himself
        (for the latter cp. Ammonius, *In Int.* 100,19-21). As Boethius, *In Int.* II,155,26ff
        (Meiser, *editio secunda*) explains, Herminus and Alexander used examples like
        'man is rational – man is not rational' to show that in certain cases undetermined
        sentences are equivalent with contrary sentences. Porphyry, however, though
        admitting that this interpretation has "some reason" rejects it for the reason that it is
        not in accordance with Aristotle's text. He follows Aspasius (1st-2nd century A.D.)
        who showed that sometimes the negation of a predicate (e.g. *non est sanus*) has the
        same meaning as the affirmation of its contrary (e.g. *aeger est*). Therefore the
        undetermined sentences which use this kind of predicates signify contrary things.
        However, this does not mean that they are contrary sentences. It seems that this line
        of interpretation was taken by Ammonius, Boethius (*ibidem* ed. sec. 159,26ff;
        160,12ff), Stephanus of Alexandria (6th-7th century A.D.), *In Int.* 28,23-36 (ed.
        Hayduck) and the Anonymus, *In Int.* 45,3-46,5 (ed. Tarán).

together, nor in the second case, where they can be false together, can it be said that they divide the true and the false.

Further, the passages Weidemann uses to support his interpretation, viz. *Int.* 17b34-7, *An. Pr.* I.4, 26a29ff., I.7, 29a27-9, do not show that Aristotle considers undetermineds as ambiguous sentences, but rather as equivalent to particulars. Aristotle mentions, however, another conception in which the negative undetermined would be equivalent to the negative general, but he explicitly rejects it (*Int.* 17b34-7). This is the reason why Aristotle emphasizes that undetermineds are not contraries; in effect they are subcontraries.

Ammonius interprets Aristotle in the same manner we did. Following Porphyry (cp. 99,8-100,29), who criticized Alexander's misunderstanding of Aristotle's intentions (100,19), he shows in a long passage (111,10-113,11) that the conception according to which undetermineds are (or are capable of being) equivalent to general sentences, which had been maintained in antiquity, is erroneous, and he tries to prove that the conception (held by Aristotle) according to which undetermineds are equivalent to particulars is the correct one. But how does he explain from this supposition Aristotle's claim that undetermineds do not always divide the true and false? Do they ever divide the true and the false?

The answer Ammonius gives is more convincing than the modern interpretation. He uses his customary method of considering the truth of sentences in different modal domains. Thus he establishes that in necessary matter and in impossible matter opposite undetermineds are both true. This is what Aristotle intends to express when he claims that they do not always divide the true and the false. According to Ammonius 'not always' means 'not in all the modal matters'.

Aristotle's introduction of pairs of opposite undetermineds has incited vigorous criticism from modern interpreters and commentators (cp. Brandt 1965, 71, Ackrill 1963, 129 and Weidemann 1994, 206-7). Aristotle is especially criticized for using the term ἀντίφασις ('contradiction') for such a pair and hence disregarding the definition he gave for this term in chapter 6. Ammonius in his commentary tries to protect Aristotle from all criticism. Regarding the claim that Aristotle, in calling the opposition of undetermineds ἀντίφασις, goes against his definition of the term, a claim apparently made in antiquity, Ammonius asserts (121,29-34) that this term has two senses: first, a more restricted sense which is more in line with the definitions given in the *Categories* and *Analytics*, and secondly a broader sense meaning 'merely any opposition of affirmative to negative sentences which have the same subject and predicate.' One can see that this second sense corresponds to the definition of ἀντίθεσις ('opposition') according to the λέξις, that we have discussed earlier. Thus Ammonius defends Aristotle against those accusing him of contradicting himself by stressing that when Aristotle denies that every ἀντίφασις has one side true and the other false, he is referring to the lexical sense of the term rather than the logical. This point is important for understanding the commentary he gives on the beginning of chapter 9.

IV.3 Commentary on Chapter 9

Lemma 1 (18a28-34)

This first lemma is only six lines long, but Ammonius' commentary on it takes up nearly half his text concerning chapter 9. This is due to the fact, already mentioned, that in his commentary Ammonius not only wants to present the thought of Aristotle, but also intends to introduce views he holds regarding the problems treated by the Stagirite.

The commentary on the first lemma includes no fewer than twelve paragraphs. The structure of the text is as follows. In paragraphs 1 and 2, Ammonius stresses the link between chapter 9 of *De Interpretatione* and earlier chapters, especially chapter 7, which includes the theory outlining the division of sentence-oppositions that is presupposed in chapter 9.

The commentary specifically devoted to the first lemma is found in paragraph 3. In paragraph 4, Ammonius explains the importance of the question discussed in the lemma for all philosophy and particularly for moral philosophy.

The object of paragraphs 5-11 is to explain and refute two arguments for universal necessitarianism. These arguments are not found in Aristotle's text and relate to it only in a general way.

In paragraph 12, Ammonius returns to the text of Aristotle and restates the commentary given in paragraph 3 in the light of the conclusions of paragraphs 5-11. This may reveal the original division of Ammonius lectures into '$\theta\epsilon\omega\rho\iota\alpha$' and '$\lambda\epsilon\xi\iota\varsigma$', paragraph 12 corresponding to the '$\lambda\epsilon\xi\iota\varsigma$' i.e. explanation of the text of Aristotle.[163]

Before explaining in detail how Ammonius understands the first lines of chapter 9, we will sketch the interpretation of Aristotle's text that prevails today. This will throw the singularity of Ammonius's procedure into greater relief.

Most current interpretations (cp. H. Weidemann 1994, 225-6, J. Ackrill 1963, 133) treat the formulation of the fundamental logical principle in *Int.*18a28-9 as ambiguous: Aristotle either means that necessarily for two contradictory sentences one is true and the other false—

T(13) $N\{(T[Cp] \bullet F[C{\sim}p]) \succ\!\!\prec (F[Cp] \bullet T[C{\sim}p])\}$,
T(11) $N\{(T[Cp] \succ\!\!\prec T[C{\sim}p]) \bullet (F[Cp] \succ\!\!\prec F[C{\sim}p])\}$

—or that each must be true or false, i.e. that each necessarily possesses one of two truth values:

---

163   Cp. D. Blank 1996, 2.

T(10)   N{(T[Cp] ›-‹ F[Cp]) • (T[C~p] ›-‹ F[C~p])}.

The standard interpretation (cp. H. Weidemann 1994, 226, J. Ackrill 1963, 136, D. Frede 1970, 9-12) gives preference to the latter interpretation arguing as follows: Aristotle says at 18a28-9 that the principle in question is valid for all sentences concerning the present and past. He then (18a29-33) turns to a review of the different sorts of sentences falling under this class, i.e. the universal, the singular and the undetermined sentences, and determines for each sort of pairs of opposites whether the two sentences divide the true and the false. He says that universals (he must mean along each diagonal) and singulars always have one sentence true and the other false, while for undetermineds this is not necessarily so. Consequently, the principle stated at 18a28-9 cannot be the same as the principle formulated in 18a29-33, the first being valid for all assertoric sentences and the last only for universal and singular sentences. Therefore 18a28-9 must be referring to T(10), while 18a29-33 contains T(13) or T(11). As a result, the principle whose validity Aristotle denies for SFCSs at 18a33 must also be T(10). Thus the standard interpretation finds its first confirmation in a reading of the first passage of chapter 9. This reading, however, has been called into question by the supporters of the non-standard interpretation (cp. G. Fine 1984, 38-40, 46 note 44, L. Judson 1988, 9-10), which hold that the two passages refer exactly to the same principle, i.e. to T(11) or T(13). Therefore this must be the principle stated at 18a28-9, whose validity Aristotle denies at 18a33 for SFCSs.

Concerning this controversy it must be noted, however, that according to classical propositional logic T(10) and T(11) are equivalent because negation is defined as an operator that changes the truth value of a proposition from true to false and from false to true. It is only due to the unfortunate subsumption of the pair of undetermined opposites under the genus ἀντιφάσεις, 'contradictories', which as we've seen is done for purely lexical reasons, that Aristotle can deny that T(11) is valid for all ἀντιφάσεις. But this does not mean that he denies the validity of T(11) for all ἀντιφάσεις formed according to the principle that one sentence affirms what the other denies. Thus it seems to us impossible to end the controversy between the standard and non-standard interpretations solely on the basis of the first passage of chapter 9.

In this context, it is interesting to point out that Ammonius considers—he stresses this as early as the first paragraph—that the problem of chapter 9 is to determine whether the pair of opposite SFCSs divide the truth values, as principle T(11) intends. Principle T(10), on the contrary, is not even mentioned. To this extent, already here he shows himself close to the non-standard interpretation.

Paragraph 1

This paragraph serves as a preparation for what follows. It is divided into two parts.

(a) (128,21-30). In this passage Ammonius establishes the link between the main topic of chapter 9 and what Aristotle has explained in chapter 7. He explains correctly that Aristotle introduces here a division of sentences according to time which is a consequence of the fact that the verb signifies time, and a division of sentences according to differences in subject. (For details of this theory see our interpretation of Ammonius' commentary on chapter 7 above.)

(b) (128,30-129,4). Ammonius at first takes up the list of species of pairs of opposite sentences found in Aristotle (*Int.* 18a29-33), such as the two diagonals, the pair of undetermineds and the pair of singular sentences. This has nothing to do with the list of four species of oppositions he himself established in his commentary on chapter 7 (cp. 90,5-10 and our commentary on this, p.139) applying strictly lexico-grammatical criteria, but is the list of pairs of opposites that, according to Aristotle, constitute ἀντιφάσεις, 'contradictories'. The term ἀντίθεσις 'opposition' therefore means in this context 'contradictory opposition' and not as usually 'grammatical opposition'. It may be disturbing that Ammonius includes in his list the undetermineds as well despite the fact that he has recognized in his commentary on chapter 7 that they carry the name ἀντιφάσεις only for grammatical reasons. But he certainly does so in order to accord with Aristotle's text.

Next he specifies in which of the four species of oppositions time plays an important role, viz. in determining whether the sentences in each opposition divide the truth values (one true, the other false). Ammonius attributes to Aristotle the claim that, in regard to the division of truth values, the first three species always behave in the same way—regardless of time. The only case for which time makes a difference is the case of singular sentences. But contrary to what Ammonius says, this claim is not explicitly stated in Aristotle's text. Nor does it square with Aristotle's procedure in the passage in which the species of oppositions are quite secondary, whereas the contrast between the present or past (ἐπὶ μέν, 18a28) and the future (ἐπὶ δέ, 18a33) plays a pivotal role. It must be admitted, however, that the claim attributed to Aristotle is not foreign to what he says; on the contrary, it is its logical consequence.

Paragraph 2

Paragraph 2 outlines the behavior of 'diagonal' sentences and the opposition of undetermineds regarding the division of truth values. For this Ammonius uses the same method used in his commentary on chapter 7: he first determines the truth or falsity of these sentences in different modal matters to see whether the opposites can be true or false together or if they always divide the truth values. As far as the results of this analysis are concerned, Ammonius repeats what he said in his commentary on chapter 7. The only difference is that he strives to show that, in the three time dimensions, the three species of oppositions behave in the same way, and hence there is no reason to analyze them according to differences in time. Thus it is interesting to point out that he shows this—though hypothetically—even for the case where the negative undetermined sentence does not signify the same thing as the negative particular, but is equivalent to the negative general—a hypothesis that, nevertheless, he rejected in his commentary on chapter 7.

Paragraph 3

The subject of this paragraph is the behavior of pairs of opposing singular sentences with respect to the division of truth values. For determining this behavior, Ammonius uses, as before, the distinction in modal matters.

Ammonius stresses this at the beginning of the paragraph (130,1-11) because the opposition of singular sentences behaves differently in different times, unlike the three species of oppositions treated in paragraph 2. This proves true, however, only for the contingent matter, not for the necessary or impossible. In the latter two, the opposition of singular sentences behaves like the diagonals, i.e. they divide the true and the false regardless of the time to which they refer, and—as Ammonius stresses—in a 'definite' (ὡρισμένως) way. This expression, here encountered for the first time in Ammonius' text, we will be returning to later.

In contingent matter, the singular sentences behave in the same fashion, but only when they are about the present or past. The interesting case is the opposition of singular sentences regarding a future and contingent state of affairs. Ammonius develops Aristotle's claim on the subject saying that these sentences also divide the true and the false, but in a different way. For the latter he later will use the technical term 'in an infinite way' (ἀορίστως). This is the meaning he gives to Aristotle's phrase at 18a33-4: ἐπὶ δὲ τῶν καθ᾽ ἕκαστα καὶ μελλόντων οὐχ ὁμοίως 'But in the case of future singulars it is not the same', in allusion to the passage (among others) at 19a29-b4 at the end of chapter 9.

The meaning of the expression by which Ammonius denies the 'definite division of true and false' (διαιρεῖν ὡρισμένως τὸ ἀληθὲς καὶ τὸ ψεῦδος) is not clear. It can be interpreted in accordance with either the standard or non-standard interpretation. By the former, an SFCS does not possess a truth value until the realization of the event it is about, and the term ἀορίστως means that the truth value it will receive is not determinate before this moment. If, on the contrary, one follows the non-standard interpretation, the term ἀορίστως means that an SFCS can possibly have a truth value opposite to what it *de facto* possesses. Under this hypothesis an SFCS is, at the moment of its enunciation, already true or false, but in a contingent way.[164]

The text of paragraph 3 has been cited by defenders of the standard interpretation to show that Ammonius holds this line (D. Frede 1985, 45 note 26;

---

[164]   For these distinctions, cp. the essay in this volume '"In a Definite Way True". On the modalization of Truth-Values in Ammonius', where G. Seel tries to show that it is unlikely that Ammonius would be a supporter of the standard interpretation.

H. Weidemann 1993, 303; R. Gaskin 1995, 156-58). But—as G. Seel shows in the essay cited (cp. pp.241-242)—this paragraph does not offer a sufficient basis for such an interpretation.

What stands out most clearly in paragraph 3 is Ammonius' claim that Aristotle maintains that SFCSs divide their truth values, but in a different way than present or past singular statements (130,20-3). But the explication of this Ammonius gives later is compatible with the non-standard interpretation as well as the standard.

1. Ammonius says that before the moment the event the SFCS's are concerned with is actually realized, one cannot say *in a determinate way* which of the two sentences will be true and which will be false. Thus there are two possibilities for the distribution of truth values. But this does not necessarily mean that the SFCS's do not have truth values before the occurrence of the event. Ammonius only speaks of the ignorance of the speaker regarding the attribution of these values, an ignorance that can be explained by the fact that no SFCS possesses its truth value in a necessary way.[165]

2. The future ἀληθεύσει/ψεύσεται, 'will be true/will be false', could be interpreted as a way of indicating the fact that no SFCS has a truth value at the moment of its enunciation, but acquires it only at the (still future) moment of the actualization of the state of affairs it is about. In fact, Richard Sorabji (1998, 11) considers this the only 'source of support' for the standard interpretation. But it is also possible that what we have here—e.g. at 130,15 and 17—is merely a rhetorical use of the future tense[166] that has no temporal connotation, as we find at 130,15 and 17 as well.

3. Finally, Ammonius' claim that before the occurrence of the event both its actualization and its non-actualization are possible is also compatible with both interpretations. For according to the non-standard interpretation, the fact that one of the two sentences is true and that the predicted event will be actualized does not away with the fact that another outcome of the process going on in the world is equally possible. Therefore the decision between the standard and the non-standard interpretation must be based on better reasons.

Paragraph 4

In this paragraph, Ammonius shows the importance of the issue of future contingents for all the philosophical disciplines, viz. ethics, physics, logic and metaphysics.

---

[165]   R. Gaskin 1995, 157 argues that the sense of this passage cannot be merely epistemic. The argument he gives, i.e. that Ammonius has no interest in offering an epistemic reading of *Int.* 9, is, however, not very convincing.

[166]   This use is found e.g. in Plato, *Resp.* II 376c. Cp. also R. Gaskin 1995, 157 note 50.

Paragraph 5

At the beginning of the paragraph, Ammonius announces the exposition and resolution of two arguments for necessitarianism. These are a) the 'Reaper' Argument which he analyses in the present paragraph and b) the argument from divine knowledge which occupies the paragraphs 6 to 10. Ammonius characterises the first as 'based on the meaning of words' and the latter as 'more based on the nature of the things'. Neither argument is found in Aristotle.[167] This shows how much the commentary on Aristotle's text is a welcome opportunity to Ammonius to deal with necessitarianism quite generally and to offer an overall refutation of the arguments for necessitarianism found in Aristotle's text or elsewhere.[168]

The 'Reaper' Argument[169] (along with the arguments reported by Aristotle in *Int.* 9 and the 'Master' Argument) is one of the famous demonstrations of necessitarianism developed in ancient philosophy, probably among the school of Dialecticians.[170] It is in our text that one finds its most complete and probably also most authentic version. The two other sources of the text are (a) the commentary of Stephanus of Alexandria on *Int.* (*Stephani in librum Aristotelis de Interpretatione commentarium*, ed. Hayduck, Berlin 1885, 34,34-35,10); and (b) the commentary of an anonymous Neoplatonist (*Anonymi commentarius in Aristotelis de Interpretatione*, ed. L. Tarán under the title *Anonymous commentary on Aristotle's De Interpretatione [codex parisinus graecus 2064]*, Meisenheim am Glan 1978, 54,8-55,5 FDS 1253). Cicero, *De Fato* 21 very likely contains indirect testimony of the Reaper Argument since the reasoning there that 'preoccupied Epicurus' corresponds to the version given by Stephanus.

Ammonius presents the argument as an ἀπορία (131,20),[171] others place it in the class of sophisms (σοφίσματα).[172] As said in our Introduction, for Hellenistic philosophers an ἀπορία is a set of sentences, each evidently true by itself, but incompatible together. A sophism, on the other hand, is an apparently sound argument that has as its conclusion a sentence whose contradiction is evident.[173] For the Dialecticians and the Stoics, ἀπορίαι and sophisms were the subject of an

---

[167]   J. Vuillemin 1984, 157, note 11—wrongly—considers Ammonius' characterisation as referring to the two arguments for necessitarianism found in Aristotle.

[168]   Therefore R. Sorabji 1998, 3—rightly—calls Ammonius' commentary 'a treatise on determinism'.

[169]   A detailed analysis of the argument is found in G. Seel 1993.

[170]   Cp. A. Long and D. Sedley 1987, 234: 'The mowing argument, a clearly deterministic argument, issuing from Diodorus' dialectical school, which they apparently treated as a companion piece to the Master Argument ... .' Cp. also G. Seel 1993.

[171]   In his opusculum 'Συμπόσιον ἢ Λαπίθαι' Lucian mentions the 'reaper' together with the 'horned' and the 'sorites' as exemples of an ἀπορία (*Symposium* 23 [vol.1 p.153 MacLeod]; FDS 1208).

[172]   Cp. Diogenes Laertius, 7.44.

[173]   Concerning the Stoic definitions of ἀπορία and sophism, and their relation, cp. G. Seel 1993, who explains why the 'Reaper' was placed in these two classes.

endeavor they called λύσις, 'solution,' which involved, in the case of ἀπορία, showing that one of the conflicting sentences is false and, in the case of sophism, discovering the error made in deducing the false conclusion. In following this tradition, Ammonius strives to highlight the error made in the Reaper Argument and to show that the conclusion's contrary must be accepted. Nevertheless, he is wrong to consider this problem so easily solved (131,32). For one thing, such an easy solution contrasts sharply with the reputation the argument had in Antiquity, a reputation best illustrated by the story told by Diogenes Laertius (VII,25; FDS 107), that, in order to learn this argument from a certain dialectician, Zeno was ready to pay him double the price he was charging. It would be unwise, therefore, to underestimate the force of the argument by presenting it as a paralogism whose falsity is blindingly obvious.[174]

The argument is a two stage chain of syllogisms: (1) The first stage is found in the lines 131,25-31. It has the form of a syllogism involving two major premises P(I) and P(II) constructed in parallel (131,25-7), a minor premise P(III) introduced by an ἀλλὰ μὴν, 'but in fact...' (131,27-8), and a conclusion C(I) (131,28). The lines 131,28-31 give an explication of the resulting transition from premises to conclusion. (2) The conclusion of the first stage then forms the minor premise of the second stage, whose major premise is found in 131,31, and whose conclusion C(II) is reached in 131,31-2.

The interpretation we give of the argument calls for the following remarks:

(a) Ammonius' reasoning concerns a concrete example, viz. a peasant beginning to sow in the spring who is in a state of uncertainty as to whether he will reap in the autumn. The example is well chosen because it is in such a case that the hypothesis at issue, i.e. that a future event is contingent, is most likely true. If, then, one succeeds in proving the necessity of the future event even in this case, then a fortiori the contingency of any future event is refuted. Thus the argument about the reaper turns out to be a proof for universal necessitarianism, and it has always rightly been considered as such.

(b) Modern modal and temporal logic[175] customarily uses double temporal indexation, one index bearing on the modal operator, the other on the state of affairs in question. This clarification enables one to avoid the ambiguities that often confuse the discussion of determinism. The ancients, however, despite the fact they were not unaware of these distinctions, were unable to make use of this technique in formulating modal statements, and were generally content to use finite verbs (like ἐνδέχεται, 'it is possible...') with an infinitive, or nominal expressions (like ἀνάγκη, 'it is necessary...') with an infinitive, or adverbial expressions (like ἀναγκαίως, 'necessarily'). Thus the use of these expressions by

---

[174]   In R. Sorabji's reconstruction (1998, 4-5) the argument appears to be a plain fallacy resulting from the ambiguity of the term 'τάχα', though that ambiguity is not easy to discover.

[175]   Cp. N. Rescher and A. Urquhart 1971; C.E. Hughes and M.J. Cresswell 1968; A.N. Prior 1957 and 1967. For the application of this pr ocedure in the interpretation of Aristotle's theory of modalities see G. Seel 1982a, 190-256.

Ammonius does not allow us to know with certainty to which period of time or moment the modal operator and the state of affairs are meant to be related. This requires us to consider several possible interpretations each time they are used.

(c) One peculiarity of the argument is that to indicate modal operators two expressions are used that are rarely found in the context of modal theory, the adverbs τάχα and πάντως. Interpreting these two words poses a problem. According to Liddell & Scott, the adverb τάχα is used 'to express any sort of contingency from probability to bare possibility'. According to this explanation, the word τάχα with a finite verb can be considered equivalent to the finite form of ἐνδέχεσθαι with an infinitive. If the adverb τάχα expresses contingency, the opposite adverb πάντως can only indicate the necessity of the given event. There is, however, still another possibility for interpreting these two adverbs. As confirmed in a passage of Sextus Empiricus (P. I 194-5), the adverb τάχα serves to express the uncertainty (subjective or objective) as to the realization of a future state of affairs (ibid. 195). Consequently the opposite word (πάντως) expresses (subjective or objective) certainty concerning this event. If the context in which Ammonius uses these words is considered, one realizes that the first interpretation would render the Reaper Argument unimportant and its articulation in two stages useless since the argument's conclusion would be trivial and already reached at the end of the first stage. This is why we hold the second interpretation, taking the adverb τάχα as an expression of the objective state of indecision[176] about the issue of a process, and the adverb πάντως as an expression of the opposite state, i.e. where the issue is decided no matter what else happens.[177]

First Stage

From what we said above about the character of aporias and sophisms, it is clear that the premises of the argument should be formulated in such a way that, though they are untrue, they could be mistaken for true sentences. Let us first consider the two parallel premises P(I) and P(II), which are found in lines 131,25-7.

---

[176]   Cp. M. Mignucci in this volume, 264ff.

[177]   R. Sorabji 1998, 4-5 gives a different interpretation of the meaning of τάχα and πάντως. He thinks that both terms are ambiguous. The former can be used either to make a 'guarded statement' about a future event, or to state a present possibility. Consequently, the latter either serves to state something without any guard or expresses the necessity of an event. According to R. Sorabji the author of the argument takes advantage of this ambiguity to pass from the denial of a guarded statement to the affirmation of necessity. According to our interpretation, however, the argument does not simply exploit an ambiguity of the terms it uses, but is a serious proof of determinism and necessitarianism. R. Gaskin 1995, 353-54 also tries to determine the meaning of the terms involved in the 'Reaper'-Argument concentrating, though, his task on the meaning of πάντως. He thinks that it either 'simply reinforces' the future statement, without modalising it, or records the necessity of the future event. However, he avoids deciding this alternative.

By our interpretation,[178] P(I) says: 'If you are going to reap, it is not undecided whether you will reap or won't reap; it is decided that you will reap.' P(II) says: 'If you are not going to reap, it is not undecided whether you will reap or won't reap; it is decided that you won't reap.' Here our interpretation of τάχα and πάντως proves convincing. By the semantics we are adopting, it *prima facie* seems unacceptable to use at the same time and with the same subject the indicative alone and the indicative with τάχα. Now, the *antecedens* of P(I) poses the hypothesis that someone is going to reap. Under this hypothesis, one cannot say it is undecided whether he will reap or not, but one is obliged to say it is decided that he will reap. A similar account applies to P(II). The two premises thus are deemed analytically true as a function of the semantics of the expressions used. If, on the other hand, τάχα and πάντως were assumed to indicate contingency and necessity, P(I) and P(II) would be very strong synthetic affirmations, which adversaries of determinism would be little disposed to accept.

The problem mentioned in (b) still remains to be solved. In fact, we don't know whether the expression 'you are going to reap' must be read as (i) 'it is now a fact that you will be reaping at a given future moment'; or (ii) 'it will be a fact at a given moment in the future that you are reaping at that very moment in the future.' In the first case, the premise P(I) is read thus:[179]

---

[178] Our interpretation differs from the (neutral!) translation given in our presentation of the text.

[179] In our formalization, 'tn' indicates the present moment, 'tf' indicates a certain instant in the future. The symbol 'r' represents the state of affairs 'you are reaping'. Consequently, the expressions '$C_{tn}C_{tf}r$', '$U_{tn}C_{tf}r$', etc. do not represent propositions in the modern sense, but rather statements, which in their logical properties resemble the ἀξιώματα of the Stoics. Thus the symbols for logical connectives represent not so much modern connectives as those of Stoic logic. We use the following expressions in the senses indicated:

$C_{tn}C_{tf}r$: it is now a fact that you will be reaping at the future moment tf

$C_{tf}C_{tf}r$: it will be a fact at the future moment tf that you will be reaping at the moment tf

$U_{tn}C_{tf}r$: it is now undecided whether you will be reaping at the future moment tf

$U_{tf}C_{tf}r$: it will be undecided at the future moment tf whether you will be reaping at the moment tf

$D_{tn}C_{tf}r$: it is now decided that you will be reaping at the future moment tf

$D_{tf}C_{tf}r$: it will be decided at future moment t that you will be reaping at the moment tf

$K_{tn}C_{tf}r$: it is now possible but not necessary (contingent) that you will be reaping at the future moment tf

$K_{tf}C_{tf}r$: it will be possible but not necessary (contingent) that you will be reaping at the future moment tf

$N_{tn}C_{tf}r$: it is now necessary that you will be reaping at the future moment tf

$N_{tf}C_{tf}r$: it will be necessary at the future moment tf that you will be reaping at moment tf.

P(Ia) $C_{tn}C_{tf} r \rightarrow [\neg(U_{tn}C_{tf} r \cdot U_{tn}C_{tf} \sim r) \cdot D_{tn}C_{tf} r]$[180]

With the other reading, we obtain:

P(Ib) $C_{tf}C_{tf} r \rightarrow [\neg(U_{tf}C_{tf} r \cdot U_{tf}C_{tf} \sim r) \cdot D_{tf}C_{tf} r]$

The text itself does not permit us to decide between these. But if we consider the point of the argument, everything favors the first possibility. For with the reading (Ib), the premise I is surely true analytically, but it is difficult to see how any deterministic consequences flow from it. Moreover, with this reading, it is difficult to understand why the author would have chosen the future tense instead of the present. With reading (Ia), on the other hand, this choice is perfectly understandable: it is only about future events that one can reasonably ask whether or not their realization has already been decided at the present moment. Regarding this question, then, the first premise says that, if the future realization of the event is already a fact, the decision about its future realization now has already occurred. This claim, as we shall see again, has deterministic consequences. Moreover, there are semantic reasons that urge to accept it. This is why we prefer the reading P(Ia).

The same reasons are valid for the second premise, which we formulate thus:

P(IIa) $C_{tn}C_{tf} \sim r \rightarrow [\neg(U_{tn}C_{tf} r \cdot U_{tn}C_{tf} \sim r) \cdot D_{tn}C_{tf} \sim r]$

The third premise presents the same difficulties with regard to the temporal index. Here also we see two possible readings:

P(IIIa) $N(C_{tn}C_{tf} r \succ\!\!\prec C_{tn}C_{tf} \sim r)$ or
P(IIIb) $N(C_{tf}C_{tf} r \succ\!\!\prec C_{tf}C_{tf} \sim r)$

But arguments similar to those that led us to choose P(Ia) and P(IIa) favor P(IIIa). To be sure, P(IIIb) is not to be confused with $C_{tf}C_{tf} r \succ\!\!\prec \neg C_{tf}C_{tf} r$, which is a law of propositional logic and thus analytically true. But it is equivalent to this. Consequently, P(IIIb) is analytically true. It presents, however, a claim that is too weak to rest a demonstration of determinism on it. P(IIIa), on the other hand, is neither equivalent to $C_{tn}C_{tf} r \succ\!\!\prec \neg C_{tn}C_{tf} r$ nor can it be deduced from this tautology. Furthermore it contains a principle that is strong enough to give, along with P(Ia) and P(IIa) as supplementary premises, consequences that are deterministic. This is why we prefer P(IIIa). Moreover it is sufficiently evident at first glance to figure in an ἀπορία. Among the ancients, Aristotle—always according to the standard interpretation—and Epicurus[181] seem to be the only ones to have refuted it. Ammonius and the anonymous commentator have undoubtedly accepted it because they did not question it in their refutation of the 'Reaper' Argument. On

---

[180]   The text also admits of the following reading for P(Ia): $C_{tn}C_{tf}r \rightarrow [\neg U_{tn}C_{tf}r \cdot \neg U_{tn}C_{tf}\sim r \cdot D_{tn}C_{tf}r]$ P(Ia) can also be changed into a conjunction of two implications: $C_{tn}C_{tf}r \rightarrow \neg(U_{tn}C_{tf}r \cdot U_{tn}C_{tf}\sim r) \cdot C_{tn}C_{tf}r \rightarrow D_{tn}C_{tf}r$

[181]   Cp. Cicero, *De Fato* 21.

the other hand, it is not out of the question that a confusion between P(IIIa) and P(IIIb) may have favored the acceptance of P(IIIa).

After interpreting the premises in accordance with the first reading, it would be inconsistent to interpret the conclusion according to the second. As a result, we formulate it thus:

C(I) $\neg(U_{tn}C_{tf}\, r \bullet U_{tn}C_{tf} \sim r)$

The first stage of the demonstration, then, can be seen to have the following structure:

$$p \rightarrow q$$
$$r \rightarrow q$$
$$p \vee r$$
$$q$$

This type of argument is relatively common in ancient literature. M. Frede 1974, 182 mentions the following passages in Sextus: *P.* II 186; *M.* VIII 281-4; 292-6; 466-9; IX 205-6. A concise explanation for the deductive strength of this type of reasoning is also found in Sextus. He says (*P.* II 186-7) that dogmatics use the following reasoning: 'That which follows from two contradictory statements is not only true, but necessarily true.'

Ammonius, too, seems to have felt the need to explain the structure of the argument. In fact, he gives it a very enigmatic justification (131,28-31). He seems to presuppose a kind of logical space, in which the undecided state of affairs is to be found somewhere. Next, using the premisses of the argument, he successively narrows this space until there no longer remains any place for what is undecided. The logical space he starts from is defined by P(IIIa). Thus the undecidedness of the event must be compatible with one of the alternatives $C_{tn}C_{tf}\, r >\!-\!< C_{tn}C_{tf} \sim r$. But P(Ia) and P(IIa) preclude its compatibility with either of these, so the mode of undecidedness has no place any more.

One can also show that the argument is correct by following the procedure the Stoics called ἀνάλυσις, i.e. its reduction to Stoic indemonstrables. This has been done in regard to its general form by M. Frede 1974, 187. Thus the formal validity of the first stage of the 'Reaper' Argument cannot be doubted.

Second stage

The conclusion of the first stage, namely, the claim that it is now already decided whether or not you will be reaping, is not identical to the conclusion the author wants to lead us to, namely, the claim that there is no contingent event. To pass from one to the other, a supplementary principle is needed that establishes the logical relation between undecidedness and contingency. This principle is formulated in the brief remark (131,31) that it was the word 'perhaps' that introduced contingency.

The meaning of this remark is far from clear. We see three possibilities for interpreting it:

$$P(IVa) \quad (U_{tn}C_{tf}\, r \bullet U_{tn}C_{tf} \sim r) \leftrightarrow (K_{tn}C_{tf}\, r \bullet K_{tn}C_{tf} \sim r)$$
$$P(IVb) \quad (U_{tn}C_{tf}\, r \bullet U_{tn}C_{tf} \sim r) \rightarrow (K_{tn}C_{tf}\, r \bullet K_{tn}C_{tf} \sim r)$$
$$P(IVc) \quad (U_{tn}C_{tf}\, r \bullet U_{tn}C_{tf} \sim r) \leftarrow (K_{tn}C_{tf}\, r \bullet K_{tn}C_{tf} \sim r)$$

P(IVb) affirms that undecidedness regarding the realization of an event presupposes the contingency of the event. This claim is no doubt true because if a future event is necessary, it is no longer open whether or not it will be realized. But this reading has the disadvantage of not permitting the deduction of the necessitarian position. In fact, the negation of the antecedent of an implication does not entail the negation of the consequent. Thus from C(I) and P(IVb) we will not obtain the conclusion, expressed in 131,31-2, that the contingency of the future event is eliminated.

The reading according to P(IVc), on the other hand, allows this conclusion to be reached quite readily in accordance with the Stoic method of the second indemonstrable. But P(IVc) has not the plausibility of P(IVb). In fact, P(IVc) says that the future event is contingent only if its realization is not yet decided. If this were true, a future contingent event would lose its contingency at the moment its realization is decided. This, however, is difficult to accept because it denies that there are any contingent facts.[182]

We find ourselves, therefore, facing the following dilemma: either we hold to P(IVb) and hence deem the Reaper Argument fallacious despite its reputation in Antiquity, or else we accept P(IVc) as the sense intended in the remark at 131,31; but in this case the argument rests on a very strong assumption. Since in his refutation, Ammonius seems to accept P(IVc),[183] we hold this as the correct interpretation. With this hypothesis, we obtain the following polysyllogism as the interpretation of the Reaper Argument reported by Ammonius:

First stage:
$$P(Ia) \quad C_{tn}C_{tf}\, r \rightarrow [\neg(U_{tn}C_{tf}\, r \bullet U_{tn}C_{tf} \sim r) \bullet D_{tn}C_{tf}\, r]$$
$$P(IIa) \quad C_{tn}C_{tf} \sim r \rightarrow [\neg(U_{tn}C_{tf}\, r \bullet U_{tn}C_{tf} \sim r) \bullet D_{tn}C_{tf} \sim r]$$
$$P(IIIa) \quad N(C_{tn}C_{tf}\, r \succ\!\!\prec C_{tn}C_{tf} \sim r)$$

$$\overline{C(I) \quad \neg(U_{tn}C_{tf}\, r \bullet U_{tn}C_{tf} \sim r)}$$

Second stage:
$$P(IVc) \quad (U_{tn}C_{tf}\, r \bullet U_{tn}C_{tf} \sim r) \leftarrow (K_{tn}C_{tf}\, r \bullet K_{tn}C_{tf} \sim r)$$
$$C(I) \quad \neg(U_{tn}C_{tf}\, r \bullet U_{tn}C_{tf} \sim r)$$

$$\overline{C(II) \quad \neg(K_{tn}C_{tf}\, r \bullet K_{tn}C_{tf} \sim r)}$$

---

[182] It seems that Aristotle and Ammonius maintained this claim or a claim that comes very close to it. For both accepted the principle of necessity of facts, F(04). However, they distinguish conditioned necessity according to F(04) and unconditioned necessity. In the sense of the latter there are unnecessary facts. Cp. Ammonius, *In Int* 153,32-155,8.

[183] Cp. our commentary on chapter 9, paragraph 17 below pp.186-189.

In our interpretation, the argument of the reaper is confirmed formally correct.

The first stage of the argument already is a proof of determinism according to the definition of this term given in our Introduction (cp. p.19 above). Therefore, as I have argued elsewhere,[184] it is not excluded that the original version consisted of the first step alone. In fact, both Diodorus Cronus and the Stoics could have accepted the first step while they had semantic reasons to reject the second. So, the second step could have been added to the first by people who wanted to show that the Stoics could not escape necessitarianism given their deterministic convictions.

Refutation

The only way to refute a formally correct argument is to raise doubts about the truth at least of one of its premises. However, this is not what Ammonius actually does. Instead of refuting one of the premises of his adversaries he attacks their position directly, arguing first that it rests on a *petitio principii* and second that it is inconsistent.

Ammonius takes P(Ia) as starting point of his argument (131,33-4). He then sets up a complete disjunction with regard to the antecedent of this implication. The fact of reaping in the future is either a contingent fact or a necessary fact. This gives:

$$A(PV) \qquad C_{tn}C_{tf}r \rightarrow (N_{tn}C_{tf}r \rightarrowtail K_{tn}C_{tf}r)^{185}$$

This disjunction allows Ammonius to catch his opponents in a dilemma both of whose alternatives ($N_{tn}C_{tf}r$ and $K_{tn}C_{tf}r$) present, according to him, consequences unfavourable to their position. If they agree to the second alternative, they are accepting right from the beginning the anti-necessitarian position, that there are contingent facts. His adversaries, then, must choose the first. To this move Ammonius addresses a double criticism: First he reproaches his adversaries for committing a *petitio principii* (132,2-3) in doing so, second he argues that this thesis is incompatible with P(IIIa) (132,3-6). Let us evaluate these objections one after the other.

1. By urging his adversaries to reformulate their first premise specifying the mode of the future event Ammonius follows a strategy that will prove effective for the solution of Aristotle's ἀπορία as well (cp. pp.187f. below). In the present context this move allows him to avoid any decision whether to accept or reject the first premise and to push his adversaries to commit a *petitio principii*. The necessitarians, however, could answer this by sticking to their first premise and in turn asking Ammonius whether he accepts or rejects it. Consequently, they are not obliged to present their thesis as something one has to accept without argument as

---

[184]   Cp. G. Seel 1993.

[185]   It is clear that one could also formulate an analogous proposition for the second premise.

Ammonius claims, rather they may insist that they deduced this position in due form. In fact,—as Richard Sorabji rightly remarks (1998,5)—the author of the argument instead of simply assuming his thesis gives an argument that is supposed to prove his point. This argument, however, does not simply exploit an ambiguity of the term 'τάχα ', as Sorabji thinks,—in this case it would be a fallacy right from the beginning—it rather deduces this conclusion from the premises presumed in our reconstruction. Therefore Ammonius takes his task as too easy, by neglecting to criticise these premises.

Nevertheless it is revealing to ask which premise he would probably have objected to, had he tried to refute the argument in the normal way. As he certainly accepted P(IIIa) the only premises he could raise doubts about are P(Ia) and P(IIa) on the one hand and P(IVc) on the other. As we can see in his refutation of the second necessitarian argument reported by Aristotle (cp. *In Int.* 149,9-11 and our commentary on *In Int* 9, 145,9-19, pp.185ff. below), Ammonius denies that sentences affirming that a future contingent event will certainly (πάντως) occur tell the truth. The same point results from the last paragraph of his commentary on chapter 9 (cp. 154,34). We therefore have good reasons to think that he would have rejected P(Ia) and P(IIa). On the other hand, the very same passages let us surmise that he was prepared to accept that decided events are necessary events (cp. again 145,9-12 and 154,3-20 and our commentary p.186 and pp.203f.). This means that he would have to accept P(IVc).[186]

2. For Ammonius it was not enough to accuse his opponents of committing a *petitio principii*. He further tried to show that the conclusion of the argument is plainly false and that its adherents must accept the contrary. To succeed in this, he maintains that if one accepts the necessity of the event, one is no longer authorized to use P(IIIa) (132,3-6). He seems convinced that the necessity of an event precludes the disjunction between its realization and the realization of its contradictory: $N_{tn}C_{tf}$ r → ¬($C_{tn}C_{tf}$ r ⟩-⟨ $C_{tn}C_{tf}$ ~r).

In our opinion, Ammonius' claim rests on an ambiguity in the expression 'you will reap or you will not reap'. In everyday language, this expression very often amounts to 'perhaps you will reap, perhaps you will not reap' which, as we have seen, describes a state of indecision as to the realization of the future event. Taken this way, the expression is incompatible with the necessity of the fact in question. But if the 'or' in the expression is interpreted as a connective in propositional logic, the expression means either 'only one of both: you will reap or you will not reap' (exclusive 'or') or ' at least one of both: you will reap or you will not reap' (non-exclusive 'or'). Taken in one of these senses, the expression 'you will reap or you will not reap' is perfectly compatible with the necessity that you will reap.

To judge Ammonius' reproach, we must decide which meaning the author of the 'Reaper' Argument has probably given to the expression 'or' in the second

---

[186]   In G. Seel 1993, 316 I conjectured that Ammonius would have rejected P(IVc), but not P(Ia) and P(IIa). However, I do not think any more that this is correct.

premise. Now the everyday sense of the expression can be rejected. In fact, only an exclusive 'or' allows us to obtain the desired result by means of P(IIIa). Nor is it possible that the author would have allowed any ambiguity to hang over the meaning of 'or', as R. Sorabji (1998,5) seems to admit. If, as we have conjectured,[187] the Reaper Argument was fashioned by a Dialectician, the possibility its creator had not mastered the use of propositional connectives can virtually be eliminated. The Dialecticians are known as the fathers of propositional logic.[188] It is perhaps revealing that in P(IIIa) (131,28) we have an ἤτοι... ἤ ... ('either...or...', with ἤτοι as a mild emphatic), an expression Chrysippus had reserved for stating an exclusive disjunction in the technical sense, while Ammonius uses in his refutation (132,6) an ἤ ... ἤ ... ('either...or...'), which can easily be interpreted in the everyday sense. Further, it is surprising that Ammonius should have turned to such an argument, in view of the fact that he seems to have known the truth-functional definition of disjunction (cp. *In An. Pr*. 9,4; 68,30).

Thus Ammonius has not, as he supposes, refuted the argument of the reaper. He has neither shown that the necessitarian assumes his thesis by *petitio principii* nor demonstrated that it is incompatible with one of the premises of his argument. He has, however, introduced a strategy that allows him both to escape the cogs of his adversary's argument and to catch him in a dilemma in turn, in case he accepted this strategy. Of course, as well as Ammonius is under no constraint to accept the premises of the Reaper Argument, the author of the latter is not obliged to accept Ammonius' counter-strategy. This means that there is a deadlock in the debate. This at least Ammonius has achieved.

Paragraphs 6-10

This long passage is entirely devoted to the exposition and refutation of the argument for necessitarianism based on the knowledge of the gods. The size of this exposition shows the complexity and importance of this argument. It is probably Stoic in origin.[189] The passage is divided thus: (a) exposition and explication of the argument (paragraphs 6-8); (b) refutation of the argument (paragraphs 9-11).

(a) The structure of the argument is as follows:

---

[187]   Cp. G. Seel 1993.

[188]   Cp. T. Ebert 1991.

[189]   Cp. the evidence from the anonymous commentary on *De Interpretatione*, L. Tarán, op. cit. p. 54, 8-11, and particularly Alexander of Aphrodisias, *De Fato*, 30, 200. 12ff. Cp. also Calcidius, *In Tim*., ch. 169. The form given here is however later, because it presupposes the distinction between definite and indefinite foreknowledge we find in Iamblichus. R. Sharples drew my attention to this point. See also Richard Sorabji 1998, 5.

(1) The starting point is the complete disjunction of the three following propositions:

A: The gods know contingent events in a definite manner.

B: The gods do not know all contingent events.

C: The gods know contingent events in the way that men know them, i.e. in an indefinite manner.[190]

Thus we get: A ∨ B ∨ C.

(2) Then we proceed through a meandering argument to a reduction to the absurd of 'B' and 'C' (132,21).

(3) Finally the truth of 'A' is inferred from the impossibility of 'B' and 'C', by *tollendo ponens* (134,2).

(4) This conclusion from the first syllogism is treated as a premise in a second argument whose conclusion is the thesis of universal necessitarianism. To reach it, a supplementary premise is needed according to which the definite knowledge of presumably contingent events implies their necessity:

This premise is stated and defended in the passage at 135,1-7. The argument advanced for this claim consists in showing that supposing an event known by the gods does not come about implies the gods are deceived about this event, which contradicts A (cp. 135,7).

(5) From A and this second premise, one could directly infer universal necessitarianism. But the author of the argument has chosen to turn once again to a demonstration through *tollendo ponens*. For this he sets up the following disjunction: either all events come about necessarily and corresponding to divine knowledge, or not all events are known by the gods. This disjunction results from the argument for the claim that divine knowledge implies necessitarianism. Since the first half of the disjunction results in the contingent being done away with, the impossibility of the second half, which has been demonstrated in the first syllogism, is sufficient for proving universal necessitarianism.

(b) The refutation of the argument occupies paragraphs 9-11. As Ammonius notes (135,4), it is borrowed from Iamblichus. To refute the conclusion of a demonstration, there are two alternatives: one can either deny that the reasoning was correct, or question the material truth of the premises used. Since Ammonius apparently considers the reasoning of the second proof correct, it remains for him to call into question one of the premises. As we shall see in detail, the premise he attacks says that the definite knowledge of events possessed by the gods implies universal necessitarianism, i.e. $A\rightarrow(p)(Cp\rightarrow NCp)$.

To refute this claim, Ammonius begins with distinctions commonly accepted in Neoplatonism, between different levels of knowing and different levels of things known.[191] Regarding these levels, he distinguishes three possible cases: (i) the level of knowing is superior to the level of the known; (ii) the level of

---

190   As 133,29 and 133,16 show, Ammonius means by 'indefinite knowledge' conjectural knowledge. Cp. R. Sorabji 1998, 5.

191   Among the Neoplatonists Plotinus and Porphyry seem to ignore this distinction; the first to have used it was Iamblichus. Cp. R. Sorabji 1998, 5 note 13.

knowing is equal to the level of the known; (iii) the level of the knowing is inferior to the level of the known. The introduction and explication of these cases occupies *paragraph 9*.

In *paragraph 10* (136,1-137,11), Ammonius refutes the claim itself. As a first step, he applies the theory of levels of knowing/known to the case of divine knowledge of contingents, saying (136,11-2) that this is an instance of (i). On this basis, Ammonius infers that contingent states of affairs have an indefinite nature and can thus come to be the case or not, while the gods know them in a definite way. If this is conceded, one must accept Ammonius' conclusion: the fact the gods know in a definite way the things we call contingent does not imply that those things are actualized necessarily.

With this result, the goal of the demonstration is reached. Nevertheless, Ammonius gives an additional argument based on a principle held by Aristotle as well. According to this principle, the statement affirming a fact is true because the fact is actualized, but the fact does not owe its actualization to the truth of the statement (cp. 149,25-8). By the same token, the definite knowledge the gods have of an event is not the cause of its necessary actualization; on the contrary, the gods know an event because it is actualized (cp. 136,27-30). But how can the gods have a definite knowledge of an indefinite event? Ammonius has an explanation for this that is quite satisfactory. In time, there exists a limit beyond which the event loses its indefinite character. In effect, when the instant to which the event is tied has become the present instant, the formerly open question of whether the event will be actualized or not is decided, as the ontological law of non-contradiction plainly demands. Since the gods have a non-temporal knowledge of what happens at every instant, they know all at once both that the actualization of the event is indefinite until its instant becomes the present instant and that then its actualization is definite. Thus they have definite knowledge of the former indefinite event having become definite.

Ammonius tries to render the theory of definite knowledge of the indefinite more plausible by noting that man can also, in particular cases, have a definite knowledge of an indefinite fact. But the example he gives shows that this is only possible when the fact is no longer indefinite in the strict sense of the word but made definite by anterior causes. The movement of a sphere on a plane can be contingent in the omnitemporal sense of the term, but once the plane is inclined the movement becomes inevitable and can hence be known in a definite way. Ammonius, then, seems to allow that facts tied to a precise instant can change their modalities. He accepts the following formula:

> There are states of affairs p and moments t', t" and t''' such that it is contingent at t' that p is the case at t''', but necessary at t" that p is the case at t'''.
>
> $\exists p \exists t' \exists t'' \exists t''' [t' < t'' < t''' \to (K_{t'} C_{t'''} p \bullet N_{t''} C_{t'''} p)]$

The analogy of this example with divine knowledge, however, is precarious because we have a definite knowledge of the contingent only when the contingent is no longer indefinite, whereas the gods have this knowledge in a timeless manner.[192]

In summary paragraph 10 contains three important claims:

1. The definite character of the knowing does not imply the definite character of the known.
2. The indefinite character of the known does not entail the indefinite character of the knowing.
3. The states of affairs which are contingent (in the omnitemporal sense of the term) can change their temporal modal status.

Taken together, these three claims are sufficient to refute the second argument for necessitarianism.

What are the conclusions to be drawn from Ammonius' arguments in paragraphs 9-12 concerning the question of whether an SFCS possesses a truth value? Three levels must be distinguished in Ammonius' discussion:

1. The level of knowledge that gods or men have of events.
2. The level of statements through which this knowledge is articulated (at least) by humans.
3. The level of states of affairs the statements are about and which are the objects of the knowledge.

In the paragraphs we have analyzed, Ammonius does not speak of sentences or their truth values, but only of levels 1 and 3. Further, it is very doubtful that divine knowledge exists in the form of sentences or statements, because Ammonius, following the Platonic tradition, characterizes it as 'one, determinate and immutable' (*In Int.* 135,3). In any case divine knowledge does not exist in the form of past, present or future tense sentences, because the gods know 'divisible (μεριστά) things indivisibly (ἀμερίστως) and without extension (ἀδιαστάτως), as well as multiplied (πεπληθυσμένα) things by a single act (ἐνοειδῶς), temporal (ἔγχρονα) things eternally (αἰωνίως), and generated (γεννητά) things ungeneratedly (ἀγεννήτως)' (136,15-7). Thus we cannot move immediately from the description of divine knowledge to attributing truth values to SFCSs. It is, however, possible to surmise such a conclusion from a consideration of the relation between the first and third levels. The gods knowing in an atemporal and determinate way a contingent event that for humans is a future event presupposes that that event is a fact. For it is due to its status as a fact that the gods can know it. Thus Ammonius emphasizes: 'But since, having a contingent and ambiguous nature, they [events] will have an end (πέρας) which will in any case (πάντως) be either so or so, it is necessary that the gods know how they will occur' (136,27-30). Although Ammonius uses future tense here saying 'how they will occur', this is not to say that he believes the gods use this type of sentence: he is simply translating divine knowledge into human language. But at any rate, the fact he considers that

---

temporal and uncertain human statements correspond to atemporal and certain divine knowledge concerning the same fact allows us to draw from Ammonius' claims a conclusion regarding the former. If what the gods know is an event which, from our perspective, is situated in the future such that, from our perspective, there is a present fact about a future event, the human statement predicting this event will not be deprived of a truth value, unless one holds that only an event that is simultaneous with the statement can function as its 'truthmaker'. But this is not Ammonius' position (cp. Seel's essay in this volume, pp.238ff.). Thus, regarding the three levels, we have the following situation:

1. On the level of knowledge, there is:
   (a) a divine knowledge that is atemporal and definite (the gods know the outcome of a course of events), but does not take the form of a sentence, and
   (b) a human knowledge that is temporal and indefinite, i.e. only conjectural (we do not know for sure which outcome the course of events has, nor do we know for sure which of two SFCSs is true).
2. On the level of sentences, we have two contradictory SFCSs, each of which has a truth value. The statement correctly predicting the event is true, the other false. This truth-value, however, is only an indefinite one, because the predicted event is contingent.
3. On the level of facts there is a fact about a contingent event tied to a precise moment which is, from the human perspective, situated in the future. This fact is from the human perspective an 'indefinite' fact about a future event and from the divine perspective a 'definite' fact (137,1) about a temporally ordered event.

Paragraph 11

Paragraph 11 is devoted to the exposition of two arguments against necessitarianism. The first is presented as a twofold response to an anonymous objection to Ammonius' claim that the gods know contingent events in a definite way. According to Ammonius, some have tried to refute this claim by noting the ambiguity of oracles.[193] To this Syrianus, whose authority Ammonius cites here, would make two objections: (1) that whatever can be said about oracles would not be valid for divine knowledge itself (137,16-7) and (2) that by rendering the oracles ambiguous the gods involve our intelligence and treat us as self-movers, which in itself excludes determinism (137,20-5).

---

[193]   Cp. Alexander, *De Fato* 29, 200,4-12 (Bruns), who gives an example of such ambiguity; though the case Alexander is referring to concerns prophecies deliberately left vague to avoid that people hearing them will do the opposite. I owe this precision to R. Sharples.

The second argument is a refutation of necessitarianism Ammonius carries out by raising a dilemma. Since it concerns an enthymeme that is not clearly expressed, we first suggest a reconstruction.

Ammonius considers a particular kind of event: the act of forming or stating an opinion about necessitarianism. Let us call this kind of event (OD). He first distinguishes two species of this kind of event:

(N) x affirms at moment y that all events are necessary (ὅτι πάντα ἠνάγκασται, 137,26-7).

(L) x affirms at moment y that many events are in our power (ὅτι πολλά ἐστιν ἐφ' ἡμῖν, 137,29-30).

As we shall see, for Ammonius (L) implies the more general claim that there are contingent events. This contradicts the claim found in (N). Since Ammonius intends to refute the latter, it would have been more consequent for him to describe the event opposed to (N) as the affirmation of the contradictory claim. This would be the event (C):

(C) x affirms at moment y that there are some contingent events.

Ammonius then asks which of the following two claims is made by the adherents of necessitarianism, implying that necessitarians have only two alternatives:

Claim (I)   Events of type (N) are necessary.
Claim (II) Events of type (OD) are in our power.

Since Ammonius clearly wants to construct a dilemma, and since it is essential for this type of argument that the disjunction it depends on be complete, he could have formulated the alternatives better by precluding any third possibility from the start. He should have been careful to ensure that the subjects be identical and the predicates contradictory, as in these two pairs of claims:

(I')   (OD) events are necessary.
(II') (OD) events are contingent.
(I")   (N) events are necessary.
(II") (N) events are contingent.

Ammonius' choice of pair (I)-(II) instead of the latter two pairs can be explained, however, by the following convictions that one can assume he holds:

(a) Events of type (OD) all possess the same modality, whatever the contents of the given opinion.

(b) An event of type (OD) is contingent if and only if its actualization is in our power.

In effect, if these claims are correct, the defect in the formulation of the alternatives, which we have criticized, has no negative consequences for the construction of the dilemma.

Next, Ammonius can show (137,28-30) that both possibilities (I) and (II) present problems for the necessitarians. If they maintain claim (II), they accept a particular case of what necessitarianism denies in general and thus contradict themselves. If, on the other hand, they were to hold claim (I), they cannot explain how some can hold the opposite of necessitarianism, i.e. how events of type (L) are possible. Since there are in fact such events, the necessitarian is defeated in the case of the second possibility as well.

One may doubt, however, whether Ammonius' argument truly reaches its goal. While the conclusion drawn from the second leg of the dilemma is quite clear, it is difficult to see why the necessitarians could not explain type (L) events as necessary events on the same footing as type (N) events. Obviously for this reason Ammonius adds (137,30-2) an argument that purports to reduce to absurdity any such explanation. If the events of type (L) were necessary, it would be because of nature's necessary chain of cause and effect that we would be compelled to deny our acts were products of nature and to attribute them wrongly to ourselves. Ammonius regards this as preposterous. He is assuming that nature pursues her own ends without doing anything contrary to them, a claim that was widespread in antiquity[194] and which Ammonius explicitly states in our text at 138,5-6.

It must be asked, however, whether it is truly a consequence of the necessitarian position that nature contradicts herself. The Stoics could raise two objections: (1) Whoever asserts that our actions are in our power, i.e. who produces an (L) event, is not compelled to deny that they are necessities due to fate. In fact, the Stoics argue that an action can be entirely in our power (ἐφ' ἡμῖν) and at the same time be an effect of the causal chain (of fate). To do this, they give a weak meaning to the phrase 'in our power' and they regard fate as the causal chain that in fact determines interior events (e.g. assent to a theoretical or practical axiom) as well as exterior. In fact, for an action to be considered within our power it is enough, according to them, to exclude the case either of an exterior cause preventing us from accomplishing it, or of it being accomplished without our intervention. Its being accomplished with our deliberate cooperation does not preclude the possibility that the internal cause triggering it (our assent to a practical axiom) is itself the effect of a prior cause (our character) that is necessary.[195] Thus, in producing by necessity both (N) events and (L) events, nature would not produce neither contradictory nor false opinions. (2) But even if the opinions formed in (L) events were false, nature would not necessarily act

---

[194]   That nature does nothing in vain can be found in Plato, *Tim.* 33d; it is one of the principles of Aristotelian physics. Cp., for example, *PA* 2.13, 658a8; 3.1, 661b23; 4.12, 694a15; *De Anima* 3.7 431a31, 432b21-23, 434a31-32. See A. Mansion 1945, 234, n. 26. Alexander of Aphrodisias, *De Fato* 11, 179, 24-26 (Bruns), notes that it was accepted by nearly all philosophers (the Epicureans would be an exception). Alexander already connects the principle with the problem of deliberation. This principle was adopted by all Neoplatonists as well. For references in Proclus and other Neoplatonists cp. the note in A.-P. Segonds (1985/86) vol. 2, 383 n.2 and 226.

[195]   For the Stoic conception of 'that which depends on us' and its relation to the concept of fate see S. Bobzien 1998a, 276-314.

against her own ends by producing them. For the erroneous opinions held by some that their actions are in their power could cause their decision to bring about certain ends and thus cause the actions leading to these ends that nature could not attain in any other way. Therefore by producing false opinions in us nature could perfectly well be promoting her own ends. If this is true, it would not be absurd for nature, acting by necessity, to bring about false opinions as one of its ways of actualizing the totality of events. To the latter objection Ammonius could answer—as he actually does in paragraph 19, 148, 22ff—that in this case to promote her ends nature has at her disposal better means than deliberation and choice, namely natural impulse. So, by producing (L) events she would do something in vain.[196]

Paragraph 12

In the last paragraph concerning the first lemma, Ammonius resumes the commentary proper on this passage of Aristotle. It is mostly a restatement of what he said in paragraphs 1-3 and particularly paragraph 3. In paragraph 12, however, Ammonius follows Aristotle's text more closely.[197]

It is interesting to see what, if anything, paragraph 12 contributes that is new. We emphasize the following points:

(1) Ammonius says again that, according to Aristotle, (a) the pairs of sentences on the diagonals divide the truth values (one statement true, one false) (138,15-9) and (b) they do so in a definite manner when they are past or present. He adds that this indicates that either the affirmative sentence is true and the negative is false or the reverse (138,21-2).

(2) Ammonius stresses once again that the division of the truth-values is indefinite when the sentences are future and in contingent matter (139,13-5).

(3) Regarding the meaning of the 'in a definite/indefinite way' distinction, we learn nothing new. He says once again that one cannot know, before the end of a process, which of the two types of possible events will be actualized when the sentences about such an event divide truth values in an indefinite way. This is compatible with the standard interpretation as well as with the non-standard (see Seel's essay in this volume, 241f.).

(4) The only truly new item is the interpretation Ammonius gives the term μέλλον in Aristotle's text. Ammonius holds that here, as in GC (2.11, 337b3-7), Aristotle uses the term μέλλον, as opposed to ἐσόμενον, to mean 'what can either occur or not occur', while ἐσόμενον means 'what will occur, whatever happens' (139,2-6). Now, as Talanga (1968a, 82) has shown, it is doubtful that Aristotle uses the term μέλλον in Int. in the sense introduced in GC. But even if Ammonius

---

[196]   Cp. our commentary on paragraph 19, p.193f.

[197]   This is a remainder of the oral lecture format, in which there is a division between the explication of the doctrine (θεωρία) and the interpretation of the words (λέξις) (cp. D. Blank 1996, Introduction, p. 3, note 17)

wrongly bases his argument on Aristotle's terminology, his claim that chapter 9 is concerned with the distribution of truth values in SFCSs remains true.

Lemma 2 (18a34-9)

The second lemma contains the beginning of the 'proof' for necessitarianism reported by Aristotle. According to Ammonius, this proof is divided into two steps: (a) The first is from 18a34 to 18b9. This step contains two lemmata (2 and 3) in accordance with the principles we will explain below. (b) The second step (18b9-25) Ammonius also divides into two lemmata (4 and 5). He thinks that each of the two steps contains a proof for necessitarianism, but he considers the second more convincing than the first.

Most contemporary interpretations divide Aristotle's text in the same way as Ammonius. The only one proposing a different division is Weidemann's (1994, 240), who understands the passage at 18a34-b4 as an argument preparing the way for the two actual proofs (more properly speaking) for necessitarianism. According to him, these proofs are found at 18b5-9 and 18b9-16.

It is clear that Aristotle does not take the necessitarian argument at face value, but reports it in order to refute it. Ammonius understands this well, showing more discernment than many interpreters, ancient and modern.[198]

It has not been clearly established, however, precisely what constitutes the argument and what the refutation. To evaluate Ammonius' reconstruction of the argument, we must compare it to the standard interpretation. For this, it will be useful first of all to sketch out the general lines of the latter.

Aristotle's argument on the standard interpretation

After denying at 18a33-4 the validity of principles T(10) and T(13) for SFCSs, it says, Aristotle tries to prove their nonvalidity by a *reductio ad absurdum*. To do this, he tries to show (at 18a34-b16) that the universal validity of these principles has necessitarian consequences. These consequences are established through a bridge principle that, in the form of an implication, links necessitarianism to these two principles. According to the standard interpretation Aristotle states this fundamental bridge principle in lines 18a34-5. Experts in the standard interpretation do not agree on the interpretation of these lines (see below). But the reading that is closest to Aristotle's text[199] is clearly the following, which apparently has been adopted by Ackrill as well:

---

[198]   Cicero, for example portrays Aristotle as a determinist (cp. *De Fato* 39 and R. Sharples' commentary (1991, 186)).

[199]   We must, however, take into consideration the variant readings of the text that has come down to us.

C(31) If every sentence is either true or false, every state of affairs is either
necessary or impossible

$$\{(T[Cp] \bullet F[C{\sim}p]) \succ{\prec} (T[C{\sim}p] \bullet F[Cp])\} \rightarrow (NCp \succ{\prec} NC{\sim}p).^{200}$$

Regarding the demonstration of this claim, the standard interpretation holds that
Aristotle deduces it from principle T(11)/T(13) (stated at 18a35-7 for future
sentences), principle C(01) (stated negatively by Aristotle at 18b2-3) and
principle T(10) (stated at 18b11-13).

C(01) Necessarily: The sentence 'It is the case that p' is true if and only if it
is the case that p

$$N\{(T[Cp] \leftrightarrow Cp) \bullet (T[(C{\sim}p] \leftrightarrow C{\sim}p) \bullet (F[Cp] \leftrightarrow {\neg}Cp) \bullet (F[C{\sim}p] \leftrightarrow {\neg}C{\sim}p)\}$$

Aristotle's argument according to Ammonius

In order to understand Ammonius' commentary, it is of the greatest importance to
see that, unlike the standard interpretation, he does not begin with the assumption
that principles T(10) and T(11)/T(13) have necessitarian consequences for
Aristotle. What does have necessitarian consequences according to him is the
stronger version of the two principles:

T(9) Necessarily every proposition is either in a definite way true or in a
definite way false (Principle of definite bivalence)

$$N\{T_d[Cp] \succ{\prec} F_d[Cp]) \bullet (T_d[C{\sim}p]) \succ{\prec} F_d[C{\sim}p])\}$$

and:

T(15) Necessarily in any contradiction, one side is determinately true and
the other is determinately false:

$$N\{(T_d[Cp] \bullet F_d[C{\sim}p]) \succ{\prec} (T_d[C{\sim}p] \bullet F_d[Cp])\}.$$

In order to deduce necessitarian consequences from these principles, Ammonius
uses a bridge principle different from C(31) that he believes is found at 18a34-5.
As we shall see, this principle is C(03) which is a feebler version of C(01):

$$C(03) \ N\{(T[Cp] \rightarrow Cp) \bullet (T[C{\sim}p] \rightarrow C{\sim}p) \bullet (F[Cp] \rightarrow {\neg}Cp) \bullet (F[C{\sim}p] \rightarrow {\neg}C{\sim}p)\}.$$

---

[200]   Cp. D. Frede 1970, 13-17; 1985, 37ff., J.L. Ackrill 1963, 135 and F. von Kutschera
1986, 212. To render this formulation symbolically, we use a symbolism different
from these authors'. It is clear that Aristotle's text permits a weaker interpretation of
the consequent in which the necessity is not divided, viz. N[Cp $\succ{\prec}$ C$\sim$p]. But since
this reading does not allow the deduction of necessitarianism, it is understandable
that Ackrill and Frede set it aside. The only one among those holding the standard
interpretation to give to the thesis a weaker meaning is H. Weidemann (1954,
230-3). He understands ἀνάγκη ('necessary') at 18a35 to have the sense of
necessitas consequentiae and reads: N[(T[Cp] $\succ{\prec}$ F[Cp]) $\bullet$ (T[C$\sim$p] $\succ{\prec}$ F[C$\sim$p]) $\rightarrow$
(Cp $\succ{\prec}$ C$\sim$p)].

Moreover, for the deduction of necessitarianism Ammonius depends on the semantics of the predicates 'definitely true' and 'definitely false'.[201]

If Ammonius were right on this point, Aristotle, in order to escape necessitarianism, would have no need to reject the universal validity of principles T(10) and T(11)/T(13); it would be sufficient to attack their definite versions, T(9) and T(15).

Thus it is quite natural that the interpretation Ammonius gives lemmata 2-7 starts from the hypothesis that the *reductio ad absurdum* deployed here is aimed at the latter two principles. We find the first confirmation of this in the commentary on lemma 2, which we analyze now.

Paragraph 13

The commentary on the second lemma takes up only one paragraph. As we shall see once again, Ammonius does not stay within the strict bounds of either lemma 2 or 3, using in his commentary on lemma 2 principles found only in lemma 3. He in fact believes lemma 3 to be a confirmation of the demonstration in lemma 2 and he holds that lemma 2 contains the first complete version of the proof for necessitarianism. As we have seen, this belief is not compatible with the standard interpretation,[202] which instead holds that the first version of the proof does not reach its end until 18b5-9. On the other hand, Ammonius reconstructs a complete argument for necessitarianism in his commentary on lemma 2.

To do this he proceeds in the following way:

1. He first tries to find in the lemma principles from which the necessitarian claim can be demonstrated. First, he succeeds in identifying the principle of implication of facts by the truth of sentences that express them, C(03) (139,29-30), and the principle of the division of truth values which he here calls 'principle of contradiction', T(11) (139,32-140,1).

2. He next explains the proof that, according to him, Aristotle gives for the latter principle (140,1-11).

3. Since Ammonius is convinced that only the definite version of the principle of division of truth values, T(15), permits the demonstration of necessitarianism, he conjectures that Aristotle must be intending this version in his formulation of the principle, though Aristotle himself never mentions definite truth values (140,11-13).

4. Next (140,13-21) he tries to defend this conjecture by demonstrating that necessitarianism actually follows from the definite version of this principle.

Let us consider these points in detail:

1. The first difficulty with Ammonius' commentary results from his reading of lines 18a34-5. Taken literally, this passage indicates principle C(31), if ἀνάγκη

---

201   For a clarification of these semantics cp. G. Seel's second article in the present volume.

202   Cp. H. Weidemann 1994, 240.

('necessity') is taken distributively, or principle C(32), if one chooses non-distributed necessity, or principle C(34), if it is assumed that ἀνάγκη only express *necessitas consequentiae*[203]:

C(31) $\{(T[Cp] \bullet F[C\sim p]) \succ\!\!\prec (T[C\sim p] \bullet F[Cp])\} \rightarrow (NCp \succ\!\!\prec NC\sim p)$

C(32) $\{(T[Cp] \bullet F[C\sim p]) \succ\!\!\prec (T[C\sim p] \bullet F[Cp])\} \rightarrow N(Cp \succ\!\!\prec C\sim p),$

C(34) $N(\{(T[Cp] \bullet F[C\sim p]) \succ\!\!\prec (T[C\sim p] \bullet F[Cp])\} \rightarrow (Cp \succ\!\!\prec C\sim p)).$

But, surprisingly enough, Ammonius is reading (if we consider only paragraph 13) in these lines either principle C(03), or principle C(21):

C(03) $N\{(T[Cp] \rightarrow Cp) \bullet (T[C\sim p] \rightarrow C\sim p) \bullet (F[Cp] \rightarrow \neg Cp) \bullet (F[C\sim p] \rightarrow \neg C\sim p)\}.$

C(21) $(T[Cp] \rightarrow NCp) \bullet (T[C\sim p] \rightarrow NC\sim p) \bullet (F[Cp] \rightarrow N\neg Cp) \bullet (F[C\sim p] \rightarrow N\neg C\sim p).$

This reading does not correspond with what Aristotle's text literally says and, worse, gives it a stronger meaning than what is actually expressed, since C(03) is stronger than C(34) and C(21) is stronger than C(31).

D. Frede 1970, 17 and H. Weidemann 1994, 231, however, have argued that the meaning of 18a34-5 is not meant to be limited to C(31) or C(32) or C(34) but that the context suggests that Aristotle wants to establish a relation between the truth value of a sentence and the modality of the fact it states. As to the alternative between C(03) and C(21), Frede defends the latter while Weidemann chooses the former.

Oddly enough, both opponents cite Ammonius to justify their readings of Aristotle. Thus D. Frede 1985, 43 thinks the passage 139,29-32 must be read with the meaning of C(21), while Weidemann holds that Ammonius clearly is intending to state C(03). He acknowledges, however, that Ammonius does not clearly distinguish between C(03) and C(21) so that he attributes to C(03) the consequences that in reality only follow from C(21).

In our opinion, neither interpreter correctly grasps Ammonius' program here. Weidemann is right when he holds that the text (not only at 139,21-32 but also at 140,17-20, where the principle is stated a second time)[204] speaks clearly in favor of C(03) over C(21). He is wrong, however, in believing that Ammonius needs C(21) in order to draw the necessitarian conclusions he reaches in the second part of the paragraph. In fact, as we will see in (4), Ammonius' conception of the difference between definite and indefinite truth values allows him to reach necessitarian conclusions on the basis of principles C(03) and T(15) as well. Besides, if Ammonius accepted C(21) as a reading of 18a34-5, his distinction between a definite and indefinite division of truth values would not allow him to avoid necessitarianism, because according to C(21) the mere truth of a sentence implies the necessity of the fact it states. To be sure, our analysis presupposes our way of interpreting this distinction and is no longer useful if one accepts the

---

[203]   For these possibilities, cp. D. Frede 1970, 17; 1985, 43 and H. Weidemann 1994, 229-31.

[204]   Cp. also 140,32-4; 141,8-10; 146,18-19.

standard interpretation. But there are good reasons we have drawn upon, outside of the context of chapter 9, to reject the standard interpretation on this point. For all these reasons we retain C(03) as the precise formulation of the principle Ammonius believes can be read in Aristotle at 18a34-5.

Our interpretation of the second principle extracted by Ammonius, i.e. the principle of the division of truth values,[205] itself requires an explanation and justification regarding several unsettled points. Ammonius formulates this principle, first of all, with neutral truth values in faithfully adopting the expressions used by Aristotle. Taken literally, then, the text contains:

$$\text{T(13)} \qquad N\{(T[Cp] \bullet F[C{\sim}p]) \succ\!\!\!\prec (F[Cp] \bullet T[C{\sim}p])\}$$

In 140,13, however, Ammonius holds that Aristotle must be implying in his formulation of this principle that the truth values here are all definite values. Thus according to Ammonius, the principle that must be presupposed in the proof for necessitarianism is in fact:

$$\text{T(15)} \qquad N\{(T_d[Cp] \bullet F_d[C{\sim}p]) \succ\!\!\!\prec (T_d[C{\sim}p] \bullet F_d[Cp])\}.$$

It is in effect the confusion between T(13), which is an entirely anodyne principle, and the strong principle T(15) that according to Ammonius accounts for the degree of persuasion the argument yields. In Ammonius' text the latter is formulated and proved only for SFCSs. But since for the other types of sentences it is valid anyway, we can formulate it in a universal way, as in T(15).

The second point needing clarification is Ammonius' use of the expression ἀξίωμα τῆς ἀντιφάσεως, 'axiom of contradiction,' to indicate this principle. According to today's use, the principle of contradiction (better: of non-contradiction) says that two statements that contradict each other cannot be true together:

$$\text{T(05)} \qquad {\neg}P(T[Cp] \bullet T[C{\sim}p]).$$

The principle of division of truth values, on the other hand, is written thus:

$$\text{T(13)} \qquad N\{(T[Cp] \bullet F[C{\sim}p]) \succ\!\!\!\prec (F[Cp] \bullet T[C{\sim}p])\}.$$

The two formulas are not equivalent, the former being compatible with the co-falsity of [Cp] and [C~p]. But one must not forget that those in the Neoplatonic school had the habit of using the expression ἀξίωμα τῆς ἀντιφάσεως to designate the conjunction of the principle of non-contradiction and the principle of the excluded middle, T(04). This conjunction is written:

$$\text{T(12)} \qquad {\neg}P(T[Cp] \bullet T[C{\sim}p]) \bullet {\neg}P(F[Cp] \bullet F[C{\sim}p]).$$

Now this conjunction is equivalent to the principle of the division of truth values, unless there is the possibility—which the standard interpretation allows—that a

---

[205] That one can speak of definite truth values, and not only a definite division of truth values seems clear from 141,18-23 and 31-34.

sentence might neither be true nor false, but neutral. We have already seen that Ammonius does not accept this possibility.

The fact that Ammonius in 140,3-4, apparently to define the expression ἀξίωμα τῆς ἀντιφάσεως, uses the formula

$$N(T[Cp] \succ\!\!\prec T[C\sim p])$$

presents a problem only at first sight, because this formula, when completed by

$$N(F[Cp] \succ\!\!\prec F[C\sim p])$$

(thus giving T(11)), is equivalent to the principle of division of truth values. Ammonius' choice of this formula rather than his habitual formula is also explained by his care to stay close to the reading of Aristotle's text. In fact, this is the formula we find in Aristotle's text at 18a36-7 and at 18b7.

2. Like Aristotle, Ammonius limits the discussion of the principle of the division of truth values to the case of SFCSs, which, as has been seen, is the only case where the application of this principle is problematic. According to Ammonius, one can prove that this principle is valid for these sentences as well by showing that in a contradictory pair of such sentences both can neither be true at once nor false at once. That is, Ammonius understands Aristotle to be deducing this principle from the principles of non-contradiction and excluded middle. He recognizes, however, that only half the argument is found in lemma 2, viz. the claim that, unlike undetermineds, the pairs of SFCS contradictories cannot be true together, whereas the claim that they cannot be false together arises only later in Aristotle's text (at 18b17-25). But this does not seem to concern Ammonius.

Ammonius endeavors to reconstruct the demonstration of the first of these claims, which he believes he can find in Aristotle's text. This demonstration is a sort of *reductio ad absurdum* of the contradictorily opposed claim. It depends on the principle of the implication of a fact by the truth of the sentence affirming it, C(03). If a pair of SFCSs could be true together, it would follow, due to C(03), that one state of affairs, e.g. that Socrates is bathing, and the contradictorily opposed state would be the case at the same time. Thus

F(11) $N(Cp \succ\!\!\prec C\sim p)$

would be denied. To avoid this absurdity, we must accept that both SFCSs cannot be true together (cp. 140,8-10 and the analogous argument at 146,8-17).

Thus Ammonius uses F(11) in his reconstruction of the argument. He seems, however, not to have realized that this principle is found in the lines 18a38-9. Unlike most contemporary interpreters (cp. Weidemann 1994, 233; Ackrill 1963, 135), he interprets these lines as an expression of the claim to be proven itself, i.e. that in the case of future contingents, the truth of an affirmation and its negation do not occur at the same time. Ammonius says the same thing in the parallel passage 145,31-146,2, a passage that also shows (cp. 145,29-31) that he assumes that the authors of the necessitarian argument wrongly consider the argument raised at 18a35-39 to be a proof not of the principle of plain division of truth values, but rather of the principle of definite division of truth values.

It should be stressed that Ammonius never mentions that Aristotle at 18b37-38 introduces as a thesis of his adversaries the claim that each affirmation and each negation is either true or false. Aristotle clearly considers this a prerequisite and one of the premises of their demonstration of the principle of the division of truth values. For, if the first claim did not hold, i.e. if sentences could be neutral (neither true nor false), the demonstration would not be successful. The standard interpretation holding that Aristotle recognized a third truth value is based on this observation.[206] Ammonius, however, does not consider the possibility of a neutral truth-value. This is why 18b37-8 does not attract his attention.

3. Taken literally, φησι, 'he says', at 140,13 indicates that Aristotle attributes to the necessitarians the claim that the contradictory pairs of SFCSs do not divide their truth values in an indefinite way, but in a definite one. Actually, the term ὡρισμένως, 'definitely', is nowhere found in Aristotle's text. We do not think this has escaped Ammonius' attention. This is why in adopting an interpretation that tries to save the coherence of the text (by the 'principle of charity') we have translated φησι as 'he means' rather than 'he says'. Ammonius tries to show (ἐπιδείξομεν) that the authors of the argument assume a definite division of truth values. As we shall see, he does this at 141,18-25 in explicitly giving a demonstration of this claim.

4. To demonstrate that in fact a definite division of truth values has necessitarian consequences, Ammonius bases his reasoning on a concrete example of a pair of SFCSs. He begins with the supposition that of two soothsayers predicting the future of a sick person, one says he will recover, the other that he will not. The argumentation, which in its structure resembles the Reaper Argument, is as follows (g = the sick person recovers):

lines	premises/conclusion	by which principle
(1) (140,16-17)	$N\{(T_d[Cg] \bullet F_d[C{\sim}g]) \succ{-}\prec$ $(F_d[Cg] \bullet T_d[C{\sim}g])\}$	T(15)
(2) (140,17-20)		
a)	$(T_d[Cg]{\rightarrow}NCg) \bullet (T_d[C{\sim}g]{\rightarrow}NC{\sim}g)$	C(22)
b)	$NC{\sim}g \leftrightarrow \neg PCg$	M(11)
(3) (140,20-1)	$NCg \succ{-}\prec \neg PCg$	T(15), C(22), M(12), M(13)
(4) (140,21)	$\neg KCg$	M(12), M(13)

---

[206] Cp. J. Lukasiewicz 1930 and 1973; see also N. Kretzmann 1998, 24-25.

The simplest way to explain the second premise is to understand it as a consequence of the principle C(22). That is what we did in our reconstruction.

C(22) $(T_d[Cp] \rightarrow NCp) \bullet (T_d[C{\sim}p] \rightarrow NC{\sim}p) \bullet (F_d[Cp] \rightarrow N{\neg}Cp) \bullet$
           $(F_d[C{\sim}p] \rightarrow N{\neg}C{\sim}p).$

It is curious, however, that Ammonius never mentions this principle in his text. To be sure, C(22) is a law that is true analytically if our hypothesis on the semantics of the expressions 'definitely true' and 'definitely false' is accurate. Thus Ammonius could think he could dispense with stating it explicitly. On the other hand we must take into account the fact that Ammonius does not at all dispense with justifying his second premise. But instead of establishing it on the basis of C(22), he justifies it (140,18-9) by means of C(03). This requires an explanation, because C(03) on first glance does not seem strong enough to serve as the grounds for the second premise.

How can a demonstration of the second premise be reconstructed on the basis of C(03)? It could be supposed that Ammonius accepted the following principle:

M(14) $(T[Cp] \rightarrow Cp) \rightarrow (NT[Cp] \rightarrow NCp).$

M(14) allows us to pass from C(03) to a modalized principle of correspondence:

C(24) $(NT[Cp] \rightarrow NCp) \bullet (NT[C{\sim}p] \rightarrow NC{\sim}p) \bullet (NF[Cp] \rightarrow N{\neg}Cp) \bullet$
           $(NF[C{\sim}p] \rightarrow N{\neg}C{\sim}p).$

Now the semantics of the expressions 'definitely true' and 'definitely false' have as a consequence the following equivalencies.[207]

$$(T_d[Cp] \leftrightarrow NT[Cp]) \bullet (F_d[Cp] \leftrightarrow NF[Cp]).$$

Ammonius can then substitute 'it is necessarily true that the sick person recovers' for 'it is definitely true that the sick person recovers'. This substitution permits the use of C(24) in the deduction of the necessity of the recovering or of the not recovering. Since C(24) is, by M(14), a consequence of C(03), Ammonius is not wrong to cite the latter principle to justify his second premise.

Lemma 3 (18a39-b9)

According to the unanimous opinion of modern interpreters, Aristotle completes the first argument for necessitarianism in the third lemma. Ammonius, however, maintains that this argument has already been concluded in lemma 2 and, as a result, he sees in the third lemma only a confirmation and explication of what has already been proved.

---

[207]   Cp. G. Seel's second article in this volume, 243-245.

The commentary on the third lemma takes up paragraphs 14 and 15. Paragraph 14 comments on Aristotle's text up to 18b4, paragraph 15 comments on the conclusion drawn at 18b5-9 and gives in its second part an explication of the different sorts of contingent.

Paragraph 14

In this paragraph Ammonius explains how Aristotle deduces 'as if from a syllogism' (cp. 141,18: ὥσπερ ἐκ συλλογισμοῦ) the principle of correspondence and the principle of the definite division of truth values, which form the basis of the first proof for necessitarianism, sketched in the previous paragraph.

Paragraph 14 is divided into three parts:

(1). First, Ammonius comments on lines 18a39-b3 (140,32-147,17). He sees there (a) a confirmation, supported by examples, of the principle of the implication of facts by the truth of sentences and (b) its complementary principle, the principle of implication of the truth of sentences by the facts; thus he obtains from both the *principle of correspondence* in its entirety.

(2). Next (141,18-25) Ammonius interprets lines 18b4-5. According to him, they include a deduction of the principle of the definite division of truth values from the principle of correspondence.

(3). Finally (141,25-30), Ammonius returns to 18b2-3, which he understands as a formulation of the principle of correspondence for the case of false sentences, which has not been discussed earlier.

Regarding (1): Weidemann (1994, 236)—like Ammonius—sees in lines 18a39-b2 a confirmation of what has been shown before. But unlike Ammonius, he identifies this as the principle of non-contradiction and the principle of excluded middle which, according to him, are demonstrated from the principle of correspondence. In this interpretation, Weidemann assumes that the εἰ ('if') in line a39 refers back to the εἰ in a34 and that ἤ ('or') is a non-exclusive 'or' in a39 and an exclusive 'or' in the two following lines. But Ammonius' reading, which stipulates that it is the principle of correspondence that is being confirmed in these lines, has the ἤ indicate an exclusive 'or' in all the occurrences, and further assumes that the εἰ in a39 refers to a35. This reading follows Aristotle's text more closely than Weidemann's, as well as avoiding the improbable assumption that the 'or' is non-exclusive in a39.

Ammonius distinguishes two partial principles which together constitute the principle of correspondence. He says (140,32-4) that Aristotle first demonstrates the principle of the implication of facts by the truth of the sentences, and then (141,6-8) he adds the principle of the implication of the truth of the sentences by the facts, thus obtaining the complete principle of correspondence. These two principles can be formulated thus:

C(03) $N\{(T[Cp] \rightarrow Cp) \bullet (T[C{\sim}p] \rightarrow C{\sim}p) \bullet (F[Cp] \rightarrow \neg Cp) \bullet (F[C{\sim}p] \rightarrow \neg C{\sim}p)\}$

and

C(04) $N\{(Cp \rightarrow T[Cp]) \bullet (C\sim p \rightarrow T[C\sim p]) \bullet (\neg Cp \rightarrow F[Cp]) \bullet (\neg C\sim p \rightarrow F[C\sim p])\}$

Versions of the first partial principle that are apparently quite different are found in the text of this paragraph, just as in the preceding paragraph. At 140,32-4, it is formulated without any modal operator; at 141,4-6, where it is supported by the cloak example, ἀνάγκη ('it is necessary that') is added before the consequent of the conditional sentence. And finally at 141,8-10, where Ammonius presents the principle of correspondence in its entirety (i.e. the conjunction of the two partial principles), he places the modal operator before the conditional sentence.

It is clear, however, that the three formulations can only be referring to a single principle and that this can only be C(03), for the following reasons:

(i). Ammonius (140,32) leaves no doubt that the first partial principle is identical to the first principle treated in the preceding paragraph, viz. C(03).

(ii). It is very probable that the version chosen at 141,8-10 for the formulation of the complete principle of correspondence expresses best Ammonius' intended meaning.

(iii). The ἀνάγκη at 141,4-6 poses no problem for this interpretation because, as we have already seen, even placed before the consequent, it can quite easily express *necessitas consequentiae*—both in Ammonius or Aristotle (for the latter, cp. again Weidemann 1994, 230-1, 235).

(iv). Only under this assumption can we understand how Ammonius could at 140,32-4 do without a modal operator for expressing the same principle.

Thus we hold C(03) as the best formalization of the first partial principle.

As for the second partial principle, we find no explicit formulation in the text. Ammonius merely remarks (141,6-8) that the first partial principle is convertible. Consequently, the second principle, which results from this conversion, will correspond to our C(04). The joining together of the two principles, an abridged version of which is given at 141,8-10, must then be formalized in the following fashion:

C(01) $N\{(T[Cp] \leftrightarrow Cp) \bullet (T[C\sim p] \leftrightarrow C\sim p) \bullet (F[Cp] \leftrightarrow \neg Cp) \bullet$
          $(F([C\sim p] \leftrightarrow \neg C\sim p)\}$

It is difficult to understand, however, to what extent Aristotle's argument in this passage is like a syllogistic deduction, as Ammonius maintains.

It is interesting to see that Ammonius considers the fact Aristotle uses the past ἦν ('was') in 18b2 worthy of comment. He thinks that here Aristotle is trying to say that facts imply the truth of affirmative sentences not only in cases where fact and statement are simultaneous but also where the statement precedes the fact (141,10-17). This gives the principle:

C(13) $(t')(t'')(p)\{(t'' < t' \bullet C_{t'}p \bullet [C_{t'}p]_{t'}) \rightarrow T_{t'}[C_{t'}p]\}$

Ammonius thinks that this principle will play a role in the second proof for necessitarianism. Among contemporary interpreters, only Donini 1989, 6 note 15 agrees with Ammonius. Weidemann 1994, 237, on the other hand, holds that the imperfect $\tilde{\eta}\nu$ has nothing to do with the second proof but serves here simply to refer back to an item already mentioned. Though the text does not permit us to decide between the two interpretations we find Ammonius' conjecture quite convincing.

The deduction that Ammonius sketches at 141,18-25 is of the greatest interest. It is probably in these lines that he fulfills the promise given at 140,13 of showing that the argument for necessitarianism depends on the tacit assumption that SFCSs divide truth values in a definite way (one definitely true, one definitely false). In fact, he reaffirms this claim at 141,20 in remarking that the authors of this argument *rightly* imply definite truth values—rightly because he believes that one can prove that their argument actually requires it. This proof is sketched by Ammonius in the lines that follow.

T(15), then, is the claim to prove. Like the proof of T(13) sketched at 140, 4-13, the demonstration for this uses the principle of division of facts, F(11). But this time the demonstration does not proceed by a reduction to the absurd. F(11) serves as a premise from which the claim to be proven can be directly deduced. To do this Ammonius introduces a second premise containing a very strong principle of correspondence, namely C(02), which appears here for the first time in Ammonius' text. The demonstration has the following structure:

lines	premises/conclusions	by which principle
141, 20-21	$N(Cp \succ\prec C\sim p)$	F(11)
141, 21-23	$(Cp \to T_d[Cp]) \bullet (C\sim p \to T_d[C\sim p])$	C(02)
intermediate conclusion (unstated)	$N(T_d[Cp]) \succ\prec T_d[C\sim p])$	T(14)
141, 24-25	$N\{(T_d[Cp] \bullet F_d[C\sim p]) \succ\prec T_d[C\sim p]) \bullet F_d[Cp])\}$	T(15)

If on the other hand one adopts the standard interpretation, the demonstration given by Ammonius will be read in the following way:

lines	premises/conclusions	by which principle
141,20-1	$N(Cp \succ\prec C\sim p)$	F(11)
141,21-3	$(Cp \to T[Cp]) \bullet (C\sim p \to T[C\sim p])$	C(04)
intermediate conclusion (unstated)	$N(T[Cp]) \succ\prec T[C\sim p])$	T(11)
141,24-5	$N\{(T[Cp] \bullet F[C\sim p]) \succ\prec (T[C\sim p]) \bullet F[Cp])\}$	T(13)

By this interpretation, the proof given at 141,20-5 leads to the same result as the proof sketched at 140,4-13. If it were correct, it would be difficult to understand why Ammonius announced at 140,13 a supplementary demonstration of the fact that SFCSs divide their truth values in a definite way. This clearly speaks against the standard interpretation.

But the non-standard interpretation has its own difficulties. It must explain how Ammonius can impute to necessitarians a principle as strong as C(02). To do this, it must be noted that Ammonius considers the fact in question as a present fact about which a predication has been made in the past. Therefore the principle of the necessity of facts T(03) applies to it. Consequently necessitarians have been able to consider a given situation not only as a fact, but as a necessary fact. By C(23) such a fact has the implication that the sentence predicating it is true in a definite manner. Thus necessitarians are able to substitute C(02) for C(23). The only objection that could be raised is that the necessity of facts principle F(03) does not figure in the immediate context and will not be introduced (and refuted!) until paragraph 17 (cp. 145,9-12), when the second necessitarianism-argument is refuted. In fact, Ammonius considers the second argument a sharper and clearer means of demonstrating what paragraph 14 had already concluded, namely, the principle of the definite division of truth values, T(15) (cp. 144,9-14). This close affinity of the two arguments is further underscored by the fact that Ammonius does not give a refutation of the first argument, as if he considered the refutation of the second as also applicable to the first. But, as we will show in Ammonius' reconstruction of the second argument, even though in the argument itself principle F(03) is not made explicit either, he regards it as the indispensable basis on which the entire demonstration depends and which thus must be called into question if the demonstration is to be refuted (cp. 145,9-12 and 152,33-153, 7). It is very likely, then, that Ammonius is reasoning along the same lines as regards the first argument. Thus, although he finds nothing wrong with C(23), he does not accept C(02). He will accuse the necessitarians, then, of wrongly substituting the latter for C(23) on the basis of F(03).

Paragraph 15

The text that Ammonius comments on in this paragraph (lines 18b5-9) contains the conclusion of the first necessitarianism argument. He interprets this conclusion as expressing the claim that the contingent is to be done away with (141,34-5). Interestingly, Ammonius emphasizes that this conclusion follows immediately (αὐτόθεν) from the validity of the principle of the definite division of truth values T(15) for SFCSs. This is accurate only if the non-standard interpretation is adopted, because according to this C(25) is an analytically true law. The standard interpretation, on the contrary, will have difficulty explaining this αὐτόθεν because necessitarianism cannot be deduced from principle T(13) alone.[208]

The rest of the paragraph (beginning at 142,1) contains an explanation of the different sorts of contingent. The appearance in Aristotle's text of the phrases ἀπὸ τύχης, "by chance," and ὁπότερ' ἔτυχεν, "however it chances" serves as an opportunity to expound this kind of events in a systematic way based on the Neoplatonic doctrine of levels of being. In fact, following the conclusion that contingency is to be denied, Aristotle introduces two types of contingents, namely ἀπὸ τύχης and ὁπότερ' ἔτυχεν (18b5-6). These two expressions are often used as synonyms by Aristotle (cp. *An. Pr.* 1.13, 32b12-13, b17) but, as Weidemann 1994, 143-44 has shown, in *De Interpretatione* 9 the latter refers to events with an equal probability of occurrence and non-occurrence, while the former refers to contingent events that occur due only to an exceptional constellation of causal factors.

Ammonius proposes a complete, and much more complicated, division of the contingent according to frequency of events and also according to their causes. Under the first heading, he distinguishes (a) what happens for the most part, (b) what happens for the lesser part, and (c) what happens with equal frequency (142,1-5).[209] To be sure, this distinction is not found in the lemma being commented on, but does correspond to the sort of conception Aristotle develops in the *Topics* (2.6, 112b1-15). Then Ammonius subdivides these types of contingents according to their cause. The contingent happening most often is caused either by nature or by art (142,5-13). The more rarely occurring contingent is caused either by chance (κατὰ τύχην) or by spontaneity (ἀπὸ ταὐτομάτου) (142,13-143,1). Events ἀπὸ τύχης are positive events happening despite one's expectation or intention, because of a happy constellation of causes. Events ἀπὸ ταὐτομάτου, on the other hand, happen due to a constellation of causes in nature, i.e. apart from human action. The contingent that happens just as frequently as not depends on a single sort of cause, human choice (143,1-3). The theory of different causes of the contingent explained here by Ammonius does not correspond in every aspect to the Aristotelian conception (cp. again H. Weidemann 1994, 243-244).

Ammonius adds that the latter type of contingent, i.e. the one which does as frequently occur as not occur, is called ὁπότερον ἔτυχε (143,3-6). According to Weidemann's analysis (1954, 243), in *De Interpretatione* Aristotle uses this expression to mean the same thing. On the contrary Ammonius thinks that Aristotle uses it for all contingents—and he criticizes him for doing so, since ὁπότερον ἔτυχε is, according to Ammonius, only the 'core' of the contingent (143,20-2).

Weidemann 1994, 245-6 rightly stresses that this division of the contingent into subclasses would not fit in the context of chapter 9 if a simple statistical

---

[208]   See also R. Sorabji 1998, 11.
[209]   For the three-fold division of the contingent cp. P. Donini 1989, 65-70 and S. Bobzien 1998c, 150.

classification were all that mattered. But as we shall soon see, Ammonius, like
Aristotle, is convinced that statistical classification of event types has implications
for the modality (probability) of the singular event that belongs to one of these
classes.

Lemma 4 (18b9-16)

This lemma contains the second argument for necessitarianism. Ammonius
understands that here Aristotle gives a clearer version of the demonstration and
proceeds in a more elaborate manner (144,13-4). The editor's division of the
commentary into two paragraphs corresponds to its internal structure: in the first,
Ammonius explicates Aristotle's text; in the second, he gives his own refutation
of the argument for necessitarianism.

Paragraph 16

Let us first determine how the second argument differs from the first and then see
to what extent Ammonius recognizes this difference. In view of the great diversity
of interpretations for the second argument (cp. Weidemann 1994, 248-63), we
must limit ourselves to presenting our own opinion:

1. First of all, the second argument differs from the first in that the principle
of the division of truth values, so important in the first argument, is absent in the
second.

2. Further, in the second two new principles are found that are absent in the
first argument. These are:

(a) the principle of the retrogradation of truth formulated at 18b9-11:

$$C(13) \qquad (t')(t'')(p)\{(t' < t'' \bullet C_{t'}p \bullet [C_{t'}p]_{t'}) \rightarrow T_{t''}[C_{t'}p]\}$$

and

(b)   the principle of simultaneity of the truth of statement and the
         corresponding fact, which appears at 18b11-13:

$$C(11) \qquad (t')(t'')(p)\{(t'' \leq t' \bullet T_{t''}[C_{t'}p]) \rightarrow C_{t''}C_{t'}p\}.$$

Our claim, which stipulates that 18b11-13 contains the principle $C(11)$,
requires a justification since interpreters are much divided on the issue.[210] The
following arguments support our claim:

1. It accounts for the fact that the argument reported by Aristotle contains
four steps. In fact, according to our interpretation, each of these four steps
contains an indispensable new item for the argument, while by the standard

---

[210]   The problem is how to interpret the οὐχ οἶόν τε in lines 12 and 13. Mostly the
        expression is given a modal meaning ('impossible'). The expression can, however,
        have a non-modal meaning as well (cp. Liddell-Scott).

interpretation, the third step is only a reformulation of the result obtained in the second.

2. According to Aristotle (cp. *Int.* 19a23-6) the two necessitarianism arguments depend on a misguided use of the principle of the necessity of facts and not, as some interpreters have claimed (cp. G. Anscombe 1968, 19; S. Haack 1974, 77-9; G. Fine 1984, 23, 36-8; M. Lowe 1980, 55-62), on the principle of the implication of the necessity of the fact by the truth of the sentence stating it. But C(11) does allow the application of the principle of the necessity of facts, the validity of which is normally limited strictly to present or past facts, to future facts as well. Thus a reconstruction of the second argument is possible that avoids having to fault its authors for mistakes as serious as confusing *necessitas consequentiae* with *necessitas consequentis*.

The role that the principle of retrogradation of truth plays in the second argument is just as controversial among interpreters (cp. H. Weidemann 1994, 250-61). In our opinion, this role is as follows. For each future event, one can imagine an infinite series of statements predicting it. Each statement is itself an event taking place in a different period of time.

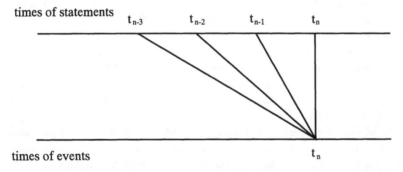

Now according to the principle of the division of truth values each element of this series is either true or false. But this division does not allow us to conclude that all the members of the series carry the same truth value. Thus in the series of sentences the possibility of both true and false ones is not precluded. If this were the case, it could be deduced by means of the principles used by Aristotle that the given event is necessary at one moment and impossible at another moment. Such a situation is clearly troublesome. To be sure, there would be no instant prior to the event at which it would be a future contingent event, which accords with necessitarianism. But the fact the same event is sometimes necessary and sometimes impossible is at odds with it. One could certainly prove that the very concepts of necessity and impossibility preclude such a case. But the principle of retrogradation of truth solves the problem in a very simple way since it ensures that all the sentences in the series have the same truth value, and consequently that the event that is actualized is at every instant in its 'past' a necessary future event

—this due to the principle that the truth of the sentence entails the necessity of the corresponding event (cp. D. Frede 1985, 55).

On this basis, we can reconstruct the second argument for determinism in this way: Let n be the state of affairs 'a white child is born', t_n be the present instant, $t' = t_n$ and $t'' \leq t'$. Then we can formulate the argument in the following way:

Steps	Claims obtained	by which principle
	$C_{t'}n$	beginning claim
1st	$(t'')(T_{t'}[C_{t'}n])$	C(13)
2nd	$(t'')(\neg C_{t''}\neg C_{t'}n)$	C(11), C(12)
3rd	$(t'')(\neg P_{t''}\neg C_{t''}\neg C_{t'}n)$	F(14), F(16)
4th	$(t'')(N_{t''}C_{t''}C_{t'}n)$	M(11)

There is no problem in writing $(t'')(N_{t'}C_{t'}n)$ for $(t'')(N_{t''}C_{t''}C_{t'}n)$.

Let us now see to what extent Ammonius understands the subtlety of the argument reported by Aristotle. It must first of all be emphasized that he explicitly states that the first argument lacks clarity and that therefore Aristotle tries in a second proof to deduce the same conclusion more clearly from a new starting point (144,9-14). But it is doubtful that he fully understood the difference between the two arguments.

1. Ammonius does not see that the principle of the definite division of truth values no longer plays any role in the second argument. On the contrary, he holds that just as in the first argument this principle is the principal goal of the deduction, and when it is reached the rejection of the contingent immediately follows (144,9-12).

2. In the other part of the paragraph (beginning at 144,14) Ammonius closely follows Aristotle's text. He notes here that the goal of the demonstration is actually the claim that everything is necessary. This difference in the identification of the goal of the deduction is explained by the fact, already shown in numerous places, that Ammonius allows his own thinking to interfere with his commentary on Aristotle's text.

3. Regarding the principle of retrogradation of truth, Ammonius sees with great clarity that what is established by this principle is the truth of an infinite series of statements each different from the others and not, as Hintikka believes (1973, 147-178 and particularly 166, note 26), the omnitemporal truth of a single statement.[211] He also notes that this principle presents the new element introduced in the discussion (cp. 144,14). But it is highly doubtful that he understands the true import of this new element. When he explains at 144,19-21 the reason the truth of a past statement makes the predicted event necessary, he does not refer to an infinite series of statements, but rather seems to have in mind just one. Thus it appears that for Ammonius what is new in the second argument is not the

---

[211]   Cp. G. Seel's second article in this volume, 237-239.

introduction of an *infinite series* of past statements, but rather the introduction of *past* statements. Thus he reconstructs the second argument as if it were perfectly parallel to the first, only that now the principle of correspondence is applied to past statements.

4. For the same reasons Ammonius does not call into service C(11) in his reconstruction. In fact, he considers the expression οὐχ οἷόν τε to mean 'impossible' (144,26-7) and hence is content with just three steps rather than four. Thus the difference between the second and third steps, so important in our reconstruction, completely disappears. Ammonius does not use in his reconstruction the principle of the necessity of facts either, but grounds the demonstration directly on principle C(21), thus adhering to the dominant line of interpretation, some modern versions of which we have mentioned above. He does not explain how the authors of the argument justify C(21), but his general line of interpretation lets us conjecture that he believes they have wrongly substituted principle C(21) for the correct and anodyne C(22) supposing that 'being true' is the same as 'being definitely true'.

5. Finally if one asks what grounds Ammonius has for holding (at 144,9-11) that the second argument amounts to a demonstration of the principle of the definite division of truth values, it is difficult to know how to respond. Unlike in the passage at 143,17-26 (cp. above pp. 180f.), in paragraph 16 the word ὡρισμένως, 'definitely', does not appear anywhere in the argument as reconstructed by Ammonius. Thus to respond to this question, we have only the two following options. Either Ammonius regards the second necessitarianism argument as identical to the argument sketched at 143,20-5, or he considers the demonstration to be indirect, assuming that the argument used is valid only if all the truth values are definite. Because it seems the more plausible, we hold to the latter option.

Paragraph 17

In this brief paragraph, Ammonius presents his refutation of the second necessitarianism argument, which (as we shall see) has repercussions for the first argument as well. The text is of great importance since the method Ammonius uses to criticize this argument permits us for the first time to decide on solid grounds whether he adheres to the standard interpretation.

Ammonius first of all makes two negative statements (145,9-12), thus denying the validity of two principles which he apparently considers decisive for the validity of the second proof. In the formulation of the first principle he uses the adverb πάντως, 'in any case', which when placed before the predicate indicates either that the given state of affairs is a settled fact or that it is a necessary fact (cp. our discussion above on the semantics of this expression in our commentary on paragraph 5). In our reconstruction of the 'Reaper' Argument, we opted for the first meaning. For the same reasons we accept this interpretation in the present context too.

If πάντως means 'settled' or 'decided', the first principle whose validity Ammonius denies means this:

C(40)   If a state of affairs is now actualized or has already been actualized, the prediction made before the instant of its actualization saying that it is decided (at the moment of its being stated) that this state of affairs will be the case at the later moment – this statement is true. Or:

$$(t') (t'') (p) \{(t'' < t' \bullet C_{t'}p \bullet [D_{t''}C_{t'}p]_{t''}) \to T_{t'}[D_{t''}C_{t'}p]\}$$

Ammonius justifies his rejection of this principle (cp. γάρ in 145,11) by denying the validity of another principle (145,11-12). This second principle is a variation of the principle of the necessity of facts.

F(03)   If p is the case at t', at any time before t' it was necessary for p to occur at t'.

$$(t')(t'')(p)\{(t'' < t' \bullet C_{t'}p) \to N_{t''}C_{t'}p\}$$

He must understand that the non-validity of F(03) is a reason for the non-validity of C(40). This implication, however, needs an explanation. If a fact is necessary the sentence stating its necessity is true, according to the principle of correspondence. Therefore, if a present fact implies its prior necessity, it also implies the truth of the sentence stating that it will necessarily be the case and vice versa. So F(03) is equivalent with the following principle.

C(41)   If a state of affairs is now actualized or has already been actualized, the prediction statement made before the instant of its actualization, saying that it is necessary (at the moment of its being stated) that this state of affairs will be the case at the later moment, is true. Or:

$$(t')(t'')(p)\{(t'' < t' \bullet C_{t'}p \bullet [N_{t''}C_{t'}p]_{t''}) \to T_{t'}[N_{t''}C_{t'}p]\}$$

Now, let us, for a moment, have a look back to the Reaper Argument (cp. above p.158). There we argued that Ammonius could have accepted P(IVc).

P(IVc) $(U_{tn}C_{tf}r \bullet Ut_{n}C_{tf} \sim r) \leftarrow (K_{tn}C_{tf}r \bullet K_{tn}C_{tf} \sim r)$

On the basis of the premises of the Reaper Argument P(IVc) is equivalent with the following principle.

$$(D_{tn}C_{tf}p \to N_{tn}C_{tf}p) \bullet (D_{tn}C_{tf} \sim p \to N_{tn}C_{tf} \sim p)$$

This, in turn, amounts to the following general principle.

M(5) $(t')(t'')(p)(\{(t'' < t' \cdot D_{t'}C_{t'}p) \to N_{t'}C_{t'}p\}$

Using M(5) one can easily show that C(40) implies C(41). Therefore, if the non-validity of F(03) implies the non-validity of C(41), it also implies the non-validity of C(40). We see from this that Ammonius' justification is perfectly sound and consistent with his treatment of the Reaper Argument.

However, neither C(40) nor F(03) played an explicit role in Ammonius' reconstruction of the second necessitarianism argument. Therefore we have to explain why he believes that their negation undermines that argument. In the argument one deduces from a present fact through intermediate steps the past necessity of that fact. Now, if that conclusion is correctly deduced, the present actuality of any state of affairs implies the prior necessity of its future realization. That is exactly what F(03) affirms. So, by denying F(03) Ammonius in fact doubts the correctness of the second argument. Ammonius is convinced (he says that at 145,18-9) that Aristotle is going to take the same step showing that the necessitarians are not allowed to substitute the false principle F(03) to a principle resembling it, namely F(04), which he considers valid.[212]

F(04) $(t')(t'')(p)\{(t'' \geq t' \cdot C_{t'}p) \to N_{t''}C_{t'}p\}$

Given the logical relation between F(03) and C(40), denying F(03) and denying C(40) is finally the same move, i.e. doubting the validity of the second argument in its totality. So, why did Ammonius introduce the rather complex principle C(40), which contains a modalized sentence, at all? The answer will be given when we now analyze Ammonius' way of refuting the argument.

So far Ammonius has only doubted the validity of the second argument, but has not given an argument that demonstrates the negation of its conclusion. He tries to do this in lines 145,12-6. Ammonius uses a tactic he has already employed in his refutation of the 'Reaper' Argument (cp. above, pp.159f.). He substitutes for the neutral SFCS, which was the object of the controversy in the preceding paragraph, an alternative of modal sentences. Whoever uses the neutral sentence (c) 'he will be born a pale child' is deliberately leaving it in the dark whether he really means (a) 'he will necessarily be born a pale child' or (b) 'he will contingently be born a pale child.' Assuming the instant of the statement t'' occurs before the instant of the actualization of the event t', we can write:

(a) $C_{t'}C_{t}n \cdot N_{t''}C_{t}n$
(b) $C_{t'}C_{t}n \cdot K_{t''}C_{t}n$
(c) $C_{t'}C_{t}n$

To be sure, sentence (c) must be stated along with one of the two others; both are compatible with it. But if (a) is true, (c) is definitely true, and if (b) is true, (c) is true in a indefinite way. The neutrality of (c) does not allow this difference to appear. Because of this, necessitarians can avoid to specify the way sentences of type (c) possess their truth-values and tacitly suppose that all truth-values are definite ones. This, again, allows them to substitute principle C(21) for the correct principle C(22) and use the former in order to deduce the necessity of the fact from the truth of the sentence predicting the fact. This means that they obtain their conclusion surreptitiously, covering up the fact they commit a *petitio principii*. By obliging them to choose between (a) and (b), Ammonius makes the *petitio*

---

[212]   Aristotle in fact makes this claim at 19a23ff.

principii obvious. Of course, the determinists can still stick to their position, but they cannot pretend to have proved it.

Ammonius, on the other hand, insists that 'the birth of a pale child' is actually a contingent event. Thus, according to him, (b) is true and (a) is false (145,12-4). But he makes no effort to prove that. He might think he does not need to, as long as the necessitarians have no proof of the contrary either. But if he is right, C(40) and F(03) are false and the second argument loses its foundation.

At the end of the paragraph (145,16-9), Ammonius clarifies the epistemological foundations of statements (a) and (b). He requires, in effect, that the validity of type (a) statements not be decided on the basis of an event that has already occurred, but by deciding before it has happened whether it is going to happen by necessity. In fact, once the event has occurred, type (a) statements are no longer in danger of being shown false. Before the end of the process that produces the event, on the other hand, type (a) statements can be falsified because the type of event, if it is contingent, could still not occur. This is why in this case one only dares to make a type (a) statement if there are reasons to believe the type of event will necessarily occur. These reasons can only be the knowledge that the causes of the future type of event already exist at the moment the statement is made and the knowledge of the causal tie linking these causes and the type of event (regarding this, cp. 137,1ff and our commentary on paragraph 10 on p.163 above).

It is interesting to compare Ammonius' refutation of the second necessitarianism argument to his refutation of the Reaper Argument. As we already emphasized both refutations use the same method, consisting of modalizing plain sentences and of showing that not only one but two different modalizations are possible of which only one has necessitarian consequences. In the case of the Reaper Argument Ammonius explicitly argues that the necessitarians by choosing the modalization convenient to their purpose would commit a *petitio principii*. As we have seen, in the present case the same blame is implicit in Ammonius' argument. It is important to note also that in his refutation of the second necessitarian argument Ammonius denies explicitly the first two premises of the Reaper Argument and he seems to admit that these premises in fact have necessitarian consequences. So we find in this paragraph an indirect confirmation of our reconstruction of the Reaper Argument given above.

The positions defended by Ammonius in this paragraph permit us to determine whether or not he holds the standard interpretation. Two points are relevant to this.

1. If Ammonius accepted the standard interpretation, in order to criticize the second argument, he would call into question the validity of the correspondence principle for SFCSs. But he does no such thing. On the contrary, the strategy he pursues in paragraph 17 precisely corresponds with what one would expect if he was a supporter of the non-standard interpretation.

2. Moreover, paragraph 17 contains a clear proof that Ammonius attributes truth values to SFCSs. An example is devised in which the event predicted in sentence (c) is a present contingent fact. It is time and not prior necessitating

causes that has put it into being (cp. 145,11-2). In our opinion, this means that in order to explain this fact, one must appeal to the ontological principle of non-contradiction which requires that at every present moment only one of two contradictory states of affairs can, and exactly one must, be the case. Now Ammonius stresses that statement (b), affirming that the fact is going to take place contingently, is true (145,13-4 and 15-6).[213] This seems to exclude Ammonius' denying a truth value to statement (c), which predicts the same event but without specifying its modality. If (b) is true, (c) is as well because (b) implies (c).

3. Unfortunately Ammonius in the paragraph does not explicitly discuss the specific manner in which sentences (a), (b) and (c) possess their truth-values. According to our interpretation, the simple truth of (a) entails the definite truth of (c) and the simple truth of (b) has the consequence that (c) is true in an indefinite way. But despite the fact Ammonius used these distinctions throughout his restatements of the first and second necessitarianism arguments, in his refutation of the latter, this distinction no longer appears. One must wait till the following paragraph for its reappearance.

Lemma 5 (18b16-25)

Paragraph 18

In this lemma Aristotle returns to a question raised in the second lemma (cp. above, p.174), the question of whether SFCSs can be false together and if not, why not. This is why J. Ackrill 1963, 137 and D. Frede 1970, 86 suspect that the passage was wrongly placed here and should be relocated to the passage 18a34-b4. H. Weidemann 1994, 268 objects to this proposal because it would seriously muddle the argument which, among other things, presupposes the result obtained at 18b5-16.

Regarding the goal of the argument, interpreters are not in agreement either. Ackrill *loc. cit.* thinks that Aristotle is intending to refute for the first time the claim that two contradictory SFCSs can be false together. And he accuses him of committing a *petitio principii* in this demonstration. But to support him against this charge, Weidemann (1994, 264-5) suggests that the goal of the demonstration is only to show that, even if the two statements could be false together, it would still lead to determinist consequences. But according to Ackrill this point is pursued in a second argument.

Ammonius also locates the passage in the context of the second lemma. But unlike modern interpreters, he does not think for a moment that it could be misplaced, because he doesn't think it odd or unusual to return later to a question left unanswered.

---

213   One cannot cite in support of the opposite claim the future ἀληθεύσει, 'will speak the truth', at 145,13. This has only rhetorical value, as ἠλήθευε in 145,15 confirms, and we should not be tempted to follow this false path.

Concerning the goal of the argument, he holds (as does Ackrill) that Aristotle first of all intends to prove that SFCS contradictories cannot be false together, and that he shows in a second argument that even if this were correct, it would not permit an escape from necessitarianism (cp. 146,5-6).

The beginning of the paragraph confirms what we have said concerning paragraph 13. Ammonius is convinced that Aristotle presupposes definite truth values in the demonstration he gives for the principle of division of truth-values. Ammonius, then, understands lines 18a35-9 as a faulty demonstration of the principle of the *definite* division of truth values. He had already declared in paragraph 13 that this demonstration was incomplete and was to be completed later. He finds this completion, correctly, in the fifth lemma. According to him, SFCS contradictories are either true together or false together or they divide truth values. In order to prove the last, the other two possibilities must be excluded. The possibility of being true together has already been rejected in the second lemma. The possibility of SFCS contradictories being false together remains to be refuted.

To do this, Aristotle (according to Ammonius) advances three arguments:

1. This hypothesis is incompatible with the principle of non-contradiction (146,11-3).
2. The hypothesis has the consequence that the state of affairs the SFCS describes will at the same time be the case and not be the case (145,13-5).
3. This in turn implies the necessity that the given state of affairs will be the case and not be the case (146,15-6).

Thus it is by a reduction to the absurd that the hypothesis of co-falsity of SFCSs is refuted (146,16-7). At the same time it is shown that, even if the hypothesis were valid, one could not escape necessitarianism, as the third argument proves.

Concerning 1: Ammonius' claim that the co-falsity of SFCSs does away with the 'principle of contradiction' is accurate, if this expression is understood in a Neoplatonic way to refer to both the principle of non-contradiction and the principle of excluded middle.[214] It should be noted, however, that Ammonius is mistaken when he maintains that Aristotle advances this argument. In fact, Aristotle does not mention the principle of contradiction. At most, it could be said

---

[214] Syrianus, *In Aristotelis Metaphysica commentaria*, CAG VI.1, 18,6, commenting on *Metaph*. III 996b24 ff explains that the ancients (παρὰ τοῖς πρεσβυτέροις) held two things concerning the principle of contradiction: first that the contradictory sentences can never both be wrong about anything and second that it is impossible that both are true at the same time. He adds that in his own day the expression is used in both ways and that he and the members of his school think that the second is simply true whereas the first is valid with qualification (it is not valid of the highest entity). See also Simplicius, *In Aristotelis Physicorum libros commentaria*, CAG IX, 21,25-29; 240,13-20; X, 985,17-20; 1021,3-4, and Ammonius' own paragraph 13, 139,32-140,4.

that he uses it, which in fact earns him the accusation of *petitio principii*. Ammonius' interpretation avoids this criticism.

Concerning 2: Ammonius stresses that Aristotle, to derive the conclusion that a state of affairs will at the same time be the case and not be the case, uses the principle introduced in the second lemma that the truth of the sentences implies the actualization of the predicted events (146,17-9), i.e. principle C(11).

Concerning 3: Actually, in lines 22-29 Ammonius attributes to Aristotle a deduction whose conclusion he states at 25-26, quoting from Aristotle's text (18b22-3): 'But if it will neither be nor not be tomorrow, there would be no <event of the kind> "however it chances"'. Ammonius interprets this as meaning that the hypothesis that anything is contingent must be denied if two contradictory sentences can be false together. The reason why one must renounce this hypothesis is—according to Ammonius—that the co-falsity of two contradictory sentences implies that the same thing at the same time both of necessity occurs and of necessity does not occur (15-16). The two premises which Ammonius says lead to this conclusion are described by him somewhat ambiguously. Our interpretation is that the first principle mentioned (τούτῳ τῷ θεωρήματι 146,24) is the one which follows from the example given in 21-22 and which—according to Ammonius—is not stated by Aristotle, i.e. the principle that from false sentences the non-existence of the thing stated follows (24); and that the second principle, which is described as the principle 'left out' (25) is the one which Aristotle left out when he discussed the possibility of two contradictory sentences being true together (18a34-b4), i.e. the theorem which says that they can be false together, which is actually at stake in the present paragraph and which Ammonius said (140,10-1) Aristotle would add later.

Ammonius does not explain to us exactly how he thinks Aristotle derives the conclusion that the notion of the contingent is to be done away with. He could get it either through principle C(22), assuming definite truth values, or directly from the second argument through the principle of the necessity of facts, F(03). Aristotle's text is unclear on this. Weidemann (1994, 268) thinks that both the δεῖ in b21 and the δέοι in b24 (both = 'it is necessary that...') indicate *necessitas consequentis*. Thus Aristotle would use principle C(12) to reach this conclusion. But it is equally possible that the two terms indicate *necessitas consequentiae*. In this case, the decisive step would be found in lines 18b22-5. The contingency of the event assumes it might actually take place or might not. But if the event neither has nor has not taken place, there is no contingency.

Lemma 6 (18b26-19a6)

In this lemma Aristotle passes from the exposition of the necessitarianism argument to reasons for rejecting it. He points out absurd consequences of the argument, mentions the uselessness of deliberation and individual initiative if necessitarianism were true, and returns to the theme of the retrogradation of truth. The lemma is commented on in paragraphs 19 and 20.

Paragraph 19

Weidemann 1994, 269 maintains that the absurd consequences Aristotle talks about at 18b26 are not those mentioned at 18b25 (that a sea battle must at the same time happen and not happen) but are those following when one applies the principle of the division of truth values to SFCSs and doing so concludes to the nonexistence of the contingent (cp. also Ackrill 1963, 137).

Ammonius' opinion on this point is not perfectly clear. On the one hand, he seems to recognize (as does Ackrill) that the absurdity involved here is that of denying contingency (147,22-5), the absurdity of which Aristotle has not yet demonstrated. Demonstrating this absurdity, then, would be one of the objects of this passage. But on the other hand, Ammonius says (147,25-8) that Aristotle adds certain further consequences which he calls 'absurdities' even though he has not yet demonstrated their absurdity. These consequences must include the fact that necessitarianism renders human initiative superfluous.

Ammonius also considers an absurdity the entire argument that leads to the denial of contingency (147,30), and he thinks that Aristotle refutes this argument in two ways:

(a) by demonstrating the impossibility, i.e. the unacceptability, of what follows from it;

(b) by demonstrating that the premises it is grounded on are false.

Thus he attributes to Aristotle's text a structure conforming to the two methods Neoplatonists used to refute an argument, i.e. ἔνστασις 'objection' and ἀντιπαράστασις 'counter-objection, rejoinder'. If you follow the first you do not accept the argument at all, but refuse to agree to its premises. If you apply the second you accept the premises of the argument and then show that they are not able to demolish your thesis or else have inacceptable consequences (cp. Ammonius *In Cat.* 52,22-53,5).

The last task is, according to Ammonius, accomplished in the present lemma; the first 'a little later', he says, i.e. in the eighth and final lemma (cp. 152,23ff.).

In characterizing the logical structure of the last type of refutation, Ammonius seems to be attributing to Aristotle an argument patterned after the second indemonstrable of the Stoics, viz. *modus tollendo tollens* (cp. Sextus Empiricus, *M.* VIII, 225), which has as premises (a) a conditional statement $p \to q$, (b) the negation of the consequent of this conditional and, as a conclusion, the negation of the antecedent. If, from the affirmation that SFCSs divide their truth values in a determinate way, the claim follows that everything happens by necessity (an implication Ammonius considers sound), and if the evidence (cp. ἐνάργεια 148,3) confirms the negation of this claim, i.e. that there are contingent events, then one can deduce the negation of the claim that SFCSs divide their truth values in a definite way.

In the second part of the paragraph (148,5ff.), Ammonius interprets the actual argument used by Aristotle to reach this conclusion. Nevertheless, as he often does, he fails to stick to the letter of Aristotle's text, constructing his own argument based on Aristotle's. In lines 18b31-3, Aristotle says simply that the necessity of events renders our deliberations and our strivings useless. This seems to be a precursor of the argument called ἀργὸς λόγος ('lazy argument'), which was made later for refuting Stoic fatalism (cp. Cicero, *De Fato* 29).[215] Ammonius, on the other hand, strengthens this argument by introducing the theorem 'nature does nothing in vain' into it.

In paragraph 20 (149,1-3) Ammonius gives an example of the type of argument used by Aristotle which shows that he considers it quite similar to the Lazy Argument: 'If we intend to sail from Egypt to Athens, we need not go down into the harbor, seek a ship, or stow our baggage. In fact, even if we have done none of these things, it is necessary for us to arrive in Athens.' We know from Cicero, *De Fato* 30 that Chrysippus brilliantly showed the failure of such an argument through his theory of *confatalia*: if it had been determined by *fatum* that someone would go to Athens, it was also determined that earlier he would have gone searching for a boat, etc.

The argument developed by Ammonius from the Lazy Argument, however, is not so easily defeated because of the introduction of an additional principle that strengthens it. It involves the principle, already used in paragraph 11 (cp. p.167 above), that nature does nothing in vain.[216] Aristotle affirms this principle elsewhere (cp. the preceding note), but does not mention it at all in our present context. For Ammonius, the force of this principle rests on two facts: its validity is beyond doubt (148,16-18) and the determinists (surely the Stoics above all) must accept it (148,19-22).

The introduction of this principle permits Ammonius to incorporate Aristotle's argument into an argument that is more complex and stronger: nature has made us capable of deliberation but, as the Lazy Argument shows, this ability is useless because, according to the determinists, this same nature 'has left nothing in our power'. Thus nature would be doing something in vain (cp. 148,22-4).

It is interesting that after this argument, Ammonius mentions a counter-argument which resembles Chrysippus' counter to the Lazy Argument.[217] Someone could reply that nature uses our capacity to deliberate (διάνοια) as a tool for realizing various states of affairs (if we read with FG πραγμάτων)[218] (148,24-5). In other words, it is not in vain that she gave us the ability to deliberate because she uses it to realize the ends she pursues by means of our actions. If this objection were valid, it would defeat Ammonius' argument. So he

---

215 On the question of determining whether the argument used by Aristotle is identical in its structure to the Lazy Argument, cp. H. Weidemann 1994, 271-2. Cp. also S. Bobzien 1998a, 182ff. Alexander, *De Fato* 11, 178,8-180,2 (Bruns) develops a similar argument.

216 Above, n.194.

217 For the Lazy Argument and Chrysippus' counter cp. again S. Bobzien 1998a, 182ff.

218 In our translation we follow Busse who reads πράξεων. Thus we translate: 'to bring about our actions' instead of 'to bring about states of affairs', but this difference does not affect the overall meaning of the counter-argument.

attempts to show (148,25-8) that the assumption it is based on is false. The argument is as follows: if nature had wanted to use our practical intelligence to realize her own ends, she would have had to do it in such a way that we would ourselves be disposed toward the actions we have been assigned, as is the case for creatures actually impelled by nature. To this one can add that, instead of giving us such an impulse, nature gave us the ability to deliberate with the result that we are in charge of whether a given action is done or not. Thus nature risks having something occur that she doesn't intend.[219] Consequently, Ammonius can maintain that, given the hypothesis of determinism, nature has done something in vain in giving us the ability to deliberate.

He tries to support the claim that nature does not use deliberation, by claiming that when we imitate the production of nature in the arts, we no longer proceed by deliberation. This is of course a dubious point, but it seems to have been accepted by some ancient philosophers.

Is Ammonius' response convincing? In our opinion, this depends entirely on one's conception of the deliberation capacity. If it is conceived as Ammonius does, as in effect the freedom to act or not to act, his argument is sound. If, however, one conceives of it as the Stoics do, as a capacity whose effects are determined by prior causes, nature certainly can make use of such a capacity to attain her own ends.

Paragraph 20

Ammonius comments here on two items treated in the second part of the lemma: (a) the claim that necessitarianism renders our deliberation useless (148,32-149,15), and (b) the question of whether a statement effectively predicting an event is required for the validity of the argument for the necessity of the predicted event (149,15-34).

(a) The uselessness of deliberation has already been discussed in the preceding paragraph. Ammonius presents here two types of deliberation, one concerned with means, the end being fixed (deliberation on the means of getting to a given destination), the other concerned with the end itself (Achilles deciding between glory and longevity, cp. *Iliad* 9, 412-16). It is worth noting that Ammonius proposes as a criterion for making this choice the *degree of value* of the end in question.

(b) The passage 18b36-19a1, which Ammonius comments on at 149,15-34, is currently considered as a parenthetical remark (H. Weidemann 1994, 272). Ammonius restates it as a possible objection to the second necessitarianism argument, which is succinctly reformulated in lines 18b33-6. In fact, one could

---

[219]   This, however, presupposes that deliberation is concerned with ends and not only with means. Though it seems that Aristotle himself limited it to the latter (cp. *EN*, III, 1113b2-5; VI, 1142b28-33) in the Hellenistic period this limitation is not observed any more.

object that the predictions on which the argument is based have never been made and therefore the necessity of the corresponding event does not follow. Ammonius rightly understands that Aristotle's remark at 18b36-37 counters this objection. In fact, Aristotle argues that an actual prediction is not necessary. For the argument to be valid, all is needed is a true sentence. Whether it is enunciated or not does not make any difference in this regard (18b37-38). According to Aristotle, the claim that an actual enunciation is necessary depends on a conclusion wrongly derived from the rule that a fact and the true sentence affirming it imply each other. It cannot be inferred from this rule that the true sentence is the cause of the event it predicts. Ammonius perfectly understands Aristotle's point, he is right to refer to *Cat.* 12, 14b8-23, where Aristotle makes this point clear: a true statement is in no way the cause of the existence of something, but its existence is the cause of the fact the statement is true. According to Ammonius, this is why the necessitarianism argument does not presuppose the enunciation of the prediction.

Given Ammonius' conception of the ἀποφαντικὸς λόγος as a speech event (cp. Seel's article in this volume pp.218ff.) this claim, however, is not without problems in his case. For, strictly speaking, for Ammonius there are no truth-bearers that are not enunciated and consequently no predictions that are not uttered. Accordingly Ammonius speaks of 'prophecies which are said' (149,31) in his concluding statement. However, how can he nevertheless agree with Aristotle that it makes no difference whether they are enunciated or not? Ammonius resolves the problem by distinguishing two modalities of these speech-acts. He renders Aristotle's claim specifying that the argument holds, whether the prophecies are said *actually or (only) potentially* (149,31-32). So the entities he speaks about are still speech events, but by distinguishing actual and potential events he can reach the same conclusion as Aristotle.

Weidemann 1994, 272 holds that at *Int.* 18b36-19a1 Aristotle is stressing the fact that the truth of a sentence in the future tense depends on the present existence of causes which make the occurrence of the predicted event necessary; to support this he cites *Metaph.* VI 3. One may doubt that what Aristotle says in this chapter actually supports this claim. But, however this may be, Ammonius never mentions such prior causes in the context of his theory of truth. In fact, if and only if one starts from the assumption that the truth-makers of future sentences are the causes given at the same instant as their enunciation, Weidemann's interpretation is valid. But, as we shall see, (cp. below pp.239f.) Ammonius does not hold this hypothesis.

Lemma 7 (19a7-22)

The structure of Aristotle's text is as follows. It consists of a conditional proposition whose antecedent is formulated at 19a7 (εἰ δὴ ταῦτα ἀδύνατα, 'if this is impossible...') and the consequent appears at 19a18 (φανερὸν οὖν [ἄρα Arist.], 'Now, it is clear that...'). The long passage (19a7-18) beginning with ὁρῶμεν γάρ,

'For we see that ... ', is meant to support the claim of the antecedent (cp. H. Bonitz 1969, 135 ff.; H. Weidemann 1994, 274).

Ammonius devotes two paragraphs to this lemma. In the first, he reaffirms Aristotle's claim that there are contingent things and gives examples of this. In the second, he gives a Neoplatonic explication of the three types of things Aristotle distinguishes, necessary things, impossible things and contingent things.

Paragraph 21

The *reductio* argument that Aristotle attempts requires that the consequences of the claim to be refuted be impossible. Aristotle shows this impossibility by listing a number of facts that contradict these consequences. Although Ammonius understands perfectly the structure of Aristotle's argument, he seems to be in error regarding passages where Aristotle sets out the various stages in the demonstration. Thus he claims (150,16-7) that Aristotle has already proved the impossibility of these consequences. But as γάρ, 'for,' at 19a7 makes clear, Aristotle in this passage is concerned with demonstrating this very impossibility. It is interesting to note that Ammonius adds a series of actions not mentioned by Aristotle that would be impossible or 'in vain' if necessitarianism were true: praising, blaming, practising virtue or vice.

Paragraph 22

This paragraph is devoted to the classification of different types of entities (states of affairs). Following Aristotle, Ammonius distinguishes entities that always exist, entities that never exist, and those that sometimes exist and sometimes not. He assigns to the first type of entities the mode of necessity, the second impossibility, the third contingency. Ammonius explains why an eternal being exists necessarily: always perfect, such a being has all the qualities belonging to its essence. According to him, it follows that such a being cannot not exist. The lack of perfection of contingent beings explains why they are subject to generation and corruption. This explanation conforms to Aristotelian theory.

Aristotle affirms that the generation of contingent beings is itself contingent (19a11). This claim is very important: it establishes a link between two types of modalities, namely, the modalities tied to the totality of moments (omnitemporal modality) and the modality tied to moments or periods that are limited. Let us briefly explain the difference between the two types of modality.

1. If an entity possesses the first type of necessity, it is necessary that it exists at every moment, if it possesses the second type of necessity, it is necessary now that it exists at one precise moment or period of time. For the mode of impossibility the analogous determinations hold.

2.   If an entity possesses the first type of contingency, it is possible that it
       exists at a part of the totality of moments and that it does not exist at a
       part of that totality. According to Aristotle this means that a contingent
       entity does not have the possibility to exist at all moments and lacks
       the possibility not to exist at all moments as well.[220] If, however, an
       entity is contingent according to the second type of modality it is
       possible at the present moment that it exists at a precise moment or
       period of time and that it does not exist at the very same moment or
       period of time.[221]

Aristotle holds (cp. ὥστε in 19a11) that the first type of contingency implies the
second, so that the first type of necessity implies a necessity of the second type
(cp. Seel 1982a, 248-51). This claim is quite debatable because it is difficult to
see why there cannot be entities having the first type of contingency whose
genesis is at a certain moment necessary in accordance with the second type of
necessity. The reason Aristotle does not accept this possibility are found in his
conception of causality (cp. G. Seel 1982a, 360 ff.) which we cannot explain here.
Ammonius, on the other hand, accepts Aristotle's conception without debate
because he reports it as a triviality (151,25-8).
       We shall see the importance of this conception of the modalities in the
interpretation of the next lemma. The conception comes down to this: the real
topic of the discussion that chapter 9 of *De Interpretatione* is concerned with is
necessity of the second type. It is thus surprising to see that Ammonius as well as
Aristotle use statistical distributions for characterizing the modalities in question,
because such a characterization is suitable for the first type of modality, but not at
all for the second. This procedure can be explained, however, if one takes into
account the logical relations that the two philosophers say link the modalities of
the second type with those of the first.
       One further remark by Ammonius at the end of the paragraph (152,9-11)
merits our attention. He says that assertions (ἀποφάνσεις) behave regarding their
truth values in the same way states of affairs do (regarding their values 'being the
case' and 'not being the case', it should be added). This means that all the modal
distinctions that have been introduced in this paragraph for distinguishing modes
of being the case can be also used for distinguishing modes of being true or false.
This is a very important step that Ammonius makes here. We shall see that he
makes extensive use of the modalities of true and false in his interpretation of the
following lemma. This procedure is all the more surprising for having no parallel
in Aristotle's text.

---

[220]   Cp. *Cael.* I.12 282a5-9. For details, cp. G. Seel 1982a, 222-3.
[221]   Cp. G. Seel 1982a, 233-56.

Lemma 8 (19a23-b4)

All interpreters agree that the eighth lemma contains the most conclusive passage of chapter 9, in which Aristotle tries to refute the arguments for necessitarianism that he presented earlier. But as to how he proceeds in this there is much disagreement. In this debate the fundamental dispute is between the standard and non-standard interpretations, which we presented at the beginning of our introduction (cp. pp.17-18 above and the treatment of this dispute in Seel's article in this volume, pp.235-236). For the details of the controversies concerning the passage 19a23-b4 again cp. Weidemann (1994, 279-99). Ammonius' commentary on this passage is thus of great importance, and particularly the question of whether or not he gives a non-standard interpretation of Aristotle's procedure.

Ammonius understands Aristotle's argument in this lemma as an internal refutation (cp. the term ἐνιστάμενος, in 153,7, which refers to ἔνστασις, the primary Neoplatonic method of refuting an argument; cp. p.192 above), which is added to the external refutation developed in the preceding two lemmas and which thus completes Aristotle's argument. The external refutation was, as we saw, a *reductio ad absurdum*. Now the task is to show that the argument for necessitarianism is not founded on sound premises, and thus fallacious. One remark at the beginning of paragraph 23 (153,9-10) shows where Ammonius suspects the error is committed in the argument. He tells us that Aristotle examines 'how <statements which bear on the future> do have the <property> of being necessarily true and how they do not'. This remark, however, tells more about Ammonius' procedure than about Aristotle's. The latter, in fact, does not make use of any differences in modes of truth. Ammonius, on the other hand, not only introduces such modalities in the course of his analysis, but also effectively grounds the refutation he proposes on the differences in modes of truth values, of which the difference between 'definitely true' and 'indefinitely true' is the most important, but not the only one.

Weidemann correctly divides the passage 19a23-b4 into three parts: 19a23-32, 19a32-9 and 19a39-b4. The three paragraphs into which Ammonius divides his commentary do not at all coincide with these three parts, nor is it clear to what extent he follows the logical structure of Aristotle's text. If any correspondence can be determined between Ammonius' three paragraphs and passages in the lemma, the following is the most probable: paragraph 23 - 19a23-8; paragraph 24 - 19a28-33; paragraph 25 - 19a33-b4.

Paragraph 23

The controversy mentioned above starts off with the interpretation of the first passage, 19a23-5: What concepts of necessity is Aristotle distinguishing here? In today's secondary literature, one generally finds two responses:

1. the claim that Aristotle distinguishes here between *necessitas consequentiae* and *necessitas consequentis*, a claim held by G. Fine 1984, 24 ff. and others.
2. the claim that the two concepts distinguished here are the concept of necessity that is doubly linked to the present moment and the concept of omnitemporal necessity; this is held by such interpreters as S. McCall 1969, D. Frede 1972 and 1985, H. Weidemann 1980 and 1994, G. Seel 1982, S. Waterlow 1982, J. Vuillemin 1983b and 1984 and G. von Wright 1984.

Ammonius also understands that the key to the Aristotelian refutation is the distinction between two types of necessity.[222] He clearly interprets this distinction along the lines of the second claim (cp. 153,13-22), assuming (too restrictively) that the two modes are concerned with the way a property holds of a subject. He defines absolute and primary necessity as that whereby properties hold always of a subject so that it cannot exist without them. But he adds that there are two cases where this necessity applies: (a) where the subject is itself eternal, and (b) where the existence of the subject is limited in time. This is why the definition modern interpreters give of this first type of necessity is not applicable to absolute and primary necessity as it is conceived by Ammonius. The modern definition is as follows:

$$N_a Cp \leftrightarrow_{def} (t)\, C_t p$$

Ammonius probably intends to be consistent with Aristotelian theory as presented in *Cat.* 10, 13a8-17, according to which a predicate can necessarily be said of a subject without the state of affairs thus described itself existing necessarily, as is the case with fire necessarily being hot and Socrates necessarily being an animal.

Qualified necessity, on the other hand, is defined by Ammonius entirely in agreement with contemporary interpretation as the necessity that a property holds of a subject as long as it is predicated of the subject in accordance with the truth. By this formulation, Ammonius does not mean that the second type of necessity depends on the truth of a sentence but rather, just as in the modern interpretation, on the corresponding fact. The examples of such necessity that he gives at 153,22-5 show this clearly. It can thus be defined in the following way:

$$(t')(t'')(\, N_{bt'}\, C_{t'}p \leftrightarrow_{def} t' = t'' \bullet C_{t'}p)$$

We will henceforth call the first type of necessity 'absolute necessity' and the second 'conditional necessity'.

It is interesting to note that Ammonius feels himself obligated to give a defense of the Aristotelian claim that as long as a state of affairs is the case, it is, by the second type of necessity, necessary that it be the case. So he argues:

---

[222]   As R. Sharples has reminded me, these distinctions were to play an important rôle in Arabic logic. Cp. N. Rescher 1967 and R. Sharples 1978b.

someone who is not walking cannot walk, while he is not walking. Here Ammonius is apparently making use of the ontological principle of non-contradiction, i.e. that it is impossible that a state of affairs and its contradictory both be the case at the same time:

$$(t') \, (t'') \, \{t' = t'' \to \neg P(C_{t'}p \bullet C_{t''}\sim p)\}$$

But Ammonius is wrong to apply this principle to the Aristotelian claim. The latter is not concerned with the question of whether two contradictory states of affairs can be the case at the same time, but with whether the existence of a certain state of affairs precludes the possibility that at the same moment it might not exist. In other words, Aristotle holds the claim (a) and not (b):

(a) $C_{t'}p \to \neg P_{t'}C_{t'}\sim p$

(b) $C_{t'}p \to \neg P_{t'}(C_{t'}p \bullet C_{t'}\sim p).$

While (b) follows analytically from the ontological principle of non-contradiction (a) is a much stronger principle of modal logic, which cannot be deduced from the principle of non-contradiction. Thus Ammonius' argument is not acceptable. But it seems his error is not easy to avoid: one encounters it in our own day as well.[223]

The last point to be raised about this paragraph is that Ammonius already presents the modal treatment of truth values that he is going to develop in the next paragraph. He applies the adverbial expression ἁπλῶς, 'absolutely', not only to modes of being and to being, but also to being true (153,30-154,2). He supposedly would accept this definition for the expression 'being absolutely true': a sentence is absolutely true if and only if the state of affairs it affirms is necessarily the case, i.e. by absolute and primary necessity. We shall see in the next paragraph that he gives a similar account of the expression 'being definitely true' though, as we shall see, this does not mean that only those sentences which are absolutely true are definitely true.

Paragraph 24

On the basis of the distinctions elaborated in the preceding paragraph, Ammonius in this paragraph makes two related points:

1. He enlarges the scope of modalities so that the modes of being true correspond with the various modes of being the case distinguished in paragraph 23, adding modes that are here introduced for the first time.

2. He differentiates among necessarily true sentences by the sort of necessity they have (absolute vs. conditional necessity); and tells why each of three types of sentences possesses its mode of being true: (a) complex sentences of a disjunctive form, which he calls ἀντιφάσεις, 'contradictions', (b) simple sentences about

---

[223]   Cp. U. Wolf 1979, 115 and G. Seel's criticism (1983, 88 n. 4). Cp. also our discussion of R. Gaskin's 'modality relative to the facts' principle (p.20 above) which would, if sound, allow such a deduction.

non-contingent states of affairs, and (c) simple sentences about contingent states of affairs of the present or past. These are the concepts of modality that permit him in paragraph 25 to develop his refutation of the argument for necessitarianism.

To enlarge the scope of modalities, Ammonius uses the principle of correspondence he has already briefly mentioned in paragraph 23 (153,11-13). To do so, however, he must enlarge its scope of application. Before, we rendered the principle of correspondence thus:

$$C(01) \qquad N\{(T[Cp] \leftrightarrow Cp) \bullet (T[C\sim p] \leftrightarrow C\sim p) \bullet (F[Cp] \leftrightarrow \neg Cp) \bullet (F([C\sim p] \leftrightarrow \neg C\sim p)\}$$

This principle makes truth values correspond to facts and non-facts. To introduce modalities of truth values, however, Ammonius needs a principle that makes modes of truth values correspond to modes of facts and non-facts. At the beginning of paragraph (154,34) he introduces just such a principle of correspondence, though only for the mode of necessity; and he reformulates the principle with a small variation at the end (154,16-20).

Let us see first of all to what extent this step is justified by Aristotle's text, or to what extent it misrepresents it. To justify it, Ammonius can refer to 19a33, where Aristotle formulates his principle of correspondence thus: ὁμοίως οἱ λόγοι ἀληθεῖς ὥσπερ τὰ πράγματα, 'the sentences are true in the way that the things are'. The meaning of this abbreviated formula is a matter of controversy (cp. H. Weidemann 1994, 292-4). Weidemann suggests, not unreasonably, that it has this sense: 'sentences behave regarding their being true just as things behave.' To make the meaning entirely clear, however, we would have to add: 'just as things behave regarding their being the case.' Interpreted this way, Aristotle's formula corresponds to C(01). But without being broadened, it does not permit the modes of being true to correspond to modes of being the case, contrary to what Ammonius intends. Nevertheless, as Weidemann is right to emphasize, *Int.* 19a33 should be considered in the context of 19a32-5. This clearly shows that Aristotle uses the principle formulated at 19a33 to justify a correspondence between the contingency of being the case and the contingency of being true. Certainly then, he would also admit a correspondence between the necessity of being the case and the necessity of being true.

Thus Ammonius is not completely wrong in asserting at the beginning of paragraph 24 that Aristotle says that the mode of necessity behaves regarding truth in sentences in a similar manner to what he said regarding (the existence of) the things. The only difference is that Aristotle makes this analogy for the mode of contingency (ὁπότερ' ἔτυχε, "however it chances") and not, as Ammonius supposes, for necessity.[224] But this difference is not as important as it seems once the principle of modalization of truth values is introduced.

---

[224]   D. Frede 1985, 46-9, in criticizing G. Anscombe's interpretation (cp. 1956, 1-15)

Since two types of necessity are involved, absolute and conditional, we must render the principle of correspondence used by Ammonius with two different formulae:

C(28) $(N_aT[Cp] \leftrightarrow N_aCp) \bullet (N_aT[C\sim p] \leftrightarrow N_aC\sim p) \bullet (N_aF[Cp] \leftrightarrow N_a\neg Cp)$
          $\bullet (N_aF[C\sim p] \leftrightarrow N_a\neg C\sim p)$

C(29) $(N_bT[Cp] \leftrightarrow N_bCp) \bullet (N_bT[C\sim p] \leftrightarrow N_bC\sim p) \bullet (N_bF[Cp] \leftrightarrow N_b\neg Cp)$
          $\bullet (N_bF[C\sim p] \leftrightarrow N_b\neg C\sim p)$.

If we consider the meaning of the expression 'conditionally necessary' established above, we can replace C(29) with the following:

$$N_{t'}T_{t'}[C_{t'}]_{t'} \leftrightarrow N_{t'}C_{t'}p$$

But since Ammonius would accept that past singular contingent statements are also necessarily true in a conditional way, we can broaden this formula to obtain:

C(30) $(t')(t''){t'' \leq t' \rightarrow (N_{t'}T_{t'}[C_{t'}p]_{t'} \leftrightarrow N_{t'}C_{t'}p)}$

This formula can be completed in an analogous way for the negation of sentences and the value 'false'.

Thanks to these principles of correspondence, Ammonius infers (154,4-16) two types of being necessarily true from the different necessities of being the case distinguished in paragraph 23: absolute necessity of being true and conditional necessity of being true. But since the reasons for a sentence to be necessarily true by absolute necessity can differ on an essential point, he distinguishes a total of three groups of sentences that are true in a necessary way:

1. The first group is disjunctive sentences like 'Socrates is either walking or not walking' and 'Fire is either hot or not hot' (cp. 154,4-12).These sentences are true by absolute necessity.[225] But this necessity of being true is independent of the nature and even the existence of the things mentioned. Thus one is tempted to qualify this type of necessity as logical necessity. But such a characterization does not exactly correspond to what Ammonius has in mind. It is not only for logical reasons, as we say currently, that all such sentences are necessarily true. Rather,

---

     attributing to Aristotle the distinction between 'true' and 'necessarily true', holds that 'nowhere else (than in 19a38-9, 18a39, b2, b10, 19a19-21 [where in fact, as she says, we fail to find it, G.S.!]) do we find a distinction between truth and necessary truth or any other modalization of true or false in Aristotle.' This is invalidated (at least the last phrase) by our passage. But it is true that Aristotle makes far less conspicuous use of this modalization than the commentators who, probably influenced by the Stoics (cp. Alexander of Aphrodisias, *De Fato* 10, 177,3ff.), make it the key to their interpretation.

225   D. Frede, 1985 77-78 holds that for Aristotle disjunctive sentences do not have the status of assertive sentences at all and hence have no truth-values. As 17a20-22 shows, Aristotle, however admits 'composite sentences' and in 17a8-9 he seems to include these under the 'assertive sentences'.

they are true, by the principle of correspondence, because the disjunctive states of affairs they are about are necessarily the case.[226]

In introducing this type of necessary truth found in disjunctive sentences, Ammonius is evidently referring to *Int.* 19a27-9, where Aristotle mentions a disjunction of the type Cp ⟩-⟨ ¬Cp. For one group of interpreters, he is warning against the illegitimate inference from N(Cp ⟩-⟨ ¬Cp) to NCp ⟩-⟨ N¬Cp (cp. D. Frede, 1985, 69-75). Be that as it may, one thing is clear (as D. Frede 1985, 74 is right to hold): in *Int.* 19a27-9 only a disjunction of events is involved and not, as in Ammonius, a disjunction of events and a disjunctive sentence. It seems to us, however, that Aristotle, according to 19a32-5, would have to accept this extension.

2. The second group of sentences is introduced at 154,12-13, but examples have already appeared earlier (153,15-19); these are simple sentences like 'this fire is hot.' These also have their truth values by absolute necessity. But unlike disjunctive sentences, their value is not always the value 'true', since there are some sentences of this group that are necessarily false. This is so, Ammonius tells us at 154,9-12, because it is due to the nature of things that these sentences possess their truth values. The sentence 'this fire is hot' is necessarily true, because the nature of fire does not admit of being cold, whereas the disjunction 'Socrates is walking or not walking' is true independently of the nature of things and is simply due to the disjunctive form of the sentence and of the fact it bears on.

3. The third group of necessarily true or false sentences is introduced at 154,14-16. Ammonius gives as examples the sentences 'Socrates is walking', 'Socrates is not walking'. These sentences are necessarily true as long as the state of affairs they bear on are the case. Thus they involve the conditional necessity of being true or being false, which corresponds to the conditional necessity of being the case or not being the case which the given states of affairs possess.

In 154,10-12, Ammonius inserts in his explication of the necessity of disjunctive sentences a concessive clause that is very important in allowing us for the first time to ascertain with some reliability the meaning of the expressions 'true in a determinate way' and 'true in a non-determinate way'. We translate: 'even if it happens in such cases [disjunctive sentences] that, due to the nature of the thing, just one of the two parts of the contradiction is true in a definite manner, and not only the contradiction as a whole'.

We draw from this remark the following conclusions:

1. Ammonius distinguishes two cases: (a) the entire disjunction and one of its parts are true in a definite way; (b) only the entire disjunction and none of its parts is true in a definite way. For reasons of symmetry, one can conjecture that in case (a) one part is true in a definite way and the other false in a definite way, and

---

[226] Cp. *In Int.* 81,18-82,2 and in particular 81,18-19 as discussed in G. Seel's first article in this volume, 228-233.

in case (b) one part is true in a indefinite way and the other false in a indefinite way.

2. Since in every case mentioned where a sentence, whether simple or complex, has a definite truth value, it also has it by absolute necessity and in every case mentioned where a sentence has a indefinite truth value, there is no absolute necessity that it have this value, we are tempted to conclude that, according to Ammonius, (1) a sentence has its truth value in a definite way if and only if it has this value by absolute necessity, and (2) a sentence has its truth value in a indefinite way if and only if it has this value without having it by absolute necessity.

Since sentences which have their truth values by absolute necessity affirm facts which are necessary in an absolute way and sentences without such values report contingent facts, we may conjecture further that according to Ammonius (1a) a sentence has a definite truth value if and only if it reports a fact that is necessary in an absolute way, and (2a) a sentence has a indefinite truth value if and only if it reports a contingent fact.

A serious problem is raised, however, by this double conjecture. If it were valid, sentences about the present that are true—and, consequently, necessarily true by conditional necessity—would not have a definite truth value if they were reporting contingent facts. This is at odds with Ammonius' assertion in paragraphs 3 (130,20-3) and 12 (138,31-4; 139,10-15) that only singular statements about contingent future matters have no definite truth value. To take this into account, we must correct our conjecture thus: (1b) a sentence has a definite truth value if and only if it has this truth value necessarily—either by absolute or conditional necessity—; and (2b) a sentence has a indefinite truth value if and only if it has a truth value that is not necessary in any way.

This last conjecture, which we consider correct, does not contradict the text of paragraph 24, since at 154,10-12 Ammonius says only that all sentences that are necessarily true by absolute necessity are also definitely true, but does not say that this is the only case of a sentence having a definite truth value. Thus it is quite possible for a sentence to have a definite truth value not 'because of the nature of the thing', but because the time in which the thing is situated is the present or the past. We shall see supplementary evidence for our conjecture in the following paragraph.

In the final passage (154,16-20), Ammonius defends his procedure by mentioning once again the principle of correspondence he relies on. He reaffirms that the mode of truth that sentences have depends first of all on the nature of the things the sentences refer to.

Paragraph 25

In this last paragraph of his commentary on chapter 9 Ammonius gives his solution to the necessitarian ἀπορία, an original solution that he nonetheless considers faithful to Aristotle. The paragraph is divided into three parts.

1. Ammonius first of all (154,21-8) presents a new version of the necessitarianism argument based on the modal concepts introduced in the preceding two paragraphs.
2. Then (154,28-34) he gives his own refutation of this argument.
3. Finally (154,34-155,8) he gives further explication of his position concerning truth values for SFCSs.

1. At the beginning of the paragraph Ammonius engages in a fictional dialogue with his reader. He poses the question of how the modal distinctions contribute to the refutation of the argument for necessitarianism. In fact in introducing them Ammonius was digressing a bit from Aristotle's text. But to show their relevance, he digresses even more, constructing on the basis of these modal concepts a new necessitarian proof not found anywhere in Aristotle's text, and which he invents out of whole cloth.

This proof is in the passage 154,22-8. The text is relatively complex and partly obscure. We shall try first of all to reconstruct the argument.

Ammonius mentions at 154,22-7 three principles:

(A)   If a sentence is necessarily true, this necessity is absolute necessity (154,22-3):

T(17) $NT[Cp] \rightarrow N_aT[Cp]$

(B)   If a statement about the present or past is true, it is necessarily true (154,24-6):

T(18) $(t')(t'')([Cp])\{(t' \leq t'' \bullet T_{t'}[C_{t'}p]_{t'}) \rightarrow NT_{t'}[C_{t'}p]_{t''}\}$

(C)   If a statement about the future is true, it is necessarily true (154,26-7):

T(20) $(t')(t'')([Cp])\{(t'>t'' \bullet T_{t'}[C_{t'}p]_{t'}) \rightarrow NT_{t'}[C_{t'}p]_{t''}\}$

Concerning the logical relations among these three principles, Ammonius tells us this: If (A) is valid, the logical step from (B) to (C) is also valid. The result of this step can be formulated thus:

(D)   If a sentence about the present or past is true, it is not only this sentence that is necessarily true, but also the sentence about the future which stated the same fact earlier:

T(21) $(t')(t'')(t''')([Cp])\{(t''' < t' \leq t'' \bullet T_{t'}[C_{t'}p]_{t'}) \rightarrow (NT_{t'}[C_{t'}p]_{t''} \bullet NT_{t''}[C_{t'}p]_{t'''})\}$

Thus Ammonius believes that (D) is the logical consequence of (A). To understand this claim, we must show how the logical move from (B) to (C) is effected by means of (A):

1.   By means of (A), we can move from (B) to (B'):

(B') $(t')(t'')([Cp])\{(t' \leq t'' \bullet T_{t'}[C_{t'}p]_{t'}) \rightarrow N_aT_{t'}[C_{t'}p]_{t''}\}$

2. Now, as we have seen in the preceding paragraph, if a sentence about the present or the past is necessarily true by absolute necessity, a sentence about the

future which stated the same fact earlier has this truth-value by absolute necessity
as well. For, in the case of absolute necessity the difference between statements
about the present or the past and statements about the future does not matter at all.
Thus, we get the following principle:

(G) $(t')(t'')(t''')([Cp])\{(t''' < t' \le t'' \bullet N_a T_{t'}[C_t p]_{t'}) \to N_a T_{t''}[C_t p]_{t'''}\}$

By (G) we can then move from (B′) to (C′):

(C′) $(t')(t'')([Cp])\{(t' > t'' \bullet T_{t'}[C_t p]_{t'}) \to N_a T_{t'}[C_t p]_{t'}\}$

Finally we obtain (C) from (C').

Therefore, Ammonius is right to say that (D) is valid if (A) is. But he would
be even more correct to say that (D) is valid only if (A) is. For, as we shall see,
without (A) none of these logical moves can be effected.

Ammonius concludes his reformulation of the argument for necessitarianism
by briefly noting that the suppression of the contingent can be derived from (C)
(154,27-8). But he gives no indication as to how this can be done. So again we
must resort to a conjecture.

First of all, it is quite clear that this cannot be deduced from (C) if SFCSs do
not have one of the two truth values. Ammonius thus must be implying that the
principle of retrogradation of truth T(22) is an implicit conviction of
necessitarians:[227]

T(22)   If a sentence about present or past is true, every sentence about
            the future asserting the same fact is also true. Or:
            $(t')(t'')(t''')([Cp])\{(t''' < t' \le t'' \bullet T_{t'}[C_t p]_{t'}) \to T_{t''}[C_t p]_{t'''}\}$

It seems to us that this principle is implicitly presupposed in the passage at 154,24-7.

If, according to this principle, all SFCSs have one of the two truth values
without exception, from (C) we can conclude that they have them in a necessary
way. By (A) this necessity is an absolute necessity. To the absolute necessity of
the truth of these sentences corresponds, by C(28), the absolute necessity of the
facts asserted. Thus all facts are absolutely necessary facts. There are no
contingent facts.

2. The refutation of this demonstration that Ammonius proposes is quite
terse. He has already stressed at 154,22-4 that the necessitarian argument depends
on the premise, at least tacitly accepted, that absolute necessity of being true is the
only way to be necessarily true. Thus it is not surprising that in his refutation,
Ammonius attacks this premise. He argues (154,23-31) that the absolute necessity
of being true surely applies to the entire disjunction, but if the states of affairs are
contingent this type of necessity does not apply to any of the parts of the
disjunction when asserted separately. He is correctly referring to the
demonstration of this made in the preceding paragraph. Ammonius offers no

---

227   T(22) clearly is a principle Ammonius himself would accept, though he would reject
       a version of T(22) which uses definite truth-values instead of unqualified ones.

reason why the necessitarians accepted the dubious principle (A). Thus we are unable to reach a definite conclusion on the question of whether he actually accuses them of passing illicitly from NT[Cp ∨ C∼p] to NT[Cp] ∨ NT[C∼p] and thus transferring the absolute necessity of the former to the latter.

It is clear, however, that without principle (A) the necessitarian argument cannot be completed. If (A) is false, we cannot reach the dubious (C) from the unquestioned principle (B). In this case obviously the necessity of being true which sentences about the present or past possess is only conditional, and such necessity is strictly limited to present and past tense sentences. Therefore, from the fact that a sentence about the present is necessarily true, one cannot infer that the sentence about the future that affirms the same fact is also true in a necessary way. Thus Ammonius is right to assert at 154,31 that the necessitarians cannot reach their intended conclusion.

Regarding the debate about the truth values of SFCSs, it is interesting to note that the strategy pursued by Ammonius in his refutation is not what one would have attempted if the standard interpretation had been adopted. In that case, he would have had to attack the principle of retrogradation of truth. But as in the refutation of the other versions of the necessitarian argument, he is not doing that. This is another indication of the fact that Ammonius has not adopted the standard interpretation.[228]

3. Finally, let us see how Ammonius—in the last passage of the paragraph—explains and summarizes his position. This long sentence contains two assertions, one formulated positively, the other negatively, on truth values of sentences about the contingent—and particularly of SFCSs. Ammonius believes these two assertions follow logically from the failure of the proof for necessitarianism (cp. δῆλον ἄρα ὅτι ἀνάγκη…, 'Therefore, it is clearly necessary…', 154,34-5).

(a) Ammonius stresses the importance of the first assertion, treating it (155,1-2) as an answer to the primary question of the whole investigation. This answer is the following: Sentences concerning contingent states of affairs do not in every case (πάντως) have the property that one part of the disjunction is true in a definite way (154,35-155,1).

We can draw the following conclusions from this:

(1) There are pairs of sentences about contingent states of affairs in which one part of the disjunction is true in a definite way. These can only be sentences about the present or past which, as our analysis shows, are necessarily true in a conditional way and which thus have definite truth values.

(2) But this is not valid for all the sentences about the contingent (cp. μὴ πάντως, 'not in every case', at 154,37). The only possible exceptions are SFCSs. These are not necessarily true and hence do not have definite truth values. Does this mean that, according to Ammonius, SFCSs do not have any truth values, as those holding the standard interpretation believe? For us, the following arguments preclude such an interpretation:

---

[228]   R. Gaskin 1995, 158-59 fails to recognize this important point.

1. Ammonius considers his claim at 154,35-155,1 to be a consequence of his refutation of the necessitarianism argument and hence a consequence of the fact that principle (A) is false. That is, the truth of (A) would have the consequence that all sentences, including SFCSs, have definite truth values. The reason (A) has this consequence is the following: as we have seen, (A) entails that all sentences possess their truth values in a necessary way, and it is this necessity that is the reason they all have definite truth values. Denying the validity of (A) thus has the consequence that certain sentences do neither have necessary nor definite truth values; but this does not mean they do not have truth values at all. To accomplish his task, Ammonius does not have to deny that SFCSs have truth values, and the tack he has taken suggests it is quite unlikely he has.

2. In his refutation Ammonius has said that the parts of disjunctive sentences do not possess necessary truth values in cases where the predicate sometimes belongs to the subject and sometimes not (154,28-31). And he explicitly intends for this to apply to sentences in the future tense as well (cp. 154,31-4). The fact these sentences do not have definite truth values clearly does not mean they do not have truth values at all. On the contrary, in the case where the predicate belongs to the subject, the future tense statement affirming this can only be true, but without being necessarily true.

(b) From the construction of the final sentence, one can expect the second part (beginning with an ἀλλ', 'but') to contain the positive claim corresponding to the negation in the first part. In fact, Ammonius goes on to tell what positively characterizes sentences about the contingent focusing on the fact that they are not in every case definitely true or false. What he goes on to say, then, concerns sentences about the contingent in general and not only SFCSs. Regarding truth values of these sentences, Ammonius distinguishes two cases:

(1) The two parts of the disjunction are equally susceptible of being false and true.

(2) One of the parts is naturally more disposed to being true, the other to being false.

According to Ammonius, then, sentences about the contingent have what we would call in our modern terminology a probability[229]—between 0 and 1—of being true. This distinguishes them from the sentences about the necessary and the impossible, which have probabilities of being true of 1 in the first case and of 0 in the second. Thus the expression μᾶλλον ἀληθεύειν, 'to be rather such as to be true', does not in Ammonius refer to a 'probability of being verified' (as H. Weidemann 1994, 296 interprets the phrase in Aristotle), but simply to a probability of being true. This probability of being true does not take the place of being true, but in effect qualifies the sentence's truth value in the same way expressions like 'necessarily true' and 'impossible to be true' do. The fact that

---

[229]   Of course by saying this we do not want to attribute to Ammonius a theory of probability, we only refer to it in order to clarify his position for the modern reader.

these qualifications apply to all sentences about the contingent, and not only to SFCSs, clearly shows that they cannot supplant being true or false, since present and past tense sentences about the contingent have truth values. These qualifications, then, have nothing to do with the tenses of the sentences. They are, rather, entirely a function of the nature of the things the sentences are about. Because states of affairs have greater or lesser probability of being the case, corresponding sentences have greater or lesser probability of being true.

This interpretation is confirmed by the remark at 154,5-6, where Ammonius comments on Aristotle's phrase οὐ μέντοι ἤδη ἀληθῆ ἢ ψευδῆ (*Int.* 19a39). In our modern scholarly literature Aristotle's text gets very different interpretations, which follow from different readings of ἤδη (cp. H. Weidemann 1994, 296). Those holding the standard interpretation give ἤδη a temporal meaning, 'yet' or 'already', (cp. E. Lemmon 1956, 389), while their opponents hold that in this context it must have a logical sense meaning 'consequently' (cp. G. Anscombe 1956, 8 and 1968, 25). Now, as the remark at 154,5-6 shows, Ammonius does not understand ἤδη in any temporal sense. This is one further reason for doubting that he adheres to the standard interpretation. Ammonius holds, rather, that at 19a39 Aristotle means that sentences about the contingent do not 'have that which is true be always true nor that which is false be always false'.[230] The subject of this sentence, however, cannot be strictly speaking an assertoric sentence (ἀποφαντικὸς λόγος) in Ammonius' narrow sense. For an ἀποφαντικὸς λόγος in this sense is a speech act, which exists only for a short time and therefore could not be said to be 'not always true'.[231] With 'assertoric sentences about the contingent' Ammonius here must rather mean λόγοι in the sense of λέξεις.[232] In fact the same λέξις can be used on several occasions. Thus one can say of a λέξις that, if it is once used in order to make a true statement, it is not therefore always used in the making of true statements. Whether it is clearly depends on the subject matter the statement is about. In cases of the necessary or impossible, the use of a given λέξις always yields either a true statement or a false statement. This statement, then, is straightaway true or straightaway false. If the λέξις is used in reference to contingent matter, on the contrary, it does not always yield a true statement. Thus the statement, if true, is not true straightaway. In our opinion, Ammonius interprets the ἤδη in this way.

This confirms our interpretation of the expression μᾶλλον ἀληθεύειν. It is the statistical distribution of facts that, on the one hand, determines whether a contingent or necessary fact is involved and, on the other, decides the manner and probability of being true for statements about these different subject matters. (For further clarification cp. Seel's second article in this volume, 244-245).

---

[230] One might, of course, doubt that this is a possible interpretation of Aristotle's ἤδη. For this point see also the article of M. Mignucci in this volume, 274-279.

[231] Cp. G. Seel's first article in this volume, 218-219.

[232] Cp. M. Mignucci's article in this volume, 278-279, giving a different explanation of 'not always true'.

Part V

Essays

by Mario Mignucci and Gerhard Seel

V.1. Ammonius' Semantics of the Assertoric Sentence*

by Gerhard Seel

According to today's semantics a proposition is necessarily related to two entities different from it. In so far as it signifies something it is related to its meaning or reference, in so far as it is true or false it stands in a necessary relation with its truth-maker or its falsity-maker. In order to make sure that a proposition can be false without thereby losing its meaning modern semantics has to show that the meaning and the truth-maker of a proposition do not coincide. For otherwise propositions would be necessarily true for the simple reason that they have meaning.

The purpose of this essay is to find out how Ammonius managed to meet this requirement for his bearers of truth values, i.e. assertoric sentences. In order to accomplish this task I shall try to clarify first Ammonius' conception of the assertoric sentence, its meaning, truth and falsity and its truth-makers and falsity-makers. This investigation, of high interest in itself, will also be very helpful to understand Ammonius' commentary on Aristotle's *De interpretatione* 9. For here the crucial question is whether each assertoric sentence about future contingent events is either true or false in the very same way the other kinds of assertoric sentences are. This, of course, can only be answered, if one knows the manner in which assertoric sentences normally have their truth-values. So I shall try to find out, how Ammonius would have answered the following four questions:

1. Which are the entities that bear truth-values?
2. What are the identity criteria of these entities?
3. What is the meaning of these entities?
4. What are the truth-makers and falsity-makers for these entities?

This, of course, is not always obvious from Ammonius' text and therefore needs conjectures and reconstructions in some cases.

---

*   This and the following essay have been translated from German by David Blank.

V.1.1 Which entities bear truth-values?

Ammonius poses this question explicitly in his commentary on *Int.* 1, 16a3-9.[233] The candidates he names for the rôle of bearer of truth-values are: a) things (τὰ πράγματα),[234] b) thoughts (τὰ νοήματα), c) vocal sounds (αἱ φωναί). At the same time, he allows for the possibility that one, two, or all of these turn out to be bearers of truth-values. In case significant vocal sounds are bearers of truth-values, he asks more specifically what sort of vocal sounds these are: subject terms (ὀνόματα, i.e. 'names'), predicate terms (ῥήματα, i.e. 'verbs'), or the (assertoric) sentences composed of these (*In Int.* 17,31-18,2).

The distinction between a), b), and c) refers to the four levels which Aristotle distinguishes in *Int.* 1, 16a3-9, i.e. (from bottom to top), the levels of the things (πράγματα), the affections in the soul (παθήματα τῆς ψυχῆς)—which Ammonius equates with the thoughts (νοήματα)—, the vocal sounds (φωναί), and finally the letters (γραφόμενα).[235] Ammonius explains this distinction at *In Int.* 18,23-19,34, where the description of the functions he ascribes to the various levels is of particular interest. Thoughts, namely, have the function of knowing the things (τὴν τῶν πραγμάτων κατάληψιν). Here 'knowing' is understood as a kind of imaging of things in the soul, in such a way that 'they are actually (ὄντως)[236] thoughts when they are, so to speak, in harmony with the things themselves' (18,28-29). The entities of the second level (vocal sounds) have the function of being 'enunciative of thoughts' (τῶν νοημάτων εἰσὶν ἐξαγγελτικαί). Finally, letters are supposed 'to preserve the memory of vocal sounds' (διαφυλάττειν τὴν μνήμην τῶν φωνῶν: 18,35-19,1). It is important to bear in mind that Ammonius conceives of the relation obtaining between an entity of a higher level and one of the next lower level as a semantic relation:[237] vocal sounds refer first and immediately to thoughts and by means of them (i.e., by their relations to things) then to things. In the reverse order: thoughts refer immediately to things (cp. 24,9), vocal sounds refer to things only by means of thoughts, and finally letters refer to things by means of vocal sounds and thoughts (24,5-9). The semantic relation is thus conceived as transitive.

Now, it is important for the investigation of the truthbearer that Ammonius (following Aristotle) allows only to thoughts the property of being likenesses of things (ὁμοιώματα τῶν πραγμάτων: 19,32-33 and *passim*) or images (εἰκόνες) of things (20,21).[238] Thus, while semantic relations exist between all four levels, an

---

[233] Cp. *In Int.* 17, 29-30: 'among which of the things which are in any way should one look for truth and falsity' (ἐν τίσι τῶν ὁπωσοῦν ὄντων χρὴ ζητεῖν τὴν ἀλήθειαν καὶ τὸ ψεῦδος).

[234] As we shall see later, these are either simple or compound things.

[235] Ammonius does not mention these in this passage, but he does not neglect them in his theory, as the following passage shows.

[236] D. Blank translates 'truly'.

[237] Cp. 17, 25-28 and 24, 5-9.

[238] Cp. Ammonius' distinction between symbols and likenesses (39,33-40,30). Ammonius—in order to accommodate Plato's *Cratylus* (cp.430a ff.)—is however

imaging relation, which is based on similarity, holds only between the first and second levels. Since the truth relation, as we shall see, is also based on a similarity relation or is even identical with a specific similarity relation, Ammonius consequently seeks the original bearer of truth-values on the level of thoughts (18,6-7). However, the entities of the third and fourth levels are, due to the semantic relation which binds them to entities of the second level, also possible bearers of truth-values, although only in an indirect way. Entities of the first level, on the other hand, do not have any truth-value:[239] on this level we should rather seek the truth-makers and falsity-makers.

Let us now consider Ammonius' second question, which is even more important than the first. Are the bearers of truth-values simple vocal sounds like names and verbs, or compound vocal sounds like sentences? The distinction between simple and compound vocal sounds results from the idea that a sentence arises from a certain kind of composition of a name and a verb. Since vocal sounds signify thoughts and the truth-bearer is to be found on both levels, the one of sounds and the one of thoughts, the same question must be asked concerning simple and compound thoughts.

Concerning this question Aristotle holds that simple thoughts are true in any case and cannot be false and that the only entities that can have both values are compound thoughts (*De anima* 3.6,430a26-28; b26-30). Ammonius, however, departs from Aristotle's position. As *In Int.* 27,30-28,1 shows, he considers that the *De anima* passages, together with *Metaph.* XII.9, 1074b15ff., deal with the truth of intelligent cognition of the most simple, truly existent things and not with the 'truth which subsists in linguistic processes'. Therefore he is convinced that concerning the latter Aristotle denies that simple thoughts have truth-values. In any case, he is convinced that among the entities mentioned before the only possible bearers of truth-values are compound thoughts. Thus he gives the following answer to our question (18,4-10): "In fact, some of these <thoughts> are simple, signified by simple vocal sounds and admitting neither truth nor falsity, while the compound ones are concerned with compound things, signified by compound vocal sounds and admitting falsity and truth." He seems to believe that this answer is in agreement with what Aristotle says at *Int.* 17a24.

But that answer is not yet complete. As there are many kinds of compound vocal sounds and compound thoughts, i.e. vocative, optative, interrogative, imperative and assertoric sentences, Ammonius has to specify whether all or only some of them are bearers of truth-values.[240] He does so at *In Int.* 27,12-14 saying

---

prepared to call the name *qua* vocal sound 'artificial likeness' (ὁμοίωμα τεχνητόν) 40,17.

[239] Cp. 18,10-12, and especially 21,16-17: 'However, things would be called neither true nor false by themselves' (αὐτὰ δὲ καθ' αὐτὰ τὰ πράγματα οὔτε ἀληθῆ λέγοιτο ἂν οὔτε ψευδῆ). This is in agreement with Aristotle's position (cp. *Metaph.* VI, 1027b25- 28).

[240] Cp. 64,26-65,30, where Ammonius insists that the assertoric sentence is only one species of the simple sentence, the others being the vocative, optative, interrogative and the imperative sentence.

that "the combination or division must be concerned with 'belonging' (ὑπαρκτικήν), that is, it must reveal that one item belongs or does not belong to another, a character seen only with regard to the assertoric sentence" (περὶ μόνον τὸν ἀποφαντικὸν λόγον).[241] So it is only this kind of compound vocal sound and compound thought which is a bearer of truth-values.[242]

Ammonius offers as a first reason for this the fact that the other compound sentences belong to the appetitive part of the soul, while the assertoric sentence is the only type of sentence belonging to the knowing part of the soul (*In Int.* 5,1-23) "It <the assertoric sentence> is annunciative of the knowledge of things which, truly or seemingly, arises within us. This is also why only this type <of sentence> is receptive of truth or falsity and none of the others is" (5,14-17). We shall see later, how the property of being receptive of truth and falsity is a consequence of the fact that assertoric sentences reveal that one item belongs or does not belong to another.

Now, the assertoric sentence is not only a possible bearer of truth-values, it necessarily has one of them. In fact, assertoric sentences are *essentially* bearers of truth-values, so that the assertoric sentence can practically be defined as that which is either true or false (80,24-26). At first glance, this seems surprising. For if the truth relation is based on a similarity relation, as we have suggested above, one cannot understand why simple thoughts, which are also images of the relevant things,[243] cannot also be true and false. It is thus interesting to see how Ammonius justifies his answer. But before we turn to this question, we should first explain how Ammonius makes sure of the identity of an assertoric sentence.

V.1.2 What are the identity criteria of the assertoric sentence?

As the texts show, Ammonius has several criteria of identity for the ἀποφαντικὸς λόγος which form an ordered series and only when taken together allow a decision as to its identity. The first thing which could be counted as an identity criterion for an ἀποφαντικὸς λόγος is its λέξις or expression.[244] But in his commentary on *Int.*

---

241   It is important to note that Ammonius uses the expression 'assertoric sentence' in two ways. When he wants to refer to the bearer of a truth-value quite generally, he uses this expression in an undifferentiated way on all three levels. In this sense there is *one* sentence which appears in three forms: in the soul, in speech, and in writing (cp. 22, 12-16). When he wants to emphasize the difference between thinking and speaking, on the other hand, he uses 'thought' (νόημα) or 'belief' (δόξα) for what is thought and meant, reserving 'sentence' for what is spoken.

242   Cp. also *In Int.* 27, 21-24.

243   Cp. 20, 23-26 and 26, 12-27.

244   On the distinction between λέξις and λόγος cp. especially *In Int.* 12,30-13,18. Ammonius qualifies the relation at one point, with reference to Aristotle's *Poetics*, in such a way that the λόγος is a part of the λέξις (13,1); at another point, referring to the third book of Plato's *Republic*, he qualifies it in such a way that the λόγος is the thought and the λέξις its expression (13,13-14). It is in the second way that we speak of λέξις here. Cp. 40,15-17: the λέξις falls under the category of quantity.

17a5 (cp. *In Int.* 72,11-73,14) Ammonius shows that, while the expression of an assertoric sentence allows us to distinguish between simple and complex, as well as between primary and secondary assertions (i.e., κατάφασις and ἀπόφασις), it is insufficient to ascertain whether we are dealing with one or more ἀποφαντικοὶ λόγοι. This is, of course, due to the fact that linguistic signs can be ambiguous, in that the same expression can signify a plurality of things. If one took the expression as the necessary and sufficient identity criterion of the ἀποφαντικὸς λόγος, that would (as Ammonius correctly sees at 73,11-14) have the unfortunate consequence that one and the same sentence could be at once true and false.

But since Ammonius certainly saw that the reverse is also possible, i.e., that different λέξεις can express the same λόγος,[245] one can conclude indirectly that for him the expression cannot even be a necessary identity criterion of the ἀποφαντικὸς λόγος. What does Ammonius suggest instead?

In the above-mentioned passage *In Int.* 73,3-14 Ammonius assumes that Aristotle's doctrine is that 'where each of the terms (ὅροι) comprising the sentence indicates some one nature (μιᾶς τινος φύσεως ἐστι δηλωτικός), we say this sentence is one .... But when either one of the terms happens to signify several things, we say that these sentences are several'. Thus Ammonius' view, is clearly that the meaning of the two simple terms which the ἀποφαντικὸς λόγος is composed of functions as the criterion of its identity.

Strictly speaking, however, this is merely a necessary, and not yet a sufficient criterion for the identity of an ἀποφαντικὸς λόγος. For an affirmative sentence and the negative sentence contradictorily opposed to it are not identical,[246] although they share the two simple terms which signify the same thing (cp. 84,13-25 and 26-35). Thus, one must additionally demand that the meaning of the ἀποφαντικὸς λόγος itself, which results from the intentional signification of the subject and predicate terms and the formal signification of the copula, be the same.[247]

If this were the identity criterion, this would have the following consequences: two assertoric sentences thought and uttered by different persons are one and the same ἀποφαντικὸς λόγος whenever what is meant by both speakers is the same. The same holds for assertoric sentences uttered one after the other by one and the same speaker. If I say, for example, on 13 June, 1993 'The day after

---

[245]   This can be concluded from his commentary on the *Categories* (15,16-16,6), where, under the heading of πολυωνυμία, he considers the possibility that several ὀνόματα signify the same concept.

[246]   Cp. Ammonius' disagreement (*In Int.* 80,15-35) with Alexander's thesis that the expression ἀπόφανσις is used homonymously. Ammonius holds with Porphyry that the expression ἀπόφανσις stands for the genus of the simple assertoric sentence and that the affirmative and negative assertoric sentence are the species which fall under that genus. This is sufficient to show that according to Ammonius κατάφασις and ἀπόφασις cannot be identical.

[247]   Cp. also the doctrine attributed to Plato at 48,26-27: 'that the one signifying one identical thing is one identical sentence' (ἕνα λόγον εἶναι τὸν ἑνὸς πράγματος ὄντα σημαντικόν). Our translation differs from D. Blank's.

tomorrow there will be a colloquium' and on 14 June, 1993 'Tomorrow there will be a colloquium', these are different speech acts expressed in different ways, but since what is meant is one and the same thing, there would have to be one and the same ἀποφαντικὸς λόγος, according to the identity criterion analyzed above.

Despite its plausibility we have good reason to doubt that Ammonius would have accepted this position. Our doubts arise especially from Ammonius' commentary on *Categories* 4b4-13 (cp. *In Cat.* 53,20-24). In that passage Aristotle is concerned with the question whether other entities besides primary substances can take on opposing qualifications, i.e., whether they are 'receptive of contraries' (δεκτικὰ τῶν ἐναντίων). Sentence (λόγος) and belief (δόξα) are serious contenders for this title. For the sentence 'Socrates is sitting' changes its truth-value if Socrates stands up in the meanwhile (cp. 4a34-b2). Aristotle himself, who does not deny the change of truth-values,[248] secures the special status of substance with reference to the following difference: substances can change absolute (one-place) qualities and can thereby be changed themselves for example, when they go from 'hot' to 'cold'. The sentence and belief, on the other hand, are not themselves changed when they switch from 'true' to 'false'. Rather this change merely reflects a change in the facts which are their truth- or falsity-makers. For, according to Aristotle's theory of truth, the predicate 'true' means that the sentence it is attributed to stands in a relation of correspondence to the given fact.

While he sees Aristotle's argument as a possible strategy to secure the special status of substance, Ammonius makes it clear that it concedes too much to the enemy. 'In truth', as he says at *In Cat.* 53,20-21, 'they (λόγος and δόξα) cannot accept any opposing qualifications at all'. The reason he gives is that the sentence and the belief can not continue to exist as identical entities when the facts or the truth-values change, but rather 'are destroyed at the same time as they are uttered' (*In Cat.* 53,24).[249]

This not only excludes that an ἀποφαντικὸς λόγος changes its truth-value, but also makes it impossible to consider an expression thought and uttered by different speakers, or even by the same speaker at different times as one and the same assertoric sentence even if it has the same meaning. Furthermore, as the parallel treatment of λόγος and δόξα shows, there is, according to Ammonius, not even a mental entity of the type ἀποφαντικὸς λόγος which remains identical in the soul of a rational being over a longer period of time. While Ammonius admits that the types of simple things (i.e., names and verbs) are stored in the passive intellect[250] and lie there ready to be called-up for inclusion in an ἀποφαντικὸς λόγος, the ἀποφαντικὸς λόγος itself is formed anew each time and exists only for the length of the act in which it is thought. This means that an ἀποφαντικὸς λόγος

---

248   Cp. *Cael.* 1.12, 283b6ff. and *Metaph.* X, 1051b13-16.

249   This position is confirmed by *In Cat.* 60,10-12, where it is said of λόγος that 'it has its existence in being said' (ἐν τῷ λέγεσθαι τὸ εἶναι ἔχει). Analogously, the δόξα has its existence in being thought.

250   Cp., e.g., Ammonius' remarks on Aristotle's *De anima* at *In Int.* 6, 9-12.

has the mode of existence of a thought-event and speech-event which is bound spatially and temporally to the particular thinker and speaker.[251] In modern terms, it is a token rather than a type.[252] This adds a second identity criterion to the first, which thus turns out to be only a necessary, but not a sufficient condition for the identity of an ἀποφαντικὸς λόγος. Only taken together do these criteria allow a decision about the identity of an ἀποφαντικὸς λόγος.

To be sure, this seems to be a very unusual conception of assertoric sentences for antiquity. One might doubt that Ammonius actually had it because the text of his commentary on the categories is only transmitted ἀπὸ φωνῆς and could thus rely on a misunderstanding of a student. But the fact that other Neoplatonists have the same position speaks rather against this.[253] It is also rather unlikely that Ammonius was the inventor of that position though we do not know who it actually was.[254]

Now, however, it needs explaining how the communication of ἀποφαντικοὶ λόγοι is possible, that is, how it is possible for two different thinkers and speakers to agree in their opinions, although the assertoric sentences which they produce for this purpose are not identical. Ammonius does not answer this question explicitly. The solution of the problem can, however, in the circumstances, only lie in the fact that there are relations of similarity[255] between the different ἀποφαντικοὶ λόγοι, and that these are understood by the speakers and confirmed through agreement. In the case of true assertoric sentences which represent the same fact it is not difficult to assume such a similarity. Since each of the sentences agrees with the fact, they must also agree with one another, and this agreement can be ascertained by each of the two speakers by means of the semantic rules for the expressions used. However, in the case of two false sentences the matter is much more difficult. For it seems that nothing in the real world corresponds to these sentences, and so here the *tertium comparationis* is missing. Nonetheless, such relations of similarity must also exist between two false assertoric sentences,

---

251   Although this position results clearly from the passage of *In Cat.* we have just analyzed, it seems that in certain other contexts (e.g., *In Int.* 154, 5-6; see the commentary there) Ammonius attributes to an unambiguous λέξις the status of an ἀποφαντικὸς λόγος (in a secondary sense).

252   This is confirmed indirectly by the fact that Ammonius speaks of 'truth which subsists in linguistic processes' (τὴν ἐν ταῖς λεκτικαῖς ὑφισταμένην κινήσεσιν), *In Int.* 27,34.

253   Cp. *Olympiodori Prolegomena et in Categorias Commentarium*, *CAG* vol. XII 1902, 79,25-28; *Anonymi Paraphrasis Categoriarum*, *CAG* vol. XXIII, pars II 1883, 18,33-34; *Eliae in Porphyrii Isagogen et Aristotelis Categorias Commentaria*, *CAG* vol. XVIII 1900, 183,34-184,8; *Philoponi (olim Ammonii) in Aristotelis Categorias Commentarium*, *CAG* vol. XIII 1898, 82,19-23.

254   Paolo Crivelli has called my attention to the fact that in *Cat.* 6, 4b32-35 Aristotle counts λόγος among the discrete quantities and in 5a33-35 he affirms: 'none of its (λόγος) parts endures, once it has been uttered it can no longer be recaptured'. So Aristotle himself could very well have been the origin of our doctrine. It may have come to Ammonius through Porphyry's commentary on the *Categories*.

255   Cp. above, p.217.

since two thinkers and speakers can obviously agree even in error. The question is how one can ascertain this agreement with relative certainty. As long as no satisfactory answer to the question about the meaning of false assertoric sentences has been found, this question must also remain open. In the next section we shall attempt to reconstruct what appears to have been Ammonius' solution to this problem.

V.1.3 What is the meaning of an assertoric sentence?

We have seen that the meaning of an assertoric sentence is part of its identity criterion. This is not the only reason why it is important to clarify how Ammonius characterizes the meaning of an assertoric sentence. In fact, this characterization will also help us to see, why assertoric sentences and only assertoric sentences are bearers of truth-values.

Let us first clarify quite generally what type of relation Ammonius intends when he says that simple and compound thoughts 'signify' (σημαίνειν) simple and compound things (e.g. *In Int.* 24,5-12). The semantic relation which obtains between thoughts and things is, as we have already seen, specified by Ammonius as an imaging relation, i.e., thoughts stand to the corresponding things as images to their model (cp. 20,20-21: "each thought must rather be an image of the thing of which it is the thought, graven in the soul as if in a tablet, given that thinking (νοεῖν) is nothing other than having received the form of what is thought or made it accessible" [ἀνάγκη τῶν νοημάτων ἕκαστον εἰκόνα εἶναι τοῦ πράγματος, οὗ ἂν ἦ νόημα, ὥσπερ ἐν πίνακι τῇ ψυχῇ γεγραμμένον]). That means that there is a relation of similarity between the thoughts and the things. Ammonius speaks, following Aristotle, of the thoughts being 'likenesses' (ὁμοιώματα) of the things. A likeness has the function "to copy (ἀπεικονίζεσθαι) the very nature of a thing as far as possible and it is not in our power to change it (for if the painted likeness of Socrates in a picture does not have his baldness, snub nose and bulging eyes, it would not be called his likeness)" (*In Int.* 20,1-6). Strictly speaking that means that—at least in the normal case—thoughts are copies of some pre-existing original.[256] They depend on that original in order to have meaning. This relation Ammonius specifies as one-to-one (20,19-20: "It is, however, impossible to think of one and the same thing with ever different thoughts" [τὸ μέντοι ἓν καὶ ταὐτὸν πρᾶγμα δι' ἄλλων καὶ ἄλλων νοημάτων ἐπινοεῖν ἀδύνατον]).[257] Strictly speaking,

---

[256]   Cp. also *In Cat.* 9,17-10,9 where Ammonius emphasizes the fact, that vocal sounds signify things by means of thoughts. These things (πράγματα) are conceived of as actually existing things. The case of things which exist "in bare thought" (ἐν ψιλῇ ἐπινοίᾳ) (9,26) is mentioned by Ammonius only in order to exclude them from the scope of Aristotle's theory. Cp. also *In Int.* 18,28-29 where he stresses that only thoughts in harmony with the things themselves are actually thoughts. This implicitly means that the others are not thoughts in the full sense of the term.

[257]   Ammonius wants to show that the thoughts are the same for all human beings (the

this excludes that a thought, insofar as it has meaning, could ever fail to correspond to the thing imaged by it. If it has meaning, the thought necessarily corresponds to one and only one thing, and this is the thing which it images. Thus, it makes no sense to say of a meaningful thought that it does not agree with this thing, just as one cannot sensibly say of a photograph that it does not agree with what is pictured by it. The alternative to this is simply that a thought has no meaning at all, in which case it images nothing and thus no longer corresponds to any thing. Then we are no longer dealing at all with an entity which satisfies Ammonius' definition of a thought.

Now, as we have already seen, what is signified by a simple thought is a 'simple thing' and what is signified by a compound thought is a 'compound thing' (συνθετὸν πρᾶγμα) *In Int.* 21,1-10. But what exactly are these 'simple things' and what the 'compound things'?

The answer to the first question is complicated by the fact that—in virtue of the distinction of names and verbs and following Aristotle—Ammonius distinguishes two kinds of simple things and by the fact that the descriptions he gives of these differ slightly from each other. The things signified by names are existing individual substances.[258] The example mostly given by Ammonius is 'Socrates' (cp. *In Int.* 20,34-21,1). The things signified by verbs are potential properties of individual substances.[259] Examples are 'walking' or 'pale'.[260]

Much more difficult than the answer to the first question is the task to clarify what Ammonius means by 'compound thing' (συνθετὸν πρᾶγμα). The example he gives at 21,1 is 'the running Socrates' and he explains this example saying that "here the substance of Socrates has taken on the activity consisting in running". This could mean two quite different things:

1. Ammonius' 'compound thing' could correspond to what we today call a 'state of affairs'. States of affairs are those entities we describe by a that-clause in sentences like: 'It is the case that Socrates runs' or 'It is the case that Socrates does not run'. States of affairs are unreal entities which exist in a Platonic world of ideas and of which if taken as such one cannot tell whether or not a fact

---

same in content and structure, not numerically the same) and therefore—in contrast to vocal sounds—are 'by nature' (φύσει); cp. *In Int.* 24,10-16.

[258] Cp. the definition of the term 'name': "a symbol <made> of a vocal sound which is significant by convention without time, of which no part is significant when separated, *indicative of the existence of a thing whatsoever or of a person*" (*In Int.* 40,4-6; our translation differs slightly from D. Blank's).

[259] Cp. *In Int.* 49,24-25 "Verbs have been said to be significant 'of things said of another', namely 'of things said of a subject or in a subject'"

[260] Cp. also *In Int.* 48,30-49,1, where Ammonius says that there are 'only two kinds of meaningful vocal sounds, name and verb, the one indicating existences, the other actions or passions, which he (Plato) called jointly 'doings' (πράξεις)'. The same point is made at 38,20-22: names mean 'some nature or person', verbs 'an action or passion'. At 40,23-27 he refers to *Cratylus* 430a ff. saying that 'the name is a representation (μίμημα) of the substance of each thing ... just as verbs are representations of what follows upon—that is, what belongs to—substances'.

corresponds to them. However, we say of a state of affairs that it is the case when there is in the real world a fact corresponding to it, and that it is not the case when there is in the real world no fact corresponding to it. In this sense states of affairs are either the case or not the case.

2. On the other hand Ammonius' 'compound thing' could correspond to a fact in the modern sense of that term i.e. to the entity referred to by the whole sentence 'It is the case that Socrates runs' or 'It is the case that Socrates does not run'.

Both conceptions allow one to explain why only compound thoughts but not simple ones are bearers of truth-values, but these explanations are quite different, depending on the two conceptions.

1. If simple thoughts were bearers of truth-values, the entities which make them true would be identical with their meaning. From that it would follow that meaningful simple thoughts could not be false at all. It seems indeed that Aristotle drew this conclusion (cp. *De Anima* 3,6, 430a26-28 and b26-30). [261] Ammonius, however, wholly denied that simple thoughts are bearers of truth-values, as we have seen before. Compound thoughts, on the other hand, if they signify compound things in the sense of 'states of affairs', do not risk being necessarily true. States of affairs consist of at least two simple things and the relation which obtains between them. And this relation can be either that of joining or that of separation. To image a compound thing, then, it is not enough to image the simple things from which it is made: the relation which obtains between them must also be imaged. This allows room for mistakes when the image exhibits the wrong relation.

It follows from this that a compound thought can be false as a whole, without the simple thoughts of which it is composed losing their meanings. If one conceived the meaning of the compound thoughts as a function, of a) the meanings of the simple thoughts of which they are composed and b) the relation it establishes between them, one could say that false compound thoughts are by no means without meaning. This would further mean that compound thoughts, regardless of their meaning, could be true or false, or, in other words, that the meaning of compound thoughts does not necessarily coincide with their truth-maker. Now, if one conceives of truth as a non-necessary property of thoughts, i.e. as a property to which there is a real alternative, then it clearly follows from what has been said that only compound thoughts can be bearers of truth-values and that they are necessarily bearers of one of the two truth-values.

2. The explanation why compound thoughts are not necessarily true is quite different when they signify facts and not states of affairs. In this case the falsity of a sentence would not result from the fact that in the description of the compound thing it gives the wrong relation of the two simple things, but rather from the fact that it states that a certain state of affairs is the case which is not the case. Thus while in the first case the error concerns the relation of the simple things itself, in the second it has to do with the ontological status of this relation.

---

[261]   Cp. above p.215.

It is most important for our overall purpose to find out which of the two conceptions of the meaning of assertoric sentences is the one corresponding most closely to Ammonius' semantics. There are four ways to clarify this point.

1. We can see how Ammonius actually justifies his thesis that only compound thoughts are bearers of truth-values.

2. As one of his answers presupposes the distinction between facts and states of affairs, as we shall see, we could try to find out if Ammonius actually makes such a distinction. This again can best be done by clarifying the very function(s) he attributes to the third linguistic part of the assertoric sentence, namely the expressions ἔστιν and οὐκ ἔστιν.

3. Since to either conception of the meaning of an assertoric sentence a different conception of truth and falsity corresponds we can try to answer our question by clarifying Ammonius' conception of truth and falsity.

4. Finally, since the conception of truth and falsity depends itself on the conception of the truth-maker and the falsity-maker, we can try to find out how Ammonius conceives of the latter.

I shall follow up these points one after the other—the first three in this section, the last in my final section. So the final answer to our question will only be given after the accomplishment of the fourth inquiry.

Ad 1. Ammonius himself has no argument for the thesis that only compound thoughts can be bearers of truth-values, but he reports such an argument at 56,14-57,18 in his explanation of Porphyry's conception of the function of the copula. Since he presents Porphyry's position without contradicting it, we may assume that he shared it. The argument runs: 'Now, the <statement of Aristotle> 'For <the verb> is not a sign of the being or not being of the thing', is the same as saying that the verb said by itself is not significant either of the thing's being, that is, <of the being of> the thing signified by it, which affirmation usually signifies, nor of its not being, which is indicated by negation' (56, 29-32).[262] (We may assume that what is said of the verb, i.e. the predicate term is *a fortiori* true of the subject term.) The passage means that the affirmative or negative sentence has not only a thing as its meaning—which must, according to what has been said before, be a compound thing—but also means that this thing either is or is not the case, while simple thoughts signify only a simple thing and nothing more. This is seen by Ammonius/Porphyry as the reason why only the former can receive the values 'true' and 'false', while the latter cannot (cp. 56,23-28).

What exactly is meant by saying that the affirmative sentence signifies the existence and the negative sentence the non-existence of the thing (πρᾶγμα) they signify? In my view, the most plausible answer is that the thing they signify is a state of affairs and that by 'signifying the existence or non-existence of that thing' Ammonius/Porphyry want to say that the assertoric sentence states that this state

---

[262]   Aristotle's text (16b22) as established by Minio-Paulello has οὐ γάρ. This is also the reading that Porphyry accepted. Ammonius mentions, however, a different reading with οὐδὲ γάρ (56, 14-17). Cp. also D. Blank 1996, 152 note 217.

of affairs is the case or is not the case. This answer, however, presupposes that Ammonius/Porphyry distinguished between 'thinking a state of affairs' and 'asserting that a state of affairs is the case'. Before deciding the case we must therefore clarify this last point.

Ad 2. I should first emphasize that for a user of ancient Greek it was not at all obvious that there was a difference between describing states of affairs and asserting facts, as it is not for the user of today's ordinary English either. For in classical Greek the assertive and descriptive functions do usually not belong to different expressions,[263] with the effect that one could hardly describe states of affairs without at the same time asserting that they are or are not the case.

To be sure, there are expressions like 'it is possible to ... ' (ἔστιν ὥστε + infinitive: e.g. *Phaedo* 93b4, 103e2) in which the assertive and descriptive functions belong to different expressions. One should also mention the expression τὸ [πρᾶγμα] σὲ καθῆσθαι, which Aristotle suggests in *Metaphysics* V 1024b17 ff.,[264] as well as modal expressions of the type '(it is) necessary (ἀναγκαῖον) + infinitive', '(it is) possible (δυνατόν) + infinitive'. But commonly the Greek language uses definite verbs, and these always have both a descriptive and an assertive function at the same time. Thus, while it is in principle possible to describe a state of affairs without asserting that it is the case, the normal practice is not to make such a distinction.

Now it is very interesting to inquire, whether in his own semantical analyses of the Greek language Ammonius is aware of the fact that definite verbs have two functions at the same time. For such an awareness could very well have let him discover the difference between states of affairs and facts.

Ammonius' commentary on *Int.* 16b19-25 offers a good point of departure for our purpose. Of interest to us is, first, the conception (already held by Aristotle: cp. *Int.* 21b9-10) that the finite verb can be analyzed into a participle and a finite form of the verb 'to be' (εἶναι: *In Int.* 55,23-28). This opens the possibility of analyzing the affirmative assertoric sentence 'Σωκράτης τρέχει' into the sentence 'Σωκράτης τρέχων ἐστίν' and the negative assertoric sentence 'Σωκράτης οὐ τρέχει' into the sentence 'Σωκράτης τρέχων οὐκ ἔστιν'[265] and then to inquire into the functions of the different parts of the sentence analyzed in this way. Of special interest is, of course, the semantic function which the expressions 'is' and 'is not' have in the context of the assertoric sentence as a whole.

Before investigating the semantic functions of 'is' and 'is not' in the context of the assertoric sentence, Ammonius asks the preliminary question, what they signify 'when said by themselves' (*In Int.* 55,21). He gives a negative and a positive answer to it. Said by themselves these expressions as well as any other verb do not signify anything true or false (55,21). They immediately signify 'being so' [ὑπάρχειν] or 'not being so' [μὴ ὑπάρχειν]. Since the verb ὑπάρχειν is

---

263   Cp. C.H. Kahn, 1972; 1973 and 1986.
264   Cp. also *Top.* III.1, 116a32, τὸ τοὺς φίλους δικαίους εἶναι. Here this πρᾶγμα is presented as preferable (αἱρετώτερον) to another πρᾶγμα.
265   Of course, this can not be done in English without changing the meaning of the sentence.

used by Ammonius both in sentences of the form 'The A belongs to the B' (τὸ Α τῷ Β ὑπάρχει), which means that the property A is correctly attributed to the subject B, and in sentences of the form 'The thing A exists' (τὸ πρᾶγμα Α ὑπάρχει), exactly what is meant in 55,20 is unclear. If the first is meant, the semantic function of the third part of the ἀποφαντικὸς λόγος is limited to creating the relation of belonging or not-belonging between the other two parts. If, however, the latter is intended, its function consists in saying of something already compounded that it is the case.

We shall try to decide this when we now turn to the semantic function of these expressions when they are used—not by themselves, but—in the frame of an assertoric sentence. What is accomplished semantically by means of the addition of 'is' or 'is not' to the two other parts of the assertoric sentence? In fact, we find in Ammonius' text rather detailed and clear statements on the semantic function of the expressions 'is' and 'is not' in the overall structure of the ἀποφαντικὸς λόγος. But here Ammonius makes our job difficult by first hiding his own view behind those of Porphyry and Alexander, who interpret Aristotle's phrase 'it additionally signifies some composition' in different ways, and then leaving it up to the reader which of the two he should accept. This difference, however, does not affect our main question.

The view of Porphyry seems to be the result of a critique of that of Alexander. We shall therefore examine the latter first. Alexander distinguishes two meanings (two semantic functions) the expressions 'is' and 'is not' can have when they are part of an ἀποφαντικὸς λόγος. Thus, he understood 'additionally signifies' (προσσημαίνει) in the sense of 'has a second meaning'.

1. These expressions can be used as names like the other verbs. In this case they signify 'participation in' or 'deprivation of being' (57,25-27). In his commentary on the *Prior Analytics* Alexander explains this use of ἔστιν saying that the sentence 'Σωκράτης ἔστιν' has the same meaning as 'Σωκράτης ὄν ἐστιν' (*In An. Pr.* 15, 17-18).

2. According to their second semantic function these expressions signify the predicate's joining with the subject of a sentence (57,27-29). Whereas according to their first semantic function the expressions 'is' and 'is not' have quite different meanings the second semantic function is the same in both cases (57,29-33). Quoting *De Anima* III.6, 430b2 Ammonius[266] makes clear that Alexander must mean the function of the synthesis of the two other terms, notwithstanding that the synthesis is either συμπλοκή in the case of a positive predicate or διαίρεσις in the case of a negative predicate.

According to Alexander, the second semantic function is responsible for the completeness of the sentence and for its character as bearer of one of the

---

266   It is not clear where exactly Ammonius' report of Alexander's theory ends and
       where his own commentary starts. However, as in 57,28 the term συμπλοκή is used
       to describe the second semantic function, while in 57,30-32 the term σύνθεσις stands
       for that function and συμπλοκή refers to one of its modes, we consider the latter
       passage as part of Ammonius' commentary.

truth-values (57,28-9; cp. also Alexander of Aphrodisias, *In An. Pr.* 15,6-14).
Unfortunately Ammonius does not say why exactly Alexander made this character
depend on the synthesis-function and we did not find any answer to this question
elsewhere in Alexander's writings either.

Porphyry has a different view of 'additionally signifies some composition'
(προσσημαίνει σύνθεσίν τινα). He interprets this expression as 'when joined with
something else it signifies a composition which is now receptive of falsity and
truth' (57,14-18). Thus 'additionally' does not refer to a first meaning of 'is' and
'is not' but to the procedure of joining these expressions to the subject and the
predicate. Except this, Porphyry's view apparently does not differ much from
Alexander's. When added appropriately to a subject-term and a predicate term 'is'
and 'is not' have the semantic function of effecting a synthesis between these and
thus creating a new entity, i.e. an assertoric sentence, which is as such true or
false. However, unlike in the case of Alexander, we can indicate Porphyry's
reasons for this position and thus answer our main question. As we have seen
before, Porphyry insists (cp. 56,28-33) that the affirmative assertoric sentence
expresses the being of a thing, and the negative assertoric sentence expresses its
not-being. Therefore 'to belong to a subject as a qualification' can not be neutral
with respect to the alternatives 'to belong to a subject in actuality/to belong to a
subject only in thought'. Rather the synthesis of a predicate expression with a
subject expression always means, according to Porphyry, that the qualification of
the predicate actually belongs to the subject.

Now, what can one conclude from this about Ammonius' view on this
point? There can be no doubt that Ammonius generally sympathizes rather with
Porphyry, even though he differs from him in certain points of detail (cp.
56,14-18). This is also the case in our question. The following passage shows that
in fact Ammonius interpreted 'belong' in the sense of 'belong in actuality'
(52,13-16): 'For nothing prevents something from being truly predicated even of
what is not, as not belonging to it or not being such as to belong <to it>—as when
I say "The hippocentaur is not healthy" or " <the hippocentaur> is not ill"—but it
is impossible for something to belong to what is not'. The explanation is
obviously valid only if 'belong' means 'belong in actuality'. For, in thought, a
predicate such as 'being ill' or 'being healthy' can indeed belong to a
hippocentaur, regardless of the non-existence of the latter. Thus, Ammonius
follows Porphyry's line on this decisive point.

Ammonius' analysis of the semantic functions of the expressions 'is' and 'is
not' amounts to the following points:

1. These expressions have two semantic functions: (a) to join or to separate
the two other parts of the assertoric sentence, (b) to assert that these relations hold
actually between the two ontological entities signified by the two other parts of
the assertoric sentence.

2. These two semantic functions go always and necessarily together.
Therefore it is impossible to think a state of affairs without asserting that it is or
that it is not the case.

3. The meaning of the assertoric sentence as a whole therefore is not simply a state of affairs, but a fact, i.e. the 'being-the-case of a state of affairs'.

But this semantic analysis of ordinary Greek does not hinder Ammonius' distinguishing 'states of affairs' and 'facts' in his philosophical metalanguage. A clear example of this is given by expressions such as: 'it is not the sentence which is the cause of the thing's being (τῷ πράγματι τοῦ εἶναι αἴτιος), but the existence of the thing (ἡ τοῦ πράγματος ὕπαρξις) which is responsible for the sentence being true' (149,27-28), 'inasmuch as the thing about which one is speaking has already occurred' (τοῦ πράγματος ἐκβεβηκότος περὶ οὗ ὁ λόγος 130,12-13), 'since the thing has not already occurred but can both occur and not occur'[267] (μήπω τοῦ πράγματος ἐκβεβηκότος δυναμένου δὲ καὶ ἐκβῆναι καὶ μὴ ἐκβῆναι 130,25-26), 'existence/non-existence of the things' (ὕπαρξιν/ἀνύπαρξιν τῶν πραγμάτων 139,30); the list could be extended. For, that of which the existence or non-existence, the occurrence or the possibility of occurring and not occurring is said in these expressions is neither a substance nor a fact—it would be a contradiction to say of a fact that it does not exist—but a state of affairs. There are also, as we shall see, systematic reasons which force Ammonius to distinguish at least in his metalanguage between states of affairs on the one hand and facts or non-facts on the other. Otherwise, there is no satisfactory solution for the problem mentioned above of the meaning of false statements. This we shall see when we in our last section address Ammonius' answer to that question.

Ad 3. But let us first see how Ammonius' conception of truth squares with this analysis of the signification of an assertoric sentence. Ammonius gives two different answers to the question under which conditions an assertoric sentence is true. We first find passages like *In Int.* 26,27-30 where he says that "when the thing should happen to be in the very state the faculty of thinking believes it to be in then the thought will be true".[268] Passages like this amount to defining truth and falsity as a relation of correspondence or non-correspondence between thoughts and things thought regarding the question of how the things are. This definition of truth would fit the conception of the meaning of the assertoric sentence we tentatively took into consideration at the beginning, i.e. the hypothesis, that the meaning of an assertoric sentence is a state of affairs. We rejected this hypothesis, however, because it did not square with the theory of Porphyry to which Ammonius, too, adheres.

On the other hand there are passages such as 21,13-16, where Ammonius lays stress not on saying how the things are, but that they are so. In these places truth seems to be defined as the agreement of the statement that something is the case with the corresponding fact that it is the case. This, of course, would very well square with Porphyry's conception of the meaning of an assertoric sentence.

---

[267]   Here by πρᾶγμα Ammonius clearly means a type of event which is a kind of state of affairs.

[268]   τότε γὰρ ἂν μὲν ... . Our translation differs from D. Blank's. A similar answer is given at 55,13-14: "one who says how what is is and how it is by nature speaks the truth". Again our translation differs from D. Blank's.

Therefore Ammonius should give preference to the latter conception of truth. It is the only one which is consistent with his semantics of the assertoric sentence.

V.1.4 What are the truth-makers and falsity-makers of an assertoric sentence?

But whichever of the two conceptions of meaning and truth one finally attributes to Ammonius, in both cases he faces a fundamental ἀπορία. For if he holds that truth is the correspondence of a compound thought with a compound thing, the truth-maker of the compound thought is nothing else but the compound thing thought, i.e. the meaning of the thought. Thus truth-maker and signification of an assertoric sentence prove to be identical. We come to the same conclusion in the case of the second conception of truth and meaning. For if Ammonius holds that truth is the correspondence of the statement that a compound thing exists to the existence of that compound thing, the truth-maker of the statement is the fact stated and that fact is also the meaning of the statement. So again truth-maker and meaning are identical. But this identity seems to have disastrous consequences for the meaning of false assertoric sentences. For if the truth-maker and the meaning of an assertoric sentence coincide, false assertoric sentences, which have no truth-maker, will have no meaning either and thus be no real thoughts any more.[269] To avoid these consequences Ammonius must find a way to show that on the one hand there is no thoroughgoing identity of truth-maker and meaning and that on the other hand false assertoric sentences as well as true ones still refer to something 'in the world' and not to a purely spurious entity.

The solution to this ἀπορία can be found in the paragraph 81,13-82,13 where Ammonius—commenting on *Int.* 17a26-37—explains the different references of affirmations, negations and contradictions. We have already seen that Ammonius distinguishes two kinds of simple assertoric sentences, viz. affirmative (καταφάσεις) and negative (ἀποφάσεις) ones. One can make a negative assertion out of a positive one by adding a negative particle (ἀρνητικὸν μόριον) to it (67,26-27) or, more precisely, to its predicate. In this way arise pairs of ἀποφαντικοὶ λόγοι whose members differ only in respect of their formal semantic element, i.e. in respect of the expressions 'is' (ἔστι) and 'is not' (οὐκ ἔστι), while having the same subject and predicate.[270] Aristotle calls such pairs 'contradictions' (ἀντιφάσεις: 18b37, cp. 17a31-34). But Ammonius uses this term at first to indicate the logical relation which obtains between the members of such pairs. He defines this relation as the 'conflict (μάχη) of an affirmation and a negation which always divide the true and the false so that when one of them is false the other is true, and vice-versa' (81,14-16). We are dealing, therefore, with the relation of contradiction familiar to us from propositional logic, and the cited passage gives us reason to suppose that Ammonius would have accepted its modern

---

269   Cp. Ammonius, *In Cat.* 9,25-10,1 τὰ μὲν ἐν ψιλῇ ἐπινοίᾳ ἐστίν, ..., τὰ δὲ καὶ ὄντως ὑφεστῶτά ἐστιν.

270   Cp. 84,6-25. We leave aside the case of indefinite predicates.

truth-functional definition.[271] At the very least the passage allows the conclusion that Ammonius agrees with the following formula:

T(16) $(T[Cp] \rightarrow F[C\sim p]) \bullet (F[Cp] \rightarrow T[C\sim p]) \bullet (T[C\sim p] \rightarrow F[Cp]) \bullet$
          $(F[C\sim p] \rightarrow T[Cp]).$

Ammonius goes on to say that the division of the truth-values results from the fact that 'there is a conflict between false negation and true affirmation and between false affirmation and true negation' (81,16-18). As the following remarks show, this means that always exactly one of the two members of such a pair is true and exactly one is false (cp. also 85,2-3; 121,22-23; 26,21-22). This can be formulated as follows:[272]

T (11) $N\{(T[Cp] \succ\!\!\prec T[C\sim p]) \bullet (F[Cp] \succ\!\!\prec F[C\sim p])\}.$

To show this Ammonius now introduces (with reference to *Int.* 17a26-29) a further important distinction: he contrasts each pair of contradictory sentences with a pair of contradictory possible compound things (81,18-26). In addition, he emphasizes that the first set represent alternative possibilities of speech-acts available to a speaker (81,24-26), while the second represent alternative possibilities for how the things are.[273]

The introduction of pairs of things (πράγματα) which are contradictorily related to one another brings a lot of consequences which Ammonius may not draw expressly, but with which he must reckon in his further discussions. The first consists in the fact that on the level of the πράγματα there are also two entities which are related analogously to the pairs of positive and negative assertoric sentences: as the assertoric sentences are either true or false, so are the πράγματα either the case (Ammonius speaks of 'what really holds' [τὸ ὄντως ὕπαρξον] at 81,28-29) or not the case (τὸ μὴ ὕπαρχον at 82,1). As exactly one sentence of each pair is true, so is exactly one πρᾶγμα of each pair the case. If we ask what exactly Ammonius understands by the expression πρᾶγμα in this context, the only answer is that this expression must mean something which corresponds to modern states of affairs. By introducing pairs of contradictory πράγματα, then, Ammonius has *de facto* conceded the difference between a state of affairs and a fact.

The two pairs of entities distinguished by Ammonius can be shown in the following table:

---

[271]   The proponents of the thesis that Ammonius is an adherent of the standard interpretation will not, however, admit this—at least not without qualification. Cp. above, pp.147-148.

[272]   For the corresponding Aristotelian position cp. *Metaph.* IV 1008a34-b1, 1011b13-1012b2; *Int.* 12 21b17.

[273]   Cp. also *In Cat.* 10,11-16.

Level of Thoughts	[p]	[~p]
Level of Things	p	~p

Table 1

Now, between these entities there are, according to Ammonius, four possible constellations (συμπλοκαί: 81,26-82,2):

1. p is the case (ὄντως ὑπάρχει) and we say that p is the case.
2. p is the case and we say that p is not the case.
3. p is not the case and we say that p is the case.
4. p is not the case and we say that p is not the case.

Of these four possible constellations, the first and fourth lead to a true, the second and third to a false statement (82,2-12).

This too can be represented in a table, although Ammonius' text lists only the facts and omits the non-facts:

	Facts	Non-Facts	Assertoric sentences	Truth-Values of assertoric sentences
1	p	~p	[Cp]	t
2	p	~p	[C~p]	f
3	~p	p	[Cp]	f
4	~p	p	[C~p]	t

Table 2

The following important points arise from Ammonius' discussion:

1. There are positive and negative sentences.
2. There are positive and negative facts.
3. For every true sentence there is a contradictorily opposed false sentence.
4. For every fact there is a contradictorily opposed non-fact.
5. Positive facts make positive sentences true, negative ones false.
6. Negative facts make negative sentences true, positive ones false.
7. Positive non-facts make positive sentences false, negative ones true.
8. Negative non-facts make negative sentences false, positive ones true.

From these points it clearly follows that not only facts, but also non-facts are truth-makers and falsity-makers of assertoric sentences. If we have a closer look at table 2 we should even say that the truth-maker or the falsity-maker of an assertoric sentence is in each case the whole constellation of a fact and a non-fact figuring on the same line on table 2. Therefore the meaning of either true or false assertoric sentences cannot simply be identical with their truth-makers or their falsity-makers. But in this respect there is an important difference between true and false sentences. We have seen that Ammonius—following Porphyry—distinguishes two elements in the meaning of an assertoric sentence: a) the thing (πρᾶγμα) 'the sentence is about' (περὶ οὗ ὁ λόγος, 130,12-13) and b) the affirmation that this thing is the case. In today's semantics one would call these the 'intentional' and the 'formal' element of the meaning of an assertoric sentence. Now, in the case of true assertoric sentences both the intentional and the formal element agree with the fact, which is their truth-maker. Therefore we can say that the meaning of true sentences simply is the fact which makes them true. On the other hand in the case of false assertoric sentences things are much more complicated. As we can see from table 2 the intentional element of a false sentence is identical with the non-fact which makes it false. But since a false sentence declares the non-fact to be a fact by means of its formal element in this case the formal element of the meaning does not agree with the non-fact the sentence is about. This is the reason why the meaning of a false assertoric sentence cannot be simply identical with its falsity-maker. Nevertheless Ammonius can say that a false assertoric sentence depicts a non-fact falsely declaring it a fact. To sum up, Ammonius holds that true sentences imitate the facts, while false sentences are 'an image of non-existence' (τὸ ψεῦδος εἰκών ἐστι τῆς ἀνυπαρξίας, 92,7-9).

I have already noted that Ammonius does not draw these consequences *expressis verbis*, but that we are dealing with conclusions drawn by us from his distinctions. However, since these consequences would also allow Ammonius to solve the problem of the semantics of false sentences, we may assume that he would have accepted them. That Ammonius could not have turned away from this solution can also be seen in another passage, to which we now turn.

At 154,7-12, a passage we examine in its own right in our commentary, (following Aristotle: *Int.* 19a27-29) Ammonius examines the possibility of using a pair of contradictory sentences to form a complex sentence of the form [C(p ›-‹ ~p)].[274] Departing from his previous usage, he then calls this new complex sentence 'contradiction' (ἀντίφασις). Now, this complex sentence is necessarily true (154,8-9; 28-29).[275] According to the fundamental assumptions of the theory, there must be a truth-maker for this sentence which can only consist in the fact that either p or ~p is the case (cp. 154,16-20): C(p ›-‹ ~p). This, then, is the fundamental fact of the world. The world is so constructed that one of the two πράγματα which form a contradictory pair is necessarily a fact and the other a non-fact. These πράγματα—i.e. those for which the expressions p and ~p stand in

---

[274]   Read: It is the case that either p or ~p. This is equivalent to [Cp ›-‹ C~p].

[275]   D. Frede 1985, 77 emphasizes that the thesis that there is such a complex and necessarily true sentence is not to be found in Aristotle. However this may be for Aristotle (cp. our commentary pp.202-203), it is certainly not the case for Ammonius.

the complex assertoric sentence [C(p >-< ~p)]—must be states of affairs; for it would be redundant to say of facts or non-facts that one is a fact and the other is a non-fact. Here we have a further proof that Ammonius would have accepted the ontology we attributed to him above. We may express this—slightly altering Wittgenstein's formula—by the following principle: 'the world is the sum of facts and non-facts'.

However, something else arises from the passage as well: in all sentences of the form [C(p >-< ~p)] the truth-maker coincides with the meaning. Since sentences of this form are necessarily true, they cannot be empty of meaning. But it would be inconsequent to admit that the complex sentence has a meaning, while maintaining that one of the simple sentences on the basis of which it is formed has not. If the complex sentence of the form [C(p >-< ~p)] has a meaning, so do simple sentences of the form [Cp] and [C~p]. Yet in the latter, unlike in the former, the truth-makers and falsity-makers do not necessarily coincide with the meaning. This forces us to equate the meaning of a false sentence, in respect of its intentional element, with its falsity-maker, while the formal element, i.e. the is-the-case-operator, has no correspondent in the falsity-maker.

According to this conception the world is at every moment composed of conjunctions of three entities: a fact of the form C(p >-< ~p), a fact p and a non-fact ~p (of course, ~p can also be the fact and p the non-fact). The first makes the relevant disjunctive sentence true and is at the same time its meaning; the second makes [Cp] true and is at the same time its meaning; and the third is the meaning of the intentional element of [C~p], but makes it false because the sentence wrongly uses an 'it-is-the-case-operator' while the corresponding state of affairs is not the case.

This result sheds also some light on our main question, i.e. the question of whether Ammonius holds that assertoric sentences about future contingent facts have no truth-value. If he adhered to this position, assertoric sentences about future contingent facts would differ from all the other assertoric sentences in such a fundamental way that they could hardly be called 'assertoric sentences' any more. But, it is very unlikely that Ammonius would have accepted this for the following reasons. However uncertain the future may be, one thing is unquestionable: of two contingent future states of affairs p and ~p exactly one will be the case. Therefore Ammonius - as we will show later - accepts the truth of the principle (p){C(p >-< ~p)} for future contingent states of affairs. That means that according to Ammonius there is a fact of the form C(p >-< ~p) which makes the disjunctive statement about future contingent states of affairs of the form [C(p >-< ~p)] true. But if Ammonius accepts the truth of the disjunction, how could he deny that the sentences of the form [Cp] and [C~p] have truth values? He could only do so, if he were prepared to accept that these sentences have no meaning and, as we will see, this is very unlikely, given his general semantics of assertoric sentences.

I should add one final point: As we have seen, Ammonius holds that assertoric sentences exist only during the period of their utterance. This means in the case of future sentences that the event the sentence is about is tied to another moment than the utterance and therefore the existence of the sentence. At the moment when the event happens the sentence does not exist any more and at the moment when the sentence exists the event has not yet occurred. So, if Ammonius simply considered the event the sentence is about as its truth-maker or falsity-maker, he would be obliged to admit that at the moment of their utterance future sentences have no truth-maker or falsity-maker and consequently no meaning. The same point can be made about past sentences. The only way to overcome these difficulties consists in saying that the truth-maker or the falsity-maker of future sentences is the fact or non-fact about the future event which is present at the moment of the utterance. In the following essay I shall attempt to clarify this point further.

V.2 'In a Definite Way True'
Truth-Values and their Modalization in Ammonius

by Gerhard Seel

A battle is underway among interpreters of Aristotle over whether Aristotle in *Int.* 9, in order to avoid universal necessitarianism, denies the validity of the Principle of Bivalence for assertoric sentences[276] about future contingent events. If one affirms that this is so, one is an adherent of the 'Standard Interpretation'; if one denies it, one holds a 'Non-Standard Interpretation'.[277] Recently, a secondary debate has developed atop this fundamental one: did ancient and mediaeval commentators on Aristotle, such as Alexander of Aphrodisias, Ammonius, Boethius, Al-Farabi, and Thomas Aquinas, interpret Aristotle according to the Standard Interpretation or not? In what follows, I shall attempt to decide this question in the case of Ammonius.

Ammonius locates the peculiarity of SFCSs in the fact that, while a pair of contradictorily opposed sentences of this kind—like the contradictory pairs of all other kinds of sentences—divide the two truth-values between them, they nonetheless do this not in a 'definite' way (ὡρισμένως, ἀφωρισμένως), but rather in an 'indefinite' way (ἀορίστως).[278] He is convinced that the necessitarian arguments opposed by Aristotle in *Int.* 9 all rest on the unspoken assumption that contradictory pairs of this kind too divide the truth-values in a definite way, and that Aristotle's refutation depends on the proof that this is not the case.[279] Therefore, it is of overriding importance for understanding Ammonius' interpretation of the necessitarian proofs and their refutation to find out just what Ammonius meant by this distinction.

If Ammonius read Aristotle according to the Standard Interpretation, then by saying that they do not divide the truth-values 'in a definite way', Ammonius means that neither of the contradictory sentences has one of the two truth-values

---

[276] Ammonius, like Aristotle, uses the term 'sentence' (λόγος) throughout his commentary mostly for the specific type of sentence which he qualifies as an 'assertoric sentence' (ἀποφαντικὸς λόγος); in the following, 'sentence' should always be taken to mean 'assertoric sentence'.

[277] The Standard Interpretation is also known under the name 'traditional interpretation'. On both interpretations and their adherents, see H. Weidemann 1994, 300-302. See also our Introduction.

[278] Cp. *In Int.* 130,1-11.

[279] *In Int.* 141,31-35.

at the time of its utterance, but rather receives one of them just at the moment at which the prophecy says the event will occur (i.e., the moment to which the event 'is bound'). If he held the Non-Standard Interpretation of Aristotle, on the other hand, then by this qualification Ammonius wants to say that each of the two sentences does indeed have a truth-value right from the moment of its utterance, but in such a way that it is not fixed in advance which truth-value belongs to it, so that it could also have the opposite truth-value.[280]

Let us first clarify the difference between the Non-Standard Interpretation and the Standard Interpretation. Provided that each sentence is either true or false, the truth-value of any pair of sentences [Cp] and [Cq] falls into one of the four constellations shown in the following table:

	[Cp]	[Cq]
1	t	t
2	t	f
3	f	t
4	f	f

If [Cp] and [Cq] are contradictorily opposed sentences, only cases 2 or 3 can arise, and—in accordance with the assumption that each of the two sentences is either true or false—exactly one of these two cases occurs. This is what Ammonius normally means when he says, following Aristotle, that two sentences divide the truth-values.[281]

Now the Standard Interpretation interprets the distinction between definite and indefinite division of the truth-values as follows: a pair of sentences divides the truth-values if and only if cases 1 and 4 do not occur; a pair of sentences divides the truth-values in a definite way if and only if it is decided which of the other two cases (2 or 3) obtains; a pair of sentences divides the truth-values in an indefinite way if and only if it is undecided which of the other two cases (2 or 3) obtains. Of course, the latter means that neither obtains and therefore neither of the sentences has a truth-value at the moment of its utterance.

If Ammonius used the terms ἀφωρισμένως/ὡρισμένως and ἀορίστως in this sense, he would maintain that in the case of singular future contingent sentences (SFCSs) neither of two contradictory sentences has one of the two truth-values until the moment the predicted event is bound to has become the present moment, and that after that each sentence has exactly one of the two truth-values. Accordingly, the sentences would change their status from 'indefinite whether true

---

280   For the two positions I refer again to H. Weidemann 1994, 300-302.
281   Cp. *In Int.* 91,18-19.

or false' to 'true' or to 'false'. This is precisely the doctrine attributed to Ammonius by the Standard Interpretation.[282]

The Non-Standard Interpretation interprets the distinction between the two ways of dividing the truth-values quite differently. All sentences—including singular future contingents—already at the time of their utterance possess one of the two truth-values, so that there has always already been a decision between cases 2 and 3. A contradictory pair of such sentences divides the truth-values 'in a definite way' when it is impossible that the truth-values be distributed differently; it divides the truth-values 'in an indefinite way', on the other hand, when the actual distribution is not fixed beforehand in a necessary manner and thus could have turned out differently. When the moment the predicted event is bound to has become the present moment, a change of the status of the sentences takes place according to the Non-Standard-Interpretation as well. This change, however, is not from 'undecided whether true or false' to 'true', but rather from 'indefinitely true' to 'definitely true' both including 'being true'.

The distinction between the two views can also be understood as a difference in the conception of the truth-maker. According to the Standard Interpretation, future sentences have a truth-maker only when at the time of their utterance a constellation of actual factors (actual causes) is present, which already at that time makes the later occurrence of the predicted future event necessary. Since in the case of future contingent events no such constellation of causes is present at the time a prediction is uttered, predictions of such events, having no truth-maker, can in principle have no truth-value. They receive both only with the presence of a necessitating constellation of causes, i.e., at the latest in the moment to which the event is tied.

The Non-Standard Interpretation, on the other hand, insists that the real future event or a present fact about it functions, regardless of whether or not its occurrence was already necessary earlier, as truth-maker for predictions made about it. Accordingly, SFCSs do not wait for the predicted event in order to receive a truth-value; rather, they already have a truth-value at the time of their utterance, but they have it in an indefinite way, since it is the contingent outcome of the actual process and not a necessary outcome which makes them true or false.[283]

Adherents of the Standard Interpretation[284] have argued that the 'weaker conception of truth' implied by the Non-Standard Interpretation was first developed in the New Academy[285] and therefore lay 'totally outside of Aristotle's horizon'. However that may be, the weaker conception of truth certainly did not lie outside of Ammonius' horizon. Therefore, nothing excludes the possibility that Ammonius ascribed the weaker conception of truth to Aristotle and interpreted his confrontation with necessitarianism on that basis.

---

282   Cp. D. Frede 1985, 42-44, H. Weidemann 1994, 303 and R. Gaskin 1995, 148ff.
283   On this point, see the paper of M. Mignucci in the present volume.
284   Cp. H. Weidemann 1994, 259-260.
285   Cp. Cicero, *De Fato* IX 18-20, XII 27-28, XIV 32-XV 33, XVI 38.

But there is still another possibility not taken into account by the adherents of the Standard Interpretation. Ammonius could have accepted the requirement that the truth- and falsity-makers of future sentences be simultaneous with the utterance of these sentences and then have argued that these truth- and falsity-makers must not consist in present causes of future events but can consist in present facts and non-facts about future events. In this way—as we shall see—the 'weak conception of truth' would lose some of its oddities.

Let us now see with which of these views Ammonius' semantics of the assertoric sentence—as analyzed in the preceding essay—squares best. According to the Standard Interpretation, an SFCS changes its truth status when it loses its original neutrality in favour of truth or falsity. This change of status presupposes the following:

1. The identity of the sentence cannot depend upon its truth-maker. For, if that entity which determines the value-status of a sentence at the same time also determined its identity, a change of the first entity would have the consequence that we were no longer dealing with the same sentence, not that the same sentence altered its value-status.

2. The sentence must exist as the identical entity over a relatively long period of time, so that it is possible to have a period of time in which it has one status and a period in which it has the other.

The Stoic ἀξίωμα easily fulfils both these conditions.[286] However, we have shown above that the ἀποφαντικὸς λόγος, as Ammonius conceives of it, fulfils them only in part. For the first condition we have seen that the signification of an ἀποφαντικὸς λόγος—which is one of its identity-conditions—does not necessarily coincide with its truth-maker. Since a truth-maker can in principle be replaced by a falsity-maker and vice-versa, an ἀποφαντικὸς λόγος could change its truth-value. That assumes, however, that during the time in which this change occurs the identical ἀποφαντικὸς λόγος continues to exist. This condition is, as we have seen, not met by an ἀποφαντικὸς λόγος, according to Ammonius. For an ἀποφαντικὸς λόγος loses its existence already in the instant immediately following its realization. This last point makes it unlikely that Ammonius was an adherent of the Standard Interpretation.

Of course, the proponents of the opposing thesis still have one possible defence of their position. They can argue that the thesis that a contingent future sentence becomes true only at the moment to which the predicted event is tied does not mean that this statement is or can be made a second time at exactly this moment—that makes no sense for the simple reason that one would at this moment need to make a present-tense statement, not a future one; rather, they would argue, the statement acquires for the first time at this moment its truth-value as that one statement which was made in the past and which one may remember.

---

[286]   Cp. M. Frede 1974, 44-48.

When, for example, a sea battle occurs today, and yesterday someone made the prediction that 'Tomorrow there will be a sea battle', this speech- and thought-event (according to this variant of the Standard Interpretation) possessed neither of the truth-values yesterday, but today has acquired the truth-value 'true' as this event of yesterday. This conception is plausible in its own right, but it is doubtful whether it is actually Ammonius' conception.

We have seen in the preceding essay (228ff.) that the signification of an ἀποφαντικὸς λόγος is only guaranteed by the fact that at the time of its utterance there is something which makes it true or false. Now, the Standard Interpretation says that contingent future sentences have neither a truth-maker nor a falsity-maker at the time of their utterance. From this Ammonius would have had to conclude, because of his semantics, that contingent future sentences have no signification at the time of their utterance and thus are not real sentences. But he does not say this anywhere. Rather, he always includes SFCSs in the class of real assertoric sentences.[287]

This is a stronger objection to the view that Ammonius held the Standard Interpretation than the simple point that he defines the ἀποφαντικὸς λόγος as something that is either true or false. For Aristotle also does this, and nevertheless there is still good reason to interpret his discussion in *Int.* 9 in accordance with the Standard Interpretation. Those who do that have simply to argue that this definition was made in ignorance of the problematic of chapter 9. Such an argument, however, can hardly be used in the case of Ammonius. For it is quite implausible that Ammonius as if by accident lists entities under the class of ἀποφαντικὸς λόγος which are, according to his own semantics, empty of signification.

However, one who brings the above objection against attributing the Standard Interpretation to Ammonius must, for his part, show that Ammonius has reason to assume that even contingent future sentences possess a truth- or falsity-maker. That truth- or falsity-maker cannot, of course, be an event or state of affairs which is bound to the time the future sentence is uttered. For we have seen[288] that the truth- or falsity-maker of an ἀποφαντικὸς λόγος is identical with the state of affairs the sentence is about and in the case of a future sentence this is obviously an event which is bound to a later time than the time of the utterance of the sentence. To attribute the Non-Standard Interpretation to Ammonius, one must therefore assume that, according to Ammonius, the truth- and falsity-makers of future sentences are, at the time of their utterance, still future events.

Against this one might argue that in principle future events cannot make a present sentence true or false. There are two possible ways to argue for this. The first is to say that the truth- or falsity-maker must quite generally be tied to the time of the utterance of the sentence which it makes true or false. However, this

---

[287]   Cp. 130,1-26.

[288]   Cp. the preceding essay, 228ff.

position is quite untenable: to accept it would require the admission that past sentences too have no truth-value.

To avoid being misunderstood, to say that the truth- or falsity-maker of an assertoric sentence may be tied to a time different from the utterance of the sentence is not the same as to say that the truth- or falsity-maker may exist at a time different from the utterance of the sentence. According to our interpretation, Ammonius would have accepted the first and denied the latter, holding that there are present facts about future events as there are present facts about past events. Of course, the exact formulation of this position requires the tools of modern temporal logic, which Ammonius obviously did not dispose of. So we do not hold that he actually said this but rather that the consistency of what he actually said requires such a reconstruction.

Against this reconstruction though there is still another possible objection. One may argue that unlike present facts about past events there can be no present facts about future events, because future events are ontologically uncertain, i.e. because it is at present completely open which of the two mutually exclusive types of event which are still possible at the present time will actually be realized. This objection is more serious than the first. To meet it, however, we need not prove that the conception of facts it assumes is false, but merely that that there is an alternative to it and that Ammonius adheres to that alternative.

The objection presupposes that in order to have a present fact about a future event we need a present constellation of causes that bring the event about and thus decide already now the outcome of the future course of events. Thus present facts about future events are causally linked to the event they are about. However, as we have seen in the Introduction (28ff.), this is not the only way present facts about future events can be conceived of. One may equally well think that there is a present fact about a future event not with regard to the present state of the world but simply with regard to the real future state of the world. If, from an atemporal point of view, at the precise period of world history that we designate from our temporal point of view with the expression 'tomorrow' there is a real event of the type 'sea-battle' then there is, again from our temporal point of view, a present fact about this event. This fact brings by no means the future event about, rather it simply reflects it. It is clear that present facts about future events, when conceived of in this way, are perfectly compatible with the openness and undecidedness of the future course of events. Therefore somebody who is convinced of the latter is under no constraint to renounce to the former.

What grounds do we have for the contention that Ammonius actually shared the second conception and rejected the first? Our first reason is semantic: The first conception is, as we have seen, incompatible with Ammonius' semantics. For it has the consequence that contingent future sentences are empty of signification, or at least undetermined in their signification. Our second reason is taken from his refutation of the 'Reaper' Argument and the necessitarian argument reported by Aristotle (cp. above 159ff. and 185ff.). As we have seen, Ammonius accepts present facts about future events, like your reaping or the birth of a pale child, that do not occur in every case (πάντως). We must keep in mind that for these events it is at the present moment undecided and open whether they will occur or not. Therefore he would contradict himself if he accepted the first conception of facts about future events.

We have a further reason to exclude Ammonius' having adopted the first conception: since it immediately excludes necessitarianism, one would expect it to be deployed by its adherents when they set out to refuse arguments for necessitarianism. However, nowhere in his various refutations of necessitarian arguments does Ammonius rely on such a conception.

From the point of view of the consistency of Ammonius' theory, therefore, there are strong grounds to attribute the Non-Standard Interpretation to Ammonius. Yet these grounds would be irrelevant if one could prove that Ammonius actually uses the expressions 'in a definite way' (ἀφωρισμένως) and 'in an indefinite way' (ἀορίστως) in accordance with the Standard Interpretation. What does an analysis of Ammonius' usage reveal?

Ammonius uses the expressions ἀφωρισμένως and ἀορίστως in three areas: a) in the area of being; b) in the area of knowledge; c) in the narrower area of the ἀποφαντικὸς λόγος. We are, of course, primarily interested in the usage of these expressions in the last area. Unfortunately, in none of the passages where they are used (there are over two dozen in all) does the context allow us to decide the question definitively. The only thing which can be adduced in favour of giving Ammonius the Non-Standard Interpretation is the fact that he not only says that pairs of contradictory sentences divide the truth-values in a definite way, but also that individual members of such pairs are true or false in a definite way (cp. 141,20; 141,22; 33; 143,18-19; 148,9; 149,17; 151,1; 154,11). This does not yield a good sense if one assumes the Standard Interpretation. For according to that interpretation, one can say about members of pairs which divide the truth-values in a definite way merely that they are true or false; the qualification 'in a definite way' applies in this case only to the way in which two sentences divide the truth-values, not to the way they have them. All that the proponents of the Standard Interpretation can do, then, is to argue that the latter is what is actually meant in all the passages named. While this may be possible, it is not very probable.

If the passages which directly concern the usage of ἀφωρισμένως and ἀορίστως as qualifications of the division or belonging of the truth-values are insufficient to decide the question, the next step is to consider the usage of these terms in the other areas in order to clarify by way of analogy their signification in this area. The area of knowledge seems the likely place to begin, since it is closest to the area of the ἀποφαντικὸς λόγος.

One must, however, remember that, according to Ammonius, the status of an ἀποφαντικὸς λόγος is not actually determined by the way in which one knows something, but rather by the status of the things which it is about. Therefore, investigating the usage of the expressions in question in the area of knowledge only makes sense if the status of the knowledge reveals something about the status of the things.

In fact, those who ascribe the Standard Interpretation to Ammonius have taken this for granted when they have concluded from the impossibility of knowing contingent future events to the indeterminacy of these events themselves, and then from the indeterminacy of the events to the undecidedness of the truth-values the sentences predicting the events will have. They then used this conclusion to interpret the difference between the two ways of dividing the truth-values. Let us evaluate the two inferences one after the other.

1. The way to this interpretation is opened by what Ammonius says at 130,20-26 and 139,19-20.[289] Here Ammonius explains the thesis that pairs of contingent future sentences divide the truth-values *in an indefinite way* by pointing out that before the event (πρὸ τῆς τοῦ πράγματος ἐκβάσεως) one cannot say or know which of the two sentences will be true and which false. Dorothea Frede,[290] H. Weidemann[291] and more recently R. Gaskin[292] interpret this as if Ammonius meant to say that the occurrence of the event itself was indefinite in this sense and thus open. It is, however, too hasty to conclude from the indefiniteness of the knowledge of the things to the indefiniteness of the things themselves.

On the contrary, Ammonius emphasizes that there can be both an indefinite knowledge of definite things and also a definite knowledge of indefinite (contingent) things. The first is clearly found in *In Cat.* 79, 16-19. There Ammonius gives the example that Socrates is covered up and only his hand is visible, saying that in this case one knows in a definite way (ὡρισμένως) that this is a hand, but not whose hand it is. It is clear, however, that the thing itself is not indefinite, for it is not undetermined whether it is the hand of Socrates or not. Of course, Ammonius does not want to say that things we cannot know are always determined. For the second there are several supporting passages in the discussion of the knowledge of the gods (*In Int.* 132,8-137,11). Thus, Ammonius says (136,30-137,3): 'And the same thing is contingent in its own nature and is no longer indefinite (ἀόριστον), but rather definite (ὡρισμένον) in the gods' knowledge. It is clearly possible for the contingent sometimes to be known in a definite manner even by our own knowledge'. From this it clearly results that according to Ammonius there is definite knowledge of indefinite things and indefinite knowledge of definite things as well as, of course, definite knowledge of definite things and indefinite knowledge of indefinite things. Therefore, it is impermissible to conclude from the status of the knowledge to the status of the things or, in the other direction, from the status of the things to that of the knowledge. This prevents using the passages at 130,20-26 and 139,12-20 in order to deduce the status of the things known from the status of our knowledge.

2. To be sure, this does not exclude that in fact Ammonius wanted to say in these passages that the events themselves are uncertain and undecided. However,

---

[289]   Cp. D. Frede 1985, 44-45; H. Weidemann 1994, 303 and R. Gaskin 1995, 157.

[290]   D. Frede 1985, 45 n. 26.

[291]   H. Weidemann 1994, 303.

[292]   R. Gaskin 1995, 157.

even if D. Frede, H. Weidemann and R. Gaskin were right in this point still it would not follow that Ammonius uses the terms ἀφωρισμένως and ἀορίστως in the sense of the Standard Interpretation. To be sure, H. Weidemann is right when he affirms that "the division of the truth-values is, according to Ammonius, indefinite in such a pair of sentences, because both what is foretold in the one and also what is foretold in the other of its two members can just as easily occur as not occur".[293] He is however wrong when he continues "so that it is not yet determined which of the two members will prove true and which false".[294] For, according to the alternative conception of facts we explained before (239), the openness and undecidedness of the future course of events does by no means prevent there being present facts about these events. Given these facts, it is perfectly determined which of the two members is true and which false.[295] As we have shown before, it is highly probable that Ammonius adopted this conception which was first introduced by Carneades (cp. our Introduction, 28). Thus we can conclude that neither the inference from the indefiniteness of our knowledge to the indefiniteness of the events nor the inference from the latter to the undecidedness of the truth-values is sound.

As a last option we can try to clarify the signification of the expressions ὡρισμένως and ἀορίστως in the other areas by using the signification they have when they are used to distinguish modes of predication. For Ammonius uses these expressions not only to qualify the division of truth-values and the coming to be and the occurrence of events (cp. 131,7), but also to describe the way in which a quality belongs to a substance (cp. *In Cat.* 99,19–100,2).

Apparently, the latter is the original usage of this pair of expressions, from which the others are all derived. Therefore, we shall devote special attention to it. In fact, Aristotle uses (*Cat.* 10, 13a8-17)[296] the expressions ἀφωρισμένως and οὐκ ἀφωρισμένως to make a distinction among ways in which a quality belongs to a subject: a quality belongs 'in a definite way' to a substance when it belongs to it necessarily, and 'not in a definite way' when it belongs to it not necessarily, but rather as it so happens.

In his commentary, Ammonius makes *de facto* the same distinction. He exemplifies 'belonging in a definite way' just as Aristotle does, using the example of heat, which necessarily belongs to fire, to which he adds the explanation that of the two contrary qualities 'hot' and 'cold' heat belongs to fire in a definite way 'and not at some time the other of the two' (*In Cat.* 99,28). For the qualities 'blind' and 'sighted' on the other hand the situation is quite different: if one of these belongs to a substance, it does not do so in a definite way, but rather 'however it so happens' (100,1-2).

---

[293]   H. Weidemann 1994, 303; the translation is ours.
[294]   H. Weidemann 1994, 303; the translation is ours.
[295]   One must keep in mind that Ammonius says that 'which one of these will be the true one it is not possible to *know*' (our emphasis), he does not say that neither of them is true now and just one will receive the value 'true' later.
[296]   J.P. Schneider has called this passage to my attention. Cp. N. Kretzmann 1998, 28.

This text clearly indicates that whenever a quality belongs necessarily to a substance, which means that it does so for the entire length of its existence, Aristotle and Ammonius say that the quality belongs to the substance 'in a definite way', and when a quality belongs contingently to a substance, meaning that it does not always belong to it, both say that it belongs to it 'not in a definite way'. However, one should not too quickly infer that the expressions 'belongs necessarily' and 'belongs in a definite way' mean the same thing. The expression 'in a definite way', rather, always refers to a plurality of mutually exclusive possible qualifications of a substance and says that *it is determined beforehand* which of these actually belongs to the substance. The reason for this determination, of course, lies in the necessity of the belonging of one of the qualifications. But in order to affirm this one must presuppose that the two expressions do not mean the same thing.[297]

In ascribing to Ammonius the Non-Standard Interpretation we can use this passage to conclude by analogy from the signification of the two expressions when they qualify how a quality belongs to a subject to their signification in the qualification of how truth-values belong to sentences. Such a procedure, indeed, is suggested by the fact that the ἀποφαντικὸς λόγος corresponds to the substance, the two truth-values to the two mutually exclusive qualities, and 'belonging necessarily' to 'being necessarily true'. What results from such a procedure?

1. If a qualification belongs in an indefinite way to a substance, this does not mean that it does not belong yet, although perhaps it will at some later time; rather, it means that it presently belongs to it in actuality. By analogy one can conclude from this that when an ἀποφαντικὸς λόγος is true in an indefinite way, it is at present already true and does not need to wait for the assignment of a truth-value.

2. If a qualification belongs in a definite way to a substance, it is necessary that this qualification belongs to it; if, on the other hand, it belongs to it in an indefinite way, it is contingent that it belongs to it. By analogy one can say of an ἀποφαντικὸς λόγος that it is true in a definite way if it is necessary that it is true and that it is true in an indefinite way if it is contingent that it is true.[298]

To my knowledge, Richard Gaskin was the first to use the passage from the Categories to determine by analogy the meaning of the crucial terms ὡρισμένως

---

[297] R. Gaskin 1995, 154 argues that the inference from definite truth to necessity which both Ammonius and Boethius accept and defend would be completely superfluous if 'definitely' already meant 'necessarily'. I agree with R. Gaskin on this point. Therefore it is important to emphasize that according to the interpretation given above 'definitely' and 'necessarily' *are not* synonymous.

[298] It is obvious that these two points speak clearly in favor of attributing the Non-Standard Interpretation to Ammonius. Therefore, it is surprising that neither Dorothea Frede nor Hermann Weidemann nor Norman Kretzmann are shaken by it, although all admit that this expression originates in Aristotle's *Categories*. Richard Gaskin is the only scholar who treats the passage in detail (1995, 168-171). He comes, however, to the conclusion that ἀφωρισμένως means that the truth values are not yet distributed. For my criticism see below.

and ἀορίστως. So he employed the same tool I did, coming, however, to the opposite result. He argues that the expressions ὡρισμένως and οὐκ ὡρισμένως which correspond to the terms used by Ammonius serve here "to indicate distribution of truth-values within a disjunction" (169). Accordingly the first signifies that the predicate (e.g. 'blind') has already been attributed to the subject and the second that it has not yet been attributed and that, however, one or the other ('blind' or 'sighted') will be attributed, though it is still open which one. In this way he gives strong support to his general claim that SFCSs do not possess truth-values but have the non-truth-functional value of being either-true-or-false.[299]

To support his position he has to place stress on the temporal distinctions (ποτέ, ἤδη) present in this passage, since it is crucial for him to distinguish a moment when the predicate has not yet been attributed and a later moment when it has. However, though Aristotle conceives of such a distinction, he does not use it in order to characterize the meaning of our crucial terms. He never says that when neither of the predicates ('blind' and 'sighted') does belong to the subject they both belong to it in an indefinite manner. Rather he uses the term οὐκ ὡρισμένως in 13a9-11 to indicate that as soon as one of the predicates belongs to the subject it does not belong to it in a definite way, but as it chances. Clearly here the indefinite attribution goes together with attribution and not with the case when the way of the attribution is still open. Therefore we stick to our construal of the passage, notwithstanding Gaskin's counter-argument.[300]

Now, one can certainly object that the analogy is deficient in two essential points: first, the two qualities are related only as contraries, while the two truth-values are contradictorily related, at least as long as the principle of bivalence is accepted; second, a substance can change its qualification, while (as we showed above) that is something an ἀποφαντικὸς λόγος cannot do. The second point is especially serious, since it appears to exclude that the quality of being necessarily true belong to an ἀποφαντικὸς λόγος. For what would the expression 'necessarily true' mean? The usual statistical procedure for defining the modes fails here. Indeed, it is impermissible to say that an ἀποφαντικὸς λόγος is necessarily true if and only if it is always true. Due to their ephemeral nature, it holds for all ἀποφαντικοὶ λόγοι that if they are ever true, they are always true.

This difficulty is easily overcome when one carefully observes how Ammonius himself defines the expressions 'necessarily true', 'contingently true', etc. According to Ammonius, an ἀποφαντικὸς λόγος is necessarily true if and only if the πρᾶγμα whose being the case it states is necessarily the case, and it is contingently true if and only if the relevant πρᾶγμα is contingently the case (cp.

---

[299]   Cp. our Introduction pp.34-35.
[300]   Our interpretation is "unattractive" to Gaskin (170) because, as he believes, it makes the terms ἀφωρισμένως and ἀναγκαίως synonymous. This is, however, a misunderstanding. For, as I already emphasized, in my understanding these terms are not synonymous though they may have the same extension.

In Int. 154,3-20).[301] The fact that assertoric sentences cannot change their truth-value, therefore, does not prevent a sensible distinction between 'necessarily true' and 'contingently true'. Necessarily true sentences are like arrows shot from close range at a galloping herd of buffalo: they cannot miss their target. Contingently true sentences, on the other hand, are like arrows that have hit their target, although they could also have missed it.

In our refutation of the Standard Interpretation we presupposed so far that Ammonius conceived of the ἀποφαντικὸς λόγος exactly the way we attributed to him in our first essay. Therefore we shall finally examine if the conclusion we draw would not be valid any more if this presupposition were false. We have to distinguish two points that played a rôle in our argument: 1. The thesis that Ammonius conceives of the ἀποφαντικὸς λόγος as a speech event and not as a type of such an event (λέξις), 2. The thesis that a ἀποφαντικὸς λόγος needs to have a truth-maker or a falsity-maker in order to have a signification. Let us deal with the first point first.

As we have seen in our first essay the conception of the ἀποφαντικὸς λόγος as a speech act is clearly found in Ammonius' commentary on the *Categories*. However it is doubtful if it is present in the other texts and especially in the commentary on the *De interpretatione* as well. We admitted already (cp. p.219, note 251) that in some passages of this text at least Ammonius seems to conceive of the ἀποφαντικὸς λόγος as an unambiguous λέξις. Nevertheless, this would not undermine our argument, as long as the rest of the semantical theory we attributed to him is not doubtful. For, according to this theory, an unambiguous λέξις could not have a (possibly changing) signification during the period of its existence without having a truth-maker or a falsity-maker at each moment of this period. So our argument relies entirely on the second point.

Let us imagine for the sake of argument that Ammonius had a different semantical theory according to which a ἀποφαντικὸς λόγος has meaning without having a truth-maker or a falsity-maker. In this case he could of course accept that a certain kind of ἀποφαντικοὶ λόγοι have at a first time no truth-value at all and get one of them at a later moment as indeed the Standard Interpretation affirms, but he still would not be obliged to do so. He could equally well accept the principle of bivalence in its full strength, but for other reasons. So while a different semantical conception would indeed undermine our first argument it would not by the same token provide an additional argument to the holders of the Standard Interpretation. Needless to say, that we would need some textual evidence for that alternative semantical theory, in order to consider it seriously.

Finally one should not forget that this discussion concerns only our first argument and leaves completely unaffected the two others. So, even if Ammonius held a different semantical theory which would allow him to accept the Standard

---

[301]   The objection of F.W. Zimmermann 1981, lxviii 'a distinction between a definite and an indefinite kind of truth was not intended' must therefore (*pace* H. Weidemann 1994, 304) be rejected.

Interpretation, we could still ask why he took no advantage of this, when he tried to refuse necessitarianism. Secondly and finally, the evidence of his use of the expressions ἀφωρισμένως and οὐκ ἀφωρισμένως would still exclude his agreeing with the Standard Interpretation of future contingent sentences.

The result of our investigation can be summed up briefly:

1. Everything points to the conclusion that Ammonius uses the expressions 'true in a definite way' (ὡρισμένως ἀληθές) and 'true in an indefinite way' (ἀορίστως ἀληθές) in order to distinguish modes of truth-values' actually belonging`, not (as would have to be maintained in order to ascribe the Standard Interpretation to Ammonius) to indicate the difference between the not-yet-belonging and the already-belonging of a truth-value.

2. If this is so, then Aristotle's suggested solution of the necessitarianism problem, according to Ammonius, is not that SFCSs have no truth-value at all, but rather that the truth-value which they have belongs to them not 'in a definite way' and therefore not necessarily.

3. To attribute the Standard Interpretation to Ammonius, one cannot rely on his linguistic usage, nor does the Standard Interpretation correspond to what Ammonius actually does in his refutation of the proofs of necessitarianism. This last point is decisively proved in his commentary on *Int.* 9 (cp. our commentary above).

V.3 Ammonius and the Problem of Future Contingent Truth

by Mario Mignucci

V.3.1

The problems raised by future contingent propositions[302] are many and some of them have to do with the question of determinism. One might argue as follows. If it is now true that a sea-battle will take place tomorrow, it cannot be the case that the sea-battle does not occur tomorrow, otherwise it would not be true today that there will be a sea-battle tomorrow. That there will be a sea-battle tomorrow has always been fixed and determined. The future in this way appears to be unpreventable and necessary. Therefore, the question can be raised whether it is legitimate to speak of contingency in a proper sense in relation to the events of the world.

Aristotle recognised the existence of truly contingent events and corresponding truly contingent propositions and he tried to avoid the deterministic consequences derived from admitting true future propositions.[303] According to many scholars his answer to the deterministic argument would be that future contingent propositions are neither true nor false before the time to which the events expressed by them refer. So the famous Aristotelian proposition

(1)   There will be a sea-battle tomorrow

can be properly described as neither true nor false before tomorrow. Unfortunately, this interpretation, which is usually called 'the traditional interpretation', is not shared by all scholars and it may be not Aristotle's view.[304] I am not concerned with Aristotle. What is relevant to me is that, in my view, Ammonius cannot be labelled as a follower of the traditional interpretation. This position is not new, since it has been convincingly defended by Richard Sorabji and Robert Sharples, and, more recently, by Gerhard Seel in a very subtle way.[305]

---

[302]   I use the term 'proposition' to translate the Greek term ἀποφαντικὸς λόγος. It corresponds to what is called 'assertoric sentence' in the rest of this book.

[303]   This question is faced by Aristotle in *Int.* 9. As is well known, the literature on this chapter is immense. The bibliography up to 1973 can be found in V. Celluprica 1977. Further bibliographical references are available in D. Frede 1985, 84-87; J. Talanga 1986a, 169-185, and H. Weidemann 1994, 97-131.

[304]   One of the best-argued presentations of the traditional interpretation is due to R. Sorabji 1980b, 91ff. Different views have recently been proposed by G. Fine 1984, 23-48; J. van Rijen 1989; J. van Eck 1988, 19-38.

[305]   Cp. R. Sorabji 1980b, 92-93; R. Sharples 1978a, 263-264; G. Seel 2001.

However, Dorothea Frede in a recent article published after Sorabji's and Sharples' works still attributes the traditional interpretation to Ammonius[306] and Richard Gaskin in a very detailed book on Aristotle's sea-battle and its ancient interpretations has offered a solution which can be labelled as a variant of the traditional position.[307] Thus, I think that we must pause a little to reconsider this problem.

The core of Ammonius' solution consists in the distinction he proposes between what is definitely and indefinitely true or false. To have an idea of the way in which the distinction is formulated by Ammonius we can read the following passage:

> (A) In the future time, on the other hand, <Aristotle> says that the singular propositions still divide the true and the false even so, but no longer in the same way as the propositions taken in the present or past time: it is no longer possible to say which of them will be true and which will be false in a definite way (ὡρισμένως), since the thing has not already occurred but can both occur and not occur.[308]

Propositions which do not divide truth and falsity in a definite way are said by Ammonius to be indefinitely (ἀορίστως) true or false:

> (B) This is actually the object of the present investigation: whether every contradiction divides the true and the false in a definite manner (ὡρισμένως), or whether there is also a contradiction which divides them in an indefinite manner (ἀορίστως).[309]

The metaphor of dividing truth and falsity is customary among Aristotle's commentators and can easily be explained by reference to the Principle of Bivalence. The Principle of Bivalence is usually distinguished from the Law of the Excluded Middle. The latter says that a proposition either is a fact or is not a fact. We can express it by stating

(EM*)   P ∨ ¬P

If we introduce a truth predicate, 'T', we can restate (EM*) as

(EM)   T[P] ∨ ¬T[P]

Lukasiewicz had briefly expressed the same view in a famous article (cp. J. Lukasiewicz 1930: (1967, 64)).

[306] Cp. D. Frede 1985, 43-45. She repeats here the interpretation already proposed in her book on Aristotle's sea-battle published in 1970, 24-27. On the same line is J. Talanga 1986a, 144-145 and also 1986c, 306-7. More recently H. Weidemann 1994, 302-4 has sided with D. Frede.

[307] R. Gaskin 1995. Chapter 12 is dedicated to the interpretation of the ancient commentators, especially Boethius and Ammonius.

[308] In Int. 130,20-26. A perhaps better translation of the last sentence of our passage is: "it is no longer possible to say in a definite way which of them will be true ..." as, in fact, the translation given in this volume has it.

[309] In Int. 131,2-4.

and take (EM) as the Law of the Excluded Middle in this extended language. On the other hand, the Principle of Bivalence asserts that a proposition is either true or false, i.e.

(PB) $T[P] \lor F[P]$[310]

Thus, we can say that a pair of contradictory propositions, e.g. P and ¬P, divide truth and falsity if they are such that one is true and the other false, i.e. if they satisfy (PB).

According to Ammonius, future contingent propositions divide the true and the false in an indefinite way. He is explicit on this point. Commenting on the beginning of *De Interpretatione* Chapter 9 he first recalls that Aristotle had said that some antithetical propositions do not divide the true and the false. Then he attributes to Aristotle the purpose of establishing which propositions are opposed in such a way that they always divide the true and the false, but in an indefinite and not in a definite way:

> (C) Consequent to this, then, he <Aristotle> adds (18a33-34) what sort of affirmative sentence is opposed to what sort of negative sentence in such a way that they always divide the true and the false, not in a definite, however, but in an indefinite manner (διαιρεῖν μὲν αὐτὰς ἀεὶ τό τε ἀληθὲς καὶ τὸ ψεῦδος, οὐ μέντοι ἀφωρισμένως ἀλλ' ἀορίστως).[311]

In Ammonius' view, the result of this analysis would be that a pair of singular propositions antithetically opposed in the present and past tense and a pair of contradictorily quantified statements divide the true and the false in a definite way, while the corresponding non-quantified propositions in contingent matter do not divide the true and the false. In other words, the former but not the latter satisfy (PB).[312] Contradictorily quantified and non-quantified propositions put in the future tense behave in the same way as present-tensed statements with respect to truth and falsity.[313]

The story is different with singular statements in the future. If they are in necessary or impossible matter they divide the true and the false in a definite way,[314] while if they are in a contingent matter, they:

> (D) always divide the true and the false, but in an indefinite, not in a definite manner (διαιροῦσι μὲν πάντως τὸ ἀληθὲς καὶ τὸ ψεῦδος, οὐ μέντοι ἀφωρισμένως ἀλλ' ἀορίστως); it is necessary that Socrates bathe or not bathe tomorrow, and it is impossible that either both or neither happen.[315]

---

[310]   As is obvious, an equivalent formulation of (PB) is (PB†) $T[P] \lor T[\neg P]$

[311]   *In Int.* 138,15-17.

[312]   *In Int.* 138,17-28. Pairs of non-quantified propositions antithetically opposed such as "man is white" and "man is not white" do not satisfy (PB) because "man is not white" is not the logical negation of "man is white".

[313]   *In Int.* 138,28-34.

[314]   *In Int.* 139,6 ff.

[315]   *In Int.* 139,14-17. See also *In Int.* 139,32-140,4; 140,11-13.

It is easy to guess that πάντως here corresponds to ἀεί of text (C). Therefore, singular future contingent propositions are different from non-quantified statements because the latter do not divide the true and the false, and they are different from present- or past-tensed singular statements because they divide the true and the false in an indefinite way. The conclusion seems to be that in Ammonius' interpretation singular future contingent propositions do divide the true and the false and in this way they satisfy (PB), although in a peculiar way.

As I have said, the view that singular future contingent propositions divide the true and the false has been resisted by several scholars, who attribute to Ammonius the traditional view. According to it, Ammonius would have restricted the validity of (PB). It is not true in general to claim that every proposition is either true or false. Future contingent statements are neither true nor false and in this sense they would constitute an exception to (PB). Dorothea Frede for instance thinks that Ammonius' speaking of indefinitely true or false propositions is only "a diplomatic way" of saying that the Bivalence admits of exceptions.[316] That is difficult to accept because there is no reason to believe that Ammonius had to be diplomatic or that he was not in a position to spell out his view in a proper and clear way.

Richard Gaskin, on the other hand, has a more refined argument. His view is that Ammonius and Boethius do say that future contingent propositions divide the true and the false, but by adding 'indefinitely' they make clear that these propositions are not either true or alternatively false, but either-true-or-false, where by this expression a third truth-value is meant. For instance if we state: "Alexander will go to the market tomorrow", which is by hypothesis a singular future contingent proposition, we cannot say that this proposition is true or that is it false. What we can say is that it is either-true-or-false, and we are not allowed to split the disjunction.[317] In this way (PB) is still restricted as in the traditional interpretation and something logically equivalent to truth-value gaps is attributed to Ammonius.[318]

I am not sure that I have clearly understood what Gaskin means when he acknowledges that Ammonius says that pairs of future contingent antithetical propositions contradictorily opposed divide the true and the false, and he interprets this as a claim that each member of them is either-true-or-false, but not either true or alternatively false.[319] Let us examine the point.

---

316   D. Frede 1985, 43; 1970, 25.
317   R. Gaskin 1995, 148ff.; 156-158.
318   As Gaskin says, his interpretation is logically equivalent to the traditional one (R. Gaskin 1995, 149).
319   R. Gaskin 1995, 157: "The claim must be that it is *in principle* impossible to assign truth to one member of a FCA [a future contingent ἀντίφασις] and falsity to the other: it is metaphysically indeterminate which way round the truth-values go. But Ammonius has just said that the members do divide the true and the false as do statements about the present and the past. Hence the position must be that FCSs [future contingent statements] divide the true and the false to the extent of being either-true-or-false, but not to the extent of being either true, or alternatively false".

If the metaphor of dividing truth and falsity has to be interpreted in the way we have done, by putting it into relation with (PB), it looks obvious to state that two antithetical propositions P and P* divide the true and the false if, and only if, one of them is true and the other is false. They do not divide the true and the false if it may happen that they are either both true or both false. Therefore, it seems that the necessary conditions required for P and P* to divide the true and the false are that (i) the truth-value *True* or the truth-value *False* is assigned to P and P* and (ii) an opposite truth-value assigned to them, in the sense that if P is true, P* is false and if P* is false, P* is true.

Consider now a pair of antithetical future contingent propositions such as "Socrates will bathe tomorrow" and "Socrates will not bathe tomorrow". According to Gaskin the same truth-value is assigned to both propositions, namely the *Either-true-or-false* truth-value. This truth-value is a truth-value different from *True* and *False*. If a proposition P is either-true-or-false it is not true (false). Therefore, how can "Socrates will bathe tomorrow" and "Socrates will not bathe tomorrow" be said to divide the true and the false? Truth and falsity as such are not involved nor are truth-values (whatever they are) divided.

I think that Gaskin would answer this objection by pointing out that when Ammonius and Boethius say that future contingent statements divide the true and the false in an indefinite way they are simply contrasting these statements to singular present or past propositions: the latter *do* really divide the true and the false; the former divide the true and the false in the way in which they are able to do it, i.e. indefinitely. But again why should Ammonius have described this situation as a division of truth-values, if there is no such division? Non-quantified antithetical propositions in contingent matter are said not to divide the true and the false. It would have been far less confusing if Ammonius had referred to the situation of these pairs to single out the peculiarity of future contingent statements.[320] On the contrary, Ammonius sharply distinguishes between the case of non-quantified propositions and the case of future contingent ones. The former can both be true (or false), while the latter rule out this possibility.

One might reply that a pair of future contingent propositions contradictorily opposed can be neither true nor false together,[321] and this may very well depend on their possessing a third truth-value (or no truth-value at all). Propositions which divide the true and the false are such because they can be neither true nor false together. Therefore, pairs of future contingent propositions contradictorily opposed, P and P*, *do* in some sense divide the true and the false as well. But division of truth and falsity for P and P* does not consist simply in their being neither true nor false together. If a division takes place, P and P* must receive a truth-value, this truth-value must be either *True* or *False*, and True and False must

---

[320] R. Gaskin 1995, 155 says that: "definite truth just is (divided) truth, and 'indefinitely true' means 'divides truth and falsity indefinitely with its negation'". But again if truth is divided from falsity "with its negation" there is no division at all.

[321] *In Int.* 140,4-11.

be split in such a way that if P is true, then P* is false or *vice-versa*. In other words, (PB) implies not only ¬(T[P] • T[P*]) and ¬(F[P] • F[P*]) but also ¬(¬T[P] • ¬T[P*]) and ¬(¬F[P] • ¬F[P*]). In a bivalent logic the two pairs of formulas are equivalent, but this is not the case if we admit the possibility that P and P* have a third truth-value. If P and P* are *Either-true-or-false*, ¬(¬T[P] • ¬T[P*]) and ¬(¬F[P] • ¬F[P*]) do not hold.

Nor is it a good way of avoiding the view imposed by the evidence of the texts to claim that in the case of future contingent propositions an indefinite division and not a simple division is in question, i.e. a division *sui generis*, which cannot be counted as a proper and simple division. There are many passages, especially in Boethius, where it is pretty clear that indefiniteness attaches to truth-values and not to the division of truth and falsity.[322] This can only mean that indefinite division must be understood as the operation by which the members of a pair of future contingent propositions contradictorily opposed receive different truth-values, namely indefinite truth and indefinite falsity, which are opposed and mutually exclusive.[323]

---

[322]   See e.g. Boethius, *In Int., sec. ed.* 208,7 ff. (text (F)), where indefiniteness is clearly attached to the truth-values of future contingent propositions and not to the way in which truth and falsity is divided among pairs of antithetical items. See also the following footnote.

[323]   R. Gaskin 1995, 151 points out that Boethius, *In Int., pr. ed.* 107,20 ff. characterises truth and falsity of future contingent propositions as *indiscreta* (108,4). But it can hardly be true that this means that we cannot divide the true and false in a pair of future contingent propositions contradictorily opposed, because Boethius, before saying that their truth and falsity is *indiscreta* claims that: *in his vero in quibus contingens est futurum, id est variabile and instabile*, totum quidem corpus contradictionis veritatem falsitatemque partitur, *sed haec veritas atque falsitas indiscreta est atque volubilis* (108,1-5). The sentence which I have emphasised corresponds exactly to what he says about past- and present-tensed propositions: in *praeteritis atque praesentibus* et *totum contradictionis corpus in veritatem falsitatemque dividitur* et *vera una est definite* (107,24-27). The *et ... et* construction shows that two conditions are laid down for past- and present-tensed contingent propositions: the members of a contradictory pair of them (i) divide truth and falsity and (ii) one is definitely true and the other definitely false. It is natural to suppose that a parallel double condition holds for future contingent contradictory pairs: their members (i) divide truth and falsity and (ii) one is indefinitely true and the other indefinitely false. The fact that *definite* is sometimes glossed by Boethius with *divise* (*In Int., pr. ed.* 126,7-8), or *constitute* (123,21-22), or *simpliciter* (124,5) does not offer evidence for Gaskin's interpretation. *Sec. ed.* 189,5 ff. explains quite well the origin of this terminology. Past- and present- tensed contingent propositions pick up events which are stable and definite (*res ipsae stabiles sunt et definitae*: 189,6-7) in the sense that they cannot be different from what they are since they have already happened (*quod factum est non est non factum...idcirco de eo quod factum est verum est dicere* definite, *quoniam factum est, falsum est dicere, quoniam factum non est*: 189,7-10). On the other hand, future contingent propositions refer to events which can be and can be not. In this sense the truth-value of these propositions is not yet stable and settled or even *divisus* because the possibility of the opposite is not ruled out (191,10-192,5). What makes a future contingent proposition *indefinita* or *incerta* or *instabilis* is that it picks up a contingent outcome which is not yet settled and

Gaskin's interpretation is not at ease with some specific passages. He equates, I think correctly, Boethius and Ammonius' interpretations, in the sense that for him they hold the same view. Therefore, he feels entitled to corroborate his interpretation of the one with texts coming from the other.[324] Take for instance Boethius' commentary on 18b17-25, where Aristotle rejects the view that the elements of a pair of future contingent statements contradictorily opposed have to be both considered as non-true.[325] In Gaskin's view Boethius would be attacking here the Stoic interpretation of Aristotle, according to which Aristotle would have maintained that future contingent propositions are neither true nor false.[326] It is difficult to understand why Boethius should have insisted on criticising a position which, according to Gaskin, is logically equivalent to his and differs from his only from a rhetorical point of view.[327]

However, consider Boethius' argument. He says that to claim that both members P and P* of a pair of future contingent propositions contradictorily opposed are not true does not differ from claiming that they are both false. But this cannot be the case because P and P* are in a contradictory relation and a pair of contradictory propositions cannot be both false.[328] Now suppose that he held the view that future contingent propositions have the truth-value *Either-true-or-false* different from *True* and *False*, and that we wanted to reject the position that future contingent propositions are neither true nor false. How could he have argued against such a view by claiming that to hold that a pair of future contingent propositions contradictorily opposed are both non-true amounts to stating that they are both false? Not only would this equivalence immediately be rejected by people admitting truth-value gaps but Boethius himself would have to deny it. If P is neither true nor false or it has a truth-value different from *True* and *False* it is easy to see that F[P] does not follow from ¬T[P]. Boethius' criticism would be pointless and inconsistent.[329]

To explain the text, Gaskin thinks that Boethius here treats truth-value gaps or the introduction of a third truth-value in bivalent terms and because of this he is

---

therefore contains an intrinsic indeterminacy: it may be different.

[324]   As is known, Boethius does not depend directly on Ammonius for his commentary on the *De Interpretatione*, but the similarity of their treatment of future contingent propositions strongly suggests that they draw their inspiration from a common source. Courcelle's thesis according to which Ammonius would have been Boethius' main source (cp. P. Courcelle 1948, 264) is nowadays rejected by all scholars. The view that both commentators depend on a common source has been proposed by J. Shiel 1958, 228-234 and is shared by L. Obertello 1974, I, 522-544, F.W. Zimmermann 1981, lxxxviii and N. Kretzmann 1987, 66-67.

[325]   Boethius, *In Int.*, sec. ed. 214, 25 ff.

[326]   Boethius, *In Int.*, sec. ed. 208, 17.

[327]   Cp. R. Gaskin 1995, 149.

[328]   Boethius, *In Int.*, sec. ed. 214,25-215,11.

[329]   Strangely enough, R. Gaskin 1995, 160 seems to hold the same: "In his first commentary, Boethius writes briefly but in a way which clearly rejects the anti-realistic solution: he regards 'neither true' as equivalent to 'both false'".

entitled to equate ¬T[P] with F[P].[330] I must confess that I do not understand Gaskin's point. The only sense I can make of it is that Boethius might have contrasted here the view attributed by the Stoics to Aristotle, according to which future contingent propositions are neither true nor false, with his alleged interpretation by which they are either-true-or-false. But were it so, it would be hard to understand how in the argument the implications from ¬T[P] to F[P] and from ¬T[P*] to F[P*] can be explained.[331]

Boethius' point seems to be different, because in his interpretation it is in some sense true to claim that the members of a pair of antithetical future contingent propositions are both non-true:

> (E) If those who have thought that Aristotle maintains that both propositions in the future are false would carefully read what he is saying here, they would never fall victim of such gross errors. For it is not the same to say that neither is true and to say that neither is true in a definite way. That there is going to be a sea-battle tomorrow and that there is not going to be one tomorrow are not said in such a way that both are altogether false, but that neither is true in a definite way, in such a way that either of them is false in a definite way. Rather, this one is indeed true and that one false, not one of them in a definite way however, but either you take in a contingent way.[332]

---

330   Cp. R. Gaskin 1995, 161: "But, in any case, for anyone who, like Boethius, finds truth-value gaps repugnant (at least that is his official line, although as we have seen he cannot strictly avoid them), the postulation of such gaps, or of a third truth-value, is likely to be heard in bivalent terms, the gap, or third value, being assimilated to one of the two standard values. Boethius thus recognises no difference between a 'neither member true' and 'both member false' solution". It is difficult to understand how the introduction of a truth-value gap, or a third truth-value, can "be heard in bivalent terms".

331   I suspect that R. Gaskin's view depends on his interpretation of the way in which Boethius (In Int., sec. ed. 208,17) reports the Stoic position. Boethius says: "Some people (the Stoics among them) believed that Aristotle says that future contingent propositions are neither true nor false. They took his statement that <the contingent> is no more disposed to being than to not being as a statement that there is no difference between considering <the corresponding propositions> true and considering them false. For they thought that these propositions are neither true nor false. But falsely." The statement that "there is no difference between considering <the corresponding propositions> true and considering them false" (nihil eas interesset falsas an veras putari: 208,5-6) cannot be interpreted, in my view, as implying that a future contingent proposition is true if and only if it is false, but as saying that there is no reason to consider it more true than false, since it has no truth-value at all. Therefore, Boethius is not claiming that the view attributed to Aristotle by the Stoics entails that a pair of future contingent propositions contradictorily opposed, being no more true than false, are both false. I do not see any reason to ascribe such a nonsense to Boethius. For the translations of Boethius I have basically followed those of N. Kretzmann in: D. Blank and N. Kretzmann (transl.) 1998, 129 ff.

332   Boethius, In Int., sec. ed.. 215,16-26. The text is not completely certain and I have basically followed Norman Kretzmann (1998, ad loc.).

The point seems to me sufficiently clear. Of a pair of future contingent propositions contradictorily opposed, P and P*, we are allowed to maintain that they are both not true, if and only if this claim amounts to saying that they are both not true in a definite way. If neither P nor P* are true in a definite way we cannot infer that they are both false, which would be absurd, since their not being true in a definite way is consistent with the fact that one of them is indefinitely true and the other indefinitely false. It comes out quite clearly that the distinction between 'being not true' and 'being not true in a definite way' is essential for Boethius. To say simply that P and P* are both not true entails that they are both false, which is absurd in Boethius' view. On the other hand, to maintain that P and P* are both not true in a definite way does not imply that they are both false. This claim is consistent with the view that P and P* are one true and the other false but in an indefinite way.[333]

The conclusion of this discussion is that Ammonius cannot be ranked among the partisans of the traditional interpretation (in the version proposed by Gaskin either). What I claim therefore is that the distinction between definitely and indefinitely true (false) propositions is not a distinction between propositions which possess and propositions which do not possess a truth-value (or possess a truth-value different from the two standard ones). Thus, we are allowed to say that not only definitely true, but also indefinitely true propositions are true. This means that a proposition which is indefinitely true cannot be labelled as allegedly true or quasi-true. It is really true no more and no less than any other true proposition. Indefiniteness (or definiteness) qualifies the way in which a proposition is true just as biped and quadruped determine types of animals. A biped is no less an animal than a quadruped and a proposition is no less true or false than any other proposition for being qualified as indefinitely true or false. This point is clearly made by Boethius. For instance, in criticising the Stoic position he states:

> (F) Aristotle does not say that, i.e. that both <members of a contradiction> are neither true nor false, but that each of them is true or false, not however in a definite way as in the case of past and present propositions. The nature of sentences is in some sense dual: some sentences are such that not only the true and the false is found in them, but also one of them is true in a definite way and the other is false in a definite way; in other sentences one is true and the other false, but in an indefinite and mutable way and this happens because of their nature, not with respect to what we do not know and we know.[334]

It seems clear to me that here Boethius claims that there are propositions which are not only true but also true in a definite way. Since 'being true' is distinguished from and coupled to 'being true in a definite way', we are entitled to interpret

---

[333]   The distinction between 'being not true', which is equivalent to 'being false', and 'being not true in a definite way', which does not imply 'being false', is disturbing for Gaskin's interpretation because he argues for an equivalence between 'true' and 'definitely true' (cp. e.g. R. Gaskin 1995, 153).

[334]   Boethius, *In Int.*, *sec. ed.*, 208,7-18.

'being true, but in an indefinite way' in the same way: there are propositions which are true and true in a indefinite way. Our passage shows also that for Boethius (and Ammonius) (PB) holds not only for past and present, but also for future contingent propositions. Since a future contingent proposition is either true in a indefinite way or false in an indefinite way, and a proposition which is indefinitely true (false) is also true (false), (PB) applies unconditionally to future contingent statements.[335]

V.3.2

Even if we agree that Ammonius cannot be ranked among the supporters of the traditional interpretation, the problem remains to understand what the distinction between indefinite and definite truth (falsity) amounts to.

A long journey awaits us and as a beginning we must devote a little space to describing the character of the critical propositions discussed in *De Interpretatione*, Chapter 9. According to Ammonius they are temporally qualified with reference to the future, in the sense that they refer to future events.[336] From this point of view he seems just to repeat Aristotle. What is more interesting is that Ammonius states more clearly than Aristotle does that the propositions in question are not only future but also contingent. From Aristotle employing the expression ἐπὶ δὲ τῶν καθ' ἔκαστα καὶ μελλόντων[337] for qualifying what is at issue, where μελλόντων instead of ἐσομένων is used, he infers that the events and propositions in question are contingent events and contingent propositions,[338] or better, following Ammonius' way of putting it, propositions in contingent matter (κατὰ τὴν ἐνδεχομένην ὕλην).[339] This means that the propositions in question are not propositions whose contingency is explicitly stated, but propositions which are said to be contingent because they refer to contingent events.

---

335 To avoid this conclusion the supporters of the traditional interpretation are compelled to distinguish between the Principle of Bivalence and the Law of the Excluded Middle. I am not at all sure that evidence for such a distinction can be found in the texts. When for instance Boethius says that past and present-tensed contingent propositions and future contingent ones are similar in that *in his autem adfirmatio est aut negatio* (*In Int.*, sec. ed. 191,24-25) or when Ammonius (*In Int.* 139,14-17) claims that a pair of future contingent propositions contradictorily opposed "always divide the true and false, but in an indefinite, not in a definite manner; for (γάρ) it is necessary that Socrates bathe or not bathe tomorrow, and it is impossible that either both or neither happen" it is hard to believe that they endorse the Law of the Excluded Middle, but not the Principle of Bivalence. The γάρ in the Ammonius passage is against this hypothesis.

336 Although Ammonius does not say so explicitly, I assume that he would not have counted as a proposition concerning the future a sentence such as: "it will be true tomorrow that three years ago Philip had a car accident".

337 *Int.* 9, 18a33.

338 *In Int.* 138.34 ff.

339 See e.g. *In Int.* 139,10.

Moreover, Ammonius underlines that the propositions discussed by Aristotle are singular. This is the straightforward and obvious interpretation of Aristotle's ἐπὶ δὲ τῶν καθ᾽ ἕκαστα at 18a33. What is strange is that Aristotle's main example is our (1) (cp. above p.247), which is not a singular proposition in its most direct construction, since it does not refer to a particular sea-battle. In fact Ammonius never quotes (1)[340] and he prefers examples such as

(2)   Socrates will bathe tomorrow

In (2) a pseudo-date (tomorrow) is used, but there are also examples where the futurity of the event in question is left open as in

(3)   This sick person will recover[341]

However, most of his examples *do* contain a pseudo-date.[342]

As is easy to see, Ammonius assumes that there is a correlation between contingency, futurity and the way in which a proposition is qualified in its truth-value. Past and present propositions about any matter, that is past and present-tensed propositions which can be truly qualified as necessary or contingent, divide truth and falsity in a definite way and in this sense they are definitely true or false.[343] On the other hand, being indefinite in its truth-value is something that can only happen to a proposition concerning the future. However, not every proposition concerning a future event is indefinite in its truth-value. If the event referred to is necessary the proposition expressing such an event is definitely true or false.[344] But the same happens for a contingent event, when all conditions for its realisation are given. The following passage makes the point to some extent. Ammonius claims that in some case we can have a definite knowledge of future events. He says:

> (G) It is clearly possible for the contingent sometimes to be known in a definite manner (ὡρισμένως) even by our own knowledge, namely when it is no longer contingent properly speaking, but necessarily follows from the causes leading the way to its own generation: it is possible, for example, for a sphere which rests on a horizontal surface while the surface keeps the same position, to be moved by something or not, but when the surface is tilted it is impossible for it not to be moved.[345]

The example of the sphere shows what kind of contingency is at issue with future propositions. A sphere resting on an horizontal surface may be moved or

---

[340]   As far as I remember the only exception is at *In Int.* 154,32. However, he considers a proposition such as "a white baby will be born tomorrow" (e.g. *In Int.* 144,15-16), which seems to be of the same type as (1). For "historical" reasons I take the liberty of referring to (1) as a future contingent proposition.

[341]   *In Int.* 140,15-16.

[342]   I take the terminology of 'pseudo-dates' from N. Rescher and A. Urquhart 1971, 27.

[343]   *In Int.* 130,1-20.

[344]   *In Int.* 130,1-5.

[345]   *In Int.* 137,1-7.

not. It depends, for instance, on the decision of someone. Before the decision is taken, it is open whether the sphere will be moved or not. But if the surface on which the sphere rests is tilted, its moving cannot be prevented and in this sense it is no longer open whether it moves or not. Since no past and present events can be changed, only the future is open, at least for those events for which the causally sufficient conditions for their being or not being are not yet given. This text implies that one and the same proposition can be treated as necessary or contingent according to the different situations to which it is tied. If today, before the starting of the battle, the decision of the admirals is taken and this makes the event unpreventable, today (1) is no longer a contingent proposition. On the other hand, before the admirals' decision, the future of the battle is still open and in this sense it is contingent that the battle will take place.

In our passage what is in question is definite or indefinite knowledge, a notion which is not the same as having a definite or indefinite truth-value. However, one might assume that *we can* have definite knowledge of a proposition P only if P has a definite truth-value.[346] Under this assumption, the text implies that a future proposition concerning a contingent event may take a definite truth-value when all conditions for the realisation of the event are given and it becomes unpreventable. This explains why present and past propositions are said to have a definite truth-value. The events that they express are fixed. It is no longer open whether a sea-battle occurred yesterday: either it happened or not, since the past and the present cannot be changed. To make the point in a different way, when a proposition has a truth-value which cannot be different it is a necessary proposition and it has a definite truth-value. On the other hand, a future proposition concerning a contingent event has a truth-value which might be different and for this reason it is true or false in an indefinite way.

This analysis suggests a further point about the way in which propositions such as (1) and (2) must be treated.[347] A proposition concerning the past or the present is said to be necessary. The kind of necessity implied by it is not logical necessity, but a sort of historical necessity, the same necessity which is attributed to a contingent event when all conditions for its realisation are given. The historical necessity of a proposition entails that it cannot be otherwise: either it is true or it is false, and this holds without any possible change. Consider now a proposition such as

(4)   Yesterday a sea-battle occurred

---

[346]   The question of how the Gods can have a definite knowledge of contingent events is a different question (cp. Ammonius, *In Int.* 135,12 ff.). On this problem see M. Mignucci 1985, 219-246.

[347]   We leave aside (3) where no pseudo-date is expressed. However, (3) can be treated in the same way as dated future contingent propositions if we assume that after the disappearance of the particular referred to (this sick person) the proposition denying the predicate of him becomes in any case definitely true.

According to Ammonius' account, (4) is a proposition about the past and it cannot change its truth-value. But this may not be true if we assign to 'yesterday' the meaning of a pseudo-date. Suppose that (4) is uttered today and that it is true. This means that yesterday a sea-battle took place. Thus, it is not true tomorrow unless a sea-battle occurs today, and so on for every day. To attribute an unchangeable truth-value to (4) we must take 'yesterday' as referring to a fixed date. Suppose that 'yesterday' is a way of referring to the 29th February 2000. Then, one might reasonably claim that the proposition

(5)   A sea-battle occurred on the 29th February 2000

is definitely true or false at any time after this date.

The same point is made by Ammonius by discussing the so-called deterministic objection. According to him this objection can be put as follows:

> (H) <Aristotle> speaks as though making his argument from a new beginning. "Further, if something is pale now",[348] like a new-born child, "it was true to say"[349] on the previous day that tomorrow a pale child would be born—actually, no more on the previous day than at any previous time at all. For what is strange <in this>? If we speak truly each time we say in advance that something will be, *this thing is not such as not to be going to be*, just as neither *is something such as not to be*, if we say truly that it exists. Thus, it was impossible for the pale child not to be born, because the prediction made about it in indefinite preceding time was true.[350]

The proposition which the determinist thinks to be true at any time cannot be

A pale child will be born tomorrow

since two days before the event (6) will be true only under the condition that two pale children are born in the following two days.

To overcome this difficulty we can proceed in this way. Let us introduce a temporal constant in the propositions we are going to consider, say τ, and state as a correspondent of proposition (1)

(1*)   A sea-battle occurs at τ

where τ is a date and 'occurs' has to be taken atemporally. We can generalise and formalise (1*) in several ways. A possible one is to introduce atemporal states of affairs p, q, r and so on, and an operator C, which, applied to a state of affairs p, says that p is the case.[351] The being the case which is expressed by applying C to p can be temporally qualified, e.g. by a temporal constant τ. Therefore, we can take

(7) $C_\tau p$

---

348   These are Aristotle's words: *Int.* 9, 18b9-10.
349   Again Aristotle's words: *Int.* 9, 18b10.
350   *In Int.* 144,14-21.
351   In this context we do not need to make a distinction between states of affairs and events, if they are both to be taken atemporally. In the following, we will indifferently call what is denoted by 'p' a state of affairs or an event.

as the form of (1*). Needless to say, (1*) and (7) do not express futurity and in this sense they do not correspond to (1). We can consider the reference to the future expressed by (1) as depending on the relation there is between the time of utterance of (1) and the time indicated in (1*). In this perspective, (1*) represents the content of (1), and this content is located in the future with respect to the present of the utterance being evaluated as true or false at the time of its utterance. To make the same point in other words, the truth-value of (1) is the truth-value that (1*) takes when it is evaluated at the time in which (1) is uttered. The time of utterance of (1) represents the time at which (1*) is evaluated as true or false, and this means that the truth value assigned to (1) is the truth value assigned to (1*) under the assumption that (1*) is evaluated at tn = τ-1 (where 'τ-1' stands for 'the day before τ').

By this analysis I do not claim that in general propositions containing pseudo-dates can be reduced to propositions in which any relevant reference to time is made by real dates, and that the so-called 'A-series' can be reduced to the B-series.[352] My point is simpler and weaker. In order to make sense of some of the ways in which Ammonius uses propositions like (1) and (2) it is convenient to read them in the above way.

V.3.3

Before offering a positive interpretation of the distinction between definitely and indefinitely true (false) propositions we have to reject a temptation which is too easy. Suppose that a singular contingent state of affairs is the case at τ, i.e. $C_\tau p$. Therefore, according to Ammonius, at any time before τ, say at ρ, $C_\tau p$ is true and indefinitely true. One might try to explain this mysterious reference to an indefinite truth by connecting it to an epistemological situation. Before τ $C_\tau p$ has a truth-value which is indefinite because we are not able to state or grasp it. On this view, indefiniteness does not depend on the objective state of the events and propositions, but on our inability to grasp them adequately. Were we gods, there would be no indefinite truth-value.

There are some texts which may be invoked as evidence for this interpretation. Consider the final part of text (A). In our translation we have taken ὡρισμένως (definitely) to refer to the being true or false of a proposition by analogy with the many passages where ὡρισμένως specifies the truth-value of propositions. But it would probably be more natural to refer ὡρισμένως to ἔστι εἰπεῖν ("it is possible to say"). If so, it is the possibility of saying that a proposition is true or false which is not yet defined. In another passage, in order to explain why "Socrates will bathe tomorrow" and "Socrates will not bathe tomorrow" are one true and the other false but in an indefinite way, Ammonius says that "which

---

352   As is well known, a debate is going on among philosophers on this subject. A useful discussion of the question can be found in R. Sorabji 1983, 33ff.

of these will be the true one it is not possible to know before the outcome of the matter"[353] Once again, the fact of having an indefinite truth-value is explained by reference to an epistemological situation. In a parallel way, with reference to a pair of contradictory propositions concerning the past or the present, their having a definite truth-value is explained by saying that "inasmuch as the thing about which one is speaking has already occurred, the true and false singular propositions are obvious".[354] One might take this statement as asserting that a present or past proposition is definitely true or false *because* its truth-value is clear, i.e. can be grasped.

Although this interpretation is attractive for its simplicity, it must be rejected. First of all, the distinction between definitely and indefinitely true (false) propositions is appealed to in order to avoid determinism. But a purely epistemic undecidability cannot do the job. In this perspective, although I cannot decide about the truth or falsity of C$_τ$p before τ, say at ε, C$_τ$p nevertheless has a fixed truth-value at ε and this is sufficient for triggering off the deterministic argument. In order to escape determinism we need to interpret the distinction between definitely and indefinitely true or false propositions as an ontological distinction. Moreover, Ammonius more than once points out that contingent things have an indefinite nature[355] and it is easy to guess that the indefinite truth-value assigned to propositions depends on the indefinite nature of the events expressed by them. This interpretation is confirmed by some statements made by Boethius, where the epistemological interpretation is overtly rejected.[356]

The conclusion is that we must look for a different interpretation of Ammonius' distinction. The lack of knowledge or unclarity we have about the truth-value of future contingent propositions is a consequence of their not having a definite status with respect to truth and falsity. Contingent propositions about the future are indefinitely true or false not because the future is hidden or unknown to our mind, but because the ontological status of the facts they refer to is not yet established. What is uncertain is not the possibility of knowing before tomorrow that Socrates will bathe tomorrow, but the event itself since it is put in the future and it is contingent.[357]

---

[353]   *In Int.* 139, 17-18.
[354]   *In Int.* 130,11-14.
[355]   E.g. *In Int.* 136,12-13.
[356]   Boethius, *In Int.*, *sec. ed.*, 208,11-18; 245,19-28.
[357]   From the fact that the prohibition against assigning a definite truth-value to future contingent propositions is sometimes spelled out in epistemic terms R. Gaskin 1995, 149 and 157 infers that future contingent statements are metaphysically indeterminate and therefore have an indefinite truth-value. Commenting on our text (A) he says: "Aristotle, on Ammonius' interpretation, says that FCSs [i.e. future contingent statements] do divide the true and the false just as present and past-tensed statements do ... But they do not divide the true and false in the same way ... For unlike the case of statements about the present and the past, it is not possible to say definitely which member is true and which false ... That impossibility cannot be merely epistemic ... Rather, the claim must be that it is *in principle* impossible to assign truth to one member of a FCA [future

V.3.4

To provide a positive interpretation of the distinction between definitely and indefinitely true or false propositions is difficult, because Ammonius never defines or explains it, but introduces it as something already known to the reader. We have seen that the distinction between past and future contingent propositions depends on the way in which they divide truth and falsity. Past propositions are definitely true or definitely false, while future propositions are indefinitely true or indefinitely false, and this means that they are true or they are false, plus something else, i.e. their being indefinite. Moreover, a proposition, which is now evaluated as true and indefinite, may be evaluated tomorrow as true and definite. This means that characterising the truth-value of a proposition as definite or indefinite depends essentially on the time at which the proposition is uttered or evaluated.

How can we explain all this? One might be tempted to answer this question in the following way. Consider the passages, taken especially from Boethius, where the commentators insist on characterising indefinite truth (falsity) as changeable (*volubilis* says Boethius in one place) and definite truth (falsity) as stable (*constituta*).[358] Moreover, Ammonius clearly states, as we have seen, that a proposition can only be called true (false) in a definite way when the objective conditions for its truth (falsity) are there, i.e. when the appropriate states of affairs obtain or are causally necessitated by other states of affairs already established, and a proposition is true (false) in an indefinite way only if such conditions are

---

contingent ἀντίφασις] and falsity to the other: it is metaphysically indeterminate which way round the truth-values go." (157) Gaskin connects ὡρισμένως to ἔστιν εἰπεῖν, which is, as we have seen, possible and perhaps natural. But even if we read the text as a claim that it is impossible to say in a definite way which of two future contingent statements contradictorily opposed is true and which is false, I do not think that we can infer from this that the two propositions of the pair are neither true nor false. The parallel passages show that 'saying in a definite way which of a pair is true or false' is only possible when we can say which is true in a definite way and which is false in a definite way. Therefore, the metaphysical impossibility involved is not the impossibility of being true or false, but the impossibility of being definitely true or definitely false. This is confirmed also by Boethius' evidence. When he says that of a pair of future contingent propositions contradictorily opposed, $C_\tau p$ and $C_\tau p^*$, nobody knows which is true and which is false, he does not mean that they do not have a truth-value: "For instance if we say: 'the Franks will overcome the Goths' and someone puts forward the negation: 'the Franks will not overcome the Goths', one of these propositions is true and the other is false, but nobody knows before the result which one is true and which one is false" (*In Int.*, sec. ed. 184, 22-26). If, as Gaskin claims (150), Boethius meant that "it is simply metaphysically indeterminate which member is true" he would contradict himself: $C_\tau p$ and $C_\tau p^*$ *do* have a truth-value (*una quidem vera est, una falsa*: 184, 24). The only way to interpret this and other similar passages safely is by taking them to mean that before the happening of the events which the propositions refer to, it is metaphysically impossible to state whether $C_\tau p$ or $C_\tau p^*$ will be *definitely* true or false.

358   See e.g. Boethius, *In Int.*, *pr. ed.*, 108,4-5; 123,20-22; 124,6-7; *sec. ed.* 190,7.

not yet given. When a proposition such as (1*), or better C$_\tau$p, is evaluated before τ, say at ρ, its truth-conditions are not yet established. However, it is said to be true or false. Therefore, we might imagine that the attribution of a truth-value to C$_\tau$p at ρ is *arbitrary*, so that one might claim that to be indefinitely true for a proposition means to be true under an arbitrary assignation. Take a pair of contingent propositions C$_\tau$p and C$_\tau$p* contradictorily opposed and evaluate them before at ρ (ρ<τ). Since by hypothesis these conditions are lacking at ρ there is no other way to assign a truth-value to C$_\tau$p and C$_\tau$p* at ρ than by an arbitrary imposition. Imagine we assign the value *True* to C$_\tau$p at ρ. If C$_\tau$p* is by hypothesis the negation of C$_\tau$p we have to assign the value *False* to it at ρ simply because of the logical form of these statements. In this way the Principle of Bivalence, which is accepted without restriction by Ammonius and Boethius, applies also to future contingent propositions. At a certain point of the history of the world, e.g. at τ, the truth-conditions for the truth or falsity of C$_\tau$p (and its negation C$_\tau$p*) show up. At that time we can easily adjust the truth-value assignation to this pair, and say that e.g. C$_\tau$p is true and C$_\tau$p* is false at τ, or *vice-versa*, according to the nature of things. Since the attribution of a truth-value to C$_\tau$p and C$_\tau$p* at τ depends no longer on an arbitrary imposition but is led by the presence of a matter of fact situation, we are allowed to say that C$_\tau$p and C$_\tau$p* have a stable and fixed truth-value at τ, which cannot change for any future evaluation of this pair, i.e. for any time equal or greater than τ. In this sense C$_\tau$p and C$_\tau$p* are true or false in a definite way at τ and they divide the true and the false accordingly.

This picture raises some general problems, which are philosophically interesting but not relevant here, and, as far I can see, it is not inconsistent with the answer to the fatalist's argument that Ammonius and Boethius offer as an interpretation of Aristotle's point of view. However, it shares with the traditional interpretation a disadvantage, which in my view is crucial. If future contingent propositions have no truth-value, or an arbitrary one, predictions are pointless. Consider a proposition such as (1) and suppose that this proposition has an arbitrary truth-value (or no truth-value at all), where its arbitrariness does not depend on epistemic conditions but is "ontologically" determined. Anyone who agrees on this would refrain from seriously predicting that tomorrow there will be a sea-battle, since what seems to be a necessary condition for performing a prediction is that the prediction can, at least in principle, be true.

It is obvious that the kind of prediction considered here has nothing to do with those predictions that we would nowadays call scientific predictions, which are not about contingent events, but about events which are submitted to laws of some sort. Propositions about such events are definitely true or false even before the time to which the events expressed by them refer. In Ammonius' account predictions refer to events which by definition are not submitted to any law. Nor are they referring to contingent events which are no longer contingent, because a causal chain has taken place which makes the originally contingent event unpreventable.[359] Ammonius' predictions concern really contingent future events. One might think that it is no great harm if such predictions are given up. We might even feel relieved if in the ideal town ruled by logicians fortune-tellers, soothsayers and other people of this sort had no admission. But this was not Ammonius' view. As is well known, the ancient world paid a great deal of attention and gave a large place to oracles, divination, prophecies and predictions in general. Philosophers were accordingly interested in these phenomena. The general attitude was more inclined to search for a justification for predictions and oracles than to question whether, or to deny that, they are reliable. In particular, Ammonius maintains that oracles offer evidence that the Gods know contingent events,[360] and their possible ambiguities do not constitute a sufficient reason for denying that Gods' knowledge of contingent events is definite.[361] Therefore, since the possibility of human predictions is not ruled out, future contingent propositions cannot either lack a truth-value or have an arbitrary one.[362] We must look for another explanation of the distinction between indefinite and definite truth.

V.3.5

The discussion of the arbitrary assignment of truth-values to future contingent statements, although it has been concluded negatively, brings us closer to the solution of our problem, i.e. the explanation of the distinction between indefinitely and definitely true (false) propositions.

Let us consider the general view on truth held by Ammonius. He shares with many Peripatetics a correspondence conception of truth: a proposition P is true (false) if and only if the event or the state of affairs signified by P and corresponding to it is (is not) the case.[363] The obtaining (non-obtaining) of the event or state of affairs is the condition for assigning a truth-value to P. Take for instance (1*) and suppose that we consider it at τ, the date at which the sea-battle is supposed to take place. At τ (1*) receives a fixed and stable truth-value: if the

---

[359]   See text (G).

[360]   *In Int.* 135,12-14.

[361]   *In Int.* 137,12-23.

[362]   R. Gaskin 1995, 171-173 correctly points out that gods' knowledge of contingent events cannot be considered as a case of *fore*knowledge because their knowledge takes place outside time. Therefore, what they think cannot be evaluated at a certain time and, in particular, before the event which the thought refers to takes place. But he seems to go too far when (misinterpreting in my view *in Int.* 137,12-23) he says that Ammonius thinks "that oracles and prophets cannot foresee what *will* happen, but only what is likely to happen, or perhaps what will happen if advice is followed (or not)—but not then whether advice will be followed" (173, n.90). Ammonius is implying neither that *every* prophecy is useless, as 135,12-14 shows, nor that only what is no longer contingent can be an object of a true prediction.

[363]   *In Int.* 139,26 ff.; 140,32 ff. and 154,16-20.

sea-battle occurs at that time (1*) is true, otherwise it is false. Since its truth-conditions are in the world, (1*) is not only true or false, but also true or false in such a way that its truth-value cannot change. Whatever the development of the history of the world may be, the truth-value assigned to (1*) at τ remains the same. This corresponds to the intuition that what has happened or is happening cannot be changed, so that it is irrevocable in every possible development of the world. Ammonius does not say this in so many words, but it may be implied by his claiming that what is stated about the present or the past is necessarily true or necessarily false:

> (I) If he <Socrates> happens not to be bathing or to have bathed on the previous day, it is clear that the negative sentence taken in the present or the past must be true, while the affirmative sentence, since it says that what has not occurred either holds or held, must be false.[364]

If it is the case that Socrates is bathing at τ, however the world might develop from τ onwards, it remains true that Socrates be bathing at τ. Past and present events are such that they rule out the possibility that the opposite occurs in their place and the corresponding true propositions do not admit the possibility of being false. The same must be said with respect to falsity. Let us call the situation in which a contingent proposition has received a truth-value because its truth-conditions are the case a situation in which the proposition has an *assigned* or *established* or *settled* truth-value.

On the other hand, Ammonius recognises the presence of contingent events in the world.[365] This means that the course of the history of the world is not fixed and the only possible one. Our future is an open one, in the sense that it may develop in different ways. While the past and the present are fixed, there are many possible different future histories of the world, each of which shares the same past. Therefore, it may very well happen that in one possible development of the world (1*) receives the assigned truth-value *True* and in a conceivably different development it takes the assigned truth-value *False*. It may happen that according to one possible history of the world the admirals decide immediately before τ that no naval confrontation with the enemy must take place. In this case such truth-conditions are laid down that (1*) takes the assigned truth-value *False*. On the other hand, in a different possible history of the world it may happen that the decision of the admirals goes in the opposite direction and that the sea-battle occurs. Therefore, in this conceivable situation we must give the assigned truth-value *True* to (1*). However, once in a possible history of the world an assigned truth-value has been given to a proposition, it remains constant in that history. In the development of the world in which the sea-battle occurs at τ, according to the decision of the admirals, (1*) takes the assigned truth-value True and this is fixed once and for all: in that history (1*) cannot change its settled truth-value. This corresponds to Ammonius' intuition that present and past events

---

[364]   *In Int.* 130,17-20.
[365]   *In Int.* 137,25 ff.; 147,25 ff.

are necessary in the sense that they cannot be changed: *factum infectum fieri nequit*.

It should be clear that before the time in which its truth-conditions are laid down, a contingent proposition has no assigned or settled or established truth-value. Before τ (1*) has no assigned truth-value. Shall we conclude from this that before τ (1*) has no truth-value at all? Well, since the truth-conditions for (1*), by hypothesis, are not given before τ, we may be led to conclude that (1*) is neither true nor false, or that an arbitrary truth-value must be given to this statement. But this is not Ammonius' position, as we have seen. His view is that even before τ (1*) is true or false, but not in a definite way, in a way, we are tempted to say, that makes the happening of the event denoted by it inescapable, because the conditions for its being true or false are given.

A possible way to interpret his claim is as follows. As we have seen, the history of the world may develop according to different paths and it may happen that the same proposition receives different assigned truth-values in these different paths because of the different situations constituting the truth- conditions for the proposition which are supposed to take place in them. Now imagine that we are able to refer to what is happening in the "real" future history of the world, i.e. what in fact will happen, whatever that may be. What I mean is not that we are able to know what is going on in the "real" future, but simply that we are in a position to mark off among the possible developments of the world the history which will be our "real" history, i.e. the history which is not merely conceived or thought of as a counterfactual possibility, but that which, as a matter of fact, will take place and in which we are going to live and operate.[366] If (1*) will "really" take the assigned truth-value *True* at τ, then it is in some sense always true that (1*) will take such a value at τ. If the assigned truth-value *True* is assigned to (1*) at τ in the real development of the world (whatever it may be) then we are entitled to say that (1*) is *plainly* or *simply* or *factually true*. [367] In other words, (1*) is plainly true if at some time the conditions for its truth will appear in the "real" world. It does not matter whether these conditions are already there at the time of the evaluation of our proposition. The important point is that they will at some time come out in the "real" history of the world to which we can refer even if it is not yet at our back, in the past. The same can be said, *mutatis mutandis*, for *plain* or *simple* or *factual falsity*.

It is easy to see that the notions of truth and falsity involved in plain truth or falsity are to some extent atemporal, in the sense that they do not intrinsically depend on the time of utterance or evaluation of the propositions at issue. To qualify a proposition P as simply true or false it is sufficient to be sure that P takes an assigned truth-value in the real history of the world. If a sea-battle occurs at τ,

---

[366]   One might challenge this claim as something which is against the view that the future is completely open before us. So e.g. N. Belnap 1992, 385-434.

[367]   In speaking of 'plain (or simple) truth (falsity)' I have been inspired by the terminology of von Wright, who uses the expression 'plain truth' (cp. G. von Wright 1984, 5).

the proposition expressing that this event occurs at τ receives the assigned truth-value *True* at τ and before τ it has no assigned truth-value. But its being true, i.e. its expressing conformity to an event, is something which does not depend on the time at which P is uttered. To ensure the possibility of such a correspondence we have just to admit that we are allowed to refer to the series of events which take place in the chain of "real" events. We do not need to wait until the conditions which allow us to attribute an assigned truth-value to a proposition are laid down in order to attach a simple truth-value to it. In this sense plain truth and plain falsity are not intrinsically related to time.[368] Needless to say, it is with respect to simple truth and falsity that Ammonius can maintain that the Principle of Bivalence holds in every case, and that an indefinitely true proposition no more and no less than a definitely true one is (plainly) true.

We are now in a position to characterise indefinitely and definitely true or false propositions. Here the time at which the proposition is uttered with respect to the time of the event expressed by it is crucial and this makes a relevant difference with respect to the attribution of simple truth (falsity) to it. Consider the case of a definitely true proposition. As we have seen, a definitely true proposition is true, i.e., in our terminology, is simply true. On the other hand, a definitely true proposition is in some way unalterable, in the sense that its truth-value cannot change. Therefore, a definitely true proposition is such that it is evaluated as true when an assigned truth-value has been given to it, since from this moment onwards its truth cannot change. By stating that our proposition is simply true we say that the event denoted by it is an event of the "real" world; by positing that it is evaluated only when its assigned truth-value has been given to it, we account for its necessity and unpreventability.

A characterisation of an indefinitely true proposition can easily be worked out from what has been said about definitely true propositions. An indefinitely true proposition is a contingent proposition, i.e. a proposition which denotes an event whose outcome is not yet fixed, and which at the same time is a simply true proposition. Therefore, its evaluation must take place before it receives an assigned truth-value. On the other hand, it is a simply true proposition. With reference to (1*) we say that this proposition is indefinitely true if (i) it is evaluated before τ, (ii) it is simply true (i.e. there are in the "real" future the objective conditions for its truth), but (iii) there is also an "unreal" development of the world in which conditions are given according to which (1*) turns out to be false.[369]

---

[368] This view has recently been developed by G. von Wright 1984, 6.

[369] This characterisation of definite and indefinite truth shows quite clearly that my interpretation does not consist in equating indefinite truth with contingent truth and definite truth with necessary truth, *pace* R. Gaskin 1995, 148 n.12. It relies on a philosophically committed analysis of the notion of truth as in some sense an atemporally determinable notion and on the assumption that we can refer to the "real" future. Therefore, in my interpretation 'definitely' and 'indefinitely true' cannot be taken as synonymous with, but only as entailing, 'necessarily' and 'contingently true'.

Our characterisation of definitely and indefinitely true propositions is able to explain in a simple way Ammonius' claim that present or past propositions are definitely true or false, while future contingent ones are indefinitely true or false. Consider again (1*) and suppose that we evaluate it before τ, let us say at ρ ($\rho < \tau$), when the conditions which make (1*) true or false in an assigned way are not yet present. Therefore, there are two possible developments of the world starting from ρ. One development leads to a situation such that (1*) becomes true (in an assigned way); the other development makes (1*) false (again in an assigned way). Suppose that the "real" development contains the conditions for the truth of (1*). Thus, (1*) is indefinitely true at ρ and it leaves the possibility open for its falsity. On the other hand, consider (1*) at τ or afterward. At that moment its truth-conditions are there and it receives an assigned truth-value. Suppose again that in the "real" path (1*) receives the assigned truth-value *True*. Thus, (1*) is definitely true at τ (and afterwards) and its possibility of becoming false is ruled out, because it refers to a fixed event in whose future no possibility of changing is left open.

V.3.6

We can put our interpretation in a more rigorous form. Let us first try to specify the context in which a formal characterisation of the notions of definite and indefinite truth can be made. Since propositions are definitely or indefinitely true or false with respect to the time in which they are uttered or considered and the situation of the world in which they are stated, we are allowed to express the predicates 'definitely true' and 'indefinitely true' of a proposition P as three-place predicates whose parameters are (i) the time in which P is uttered or considered, (ii) the state of the world in which P is evaluated and, of course, (iii) P itself. However, to make things easier, we can conflate parameters (i) and (ii) and take the time in which P is uttered or considered to be the same as the time of the situation of the world with respect to which P is evaluated. Therefore, we can express the predicates 'definitely true' and 'indefinitely true' as two-place predicates and write '$T_d([P], S_i)$' to say that P is definitely true with respect to the situation of the world S_i. Similarly, '$T_i([P], S_i)$' is a way to express that P is indefinitely true with respect to S_i.

We have next to say how time must be conceived of. Since contingency has to be taken as the open part of our future and linked to time, we can picture the world as a branching structure or a tree whose nodes represent possible states and its paths possible histories of it. Time can be interpreted as an order relation on the different stages of possible states of the world.[370] To make things easier we may think of the history of a single proposition and represent it by means of an ordinary binary tree as follows:

---

370   Cp. N. Rescher and A. Urquhart 1971, 125ff.

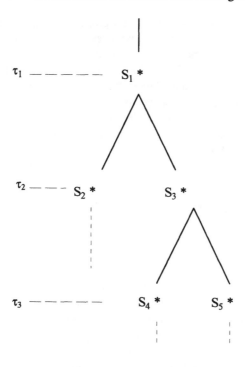

Fig. (I)

S_1-S_5 are *nodes* and the lines going through nodes are *paths* of the tree.

We can express the relation between time and the nodes of a tree by introducing the notion of level and by saying that an instant τ_i is the level of a node S_j. With reference to Fig. (I) we can state for instance that

(8) $t_2 = Lv(S_2) = Lv(S_3)$

It is easy to define in a rigorous way what 'being a possible development of S_i' means for a node S_j in such a structure. This notion is the intuitive counterpart of the relation of accessibility, which is well known to modal logicians. We represent it by 'Dev(S_j,S_i)' and we take it to be reflexive and transitive.[371] For instance with respect to (I) we can say that S_5 is a development of S_1, because there is a backward path going from S_5 to S_1 through S_3, while S_4 is not a development of S_2 because there is no such backward path. Therefore, it is with respect to structures such as (I) that we have to define what it is for a proposition to be definitely or indefinitely true or false.

---

[371]   For the notion of accessibility cp. G.E. Hughes and M.J. Cresswell 1968, 75-80. Since the accessibility relation used here is supposed to be reflexive and transitive, the modal system involved is at least as strong as S4.

Let us now try to define what it is for a proposition $C_\tau p$, which is supposed to denote a contingent event, to be true with respect to a given situation of the world S_i. According to Ammonius' correspondentistic view about truth, if we consider $C_\tau p$ in S_i and S_i is on a level which is equal to or greater than τ, we must assign to $C_\tau p$ either the truth value *True* or the truth value *False* according to the situation of the world we are referring to. Thus, $C_\tau p$ in $S_i(Lv(S_i) \geq \tau)$ has the *assigned* truth value *True* or the *assigned* truth-value *False*. Let us write 'Ass($[C_\tau p]$, S_i)=1' for 'the truth-value *True* is assigned to $C_\tau p$ in the node S_i'. In a similar way, we state 'Ass($[C_\tau p]$, S_i)=0' for 'the truth-value *False* is assigned to $C_\tau p$ in the node S_i' or, what is the same, 'the truth-value *True* is assigned to $\neg C_\tau p$ in S_i'.[372] Formally, we have

(T*) $T^*([C_\tau p], S_i) =_{df} \text{Ass}([C_\tau p], S_i)=1$

and

(F*) $F^*([C_\tau p], S_i) =_{df} \text{Ass}([C_\tau p], S_i)=0$[373]

As we have seen, what is important to underline is that an assigned truth value can be given to a proposition if, and only if, the conditions for assigning such a truth value to it are established, i.e. if the events referred to by the propositions occur or are at least somewhat implied by the due course of the events. If we have to do with a contingent proposition, i.e. a proposition in which the event denoted by it is not established before the happening of the event itself, it is reasonable to state that no assigned truth-value can be attributed to $C_\tau p$ before τ, i.e. in a node which is on a level preceding τ.[374] Therefore, we are allowed to state

(PA) $T^*([C_\tau p], S_i) \vee F^*([C_\tau p], S_i) \rightarrow Lv(S_i) \geq \tau$

In other words, if an assigned truth value is given to $C_\tau p$ with respect to a situation S_i, then the level of S_i must be either the same or greater than τ.

It is easy to understand that if a truth-value is assigned to $C_\tau p$ in S_i, this truth-value remains constant in any node developing from S_i. Past and present events are such that they rule out the possibility that the opposite occurs in their place and the corresponding true propositions do not admit the possibility of being false. The same must be said with respect to the falsity. Therefore

---

[372]   To be precise, we should distinguish between atomic and non-atomic propositions but for our purposes it is sufficient to consider the notion of assignment with reference to the former since no other propositions than atomic ones and their negations are considered by Ammonius.

[373]   (T*) and (F*) could be generalised to refer to any proposition P whatsoever. However, where we have not to do with future contingent propositions there is no way to distinguish between assigned and unassigned truth-values.

[374]   In principle "a sea-battle occurs at τ" might have an assigned truth-value even before τ, if the conditions which unequivocally determine the happening or not happening of this event are given at some time before τ (see text [G]). But to avoid complications we may suppose that these conditions are not given before τ.

(AT) $\quad$ $T^*([C_\tau p], S_i) \to (S_j)(\mathrm{Dev}(S_j, S_i) \to T^*([C_\tau p], S_j))$

(AF) $\quad$ $F^*([C_\tau p], S_i) \to (S_j)(\mathrm{Dev}(S_j, S_i) \to F^*([C_\tau p], S_j))$

(AT) and (AF) express the condition according to which when a truth-value is assigned to a proposition with respect to a node S_i, it remains the same in any node developing from S_i.

It is reasonable to think that when a truth-value is assigned to $C_\tau p$ in S_i, where $\mathrm{Lv}(S_i) \geq \tau$, $C_\tau p$ receives an assigned truth-value in every node which is either on the same level as S_i or after S_i, independently from its being a development or not from S_i. The conditions which allow us to attribute an assigned truth-value to $C_\tau p$ are at any rate given at τ. Whatever the situation or the history of the world may be, from τ onwards $C_\tau p$ is assignedly true or false. We can therefore state:

(AP) $\quad$ $\mathrm{Lv}(S_i) \geq \tau \to T^*([C_\tau p], S_i) \vee F^*([C_\tau p], S_i)$

which is the converse of (PA). Then, by coupling (PA) and (AP) we get the equivalence

(APA) $\quad$ $\mathrm{Lv}(S_i) \geq \tau \leftrightarrow T^*([C_\tau p], S_i) \vee F^*([C_\tau p], S_i)$

An example of what we are saying could be as follows. Since the truth-values of $[C_\tau p]$ remain constant once they are assigned, we can simplify (I) and imagine that $C_\tau p$ is given an assignation of truth-values according to Fig. (II) overleaf.

Since by hypothesis $\tau_2 = \tau$, in virtue of (APA) we can give an assigned truth-value to $C_\tau p$ with respect to S_2 and S_3. Suppose that $C_\tau p$ takes the assigned truth-value 0 in S_2 and the assigned truth-value 1 in S_3. Thus, in any node developing from S_3 $C_\tau p$ will have the assigned truth value 1 and in any node developing from S_2 it will have the assigned truth value 0 because of (AT) and (AF). On the other hand, no assigned truth-value can be given to $C_\tau p$ in S_1, because its level is τ_1, which is by hypothesis before τ, and (APA) is supposed to hold. As we have seen, we cannot infer from this that $C_\tau p$ is neither true nor false in S_1, since no truth-value can be assigned to it. Ammonius' view is that even before τ $C_\tau p$ is true or false, but not in a definite way, in a way, we are tempted to say, that makes the happening of the event denoted by it inescapable.

To give an appropriate truth-value to $C_\tau p$ in S_1 we must introduce a new truth predicate. Suppose that we are be able to refer to what is happening in the "real" future, i.e. what will in fact happen, whatever this may be. Then, $C_\tau p$ will "really" take the assigned truth value 1 at τ, and it is in some sense "always" (or better atemporally) true that $C_\tau p$ will take such a value at τ. Therefore, if the truth-value 1 is given to $C_\tau p$ in an assigned way in a node of the path which is supposed to represent the "real" history of the world (of course at or after τ), $C_\tau p$ is *plainly* or *simply* or *factually* true. Take **R** to be the path representing the "real" history of the world, and suppose that S_n, whose level is by hypothesis equal or greater than τ, belongs to **R**, i.e. that $S_n \in \mathbf{R}$. If the truth-value 1 is given to $C_\tau p$ in an assigned way in S_n, $C_\tau p$ is simply true. If '$T[C_\tau p]$' stands for '$C_\tau p$ is simply true' we can write:

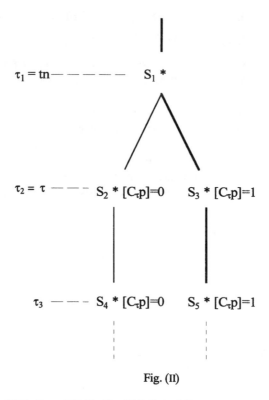

Fig. (II)

(T) $T[C_\tau p] =_{df} \exists S_i(S_i \in \mathbf{R} \bullet T^*([C_\tau p], S_i))$

If we suppose that the bold line in Fig. (II) represents the "real" path $\mathbf{R}$, we can say that $C_\tau p$ is simply true because there is at least one node on $\mathbf{R}$, namely S_3, where $C_\tau p$ takes the assigned truth-value 1. In a similar way we can characterise an atomic proposition which is simply false by assuming:

(F) $F[C_\tau p] =_{df} \exists S_i(S_i \in \mathbf{R} \bullet F^*([C_\tau p], S_i))$

The idea involved by (T) and (F) is plain and corresponds quite well to our intuition. If conditions for the truth or falsity of $C_\tau p$ will be given in the future, then $C_\tau p$ is at any time true or false, in the sense that $C_\tau p$ will take either the assigned truth value 1 or the assigned truth value 0 in the real future of the world.[375]

We are finally in a position to give a definition of indefinitely and definitely true or false propositions. As we have seen, what contributes in an essential way to characterise a definitely true proposition is that it denotes a fixed event which occurs in an inescapable way. We can express these features by saying that a definitely true proposition is a simply true proposition to which the truth-value 1

---

[375]   Also in the case of (T) and (P) generalisations can easily be made to accommodate these definitions to any proposition.

is attributed in an assigned way. By positing that it is a simply true proposition we say that the event denoted by the proposition is an event of the "real" history of the world; by giving the assigned truth value 1 to it we state that it refers to an event which cannot happen in a different way. Therefore, we write in a condensed way

$$(T_D) \qquad T_d([C_\tau p], S_i) =_{df} T^*([C_\tau p], S_i) \bullet S_i \in \mathbf{R}$$

where, as usual, '$\mathbf{R}$' denotes the "real" history of the world. An alternative characterisation of definite truth could be:

$$(T_D\dagger) \qquad T_d([C_\tau p], S_i) =_{df} T([C_\tau p] \bullet T^*([C_\tau p], S_i)$$

which is based on the fact that the assignation function which defines T^*-truth is monotonic. Therefore, $Ass([C_\tau p], S_i)=1$ implies $(S_j)(Dev(S_j, S_i) \rightarrow Ass([C_\tau p], S_j)=1)$. $(T_D\dagger)$ has the advantage over (T_D) of showing that definite truth is a kind of truth. Parallel definitions for a definitely false proposition can be given in an obvious way.

A characterisation of an indefinitely true proposition can easily be worked out from (T_D). An indefinitely true proposition is a contingent proposition, i.e. a proposition which denotes an event whose outcome is not yet settled, and at the same time is a simply true proposition. Then we can state:

$$(T_I) \qquad T_i([C_\tau p], S_i) =_{df} T([C_\tau p] \bullet \exists S_j(Dev(S_j, S_i) \bullet F^*([C_\tau p], S_j))$$

A definition of what it is for a proposition to be indefinitely false can easily be given. (T_D) obviously implies that the level of S_i, the node in which $C_\tau p$ is evaluated, must be equal or greater than τ because of (APA). On the other hand, in (T_i) the level of S_i must be less than τ. Were it equal or greater, then $C_\tau p$ should have an assigned truth value in S_i, which should remain the same in all nodes developing from S_i. But this is not the case. There is a node developing from S_i in which $C_\tau p$ takes 0 as assigned truth-value and a node in which it takes 1 as assigned truth-value. Therefore, $Lv(S_i) < \tau$ in (T_I).

To exemplify our definitions we can say with reference to Fig. (II) that $C_\tau p$ is indefinitely true at τ_1 in the node S_1, since (i) it is simply true, receiving the truth value 1 at S_3 which is on path $\mathbf{R}$, the "real" history of the world, and (ii) it is not necessarily true, since in the node S_2, which is a development from S_1, it takes the assigned truth value 0. On the other hand, $C_\tau p$ is definitely true in S_3, since in this node it has the assigned truth-value 1, and S_3 is on the "real" path $\mathbf{R}$.

V.3.7

What we have to do now is to check our interpretation of Ammonius' view against his effort to make the deterministic argument ineffective. Let us return to text (H) where the deterministic objection is summarised by the commentator. The argument can be generalised and divided in the following steps:

(i)   Suppose that $C_\tau p$ is true at τ.
(ii) If $C_\tau p$ is true at τ, it is true at ρ which is before τ.
(iii) If $C_\tau p$ is true at ρ, it is true at any time before τ.
(iv) If $C_\tau p$ is true at any time before τ, it is necessary.
(v)   Therefore $C_\tau p$ is necessary.

According to the traditional interpretation it is step (ii) that must be rejected. From the very fact that $C_\tau p$ is true at τ it does not follow that it is true at ρ and at any time before τ. If the event denoted by $C_\tau p$ is not causally determined before τ, $C_\tau p$ has no truth-value before τ. But if (ii) does not hold, the deterministic conclusion can be avoided. We have already seen a consequence of this position, i.e. the invalidation of the Principle of Bivalence, and we know that Ammonius did not want to abandon it, nor was he prepared to introduce truth-value gaps.

Ammonius not only avoided introducing truth-value gaps (or truth-values different from the standard ones) but also, as we have seen, maintained the possibility of true human predictions. Therefore in his view step (ii) must be preserved. How can he then escape the conclusion of the deterministic argument? His answer consists essentially in denying step (iv). What he says is as follows:

> (J) To this argument[376] one must reply that it was not true of what has occurred now or has already happened to say before the event that it will, in any case ($\pi\acute{a}\nu\tau\omega\varsigma$), be pale.[377] For we should not think it has happened by a necessary pre-establishment just because time has brought it into being. Thus, of those who make predictions about it, it is not the one who says that of necessity it will be pale who will speak truly, but rather the one who says all of this, \<namely\> that it will occur in a contingent manner. If this is so, it is clear that it was also possible for it not to occur, since it would not otherwise have been true that it would occur in a contingent manner. Therefore, let those who say this not judge what is still going to be[378] from what has already occurred, but let them keep it as not yet having occurred and inquire whether it will occur of necessity.[379]

Ammonius' point seems to be that predictions are possible and they do not rule out contingency.[380] Take $C_\tau p$ to denote a contingent event and suppose that it

---

376   I.e. the determinist argument developed in text (H).
377   Ammonius is here hinting at the example of the new-born pale child mentioned in text (H).
378   οἱ ταῦτα λέγοντος is probably a misprint since the sense requires λέγοντες.
379   *In Int.* 145,9-18.
380   According to R. Gaskin 1995, 155 n.39 Boethius would not "allow prediction of the simple truth of FCSs [future contingent statements], compatible with their contingency". But this does not seem to be Boethius' view, when e.g. he says:

is true at τ, so that (i) is satisfied. According to Ammonius nothing prevents us from admitting that $C_\tau p$ is true at any time before τ, in accordance with premisses (ii) and (iii) of the deterministic argument. The question is: in what sense is $C_\tau p$ true before τ, being a contingent proposition? Well, if we look at our analysis of the notions of definite and indefinite truth, the answer is clear: it is *indefinitely* true. Because of (i) $C_\tau p$ takes the assigned truth-value 1 at τ. Since by hypothesis the event denoted by $C_\tau p$ is the case in the real history of the world, it is simply true. It is precisely this situation which allows the possibility of $C_\tau p$ being truly predicted. On the other hand, $C_\tau p$ is contingent before τ, in the sense that it leaves open the possibility of the opposite. This means that the possibility for $C_\tau p$ of being false is not ruled out, or, if you prefer, that before τ the conditions which determine the event denoted by it are not yet given. We must expect therefore that in one of the possible histories of the world different from the "real" one $C_\tau p$ takes the assigned truth-value *False*. Therefore, $C_\tau p$ is indefinitely true according to our definition.

If this interpretation is correct, the whole point of Ammonius' refutation of determinism lies in the distinction between definite and indefinite truth. If every proposition were definitely true or false before the time to which the event denoted by it refers, no contingency would be allowed in the world. As he says with reference to a pair of contradictory contingent propositions concerning the future:

> (K) If one of these <the people foretelling the event> will be speaking truly in a definite manner, and the destruction of the contingent followed from the fact that one sentence of the contradiction is true in a definite manner, then it is apparent that the contingent will disappear from among the things which exist.[381]

The claim is clear. Suppose that $C_\tau p$ is not only plainly true, but definitely true before τ, for instance at τ-1, or, more precisely, in a node S_j whose level is less than τ. Then in no node developing from S_j can the assigned truth-value *False* be given to $C_\tau p$ and in this sense the future of $C_\tau p$ is by no means open. Its truth-value situation is settled and in this way $C_\tau p$ is not different from present or past propositions. But there is no reason to assume that $C_\tau p$ should be definitely true before τ. We can assume that it is indefinitely true. Since indefinite truth does not rule out contingency, it may happen that one and the same proposition concerning the future is plainly true and contingent. In this way prediction does not imply necessity, since the fact that $C_\tau p$ is definitely true or false does not depend on its possibility of being predicted but rather on the nature of the event it denotes. In this way the deterministic argument is made ineffective.

---

[381] *oportet enim in contingentibus ita aliquid praedicere, si vera erit enuntiatio, ut dicat quidem futurum esse aliquid, sed ita, ut rursus relinquat esse possibile, ut futurum non sit. (In Int., sec. ed.* 213,7-10). I take it to mean that (i) it is possible to state a prediction; (ii) this prediction can be true; (iii) in order to be true the prediction should not be formulated as a necessary proposition, in the sense that it must have the form: 'it will be so, but it might be differently'.

381 *In Int.* 143,17-20.

One might object to this view by repeating the deterministic argument. If $C_\tau p$ is indefinitely true at S_j it is simply true. This means that $C_\tau p$ in due course will take the assigned truth-value 1 in the real history of the world. Therefore, the future of $C_\tau p$ at S_j is not at all open, since it is already decided that $C_\tau p$ will be true in the real world. In other words, the contingent state of $C_\tau p$ before τ is only apparent, since it does not play any role in the development of the real world. This difficulty, I believe, can be met by underlining the difference there is between being definitely and indefinitely true. What makes $C_\tau p$ indefinitely true before τ is that the real development of the world at the stage in which $C_\tau p$ is evaluated is not yet fixed. We may refer to the future real history of the world, but how the world will evolve is still completely open. Therefore, what we actually say when we claim that $C_\tau p$ is indefinitely true at S_j is that $C_\tau p$ is true under the condition that the world develops in a certain way. And this condition is a real condition, because at S_j the future of $C_\tau p$ is still open.

But again one might urge that at S_j $C_\tau p$ is either true or false. Then, since it is, say, true, then the "real" development of the world will be such and such and in this sense already determined. This statement would be true if $C_\tau p$ at S_j had an assigned truth-value. But this is not the case. Attributing a simple truth value to $C_\tau p$ does not depend on the fact that the course of the events is fixed in the future, but it is the consequence of admitting that there will be a future and a real history of the world, whatever it may be. In other words, what is simply true, by itself, is not part of the furniture of the world in the sense that it refers to events which are, in some sense, already there and which can be causally related to other events. That there is a sea-battle at τ is not a fact before τ nor is it causally implied by other facts which are already given, although the proposition which expresses this fact is true or false even before the actual obtaining of the fact.

To admit such a possibility, we must concede that the relation between propositions and facts is not a temporal relation. This point is important because it marks a relevant difference between the traditional interpretation and Ammonius' view. As we have seen, the traditional interpretation is based on the idea that a proposition can only be said to be true or false, when the extra-linguistic conditions for this attribution are given. In the case of future contingent propositions these conditions do not obtain. Therefore, no truth-value can be assigned to them. What comes out from this view is that truth is a totally temporal notion, i.e. a notion which can only be applied when appropriate extra-linguistic conditions are the case.

Notwithstanding its simplicity, one might feel this position unpalatable. From the fact that it is not true now that there will be a sea-battle tomorrow it cannot be inferred, according the traditional interpretation, that a sea-battle will not occur tomorrow. This looks not at all obvious and one might prefer to think of truth as something which is not completely given in time. Of course, the conditions which make a proposition true or false are given in time. It is in time that a sea-battle takes place and it is in time that an assigned truth-value is given to the corresponding proposition. But it does not follow from this that the predicate *True* can only be applied to a proposition when the corresponding extra-linguistic conditions occur. If at some time a proposition becomes true in a proper sense, we are allowed to refer to this fact even before it happens. If "there is a sea-battle at τ" is T*–true, i.e. true in an assigned way at τ, so that the conditions for its truth are given at τ, then we can refer to the plain truth of this proposition at any time whatsoever. This does not mean that the conditions which make the proposition true are given at any time. By hypothesis, they are not given before τ. Nonetheless, if a sea-battle happens at τ the proposition "there is a sea-battle at τ" is in a sense "always" or simply true because once and for all it takes the truth-value 1 at τ.

We cannot pursue any longer this inquiry which has deep and controversial philosophical implications. I would like to conclude this section by facing a further objection to our interpretation. Consider once more $C_\tau p$ with reference to figure (II). As we have seen, $C_\tau p$ is indefinitely true at S_1 and it becomes definitely true at S_3. What makes the difference between its being indefinitely and definitely true is that when $C_\tau p$ is indefinitely true, it is (simply) true and it admits the possibility (never fulfilled) of being false at a further node, while this possibility is ruled out once $C_\tau p$ becomes definitely true. Therefore, one might claim that, in some sense, if $C_\tau p$ is true, it is always true. But, according to Ammonius, what seems to be characteristic of propositions about contingent events is that they are not always true.[382] Therefore, these propositions change their truth-value, which does not happen with $C_\tau p$ in our model. Thus, one might claim that since $C_\tau p$ is not a contingent proposition, it is necessary even when it is indefinitely true, and conclude that the interpretation proposed is inadequate to express Ammonius' view.

I do not think that we should accept such a catastrophic conclusion. First of all, I am not sure that Ammonius' position about the modal operators is such that it simply allows us to equate necessity with what is always true and contingency with what is sometimes true and sometimes false. What he says is in almost all cases plainly compatible with the claim that a contingent proposition is such that it *can* have a different truth-value (even if it never changes it) and a necessary proposition is a proposition which *cannot* have a different truth-value. In this vein, a proposition which is necessary in an absolute sense is defined by him as a proposition whose predicate is in such a way always true of its subject that the subject cannot exist without the predicate.[383] Taken in this way Ammonius' view about modalities would be perfectly consistent which the claim that $C_\tau p$ is a contingent proposition and never changes its truth-value.

There is however at least one passage where Ammonius seems to hold that in some cases the contingent members of a contradictory alternative are not always true. He says:

(L) Therefore, it is clearly necessary for sentences said about contingent <things> (which he indicated by the elimination of the extremes, i.e. the

---

[382]   Cp. e.g. *In Int.* 154,34-155,6.
[383]   *In Int.* 153,13-15.

necessary and the impossible, of which he called the one *'what always exists'* and the other *'what always does not exist'*) not in every case to have one member of the contradiction be true in a definite manner—which was what we were to investigate from the beginning—but either to have both members equally receptive of truth and falsity, as what is said contingents which are however it chances, or to have one member which is rather such as to be true and the other rather such as to be false, but not to have that which is true be always true nor that which is false be always false, which he <Aristotle> indicated by 'but not already true or false'.[384]

The first part of the passage is a standard repetition of Ammonius' position: there are cases in which truth and falsity do not apply to a pair of contradictory propositions in such a way that one is definitely true and the other definitely false, and this happens with equally contingent and in most cases contingent propositions, when, of course, they are referring to future events. What is difficult is the last part of the text where Ammonius seems to claim that in the cases in question the part of a contradiction which is true is not always true and the part which is false is not always false. This seems to imply that "tomorrow there will be a sea-battle", if it is true, it not always true, and this statement is against our interpretation.

I have two possible answers to this objection. The first consists in supposing that Ammonius here uses 'always true' and 'always false' not in the proper temporal sense, but in the sense in which he says that he has taken the corresponding Aristotelian expressions at the beginning of the passage, i.e. as synonymous with 'necessary' and 'impossible'. In other words, what he claims is simply that "tomorrow there will a sea-battle" is a proposition which, if it is true, is not "always true", i.e. necessarily true, in the sense that it does not rule out the possibility of its being false. Since it does not rule out this possibility, it is not definitely true, as we have seen, and it is not necessary in an absolute way.

The second possible answer depends on taking "the member which is true is not always true" as meaning 'the member which is true is not always definitely true', which fits our interpretation very well. "Tomorrow there will a sea-battle" is obviously not always true in a definite way: if it is true, it is indefinitely true before tomorrow, and it is only after tomorrow that it becomes either definitely true or definitely false. This interpretation of the passage has the advantage of making it easier to understand the meaning of expressions such as "both members of the contradiction are equally receptive of truth and falsity" or "one member is rather such as to be true and the other is rather such as to be false" by which Ammonius refers to propositions expressing contingent events that happen as often as not or for the most part.[385] The truth and falsity which are in question here are clearly definite truth and falsity and not simple truth and falsity.[386] Therefore,

---

384   *In Int.* 154,34-155,6. The Aristotelian reference is at 19a39.
385   On what is contingent "for the most part" (ὡς ἐπὶ τὸ πολύ) and "equally" (ἐπ' ἴσης) see also *In Int.* 142,1 ff.
386   *Pace* R. Gaskin 1995, 157 n.51.

it may also be that what is not always true is meant to be what is not always true in a definite way.

V.3.8

As is easy to guess, Ammonius was not the man who invented the theory we have tried to present. He did not possess the capacity for such a creative and difficult task. Moreover, the same theory can be found in Boethius and nowadays scholars are inclined to think that Boethius did not take it from Ammonius. There are similarities between the two commentators and the more natural way of explaining them is by supposing that they drew information from the same source in an independent way.

The problem arises: what was the common source of Ammonius and Boethius? The question has been studied with reference more to Boethius than Ammonius and for the Latin commentator the answer seems to be: Porphyry.[387] However, there is no clear evidence for Ammonius. He quotes more than once Porphyry who seems to be his main source for the discussion of alternative readings of Aristotle's text.[388] Sometimes he mentions some of his views with approval[389] and in one case he says that he will follow Porphyry's theory in his exposition trying to make it clearer.[390] From this evidence we cannot even infer that Ammonius had direct access to the works of Porphyry, since it may be that his quotations were taken from a later source. In fact, his main source seems to be Proclus, who is mentioned at the beginning of the commentary in a rather solemn way as the "divine teacher", having made Ammonius' work possible by his research on Aristotle.[391] In the course of the commentary on Chapter 9 Iamblichus is quoted for the decisive step concerning the solution of the problem of how Gods can know contingent events.[392] Here the distinction between having definite and indefinite knowledge of future contingents plays an important role, but it is not clear whether this distinction has something to do with the distinction between

---

[387] Cp. M. Mignucci 1987, 38-41. What is still in dispute is whether Boethius had direct access to Porphyry's commentary on the *De Interpretatione* or he only translated a Greek codex with *marginalia* mostly taken from Porphyry. On this question, which does not affect our problem very much, see J. Shiel 1958, 356-361 and S. Ebbesen 1990, 375ff.

[388] For instance, a different reading of *Int.* 16b9-10 is attributed by Ammonius to Porphyry (*In Int.* 50,8-12) and the same happens with reference to *Int.* 16b22 (*In Int.* 56,14-18). Again, Porphyry's discussion of *Int.* 17b16 ff. is considered with his reading ἀποφαντικῶς instead of ἀντιφατικῶς at *Int.* 17b17 (*In Int.* 109,24 ff.), and a variant at *Int.* 19b24-25 is discussed by quoting Porphyry (*In Int.* 171,16).

[389] E.g. *In Int.* 32,35; 70,3 ff.; 99,8 ff.

[390] *In Int.* 94,25-28.

[391] *In Int.* 1,6-11. Strangely enough, Proclus is quoted only in another passage at 181,30 ff. (cp. Stephanus, *In Int.* 46,25-26).

[392] *In Int.* 135,14.

definitely and indefinitely true or false propositions.[393] At any rate, Iamblichus'
point was well known to Proclus,[394] and we can once more suppose that Proclus
was the direct source of Ammonius. A prudent conclusion may be that Ammonius
refers to a doctrine whose existence can be traced back to Porphyry.

However, we could try to push our inquiry a step further by asking whether
Porphyry was the creator of the doctrine. There are some testimonies which
render the answer controversial. A passage of Simplicius must be taken into
account, to which Richard Sorabji first attracted attention.[395] A certain Nicostratus
is mentioned in it, who is probably to be identified with the Nicostratus who got
an honorific inscription at Delphi and was a Platonic philosopher whose acme has
to be put in the middle of the second century AD.[396] Simplicius reports that
Nicostratus denied any truth-value to future contingent propositions, making of
him a partisan of the traditional interpretation.[397] If we are to trust Cicero's
testimony, Nicostratus was not the only ancient follower of the traditional
interpretation, since Epicurus was among its supporters.[398] After Nicostratus
Simplicius considers the position of the Peripatetics and he says:

> (M) But the Peripatetics say that the contradiction regarding the future is true or
> false, while it is by nature unseizable and uncertain which part of it[399] is true and
> which part is false. For nothing prevents us from saying the contradiction with
> respect to any time, as for instance "it will be or it will not be", and each of the
> two parts contained in it, as for instance "it will be" or "it will not be", is already
> (ἤδη) true or false in a definite way (ἀφωρισμένως) with respect to the present or
> past time. But those parts of a contradiction which are said with respect to the
> future are not yet (ἤδη) true or false, and they will be true or false. Let these
> things be sufficient against (πρός) Nicostratus.[400]

One might think that the view of the Peripatetics is not clear. On the one hand, the
fact that the adverb ἀφωρισμένως (407,10-11) is connected with ἢ ἀληθῆ ἢ ψευδῆ
lets us imagine that Ammonius' doctrine is hinted at here. On the other hand,
contingent propositions concerning past or present events are not opposed to
future propositions which have an indefinite truth-value, as one might expect, but
to propositions which are not yet true or false. That future contingent propositions
are not yet true or false would not be admitted by Ammonius and this statement
reminds us rather of the traditional interpretation. Were the Peripatetics referred
to by Simplicius followers of the traditional interpretation or partisans of the same
position Ammonius holds?

---

393   *In Int.* 135,12 ff.
394   *El. Theol.* 124 (110,10-13 Dodds); *Theol. Plat.* I 15 (69,10-12, 70,22-25, 74,9-16
       Saffrey-Westerink); *Decem Dubitationes* 6-8 (Boese).
395   Cp. R. Sorabji 1980b, 92-93.
396   Cp. K. Praechter 1973, 101-113; J. Dillon 1977, 233-236.
397   Simpl., *In Cat.* 406,13-16.
398   Cic., *De Fato* IX 18; X 21; XVI 37; *Acad.* II 97.
399   Adopting Kalbfleisch's suggestion I read at 407,7 πότερον δὲ ἔσται μόριον αὐτῆς
       ἀληθές instead of ... αὐτῶν ἀληθές. Cp. 407,9-10.
400   *In Cat.* 407,6-14.

On reflection, I would be inclined to choose the second alternative. Suppose that the Peripatetics embraced the traditional interpretation. If P is a future contingent proposition, the Principle of Bivalence does hold for P. But Simplicius at the beginning of our passage says that according to the Peripatetics "the contradiction regarding the future is true or false" and this statement can only mean that (PB) applies also to future contingent propositions. Moreover, if the Peripatetics adopted the traditional interpretation, they would have held the same view as Nicostratus. But the position of the latter is clearly opposed by Simplicius to the view of the Peripatetics.[401] The conclusion is that the Peripatetics did not embrace the traditional interpretation. How can we explain then the view Simplicius attributes to them with respect to future contingent propositions? In what sense are these propositions not yet true or false? The question is easily answered if we admit that 'not yet true or false' means 'not yet definitely true or false', i.e. if we understand ἀφωρισμένως to be connected to ἤδη μὲν οὐκ ἔστιν ἢ ἀληθῆ ἢ ψευδῆ at 407,12-13. In this way the Peripatetics must be taken as representatives of the view defended by Ammonius.[402]

Unfortunately, Simplicius does not tell us whom the Peripatetics holding the same view as Ammonius are. Nor does he give us any hint at identifying them. One might think that the Peripatetics were led to formulate their doctrine as a reaction to the position put forward by Nicostratus. If so, we have a *terminus post quem* for the origin of Ammonius' view and we might suppose that it was created before Porphyry in a Peripatetic milieu after the middle of the second century AD. The name of Alexander of Aphrodisias comes spontaneously to mind. But Simplicius' words assure neither the starting point nor the consequences of this interpretation. He uses the Peripatetic view against Nicostratus to show that his

---

[401]   This remark has been made also by R. Sharples 1978a, 263.

[402]   Richard Sorabji has suggested to me another possible interpretation of what Simplicius says. It may be that he only pointed out that future contingent propositions are such that they *eventually* get a truth-value. Their view would still be different from Nicostratus' position. I have two worries about this interpretation. First of all, is the fact that a future contingent proposition becomes true or false eventually sufficient to warrant that the Principle of Bivalence holds unconditionally? I am not sure that we can easily give a positive answer to this question. Secondly, if for a future contingent proposition it is essential to become at some time true or false, the reference to a date or fixed time becomes crucial: (1*) surely becomes either true or false at τ. But what happens with a statement such as "it will be raining" (without the addition of a date)? Suppose that tomorrow it does not rain. Can we say that it is false? Of course not, because it may be raining the day after tomorrow. Until it *does* rain we cannot attribute a truth-value to our statement, and so it may never happen that it receives a truth-value. One might retort that the interpretation of indefinitely true or false propositions is also focused on dated future contingent propositions and it cannot be extended to every kind of non-dated future-tensed statements. However, since their truth or falsity is not strictly dependent on the time of their utterance, I think that it is not impossible to accommodate the theory underlying the distinction between indefinite and definite truth (falsity) to cover also the case of "it will be raining".

position is not the only possible one. But this does not mean that the Peripatetics themselves elaborated their conception to avoid Nicostratus' view. To make things worse, the position of Alexander about future contingents which is known to us from his remaining works is far from being clear. We cannot examine this question here. It is sufficient to remember that some scholars who have studied this problem at length are inclined to think that Alexander was rather near to the traditional interpretation, although the Greek commentator is never explicit on this point.[403] Therefore, no relevant clue can be extracted from the Simplicius passage to find a way out for our question.

There is however another testimony which has led some scholars to associate the origin of Ammonius' doctrine with the Peripatetics near to Alexander.[404] I am referring to a passage in the *Quaestiones* traditionally attributed to Alexander, but in fact made up of rather heterogeneous materials.[405] This is true especially for the *Quaestio* which interests us, i.e. *Quaest*. I 4.[406] In the last part of it an allusion is made to a doctrine which is *prima facie* similar to Ammonius' position. There are two passages where ἀφωρισμένως is used in connection with the truth and falsity of a contradictory pair of future contingent propositions. The first of them runs as follows:

> (N) And further, if that is possible from which, if it is supposed that it is the case, nothing impossible results; and if, from everything of which the opposite is truly said beforehand, there results, if it is supposed that it is the case, something impossible, i.e. that the same thing both is and is not at the same time; then none of those things, of which one part of the contradiction referring to the future is true definitely (ἀφωρισμένως ἀληθές ἐστιν) would be the case contingently. But they say that in all cases one part of the contradiction is true definitely (ἀφωρισμένως ἀληθὲς εἶναι).[407]

The Greek is in a rather poor condition and it is not very easy to follow the development of the argument in favour of determinism outlined here. The main idea seems to be that if a contingent proposition such as (1*) is definitely true before τ, then it is necessary, because the hypothesis that the negation of (1*) is true entails a contradiction. What is important to underline is that in the last lines of the passage a sort of Principle of Bivalence is laid down with reference to definitely true propositions, which says that either [P] or [¬P] is definitely true. We can express it formally as follows:

---

[403] Cp. R. Sharples 1978a, 264; 1983a, 11-12. See also R. Sorabji 1980, 92-93 and especially p. 93 n. 5; D. Frede 1984, 286.

[404] Cp. D. Frede 1970, 26; R. Sharples 1978a, 264; *id.*, 1982, 38-39; R. Sorabji 1980, 93 n.10.

[405] On the *Quaestiones* see R. Sharples 1990, 83-111. In particular for *Quaest*. I 4 which will be at issue here see I. Bruns 1889; M. Mignucci 1981, 198-204; R. Sharples 1982, 23-38.

[406] Cp. R. Sharples 1982, 24-25.

[407] *Quaest*. I 4 12,13-18. Following Bruns I delete μή at 12,13 and I add συμβήσεται at 12,15. For an analysis of this passage see also I. Bruns 1889, 627-628. The translation is taken from R. Sharples 1992.

(PB*) $T_d*[P] \lor T_d*[\neg P]$

where, of course, '$T_d*[P]$' stands for 'P is definitely true'. The relevant point is to
see whether the predicate 'definitely true' which is mentioned here is the same as
the predicate used by Ammonius, i.e. whether 'T_d*' can be reduced to 'T_d'. The
simple fact that the same expression 'definitely true' is used is not a sufficient
reason to give an affirmative answer to our question. It might be that ἀφωρισμένως
ἀληθές used in the *Quaestio* has the same meaning as Ammonius' expression, but
that is neither necessary by itself nor imposed by the context. ἀφωρισμένως ἀληθές
might simply refer to what is *already* true with respect to what is not yet true.
From this point of view the deterministic argument would have its main point in
the premiss that even future contingent propositions always have a truth-value.
But if $C_\tau p$ is true even before τ then it is always true and therefore necessarily
true.[408]

   The answer of the author of the Quaestio to the deterministic argument
contains the other occurrence of ἀφωρισμένως ἀληθές. He says:

> (O) But if it is alike possible for the same thing to come to be and not to come to
> be, how is it not absurd to say, in the case of these things, that one part of the
> contradiction spoken beforehand is true definitely (ἀφωρισμένως ἀληθές), and
> the other false, when the thing in question is alike capable of both?[409]

Unfortunately, here it is not clear either what ἀφωρισμένως ἀληθές means. The
core of the answer to the deterministic argument is that it is inconsistent to
maintain that every proposition is definitely true or definitely false and that there
are contingent events. If (1*) is always true in a definite way, then there is no
possibility that the event denoted by it does not obtain. But it is absurd to reject
the existence of contingent events. Therefore, it cannot be admitted that every
proposition always has a definite truth-value. The question is: shall we infer that
future contingent propositions have an indefinite truth-value or must the
conclusion rather be that these propositions have no truth-value at all? If we give
the first answer, we have Ammonius' view and we are entitled to say that the
doctrine was born among the pupils of Alexander. On the other hand, if we prefer
the second answer, we have to reckon Alexander's school among the supporters
of the traditional interpretation and the problem of the origin of Ammonius'
theory is left in the dark. Needless to say, we would like to embrace the first
answer, because it gives a nice solution to our problem. But it would be unfair to
adopt it simply because it offers an explanation of what we are looking for. I do
not see any reason to prefer the first interpretation to the second. In our passage it
is not said to what ἀφωρισμένως ἀληθές is opposed, and it might be contrasted
either to what is indefinitely true or to what is not yet true. Consequently, the
author of the *Quaestio* might be equally a forerunner of Ammonius or a follower
of Nicostratus.

---

[408]   N. Kretzmann 1998, 27-28 expresses similar worries about the interpretation of this
          passage.

[409]   *Quaest.* I 4 13,26. Also here I follow Sharples' translation.

   Although we do not know where his view ultimately comes from, Ammonius' doctrine is far from being uninteresting in an historical and philosophical perspective. Its commitment to an atemporal theory of truth, on the one hand, and its exploiting of the notions of necessity and possibility, on the other, clearly show how ample the range of the problems involved is and how modern they are.[410]

---

[410]   This is a further revised version of a paper that appeared originally as: 'Ammonius on Future Contingent Propositions', in M. Frede and G. Striker 1996, 279-310 and, revised, as: 'Ammonius' Sea Battle', in D. Blank and N. Kretzmann 1998, 53-86.

Part VI

Bibliography

VI.1 Texts and Translations

Ackrill, J. L. 1963: *Aristotle's Categories and De Interpretatione*. Translated with Notes by J. L. Ackrill, Oxford, 1963 (reprint 1974).

Alexander of Aphrodisias 1883: *In Aristotelis Analyticorum priorum librum I commentarium*, ed. M. Wallies, Berlin (*CAG* II.1).

— 1891a: *In Aristotelis Metaphysica commentaria*, ed. M. Hayduck, Berlin (*CAG* I).

— 1891b: *In Aristotelis Topicorum libros octo commentaria*, ed. M. Wallies, Berlin (*CAG* II.2).

— 1892: *Praeter commentaria scripta minora*, in: *Supplementum aristotelicum* II, ed. I. Bruns, Berlin (*CAG* suppl. II.2) (contains the *Quaestiones*, *De Fato* and *De Mixtione*).

Ammonius 1895: *In Aristotelis Categorias commentarius*, ed. A. Busse, Berlin (*CAG* IV.4).

— 1897: *In Aristotelis De Interpretatione commentarius*, ed. A. Busse, Berlin (*CAG* IV.5).

— 1899: *In Aristotelis Analyticorum priorum librum I commentarium*, ed. M. Wallies, Berlin (*CAG* IV.6).

— 1961: *Commentaire sur le Peri Hermeneias d'Aristote, traduction de Guillaume de Moerbeke*, ed. G. Verbeke, Louvain/Paris.

— 1996: *On Aristotle on Interpretation* 1-8, translated by D. Blank, London.

— 1998: *On Aristotle on Interpretation* 9. See Blank, D. and Kretzmann, N.

[Anon.] 1883: *Paraphrasis Categoriarum*, ed. M. Hayduck, Berlin (*CAG* XXIII.2).

[Anon.] 1978: *In Aristotelis De Interpretatione commentarius*, ed. L. Tarán, *Anonymous Commentary on Aristotle's De Interpretatione (Codex Parisinus Graecus 2064)*, Meisenheim am Glan.

Apuleius 1991: *De Philosophia libri*, ed. C. Moreschini, Stuttgart/Leipzig (*Apulei opera quae supersunt*, III).

Apostle, H. G. 1980: *Aristotle's Categories and Propositions (De Interpretatione)*. Translated with Commentaries and Glossary by H. G. Apostle, Grinnell, Iowa.

Arens, H. 1984: *Aristotle's Theory of Language and its Tradition. Texts from 500 to 1750*, Amsterdam/Philadelphia.

Aristophanes 1900-1907: *Plutus*, ed. Hall, F.W. and Geldart, W.M., vols. I-II, Oxford.

Aristotle 1831-1870: *Opera*, 5 vols., ed. I. Bekker, Berlin.

— 1890a: *De Generatione et Corruptione*, ed. H.H. Joachim, Oxford.

— 1890b: *Ethica Nicomachea*, ed. I. Bywater, Oxford.

— 1936: *De Caelo*, ed. D. Allan, Oxford.

— 1950: *Physica*, ed. W. Ross, Oxford.

— 1955: *De Partibus Animalium*, ed. A.L. Peck (Loeb) London/Cambridge Mass.

— 1956a: *Categoriae et Liber de Interpretatione*, ed. L. Minio-Paluello, Oxford.

— 1956b: *De Anima*, ed. W. Ross, Oxford, 1956.

— 1957: *Metaphysica*, ed. W. Jaeger, Oxford.

— 1958: *Topica et Sophistici Elenchi*, ed. W. Ross, Oxford.

— 1959: *Ars Rhetorica*, ed. W. Ross, Oxford.

— 1963: *De mundo*, ed. E.S. Forster, Oxford.

— 1964: *Analytica Priora et Posteriora*, ed. W. Ross, Oxford.

— 1968: *De Arte Poetica Liber*, ed. R. Kassel, Oxford.

— 1991: *Ethica Eudemia*, ed. R. Walzer and J. Mingay, Oxford.

[Arist. Lat. II.1-2] 1965: *Aristoteles Latinus II 1-2: De Interpretatione vel Periermenias. Translatio Boethii, Specimina Translationum Recentiorum, edidit L. Minio-Paluello. Translatio Guillelmi de Moerbeka, edidit G. Verbeke, revisit L. Minio-Paluello*, Bruges-Paris.

Aspasius 1889: *In Aristotelis Ethica Nicomachea quae supersunt commentaria*, ed. G. Heylbut, Berlin (*CAG* XIX.1).

Averroes, *Expos.* 1562: *Aristotelis de Interpretatione liber primus/secundus ... cum Averrois Cordubensis Expositione ...*, in: *Aristotelis Opera cum Averrois Commentariis*, vol. I, pars 1, Venice (reprint Frankfurt a. M. 1962).

— *MC* 1983: *Averroes' Middle Commentary on Aristotle's De Interpretatione*. Translated, with Notes and Introduction by C. E. Butterworth, in: Butterworth, 89-187.

Basil 1857: *Homiliae in Hexaemeron*, ed. J.-P. Migne, Turnholt (*Patrologia Graeca* 27).

Bayer, K. (ed.) 1959: Cicero: De fato (*Über das Fatum*), München.

Bekker, I. 1831: *Aristoteles Graece ex recensione I. Bekker*. Edidit Academia Regia Borussica (*Aristotelis Opera*, vol. I-II), Berlin.

Blank, D. (transl.) 1996: *Ammonius on Aristotle on Interpretation 1-8*, London (*Ancient Commentators on Aristotle*, gen. ed. R. Sorabji).

Blank, D. and Kretzmann, N. (transl.) 1998: *On Determinism, Ammonius on Aristotle on Interpretation 9 with Boethius on Aristotle on Interpretation 9 (first and second commentaries)*, London (*Ancient Commentators on Aristotle*, gen. ed. R. Sorabji).

Boethius 1877/1880: *Commentarii in librum Aristotelis Peri Hermēneias*, prima editio, ed. C. Meiser, Leipzig 1877; secunda editio, ed. C. Meiser, Leipzig 1880.

— 1957: *De consolatione philosophiae*, ed. L. Bieler, Turnhout (*CCSL* 94).

— see Arist. Lat. II.1-2.

Busse, A. 1897: *Ammonius, In Aristotelis De interpretatione commentarius*, ed. A. Busse, Berlin (*CAG* IV.5).

Calcidius 1962: *Platonis Timaeus translatus commentarioque instructus*, ed. J.H. Waszink, London-Leiden (*Plato Latinus* IV).

Chrysippus: see below under PHerc 1038 and PHerc 307.

Chrysostom, John 1862: *De fato et providentia*, ed. J.-P. Migne, *PG* 50, Turnholt, 749-72.

Cicero 1903a: *Topica*, in: *M. Tullii Ciceronis Rhetorica, ii*, ed. A.S. Wilkins, Oxford.

— 1903b: *Tusculanae disputationes*, ed. M. Pohlenz, Leipzig (reprint Stuttgart, 1967).

— 1915: *De finibus bonorum et malorum*, ed. Th. Schiche, Leipzig (reprint Stuttgart, 1966).

— 1922: *Academica posteriora - Academica priora (Academicorum reliquiae cum Lucullo)*, ed. O. Plasberg, Leipzig (reprint Stuttgart, 1966).

— 1933a: *De natura deorum*, ed. W. Ax, Leipzig (reprint Stuttgart, 1968).

— 1933b: *Oratio pro L. Murena*, ed. H. Kasten, Leipzig, 1933, 1961 (reprint 1972).

— 1938: *De divinatione, De fato and Timaeus*, ed. W. Ax, Leipzig (reprint Stuttgart, 1965).

— 1975: *De fato: M. Tulli Ciceronis scripta quae manserunt omnia, fasc. 46: De divinatione, De fato, Timaeus*, ed. R. Giomini, Leipzig, 149-176.

— 1982: *Epistulae ad familiares*, ed. W.S. Watt, Oxford.

— 1991: *De officiis (On duties)*, ed. M.T. Griffin and E.M. Atkins, Cambridge.

Clement of Alexandria 1970: *Stromata VII-VIII*, ed. O. Stählin, L. Früchtel and U. Treu, Berlin (*GCS* 17).

— 1985: *Stromata I-VI*, ed. O. Stählin, L. Früchtel and U. Treu, Berlin (*CGS* 52).

Dexippus 1888: *In Aristotelis Categorias commentarium*, ed. A. Busse, Berlin (*CAG* IV.2).

Diogenes Laertius 1964: *Vitae Philosophorum*, ed. H.S. Long, 2 vols., Oxford.

Ehrig-Eggert, C. 1989: *Yahyā ibn 'Adī, Über den Nachweis der Natur des Möglichen*, Edition und Einleitung, in: *Zeitschrift für Geschichte der Arabisch-Islamischen Wissenschaften* 5 283-297 and 63-97.

— 1990: *Die Abhandlung über den Nachweis der Natur des Möglichen von Yahyā ibn 'Adī (ob. 974 A.D.)*. *Übersetzung und Kommentar*, in: *Veröffentlichungen des Instituts für Geschichte der Arabisch-Islamischen Wissenschaften*, Reihe A, Bd. 5, Frankfurt a.M.

Elias 1900: *In Porphyrii Isagogen et Aristotelis Categorias Commentaria*, ed. A. Busse, Berlin (*CAG* XVIII).

Epictetus 1916: *Dissertationes, ab Arriano digestae; Enchiridion*, ed. H. Schenkel, Leipzig.

Epicurus: See below under PHerc 679, 1056, 1191: also Arrighetti and Usener under 'Collections of Testimonies' below.

Erler, M. 1980: *Proklos Diadochos: Über die Vorsehung, das Schicksal und den freien Willen an Theodorus den Ingenieur (Mechaniker)*, translation and commentary, Meisenheim am Glan,.

Eusebius 1954-6: *Praeparatio evangelica*, ed. K. Mras, parts I-II, Berlin.

Farabi, Abu Nasar al-, 1981: *Al-Farabi's Commentary and Short Treatise on Aristotle's De Interpretatione*. Translated with an Introduction and Notes by F. W. Zimmermann, Oxford.

Galen 1896: *Institutio logica*, ed. C. Kalbfleisch, Leipzig.

— 1937: *De proprium Animi Cuiuslibet Affectuum Dignotione et Curatione*, ed. W. de Boer, Leipzig (*CMG* V.4, 1, 1).

— 1978-80: *De placitis Hippocratis et Platonis (Galen on the Doctrines of Hippocrates and Plato*. Edition, Translation and Commentary), ed. Ph. de Lacy, parts I-II, Berlin (*CMG* V.4, 1, 2).

Gellius 1968: *Noctes Atticae*, ed. P.K. Marshall, 2 vols., Oxford.

Graeser, A. 1973: *Die logischen Fragmente des Theophrast*, Berlin/New York.

Gregory of Nyssa 1952-90: *Gregorii Nysseni opera*, ed. W. Jaeger, Leipzig.

[Heliodorus] 1889: *In Aristotelis Ethica Nicomachea paraphrasis*, ed. G. Heylbut, Berlin (*CAG* XIX.1).

Hierocles 1992: Ἠθικὴ Στοιχείωσις, ed. A.A. Long and G. Bastiani, in: *Corpus dei papiri filosofici graeci et latini*, pt. 1, vol. 1. 2, Accademia toscana di scienze e lettere La Colombaria, Florence, 296-366.

Index Stoicorum Herculanensis 1952: ed. A. Traversa, Genova.

Johannes Philoponos: see under Philoponus

Josephus 1888-96: *Opera*, ed. S.A. Naber, Leipzig.

Lactantius 1890: *Divinae institutiones*, ed. S. Brandt and G. Laubmann, Vienna (*CSEL* 19).

[Lamprias]1967: *Lamprias' Catalogue*, ed. F.H. Sandbach, in: *Plutarchi Moralia*, VII, Leipzig, 1-10.

Londey, D. and Johanson, C.1987: *The Logic of Apuleius, including a complete Latin text and English translation of the Peri Hermeneias of Apuleius of Madaura (Philosophia Antiqua*, Bd. 47), Leiden, New York, Kopenhagen, Köln.

Lucian 1972-87: *Opera*, ed. M.D. MacLeod, 4 vols., Oxford.

Minio-Paluello, L. 1956: *Aristotelis Categoriae et liber de Interpretatione. Recognovit brevique adnotatione critica instruxit L. Minio-Paluello*, Oxford, 2. Aufl..

— 1961: *Aristoteles Latinus I 1-5: Categoriae vel Praedicamenta*, ed. L. Minio-Paluello, Bruges-Paris.

— 1966: *Aristoteles Latinus I 6-7: Categoriarum supplementa*, ed. L. Minio-Paluello adiuvante B. G. Dod, Bruges-Paris.

Natali, C. (ed.) 1996: *Alessandro di Afrodisia, Il destino*, prefazione, introduzione, commento, bibliografia e indici di Carlo Natali, traduzione di Carlo Natali ed Elisa Tetamo, Milano.

Nemesius 1987: De natura hominis, ed. M. Morani, Leipzig.

Obertello, L. 1974: *Severino Boezio*, 2 vols., Genova: Accademia Ligure di scienze e lettere.

Olympiodorus 1902: *Prolegomena et in Categorias Commentarium*, ed. A. Busse, Berlin (*CAG* XII).

Origen 1893: *Commentarium III in Genesim* (fragmenta) = *Philocalia* 23.1-11, 14-21, ed. J.A. Robinson, in: *The Philocalia of Origen*, Cambridge, 187.13-189.29, 202.2-207.31.

— 1899: *De oratione*, ed. P. Koetschau, Leipzig (*GCS* 3).

— 1913: *De principiis*, ed. P. Koetschau, Leipzig (*GCS* 22).

— 1967-76: *Contra Celsum*, ed. M. Borret, Paris.

Pacius, J. (1597a): *Aristotelis ... Organum, hoc est, libri omnes ad Logicam pertinentes, Graecè & Latinè*. Iul. Pacius recensuit ... Editio Secunda tot locis emendata & aucta, ut nova editio videri possit, Frankfurt a. M. (reprint Hildesheim, 1967).

— (1597b): *Iul. Pacii a Beriga in Porphyrii Isagogen, et Aristotelis Organum, Commentarius Analyticus*, Frankfurt a. M. (reprint Hildesheim, 1966).

— 1623: *Aristotelis ... Organum, hoc est, libri omnes ad Logicam pertinentes, Graecè & Latinè*. Iul. Pacius a Beriga recensuit, Hanau (reprint Frankfurt a. M. 1967).

PHerc 307: Chrysippus, Λογικὰ Ζητήματα, ed. H. von Arnim, *SVF* ii, fr. 298a.

— 679, 1056, 1191: Epicurus, ed. D.N. Sedley, 'On nature book XXVIII', *Cronache Ercolanesi* 3 (1973) 5-83.

— 1038: Chrysippus, Περὶ Προνοίας, ed. A. Gercke, in: 'Chrysippea', *Jahrbuch für klassische Philologie*, Supplbd. 14 (1885) 689-781, at 710-11.

— 1428: Philodemus, Περὶ Εὐσεβείας, ed. A. Henrichs, *Cronache Ercolanesi* 4 (1974) 5-32.

— 1670: Philodemus, ed. M. Ferrario, 'Philodemo "sulla provvidenza"?', *Cronache Ercolanesi* 2 (1972) 67-94.

Philo of Alexandria 1886-1915: *Philonis Alexandri opera quae supersunt*, ed. L. Cohn and P. Wendland, 6 vols., Berlin (repr. 1962).

Philodemus: *De providentia*. See above under PHerc 1670.

— 1978: *De signis*, ed. Ph.H. and E.A. DeLacy, Naples.

Philoponus, John 1897: *Ioannis Philoponi in Aristotelis De Anima libros commentaria*, ed. M. Hayduck, Berlin, (*CAG* XV).

— 1898: *In Aristotelis Categorias Commentarium*, ed. A. Busse, Berlin (*CAG* XIII).

— 1905: *In Aristotelis Analytica priora commentaria*, ed. M. Wallies, Berlin (*CAG* XIII.2).

— 1909: *Ioannis Philoponi in Aristotelis Analytica Posteriora commentaria cum anonymo in librum II*, ed. M. Wallies, Berlin (*CAG* XIII.3).

Plato 1900a: *Cratylus* in: *Platonis Opera* ed. J. Burnet, I, Oxford.

— 1900b: *Phaedo* in: *Platonis Opera* ed. J. Burnet, I, Oxford.

— 1901: *Parmenides* in: *Platonis Opera* ed. J. Burnet, II, Oxford.

— 1902a: *Respublica* in: *Platonis Opera* ed. J. Burnet, IV, Oxford.

— 1902b: *Timaeus* in: *Platonis Opera* ed. J. Burnet, IV, Oxford.

— 1907: *Leges* in: *Platonis Opera* ed. J. Burnet, V, Oxford.

Plotinus 1962-84: *Opera*, ed. P. Henry and H.R. Schwyzer, 3 vols., Oxford.

Plutarch 1925-67: *Plutarchi Moralia, I-VII*, ed. W.J. Paton, J. Wegehaupt, M. Pohlenz, et al., Leipzig.

— 1952a: *De communibus notitiis contra Stoicos*, ibid. VI.2, ed. M. Pohlenz and R. Westman.

— 1952b: *De Stoicorum repugnantiis*, ibid. VI.2, ed. M. Pohlenz and R. Westman.

[Plutarch] 1929: *De fato*, ibid. III, ed. W.R. Paton, M. Pohlenz and W. Sieveking.

[Plutarch] 1971: *De placitis philosophorum* (874a-911c), ibid. V.2.1, ed. J. Mau.

Porphyrius 1993: *Fragmenta*, ed. A. Smith, Stuttgart/Leipzig.

Proclus 1960: *Procli Diadochi Tria Opuscula (De decem dubitationibus circa providentiam; De providentia et fato; De malorum subsistentia)*, ed. H. Boese, Berlin.

— 1963: *The Elements of Theology*, a revised text with translation, introduction and commentary by E.R. Dodds, Oxford (2nd ed.)

— 1968: *Théologie platonicienne*, texte établi et traduit par H.D. Saffrey et L.G. Westerink, t.I, Paris.

— see also Segonds, A.P. 1985/1986.

Ptolemy 1940: *Tetrabiblos*, ed. F. Boll and E. Boer, Leipzig.

Quintilian 1970: *Institutio Oratoria*, ed. M. Winterbottom, Oxford.

Segonds, A.P.1985/86: *Proclus sur le premier Alcibiade de Platon*, texte établi et traduit par A.P. Segonds, 2 vols., Paris.

Seneca 1907: *Naturalium quaestionum libri VIII*, ed. A. Gercke, Leipzig (reprint with addenda Stuttgart 1970).

— 1922-42a: *Ad Marciam de consolatione*, in: *Sénèque, Dialogues*, ed. A. Bourgery and R. Waltz, Paris,.

— 1922-42b: *De providentia*, ibid.

— 1965: *Epistulae morales ad Lucilium*, ed. L.D. Reynolds, 2 vols., Oxford.

Sextus Empiricus 1914-61: *Opera*, ed. H. Mutschmann and J. Mau, Leipzig.

Sharples, R.W. (1983a): *Alexander of Aphrodisias On Fate*, text, translation and commentary by R.W. Sharples, London.

— 1991: *Cicero: On Fate and Boethius: Consolation of Philosophy IV.5-7, V*, Warminster.

— 1992: *Alexander of Aphrodisias, Quaestiones 1.1-2.15*, translated by R.W. Sharples, London.

Shiel, J. 1958: 'Boethius' Commentaries on Aristotle', *Mediaeval and Renaissance Studies* 4 228-234 (reprinted in: M. Fuhrmann and J. Gruber (eds.), *Boethius*, Darmstadt, 1984, 155-183, and in: R. Sorabji (ed.), *Aristotle Transformed. The Ancient Commentators and Their Influence*, London, 1990, 349-372).

Simplicius 1882: *In Aristotelis De Anima commentaria*, ed. M. Hayduck, Berlin (*CAG* XI).

— 1882-1895: *In Aristotelis Physicorum libros quattuor priores/posteriores commentaria*, ed. H. Diels, Berlin (*CAG* IX and X).

— 1907: *In Aristotelis Categorias commentarium*, ed. C. Kalbfleisch, Berlin (*CAG* VIII).

— 1995: *In Epicteti Enchiridion commentarium (Commentaire sur le Manuel d'Epictète)*, ed. I. Hadot, Leiden.

Stephanus 1885: *Stephani in librum Aristotelis De interpretatione commentarium*, ed. M. Hayduck, Berlin (*CAG* XVIII.3).

Stobaeus 1884: *Anthologii libri duo priores qui inscribi solent Eclogae physicae et ethicae*, ed. K. Wachsmuth, 2 vols., Berlin.

Syrianus 1902: *In Aristotelis Metaphysica commentaria*, ed. W. Kroll, Berlin (*CAG* VI.1).

Tarán, L. 1978: *Anonymous Commentary on Aristotle's De Interpretatione (Codex Parisinus Graecus 2064)*, Meisenheim am Glan.

Theophrastus 1973: see Graeser, A.

— 1992: *Theophrastus of Eresus, Sources for his Life, Writings, Thought and Influence*, edited by W.W. Fortenbaugh et al., parts I and II, Leiden/New York/Köln.

Tricot, J. 1997. *Aristote, Organon* I: *Catégories*, II: *De l'Interprétation*, Traduction nouvelle et notes, Nouvelle édition, Paris.

Verbeke, G. 1961: *Ammonius, Commentaire sur le Peri Hermeneias d'Aristote, traduction de Guillaume de Moerbeke*, édition critique et étude sur l'utilisation du Commentaire dans l'oeuvre de saint Thomas par G. Verbeke (*Corpus Latinum Commentariorum in Aristotelem Graecorum* II), Louvain/Paris.

Waitz, T. 1844: *Aristotelis Organon Graece*. Novis codicum auxiliis adiutus recognovit, scholiis ineditis et commentario instruxit Th. Waitz. Pars prior: *Categoriae, Hermeneutica, Analytica priora*, Leipzig, (reprint Aalen, 1965).

Weidemann, H. 1994: *Peri Hermeneias*, übersetzt und erläutert von H. Weidemann, in: *Aristoteles' Werke in deutscher Uebersetzung*, eds. E. Grumach and H. Flashar, Berlin,.

Zanatta, M. 1992: *Aristotele, Dell'interpretazione*. Introduzione, traduzione e commento di M. Zanatta [Greek-Italian edition], Milan.

Zierl, A. 1995: *Alexander von Aphrodisias, Über das Schicksal*, text, translation and commentary, Berlin.

Zimmermann, F. W. 1981: *Al-Farabi's Commentary and Short Treatise on Aristotle's De Interpretatione*, transl. and notes, Oxford.

VI.2 Collections of Testimonies

Arnim, H. von 1903-5: *Stoicorum veterum fragmenta*, I-III, Leipzig; M. Adler, *Stoicorum veterum fragmenta*, IV, indices, Leipzig, 1924.

Arrighetti, G. 1960: *Epicuro: Opere*, Turin (2nd ed. 1973).

Diels, H. 1879: *Doxographi Graeci*, Berlin (reprint 1958).

Diels, H. and Kranz, W. 1951: *Die Fragmente der Vorsokratiker* I-III, Zürich/Hildesheim.

Döring, K. 1972: *Die Megariker: Kommentierte Sammlung der Testimonien*, Amsterdam.

Edelstein, L. and Kidd, I.G. 1988: *Posidonius, I, Fragments, II-III, Commentary* by I.G. Kidd, Cambridge.

Gercke, A. 1885: 'Chrysippea', *Jahrbuch für klassische Philologie*, Supplbd. 14 689-781.

Hülser, K. 1987-8: *Die Fragmente zur Dialektik der Stoiker*, 4 vols., Stuttgart-Bad Cannstatt.

Straaten, M. van 1962: *Panaetii Rhodii Fragmenta*, Leiden.

Theiler, W. 1982: *Posidonios, Die Fragmente*, 2 vols., Berlin.

Usener, H. 1887: *Epicurea*, Leipzig.

VI.3. Secondary Literature

Amand, D. 1945: *Fatalisme et liberté dans l'antiquité grecque*, Paris/Louvain (reprint Amsterdam, 1973).

Anscombe, G. E. M. 1956: 'Aristotle and the Sea Battle. *De Interpretatione* Chapter IX', *Mind* 65 1-15; revised reprint in: Moravcsik 1968, 15-33; German translation (with an Addendum, 1969) in: Hager 1972, 211-231.

Aubenque, P. (ed.) 1980: *Concepts et catégories dans la pensée antique*, Paris.

Ax, W. 1978: 'Ψόφος, φωνή und διάλεκτος als Grundbegriffe aristotelischer Sprachreflexion', *Glotta* 56 245-271.

— 1979: 'Zum isolierten ῥῆμα in Aristoteles' *de interpretatione* 16 b 19-25', *Archiv für Geschichte der Philosophie* 61 271-279.

— 1986: *Laut, Stimme und Sprache. Studien zu drei Grundbegriffen der antiken Sprachtheorie*, Göttingen.

Barnes, J. 1985a: 'Cicero's *De Fato* and a Greek Source', in: J. Brunschwig, C. Imbert and A. Roger (eds.), *Histoire et structure*, Paris.

— 1993: 'Meaning, Saying and Thinking', in: Döring and Ebert, 47-61.

Barnes, J., Burnyeat, M. and Schofield, M. (eds.) 1980: *Doubt and Dogmatism: Studies in Hellenistic Epistemology*, Oxford.

Barnes, J. and Mignucci, M. (eds.) 1988: *Matter and Metaphysics, Fourth Symposium Hellenisticum*, Naples.

Barnes, J., Schofield, M. and Algra, K. (eds.) 1999: *The Cambridge History of Hellenistic Philosophy*, Cambridge.

Becker[-Freyseng], A. 1934: 'Zwei Beispiele für Interpolationen im Aristoteles-Text: *Hermeneutik* 13.22 b 38-23 a 26 und *Metaph.* Θ 4. 1047 b 14-30', *Hermes* 69 444-450.

— 1936: 'Bestreitet Aristoteles die Gültigkeit des "Tertium non datur" für Zukunftsaussagen? (Zum 9. Kapitel der Aristotelischen *Hermeneutik*), in: *Actes du Congrès International de Philosophie Scientifique, Paris 1935, VI: Philosophie des Mathématiques*, Paris, 69-74.

— 1938: *Die Vorgeschichte des philosophischen Terminus 'contingens'. Die Bedeutungen von 'contingere' bei Boethius und ihr Verhältnis zu den Aristotelischen Möglichkeitsbegriffen*, Heidelberg.

Belnap, N. 1992: 'Branching Space-Time', *Synthese* 92 385-434.

Blank, D. 1996: Introduction to the first volume of: *Ammonius, On Aristotle on Interpretation 1-8*, translated by D. Blank, London.

Bluck, R. S. 1963: 'On the Interpretation of Aristotle, *De Interpretatione* 12-13', *Classical Quarterly* 13 214-222.

Bobzien, S. 1986: *Die stoische Modallogik (Epistemata, Reihe Philosophie*, Bd. 32), Würzburg.

— 1993: 'Chrysippus' modal logic and its relation to Philo and Diodorus', in: Döring and Ebert, 63-84.

— 1996: 'Stoic Syllogistic', *Oxford Studies in Ancient Philosophy* 14 133-92.

— 1997: 'Stoic Conceptions of Freedom and their relation to Ethics', in: R. Sorabji (ed.), *Aristotle and After* (Bulletin of the Institute of Classical Studies suppl. 68), London, 71-89.

— 1998a: *Determinism and Freedom in Stoic Philosophy*, Oxford.

— 1998b: 'Chrysippus' theory of causes', in: K. Ierodiakonou (ed.), *Topics in Stoic Philosophy*, Oxford, 196-242.

— 1998c: 'The inadvertent conception and late birth of the free-will problem', *Phronesis* 43 133-175.

Boeft, J. den 1970: *Calcidius on Fate: his doctrine and sources*, Leiden.

Bonitz, H. 1862-1867: *Aristotelische Studien I-V*, Vienna (single volume reprint, Hildesheim, 1969).

Botros, S. 1985: 'Freedom, Causality, Fatalism and Early Stoic Philosophy', *Phronesis* 30 274-304.

Brandt, R. 1965: *Die Aristotelische Urteilslehre; Untersuchungen zur Hermeneutik*. Diss. Marburg.

Bruns, I. 1889: 'Studien zu Alexander von Aphrodisias, I. Der Begriff des Möglichen und die Stoa', *Rheinisches Museum für Philologie*, N.F. 44 619-630.

Brunschwig, J. 1969: *La proposition particulière et les preuves de nonconcluance chez Aristote* (reprint in: Menne and Öffenberger I 1982, 182-205).

— (ed.) 1978: *Les Stoiciens et leur logique: Actes du colloque des Chantilly 18/22 sept. 1976*, Paris.

Brunschwig, J. and Nussbaum, M.C. (eds.) 1993: *Passions and Perceptions*, Cambridge.

Cavini, W. 1985: 'La negazione di frase nella logica greca', in: W. Cavini, M. C. Donnini Macciò, M. S. Funghi, D. Manetti, *Studi su papiri greci di logica e medicina (Accademia Toscana di Scienze e Lettere La Colombaria, Studi LXXIV)*, Florence 7-126.

Celluprica, V. 1977a: *Il capitolo 9 del De interpretatione di Aristotele. Rassegna di studi: 1930-1973*, Bologna.

— 1977b: 'L'argomento dominatore di Diodoro Crono e il concetto di possibile di Crisippo', in: Giannantoni 1977, 55-74.

— 1984: 'Necessità Megarica e fatalità Stoica', *Elenchos* 3 361-85.

Cherniss, H. 1976: *Plutarch's Moralia* vol. XIII.2, London-Cambridge, Mass.

Cooper, J. M. 1985: 'Hypothetical Necessity', in: A. Gotthelf (ed.), *Aristotle on Nature and Living Things. Philosophical and Historical Studies presented to David M. Balme on his Seventieth Birthday*, Pittsburgh/Bristol, 151-167.

Corcoran, J. (ed.) 1974: *Ancient Logic and its Modern Interpretations*, Dordrecht.

Courcelle, P. 1948: *Les lettres grecques en Occident. De Macrobe à Cassiodore*, Paris.

Craig, W.L. 1988: *The Problem of Divine Foreknowledge and Future Contingents from Aristotle to Suarez*, Leiden.

Dancy, R. M. 1983: 'Aristotle and Existence', *Synthese* 54 409-442 (reprint in: Knuuttila and Hintikka 1986, 49-80).

Dapunt, I. 1970: 'Zur Frage der Existenzvoraussetzungen in der Logik', *Notre Dame Journal of Formal Logic* 11 89-96.

De Rijk, L.M.: see Rijk, L.M. de.

Denyer, N.C. 1981a: 'Time and Modality in Diodorus Cronus', *Theoria* 47 31-53.

— 1981b: *Time, Action and Necessity: A Proof of Free Will*, London.

Di Cesare, D. 1981: 'Die Semantik bei Aristoteles', *Sprachwissenschaft* 6 1-30.

Dickason, A. 1976: 'Aristotle, the Sea Fight and the Cloud', *Journal of the History of Philosophy* 14 11-22.

Dillon, J. 1977: *The Middle Platonists. A Study of Platonism, 80 B.C. to A.D. 220*, London.

— 1993: *Alcinous: The Handbook of Platonism*, Oxford.

Donini, P.L. 1973: 'Crisippo e la nozione del possibile', *Rivista di Filologia* 101 333-51.

— 1974a: *Tre studi sull'Aristotelismo nel II secolo*, Torino.

— 1974b: 'Psicologia ed etica in Galeno e in Alessandro di Afrodisia: il problema del determinismo', in: Donini 1974a 127-85.

— 1974/5: 'Fato e volontà umana in Crisippo', *Atti dell'Academia delle Scienze di Torino* 109 1-44.

— 1977: 'Stoici e Megarici nel de fato di Alessandro di Afrodisia?', in: Giannantoni 1977, 174-194.

— 1988: 'Plutarco e il determinismo di Crisippo', in: I. Gallo (ed.), *Aspetti dello stoicismo e dell'epicureismo in Plutarco*, Ferrara, 21-32.

— 1989: *Ethos: Aristotele e il determinismo (Culture antiche. Studi e testi, 2)*, Alessandria.

Döring, K. and Ebert, T. (eds.): *Dialektiker und Stoiker*, Stuttgart, 1993.

Dragona-Monachou, M. 1973: 'Providence and fate in Stoicism and prae-Neoplatonism: Calcidius as an authority on Cleanthes' theodicy (*SVF* 2.933)', *Philosophia* 3 (Athens) 262-306.

— 1978: *The Stoic Arguments for the Existence and the Providence of the Gods*, Athens.

Duhot, J.J. 1989: *La conception stoicienne de la causalité*, Paris.

Ebbesen, S. 1990: 'Boethius as an Aristotelian commentator', in: Sorabji 1990, 373-391.

Ebert, T. 1977: 'Zur Formulierung prädikativer Aussagen in den logischen Schriften des Aristoteles', *Phronesis* 22 123-145.

— 1985: 'Gattungen der Prädikate und Gattungen des Seienden bei Aristoteles. Zum Verhältnis von *Kat.* 4 und *Top.* I 9', *Archiv für Geschichte der Philosophie* 67 113-138.

— 1991: *Dialektiker und frühe Stoiker bei Sextus Empiricus*, Göttingen.

Eck, J. van. 1988: 'Another Interpretation of Aristotle's *De Interpretatione* IX. A Support for the so called Second Oldest or "Medieval" Interpretation', *Vivarium* 26 19-38.

Ehrig-Eggert, C.: see 'Texts and Translations'.

Englert, W.G. 1987: *Epicurus on the Swerve and Voluntary Action*, Atlanta.

Fine, G. 1984: 'Truth and Necessity in *De Interpretatione* 9', *History of Philosophy Quarterly* 1 23-47.

Flamand, J.-M. 1989: 'Apulée de Madaure', in: R. Goulet, ed., *Dictionnaire des philosophes antiques*, vol. I, 298-317.

Frede, D. 1970: *Aristoteles und die "Seeschlacht". Das Problem der Contingentia Futura in De Interpretatione 9*, Göttingen.

— 1972: 'Omne quod est quando est necesse est esse', *Archiv für Geschichte der Philosophie* 54 153-167.

— 1976: Review of Hintikka 1973, *Philosophische Rundschau* 22 237-242.

— 1982: 'The Dramatization of Determinism: Alexander of Aphrodisias' *De Fato*', *Phronesis* 27 276-98.

— 1984: 'Could Paris (Son of Priam) Have Chosen Otherwise?', *Oxford Studies in Ancient Philosophy* 2 279-92.

— 1985: 'The sea-battle reconsidered: A defence of the traditional interpretation', *Oxford Studies in Ancient Philosophy* 3 31-87.

— 1990: 'Fatalism and Future Truth', in: *Proceedings of the Boston Area Colloquium in Ancient Philosophy* 6 195-227.

Frede, M. 1974: *Die stoische Logik*, Göttingen.

Frede, M. and Striker, G. (eds.) 1996: *Rationality in Greek Thought*, Oxford.

Gaskin, R. 1993: 'Alexander's Sea Battle: a discussion of Alexander of Aphrodisias *De Fato* 10', *Phronesis* 38 75-94.

— 1995: *The Sea-Battle and the Master Argument: Aristotle and Diodorus Cronus on the Metaphysics of the Future*, Berlin.

Geach, P.T. 1950: 'Subject and Predicate', *Mind* 59 461-482.

Giannantoni, G. (ed.) 1977: *Scuole socratiche minori e filosofia elenistica*, Bologna.

Gombocz, W. L. 1988: 'Apuleius, *de interpret.* 180, 20-181, 7 (Thomas). Goldbachers Änderung der Überlieferung und die Folgen', *Wiener Studien* 101 279-292.

Görler, W. 1987: 'Hauptursachen bei Chrysipp und Cicero? Philologische Marginalien zu einem vieldiskutierten Gleichnis (*De fato* 41-44)', *Rheinisches Museum für Philologie* 130 254-74.

Gottschalk, H. B. 1990: 'The earliest Aristotelian commentators', in: Sorabji 1990, 55-81.

Gould, J.B. 1967: 'Chrysippus: on the criteria for the truth of a conditional proposition', *Phronesis* 12 152-61.

— 1970: *The Philosophy of Chrysippus*, Leiden, 1970.

— 1974: 'The Stoic Conception of Fate', *Journal of the History of Ideas* 35 17-32.

Greene, W.C. 1944: *Moira: Fate, Good, and Evil in Greek Thought*, Cambridge, Mass.

Gundel, W. 1914: *Beiträge zur Entwicklungsgeschichte der Begriffe Ananke und Heimarmene*, Giessen.

Haack, S. 1974: *Deviant Logic. Some philosophical issues*, Cambridge.

Hadot, I. 1990: 'The life and work of Simplicius in Greek and Arabic sources', in: Sorabji 1990, 275-303.

Hadot, P. 1980: 'Sur divers sens du mot pragma dans la tradition philosophique grecque', in: Aubenque, P. 1980, 309-319.

Hager, F.-P. (ed.) 1972: *Logik und Erkenntnislehre des Aristoteles (Wege der Forschung, Bd. 226)*, Darmstadt.

Hintikka, J. 1964a: 'Aristotle and the "Master Argument" of Diodorus', *American Philosophical Quarterly* 1 101-114 (reprint in: Hintikka 1973).

— 1964b: 'The Once and Future Sea Fight. Aristotle's Discussion of Future Contingents in *De Interpretatione* 9', *Philosophical Review* 73 461-492; corrected and expanded reprint in: Hintikka 1973, 147-178; German translation (with a Postscript, 1968) in: Hager 1972, 259-295.

— 1973: *Time and Necessity. Studies in Aristotle's Theory of Modality*, Oxford.

— 1977 (with U. Remes and S. Knuuttila): 'Aristotle on Modality and Determinism', *Acta Philosophica Fennica*, Vol. 29, No. 1, Amsterdam.

— 1986: 'The Varieties of Being in Aristotle', in: Knuuttila and Hintikka 1986, 81-114.

Hoffmann, J. G. E. 1869: *De hermeneuticis apud Syros Aristoteleos*, Leipzig.

Huby, P. 1970: 'An Epicurean Argument in Cicero, *De Fato* XVII 40', *Phronesis* 15 83-5.

Hughes, G.E. and Cresswell, M.J. 1968: *An Introduction to Modal Logic*, London.

Ierodiakonou, K. (ed.) 1988: *Topics in Stoic Philosophy*, Oxford.

Ioppolo, A.M. 1988: 'Le cause antecedenti in Cic. *De Fato* 40', in: Barnes and Mignucci 1988, 397-424.

Isaac, J. 1953: *Le Peri Hermeneias en Occident de Boèce à Saint Thomas*, Paris.

Isnardi Parente, M. 1980: 'Stoici, epicurei e il "motus sine causa", *Rivista Critica di Storia della Filosofia* 35 23-31.

Irwin, T. H. 1982: 'Aristotle's concept of signification', in: M. Schofield, M. C. Nussbaum (eds.), *Language and Logos. Studies in ancient Greek philosophy presented to G. E. L. Owen*, Cambridge, 241-266.

Jacobs, W.1979: 'Aristotle and Nonreferring Subjects', *Phronesis* 24 282-300.

Jaeger, H.-E. H. 1974: 'Studien zur Frühgeschichte der Hermeneutik', *Archiv für Begriffsgeschichte* 18 35-84.

Joja, A. 1969: 'La théorie de la modalité dans le "De Interpretatione"', *Revue Roumaine des sciences sociales (philosophie et logique)* 13,3 323-342.

Judson, L. 1988: 'La bataille navale d'aujourd'hui: *De Interpretatione* 9', *Revue de Philosophie Ancienne* 6 5-37.

Kahn, C. H. 1972: 'On the Terminology for Copula and Existence', in: Stern, Hourani and Brown 1972, 141-158.

— 1973: *The Verb 'Be' in Ancient Greek (The Verb 'Be' and Its Synonyms. Philosophical and Grammatical Studies*, J. W. M. Verhaar (ed.), Part 6), Dordrecht/Boston.

— 1986: 'Retrospect on the Verb "To Be" and the Concept of Being', in: Knuuttila and Hintikka 1986, 1-28.

Kirwan, C. A. 1986: 'Aristotle on the Necessity of the Present', *Oxford Studies in Ancient Philosophy* 4 (*A Festschrift for J. L. Ackrill*, M. Woods (ed.)), Oxford, 167-187.

Kneale, W. and M. 1962: *The Development of Logic*, Oxford (second edition 1975 (with corrections), 1978).

Knuuttila, S. and Hintikka, J. (eds.) 1986: *The Logic of Being. Historical Studies*, Dordrecht, Boston, Lancaster, Tokyo.

Kogan, B. S. 1985: 'Some Reflections on the Problem of Future Contingency in Al-Farabi, Avicenna and Averroes', in: Rudavsky 1985, 95-101.

Kretzmann, N. 1974: 'Aristotle on Spoken Sound Significant by Convention', in: Corcoran 1974, 3-21.

— 1987: 'Boethius and the Truth about Tomorrow's Sea Battle', in: De Rijk and Braakhuis 1987, 63-97.

— 1998: 'Boethius and the Truth about Tomorrow's Sea Battle', in: Blank, D. and Kretzmann, N. (transl.), 1998, 24-52.

Kretzmann, N., Kenny, A., Pinborg, J. (eds.) 1982: *The Cambridge History of Later Medieval Philosophy. From the Rediscovery of Aristotle to the Disintegration of Scholasticism (1100-1600)*, Cambridge.

Kühner, R. and Gerth, B. II-1/II-2, 1898-1904: *Ausführliche Grammatik der griechischen Sprache. Zweiter Teil: Satzlehre* (2 Bde.), 3. Aufl., Hannover, Leipzig (reprint Hannover, 1983).

Kullmann, W. 1974: *Wissenschaft und Methode. Interpretationen zur aristotelischen Theorie der Naturwissenschaft*, Berlin/New York.

— 1985: 'Notwendigkeit in der Natur bei Aristoteles', in: Wiesner 1985, 207-238.

Kutschera, F. von, 1986: 'Zwei modallogische Argumente für den Determinismus: Aristoteles und Diodor', *Erkenntnis* 24 203-217.

Lallot, J. 1989: *La grammaire de Denys de Thrace*, Paris.

Lemmon, E. J. 1956: Review of Anscombe 1956, *Journal of Symbolic Logic* 21 388-389.

Lloyd, A.C. 1979: 'Emotion and Decision in Stoic Psychology', in: Rist 1979, 187-202.

Londey, D. and Johanson, C.: see 'Texts and Translations'.

Long, A.A. 1970: 'Stoic Determinism and Alexander of Aphrodisias' *De Fato* I-XIV', *Archiv für Geschichte der Philosophie* 52 247-68.

— (ed.) 1971: *Problems in Stoicism*, London.

— (1971a): 'Freedom and Determinism in the Stoic Theory of Action', ibid. 173-99.

— (1971b): 'Language and Thought in Stoicism', ibid. 75-113.

— 1996: *Stoic Studies* (collected essays), Cambridge.

Long, A.A. and Sedley, D.N. (eds.) 1987: *The Hellenistic Philosophers*, 2 vols., Cambridge.

Lowe, M. F. 1980: 'Aristotle on the Sea-Battle. A Clarification', *Analysis* 40 55-59.

Lukasiewicz, J. 1930: 'Philosophical Remarks on Many-Valued Systems of Propositional Logic', in: McCall, S. (ed.), 1967, 63-64. An English translation of this paper is also available in: Borkowski, L. (ed.): *J. Lukasiewicz, Selected Works*, Amsterdam-London, 1970, 153-178. The article originally appeared in German: 'Philosophische Bemerkungen zu mehrwertigen Systemen des Aussagenkalküls', in:

Comptes Rendus des séances de la Société des Sciences et des lettres de Varsovie XXIII 1930, Classe III, 51-77 (reprint in: Pearce and Wolenski 1988, 100-119).

— 1951: *Aristotle's Syllogistic from the Standpoint of Modern Formal Logic*, Oxford (second edition 1957).

— 1973: 'Über den Determinismus' (German translation by G. Patzig), *Studia Leibnitiana* 5 5-25 (reprint in: Menne and Öffenberger III 1988, 1-21).

Lumpe, A. 1982: *Die Logik des Pseudo-Apuleius. Ein Beitrag zur Geschichte der Philosophie*, Augsburg.

Mansfeld, J. 1979: 'Providence and the destruction of the universe in early Stoic thought', in: Vermaseren, M.J. (ed.), *Studies in Hellenistic Religions*, Leiden, 129-88.

Mansion, A. 1945: *Introduction à la physique aristotélicienne*, Louvain.

McCall, S. 1967: *Polish Logic, 1920-1930*, Oxford.

— 1969: 'Time and the Physical Modalities', *The Monist* 53 426-446.

McKim, V. R. 1971/72: 'Fatalism and the Future. Aristotle's Way Out', *The Review of Metaphysics* 25 80-111.

Meyer, E. 1984: 'Der Mittlere Kommentar des Averroes zur aristotelischen Hermeneutik. Bericht über die vorliegenden Editionen', *Zeitschrift für Geschichte der Arabisch-Islamischen Wissenschaften* 1 265-287.

Menne, A. and Öffenberger, N. 1980-81: 'Über eine mehrwertige Darstellung der Oppositionstheorie nicht-modaler Urteilsarten. Zur Frage der Vorgeschichte der mehrwertigen Logik', *Filosofia* 10-11 304-327.

— (eds.) 1982-1988: *Zur modernen Deutung der aristotelischen Logik. Bd. I: Über den Folgerungsbegriff in der aristotelischen Logik, Bd. II: Formale und nicht-formale Logik bei Aristoteles, Bd. III: Modallogik und Mehrwertigkeit*, Hildesheim, Zürich, New York.

Mignucci, M. 1978: 'Sur la logique modale des Stoïciens', in: Brunschwig 1978, 317-46.

— 1981a: 'Pseudo-Alexandre critique des Stoïciens', in: *Proceedings of the World Congress on Aristotle, Thessaloniki, August 7-14, 1978*, I, Athens: Publications of the Ministry of Culture and Sciences, 198-204.

— 1981b: 'ὡς ἐπὶ τὸ πολύ et nécessaire dans la conception aristotélicienne de la science', in: Berti, E. (ed.), *Aristotle on Science: "The Posterior Analytics"* (*Studia Aristotelica*, 9), Padua, 173-203 (German translation in: Menne and Öffenberger III 1988, 105-139).

— 1983: 'La teoria della quantificazione del predicato nell'antichità classica', *Anuario Filosófico* 16 11-42.

— 1985: 'Logic and Omniscience: Alexander of Aphrodisias and Proclus', *Oxford Studies in Ancient Philosophy* 3 219-46.

— 1987: 'Boezio e il problema dei futuri contingenti', *Medioevo* 13 1-50.

— 1989: 'Truth and Modality in Late Antiquity. Boethius on Future Contingent Propositions', in: *Atti del Convegno Internazionale di Storia della Logica, Le teorie delle modalità (San Gimignano, 5.-8. Dez. 1987)*, Bologna, 47-78.

— 1996: 'Ammonius on Future Contingent Propositions', in: M. Frede and G. Striker (eds.) 1996, 279-310.

Minio-Paluello, L. 1974: 'William of Moerbeke', in: *Dictionary of Scientific Biography 9*, New York, 434-40.

Moreau, J. 1978: 'Immutabilité du vrai, necessité logique et lien causal', in: Brunschwig, J. (ed.) 1978, 347-60.

Moraux, P. 1961: 'Kritisch-Exegetisches zu Aristoteles,' *Archiv für Geschichte der Philosophie* 43 15-40.

— 1974/1983: *Der Aristotelismus bei den Griechen von Andronikos bis Alexander von Aphrodisias. Bd. 1: Die Renaissance des Aristotelismus im 1. Jh. v. Chr.*, Berlin/New

York, 1973; *Bd. 2: Der Aristotelismus im 1. und 2. Jh. n. Chr.*, Berlin/New York 1984.

Moravcsik, J. M. E. (ed.) 1968: *Aristotle. A Collection of Critical Essays*, London/ Melbourne.

Mueller, I. 1978: 'An introduction to Stoic logic', in: Rist 1978, 1-26.

Natali, C. (ed.): see 'Texts and Translations'.

Normore, C. 1982: 'Future contingents', in: Kretzmann, Kenny, Pinborg 1982, 358-381.

— 1985: 'Divine Omniscience, Omnipotence and Future Contingents, An Overview', in: Rudavsky 1985, 3-22.

Nuchelmans, G. 1973: *Theories of the Proposition. Ancient and medieval conceptions of the bearers of truth and falsity*, Amsterdam/London.

Obertello, L. 1974: see 'Texts and Translations'.

— 1981: 'Proclus, Ammonius and Boethius on divine foreknowledge', *Dionysius* 5 127-164.

Patzig, G. 1969: *Die aristotelische Syllogistik. Logisch-philologische Untersuchungen über das Buch A der „Ersten Analytiken".* 3rd revised edition, Göttingen.

Pépin, J. 1985: 'Σύμβολα, Σημεῖα, Ὁμοιώματα. A propos de *De interpretatione* 1, 16 a 3-8 et *Politique* VIII 5, 1340 a 6-39', in: Wiesner 1985, 22-44.

Pearce, D. and Wolenski, J. (eds.) 1988: *Logischer Rationalismus. Philosophische Schriften der Lemberg-Warschauer Schule*, Frankfurt a.M.

Polansky, R. and Kuczewski, M. 1990: 'Speech and Thought, Symbol and Likeness. Aristotle's *De Interpretatione* 16 a 3-9', *Apeiron* 23 51-63.

Powell, J.G.F. 1995: 'Cicero's Translations from the Greek', in: Powell, J.G.F. (ed.), *Cicero the Philosopher*, Oxford, 273-300.

Praechter, K. 1973: 'Nikostratos der Platoniker', in: Praechter, K., *Kleine Schriften*, Hildesheim-New York, 101-113.

Prior, A. N. 1957: *Time and Modality*, Oxford.

— 1967: *Past, Present, and Future*, Oxford.

Quine, W. V. 1976: 'On a So-called Paradox', *Mind* 62 (1953) 65-67 (reprint [under the title 'On a Supposed Antinomy'] in: Quine, W.V., *The Ways of Paradox and Other Essays*, Cambridge, Mass./London, 19-21).

Reesor, M.E. 1965: 'Fate and Possibility in Early Stoic Philosophy', *Phoenix* 19 285-97.

— 1978: 'Necessity and Fate in Stoic Philosophy', in: Rist 1978, 187-202.

Rehder, W. 1980: 'Über J. Hintikkas Interpretation von ἀκολουθεῖν in *De Interpretatione* 12-13', *Archiv für Geschichte der Philosophie* 62 58-66.

Rescher, N. 1963: 'An Interpretation of Aristotle's Doctrine of Future Contingency and Excluded Middle', in: Rescher, N., *Studies in the History of Arabic Logic*, Pittsburgh, 43-54.

Rescher, N. and Urquart, A. 1971: *Temporal Logic*, Vienna-New York.

Richard, M. 1950: '*Apo Phônês*', *Byzantion* 20 191-222.

Rijen, J. van. 1989: *Aspects of Aristotle's Logic of Modalities*, Dordrecht/Boston/ London.

Rijk, L.M. and Braakhuis, H.A.G. (eds.) 1987: *Logos and Pragma. Essays on the Philosophy of Language in Honour of Professor Gabriel Nuchelmans*, Nijmegen.

Rist, J.M. (ed.) 1978: *The Stoics*, Berkeley.

Rudavsky, T. (ed.) 1985: *Divine Omniscience and Omnipotence in Medieval Philosophy. Islamic, Jewish and Christian Perspectives*, Dordrecht/Boston/ Lancaster.

Ryle, G. 1954: *Dilemmas*, Cambridge (reprint 1977).

Saffrey, H.D. 1989: 'Ammonius d'Alexandrie (no. 141)', in: Goulet, R. (ed.), *Dictionnaire des philosophes antiques*, vol. I, Paris.

Sainati, V. 1968: *Storia dell' "Organon" aristotelico. I. Dai "Topici" al "De interpretatione"*, Florence.

Schreckenberger, H. 1964: Ἀνάγκη: *Untersuchungen zur Geschichte des Wortgebrauchs* (*Zetemata*, 36) Munich.

Sedley, D. 1977: 'Diodorus Cronus and Hellenistic Philosophy', *Proceedings of the Cambridge Philological Society* NS 23 74-120.

— 1982: 'On signs', in: Barnes, J., Brunschwig, J., Burnyeat, M., Schofield, M. (eds.), *Science and speculation, Studies in Hellenistic theory and practice*, Cambridge/Paris.

— 1983: 'Epicurus' refutation of determinism', in: *ΣΥΖΗΤΗΣΙΣ: Studi sull' epicureismo greco e latino offerti a Marcello Gigante*, 2 vols., Naples, 11-51.

— 1984: 'The negated conjunction', *Elenchos* 5 311-316.

— 1993: 'Chrysippus on Psychophysical Causality', in: Brunschwig and Nussbaum 1993, 313-31.

— 1996: 'Aristotle's *De interpretatione* and Ancient Semantics', in: G. Manetti (ed.), *Knowledge Through Signs. Ancient Semiotic Theories*, Turnhout.

Seel, G. 1982a: *Die Aristotelische Modaltheorie*, Berlin/New York.

— 1982b: 'Diodore domine-t-il Aristote?', *Revue de Métaphysique et de Morale* 87 293-313.

— 1983: Review of U. Wolf, *Möglichkeit und Notwendigkeit bei Aristoteles und heute*, *Archiv für Geschichte der Philosophie*, 65 81-91.

— 1993: 'Zur Geschichte und Logik des θερίζων λόγος, in ehrendem Andenken an Fernand Brunner', in: Döring and Ebert (eds.) 1993.

— 2001: 'The battle of the sea-battle, Ammonius' solution of Aristotle's puzzle', in: M. Frede and M. Mignucci (eds.), *Proceedings of the 13th Symposium Aristotelicum* (forthcoming).

Segonds, A.-Ph.: see 'Texts and Translations'.

Sharples, R.W. 1975a: 'Aristotelian and Stoic conceptions of necessity in the *De Fato* of Alexander of Aphrosidias', *Phronesis* 20 247-274.

— 1975b: 'Responsibility, chance, and not-being (Alexander of Aphrosidias *mantissa* 169-172)', *Bulletin of the Institute of Classical Studies* 22 37-63.

— 1978a: 'Alexander of Aphrodisias *De Fato*: some parallels', *Classical Quarterly* 28 243-66.

— 1978b: 'Temporally qualified necessity and possibility', *Liverpool Classical Monthly* 3 89-91.

— 1980: 'Alexander of Aphrodisias' second treatment of fate? (*de anima libri mantissa* 179-186 Bruns)', *Bulletin of the Institute of Classical Studies* 27 76-84.

— 1981: 'Necessity in the Stoic doctrine of fate', *Symbolae Osloenses* 56 81-97.

— 1982a: 'Alexander of Aphrodisias; Problems about possibility Iʹ, *Bulletin of the Institute of Classical Studies* 29 91-108.

— 1982b: 'An ancient dialogue on possibility; Alexander of Aphrodisias. *Quaestio* I.4', *Archiv für Geschichte der Philosophie* 64 23-38.

— 1983a: see 'Texts and Translations'

— 1983b: Alexander of Aphrodisias; Problems about possibility IIʹ, *Bulletin of the Institute of Classical Studies* 30 (1983) 99-110.

— 1986: 'Soft Determinism and Freedom in Early Stoicism: a reply to Botros', *Phronesis* 31 266-79.

— 1990: 'The School of Alexander?', in: Sorabji 1990, 83-111.

— 1991: see 'Texts and Translations'.

— 1992: see 'Texts and Translations'.

Shiel, J. 1958: 'Boethius' Commentaries on Aristotle', in: R. Hunt, R. Klibansky, L. Labowsky (eds.), *Medieval and Renaissance Studies* 4 217-244; reprinted in: R. Sorabji 1990 (references to the latter).

Simons, P. 1988: 'Aristotle's Concept of State of Affairs', in: O. Gigon and M. W. Fischer (eds.), *Antike Rechts- und Sozialphilosophie (Salzburger Schriften zur Rechts-, Staats- und Sozialphilosophie*, Bd. 6), Frankfurt a. M./Bern/ New York/Paris, 97-112.

Sonderegger, E. 1989: '... denn das Sein oder Nichtsein ist kein Merkmal der Sache .... Bemerkungen zu Aristoteles, *De interpretatione* 3, 16 b 22f.', *Zeitschrift für philosophische Forschung* 43 489-508.

Sorabji, R. 1980a: 'Causation, Laws and Necessity', in: Barnes et al. 1980, 250-82.

— 1980b: *Necessity, Cause, and Blame*, Ithaca/New York.

— 1983: *Time, Creation and the Continuum, Theories in Antiquity and the Early Middle Ages*, London.

— (ed.) 1990: *Aristotle Transformed*, London.

— 1998a: 'The three deterministic arguments opposed by Ammonius', in: Blank and Kretzmann (transl.) 1998, 3-15.

— 1998b: 'Boethius, Ammonius and their different Greek backgrounds', in: Blank and Kretzmann (transl.) 1998, 16-23.

Stern, S.M., Hourani, A., Brown, V. (eds.) 1972: *Islamic Philosophy and the Classical Tradition, Essays presented by his friends and pupils to Richard Walzer on his seventieth birthday*, Oxford.

Stough, C. 1978: 'Stoic Determinism and Moral Responsibility', in: Rist 1978, 203-31.

Strawson, P. F. 1952: *Introduction to Logical Theory*, London/New York.

Suermann, H. 1990: 'Die Übersetzungen des Probus und eine Theorie zur Geschichte der syrischen Übersetzung griechischer Texte', *Oriens Christianus* 74 103-114.

Talanga, J. 1986a: *Zukunftsurteile und Fatum. Eine Untersuchung über Aristoteles' De interpretatione 9 und Ciceros De fato, mit einem Überblick über die spätantiken Heimarmene-Lehren* (Habelts Dissertationsdrucke, Reihe Klass. Philologie, H. Erbse und W. Schetter (eds.), Heft 36), Bonn.

— 1986b: Review of F. W. Zimmermann 1981, *Archiv für Geschichte der Philosophie* 68 302-309.

Tarán, L. 1981: 'Proclus, Ammonius and Boethius on Divine Knowledge', *Dionysius* 5.

Theiler, W. 1946: 'Tacitus und die antike Schicksalslehre', in: O. Gigon et al. (eds.), *Phyllobolia für P. von der Muehll*, Basel, 35-90.

Thillet, P. (ed.) 1984: *Alexander of Aphrodisias: De fato (Traité du destin)*, Paris.

Thomason, R. H. 1970: 'Indeterminist time and truth-value gaps', *Theoria* 36 264-281.

Thompson, M. 1953: 'On Aristotle's Square of Opposition'; reprint in: Moravcsik 1968, 51-72.

Vegetti, M. 1991: 'Fato, Valutatione e imputabilita. Un argomento stoico in Alessandro, *De Fato* 35', *Elenchos* 12 257-70.

Verbeke, G. 1968: 'Aristotélisme et Stoicisme dans le *De Fato* d'Alexandre d'Aphrodisias', *Archiv für Geschichte der Philosophie* 50 73-100.

Voelke, A.-J. 1973: *L'idée de volonté dans le Stoicisme*, Paris.

Vuillemin, J. 1983a: 'Le carré Chrysippéen des modalités', *Dialectica* 37 235-47.

— 1983b: 'Le chapitre IX du *De Interpretatione* d'Aristote. Vers une réhabilitation de l'opinion comme connaissance probable des choses contingentes', in: *Philosophiques* 10 15-52.

— 1984: *Nécessité ou contingence: l'aporie de Diodore et les systèmes philosophiques*, Paris.

Wagner, H. 1971: 'Aristoteles, De Interpretatione 3 16 b 19-25', in: R. B. Palmer, R. Hamerton-Kelly (ed.), *Philomathes. Studies and Essays in the Humanities in Memory of Philip Merlan*, The Hague, 95-115.

Waterlow, S. 1982: *Passage and Possibility. A Study of Aristotle's Modal Concepts*, Oxford.

Wedin, M. V. 1978: 'Aristotle on the Existential Import of Singular Sentences', *Phronesis* 23 179-196.

— 1990: 'Negation and Quantification in Aristotle', *History and Philosophy of Logic* 11 131-150.

Weidemann, H. 1980: 'Überlegungen zu einer temporalen Modalanalyse', *Zeitschrift für philosophische Forschung* 34 405-422 (reprint with a postscript, 1986, in: Menne and Öffenberger III 1988, 86-104).

— 1982: 'Ansätze zu einer semantischen Theorie bei Aristoteles', *Zeitschrift für Semiotik* 4 241-257.

— 1985: 'Textkritische Bemerkungen zum siebten Kapitel der Aristotelischen 'Hermeneutik': *Int.* 7, 17 b 12-16/16-20', in: Wiesner 1985, 45-56.

— 1986: 'Aristoteles und das Problem des kausalen Determinismus (*Met.* E 3)', *Phronesis* 31 27-50.

— 1987: 'Möglichkeit und Wahrscheinlichkeit bei Aristoteles', *Studia Philosophica (Jahrbuch der Schweizerischen Philosophischen Gesellschaft)* 46 171-189.

— 1989: 'Prädikation I. (Antike, Mittelalter, Neuzeit)', *Historisches Wörterbuch der Philosophie*, Bd. 7, Basel, Darmstadt, 1194-1208.

— 1991: 'Grundzüge der Aristotelischen Sprachtheorie', in: P. Schmitter (ed.), *Sprachtheorien der abendländischen Antike (Geschichte der Sprachtheorie*, Bd. 2), Tübingen, 170-192.

— 1993: 'Zeit und Wahrheit bei Diodor', in: Döring and Ebert 1993, 319-329.

— 1994: see 'Texts and Translations'.

Westerink, L. G. 1990: 'The Alexandrian commentators and the introductions to their commentaries', in: Sorabji 1990, 325-348.

— 1994: see Texts and Translations.

White, M.J. 1979: 'Aristotle and Temporally Relative Modalities', *Analysis* 39 88-93.

— 1980: 'Necessity and Unactualized Possibilities in Aristotle', *Philosophical Studies* 38 287-298.

— 1980: 'Aristotle's temporal interpretation of necessary coming-to-be and Stoic determinism', *Phoenix* 34 208-18.

— 1981: 'Fatalism and Causal Determinism. An Aristotelian Essay', *Philosophical Quarterly* 31 231-241.

— 1983: 'Time and Determinism in the Hellenistic Philosophical Schools', *Archiv für Geschichte der Philosophie* 65 40-62.

— 1985: *Agency and Integrality*, Dordrecht.

Wieland, W. 1979: 'Aristoteles und die Seeschlacht. Zur Struktur prognostischer Aussagen', *Berichte zur Wissenschaftsgeschichte* 2 25-33.

Wiesner, J. (ed.) 1985-1987: *Aristoteles—Werk und Wirkung. Paul Moraux gewidmet*. Bd. 1: *Aristoteles und seine Schule*, Berlin/New York 1985; Bd. 2: *Kommentierung, Überlieferung, Nachleben*, Berlin/New York 1987.

Williams, C. J. F. 1978: 'True Tomorrow, Never True Today', *Philosophical Quarterly* 28 285-299.

— 1980: 'What Is, Necessarily Is, When It Is', *Analysis* 40 127-131.

Williams, D. C. 1954: 'Professor Linsky on Aristotle', *Philosophical Review* 63 253-255.

Wolf, U. 1979: *Möglichkeit und Notwendigkeit bei Aristoteles und heute*, Munich.

Wright, G. H. von. 1984: *Philosophical Papers*, vol. III: *Truth, Knowledge, and Modality*, Oxford.

Yon, A. (ed.) 1950: *Cicero: De fato (Traité du destin)*, Paris.

Zadro, A. 1979: *Tempo ed enunciati nel "De interpretatione" di Aristotele*, Padua.

Zeller, E. 1916: *Die Philosophie der Griechen in ihrer geschichtlichen Entwicklung*, III, Leipzig.

Zimmermann, A. 1971: 'Ipsum enim <'est'> nihil est" (Aristoteles, *Periherm.* I, c. 3). Thomas von Aquin über die Bedeutung der Kopula', in: A. Zimmermann (ed.), *Der Begriff der Repraesentatio im Mittelalter* (*Miscellanea Mediaevalia*, Bd. 8), Berlin/New York, 282-295.

Zimmermann, F. W. 1972: 'Some Observations on Al-Farabi and Logical Tradition', in: Stern, Hourani and Brown 1972, 517-546.

— 1981: see 'Texts and Translations'.

Part VII

Indices

VII.1 Index of Names

VII.2 Index of Passages Cited

This index does not contain the passages from Aristotle, *Int.* 7 and 9 and Ammonius, *In Int.* 86-101; 128-155 that are printed in part II and commented on in part III.

Elias
In Cat. 183,34-184,8 219 n.

Epictetus
Diss. II 19,1-10 19 n.

Homer
Iliad IX 412-416 115, 194; XIX 86-87 79

Lucian
Symp. 23 152 n.

Olympiodorus
In Cat. 79,25-28 219 n.

Parmenides
B 8,5 (D.-K.) 83 n.; B 8,6 (D.-K.) 89 n.

Philoponus
In Cat. 82,19-23 219 n.

Plato
Crat. 385b 125 n.; 430a ff. 221 n.
Leg. X 905a 83 n.
Parm. 140e ff. 83 n.
Phaed. 93b4 224; 103e2 224
Resp. II 376c 151 n.; III 392c 216 n.; V
    458d5 113 n.
Tim. 33d 167 n; 37d ff. 83 n.; 37e 89

Plutarch
Comm. not. 1081c-1082a 25 n.

Porphyry
fr. 97 (Smith) 67 n.

Proclus
De Dec. Dub. 6-8 280 n.
El. Theol. 124 110,10-13 Dodds 280 n.
Theol. Plat. I 15 (69,10-12) 280 n.; I 15
    (70,22-25) 280 n.; I 15 (74,9-16)
    280 n.

Sextus Empiricus
M. VII 211-216 27 n.; VIII 10 24, 25; VIII
    225 192; VIII 254-255 25; VIII
    281-284 157; VIII 292-296 157; VIII
    466-469 157; IX 205-206 157
P. I 194-195 154; II 186-187 157

Simplicius
In Cat. 386,6-15 53 n.; 406,13-16 29,
    280 n.; 406,21ff. 23 n.; 407,6-14
    280 n.; 407,12-13 30, 281
In Phys. 21,25-29 190; 240,13-20 190;
    985,17-20 190; 1021,3-4 190

Stephanus
In Int. 28,23-36 145 n.; 34,34-35,10 152;
    46,25-26 279 n.; 63,4ff. 133 n.

Stobaeus
Ecl. I 106,5-23 25 n.

Syrianus
In Met. 18,6 190 n.

Peripatoi

Philologisch-Historische Studien zum Aristotelismus
Herausgegeben von Wolfgang Kullmann, Robert W. Sharples und Jürgen Wiesner

Vol. 17:

Aspasius

The Earliest Extant Commentary on Aristotle's Ethics

Ed. by Antonia Alberti and Robert W. Sharples

1999. 23 x 15,5 cm. IX, 208 Seiten. Leinen. ISBN 3-11-016081-1

Vol. 16:

Christian Wildberg

John Philoponus' Criticism of Aristotle's Theory of Aether

Ed. by Paul Moreaux

1988. 23 x 15,5 cm. XIV, 274 Seiten. Leinen. ISBN 3-11-010446-6

Vol. 15:

Ilsetraut Hadot/Michel Tardieu/Philippe Hofmann

Simplicius. Sa vie, son oeuvre, sa survie

Actes du colloque international de Paris (28. Sept.–1er Oct. 1985)

Ed. par Ilsetraut Hadot

1987. 23 x 15,5 cm. X, 406 Seiten. Leinen. ISBN 3-11-010924-7

Vol. 14:

Zweifelhaftes im Corpus Aristotelicum

Studien zu einigen Dubia Akten des 9. Symposium Aristotelicum (Berlin 7.–16. September 1981)

Hrsg. von Paul Moreaux und Jürgen Wiesner

1983. 23 x 15,5 cm. XII, 401 Seiten. Leinen. ISBN 3-11-008980-7

Vol. 13:

Paul Moreaux

Le Commentaire d'Alexandre d'Aphrodise aux „Seconds Analytics" d'Aristote

1979. 23 x 15,5 cm. VIII, 157 Seiten. Leinen. ISBN 3-11-007805-8

WALTER DE GRUYTER GMBH & CO. KG
Genthiner Straße 13 · 10785 Berlin
Telefon +49-(0)30-2 60 05-0
Fax +49-(0)30-2 60 05-251
www.deGruyter.de

de Gruyter
Berlin · New York